Collected Works of Northrop Frye

VOLUME 16

Northrop Frye on Milton and Blake

The Collected Edition of the Works of Northrop Frye has been planned and is being directed by an editorial committee under the aegis of Victoria University, through its Northrop Frye Centre. The purpose of the edition is to make available authoritative texts of both published and unpublished works, based on an analysis and comparison of all available materials, and supported by scholarly apparatus, including annotation and introductions. The Northrop Frye Centre gratefully acknowledges financial support, through McMaster University, from the Michael G. DeGroote family.

Northrop Frye on Milton and Blake

VOLUME 16

Edited by Angela Esterhammer

UNIVERSITY OF TORONTO PRESS
Toronto Buffalo London

ISBN 0-8020-3919-7

Library and Archives Canada Cataloguing in Publication

Frye, Northrop, 1912–1991
Northrop Frye on Milton and Blake / edited by Angela Esterhammer.

(Collected works of Northrop Frye : v. 16)
Includes bibliographical references and index.
ISBN 0-8020-3919-7

1. Blake, William, 1757–1827 – Criticism and interpretation. 2. Milton, John, 1608–1674 – Criticism and interpretation. I. Esterhammer, Angela II. Title. III. Series.

PR3588.F79 2005 821′.7 C2005-900397-9

This volume has been published with the assistance of a grant from Victoria University.

University of Toronto Press acknowledges the financial assistance to its publishing program of the Canada Council for the Arts and the Ontario Arts Council.

University of Toronto Press acknowledges the financial support for its publishing activities of the Government of Canada through the Book Publishing Industry Development Program (BPIDP).

Contents

Essays on Blake

Preface

This volume of Northrop Frye's Collected Works contains all of his published articles, public lectures, and reviews pertaining to the works of John Milton and William Blake, as well as one unpublished typescript, the introduction to a planned *Festschrift* for Milton scholar Balachandra Rajan (no. 6). The items have been arranged chronologically according to date of first publication (in the case of articles and reviews), delivery (in the case of public lectures), or composition (in the case of unpublished material). The complete text of *The Return of Eden: Five Essays on Milton's Epics* (1965) is included here (no. 3). However, *Fearful Symmetry: A Study of William Blake* (1947), is published separately as volume 14 of the Collected Works. A few previously unpublished typescripts pertaining to Milton and Blake are included in other volumes of the Collected Works. For instance, volume 10, *Northrop Frye on Literature and Society, 1936–1989: Unpublished Papers*, contains notes for a slide lecture on "Blake's *Jerusalem*" and two talks Frye broadcast on CBC Radio in 1950, "Writer as Prophet: Milton" and "Writer as Prophet: Blake."

Headnotes to the individual items specify the copy-text, list all known reprintings in English of the item, and also note the existence of typescripts and where they can be found in the Northrop Frye Fonds in the E.J. Pratt Library of Victoria University. The copy-text chosen is generally the last edition published by Frye himself, usually in his own collections, such as *Fables of Identity* or *Spiritus Mundi*. All substantive changes to this version are noted in the list of editorial emendations.

In preparing the text, I have followed the general practice of the Collected Works in handling published material from a variety of sources. That is to say, since the conventions of spelling, typography, and to some extent punctuation derive from the different publishers' house styles rather than from Frye, they have been regularized silently throughout the volume. For instance, Canadian spellings ending in -our have been substituted for American -or ones, commas have been added before the "and" in sequences of three, titles of poems have been italicized, and capitalization conforms to the practice of other volumes in the Collected Works. Sometimes, where editors have added commas around such expressions as "of course," these have been silently removed to conform with the more characteristic usage in the typescript.

Endnotes identify the source of quotations and allusions, as far as these could be tracked down, and provide some contextualizing information. Notes provided by Frye himself are identified by [NF] following the note. Authors and titles mentioned in passing are not annotated, but life dates and date of first publication of books are provided in the index.

Acknowledgments

A number of people helped in the preparation of this volume. The articles were originally expertly typed or scanned by Alex Stephens. Graduate assistants Jianmeng He, Helen McEnroy-Smith, Diane Piccitto, and Mitchell Rowat helped track down many references and quotations. Jean O'Grady and Margaret Burgess provided invaluable guidance and assistance; thanks are due to them as well as to the librarians at the E.J. Pratt Library, Victoria University. Thanks also to those who have cheerfully answered queries and provided information: Christopher G. Brown, Robert Denham, Michael Dolzani, Donald S. Hair, Nicholas Halmi, M.J. Kidnie, Alvin A. Lee, John Leonard, Richard Nemesvari, Elias Polizoes, and Tilottama Rajan.

Credits

We wish to acknowledge the following sources for permission to reprint works previously published by them. We have not been able to determine the copyright status of all the works included in this volume, and welcome notice from any copyright holders who have been inadvertently omitted from these acknowledgments.

Huntington Library Quarterly for "Blake's Introduction to Experience," from the *Huntington Library Quarterly*, 21 (November 1957).

The Johns Hopkins University Press for "Review of Bernard Blackstone's *English Blake*," from *Modern Language Notes*, 66 (1951). Copyright © The Johns Hopkins University Press. Reprinted by permission of the Johns Hopkins University Press.

Journal of Aesthetics and Art Criticism for "Poetry and Design in William Blake," from the *Journal of Aesthetics and Art Criticism*, 10 (September 1951).

McArthur & Company Publishing Limited for "Notes for a Commentary on *Milton*," from *The Divine Vision: Studies in the Poetry and Art of William Blake*, ed. Vivian de Sola Pinto (London: Gollancz, 1957).

Museum of Fine Arts, Boston, for the frontispiece *The Archangel Raphael with Adam and Eve (Illustration to Milton's "Paradise Lost")*, 1808. Pen and watercolour on paper. Catalogue Raisonné: Butlin 536 (6). 49.8 × 39.8 cm (19 5/8 × 15 11/16 in.). Gift by subscription; 90.97.

Oxford University Press for "Review of *The Theology of William Blake,*" from *The Review of English Studies*, 1 (1950).

Random House, Inc. for "Introduction to *Selected Poetry and Prose of William Blake,*" from *Selected Poetry and Prose of William Blake*. Copyright © 1953, 1981 by Random House, Inc. Used by permission of Random House, Inc.

University of Nebraska Press for "The Road of Excess," from *Myth and Symbol: Critical Approaches and Applications* by Northrop Frye and L.C. Knights, edited by Bernice Slote. Copyright © 1963, 1991 by the University of Nebraska Press. Used by permission of the University of Nebraska Press.

University of North Carolina Press for "Literature as Context: Milton's *Lycidas,*" from *Comparative Literature: Proceedings of the Second Congress of the International Comparative Literature Association*, edited by Werner P. Friederich. Nos. 23 and 24 UNC Studies in Comparative Literature. Copyright © 1959 by the University of North Carolina Press, renewed 1987 by Werner P. Friederich. Used by permission of the publisher.

University of Toronto Press for "Agon and Logos: Revolution and Revelation," from *The Prison and the Pinnacle* (1973); for "Blake after Two Centuries," from the *University of Toronto Quarterly*, 27 (October 1957); for the "Editor's Preface" from *The Valley of Vision: Blake as Prophet and Revolutionary* (1961); for "*The Portable Blake,*" from the *University of Toronto Quarterly*, 17 (October 1947); for *The Return of Eden: Five Essays on Milton's Epics* (1965, rev. 1975); and for "The Revelation to Eve," from *Paradise Lost: A Tercentenary Tribute* (1969).

All other works are printed by courtesy of the Estate of Northrop Frye/ Victoria University.

Abbreviations

Individual Works by Milton

CD	*De Doctrina Christiana (Christian Doctrine)*
PL	*Paradise Lost*
PR	*Paradise Regained*
SA	*Samson Agonistes*

Individual Works by Blake

FZ	*Four Zoas*
J	*Jerusalem*
M	*Milton*
MHH	*The Marriage of Heaven and Hell*

Other Abbreviations and Short Titles

Ayre	John Ayre. *Northrop Frye: A Biography*. Toronto: Random House, 1989.
E	William Blake. *The Complete Poetry and Prose of William Blake*. Rev. ed. Ed. David V. Erdman. Berkeley: University of California Press, 1982.
EAC	*The Eternal Act of Creation: Essays, 1979–1990*. Ed. Robert D. Denham. Bloomington: Indiana University Press, 1993.
FI	*Fables of Identity: Studies in Poetic Mythology*. New York: Harcourt, Brace and World, 1963.
FS	*Fearful Symmetry: A Study of William Blake*. Princeton: Princeton University Press, 1947.

FS2 *Fearful Symmetry: A Study of William Blake*. Ed. Nicholas Halmi. CW, 14. Toronto: University of Toronto Press, 2004.
K William Blake. *The Complete Writings of William Blake*. Ed. Geoffrey Keynes. Nonesuch Press, 1957; rpt. Oxford: Oxford University Press, 1966.
MM *Myth and Metaphor: Selected Essays, 1974–1988*. Ed. Robert D. Denham. Charlottesville: University Press of Virginia, 1990.
NF Northrop Frye
NFF Northrop Frye Fonds, Victoria College Library.
NFHK *The Correspondence of Northrop Frye and Helen Kemp, 1932–1939*. Ed. Robert D. Denham. Toronto: University of Toronto Press, 1996.
RE *The Return of Eden: Five Essays on Milton's Epics*. Toronto: University of Toronto Press, 1965.
RW *Reading the World: Selected Writings, 1935–1976*. Ed. Robert D. Denham. New York: Peter Lang, 1990.
SE *Northrop Frye's Student Essays, 1932–1938*. Ed. Robert D. Denham. Toronto: University of Toronto Press, 1997.
SM *Spiritus Mundi: Essays on Literature, Myth, and Society*. Bloomington: Indiana University Press, 1976.
StS *The Stubborn Structure: Essays on Criticism and Society*. London: Methuen, 1970.
TS Typescript
Works John Milton. *The Works of John Milton*. 18 vols. Ed. F.A. Patterson. New York: Columbia University Press, 1931–38.

A Note on Citations from Milton and Blake

In this volume, quotations from Milton's works are cited from *The Works of John Milton*, 18 vols., ed. F.A. Patterson (New York: Columbia University Press, 1931–38). This, the "Columbia edition," is the one Frye generally used, and the one he called, at the beginning of his own edition of Milton's *"Paradise Lost" and Selected Poetry and Prose*, "the definitive modern edition." Quotations from *Paradise Lost* and *Paradise Regained* are cited by book and line number; for shorter poems, line numbers are provided when necessary; for prose quotations, volume and page numbers are given.

For Blake, Frye himself recommended (in no. 23) "the one-volume *The*

Poetry and Prose of William Blake, ed. Geoffrey Keynes (London and New York, 1927)." This 1927 edition was the basis for *The Complete Writings of William Blake*, ed. Geoffrey Keynes (Nonesuch Press, 1957; rpt. Oxford: Oxford University Press, 1966). As the edition most readily available to readers, the 1957/1966 edition is the one cited here unless otherwise indicated. The Keynes edition ("K") is almost inevitably the one Frye quotes and uses as a guide for spelling, capitalization, and punctuation, as well as for the variable numbering of plates or ordering of manuscript pages in Blake's work. An interesting exception to the use of Keynes is no. 22 in this volume, "The Keys to the Gates," an essay written in the mid-1960s when David V. Erdman's edition of Blake's work was first published as *The Poetry and Prose* of *William Blake* (Garden City, N.Y.: Doubleday, 1965). The Erdman edition retains Blake's idiosyncratic spelling and punctuation where Keynes had often normalized it; in its revised version, *The Complete Poetry and Prose of William Blake* (Berkeley: University of California Press, 1982), Erdman ("E") has become the standard edition for Blake scholarship. The only time Frye's copy-texts cite the Erdman edition, rather than Keynes, is in the case of longer quotations from the prophetic books in the aforementioned essay (no. 22). For shorter phrases and quotations from Blake's lyrics and prose, Frye follows the more normalized Keynes edition, and in later essays he continues to cite from Keynes. In the present volume, quotations from Blake follow the Keynes edition except where otherwise indicated, and page references are given to both "K" and "E," as well as plate and line numbers in the case of the engraved prophetic books.

In some essays, the published version prepared by Frye provides references only for the more significant quotations. In these cases, Frye's references have been retained in parentheses ( ) and supplemented by references for the remaining quotations in square brackets [ ]. Frye's own occasional square brackets have been replaced with braces { } to distinguish them from editorial interpolations. In no. 15, which is unique in this volume in being a detailed commentary on a single text by Blake, and for which Frye provided copious references to plate and line number, Frye's referencing system has been retained; most "K" and "E" page numbers are omitted since virtually all the references are to a single text, Blake's *Milton*.

For references to Blake's unengraved prophetic book *The Four Zoas*, finally, the "Night" and line numbers are given for the Keynes edition (the one Frye used), along with the page number in K. The page number in E is given as well, although Erdman's alternative numbering of the Nights, lines, and pages of Blake's manuscript has been omitted in order to avoid confusion.

Minor changes in punctuation and accidentals to make quotations conform to the standard editions have been made silently; any significant changes or corrections are noted in the list of emendations.

Introduction

Northrop Frye's writings on John Milton and William Blake span four decades, the earliest of the pieces in this volume dating from 1947, the last from 1987. The writings on Milton and those on Blake take up comparable numbers of pages, although this is a somewhat misleading comparison because the section on Milton contains the complete text of Frye's book of essays on Milton, *The Return of Eden* (1965), while his seminal book on Blake, *Fearful Symmetry* (1947), appears separately as volume 14 of the Collected Works. Perhaps surprisingly, Frye did not write extensively on Milton and Blake together. Several other twentieth-century critics focused on the complex relationship between these two challenging poets, particularly on Blake's vehement responses to the work of his predecessor; some even constructed a theory of poetry around the Milton-Blake relationship.[1] In Frye's work, the two poets occupy quite distinct places. However, both Milton and Blake are absolutely central to his concept of the imaginative structure of Western literature, thought, and society, and no other poets had greater lifelong importance for him.

Frye's "conversion" to Blake, and his less tempestuous, yet enduring, appreciation of Milton, both began during his undergraduate years at Victoria College. Inspired by Denis Saurat's *Blake and Modern Thought* (1929), and still more by the lectures of his mentor Pelham Edgar, Frye began work on Blake that included a long paper for Edgar's course during Frye's third undergraduate year. At this point he cited both Milton and Blake among his "very definite heroisms in literature"—while, however, naming Robert Browning as his favourite poet (*NFHK*, 1:84).

It was Blake who came to occupy the centre of Frye's intellectual universe, however, when he continued post-B.A. studies in theology at

Emmanuel College in 1933–34, while also taking a seminar on Blake with Herbert Davis at University College that year. Staying up all night to prepare a paper on Blake's long prophetic poem, *Milton*, Frye had what he later described as an epiphany: "I began to see glimpses of something bigger and more exciting than I had ever before realized existed in the world of the mind, and when I went out for breakfast at five-thirty on a bitterly cold morning, I was committed to a book on Blake" (Ayre, 92). The insight marked not only the inception of Frye's first book, *Fearful Symmetry*, to be tortuously written over the next thirteen years and finally published in 1947, but more specifically the realization of how thoroughly Blake's mythological universe was indebted to earlier poets, chiefly Milton, and how central both Milton and Blake were to an immense system of myth and symbolism that derived from the Bible and permeated Western culture.

Frye's engagement with Milton was less melodramatic and all-consuming, and he was never the world's foremost authority on Milton, as was arguably the case with Blake in the era of *Fearful Symmetry*. Yet his undergraduate admiration for Milton was reinforced during his first year of full-time teaching, 1935–36, when he taught a course on Milton and seventeenth-century poetry at Victoria College. During the 1940s and 1950s he was, along with A.S.P. Woodhouse, a major figure in Milton studies on the University of Toronto campus. Both of them internationally renowned scholars and powerful teachers, but doing very different kinds of work, Woodhouse and Frye attracted large numbers of undergraduate and graduate students to the study of Milton.

There is, in fact, an interesting complementary relationship between teaching and research in Frye's work on Milton and Blake. His scholarly engagement with Blake was always fueled by a personal, intellectual, and spiritual questing, which led, once Frye became famous for *Fearful Symmetry*, to more and more teaching commitments. His work on Milton tended to move in the opposite direction: beginning in the classroom, it developed into conferences, publications, and public lectures. As Frye himself notes in the introductions to several of the texts reprinted here, the Milton essays are more likely to be overviews directed toward student audiences, while the Blake essays, at least in the earlier years, are more likely to be addressed to the scholarly community—although both are challenging, in their way, and often have wider relevance than Frye's modest introductory comments would suggest. The difference may have something to do with the relative importance of Renaissance and Romantic studies during Frye's formative years: the Romantics were an unfashionable specialization in English studies during the mid-twentieth century, the Renaissance a more canonical and respected field. The shift in late-twentieth-century literary criticism and theory, whereby the Romantics attained much greater prominence, can in part be put down to changes in academic fashion, but it also has a good deal to do with Frye's own work in revolutionizing the Romantic canon and making a place for Blake within it.

Before surveying Frye's views on the two poets separately, it is worth stressing the links between Milton and Blake in his work—even if each of the pieces in this volume is concerned with either one writer or the other. Both are, for Frye, poet-prophets, the most important poet-prophets in the English tradition. Both are revolutionaries who lived in revolutionary times, and embraced the cause of political liberty because they saw it as inseparable from spiritual and religious liberty. Both are also revolutionaries of the imagination—although Blake is more blatant in presenting the reader with an idiosyncratic mythology, while Milton's departures from Christian orthodoxy appear more subtle and often need explication for a modern readership.

In his analyses of both poets, Frye returns often to a few crucial themes: liberty; the imagination; genre, especially the epic; the heroic act as the focus of epic form; and the existence of a central framework of archetypes and symbols that the work of Milton and Blake both reflects, and helps to establish. The prominence of the mythological framework in the work of these two towering poets makes them indispensable to Frye as he develops his ideas on the structure of imagery in Western literature. In the essays collected here, and increasingly in the later writings, we see his analyses of Milton the poet, and Blake the poet and artist, open out into his growing concern with the anatomy of criticism and the shape of the human imagination.

Setting the tone for his writings on Milton, inspired as they were by his experiences in the classroom, Frye's first publication on this poet (no. 1) is an introduction to a student edition of Milton's works, *"Paradise Lost" and Selected Poetry and Prose*, that Frye completed in June 1950. The anthology is a modernized text of Milton published by Holt, Rinehart and Winston. Frye's approach in the introduction is chronological: analysing the various phases of Milton's career, he constructs a continuous narrative of Milton's mental, spiritual, and poetic development in the context of his personal and political history. He considers the various genres in which Milton wrote, demonstrating the "occasional" nature of Milton's earlier poetry, which is often a response to events such as deaths or festivals, and contextualizing his political writing within the events of his age. There is a conspicuous emphasis on "the consistency of Milton's thinking" (11) over the course of his career. In this essay, Frye also writes about Milton's prosody in more detail than he ever would again. Then, in the last paragraph of the introduction, he provides a brilliant summary of what makes Milton a "visionary poet"—which also goes a long way toward showing why Milton is a poet Frye would engage with so deeply and for so long. Building on the argument he has just made about the music of Milton's verse, and the compelling reasons why "the ear predominates over the eye" in all his major poetry, Frye explains that Milton's "steady flow of powerful working words" constitutes exactly the kind of "temptation" that most of his major poetry takes as its theme. But, unlike the Satanic temptations of *Paradise Lost* and *Paradise Regained,* this temptation is an educative and redemptive one. The poetic voice entices us to accede to what seems at first to be poetic illusion, but turns out to be a more profound and accurate vision of reality than the historical and material realities we are usually willing to accept. This temptation is not to forsake the Word, but to embrace it: "Milton, the agent of the Word of God, is trying to awaken with his words a vision in us which is, in his own language, the Word of God in the heart" (23).

Frye's delineation of Milton's career reflects his simultaneous immersion in Blake and Romantic poetry, even if Blake is never mentioned in Frye's introduction to the Milton edition. He begins with the poet's function as a priest (as in Milton's early Latin poem *Elegia Sexta*) whose worldly experience pushes him into the role of political prophet. But this role is vulnerable to ironic self-delusion, as the poet-prophet is drawn into "the plight of the liberal intellectual who sees in every revolution an apocalyptic struggle of tyranny and freedom and finds it so hard to understand that revolution is a technique of transferring power from one class to another" (9–10). Frye, already immersed in visions and revisions of *Fearful Symmetry,* seems tempted to regard Milton as the "Romantic" poet that he might have been had he died a martyr at the time of the Restoration in 1660, rather than dying "in his bed" after descending from superior poetry to "a more traditional strain" of historical and religious prose (11). This fantasy of a short-lived, Romantic Milton would also, however, entail giving up *Paradise Lost* and *Paradise Regained,* the products of Milton's maturity. Frye is not prepared to do that; rather than giving in to the temptation of constructing a Romantic Milton, he comes to concentrate instead on the archetypal continuities between Milton and Blake, and the resonances in their readings of the Bible.

Although it covers traditional considerations of genre, prosody, and political history, then, Frye's first published text on Milton leaves no doubt as to where his true interests lie. The historical-political subjects of Milton's prose works are evoked only to be transcended for the sake of "greater" ethical and aesthetic issues: "it is the long-range values in his political writing that are important to us: those moments in which he looks over the head of the immediate situation to a greater vision beyond it" (10). In "Literature as Context: Milton's *Lycidas*" (no. 2), Frye intensifies his polemic against purely historicizing critics: "There are critics who can find things in the Public Records Office," he writes, "and there are critics who, like myself, could not find the Public Records Office" (34). Despite the characteristic self-deprecating irony, Frye is staking out a serious critical position: historical investigations of sources and influences are relegated to a distinctly secondary status, in favour of the autonomous mythic structure of literature.

While the awareness of this structure is already latent in the very earliest writings on Milton, Frye's focus here is primarily on the ethical dimension—that is, on a philosophy of action and responsibility. His comments on Milton's epics combine an Aristotelian view of epic as the representation and analysis of an *action* with Milton's own conviction that any true action (as opposed to a parody of action, or a failure to act) is by definition *good*: "For Milton all real acts are good, and there are no real evil acts" (no. 3, n. 56). When Frye was granted a Guggenheim fellowship in 1950 to spend a research year at Harvard, he initially planned a three-volume project on Renaissance symbolism that would include a study of Milton as the poet who analysed most fully the potential of the heroic act in epic (Ayre, 221). Although the project was never completed in this form, the ethical dimension of epic looms large in Frye's early essays on Milton.

His second Milton essay, "The Typology of *Paradise Regained*," appeared in *Modern Philology* in May 1956, and was later reprinted in a slightly revised version as the last essay in *The Return of Eden*, where it appears in the present volume. This study again reflects the concerns of the Guggenheim project he had contemplated earlier; it focuses on epic structure, and on the question of heroism in political, moral, and mythic contexts. Frye approaches these issues first from the perspective of a reader of *Paradise Regained*: Where in the poem do readers identify with Christ's heroism? At what point are we inclined to lose sympathy with him? Why is he an unusual heroic figure, and how can his heroism finally be reconciled with Christian doctrine and a typological understanding of the Bible? The climax of Frye's argument is the divine-human nature of Christ; he shows how Milton works with this concept in the poetic and ethical structure of *Paradise Regained*, especially how he focuses the reader's attention on the "necessary point" where "[Christ's] human will has been taken over by the omnipotent divine will . . . and prefigures the commending of his spirit to the Father at the instant of his death on the cross" (128). What upholds Frye's concern with heroism and true action is a preoccupation with the nature of liberty—a preoccupation that also reflects the exigencies of the mid-twentieth-century political context in which he was writing. He repeatedly distinguishes liberty, in Milton, from licence, identifying true liberty as a responsibility and even a burden. "God wills liberty for man," Frye writes (6), or even, "liberty is something that man does not want, but that God is determined he shall have" (385). The ethical-political themes of heroic action, liberty, and revolution come to the fore again, this time as components of the genre of tragedy, in Frye's 1973 essay on Milton's *Samson Agonistes* (no. 5). Both *Paradise Regained* and *Samson Agonistes* are manifestations of the "central revolutionary attitude" (177) that Milton expressed throughout his poetry and prose, an attitude inherent in the tradition of the Bible as Milton, Blake, and Frye all read it.

The Centennial lectures presented at Huron College in London, Ontario, and published in 1965 as *The Return of Eden: Five Essays on Milton's Epics* (no. 3), provided Frye with the opportunity to expand on Milton's analyses of action and liberty. Frye now begins to describe epic structure in Milton (and, before him, Virgil) in terms of a spiral: "Here the total action begins and ends, not at precisely the same point, but at the same point renewed and transformed by the heroic action itself" (44). Analysing the "total action" of *Paradise Lost*, Frye begins with Milton's definition of an act, according to which every real act is good, and "only the divine . . . can really act" (50). This is the key to the epic and ethical structure of *Paradise Lost*: "Christ, therefore, who creates the world and then recreates or redeems man, is the hero of *Paradise Lost* simply because, as the agent or acting principle of the Father, he is ultimately the only actor in the poem" (50). The principle of action, and the principle of liberty, both become absorbed into a new preoccupation with divine creation, which is a model for ideal human creativity. Creation is a major subject of the second essay in *The Return of Eden*, where Frye muses on energy and form. Because the true Creator's activity consists of "releasing energy by creating form" (69), we should properly regard creation as a liberating activity: "we ought to revise our conception of creation: it is not so much imposing form on chaos as incorporating energy in form" (68). The devils in *Paradise Lost*, by contrast, fail to understand the agency of their own creation and the principles of true artistic creation. Similarly, incautious or uneducated readers of Milton are taken in by the illusory extension of space and time, the reality of which—that is, form and energy—finds its true expression in divine and human creativity. "All superficial readers of Milton" are, in this sense, "in the position of minor devils" (56). Describing the process of reading Milton's *Paradise Lost* as the reader's progressive education, and even salvation, Frye engages in his own form of reader-response criticism. It is a more aesthetic and phenomenological version of the critical perspective that was promoted at about the same time by Stanley Fish, when he described the education of Milton's reader in moral and doctrinal terms in *Surprised by Sin: The Reader in "Paradise Lost"* (1967).

But Frye's reading of Milton—unlike Fish's, which depends on a Renaissance view of self-education—has distinctly Romantic overtones. His Centennial lectures on Milton modulate into the cadences of Blake, as when he talks about Milton's God seeing past, present, and future all at once (like Blake's Bard), or the devils "closing the gate of their own origin" (59)—open and closed gates being common images in Blake's work. More extended arguments, such as the idea that "the externalizing of the demonic and the internalizing of the divine runs through every aspect of Milton's writing" (108), also owe something to the world view of Blake, whose major works depict the externalizing of evil to the point where it can be cast off, and who proclaimed that every thing that lives is holy.

The published version of *The Return of Eden* was transcribed from tapes made by an audience member at the Centennial lectures, which Frye delivered almost *ex tempore*, using only a few index cards as his text. While they are impressive impromptu performances before large audiences, both the lectures and the published book garnered mixed reviews. Frye's disclaimer at the outset of these lectures is a reminder of the extent to which his expertise on Milton was developed through undergraduate teaching, but also of the fundamental place that Milton acquired in Frye's thought through this activity: "I am talking about Milton because I enjoy talking about Milton . . . I have been teaching him long enough to have incorporated him as a central part of my own literary experience" (36).

In *The Return of Eden*, it is clear that Milton is already a crucial component in Frye's developing concept of the unified imaginative structure that underlies human life and art. Explaining the role of "revelation" at the end of the first essay, Frye claims that "what Milton means by revelation is a consolidated, coherent, encyclopedic view of human life which defines, among other things, the function of poetry" (55). That is what *Frye* means by revelation, at any rate; and as he explores the concept of revelation at greater length in the third and fourth *Return of Eden* essays, his pronouncements on it become increasingly radical and increasingly enigmatic. "Liberty for Milton is a release of energy through revelation," we read in the fourth essay, and "revelation has to be a personal force as well as a vision," in order for our consciousness of a better, more humanized existence to issue in action (99, 100).

The aesthetic form of revelation, as Frye finds it in Milton, had already emerged explicitly in "Literature as Context: Milton's *Lycidas*" (no. 2), presented a few years earlier to the International Comparative Literature Association. For the sake of the comparative-literature audience, Frye here stresses the universalism of Milton's sources and influences: "there is no poet whose literary influences are entirely confined to his own language. Thus every problem in literary criticism is a problem in comparative literature, or simply of literature itself" (28). The last phrase marks an important turn from the idea of literatures in the plural, to the concept of literature as a universal phenomenon, which is fundamental to Frye's main argument in the essay: namely, that all literature together must be recognized as an "order of words" (32). The main title of the *Lycidas* essay, "Literature as Context," is only apparently bland. In fact, it indicates a specific and polemical critical position: Frye is beginning to insist that regarding an entire body of Literature as relevant Context is the condition of possibility for reading any individual literary work.

In 1951, as part of a symposium entitled "My Credo," Frye had published an essay on "The Archetypes of Literature" in *The Kenyon Review* (it later became the first essay in *Fables of Identity*). Eight years later, in "Literature as Context: Milton's *Lycidas*," the term "archetype" enters the writings on Milton and Blake for the first time, and Frye takes the opportunity to provide a definition: "By an archetype I mean a literary symbol, or cluster of symbols, which is used recurrently throughout literature, and thereby becomes conventional" (25). After an *explication de texte* of *Lycidas* in the literary-historical context of the pastoral elegy as a genre, Frye moves on to his more original and more passionate concern: the "framework of ideas" or "framework of images" into which Milton's poem needs to be inserted, which Frye describes as a spiritual universe comprising four levels of existence. The "framework of ideas" is a creative principle "for which there is no name" (28)—unlike the more straightforward creative principles of convention, genre, and archetype or symbol—but whose most important feature is the autonomy of literature as an order of images and ideas, independent of biographical, historical, or material concerns. The move beyond a purely historical framework accounts for the difference between a (literary) elegy such as Milton is writing on the occasion of the death of his friend, and a (non-literary) obituary: "he does not start with Edward King and his life and times, but with the conventions and archetypes that poetry requires for such a theme" (28). Later in the essay, Frye repeatedly raises historical-biographical questions such as "Who was Edward King? What was his relation to Milton? How good a poet was he?" (29)—or, How sincere was Milton in grieving over King's death? and What does the poem say about Milton's own fear of death?—but only in order to banish these questions to what Shelley would call the "intense inane." They obscure the framework of ideas that is crucial to the human creation of meaning out of experience, a framework that is most obviously expressed in literature and art.

Near the end of the essay, Frye goes further, relegating both biographical and traditional literary-historical concerns ("the place of *Lycidas* in Milton's development; its place in the history of English poetry; its place in seventeenth-century thought or history," the "jangle of echoes from other poets") to "secondary and derivative" status, and preferring instead the unified and unifying context of literature as an order of words (32–3). Finally, he introduces the term "myth" as a "short, simple, and accurate name" for the "recurring structural principle" by which every new work reshapes inherited patterns of narrative, images, conventions, and topoi (32).

As important as the definitions of myth, archetype, and the framework of ideas are to Frye's developing anatomy of criticism, he is also engaged in reminding historical-biographical critics of some Classical principles of literary criticism. This includes the independence of literature from "personal sincerity" (30). Grief, in a literary elegy, is not inarticulate, private grief, but rather "idealized" grief, as Aristotle wrote and as many of the Romantics later repeated in their own terms. "The pretence of personal sincerity is itself a literary convention"—or, as poststructuralist criticism would say, a trope. Moreover, the trope of sincerity is one that happens to be particularly distinctive of Romantic poetry; hence Frye brings forward an example from Wordsworth's Lucy poems to set alongside Milton's *Lycidas*.

In his work on Milton, Frye distinguishes between the "revolutionary" artist—who invents new paradigms—and the "conservative" artist—who makes use of inherited forms and concentrates on perfecting them. Milton belongs in the "revolutionary" category, according to this aesthetic definition as well as in political and religious terms. Frye's tendency to think of artists as either ground-breakers or form-perfecters—both "heroes" of a sort—is of a piece with his focus on heroism in the epic and other literary genres. With major essays devoted to *Lycidas, Paradise Lost, Paradise Regained*, and *Samson Agonistes*, substantial discussion of *Comus* in the 1969 essay "The Revelation to Eve" (no. 4), and wide-ranging references to Milton's shorter English and Latin poetry as well as the whole range of his political and religious prose, Frye provides an expansive interpretation of Milton's corpus. Whatever else they do, virtually all of Frye's writings on Milton consider how Milton's Christian epics and tragedy revise Classical models of heroism, relegating the latter to objects of parody. In his revolutionary versions of heroic and tragic action, Milton adapts and reworks Aristotelian categories so as to apply them to a revolutionary Christian scheme of history.

Frye's Milton, then, is a heroic Milton. The fullness of his career distinguishes him from the stereotypical Romantic hero who burns himself out by striving beyond the bounds of everyday experience—and yet Milton still emerges, in some ways, as a precursor of Romanticism. As Frye writes at the end of "The Revelation to Eve," "the revolutionary emphasis in Milton shows how near he is to the mythology of Romanticism and its later by-products, the revolutionary erotic, Promethean, and Dionysian myths of Freud, Marx, and Nietzsche" (154). More generally, after a thirteen-year agon writing *Fearful Symmetry*, Frye often understands and describes the poetry of both Milton and Blake in terms he has learned from Blake himself. Indeed, in the first of the writings on Blake collected here, a review dating from the year *Fearful Symmetry* was published, Frye politely dismisses the attitude of the "grave and thoughtful" professional critic, countering that "the best way to approach Blake is to surrender unconditionally to Blake's own terms" (187).

All of the twenty-three writings on Blake collected in the present volume post-date *Fearful Symmetry*. They represent Frye's elaboration of his ideas about Blake and his universe of the imagination for a wide variety of audiences, as well as his contributions to the role an established Blake scholar is asked to undertake in the writing of reviews, introductions, and encyclopedia entries. Throughout these writings, Frye is steeped in Blake's language and ideas: his ability to range over Milton's entire corpus when writing about any one work is outdone only by his familiarity with all of Blake's writing, which he quotes and echoes relentlessly. Except for block quotations, Frye usually does not provide references; these have been added in the present edition, in the hope that they will give a sense of the completeness of Frye's engagement with Blake's work, shown by the way he pays equally serious attention to Blake's short lyrics and his long Prophecies, his illuminated works and his fragmentary manuscripts, his artwork and his marginalia, his attempted addresses to the public and his private letters, his earnest art criticism and his often outrageous satire.

Not only is Frye immersed in Blake's language, but he is on close terms with the world of Blake scholarship. Unlike the Milton essays, several of the pieces on Blake collected here are book reviews or review articles. While Frye is, on the whole, complimentary about the achievements of fellow Blake critics such as Mark Schorer, J.G. Davies, and especially David V. Erdman, in some reviews of mid-twentieth-century Blake books he sets himself in opposition to the post-World War II tendency of critics to read Blake in the context of social questions. Frye stakes out a contrasting position, identifying himself with "the claim, advanced by many artists since the Romantic period at least, that the arts represent an autonomous and authoritative prophetic tradition which is as significant for religion as for culture" (185). Though presented here as the property of artists and the legacy of Romanticism, this claim for the autonomy of art represents Frye's own view pretty well, and foreshadows some recurring themes in his writings on Blake. First, he insists on Blake's sanity, even when many modern critics are still repeating, in different forms, the charges of Blake's own contemporaries that he was mad (and therefore unreliable and inconsistent). Second, there is a strong, articulated structure to the mythology of Blake's Prophecies, which has been recognized by the pioneering Blake critic S. Foster Damon and Frye himself, but not by most other critics. Third, Blake and Frye are in the line of those who believe that art has a prophetic authority of its own, though many critics try to assimilate the artist to social critique or political systems. Fourth, Blake needs to be read on his own terms.

In his reviews, Frye's own priorities in Blake scholarship come to the fore: he is interested in Blake's symbolism, his relation to the tradition of English literature and philosophy, and his social and ethical views—but only if these are recognized as inseparable from his views on art. When he finds these priorities, Frye praises, and when he finds them missing, he critiques their omission. Thus, he praises Bernard Blackstone for "expounding Blake and speaking from Blake's point of view," and adds that "he quotes very well" (210). Interestingly, however—and in contrast to his critique of Milton scholars for their obsession with historical detail—Frye writes a very favourable review for *Philological Quarterly* of David V. Erdman's *Blake: Prophet against Empire: A Poet's Interpretation of the History of His Own Times* (no. 14). Though Erdman's detailed delineation of historical references and contexts throughout Blake's poetry seems light-years from Frye's symbolic interpretations, the two are in sympathy in treating Blake seriously and reading him painstakingly, and Frye accordingly praises Erdman for providing the first accurate and detailed account of Blake's "historical allegory" based on primary-source research. In a similar vein, Frye praises Bernard Blackstone's *English Blake* for elucidating the background to Blake's early, satirical work, *An Island in the Moon*, which Blackstone called "an important social document" and "an outstanding success on many counts."[2] Frye, too, was among the first to call attention to *An Island in the Moon*, and take it seriously as part of Blake's intellectual development, while appreciating its biting humour.

Frye uses the satirical *Island in the Moon*, among other things, to make a point about Blake's attempted interventions in methods of artistic production and in the late-eighteenth-century economic system of patrons, commercial publishers, and creative artists. In addressing these issues, for instance in the 1951 essay "Poetry and Design in William Blake" (no. 12), Frye was ahead of the scholarly "Blake industry," which only began to give sustained consideration to such topics with the work of W.J.T. Mitchell, Morris Eaves, and Robert Essick in the 1980s. Frye's own *Fearful Symmetry* had not included extensive discussion of Blake's visual art either. But he makes up for it in some of his essays, where—perhaps through the influence of his wife Helen, an art historian—he pays more attention to Blake as an artist than was usual for Blake criticism at the time. "For one reason or another, many literary students of Blake have only the vaguest notion of what sort of pictorial basis underlies his poetry," Frye writes in his 1951 article (220). As he points out, one major reason for this ignorance is that, in the mid-twentieth century, no satisfactory reproductions of most of Blake's illuminated books were available to the general reader. In the essay, Frye gives equal weight to Blake's artistic achievement and the textual dimension of his work, and seriously addresses the relationship of image to text as it evolved over the course of Blake's career. He remarks on the effects of illustration on poetic form, as well as vice versa, noting the simultaneity and the interpenetration of Blake's composition of images with his composition of text. For Frye, the unity of art forms in Blake contributes to the vision of a "City of Art" that turns out to be an essential component of the apocalyptic level of imagery in Blake and in the Bible. It becomes clear in the "Poetry and Design" essay how important the awareness of Blake's visual art is to Frye, for Blake's graphic images provide a great deal of the evidence for the complex, yet ordered and Biblically-derived, mythological background that Frye discovers in Blake and, beyond him, in Western art and literature.

Later in his life, in the early 1980s, Frye gave two public lectures on Blake's art at the Art Gallery of Ontario. The outline for the first of these, consisting of extensive notes for a slide lecture on Blake's *Jerusalem*, is reprinted in volume 10 of the Collected Works (*Northrop Frye on Literature and Society, 1936–1989: Unpublished Papers*). The lecture, presented on 26 November 1981, covered all one hundred colour plates of *Jerusalem*; while Frye reads the images, they are necessarily, in such a synoptic overview, presented as a very rapid visual commentary on Frye's interpretation of Blake's myth. In the lecture on "Blake's Biblical Illustrations," presented on 4 February 1983 (no. 28 in the present volume), it is even more obvious that Frye is re-emphasizing the verbal in relation to the visual. "All Blake's pictorial work," he now writes, "was closely associated with books: nothing of real importance that he produced is wholly independent of some kind of verbal context." Now that Blake has become much more generally recognized as an artist than he was a generation earlier, Frye interestingly reveals how primary and enduring his own verbal orientation is, commenting, "I should imagine that a film version of a favourite novel, or even a performance of a favourite play, seldom permanently displaces the inner vision of it for most people" (403).

During the 1960s, Frye's publications and presentations on Blake all derived from the fundamental understanding of the poet that crystallized in *Fearful Symmetry*, as a radical ethical reformer dedicated to the centrality of art and imagination—these being forces that can counter the effects of restrictive rationalism, oppressive morality, and man's inhumanity to man. Themes that recur as Frye presents Blake to different audiences are Blake's recognition of the powerful psychological drives fueling war, power, and artistic creation, which in Blake's mythological universe are identified with Orc, Urizen, and Los, respectively; prophecy and art as visions of human freedom; the four levels of existence that Frye also finds in the poetry of Milton; and Blake's Biblically derived symbolism. As in his writings on Milton, Frye ascribes a striking degree of unity to the poet's entire corpus. For Blake, whose late, seemingly impenetrable prophetic books seem worlds apart from his early lyrics, this represents a particularly polemical approach. In the 1957 article "Blake's Introduction to Experience" (no. 18), Frye reads the lyrical *Introduction* to *Songs of Experience* entirely in light of the prophetic books—despite a preamble in which he points out that this is not the only way to read the poem, and that Blake's lyrics should be appreciated apart from his Prophecies. In a radio talk recorded for the BBC Open University in 1971 (no. 26), Frye begins with Blake's most accessible *Songs*, but leads his listeners onward from there into the most challenging and obscure of his unfinished Prophecies, *The Four Zoas*.

Frye's vision of Blake's work as a synchronic and systematic framework of ideas is particularly evident in two essays published in the mid-1960s. "The Keys to the Gates," published in 1966 (no. 22), is a difficult and daring study. In a journal-length article, Frye incorporates readings from all parts of the Blakean corpus, including dense passages from the prophetic books, obscure Notebook poems, and sets of illustrations together with their captions. He pays particular attention to *The Mental Traveller*, an enigmatic ballad-like poem from the so-called Pickering manuscript of Blake. "The Keys to the Gates" is also the one essay in which Frye clearly retains Blake's idiosyncratic punctuation when quoting from the prophetic books, probably at the instigation of Erdman's new edition of Blake's poetry and prose, which appeared for the first time as Frye was writing his essay. All this evidence allows Frye, with the help of arrows and diagrams, to present Blake's thought in terms of four "gates" and the "fourfold vision" that inspired him. Frye locates Blake within a vision of the imaginative universe that is present all at once in the mind. This eternal vision is itself the subject of the near-contemporaneous essay "The Road of Excess" (no. 20), which contrasts linear structures in literature with static or timeless ones.

Both "The Road of Excess" and "The Keys to the Gates" also contain some very strong statements about the cohesion (though not the identity) of creation and criticism—as well as, Frye tellingly adds, the continuity of both of these activities with teaching. "The main work of criticism is teaching, and teaching for Blake cannot be separated from creation," Frye writes in 1963 (317). In "The Keys to the Gates," Frye looks back to the process of writing *Fearful Symmetry* and evaluates its place in his own critical path: "I finished my book in the full conviction that learning to read Blake was a step, and for me a necessary step, in learning to read poetry, and to write criticism. For if poetic thought is inherently schematic, criticism must be so too" (338). In the 1969 essay "Blake's Reading of the Book of Job" (no. 25), Frye describes Blake's illustrations to the Book of Job as a creative endeavour, but equally an act of reading and criticism. It is clear that he sees himself as participating with Blake in the elucidation of Biblical myth and the process of making it relevant to the critic's or artist's own time. All of this indicates that Frye is rapidly moving onward to the framework of myth and imagery presented in *The Great Code* and *Words with Power*—a framework that is not only derived from the study of Blake and Milton, nor only an instrument for understanding their work, but that represents Frye's collaborative effort with the great poets in a vision and a critique of culture. By the time of his lecture at the Art Gallery of Ontario in 1983, Frye is talking as much about the great code of Western myth and symbolism as he is about the specifics of Blake's poetry and painting, and Blake and Frye stand together as modern rediscoverers of this framework:

> Blake was the first poet in English literature, and so far as I know the first person in the modern world, to realize that the traditional authoritarian cosmos had had it, that it no longer appealed to the intelligence or the imagination, and would have to be replaced by another model. Blake gave us a complete outline of such a model, but unfortunately nobody knew that he had done so, and one has to read thousands of pages of poetry and philosophy since his time to pick up bits and pieces of his insight. (410)

From the time of Frye's earliest writings on Blake, he notes that Blake (like Milton) lived in the real world, and that he belongs to the world beyond academe: "Much of Blake's poetry is for the common reader, and will not mislead him" (231). Several of the pieces on Blake in this volume are public lectures or radio talks for the educated lay listener—although the popular orientation does not diminish the effect that Frye's work had on Blake scholarship, and on the shape of the field of Romanticism. In his 1953 Introduction to *Selected Poetry and Prose of William Blake* (no. 13), Frye took the lead in locating Blake in the so-called "Age of Sensibility," thus distinguishing him from both the Augustan eighteenth century, and the High Romantic period—a critical re-evaluation that would be carried on in the work of Harold Bloom, among others. In the essays written during the 1960s, though, Frye emphasizes the characteristics Blake's poetry shares with that of the Romantics, including the later generation of Shelley and Keats. "Blake was the first and the most radical of the Romantics who identified the creative imagination of the poet with the creative power of God," Frye writes in "The Road of Excess" (327); his lyrics "can be used as a key to Romanticism" (334), since "what Blake did was closely related to the Romantic movement" (328). These are rather moderate statements, given that Frye himself was largely responsible for introducing Blake into the Romantic canon as the sixth of the male poets who constituted that canon for a generation after *Fearful Symmetry*. An equally important result of Frye's work on Blake was the growing effort to take the Blakean corpus seriously—in all its diversity and idiosyncracy—and to apply the same critical principles and standards to it as to the work of other poets and artists. "Blake criticism today is moving ahead rapidly after a very slow start; new editions, bibliographies, reproductions of the illuminated books, are providing the apparatus his students need," Frye writes in the Introduction to a book of critical essays on Blake in 1966 (331). He modestly makes no mention of *Fearful Symmetry*, a major factor in "providing the apparatus" and stimulating the rapid developments that by the 1960s made the field of Blake studies a criticism on the move.

In his last public lecture on Blake, presented in 1987 for the Blake Society at St. James in London, England, Frye is emphatic about Blake's achievement in the context of Western mythology:

> To have turned a metaphorical cosmos eighteen centuries old upside down in a few poems, and provided the basis for a structure that practically every major thinker for the next century would build on, was one of the most colossal imaginative feats in the history of human culture. The only draw-

> back, of course, was that no one knew Blake had done it: in fact Blake hardly realized he had done it either. (427)

Clearly, Frye realized it, and for most of his life he strove to awaken the insight in others. Looking into the indefinite future—and, as it turned out, beyond his death in 1991—Frye stressed again the immediacy and relevance of Blake's vision for the contemporary world: "And whatever the cultural interests of the year 2000 may be, it will be discovered in that year that Blake had them particularly in mind, and wrote his poems primarily to illustrate them" (336).

To an extent, this has proven true. Blake has been regarded by recent critics as "illustrating" tenets of psychoanalysis, Eastern religion, New Age thought, deconstruction, gender relations, performativity, and identity politics. At the same time, a difference has come into Blake criticism since Frye's time that he did not anticipate, or at least did not articulate. While a large number of Blake critics are still drawn into Blake's point of view—a basic sympathy with it almost seems a prerequisite for entering the challenging field of Blake studies—it is much less usual now to find critics speaking as thoroughly from Blake's perspective and from within his world as Frye did. A more sceptical spirit generally prevails. Ironically, this can make access to Frye's writing on Blake difficult for students of Blake today. One almost needs to be as thoroughly located within Blake's world as Frye was in order to understand what he is telling us about it—even if the work of Frye was the necessary underpinning that has brought the understanding of Blake's work to the point it has reached today.

Other critical perspectives have shifted as well. The discipline of comparative literature, which once would have been entirely in sympathy with Frye's treatment of literature as a universal system, is now more inclined to stress diversity, difference, and regionalism—even if it needed to come to the recognition of fundamental structures and archetypes before passing beyond them to an awareness of the different ways literary systems develop within different cultures. And historical criticism, against which Frye in his time needed to assert the concerns of an autonomous critical framework, has since re-asserted itself in a different, new-historical form in both Early Modern and Romantic scholarship. Against a post-structuralism that seemed to have become too abstract and irrelevant to real-world considerations of culture, class, identity, and gender, new historicism has sought to re-evaluate the position of writing and reading subjects. But in Frye's writings on Milton and Blake, as in the rest of his work, his genuine commitment to the human condition, to the issues confronting contemporary society, and to students as well as to nonacademic audiences, should be clear, if anything is. As he writes of the advice Adam receives from the angel Raphael in *Paradise Lost*, the "essential knowledge" needed in the human world "should be human-centred, practical, engaged knowledge" (73). That, in these writings, is what Frye provides. To paraphrase, finally, what he wrote about Blake in 1947: "if one quality in Frye is clear it is his honesty, and honest critics do not let their readers down" (188).

William Blake, *The Archangel Raphael with Adam and Eve* (*Illustration to Milton's "Paradise Lost"*), 1808.

Essays on Milton

1

Introduction to *"Paradise Lost" and Selected Poetry and Prose*

June 1950

Introduction to John Milton's "Paradise Lost" and Selected Poetry and Prose, *ed. Northrop Frye (New York: Holt, Rinehart and Winston, 1951), v–xxxvi. Frye gives the date of this introduction as June 1950.*

I Early Poetry, 1629–1640

The first poem of Milton's to show major genius, the poem generally called the *Nativity Ode,* was written during the Christmas season of 1629. Not many of us can have much idea of what it would feel like to have such a poem as that tearing itself loose from one's brain at the age of twenty-one. The shock of its emergence is recorded in a Latin poem, later known as the *Sixth Elegy,* which Milton sent to his friend Charles Diodati at that time. In this poem Milton says that the major poet must think of himself as a priest of poetry, "making augury before the wrathful gods." For "the bard (*vates*) is sacred to the gods; he is their priest; from both his hidden heart and his lips he breathes Jove."[1]

The poet's images are derived from human life, but the major poet must also use those human symbols to convey to man some inkling of the eternal worlds beyond human knowledge, "singing now the holy counsels of the gods above, and now the deep regions where the fierce dog (Cerberus) barks,"[2] to quote again from the *Sixth Elegy.* He must use all the resources of human wisdom and sensibility, but in doing so he will show how limited and finite the human perspective is. If the poet is an "augur," he must bend every effort of imagination and will to formulate the questions in which human experience ends. And when he has done all he can, he may, in those moments of involuntary inspiration that the poet can do nothing but wait for, get some of the answers.

The *Sixth Elegy* uses Classical imagery, and therefore speaks of priests and oracles. But Milton was a Christian, and for him the Christian poet follows the track of the Hebrew prophets and the Christian apostles, whose work was based on the belief in a "Word of God," a verbal revelation from God to man. Milton pictures God as surrounded by tense and waiting angels, listening constantly for messages. It is this sense of the dedication of his genius that gives Milton's poetry its deep impersonality and reserve. For his rare love poems, even for his more intimate touches of personal feeling, he seeks the shelter of Latin or Italian. His poetry is rarely inspired by his personal moods; it is usually a response to a definite occasion. A friend dies, and Milton writes an elegy; Christmas comes and he writes a *Nativity Ode*; he is asked for a masque, and he produces *Comus*; the sonnets are nearly all comments on events, personal or political.

The commonest type of occasion, up to 1640, is a death. Almost any death will do: "a fair infant dying of a cough," the university beadle, the Vice-Chancellor, are all metrically commemorated. Two great funeral poems, the English *Lycidas* and the Latin *Epitaphium Damonis*, mark the end of the early poetry. It is not hard to understand Milton's preference for elegiac subjects. Death marks the limit of knowledge as well as life: the first question that man asks at the oracle of the gods is about death. The answer that comes from the Christian oracle, the vision of resurrection and immortality, is implied or expressed at the end of all Milton's elegies. The funeral elegy, then, is for Milton one of the most concentrated forms of poetry, as it brings the human and the divine worlds into direct alignment. The relation between them must still be expressed in human imagery, however, and the traditional symbol of the mystery of death and resurrection is the cycle of nature, the daily victory of dawn over night, the annual victory of spring over winter.

Thus the hero of *Lycidas* is not so much Milton's friend Edward King as a larger being, what in paganism would be called a god, who personifies both the sun that falls into the western ocean at night and the vegetable life that dies in the autumn. In this latter aspect Lycidas is the Adonis or Tammuz whose "annual wound," as Milton calls it elsewhere [*PL*, 1.447], was the subject of a ritual lament in Mediterranean religion. Out of the lament for Adonis there developed the convention of the pastoral elegy, the lament for the death of a friend symbolized by the passing of summer. Milton's approach to his subject commits him to the use of this convention. As a poet, Lycidas is similarly linked with Orpheus, who also died young and was flung into the water, and as priest, with Peter, who would have drowned on the "Galilean lake" [*Lycidas*, l. 109] without the help of Christ. Each aspect of Lycidas poses the question of premature death as it relates to the life of man, of poetry, and of the church. The central theme and its two episodes (often absurdly called "digressions") are all contained in the figure of Christ, the young dying god who is eternally alive, the Word that contains all poetry, the head and body of the church, the Good Shepherd whose pastoral world sees no winter, the Sun of righteousness that never sets, and whose power can raise Lycidas, like Peter, out of the waves. Christ does not enter the poem as a character, but he pervades every line of it, supplying the continuous answer of revelation to the repeated questions of ignorance. And so, although Lycidas becomes the "Genius of the shore" [l. 183], a deified nature spirit like those in pagan mythology, that, for Milton, is only a minor function of what Lycidas has really become, a Christian angel, a member of those "solemn troops, and sweet Societies" [l. 179] who are in a world lifted clear of the wheel of time.

It is not only in the elegiac poems that the contrasts of night and day, and of winter and summer, represent the contrast between the human world that ends in death and the world of eternal life beyond it. The crucial importance of this symbolism meets us everywhere in Milton's poetry. His nephew even tells us, whatever significance it may have, that "his vein never happily flowed but from the autumnal equinoctial to the vernal."[3] In the *Nativity Ode*, for instance, the barren frozen world of the winter solstice, with the steady advance of the long nights haunted by the sinister and gloomy gods that man has made in his own image, is our own world, the darkness that does not comprehend the new light. The world of Moloch and Osiris is also the world of Comus, the master of illusion, whose habitat is in the night and the forest, and whose power over the Lady is broken by the nymph of the Severn River, as spring rains release life from the paralysis of winter.

But *Comus* presents a moral problem as well: it is the first of Milton's four great temptation poems. The whole of nature, the whole "fallen" world that man lives in, is the real domain of Comus, and of the false gods of the *Nativity Ode* as well; spring as well as winter, day as well as night. The natural images of dawn and spring in Milton's poetry represent something much larger than themselves: they represent the passing from the world of the temporal alternation of seasons to a world of perpetual spring. This latter is the paradisal world or "Gardens of Adonis" to which the Attendant Spirit who watches over the Lady belongs. Comus tempts the Lady's chastity with "natural" arguments: he seems to represent the free abandon of nature in contrast to the Lady's starched and sterile prurience. But the apparent situation is the opposite of the real one. The Lady's chastity is the condition of life on the upper or spiritual level: it enables one to possess the joy and freedom that will satisfy a conscious being. Comus is preaching passion, and at the core of passion lies passivity, the helpless servitude to desire that we see at the end of all lust. All passions are ruling passions, and their rule is tyranny. The conflict of the dancing Comus and the frozen Lady is the same paradoxical conflict that we get later in *Paradise Regained*. The tempter attracts all our attention and most of our sympathy because he is constantly in action, but the goal of his activity is death, and to find the principle of real energy we must turn to the motionless figure in the centre.

We have moralized on *Comus* because it shows that the ignorance and confusion of human life is, in terms of action, slavery and bondage. It is not only enlightenment that man wants from the gods, but emancipation. For Milton the capacity to emancipate man is what distinguishes Christianity. The pagans had seen clearly that man is, in Christian terms, "fallen," bound by his human nature to the state of nature, which is a state of tyranny. But they had seen only the contrast, along with the irony and tragedy which that contrast suggests. "The gods alone are free," Homer says.[4] The New Testament on the contrary insists that God wills this freedom for man as well as for himself. Thus the Christian poet, who breathes Christ rather than Jove, will, if society is relatively secure and at peace, devote himself to making poems out of the Christian vision of life; but, if society is in crisis, he will turn to prose and fight for liberty.

II Prose and Controversy, 1640–1660

After 1640, then, Milton turned to controversial prose, and to working out the conception of liberty which was the central theme of his prose. In a later pamphlet he divides liberty into three categories: religious, involving the question of church government; domestic, relating to private life; and civil, relating to public life. But liberty for him, in contrast with the Romantic poets, does not begin with man; it begins with God. God wills liberty for man, and if man submits himself to God he gains liberty, which means that "none can love freedom heartilie, but good men; the rest love not freedom, but licence."[5] The instrument of God's revelation to man is a book, the Bible or Word of God, and the messengers or prophets of God will normally be people with special capacities for handling words. But in the attaining of human liberty, God is the only free agent. Man can do nothing directly to achieve his own freedom: what he can do is to indicate his willingness to be set free by knocking down his idols, and so allow the Word of God to circulate freely in human society. The prophet is not a Utopian or a social planner, but an iconoclast, a breaker of the false images that man worships.

One obvious place to look for these images is in the Christian church itself, and Milton's first issue is an ecclesiastical one. For Milton, the church is a community in which all the members are made free and equal by their faith. In such a community the only authority is spiritual, and spiritual authority, the reverence aroused by sanctity, has, in contrast to temporal authority, no power to coerce, and cannot take the form of an institutional hierarchy, as sanctity cannot be delegated. When the principle of temporal authority enters the church, the church is being made a worldly institution. Such a corruption set in when the purely spiritual authority of the apostles was replaced by a hierarchy of bishops, Christians with temporal authority over other Christians. With such arguments as these Milton defends the Puritan system of church government against the Anglican one. The logical end of the episcopal system, Milton says, is the Papacy, and Milton thinks of the Papacy as the chief obstacle to Christian liberty within Christianity, the autonomous church which has, so to speak, swallowed the Word of God by claiming the monopoly of interpreting it. On the other hand, Milton was not a Bibliolater: the revelation of God to man does not remain in the Bible, but passes through it. The Holy Spirit builds up from it a structure of wisdom and energy in the human mind which does not override the intelligence and will already there, but emancipates and fulfils them.

For Milton the church's whole duty is to study the Bible and recognize its spiritual authority. And the Bible must be interpreted by what Milton terms the "rule of charity."[6] The Bible is designed to free man from a state of slavery, and therefore any passage in it which seems to confirm or approve the bondage of man has not been rightly understood. Churches pervaded by temporal authority could, from Milton's point of view, hardly avoid uncharitable conceptions of Scripture, and Milton found a crucial example of such an uncharitable conception in the ecclesiastical view of marriage and divorce. Milton's unfortunate first marriage may have awakened, as it certainly embittered, his interest in this subject; but it is hard to see how he could have avoided writing about the one conspicuous case in which a passage from the Gospels has been made the basis of common law.

The argument of the divorce pamphlets is, briefly: Moses allowed for divorce in the marriage law; Jesus declared marriage to be indissoluble. But Jesus' words form part of the gospel, and thus relate, not to the law of marriage, which remains unchanged, but to marriage as God sees it in relation to the free life of man: a lifetime companionship which can be "consummated," which means finished, only by the death of one of the partners. Marriage as Jesus sees it is like the innocent love of Adam and Eve before the fall, for each of whom there was, very literally, no one else. The *law* of marriage relates only to a sexual union in the fallen world, and divorce must always be a part of marriage law. For if a divorce is necessary, the gospel marriage, the lifetime companionship, is simply not there, and man can always put asunder what God has never joined together in the first place. Milton is thus not preferring the law to the gospel; he is attacking the Christian Pharisaism that makes a new law out of the gospel.

The effect of this argument is to separate still more widely the spheres of spiritual and temporal authority. The church which, by a legalistic interpretation of the gospel, perverts a reasonable law into a superstitious taboo is revealed as a force making for tyranny within the state. The next step is to redefine the two spheres so as to show that, as there is a temporal church, so there may be spiritual authority outside the church. In *Areopagitica* the conception of spiritual authority bursts out of the church and overflows into fields that the church itself usually calls "worldly." Prophets and apostles spoke in the marketplace and the court, and their descendants today may be writers of books as well as preachers. *Areopagitica* is an attack on censorship of books before publication in which Milton explains that the censor of the creative process, like the bishop and the indissoluble marriage contract, stands for the perversion of the spiritual power that frees into the temporal power that compels. The censor is the agent of the bondage of the moral law; his function is to ensure that man will hear only what he already knows. This means that he will never hear the revelation of God, which is always foreign to man's nature in every age, and always sounds disturbingly new and dangerous.

So far Milton had not committed himself on the subject of temporal authority. In fact, he never developed a positive theory of temporal government, and his political views were shaped largely by the course of events. After the execution of King Charles and the "purging" of the Long Parliament, Milton stepped forward in defence of "civil liberty," as a spokesman for the Cromwellian party; but what he defended was the regicide itself rather than the form of government established after it took place.

Nevertheless, Milton did claim to speak for the republic and the English people against the tyranny of Charles, and so he was forced to include a rudimentary theory of contract resembling the one later developed by Locke. The king, he says, is responsible to the people for his authority, and may be removed if he is irresponsible. But Milton is uneasy with this argument: "people," for him, are mostly unregenerate men who prefer tyranny to freedom anyway. It is the people of God, the free and equal society of believers, with whom temporal authority must come to terms. From a Christian point of view, tyranny is essentially a violation of Christian conscience, an attempt on the part of Caesar to seize the tribute that belongs to God. A monarchy is particularly vulnerable to this form of tyranny, because the reverence paid to the king is apt to turn him into another human idol. The more his power is withdrawn from the Christian community, the more likely this is to happen. There is thus a kind of revolutionary dynamic within the church itself that first neutralizes the anti-Christian tendencies in temporal power, and then forces temporal power to fall in line with its own pattern of a free society. For a brief moment Milton felt that the reformed Church of England was beginning to assimilate the English nation to this pattern.

Milton's objections to monarchy apply with even greater force to dictatorship; but the "judges" of the Bible indicate that a strong man may be useful in guiding an ignorant and confused populace past the initial crises of a bid for freedom. Milton accepted the Cromwellian regime as a temporary measure, with many qualifications and warnings. After Cromwell's death, he proposed that the power of holding the new republic together should be entrusted to a permanent senate, a sort of reconstituted Long Parliament. He thus never arrived at what we should now consider a liberal or democratic position, partly because, being in a revolutionary situation, he was trying to see what would fit that situation, not what would be on paper the best form of government.

From one point of view, Milton's political theories seem to be a series of helpless rationalizations of every major change that occurred, until he was finally checkmated by the Restoration. He certainly illustrates the plight of the liberal intellectual who sees in every revolution an apocalyptic struggle of tyranny and freedom and finds it so hard to understand that revolution is a technique of transferring power from one class to another. The Restoration was a perfectly logical way of showing that the wealthy and powerful class which had risen in revolt against Charles I had achieved its ends. Charles II, though he did not have as great a mind as Milton, understood that very well. But to Milton the Restoration was the deliberate refusal of the freedom which God had offered "first to his English-men."[7] The people who had had the chance of becoming a second Israel, a people chosen for the gospel instead of the law, had preferred "a captain back for Egypt,"[8] and had turned again to rolling up the same old Sisyphus stone of human history.

There is clearly a certain unreality in Milton's application of his vision to England, and it is the long-range values in his political writing that are important to us: those moments in which he looks over the head of the immediate situation to a greater vision beyond it. He saw that the only permanent support on which man can rely for preserving his freedom is education. As there can be no freedom without social responsibility and discipline, the students in Milton's treatise *Of Education* are conceived as a potential ruling class. Their education is based on the pattern which the Renaissance humanists, whom Milton is following, had derived from the great Classical writers. For the humanist, if a man wished to understand literary style, he read Cicero and Quintilian; if medicine, Hippocrates and Galen; if architecture, Vitruvius; if agriculture, Columella and Varro, and so on. There had been an end to the making of Classical books, and it was possible for a single diligent student to attain a considerable grasp of what had survived from that era. Thus the humanist ideal was encyclopedic, designed to give one a comprehensive grasp of human knowledge. The keystone of all this learning was for Milton the Bible, the end of education being "to repair the ruines of our first Parents by regaining to know God aright."[9]

The assumption in *Of Education* is that the freedom which education brings makes the individual responsible to society. The end of human learning is not a selfish or parasitic "culture," but a knowledge of social and moral questions; the end of religious learning is not contemplation but prophecy, teaching others how it is God's will that they should be free. *Areopagitica* makes the complementary assumption: that the individuals who have been made free by liberal education and Christian liberty, and are trying to free others, constitute the only freedom that society has. In the foreground of Milton's social thought, therefore, is an intellectual elite of Christian humanists, including himself, the agents of spiritual authority. But in the background is his great vision of the free nation which is the fulfilment of their work, absorbed in the serene excitement of civilized life even with an enemy at its gates, disputing of the highest and deepest secrets of religion, culture, and politics. As he says more plainly in a later pamphlet, all such words as "heretic" or "blasphemer," which mean very little except that some human mind is determined to impose its own limitations on the infinite mind of God, will soon become obsolete if people will only use the talents and the birthright that have been given them.

III The Final Period, 1660–1674

In an enlightened age like ours, a politically active poet could not possibly survive four revolutions. And there are many today who would admire Milton more if he had been executed in 1660. We should then have seen him as a man who, after showing that he could write poetry better than anyone else, walked contemptuously off into prose and died a martyr to the cause of real life. However, he was allowed to finish his work and die in his bed. As a result, though he still remains our greatest revolutionary genius, both in the content and in the form of his work, we can also see a more traditional strain in him, as we watch his life moving toward a final statement of everything he had to say.

It was an axiom of Renaissance criticism that, as there were major poets, so there were major poetic forms, in which alone a major poet's genius could find adequate expression. There was also general agreement that there were two such major forms, epic and tragedy. Milton had stated this doctrine as early as 1642, except that he divides the epic into two species: the "diffuse," the full-dress epic in twelve books, or some multiple of twelve, of which Homer and Virgil are the models, and the "brief," the model of which Milton cites as the Book of Job.[10] The models of tragedy for Milton are also Biblical as well as Classical. The close correspondence of this threefold scheme with the forms of *Paradise Lost*, *Paradise Regained*, and *Samson Agonistes*, respectively, produced so many years later, is a good illustration of the consistency of Milton's thinking. Around 1640, apparently, Milton thought that his "diffuse" epic would be, like Spenser's *Faerie Queene*, a patriotic epic with the legendary Arthur as its hero. He seems to have considered the theme of *Paradise Lost* at first as a possible subject for tragedy, and presumably it was his political disillusionment that pushed into the more conspicuous place of the diffuse epic the story of how man lost his liberty, and how he still resists all God's efforts to give it back to him. Similarly his tragedy of Samson is a grimly ironic comment on the great passage in *Areopagitica* which speaks of England as a "Nation rousing herself like a strong man after sleep, and shaking her invincible locks" [*Works,* 4:344].

Most Renaissance critics regarded the epic as a greater form than tragedy: this fact is to be connected with the humanist sense already referred to of the encyclopedic range of knowledge to be derived from the study of the Classics. For the difference between an epic and an ordinary narrative poem lies chiefly in the encyclopedic quality of the epic. The epics of Homer, Virgil, Dante, and Milton are vast syntheses of religious, philosophical, political, and even scientific ideas: they integrate not only the poet's own thinking, but the whole culture of their times. An epic of this sort can only be written in an age which possesses some kind of encyclopedic vision. For Milton, the humanist synthesis of knowledge was in its turn contained within Christianity. The Bible, as Milton saw it, transcends all secular knowledge, but comprehends it too, and is also encyclopedic, though on a far bigger scale. It begins where time begins, at the creation; it ends where time ends, in the apocalypse; and it surveys the entire life of man between these two points. Yet these two points are at the same point in the eternity of God, and thus time goes in a circle, proceeding from God and returning to him.

This last point indicates that the Bible is in form not only encyclopedic but cyclic, and the same cyclic movement is to be found in the great epics as well. The total action of the *Iliad* moves from Greece to Troy and back again; the total movement of the *Odyssey* is from Ithaca back to Ithaca; the *Aeneid* moves from the old Troy to the new one at Rome. In each case the final goal is the starting point renewed and transformed by the heroic quest which is the epic theme. Similarly the total action in *Paradise Lost* is a cyclic movement from the begetting of the Son by the Father to the reabsorption of all things in the Father, transformed by the heroic quest of Christ to release man from his bondage.

Traditionally, the epic begins at a low point in the middle of the action: the *Iliad,* at a moment of despair in the Greek camp; the *Odyssey,* at the widest point of separation of Odysseus from his home; the *Aeneid,* with the hero shipwrecked at the enemy city of Carthage. The foreground action of *Paradise Lost* is similarly at the furthest point from God, the fall of Satan and Adam. The epic picks up the thread of action in the middle, from which we can see the beginning and the end hanging down in separate strands. In *Paradise Lost* these two strands are traced out by the speeches of Raphael and Michael, which work back to the beginning and forward to the end of the total action respectively. The cyclic action of *Paradise Lost* is thus also that of the Bible itself, the whole of the Christian revelation from creation to apocalypse focused on, and implicit in, the story of one of its most important episodes, the fall of man.

Traditionally, too, the theme of the epic is heroic action, and all the conventional features that Milton takes over from the Classical epic—the similes, the battles, the set speeches, the invocations to Muses, the councils of gods and leaders—are concerned essentially with this theme. But Milton was sick of what the world calls heroism, and he no longer believed that there could be such a thing as a "Christian hero," the role that he makes Jesus reject with such contempt in *Paradise Regained*. There are three orders of existence in *Paradise Lost*: those of heaven, earth, and hell; and there are correspondingly three types of action. The essentially human act of Adam and Eve is the act of disobedience, which is not really an act at all, any more than jumping over a precipice is a real act. Adam is faced with the choice of preserving his freedom or of throwing it away, and when he throws it away his freedom to act comes to an end. With his fall human history begins, and human history is pervaded by that fundamental inertia and incapacity known as "original sin," which makes history a record of spasmodic but always unsuccessful efforts to reach peace, freedom, and justice.

The essentially divine act is the act of creation, which in *Paradise Lost* shows itself not only in the creation proper, the separation of cosmos from chaos, but in redemption, the recreation of order and reason in man out of the chaos he fell into. All the divine acts are performed by the Son of God, to whom the Father transfers all his power, retiring from the action, though not nearly far enough. The reasons for Milton's grotesque failure to portray the Father as anything better than a smug and wily old hypocrite are too complicated to examine here: we are concerned only with the fact that Christ is the real hero of *Paradise Lost*. He gets this title by default, as he is the only character in the poem who does perform a positive act; nevertheless, the only men who deserve to be called heroic are his prophets, who carry on his work even when it means ostracism or persecution. Their prototype in *Paradise Lost* is Abdiel, the faithful angel. Milton's epic thus closes up the gap between the hero and the poet who celebrates him, as for him the true hero and the true poet are engaged in the same work.

The question of Satan's heroism is quite different. The essential demonic act is rebellion, and rebellion, as distinct from mere disobedience, involves an attempt at rivalry with God. Satan could not have fallen at all without convincing himself that God was not God but *a* god, and he himself therefore another god. Hence he sets up a kingdom in hell which is a close parody of the kingdom of heaven. To the heroism of Christ, which is to show itself in *Paradise Regained* as persistence in obedience, there is opposed the heroism of Satan, who is usually the model for man when man tries to be heroic. Satan is thus the hero of a kind of mock-heroic epic within *Paradise Lost*, which incorporates the heroic mood of the non-Christian epic. Satan is the haughty Achilles, the crafty Ulysses, the knight-errant who achieves the perilous quest of chaos, and all through the first four books he is surrounded with the rumours and the panoply of war. The trouble is that such heroism is founded on pride, and pride is evil. We like to distinguish moral levels in evil: we feel that hurling defiance in the teeth of God is more admirable than, say, stealing pennies out of a blind beggar's cup. But for Milton all evil is in one piece, and Satan, merely by the compulsion of obeying his own nature, is forced to become more and more debased. By the time he has got himself disguised as a talking snake and is congratulating himself on catching Eve alone with the man of the house away, the sombre Promethean rebel of the opening books seems remote. Yet even so Milton never suggests the comic or ridiculous devil who was such a favourite of the Middle Ages. Satan may be ridiculous to God, but man cannot take God's attitude, and even as a snake or a toad he is still a gigantic and terrifying angel.

The sinister figure of Nimrod, who appears at the beginning of the last book, marks the change in human life from disobedience to rebellion. From now on man is capable of worshipping devils, of mistaking the demonic for the divine, and the sign of it is the appearance in human life of hell's parody of the kingdom of heaven, the substitution of a society of slavery and compulsion for a society of love and freedom. In heaven God is an absolute monarch whose angels wait on his will; but, for Milton, human attempts to imitate this government produce only something more like the dictatorial hierarchy of hell. Michael explains to Adam that Satan is reborn in every tyrant, every seeker of earthly power and glory, every human leader that man turns to when he turns away from God. Spiritual authority, the element in human life that tries to redeem and emancipate it, remains apart from this demonic social order, outcast and ridiculed, forced, like Christ in *Paradise Regained*, to wander starving in the wilderness, and hunted down and persecuted even there. Yet the vision of a lost paradise can never be itself quite lost, and when Adam and Eve join hands as they walk slowly out of their garden, we know that another kind of human society has already been formed, and one that no tyranny can ever penetrate.

Milton said that *Samson Agonistes* was not intended for the stage: he meant the Restoration stage, and we should not conclude that it is not a real play. The greatest contemporary dramatist, Racine, also turned at the end of his life to the same combination of Old Testament subject and Classical treatment.[11] No one can forget, in reading *Samson Agonistes*, that its author was also a blind giant in the power of Philistines, but it sums up Milton's life far more profoundly than that. The great champion of Israel is now enslaved; he cannot free himself, but he can destroy the idols of his servitude. His father appears, offering ransom; his wife, the Philistine Delilah, comes seeking reconciliation, and a giant comes to bully him. Samson beats them all off, like the poet who fought religious, domestic, and civil tyranny all in turn. He is summoned to the Philistine temple and refuses to go: it is right that he should refuse, but he has come to the end of his own will. At that point a mysterious change in his will takes place (the "peripety" or turning point in the tragic action); he goes to the temple and brings it crashing into the dust. The cowering Israelites, though free for the moment, have still to wait a long time for their redemption, and meanwhile their champion is dead. But the temple of ignorance and superstition no longer has any pillars.

According to Milton's view of the Bible, the ultimate author of the story of Samson was Christ himself, and the tragedy of Samson is thus one of Christ's parables. To the Greeks, tragedy was primarily a vision of law, of the nemesis that follows pride, of the social contract that replaces the fury of revenge in Aeschylus's *Oresteia*. For a religion concerned with deliverance from the law, the source of tragedy comes to be thought of as increasingly cruel and malignant. In the Book of Job, for instance, it is Satan; but while Satan is the ultimate source in *Samson Agonistes* too, he operates mainly through the Nimrods of human tyranny, who in this case are the Philistine lords. Samson is thus, somewhat as Christ was to be later himself, a tragic hero to his oppressed followers and simultaneously the buffoon of a Philistine carnival. As soon as God has taken charge of his will, the two aspects of the drama are reversed: the tragedy ends in triumph and the carnival in confusion. But the Israel who triumphs is not the Israel that reluctantly followed and then deserted Samson: they have little part in his victory, and will be enslaved many times again. It is the Christian Israel, the city of God, whose power to destroy tyranny Samson has vindicated, and the serene quiet in which the poem ends vibrates with the presence of the same "solemn troops, and sweet Societies" that welcome Lycidas, though nothing can actually be seen but bewildered slaves with no masters, a city wailing to its helpless gods, and a dead giant in a pile of broken stones.

IV The Poetry of Milton

Some poets—Spenser is a good example—start with experiment and end with conventional forms. Milton, like Shakespeare, begins in convention and becomes increasingly radical as he develops. The *Nativity Ode* is written in a tight, intricate stanza: the rhythm is not thereby prevented from bringing out every ripple and curve of the meaning—

> She crown'd with Olive green, came softly sliding
> Down through the turning sphear

—but it is still exactly confined to the pattern of the stanza. It is a miraculous feat of technical skill, but even Milton could not always be performing miracles. He began a complementary poem on the Passion, but abandoned it after eight stanzas, and the stanzaic poem along with it. In the lovely tripping octosyllabics of *L'Allegro* and *Il Penseroso* he escaped into a more freely moving and continuous rhythm, and one that he uses for a good part of *Comus*. From that time on he sought mainly for long-range rhythmical units, and consequently moved away from rhyme, with its emphatic recurrence of sound, to the more austere but freer patterns of blank verse. He had a keen appreciation of music, and perhaps the continuity of rhythm in music influenced his poetry: it is noteworthy that in the Preface to *Paradise Lost* he speaks of "musical delight" as consisting among other things in "the sense variously drawn out from one Verse {that is, line} into another" [*Works*, 2:6].

The epic in any case makes heavy demands on the more sustained and cumulative rhythms, and Milton may have found his twenty years of practice in writing prose also of some help. Prose gives the fullest scope for long-range rhythmical construction, and Milton, though he complains about having only the use of his "left hand" in prose,[12] took every advantage of what prose had to give him. His vast periodic sentences that almost never end, his dizzy flights of prayer and peroration, and his labyrinths of subordinate clauses, qualifying epithets, and parenthetical allusions do not always make for what we should now consider ideal prose. But they may well have played some part in developing the motor power that makes *Paradise Lost*, apart from all its other qualities, the most readable epic in English. Milton's long postponement of his epic had its reward in the almost effortless mastery of the final performance. His reference to "Easie my unpremeditated Verse" [*PL*, 9.24] is no idle boast, and from beginning to end it is clear that *Paradise Lost* was not so much written as written out.

As Milton moves from the stanza into the more linear and continuous pentameter forms, a much bigger type of stanza develops, containing a number of pentameter lines in a rhythmic unit for which the most convenient name is "verse paragraph." The opening lines of *Lycidas*, down to "Without the meed of som melodious tear" [l. 14], constitute an intricately organized verse paragraph, held together by the rhymes to "sere" in the second line and by a varied but consistent pattern of alliteration. The real secret of the unity behind its irregularity, however (the first line, for instance, is unrhymed and the fourth line is not a pentameter), defies all critical analysis. Many of the sonnets, too, are much more verse paragraphs than they are conventional sonnets. This paragraph forms a larger rhythmical unit in *Paradise Lost* too, and its presence enables Milton to handle the pentameter line with such a large number of run-on lines and medial pauses. In *Samson Agonistes* the paragraph achieves a much greater independence from the line and forms the basis for those amazing passages of recitativo which are perhaps the "freest" and most radically experimental verse that English poetry has yet reached.

The elements of versification are sound, vocabulary, rhythm, and imagery, and all four demand the closest attention from the reader of major poetry. Let us take a passage from *L'Allegro* and compare it with one from *Il Penseroso*:

> While the Cock with lively din,
> Scatters the rear of darknes thin,
> And to the stack, or the Barn dore,
> Stoutly struts his Dames before [*L'Allegro*, ll. 49–52]

To behold the wandring Moon,
Riding neer her highest noon,
Like one that had bin led astray
Through the Heav'ns wide pathles way [*Il Penseroso*, ll. 67–70]

We can see how each of these four elements helps to make the contrast between the two poems. The *L'Allegro* passage has sharp, light vowels and abrupt, explosive consonants; the *Il Penseroso* one has resonant vowels and soft liquids. *L'Allegro* has vigorous words like "scatters," "struts," and "din"; *Il Penseroso*, quiet and pensive words like "wandering" and "behold." The *L'Allegro* rhythm flutters away in the almost unscannable third line and swaggers in the fourth; the *Il Penseroso* rhythm, especially in the fourth line, is full of slow and sonorous heavy accents. The first passage describes the clucks and crows of a poultry yard at dawn; the second dwells on the silence of a moonlit night. These points are simple enough, though it takes the highest kind of genius to produce the simplicity, and the principles involved are applicable everywhere in Milton.

Every language has its own body of descriptive sounds, and every poet accepts what his language affords him as a matter of course. "S" is always a hissing letter, suitable for serpents:

And *Dipsas* (not so thick swarm'd once the Soil . . .) [*PL*, 10.526]

"R" (which Milton is said to have pronounced very hard) is a martial one:

Innumerable force of Spirits arm'd [*PL*, 1.101]

"W" is for loneliness and terror:

Through the worlds wilderness long wanderd man [*PL*, 12.313]

and the long "a" and "o" sounds (even more resonant in seventeenth-century pronunciation) herald the approach of the prince of darkness:

Mean while upon the firm opacous Globe
Of this round World, whose first convex divides
The luminous inferior Orbs, enclos'd
From *Chaos* and th' inroad of Darkness old,
Satan alighted walks [*PL*, 3.418–22]

Milton's poetry is proverbial for its resonance: the sonnet on the massacre in Piedmont, for instance, is a deeply felt and powerfully indignant poem, but this does not prevent it from being also a kind of étude, a technical exercise in sombre vowels. It is natural that we should find what makes most noise easiest to hear. This is one reason why Satan makes the strongest initial impact on the reader of *Paradise Lost*, for in the great variety of Milton's orchestration Satan gets most of the heavy brass. It is true also that the gloom and terror of hell is not less impressive for being obviously impressive. But it would be a pity to neglect the woodwinds and strings, and fail to hear how the brothers in *Comus* murmur to each other what they have read in praise of chastity; how the flowers are dropped one by one on Lycidas's grave; how the Christ child lies asleep with his legions of angels sitting quietly around him; how the fragrance of Eden is diffused over the earth by lazy breezes. The great hymn of creation in the seventh book of *Paradise Lost*, in which everything seems to dance in the joy of its deliverance from chaos and the release of its form, is a particularly wonderful example of Milton's skill in the subtler and softer harmonies:

> Forth flourish't thick the clustring Vine, forth crept
> The smelling Gourd, up stood the cornie Reed
> Embattell'd in her field: and th' humble Shrub,
> And Bush with frizl'd hair implicit: last
> Rose as in Dance the stately Trees [*PL*, 7.320–4]

Passing from the sounds to the words, we notice that Milton uses an unusually large proportion of long words of Latin origin. Also that he often uses such words in an original Latin sense different from ours: "frequent" means crowded, "horrid" means bristling, "explode" means to hiss off or drive away, and so on. Many of these Latin words have become dead robot words in our speech, with nothing left in them of the vivid concrete metaphors they once were. But Milton uses them with the whole weight of their etymology behind them, and in reading him we have to wake up this part of our vocabulary. It comes as something of a shock to read in *Paradise Regained* of "Elephants endorst with Towers" [*PL*, 3.329], because we no longer think of *dorsum*, back, in connection with the word. But in Milton "astonished" means not mildly surprised but struck with thunder; "aspect" and "influence" are still partly technical terms in astrology; and "insinuating" has its visual meaning of wriggling as well as its abstract meaning. This principle of traditional weight applies not only to words, but to phrases as well, and the reader should be warned that it is precisely in such lines as "Hee for God only, shee for God in him" [*PL*, 4.299], where Milton seems to be most typically Miltonic, that he is most likely to be quoting verbatim from the Bible.

Another feature of Milton's vocabulary, the catalogues of proper names, also needs a word of warning. There are two reasons for which these catalogues are never used. They are never used to show off Milton's learning, and they are never used as an easy way of increasing the resonance. When they are lists of strange gods, they suggest the incantation or muttered spell of the magician who commands them, as in the summoning of Sabrina in *Comus*, and, less obviously, in the roll call of baffled demons in the *Nativity Ode*. In *Paradise Lost* the rumble and crash of Satan's armies is echoed in the place names of epic and romance; the garden of Eden calls up the luxuriant and fruitful spots of earth, and the storms of advancing chaos sweep from point to point over the wastes of Asia and America. In each case the reader who has to look up several dozen references at once may miss the fact that the vagueness and strangeness of the names is exactly the poet's reason for using them. There are exceptions to this, of course: one should not miss the irony of "Vallombrosa," with its echo of "valley of shadows" in reference to hell [*PL*, 1.303], nor of the fateful epithet of Eden, "this Assyrian Garden" [*PL*, 4.285], which links it prophetically with the ferocious children of Nimrod who annihilated the Ten Tribes.

Some of the peculiar features of Milton's rhythm have been mentioned. The prosody of *Paradise Lost* has been exhaustively studied, but the general principle is that Milton can do anything he likes with the pentameter line. One may notice particularly the use of trochaic rhythms to describe failing movement:

> Hurld headlong flaming from th' Ethereal Skie [*PL*, 1.45]
>
> Exhausted, spiritless, afflicted, fall'n [*PL*, 6.852]

the placing of two strong accents together in the middle of a line to describe something ominous or foreboding:

> Which tasted works knowledge of Good and Evil [*PL*, 7.543]
>
> Deep malice to conceale, couch't with revenge [*PL*, 4.123]

the use of extra syllables to suggest relaxation or lateral movement:

> Luxuriant; mean while murmuring waters fall [*PL*, 4.260]

and the use of a weak or enjambed ending that pushes the rhythm into the next line to describe the completing of a movement:

> Intelligent of seasons, and set forth
> Thir Aierie Caravan high over Sea's
> Flying [*PL*, 7.427–9]

The long Latin words in Milton's vocabulary also have the rhythmical function of relaxing or increasing the speed. A monosyllable always means a separate accent, however slight, and a series of them produces a slow, emphatic sonority that would soon become intolerable unless relieved:

> Scarce half I seem to live, dead more then half.
> O dark, dark, dark, amid the blaze of noon,
> Irrecoverably dark [*SA*, ll. 79–81]

The same principles of variation apply to the other verse forms as well as to the pentameter, and usually the sense will warn us when a change of pace is coming:

> I can fly, or I can run
> Quickly to the green earths end,
> Where the bow'd welkin slow doth bend [*Comus*, ll. 1012–14]

Milton's imagery is more difficult to appreciate than any other aspect of his work. Except perhaps in *L'Allegro* and *Il Penseroso*, he is not one of the intensely visualizing poets: we are more conscious of degrees of light and shade than of sharply outlined objects. In this Milton is more characteristic of his age than elsewhere: in such painters as Rembrandt and Claude Lorrain, who were Milton's contemporaries, we find the same mysterious shadows and diffused brilliance that we find in Milton's hell and heaven. The relative vagueness of vision in *Paradise Lost* can hardly be due primarily to Milton's blindness, for we find it also in the early poems: in the formless shadows of the old gods retreating from the tiny point of light at the centre of the *Nativity Ode*; in the dark wood of *Comus* and in the stylized pastoral world of *Lycidas*. In *Samson Agonistes*, where the hero is blind, the vision is outside the poem: it is focused with unbearable intensity on the hero himself, whose inability to stare back is his greatest torment, an agony of humiliation that makes him, in one of the most dreadful passages in all drama, scream at Delilah that he will tear her to pieces if she touches him. The precision of Milton's poetry is aural rather than visual, musical rather than pictorial. When we read, for instance,

> Immediately the Mountains huge appeer
> Emergent, and thir broad bare backs upheave [*PL*, 7.285–6]

the mountains cannot be *seen*: it is the ear that must hear in "emergent" the splash of the water falling from them, and in the long and level monosyllables the clear blue line of the horizon. In every major poem of Milton's there is some reason why the ear predominates over the eye. In the *Nativity Ode*, it is because of the pattern of light and shade already mentioned; in *Comus*, it is because of the dark "leavie Labyrinth" [l. 277] where one listens intently for rustles and whispers; in *Lycidas*, it is because the ritual lament generalizes the imagery; in *Paradise Lost* it is because the three states of existence—heaven, hell, and paradise—all transcend visualization; in *Samson Agonistes* it is because the Classical form of the tragedy makes it a discussion or reporting of offstage events. The prominence of temptation among Milton's themes is significant too, as temptation is an attempt to persuade one through aural suggestion to seize something that is illusory.

In *Paradise Lost* Milton uses the same Ptolemaic onion-shaped universe that Dante does, with the earth at the centre and the primum mobile at the circumference. But Dante puts heaven and hell inside this universe; Milton puts them outside, and the impersonal remoteness of the Copernican universe, with its unthinkable stretches of empty space, thus forms part of his poetic vision. Dante relies on symmetry; Milton on disproportion. Satan is a colossal angel and a toad; Christ is to become a despised son of the Adam he creates; Raphael is a hero of a war that rocks heaven, yet he drops in on Adam and Eve for a cold lunch; all the armies of heaven and hell and the fate of the created universe hang on one apple, and on whether or not a hungry girl will reach for it. What holds this farrago together is nothing that the eye or mind can accept, but the steady flow of the powerful working words that, exactly like the temptations in the poems, persuade us to seize the illusion. Milton, the agent of the Word of God, is trying to awaken with his words a vision in us which is, in his own language, the Word of God in the heart, and in the possession of which we may say with Job, "I have heard thee with the hearing of the ear, but now mine eye seeth thee."[13] If we surrender to his charming and magical spell, and seize his fables of hell and paradise, they will become realities of earth, and the stories of Adam and Samson our own story. And then, perhaps, we may consider a further question:

> what if Earth
> Be but the shaddow of Heav'n, and things therein
> Each to other like, more then on earth is thought? [*PL*, 5.574–6]

2

Literature as Context: Milton's *Lycidas*

1959

From FI, *119–29. Originally published in* Comparative Literature: Proceedings of the Second Congress of the International Comparative Literature Association, *ed. Werner P. Friederich, University of North Carolina Studies in Comparative Literature, 23 (1959): 44–55. Reprinted in* Milton's "Lycidas": The Tradition and the Poem, *ed. C.A. Patrides (New York: Holt, Rinehart and Winston, 1961), 200–11.*

I should like to begin with a brief discussion of a familiar poem, Milton's *Lycidas*, in the hope that some of the inferences drawn from the analysis will be relevant to the theme of this conference. *Lycidas*, then, is an elegy in the pastoral convention, written to commemorate a young man named Edward King who was drowned at sea. The origins of the pastoral are partly Classical, the tradition that runs through Theocritus and Virgil, and partly Biblical, the imagery of the twenty-third Psalm, of Christ as the Good Shepherd, of the metaphors of "pastor" and "flock" in the church. The chief connecting link between the traditions in Milton's day was the *Fourth* or *Messianic Eclogue* of Virgil. Hence it is common enough to have pastoral images echoing both traditions at once, and not surprising to find that *Lycidas* is a Christian poem as well as a humanistic one.

In the Classical pastoral elegy the subject of the elegy is not treated as an individual but as a representative of a dying spirit of nature. The pastoral elegy seems to have some relation to the ritual of the Adonis lament, and the dead poet Bion, in Moschus's poem, is celebrated with much the same kind of imagery as Bion himself uses in his lament for Adonis. The phrase "dying god," for such a figure in later pastoral, is not an anachronism: Virgil says of Daphnis, for example, in the *Fifth Eclogue*: "deus, deus ille, Menalca."[1] Besides, Milton and his learned contemporaries, Selden, for example, or Henry Reynolds, knew at least as much about the symbolism of the "dying god" as any modern student could get out of *The Golden Bough*, which depends mainly on the same Classical sources that were available to them. The notion that twentieth-century poets differ from their predecessors in their understanding or use of myth will not bear much scrutiny. So King is given the pastoral name of Lycidas, which is equivalent to Adonis, and is associated with the cyclical rhythms of nature. Of these three are of particular importance: the daily cycle of the sun across the sky, the yearly cycle of the seasons, and the cycle of water, flowing from wells and fountains through rivers to the sea. Sunset, winter and the sea are emblems of Lycidas's death; sunrise and spring, of his resurrection. The poem begins in the morning, "Under the opening eye-lids of the morn," and ends with the sun, like Lycidas himself, dropping into the western ocean, yet due to rise again as Lycidas is to do. The imagery of the opening lines, "Shatter your leaves before the mellowing year," suggests the frosts of autumn killing the flowers, and in the great roll-call of flowers towards the end, most of them early blooming flowers like the "rathe Primrose," the spring returns. Again, the opening invocation is to the "Sisters of the sacred well," and the water imagery carries through a great variety of Greek, Italian, and English rivers to the sea in which the dead body of Lycidas lies.

Lycidas, then, is the "archetype" of Edward King. By an archetype I mean a literary symbol, or cluster of symbols, which is used recurrently throughout literature, and thereby becomes conventional. A poetic use of a flower, by itself, is not necessarily an archetype. But in a poem about the death of a young man it is conventional to associate him with a red or purple flower, usually a spring flower like the hyacinth. The historical origin of the convention may be lost in ritual, but it is a constantly latent one, not only in literature but in life, as the symbolism of the scarlet poppies in World War I shows. Hence in *Lycidas* the "sanguine flower inscrib'd with woe" is an archetype, a symbol that recurs regularly in many poems of its kind. Similarly Lycidas himself is not only the literary form of Edward King, but a conventional or recurring form, of the same family as Shelley's Adonais, the Daphnis of Theocritus and Virgil, and Milton's own Damon. King was also a clergyman and, for Milton's purposes, a poet, so, having selected the conventional archetype of King as drowned young man, Milton has then to select the conventional archetypes of King as poet and of King as priest. These are, respectively, Orpheus and Peter.

Both Orpheus and Peter have attributes that link them in imagery with Lycidas. Orpheus was also an "inchanting son" or spirit of nature; he died young, in much the same role as Adonis, and was flung into the water. Peter would have drowned too without the help of Christ; hence Peter is not named directly, but only as "The Pilot of the *Galilean* lake," just as Christ is not named directly, but only as "him that walk'd the waves." When Orpheus was torn to pieces by the Maenads, his head went floating "Down the swift *Hebrus* to the *Lesbian* shore." The theme of salvation out of water is connected with the image of the dolphin, a conventional type of Christ, and dolphins are called upon to "waft the haples youth" just before the peroration begins.

The body of the poem is arranged in the form ABACA, a main theme repeated twice with two intervening episodes, as in the musical rondo. The main theme is the drowning of Lycidas in the prime of his life; the two episodes, presided over by the figures of Orpheus and Peter, deal with the theme of premature death as it relates to poetry and to the priesthood respectively. In both the same type of image appears: the mechanical instrument of execution that brings about a sudden death, represented by the "abhorred shears" in the meditation on fame and the "grim two-handed engine"[2] in the meditation on the corruption of the church. The most difficult part of the construction is the managing of the transitions from these episodes back to the main theme. The poet does this by alluding to his great forerunners in the pastoral convention, Theocritus of Sicily, Virgil of Mantua, and the legendary Arcadians who preceded both:

> O fountain *Arethuse*, and thou honour'd floud,
> Smooth-sliding *Mincius*, crown'd with vocal reeds . . .

and later:

> Return *Alpheus*, the dread voice is past,
> That shrunk thy streams; Return *Sicilian* Muse.

The allusion has the effect of reminding the reader that this is, after all, a pastoral. But Milton also alludes to the myth of Arethusa and Alpheus, the Arcadian water-spirits who plunged underground and reappeared in Sicily, and this myth not only outlines the history of the pastoral convention, but unites the water imagery with the theme of disappearance and revival.

In pastoral elegy the poet who laments the death is often so closely associated with the dead man as to make him a kind of double or shadow of himself. Similarly Milton represents himself as intimately involved with the death of Lycidas. The theme of premature death is skilfully associated in the opening lines with the conventional apology for a "harsh and crude" poem; the poet hopes for a similar elegy when he dies, and at the end he accepts the responsibilities of survival and turns "To morrow to fresh Woods, and Pastures new," bringing the elegy to a full rich *tierce de Picardie* or major chord. By appearing himself at the beginning and end of the poem, Milton presents the poem as, in a sense, contained within the mind of the poet.

Apart from the historical convention of the pastoral, however, there is also the conventional framework of ideas or assumptions which forms the background of the poem. I call it a framework of ideas, and it may also be that, but in poetry it is rather a framework of images. It consists of four levels of existence. First is the order revealed by Christianity, the order of grace and salvation and of eternal life. Second is the order of human nature, the order represented by the Garden of Eden in the Bible and the Golden Age in Classical myth, and which man in his fallen state can, up to a point, regain through education, obedience to law, and the habit of virtue. Third is the order of physical nature, the world of animals and plants which is morally neutral but theologically "fallen." Fourth is the disorder of the unnatural, the sin and death and corruption that entered the world with the fall.

Lycidas has his connections with all of these orders. In the first place, all the images of death and resurrection are included in and identified with the body of Christ. Christ is the sun of righteousness, the tree of life, the water of life, the dying god who rose again, the saviour from the sea. On this level Lycidas enters the Christian heaven and is greeted by the "Saints above" "in solemn troops, and sweet Societies," where the language echoes the Book of Revelation. But simultaneously Lycidas achieves another apotheosis as the Genius of the shore, corresponding to the Attendant Spirit in *Comus*, whose habitation is said to be a world above our own, identified, not with the Christian heaven, but with Spenser's Gardens of Adonis. The third level of physical nature is the world of ordinary experience, where death is simply a loss, and those who mourn the death have to turn to pick up their tasks again. On this level Lycidas is merely absent, "to our moist vows deny'd," represented only by the empty bier with its flowers. It is on this level too that the poem is contained within the mind of the surviving poet, as on the Christian level it is contained within the body of Christ. Finally, the world of death and corruption holds the drowned corpse of Lycidas, which will soon come to the surface and "welter to the parching wind." This last is an unpleasant and distressing image, and Milton touches it very lightly, picking it up again in an appropriate context:

> But swoln with wind, and the rank mist they draw,
> Rot inwardly . . .

In the writing of *Lycidas* there are four creative principles of particular importance. To say that there are four does not mean, of course, that they are separable. One is convention, the reshaping of the poetic material which is appropriate to this subject. Another is genre, the choosing of the appropriate form. A third is archetype, the use of appropriate, and therefore recurrently employed, images and symbols. The fourth, for which there is no name, is the fact that the forms of literature are autonomous: that is, they do not exist outside literature. Milton is not writing an obituary: he does not start with Edward King and his life and times, but with the conventions and archetypes that poetry requires for such a theme.

Of the critical principles illustrated by this analysis, one will be no surprise to the present audience. *Lycidas* owes quite as much to Hebrew, Greek, Latin, and Italian traditions as it does to English. Even the diction, of which I have no space to speak, shows strong Italian influence. Milton was of course a learned poet, but there is no poet whose literary influences are entirely confined to his own language. Thus every problem in literary criticism is a problem in comparative literature, or simply of literature itself.

The next principle is that the provisional hypothesis which we must adopt for the study of every poem is that that poem is a unity. If, after careful and repeated testing, we are forced to conclude that it is not a unity, then we must abandon the hypothesis and look for the reasons why it is not. A good deal of bad criticism of *Lycidas* has resulted from not making enough initial effort to understand the unity of the poem. To talk of "digressions" in *Lycidas* is a typical consequence of a mistaken critical method, of backing into the poem the wrong way round. If, instead of starting with the poem, we start with a handful of peripheral facts about the poem, Milton's casual knowledge of King, his ambitions as a poet, his bitterness against the episcopacy, then of course the poem will break down into pieces corresponding precisely to those fragments of knowledge. *Lycidas* illustrates, on a small scale, what has happened on a much bigger scale in, for example, the criticism of Homer. Critics knowing something about the fragmentary nature of heroic lays and ballads approached the *Iliad* and the *Odyssey* with this knowledge in mind, and the poems obediently split up into the pieces that they wished to isolate. Other critics came along and treated the poems as imaginative unities, and today everyone knows that the second group were more convincing.

The same thing happens when our approach to "sources" becomes fragmentary or piecemeal. *Lycidas* is a dense mass of echoes from previous literature, chiefly pastoral literature. Reading through Virgil's Eclogues with *Lycidas* in mind, we can see that Milton had not simply read or studied these poems: he possessed them; they were part of the material he was shaping. The passage about the hungry sheep reminds us of at least three other passages: one in Dante's *Paradiso,* one in the Book of Ezekiel, and one near the beginning of Hesiod's *Theogony*. There are also echoes of Mantuan and Spenser, of the Gospel of John, and it is quite possible that there are even more striking parallels with poems that Milton had not read. In such cases there is not *a* source at all, no one place that the passage "comes from," or, as we say with such stupefying presumption, that the poet "had in mind." There are only archetypes, or recurring themes of literary expression, which *Lycidas* has recreated, and therefore re-echoed, yet once more.

The next principle is that the important problems of literary criticism lie within the study of literature. We notice that a law of diminishing returns sets in as soon as we move away from the poem itself. If we ask, Who is Lycidas? the answer is that he is a member of the same family as Theocritus's Daphnis, Bion's Adonis, the Old Testament's Abel, and so on. The answer goes on building up a wider comprehension of literature and a deeper knowledge of its structural principles and recurring themes. But if we ask, Who was Edward King? What was his relation to Milton? How good a poet was he? we find ourselves moving dimly in the intense inane. The same is true of minor points. If we ask, Why is the image of the two-handed engine in *Lycidas*? we can give an answer, along the lines suggested above, that illustrates how carefully the poem has been constructed. If we ask, What is the two-handed engine? there are forty-odd answers, none of them completely satisfactory; yet the fact that they are not wholly satisfactory hardly seems to be important.

Another form of the same kind of fallacy is the confusion between personal sincerity and literary sincerity. If we start with the facts that *Lycidas* is highly conventional and that Milton knew King only slightly, we may see in *Lycidas* an "artificial" poem without "real feeling" in it.[3] This red herring, though more common among third-rate Romantics, was dragged across the study of *Lycidas* by Samuel Johnson. Johnson knew better, but he happened to feel perverse about this particular poem, and so deliberately raised false issues. It would not have occurred to him, for example, to question the conventional use of Horace in the satires of Pope, or of Juvenal in his own. Personal sincerity has no place in literature, because personal sincerity as such is inarticulate. One may burst into tears at the news of a friend's death, but one can never spontaneously burst into song, however doleful a lay. *Lycidas* is a passionately sincere poem, because Milton was deeply interested in the structure and symbolism of funeral elegies, and had been practising since adolescence on every fresh corpse in sight, from the university beadle to the fair infant dying of a cough.

If we ask what inspires a poet, there are always two answers. An occasion, an experience, an event, may inspire the impulse to write. But the impulse to write can only come from previous contact with literature, and the formal inspiration, the poetic structure that crystallizes around the new event, can only be derived from other poems. Hence while every new poem is a new and unique creation, it is also a re-shaping of familiar conventions of literature, otherwise it would not be recognizable as literature at all. Literature often gives us the illusion of turning from books to life, from second-hand to direct experience, and thereby discovering new literary principles in the world outside. But this is never quite what happens. No matter how tightly Wordsworth may close the barren leaves of art and let nature be his teacher, his literary forms will be as conventional as ever, although they may echo an unaccustomed set of conventions, such as the ballad or the broadside. The pretence of personal sincerity is itself a literary convention, and Wordsworth makes many of the flat simple statements which represent, in literature, the inarticulateness of personal sincerity:

> No motion has she now, no force;
> She neither hears nor sees.[4]

But as soon as a death becomes a poetic image, that image is assimilated to other poetic images of death in nature, and hence Lucy inevitably becomes a Proserpine figure, just as King becomes an Adonis:

> Rolled round in earth's diurnal course,
> With rocks, and stones, and trees.[5]

In Whitman we have an even more extreme example than Wordsworth of a cult of personal statement and an avoidance of learned conventions. It is therefore instructive to see what happens in *When Lilacs Last in Dooryard Bloomed*. The dead man is not called by a pastoral name, but neither is he called by his historical name. He is in a coffin which is carried the length and breadth of the land; he is identified with a "powerful western fallen star";[6] he is the beloved comrade of the poet, who throws the purple flower of the lilac on his coffin; a singing bird laments the death, just as the woods and caves do in *Lycidas*. Convention, genre, archetype, and the autonomy of forms are all illustrated as clearly in Whitman as they are in Milton.

Lycidas is an occasional poem, called forth by a specific event. It seems, therefore, to be a poem with a strong external reference. Critics who cannot approach a poem except as a personal statement of the poet's thus feel that if it says little about King, it must say a good deal about Milton. So, they reason, *Lycidas* is really autobiographical, concerned with Milton's own preoccupations, including his fear of death. There can be no objection to this unless Milton's conventional involving of himself with the poem is misinterpreted as a personal intrusion into it.

For Milton was even by seventeenth-century standards an unusually professional and impersonal poet. Of all Milton's poems, the one obvious failure is the poem called *The Passion*, and if we look at the imagery of that poem we can see why. It is the only poem of Milton's in which he is preoccupied with himself in the process of writing it. "My muse," "my song," "my Harp," "my roving verse," "my Phoebus," and so on for eight stanzas until Milton abandons the poem in disgust. It is not a coincidence that Milton's one self-conscious poem should be the one that never gets off the ground. There is nothing like this in *Lycidas*: the "I" of that poem is a professional poet in his conventional shepherd disguise, and to think of him as a personal "I" is to bring *Lycidas* down to the level of *The Passion*, to make it a poem that has to be studied primarily as a biographical document rather than for its own sake. Such an approach to *Lycidas* is apt to look most plausible to those who dislike Milton, and want to see him cut down to size.

One more critical principle, and the one that I have written this paper to enunciate, seems to me to follow inevitably from the previous ones. Every poem must be examined as a unity, but no poem is an isolatable unity. Every poem is inherently connected with other poems of its kind, whether explicitly, as *Lycidas* is with Theocritus and Virgil, or implicitly, as Whitman is with the same tradition, or by anticipation, as *Lycidas* is with later pastoral elegies. And, of course, the kinds or genres of literature are not separable either, like the orders of pre-Darwinian biology. Everyone who has seriously studied literature knows that he is not simply moving from poem to poem, or from one aesthetic experience to another: he is also entering into a coherent and progressive discipline. For literature is not simply an aggregate of books and poems and plays: it is an order of words. And our total literary experience, at any given time, is not a discrete series of memories or impressions of what we have read, but an imaginatively coherent body of experience.

It is literature as an order of words, therefore, which forms the primary context of any given work of literary art. All other contexts—the place of *Lycidas* in Milton's development; its place in the history of English poetry; its place in seventeenth-century thought or history—are secondary and derivative contexts. Within the total literary order certain structural and generic principles, certain configurations of narrative and imagery, certain conventions and devices and *topoi*, occur over and over again. In every new work of literature some of these principles are reshaped.

Lycidas, we found, is informed by such a recurring structural principle. The short, simple, and accurate name for this principle is myth. The Adonis myth is what makes *Lycidas* both distinctive and traditional. Of course if we think of the Adonis myth as some kind of Platonic idea existing by itself, we shall not get far with it as a critical conception. But it is only incompetence that tries to reduce or assimilate a poem to a myth. The Adonis myth in *Lycidas* is the structure of *Lycidas*. It is in *Lycidas* in much the same way that the sonata form is in the first movement of a Mozart symphony. It is the connecting link between what makes *Lycidas* the poem it is and what unites it to other forms of poetic experience. If we attend only to the uniqueness of *Lycidas*, and analyse the ambiguities and subtleties of its diction, our method, however useful in itself, soon reaches a point of no return to the poem. If we attend only to the conventional element, our method will turn it into a scissors-and-paste collection of allusive tags. One method reduces the poem to a jangle of echoes of itself, the other to a jangle of echoes from other poets. If we have a unifying principle that holds these two tendencies together from the start, neither will get out of hand.

Myths, it is true, turn up in other disciplines, in anthropology, in psychology, in comparative religion. But the primary business of the critic is with myth as the shaping principle of a work of literature. Thus for him myth becomes much the same thing as Aristotle's *mythos*, narrative or plot, the moving formal cause which is what Aristotle called the "soul" of the work and assimilates all details in the realizing of its unity.

In its simplest English meaning a myth is a story about a god, and Lycidas is, poetically speaking, a god or spirit of nature, who eventually becomes a saint in heaven, which is as near as one can get to godhead in ordinary Christianity. The reason for treating Lycidas mythically, in this sense, is conventional, but the convention is not arbitrary or accidental. It arises from the metaphorical nature of poetic speech. We are not told simply that Lycidas has left the woods and caves, but that the woods and caves and all their echoes mourn his loss. This is the language of that curious identification of subject and object, of personality and thing, which the poet has in common with the lunatic and the lover.[7] It is the language of metaphor, recognized by Aristotle as the distinctive language of poetry. And, as we can see in such phrases as sun-god and tree-god, the language of metaphor is interdependent with the language of myth.

I have said that all problems of criticism are problems of comparative literature. But where there is comparison there must be some standard by which we can distinguish what is actually comparable from what is merely analogous. The scientists discovered long ago that to make valid comparisons you have to know what your real categories are. If you're studying natural history, for instance, no matter how fascinated you may be by anything that has eight legs, you cannot just lump together an octopus and a spider and a string quartet. In science the difference between a scientific and a pseudoscientific procedure can usually be spotted fairly soon. I wonder if literary criticism has any standards of this kind. It seems to me that a critic practically has to maintain that the Earl of Oxford wrote the plays of Shakespeare before he can be clearly recognized as making pseudocritical statements. I have read some critics on Milton who appeared to be confusing Milton with their phallic fathers, if that is the right phrase. I should call them pseudo-critics; others call them neo-Classicists. How is one to know? There is such a variety of even legitimate critics. There are critics who can find things in the Public Records Office, and there are critics who, like myself, could not find the Public Records Office. Not all critical statements or procedures can be equally valid.

The first step, I think, is to recognize the dependence of value judgments on scholarship. Scholarship, or the knowledge of literature, constantly expands and increases; value judgments are produced by a skill based on the knowledge we already have. Thus scholarship has both priority to value judgments and the power of veto over them.[8] The second step is to recognize the dependence of scholarship on a co-ordinated view of literature. A good deal of critical taxonomy lies ahead of us. We need to know much more than we do about the structural principles of literature, about myth and metaphor, conventions and genres, before we can distinguish with any authority a real from an imaginary line of influence, an illuminating from a misleading analogy, a poet's original source from his last resource. The basis of this central critical activity that gives direction to scholarship is the simple fact that every poem is a member of the class of things called poems. Some poems, including *Lycidas*, proclaim that they are conventional, in other words that their primary context is in literature. Other poems leave this inference to the critic, with an appealing if often misplaced confidence.

3

The Return of Eden: Five Essays on Milton's Epics

1965

From the book The Return of Eden: Five Essays on Milton's Epics, *published by the University of Toronto Press, 1965; paperback reprint 1975. The British edition, entitled* Five Essays on Milton's Epics *(London: Routledge & Kegan Paul, 1966), uses the same text printed in a different format, and includes an index. The first four essays were the Huron College Centennial Lectures delivered in London, Ontario, in 1963. The last essay, "Revolt in the Desert," is a revised version of the article "The Typology of 'Paradise Regained,'" published in* Modern Philology, *53 (May 1956): 227–38, and reprinted in* Milton: Modern Essays in Criticism, *ed. Arthur E. Barker (New York: Oxford University Press, 1965), 429–46, and in* Milton's Epic Poetry, *ed. C.A. Patrides (Baltimore: Penguin, 1967), 301–21.* The Return of Eden *was dedicated to A.B.B. Moore, the president of Victoria University. There is also a typescript with printer's annotations (NFF, 1988, box 22, file 5).*

Preface

The first four chapters of this book were originally the Centennial Lectures delivered at Huron College in March 1963, under the title "A Tetrachordon for *Paradise Lost.*" This title was somewhat spoiled by the addition of a revised version of an earlier paper of mine, "The Typology of *Paradise Regained,*" which appeared in *Modern Philology* in May 1956. I am indebted to Principal Morden and Professor Blissett of Huron College for many kindnesses, and to the University of Chicago Press for allowing me to reprint the substance of my article from *Modern Philology*.

The lectures at Huron College were conceived as an introduction to *Paradise Lost* for relatively inexperienced students, with the hope that they would also have something to interest the general reader. They have grown more complicated as I have rewritten them for publication, but this is still their main intention. Perhaps if I say that they are a distillation of undergraduate lecture notes their function will be more clearly understood. As is inevitable when one writes more than once on the same subject, there is some repetition with other writings of mine. The first chapter expands several points summarized in my introduction to an edition of Milton which was published in 1950 and is still in print, and the second chapter explains once more the framework of Renaissance imagery which is already explained in my *Fables of Identity* and elsewhere. However, the advantage of this repetition is that the present book is a complete argument in its own right.

N.F.
Victoria College in the
University of Toronto
September 1964

I The Story of All Things

I suppose anyone proposing to deliver a series of lectures on *Paradise Lost* ought to begin with some explanation of why he is not deterred from doing so by the number of his predecessors. If my predecessors had all failed, I could at least claim the merit of courage, like the youngest adventurer of so many folk tales who is also the brashest and most bumptious of the whole series. But many of them have succeeded better than I expect to do, and I have no knowledge of Milton sufficiently detailed to add to the body of Milton scholarship or sufficiently profound to alter its general shape. I am talking about Milton because I enjoy talking about Milton, and while I may have begun the subject of these lectures late, it was not long in choosing. Huron College is a hundred years old, and though I find, on checking the dates, that I have not been teaching Milton for quite that long, I have been teaching him long enough to have incorporated him as a central part of my own literary experience. Consequently I feel that I can approach Milton with some sense of proportion based on the fact that his proportions are gigantic. Every student of Milton has been rewarded according to his efforts and his ability: the only ones who have abjectly failed with him are those who have tried to cut him down to size—their size—and that mistake at least I will not make.

The second edition of *Paradise Lost* opened with two complimentary poems addressed to Milton, one in English by Andrew Marvell and one in Latin by Samuel Barrow. The Barrow poem begins with a rhetorical question. When you read this wonderful poem, he says, what do you read but the story of all things? For the story of all things from their first beginnings to their ultimate ends is contained within this book:

> Qui legis Amissam Paradisum, grandia magni
> Carmina *Miltoni*, quid nisi cuncta legis?
> Res cunctas, & cunctarum primordia rerum,
> Et fata, & fines continet iste liber.[1]

Implicit in what Barrow says is a standard Renaissance critical theory. It will be familiar to most readers, but I need it again because its elements reappear as structural principles in *Paradise Lost*. It was generally assumed that in literature there were inherently major genres and minor genres. Minor poets should stick to the minor genres, and should confine themselves to pastorals or to love lyrics. Minor genres were for poets of minor talents, or for professional poets learning their trade, or for poets too high in social rank to be much interested in publication or in any kind of poetic utterance beyond the kind of graceful conventional verse that is really a form of private correspondence. The major poets were those for whom the major genres were reserved; and of these, the most important in Renaissance theory were epic and tragedy.

The epic, as Renaissance critics understood it, is a narrative poem of heroic action, but a special kind of narrative. It also has an encyclopedic quality in it, distilling the essence of all the religious, philosophical, political, even scientific learning of its time, and, if completely successful, the definitive poem for its age. The epic in this sense is not a poem by a poet, but that poet's poem: he can never complete a second epic unless he is the equal of Homer, and hence the moment at which the epic poet chooses his subject is the crisis of his life. To decide to write an epic of this kind is an act of considerable courage, because if one fails, one fails on a colossal scale, and the echo of ridicule may last for centuries. One thinks of what the name "Blackmore" still suggests to students of English literature, many of whom have not read a line of Blackmore's epics.[2] Further, the epic can only be completed late in life, because of the amount of sheer scholarship it is compelled to carry. In Gabriel Harvey's phrase, major poets should be "curious universal scholars,"[3] but it takes time to mature a scholar and still more time to unite scholarship with poetic skill. Of course this theory implies that Homer was a poet of encyclopedic learning, but it was almost a critical commonplace to assume that he was: William Webbe, for example, speaks of "Homer, who as it were in one sum comprehended all knowledge, wisdom, learning and policy that was incident to the capacity of man."[4]

The epic, as a poem both narrative and encyclopedic, is to be distinguished from the long poem which is simply one or the other. A narrative poet, as such, is a story-teller, and a story-teller is in the position of a modern novelist: the more stories he tells the more successful he is. One thinks of Ariosto's *Orlando Furioso* and of the question addressed to the author by the Cardinal who was supposed to be his patron: "Where did you find all these silly stories, Messer Lodovico?" This remark, however inadequate as criticism, does indicate something of the quality of the romance genre that Ariosto was using, for the romance tends to become an endless poem, going on from one story to another until the author runs out of stories to tell. The encyclopedic poem, again, was a favourite genre of the Renaissance. The two poets of this group whom we should now rank highest, Lucretius and Dante, were somewhat disapproved of in Protestant England on ideological grounds, and a more tangible influence on Milton was *La Sepmaine* of du Bartas, which displayed so much knowledge of the creation that its author was compelled to expand the divine activity into two weeks. Some other encyclopedic poems, such as Palingenius's *Zodiac of Life*, which, as translated by Barnabe Googe, may have been one of Shakespeare's school books, were based on rather facile organizing schemes—in other words their scholarship was a matter of content rather than of poetic structure. Romances, particularly *The Faerie Queene*, could also achieve an encyclopedic quality by virtue of being allegorical, when they not only told stories but when their stories meant things in moral philosophy and political history—"Where more is meant then meets the ear," as Milton says [*Il Penseroso*, l. 120].

But although there were many encyclopedic poems and many romances and narratives, and although the authors of both genres were highly respected, still the central form with the greatest prestige was the epic. And the ideal, the huge, impossible ideal, would be a poem that derived its structure from the epic tradition of Homer and Virgil and still had the quality of universal knowledge which belonged to the encyclopedic poem and included the extra dimension of reality that was afforded by Christianity. Now, says Samuel Barrow, who would ever have thought that anyone could actually bring off such a poem? But it's been done, and by an English poet too:

> Haec qui speraret quis crederet esse futurum?
> Et tamen haec hodie terra Britanna legit.[5]

For in the seventeenth century, writing such a poem in English was still a patriotic act, with a certain amount of conscious virtue about it, as writing poetry on this side of the American border has now. The first critical statement ever made about *Paradise Lost*, therefore, tells us that *Paradise Lost* is among other things a technical tour de force of miraculous proportions.

That Milton was fully aware of the size and scope of what he was attempting, and that he shared the assumptions of his age about the importance of the epic, hardly need much demonstrating. For him, of course, the responsibilities entailed by the possession of major poetic talent were only incidentally literary: they were primarily religious. The word "talent" itself is a metaphor from a parable of Jesus that seems to associate the religious and the creative aspects of life, a parable that was never long out of Milton's mind.[6] The analogy between the Christian and the creative life extends even further. A Christian has to work hard at living a Christian life, yet the essential act of that life is the surrender of the will; a poet must work hard at his craft, yet his greatest achievements are not his, but inspired.

Milton's first major poem, the one we know as the *Nativity Ode*, ends its prelude with the self-addressed exhortation:

> And joyn thy voice unto the Angel Quire,
> From out his secret Altar toucht with hallow'd fire.

In a sense this is the key signature, so to speak, of Milton's poetry: his ambition as a poet is to join the tradition of inspired prophetic speech that began with the great commission to Isaiah.[7] When he speaks in *Paradise Lost* of wanting to justify the ways of God to men, he does not mean that he wishes to do God a favour by rationalizing one of God's favourite parables: he means that *Paradise Lost* is a sacrificial offering to God which, if it is accepted, will derive its merit from that acceptance.

The *Nativity Ode* is closely related to the *Sixth Elegy*, addressed to Diodati,[8] where Milton distinguishes the relaxed life permitted the minor poet who writes of love and pleasure from the austerity and rigorous discipline imposed by major powers. One is a secular and the other a priestly or dedicated life. The reason for the discipline is not so much moral as spiritually hygienic. To be a fit vessel of inspiration the poet must be as genuinely pure as the augur or pagan priest was ceremonially pure:

> Qualis veste nitens sacra, & lustralibus undis
> Surgis ad infensos augur iture Deos.[9]

After the first period of Milton's poetry had reached its climax with the two great funeral elegies, *Lycidas* and *Epitaphium Damonis*, Milton started making plans for poetry in the major genres—perhaps part of the meaning of the "fresh Woods, and Pastures new" at the end of *Lycidas*. His *Reason of Church Government*, in a famous passage, mentions in particular three genres, the tragedy, the "diffuse" or full-length epic, and the "brief" epic [*Works*, 3:237]. This last is still a somewhat undeveloped conception in criticism, though examples of it in English literature stretch from *Beowulf* to *The Waste Land*. One cannot help noticing the similarity between this list of three major genres and the *Samson Agonistes*, *Paradise Lost*, and *Paradise Regained* produced so many years later. At that time, Milton tells us, he was thinking of Arthur as the subject for his "diffuse" epic. But of course he had still many years to wait before he could give his full attention to writing it. The simultaneous pull in Milton's life between the impulse to get at his poem and finish it and the impulse to leave it until it ripened sufficiently to come by itself must have accounted for an emotional tension in Milton of a kind that we can hardly imagine. That the tension was there seems certain from the way in which the temptation to premature action remains so central a theme in his poetry. The tension reached a crisis with his blindness, yet his blindness, as he had perhaps begun to realize by the time he wrote *Defensio Secunda*, eventually gave him, as deafness did Beethoven, an almost preternatural concentration, and was what finally enabled him to write of heaven, hell, and the unfallen world on his own terms.

In the same passage of *The Reason of Church Government* Milton speaks of doing something for his own nation of the same kind as Homer and Virgil, "with this over and above of being a Christian" [*Works*, 3:236]. This additional advantage means for him partly a technical poetic advantage as well. For what gave the encyclopedic poem such prestige in Christian civilization was the encyclopedic shape of Christian philosophy and theology, a shape derived ultimately from the shape of the Bible. The Bible, considered in its literary aspect, is a definitive encyclopedic poem starting with the beginning of time at the creation, ending with the end of time at the Last Judgment, and surveying the entire history of man, under the symbolic names of Adam and Israel, in between. Explicitly Christian poetry had moved within this framework from earliest times. Bede's *Ecclesiastical History*, one of the authorities used by Milton for his history of Britain, tells how English poetry began with the poet Caedmon, who was ordered by an angel to sing him something. Being inspired by a Christian muse, Caedmon began promptly with a paraphrase of the first verses of Genesis on the creation, worked his way down through the Exodus and the main episodes of the Old Testament to the Incarnation, and went on to the Last Judgment and the life eternal. The dramatic cycles of the Middle Ages are another example of the effect of the shape of the Bible on English literature.

The sermon, in Milton's day, constituted a kind of oral epic tradition dealing with the same encyclopedic myth. The proverbially long Puritan sermons, divided into anything from eighteen to twenty-five divisions, usually owed their length to a survey of the divine plan of salvation as it unrolled itself from the earliest prelapsarian decrees to the eventual consummation of all things. This oral tradition has been embedded in *Paradise Lost* in the four hundred lines of the third book which constitute a sermon of this type preached by God himself. The speech of Michael, which takes up most of the last two books of *Paradise Lost*, is a summary of the Bible from the murder of Abel to the vision of John in Patmos in which the Biblical myth takes the form of a miniature epic or epyllion, and as such pulls together and restates all the major themes of the poem, like a stretto in a fugue.

Renaissance critics believed that there were major and minor genres for prose as well as for poetry, as they made much less of the technical distinction between prose and verse than we do. In prose the major genres were mainly those established by Plato: the Socratic dialogue form, and the description of the ideal commonwealth. Such works as Sidney's *Arcadia* were highly praised because they were felt to belong to this tradition, as we can see in the discussion of the *Arcadia* in the opening chapter of Fulke Greville's biography of Sidney.[10] But the Renaissance was above all a great age of educational theory, and its educational theory, to which Milton contributed, was based squarely on the two central facts of Renaissance society, the prince and the courtier or magistrate. Hence the educational treatise, which normally took the form of the ideal education of prince, courtier, or magistrate, had even greater prestige in Renaissance eyes than the description of the ideal commonwealth.

The Classical pattern for the treatise on the ideal education of the prince had been established by Xenophon in the *Cyropaedia*, which Sidney describes as "an absolute heroical poem,"[11] thus implying that it represents the prose counterpart of the encyclopedic epic. Spenser, in the letter to Raleigh which introduces *The Faerie Queene*, makes it clear that this encyclopedic prose form is also a part of the conception of his poem, and speaks of his preference for Xenophon's form to Plato's, for a practicable as compared to an impossible ideal. Milton also shows a touch of impatience with Plato and with what he calls Plato's "ayrie Burgomasters"[12] and we should expect him to be of Spenser's mind in this matter. And just as the encyclopedic shape of the Bible is condensed into the speech of Michael, so the speech of Raphael versifies a major prose genre, for the colloquy of Raphael and Adam is a Socratic dialogue without irony, a symposium with unfermented wine, a description of an ideal commonwealth ending with the expulsion of undesirables, and (for Adam is the king of men) a cyropaedia, or manual of royal discipline. It is essentially the education of Adam, and it covers a vast amount of knowledge, both natural and revealed.

The tradition of the epic was, of course, established by Homer in the *Iliad* and the *Odyssey*, but these two epics represent different structural principles. Many Classical scholars have noted that the *Iliad* is closer in form to Greek tragedy than it is to the *Odyssey*. The *Odyssey*, the more typically epic pattern, is the one followed more closely by Virgil in the *Aeneid* and by Milton in *Paradise Lost*. Of the characteristics which the *Odyssey*, the *Aeneid*, and *Paradise Lost* have in common, three are of particular importance.

In the first place, there are, in the form in which we have them, twelve books, or a multiple of twelve. Milton published the first edition of *Paradise Lost* in ten books to demonstrate his contempt for tradition, and the second edition in twelve to illustrate the actual proportions of the poem. He had been preceded in his conversion to a duodecimal system by Tasso, who had expanded the twenty cantos of *Gerusalemme Liberata* into the twenty-four of *Gerusalemme Conquistata*. Spenser, too, is preoccupied with twelves: each book has twelve cantos and the total number of books planned was either twelve or twenty-four. We shall try to suggest in a moment that the association of Milton's epic with this sacred and zodiacal number may be less arbitrary than it looks.

Secondly, the action of both the *Odyssey* and the *Aeneid* splits neatly in two. The first twelve books of the *Odyssey* deal with the wanderings of the hero, with the journey through wonderlands of marvels and terrors, the immemorial quest theme. The next twelve books never leave Ithaca (except for the katabasis at the end, in a part of the poem often considered a later addition), and their action is that of a typical comedy of recognition and intrigue, as the unknown and ridiculed beggar eventually turns out to be the returning hero. The first six books of the *Aeneid* have a similar quest pattern; the next six, the account of the struggle of Aeneas with the Italian warlords, also has the structure of romantic comedy, full of compacts, ordeals, and other traditional features of comic action, and ending in success, marriage, and the birth of a new society. In both epics the main interest shifts half way from the hero's private perils to his social context. In the letter to Raleigh, Spenser, with a reference to Tasso, also distinguishes private or princely from public or kingly virtues in the epic theme. This division of narrative between a quest theme and a theme of the settling of a social order has a Biblical parallel in the story of the Exodus, where forty years of Israel's wandering in the wilderness are followed by the conquest and settlement of the Promised Land. Milton preserves the traditional feature of a split in the middle of the action when, at the beginning of book 7, he says that the action for the second half of the poem will be confined to the earth. The order in *Paradise Lost* is the reverse of the Biblical one, as it starts with the Promised Land and ends in the wilderness; but the Biblical order is preserved when we add *Paradise Regained* to the sequence.

But of course of all the traditional epic features, the most important is that of beginning the action *in medias res*, in Horace's phrase, at a dramatically well-advanced point and then working back simultaneously to the beginning and forward to the end. If we ask beginning and end of what, the answer is, beginning and end of the total action, of which only a part may be presented in the actual poem. This total action is cyclical in shape: it almost has to be because of the nature of the quest theme. The hero goes out to do something, does it, and returns. In the *Odyssey*, the total action begins when Odysseus leaves Ithaca and goes off to the Trojan War, and it ends when he gets back to Ithaca as master of his house again. Matters are less simple in the *Iliad*, but even there the total movement of the Greeks out to Troy and back home again is clearly in the background. In the *Aeneid* there is what from Milton's point of view is a most important advance in this conception of a total cyclical action. Here the total action begins and ends, not at precisely the same point, but at the same point renewed and transformed by the heroic action itself. That is, the total action of the *Aeneid* begins when Aeneas leaves Troy collapsing in flames, losing his wife; and it ends with the new Troy established at Rome, Aeneas remarried, and the household gods of the defeated Troy set up once again in a new home. The end is the beginning as recreated by the heroism of Aeneas.

We notice that the trick of beginning the action at a dramatically well-advanced point is not done entirely at random. The *Odyssey* begins with Odysseus at the furthest point from home, on the island of Calypso, subjected to the temptations of Penelope's only formidable rival. The action of the *Aeneid* similarly begins with Aeneas's shipwreck on the shores of Carthage, the *Erbfeind* or hereditary enemy of Rome and the site of the citadel of Juno, Aeneas's implacable enemy. Similarly, the action of *Paradise Lost* begins at the furthest possible point from the presence of God, in hell. The cycle which forms the total background action of *Paradise Lost* is again the cycle of the Bible. It begins where God begins, in an eternal presence, and it ends where God ends, in an eternal presence. The foreground action begins *in medias res*, translated by Milton in his Argument as "into the midst of things," with Satan already fallen into hell, and it works from there back to the beginning and forward to the end of the total action. The foreground action deals with the conspiracy of Satan and the fall of Adam and Eve, and the two speeches of the two angels deal with the rest of the cycle. Raphael begins with what is chronologically the first event in the poem, the showing of Christ to the angels, and brings the action down to the point at which the poem begins. After Adam's fall, Michael picks up the story and summarizes the Biblical narrative through to the Last Judgment, which brings us back again to the point at which God is all in all. The epic narrative thus consists of a foreground action with two great flanking speeches where the action is reported by messengers (*angeloi*) putting it in its proper context.

We notice that in the Classical epics there are two kinds of revelation. There is the kind that comes from the gods above, when Athene or Venus appears to the hero at a crucial point with words of comfort or advice.

There is nothing mysterious about these appearances: they happen in broad daylight and their function is to illuminate the present situation. Athene appears in the disguise of Mentor to give Telemachus the kind of advice that a wise and kindly human being would also give. There is another kind of revelation which is sought from gods below. Telemachus gains it by disguising himself as a seal and catching Proteus; Odysseus gains it by a complicated and sinister ritual of sacrifice, the spilling of blood, ghosts and darkness. There are strong hints that knowledge obtained in this way is normally forbidden knowledge, and it does not illuminate a present situation: it is specifically knowledge of the future. It is knowledge about his own future that Odysseus seeks when he calls up Tiresias from hell; it is knowledge of the future of Rome that Aeneas gets when he descends, though with less ritual elaboration, into the cave guarded by the Sibyl. The association of future and forbidden knowledge is carried even further in Dante's *Inferno*, because the people in Dante's hell have knowledge of the future but not of the present.

The kind of knowledge given to Adam in Michael's speech is essentially a knowledge of the future, of what is going to happen. It is intended to be consoling, although Adam collapses twice under the ordeal of being consoled, and the fact that knowledge of the future is possible means of course that the freedom of human will has been mortally injured. The suggestion is clearly that such knowledge of the future is a part of the forbidden knowledge which Adam should never have had in the first place, knowledge which God is willing to give him but which Satan would have cheated him out of. Human life now is in large part a dialectic between revelation and the knowledge of good and evil, and this dialectic is represented in *Paradise Lost* by the contrast between God the Father and Adam after his fall. God the Father sits in heaven and foreknows what will happen, but, as he carefully explains, not forcing it to happen. Below him is Adam in a parody of that situation, foreknowing what is going to happen to the human race in consequence of his fall, but unable in the smallest degree to interfere with or alter the course of events.

The foreground action, the conspiracy of Satan and its consequences, forms a kind of mock-Telemachia in counterpoint to the main epic action to be considered in a moment, a parable of a prodigal son who does not return. Technically, however, the foreground action presents a sharp focusing of attention which brings it close to dramatic forms. The fall itself is conceived in the form of tragedy, the great rival of epic in

Renaissance theory, yet almost the antithesis of the epic, as it demanded a concentrated unity of action which seems the opposite of the epic's encyclopedic range. The ninth book represents a crystallization of Milton's earlier plans for treating the fall of man in tragic form, with Satan as a returning spirit of vengeance persuading Eve into a foreshortened compliance much as Iago does Othello. Nature, sighing through all her works, occupies the place of the chorus.

At the opening of the poem we find ourselves plunged into the darkness of hell and eventually, after our pupils have expanded, look around and see one or two lights glaring. We then realize that these are eyes, and a number of huge clouded forms begin to come out of a kind of sea and gather on a kind of shore. Throughout the first two books we move through shadowy and indefinite gloom, and then, at the opening of the third, are plunged quite as suddenly into blinding light, where only after our pupils have contracted again can we observe such details as the pavement of heaven which "impurpl'd with Celestial Roses smil'd" [*PL*, 3.364]. We feel that such intensities are appropriate to a poet who is not only blind but baroque, and who, if he never saw the shadows of Rembrandt or the sunlight of Claude, still reflects his age's interest in chiaroscuro. But the principle *ut pictura poesis*[13] can only be expressed in verbal spectacle, and we should also realize the extent to which the dramatic form of the Jonsonian masque has informed these first three books, a dark and sinister antimasque being followed by a splendid vision of ordered glory. The masque vision moves slowly from heaven down through the starry spheres to Eden; the antimasque modulates into the ludicrous disorder of the Limbo of Vanities, and disappears until it is recalled by Raphael's narrative of an earlier expulsion from heaven.

There is, then, with the dramatic foreground action and the speeches of Raphael and Michael filling in the beginning and end of the total background action, a kind of formal symmetry of a type that we might not expect in a poem that we have just called baroque. I think that this formal symmetry can be carried much further, and I should like to divide the total action in a way which I think best illustrates it. Some of the divisions take up several books and others only a few lines, but that is of no importance. Most of the shorter ones are from the Bible, and Milton expected his reader to be able to give them their due importance. Let us visualize the dial of a clock, with the presence of God where the figure twelve is. The first four figures of the dial represent the four main events of the speech of Raphael. First comes the first epiphany or manifestation of Christ, when God the Father shows his Son to the angels and demands that they worship him. This is the chronological beginning of the total action, as already remarked. Next, at two on the dial, comes the second epiphany of Christ at the end of the war in heaven, when on the third day he tramples on the rebel angels and manifests himself in triumph and wrath. The third stage is the creation of the natural order, as described by Milton in his extraordinarily skilful paraphrase of the Genesis account. The fourth phase is the creation of the human order, with the forming of the bodies of Adam and Eve, in the account of which Adam takes over from Raphael.

After this the foreground action moves across the lower part of the dial. At the figure five comes the conspiracy of Satan, ending in his pact with Sin and Death. The generation of Death from Satan is a parody of the generation of the Son from the Father which starts off the action, Death being, so to speak, the Word of Satan. At six, the nadir of the action, comes the tragic catastrophe, the fall of Adam and Eve, the fall, that is, of the human order established by God. Next, at seven, comes the fall of the natural order, which is really a part of the fall of Adam and Eve, and is described in book 10 as the triumph of Sin and Death, corresponding to Satan's pact with them at five.

The next four stages are the ones covered by the speech of Michael: they correspond to the four that we found in the speech of Raphael, but are in roughly the reverse order. First, at eight, comes the re-establishing of the natural order at the time of the flood, when it is promised with the symbol of the rainbow that seedtime and harvest will not fail until the end of the world. Next, at nine, comes the re-establishing of the human order, when the law is given to Israel and the prototype of Jesus, Joshua, who has the same name as Jesus, takes possession of the Promised Land. Next, at ten, comes the third epiphany of Christ, the Incarnation properly speaking, which again is an epiphany ending with the triumph over death and hell in a three-day battle. Next, at eleven, comes the fourth epiphany of Christ, the Last Judgment, again an epiphany of triumph and wrath, when the final separation is made between the orders of heaven and of hell. At twelve, we come back again to the point prophesied by God himself in his speech in book 3, when he says that there will come a time when he will lay by his sceptre and "God shall be All in All" [*PL*, 3.341]. The final point in the vast cycle is the same point as the beginning, yet not the same point, because, as in the *Aeneid*, the ending is the starting point renewed and transformed by the heroic quest of Christ.

Thus there can be only one cycle, not an endless series of them. To summarize:

1. First epiphany of Christ: generation of Son from Father.
2. Second epiphany of Christ: triumph after three-day conflict.
3. Establishment of the natural order in the creation.
4. Establishment of the human order: creation of Adam and Eve.
5. Epiphany of Satan, generating Sin and Death.
6. Fall of the human order.
7. Fall of the natural order: triumph of Sin and Death.
8. Re-establishment of the natural order at the end of the flood.
9. Re-establishment of the human order with the giving of the law.
10. Third epiphany of Christ: the Word as gospel.
11. Fourth epiphany of Christ: the apocalypse or Last Judgment.

There are four orders of existence in *Paradise Lost*, the divine order, the angelic order, the human order, and the demonic order. Being an epic, *Paradise Lost* has to deal with the traditional theme of the epic, which is the theme of heroic action. In order to understand what heroic action was to Milton we have to think what a Christian poet would mean by the conception of heroic action: that is, we have to ask ourselves what for Milton a hero was, and, even more important, what an act was. Milton says clearly in *The Christian Doctrine* what he means by an act. An act is the expression of the energy of a free and conscious being. Consequently all acts are good. There is no such thing, strictly speaking, as an evil act; evil or sin implies deficiency, and implies also the loss or lack of the power to act. There is a somewhat unexpected corollary of this: if all acts are good, then God is the source of all real action. At the same time, as Milton says, or rather as his sentence structure says in spite of him, it is almost impossible to avoid speaking of evil acts:

> It is called Actual Sin, not that sin is properly an action, for in reality it implies defect; but because it commonly consists in some act. For every act is in itself good; it is only its irregularity, or deviation from the line of right, which, properly speaking, is evil. [*Works*, 15:199]

What happens when Adam eats the forbidden fruit, then, is not an act, but the surrendering of the power to act. Man is free to lose his freedom, and there, obviously, his freedom stops. His position is like that of a man on the edge of a precipice—if he jumps it appears to be an act, but it is really the giving up of the possibility of action, the surrendering of himself to the law of gravitation which will take charge of him for the brief remainder of his life. In this surrendering of the power to act lies the key to Milton's conception of the behaviour of Adam. A typically fallen human act is something where the word "act" has to be in quotation marks. It is a pseudo-act, the pseudo-act of disobedience, and it is really a refusal to act at all.

Implied in this argument is a curious paradox between the dramatic and the conceptual aspects of the temptation scenes in Milton's poetry. In a temptation somebody is being persuaded to do something that looks like an act, but which is really the loss of the power to act. Consequently, the abstaining from this kind of pseudo-activity is often the sign that one possesses a genuine power of action. The Lady in *Comus*, for example, has a somewhat uninteresting dramatic role: she is, in fact, paralysed, and, dramatically, says little except an eloquent and closely reasoned paraphrase of "no." Comus attracts a good deal more of our sympathy because his arguments are specious, and therefore dramatically more interesting. Yet we have to realize that the real situation is the opposite of the dramatic one. It is Comus who represents passion, which is the opposite of action; it is the Lady who holds to the source of all freedom of action. The same situation is even more sharply manifested in the role of Jesus in *Paradise Regained*, where Jesus behaves, for four books, like a householder dealing with an importunate salesman. Yet again what is actually going on is the opposite of what appears to be going on. Satan, who seems so lively and resourceful, is the power that moves toward the cessation of all activity, a kind of personal entropy that transforms all energy into a heat-death.

The typical demonic "act" is not a real act either, but it is a much more concentrated parody of divine action. It has the quality not of disobedience but of rebellion, and it differs from the human act in that it involves rivalry, or attempted rivalry, with God. The appearance of Nimrod at the beginning of the last book of *Paradise Lost* represents the coming into human life of the demonic, of the ability to worship devils, of turning to Satan for one's conception of the kingdom and the power and the glory, instead of to God. What Satan himself manifests in *Paradise Lost* is this perverted quality of parody-heroism, of which the essential quality is destructiveness. Consequently it is to Satan and his followers that Milton assigns the conventional and Classical type of heroism. Satan, like Achilles, retires sulkily in heaven when a decision appears to be favouring another Son of God, and emerges in a torrent of wrath to wreak vengeance. Like Odysseus, he steers his way with great cunning between the Scylla-like Sin and the Charybdis-like Death; like the knights errant of romance, he goes out alone on a perilous quest to an unknown world. The remark the devils make about the war in heaven, that they have sustained the war for a day, "And if one day, why not Eternal dayes?" [*PL*, 6.424], opens up a perverted vision of eternity as a Valhalla of endless strife.

It is only the divine that can really act, by Milton's own definition of an act, and the quality of the divine act reveals itself in *Paradise Lost* as an act of creation, which becomes an act of recreation or redemption after the fall of man. Christ, therefore, who creates the world and then recreates or redeems man, is the hero of *Paradise Lost* simply because, as the agent or acting principle of the Father, he is ultimately the only actor in the poem.

The angelic order is there to provide models for human action. They have superior intellectual and physical powers which man may eventually attain, but in *Paradise Lost* they are moral models only. They form a community of service and obedience, often doing things meaningless to them except that as the will of God they have meaning. They are ministers of responsibility (Gabriel), instruction (Raphael), command (Michael), or vigilance (Uriel). The figure of the tense, waiting angels, listening for the Word to speak and motionless until it does, appears in the last line of the *Nativity Ode* and again in the last line of the sonnet on the poet's blindness. Such angels are, as the angel says to John at the end of the Bible, fellow servants of mankind: there is nothing in Milton of Rilke's "schrecklich" angel.[14]

More important than any of these, for the theme of heroism, is Abdiel, who remains faithful to God in the midst of the revolted angels. Abdiel, like many people of unimpeachable integrity, is not a very attractive character, but everything he says in the poem is of the highest importance. The speech which he makes to Satan at the time of the war in heaven indicates that he is establishing the pattern of genuine heroism that is later to be exhibited in the life of Christ, the "better part of fortitude"[15] which consists primarily in obedience and endurance and in the kind of courage that is willing to suffer under ridicule and contempt and a chorus of opposition. As Abdiel says to Satan, after being restored to the faithful angels, "my Sect thou seest" [*PL*, 6.147]. This pattern is followed in the Biblical visions which Michael shows to Adam: in the story of Enoch, the one just man who stands out against all the vice of his time, and receives the angelic reward of direct transportation to heaven, and in Noah, who is similarly the one just man of his time and is saved from an otherwise total destruction. It could have been exemplified by Lot in Sodom, which is referred to briefly by Milton. This is the pattern which is followed by the prophets and apostles, and nobody else is entitled to be called heroic.

Doubtless the faithful angels could have defeated the rebels by themselves, but the symbolism of the three-day war in heaven is designed to show that the total angelic power of action is contained in the Son of God. The angels have no strength that does not come from God, and the devils have no strength against God at all. It is difficult not to feel that the entire war in heaven is a huge practical joke to the Father, all the more of one because of the seriousness with which the devils take it. The admiring description of the size of Satan's spear and shield in book 1 has two perspectives: from man's point of view Satan is incalculably strong, but from God's point of view he is only a lubber fiend. God's own conception of strength is represented by the infant Christ of the *Nativity Ode*, the genuine form of Hercules strangling the serpent in his cradle, physically weak and yet strong enough to overcome the world.

In this world spiritual strength, being a direct gift of God, is not necessarily accompanied by physical strength, though it is normally accompanied by physical invulnerability. This condition is the condition of chastity, traditionally a magical strength in romance, and the theme of the magic of chastity runs all through Milton. The Lady cannot be hurt by Comus because of the "hidden strength" of her chastity [l. 415]. Samson owes his physical strength to his chastity, to his observance of his Nazarite vow: as he says bitterly, God hung his strength in his hair [*SA*, ll. 58–9]. He loses his chastity when he tells Delilah what his secret is. Such chastity does not in his case imply virginity or even continence: two marriages to Philistine women do not affect it, nor apparently does even a visit to a Philistine harlot, which Milton ignores, though he read about it in the Book of Judges. Adam and Eve have been given more than mortal strength by their chastity, which is also not affected by sexual intercourse: they lose their chastity only by eating of the forbidden tree. A reference to Samson in book 9 establishes the link in the symbolism of chastity between the two.

Like most morally coherent writers, Milton is careful to distinguish the human from the demonic, even when what he is showing is the relation between them. As it may be difficult to feel this distinction without examples we may take an analogy from Shakespeare. Cleopatra in Shakespeare is all the things that the critics of Milton say Eve is. She is vain and frivolous and light-minded and capricious and extravagant and irresponsible and a very bad influence on Antony, who ought to be out chasing Parthians instead of wasting his time with her. She is morally a most deplorable character, yet there is something about her which is obstinately likable. Perhaps that makes her more dangerous, but it's no good: we cannot feel that Cleopatra is evil in the way that Goneril and Regan are evil. For one thing, Cleopatra can always be unpredictable, and as long as she can be that she is human. Goneril and Regan are much closer to what is meant in religion by lost souls, and what that means dramatically is that they can no longer be unpredictable. Everything they do or say is coarse and ugly and cruel, but still it also has about it something of the stylized grandeur of the demonic, something of the quality that Milton's devils have and that his human beings do not have. At the same time Cleopatra is a part of something far more sinister than herself: this comes out in the imagery attached to Egypt, if not in the characterization attached to her. Putting the two together, what we see is the human contained by the demonic, a fascinating creature of infinite variety who is still, from another point of view, sprung from the equivocal generation of the Nile.

It is the same with Adam and Eve. Theologically and conceptually, they have committed every sin in the calendar. In *The Christian Doctrine* Milton sets it all down: there was nothing bad that they omitted to do when they ate that wretched apple:

> It comprehended at once distrust in the divine veracity, and a proportionate credulity in the assurances of Satan; unbelief; ingratitude; disobedience; gluttony; in the man excessive uxoriousness, in the woman a want of proper regard for her husband, in both an insensibility to the welfare of their offspring, and that offspring the whole human race; parricide, theft, invasion of the rights of others, sacrilege, deceit, presumption in aspiring to divine attributes, fraud in the means employed to attain the object, pride, and arrogance. [*Works,* 15:181–3]

Yet this is something that it is wholly impossible for us to feel or realize dramatically, nor does Milton attempt to make us do so. Eve may have been a silly girl but she is still our general mother, still quite obviously the same kind of human being that we are. What has happened is that human life is now attached to the demonic, this being one of the points made by Michael, especially in the vision of Nimrod, the archetypal tyrant, the tyrant being one of the clearest examples of a human being who has given himself up to the demonic.

The fact that conventional heroism, as we have it in Classical epic and medieval and Renaissance romance, is associated with the demonic in Milton means, of course, that *Paradise Lost* is a profoundly antiromantic and antiheroic poem. Most of us live our lives on a roughly human level, but if we meet with some setback, snub, imposed authority, or other humiliation we are thrown back on something that will support and console us, and unless we are saints that something is likely to be the ego. The sombre, brooding, humourless ego, with its "high disdain, from sence of injur'd merit" [*PL*, 1.98] drives us to look for compensation, perhaps by identifying ourselves with some irresistible hero. If in this state we read Milton, we shall find his Satan, so far from being the author of evil, a congenial and sympathetic figure. If we later regain a better sense of proportion, we may understand something of the profundity and accuracy of Milton's conception of evil.

Satan is a rebel, and into Satan Milton has put all the horror and distress with which he contemplated the egocentric revolutionaries of his time, who stumbled from one party to another and finally ended precisely where they had started, in a cyclical movement with no renewal. There is an almost uncanny anticipation of some of the moods of later Romanticism, also an age of egocentric revolutionaries. In particular, there is a quality in Milton's treatment of the demonic world that can only be called Wagnerian: in the unvarying nobility of the rhetoric, in the nihilistic heroic action that begins and ends in the lake of fire, in the *Götterdämmerung* motif in the music of hell:

> Others more milde,
> Retreated in a silent valley, sing
> With notes Angelical to many a Harp
> Thir own Heroic deeds and hapless fall
> By doom of Battel; and complain that Fate
> Free Vertue should enthrall to Force or Chance. [*PL*, 2.546–51]

This is not to say that Wagner is a demonic artist, any more than that Milton is a Satanist, only that there are demonic elements portrayed in

Wagner that some very evil people have found, as many have found Satan, irresistibly attractive.

The antiheroic tendency in Milton is, however, less complicated than his attitude to myth, of which it forms part. When a literary critic says that the story of the fall of man is a myth, he is not making any statement about the truth of its content, merely that it is a certain kind of story; but still his feeling about its truth is coloured by this very shift of attention from its content to its form. But Milton is never tired of stressing the difference in ethical content between the truth of the Bible and the fables of the heathen, and obviously the story of the fall would never have interested him if he had not believed it to be as literally true as the events of his own life. The story of *Paradise Lost* is a myth in the sense that the action or narrative movement (*mythos*) is provided by a divine being: the essential content is human, and as credible and plausible as Milton's source would allow him to make it. The marvels and grotesqueries of the poem, such as the building of Pandemonium or the Limbo of Vanities, are mostly demonic, and form a contrast to the central action. In modern literature a writer may use a mythical subject because it affords him an interesting and traditional story pattern, as Cocteau does in *Orphée* or Giraudoux in *Antigone*. In Tolstoy's *Resurrection* we have a purely realistic narrative which assumes a shape with the religious significance indicated in the title. Milton's attitude to myth in *Paradise Lost* is much closer, temperamentally and technically, to Tolstoy than it is to Cocteau or Giraudoux.

Myths differ from folk tales or legends in having a superior kind of importance attached to them, and this in turn makes them stick together and form mythologies. A fully developed mythology thus tends, as the Bible does, to take an encyclopedic shape. Ovid's *Metamorphoses*, for example, starts with creation and flood stories and works its way down to Julius Caesar as the Bible does to Jesus. Milton's exhaustive use of Ovid is often sympathetic, but evidently he finds in the Ovidian theme of metamorphosis, the identifying of a human figure with an object in nature, the point at which polytheism becomes obvious idolatry. The demonic action of *Paradise Lost* ends with an Ovidian metamorphosis in which the devils are changed to serpents. Satan has taken the form of the serpent; he finds in hell that he cannot get rid of it, but is still a serpent; the devils in looking at him become serpents too:

what they saw,
They felt themselvs now changing. [*PL*, 10.540–1]

There is a clear recall of the remark about idols in the 115th Psalm: "they that make them are like unto them" [Psalm 115:8].

For us, the mythological imagination is really part of the poetic imagination: the instinct to identify a human figure with a natural object, which gives mythology its sun-gods and tree-gods and ocean-gods, is the same instinct that is described by Whitman:

> There was a child went forth every day,
> And the first object he look'd upon, that object he became,
> And that object became part of him for the day or a certain part of the day,
> Or for many years or stretching cycles of years.[16]

The author of *Lycidas* would have understood this very well; but a question not relevant to Whitman is relevant to Milton: is this identifying consciousness centred in the ego, as Satan's intelligence is, or not? To identify one's consciousness directly with the works of God in our present world, for Milton, is to enter the forest of Comus on Comus's own terms, to unite ourselves to a submoral, subconscious, subhuman existence which is life to the body but death to the soul. The free intelligence must detach itself from this world and unite itself to the totality of freedom and intelligence which is God in man, shift its centre of gravity from the self to the presence of God in the self. Then it will find the identity with nature it appeared to reject: it will participate in the Creator's view of a world he made and found good. This is the relation of Adam and Eve to Eden before their fall. From Milton's point of view, the polytheistic imagination can never free itself from the labyrinths of fantasy and irony, with their fitful glimpses of inseparable good and evil. What Milton means by revelation is a consolidated, coherent, encyclopedic view of human life which defines, among other things, the function of poetry. Every act of the free intelligence, including the poetic intelligence, is an attempt to return to Eden, a world in the human form of a garden, where we may wander as we please but cannot lose our way.

II The Breaking of the Music

In looking at the total cycle of events in *Paradise Lost*, we saw that the first event chronologically is the manifestation of Christ to the angels by the Father, the event described by Raphael near the middle of book 5. There are several difficult points in this scene, and we have to walk warily. In the first place, it looks as though the Father were exhibiting his youngest upstart favourite to a better-established community who had at least the right of seniority; and in regard to Satan, as though some senile whim were making a younger Jacob supplant an Esau who had as yet done nothing to forfeit his birthright. This view of the Son of God as the latest favourite is the superficial view, and consequently it is the one that the devils take, all superficial readers of Milton being in the position of minor devils. But the superficial view is, as usual, the wrong one.

In *The Christian Doctrine*, Milton distinguishes the literal generation of the Son by the Father from the "metaphorical" generation. Where God is concerned, Milton is much more at ease with the literal than with the metaphorical, but there is a real distinction here, the nature of which is explained by Abdiel to Satan later on. Abdiel says that the Son of God is the Word of God, that is, the active agent of God, and as the agent of God, he created all things, including the angels. This may be the Son of God's first epiphany, or manifestation as an objective fact or personality, to the angels, but what the angels are really looking at, including those who are later to revolt, is their own creative principle. By refusing to understand that he is their own creative principle, by resenting or mocking his exhibition, the rebel angels are committing the sin which later reappears in human history as the sin of Ham, the sin that brought so heavy a curse of servitude on Ham and his descendants.[17]

It also appears that the epiphanized Son of God is to the angels something of what the forbidden tree is to man, a provoking object, as Milton calls it in *Areopagitica*, set in front of the angels, hung deliberately in front of their noses as a test of their obedience and as an incident in their own spiritual education. One gets the impression that in some mysterious way there is a drama going on in heaven which corresponds to the drama going on on earth, and that the angels are being educated in the same kind of epic quest that the human race is being educated in. Perhaps this is part of what Raphael means when he says to Adam that earth may be only the shadow of heaven, and that things on earth are much more like things in heaven than is generally believed by Adam's descendants. God the Father says to the angels, quoting from what is eventually going to be the second Psalm,

> This day have I begot whom I declare
> My onely Son[18] [*PL*, 5.603–4]

and to Adam, "in the day that ye eat thereof ye shall surely die."[19] In both oracles there is a mental reservation in the word "day" which angels and Adam alike are required to understand. "This day" to the angels does not mean literal begetting at that moment: "the day" to Adam does not mean literal death at that moment.

In any case, the rebel angels assume that the Son of God is a creature, because they feel that they are also sons of God. But as the Son is the manifest power of God, and as they do not recognize him as such, they are forced to go on to reject the creative power of God itself. In the *Ecclesiastical Polity*, Hooker, in attempting to deal with the question of why some angels revolted in the very presence of God, says that it could only have happened as the result of some sort of "reflex of their understanding upon themselves."[20] In Milton, the rebel angels go through a similar kind of reflex, which takes the form of a curious abstracting quality in their minds. Three aspects of this abstraction are of particular importance in understanding the poem.

In the first place, they abstract the will of God into fatalism. The Son is the will or agent of God, carrying out the divine decrees in the Father's mind: when they reject him, the conception of omnipotent will becomes separated from God, and from the sense of reason and purpose and consciousness which his presence should inspire. This separation obliterates the distinction between Creator and creature: the real creative power, Satan feels, has made him as much of a god as God, and where two gods conflict, there can be no supreme power but fate. Fate is not chance, to be presently considered, and which is the deity of chaos rather than hell. Chance is mindless and automatic: fate is a mysterious and sinister omnipotence to which a demonic being would feel himself impersonally linked, as the Son is personally linked to the Father.

Secondly, as just implied, the rebel angels abstract the personal creative power of God into an impersonal creative power, whose affiliations are with the physical and material. Their invention of gunpowder is a byproduct of the demonic instinct to turn for help from the creative power of God to the "originals of Nature" [*PL*, 6.511]. Third, and most important, they abstract the two aspects of God's creative power, energy and form, into the categories which we know as time and space. Thus in the later demonic theology, time and space are the official creative forces of the world. Space, says Satan in the council of devils, may produce new worlds. And in reply to Abdiel he says:

> We know no time when we were not as now;
> Know none before us, self-begot, self-rais'd
> By our own quick'ning power, when fatal course
> Had circl'd his full Orbe, the birth mature
> Of this our native Heav'n, Ethereal Sons. [*PL*, 5.859–63]

Raphael has already explained to Adam, when he gets to this point in his narrative, that the showing of the Son to the angels took place on a New Year's Day in the great year marked by the precession of the equinoxes, and which takes up twenty-six thousand of our years. It is obvious, therefore, that there are different levels of experiencing and comprehending time and space. In the mind of God time is always a pure present, and past, present, and future are all the same point. The ambiguity in the word "day" requires men and angels to sharpen their habitual conceptions of time to understand something of the divine view, which proceeds from a mind where a day and a thousand years are the same. With the angels, time is essentially the variety and rhythm of experience, or, as Raphael explains to Adam:

> For wee have also our Eevning and our Morn,
> Wee ours for change delectable, not need. [*PL*, 5.628–9]

The experience of time by Adam is similar, but after his fall, human beings began to experience time in the way that we still do, as a combination of a straight line and a circle. The straight line, where there is no real present and everything is annihilated in the past as we are drawn into an unknown future, is the fallen conception of time. The unfailing cycle of seedtime and harvest, established after the flood, represents the element of promise and hope in time, and imitates in its shape the circling of the spheres. To the devils below mankind, time is pure clock time, or simply one moment after another, the kind of experience dramatized by Macbeth in his "Tomorrow" speech [5.5.19–24].

Similarly with the understanding of space. To God, just as all time is an eternal present, so all space is an eternal presence. For the angels, and for man in paradise, space has that coherence of form which we attach to the word "home" in our ordinary language. To Adam after the fall, space has become an indifferent environment, and in the demonic conception of space, it has become a world of total alienation. Two famous remarks of Satan indicate this: one is "Which way I flie is Hell; my self am Hell" [*PL*, 4.75], the other is

> The mind is its own place, and in it self
> Can make a Heav'n of Hell, a Hell of Heav'n. [*PL*, 1.254–5]

The two statements represent very different moods, but are intellectually identical: they both assume a totally objective universe with nothing qualitatively different from it except the egocentric subject.

In refusing to recognize the Son as their own creative principle, then, the devils are closing the gate of their own origin. This theme of closing the gate of origin recurs all through the epic, and is the basis of the feeling which later appears in humanity as what Milton calls shame. Shame to Milton is something deeper and more sinister in human emotion than simply the instinctive desire to cover the genital organs. It is rather a state of mind which is the state of the fall itself: it might be described as the emotional response to the state of pride. It is the state later dramatized in Blake's very Miltonic lyric, *Earth's Answer*, in the *Songs of Experience*:

> Does the sower
> Sow by night,
> Or the plowman in darkness plow? [K211/E19]

In Homer's *Odyssey* Odysseus is placed asleep in a mysterious place called the Cave of the Nymphs, which is said to have two entrances, one used by the gods and the other by mortal men. The conception is similar to Homer's other conception of the two gates of dreams in the *Iliad*, the horn gate of true dreams and the ivory gate of delusory ones. The Cave of the Nymphs became an important archetype with the Neoplatonic philosopher Porphyry's commentary *De antro nympharum*, and it finds its way into the symbolism of, at least, Blake and Yeats.[21] Milton's paradise also has two entrances, one employed by God and the angels in descending what was later visualized as Jacob's ladder, and the other used by Adam when he is driven out of paradise down to the "subjected Plaine" [*PL*, 12.640]. From then on, and during the whole of human history, the gate of origin for the entire human race is shut behind us.

In contrast, the gate of heaven opens easily, as though operated by some kind of electric eye. When Raphael comes down to instruct Adam, we are told that

> at the Gate
> Of Heav'n arriv'd, the gate self-opend wide
> On golden Hinges turning. [*PL*, 5.253–5]

Similarly when the Son of God comes down to create the world in book 7:

> Heav'n op'nd wide
> Her ever during Gates, Harmonious sound
> On golden Hinges moving. [*PL*, 7.205–7]

But while the gate of heaven opens easily, it shuts easily too, if the grace its opening symbolizes is not taken advantage of. Milton says in *The Reason of Church Government*, "The doore of grace turnes upon smooth hinges wide opening to send out, but soon shutting to recall the precious offers of mercy to a nation" [*Works*, 3:225]. Man does not evolve toward grace in his own time, but must seize the eternal moment of heaven when it appears to him. The gate separating hell from chaos, by contrast, opens with great and creaking difficulty, but once open, it can never be shut until the Last Judgment, when it becomes the seal on a tomb from which there is no resurrection:

> Both *Sin*, and *Death*, and yawning *Grave* at last
> Through *Chaos* hurld, obstruct the mouth of Hell
> For ever, and seal up his ravenous Jawes. [*PL*, 10.635–7]

The conceptions of time and space, then, which are really the energy and form of God's creative power, exist on different levels, depending on the intelligence of the conceiving mind. This is a cosmological fact, and the fall, first of the rebel angels and then of man, elaborates a cosmology. Everybody who has ever had to comment on *Paradise Lost* has had to devote some time to its cosmology, often with some reluctance at having to incorporate what seems the lumber of defunct science in with the living poetry. It would however be better to think of the cosmology of *Paradise Lost* as a framework for the poem's imagery: in that way it does not become merely obsolete science but a part of the structure of the poem itself.

Traditionally, for both medieval and Renaissance poets, and in fact for most poets down to Newton's time, there are four levels of existence, corresponding, with some modifications, to the four orders of existence described in the previous chapter. There is, in the first place, the order of grace or heaven, in the sense of the place of the presence of God. Below this is the proper human order, the way in which God intended man to live, the order represented by the story of the Garden of Eden in the Bible and by the legend of the Golden Age in the Classics. This order, though, in the Psalmist's phrase, "a little lower than the angels" [Psalm 8:5], is not, at least in Milton, qualitatively different from the angelic order. Below this again is the physical order into which man is now born, the order to which animals and plants are much better adjusted than he is. Below the physical world is the world of sin and death and corruption, a level which is not really part of nature, in the sense that it was never intended to be there, although of course it permeates the physical world and causes everything alive in it to die. We notice that Christianity has adopted the worldwide primitive belief that there is no such thing as natural death, and that all death is ultimately the result of a personal and malignant agency.

Since the fall, man is born into the third of these four levels of existence, the physical world of animals and plants. He does not belong in it, but is faced from birth with a moral dialectic, and must either rise above it into his proper human home or sink below it into the state of sin, a degradation that the animal cannot reach. Education, religion, law, and the habit of virtue are the means by which man may raise himself from the physical order into which he is born to his proper human home where he belongs. That proper home is all that he can now recover of the paradise in which he was originally placed. If we keep this in mind we shall readily understand Milton's conception of the aim of education as being "to repair the ruines of our first Parents by regaining to know God aright."[22] It follows that there are two levels of nature, a physical one and a human one. The forest inhabited by Comus is the physical world in which the Lady is lost and imprisoned: Comus urges her to enter into communion with nature as lived in that world, and his proposal is exactly that of Satan to Eve: "Be wise, and taste" [l. 812]. Included in the proposal is the suggestion that such things as sexual promiscuity are innocent, because "natural." The Lady knows that *her* nature is of a different order, and that the argument from Comus's kind of nature is founded on a bad pun.

In Milton's earlier poems, including *Comus,* the starry spheres in the physical world above the earth represent all that is left of nature as God originally planned it. The heavenly bodies are made out of quintessence, which is immortal; they move in perfect circles, the only form proper to their dignity, and they are not subject to sin or decay or mutability. There is a traditional association of the angels with the heavenly bodies: a group of angels called intelligences had them under their particular jurisdiction. We see a vestige of this in *Paradise Lost* when Milton calls Uriel the Regent of the Sun. But there are certain modifications that Milton makes in the traditional picture of the universe. In the first place, heaven itself is a creation of God like the angels, and consequently heaven is a part of the order of nature. The angels in Milton are quite familiar with the conception of nature: Abdiel says to Satan, for example: "God and Nature bid the same" [*PL*, 6.176]. Then again, in *Paradise Lost*, the whole of the order of nature falls with the fall of Adam, and with the fall of nature, as described in book 10, the stars turn into beings of noxious efficacy, meeting "in Synod unbenigne" [*PL*, 10.661]. *As far as man is concerned* (I italicize this because it is a hinge of Milton's argument), the entire order of nature is now a fallen order. The washing away of the Garden of Eden in the flood symbolizes the fact that the two levels of nature cannot both exist in space, but must succeed one another in time, and that the upper level of human nature can be lived in only as an inner state of mind, not as an outward environment.

In book 8 Adam asks Raphael, or is obviously preparing to ask him, whether other parts of the starry heavens are inhabited by conscious beings, and is "doubtfully answer'd" [Argument to book 8]. We are not yet ready to explain why Milton gives so much prominence to the fact that he, and consequently Raphael, cannot answer the question, but it is clear already that the question is unanswerable, within the framework of *Paradise Lost*. To answer a question is to consolidate the mental level on which it is asked, because we can only answer a question by accepting the assumptions in the question. If we ask, Where is God? the correct answer is no answer, because the assumption in the question is wrong: the conception of space does not apply to God in this direct way. Adam is asking a question about nature, and the nature of nature, so to speak, depends on Adam's behaviour.

This is the kind of semantic problem that we meet in Milton's discussion of the creation. The opening statement of the Bible is that God made the heavens (i.e., the sky or firmament) and the earth. The reader may naturally ask, What did he make it out of? The account goes on to say that God imposed form and light on something described as waste, void, dark, watery, and deep. In Milton this something is chaos, and there is an answer to the reader's question: God made the world "out of" matter, in its chaotic state. But if the reader asks further, Who made matter? the question is semantically illegitimate. Matter is not "made"; it is not a creation at all. If we push this "What did he make it out of" question beyond its semantic limits, we have to say either "out of nothing," which is really saying that there is no answer, or "out of something coeternal with God," which for Milton is nonsense, though it is the entering wedge of Satan's conception of an independent creative power in nature. We should be better advised to go back to the Biblical statement that God made the world and start again. To make something, whether a poem out of the babble of words in our mind or a statue out of a block of marble, is to extend our presence and consciousness into an area where it has not previously been. So with God. Chaos is that into which God's presence chooses not to extend itself; creation is that into which his presence has extended itself.

The traditional diagrams of creation are those of the chain of being and of the Ptolemaic cosmos, and Milton uses what he wants from both. The chain of being is a hierarchy of existence founded on the conceptions of form and matter, the creation and that out of which the creation is made. It stretches from God, who is form without matter, down through the angels to man, who, being half spiritual and half material, is in the exact centre, the microcosmos or epitome of the whole chain, and from there through animals and plants to the mineral world, which is the limit of creation, and from there to chaos, which is as near as we can get to matter without form. In Milton everything created, that is, anything once touched by the presence of God, has implanted in it a tendency to rise upward toward its maker and seek identity with him. For mankind this is an evolution toward a purely spiritual nature. If Adam had not fallen, the evolution would have been physical in process, until, as Raphael explains, "Your bodies may at last turn all to Spirit" [*PL*, 5.497]. Now it is primarily a moral process, like that symbolized by the chastity of the Lady in *Comus*:

> Till oft convers with heav'nly habitants
> Begin to cast a beam on th' outward shape,
> The unpolluted temple of the mind,
> And turns it by degrees to the souls essence,
> Till all be made immortal. [ll. 458–62]

The Ptolemaic universe is the environment of the chain of being. God's environment is the upper Heaven or the Empyrean; the lower heaven or sky, which stretches from the primum mobile to the moon, is part of the order of nature but not—as yet—a part of man's home. It has the traditional associations with angels we have mentioned, and is the symbolic human home of regenerate man in Dante's *Paradiso*. Below the moon are the spheres of the four elements, fire, air, water, and earth. In *Paradise Lost* there appears to be no elemental sphere of fire: we may assume that the traditional sphere of fire is identified with those of the heavenly bodies and the angels guarding them. In the *Vacation Exercise* poem, written early but published later than the first edition of *Paradise Lost*, we gather that the spheres of the elements at one time played a larger role in Milton's imagination:

> Then passing through the Spherse of watchful fire,
> And mistie Regions of wide air next under,
> And hills of Snow and lofts of piled Thunder,
> May tell at length how green-ey'd *Neptune* raves,
> In Heav'ns defiance mustering all his waves. [ll. 40–4]

This passage introduces another important element in Milton's cosmology: the three regions of air. Above the lower air that we breathe is the middle air, a region of intense cold from which storms and tempests emerge, and from which Death, in one of Milton's earliest poems, descends to carry off an infant dying of a cough. This deathly region could not have existed before the fall: it marks the limit of Satan's conquest of the order of nature and his present headquarters in human life. This is why Paul speaks of him as prince of the power of the air, why witches and other devotees of evil have the power of raising tempests, and why the heathen associated their gods with such places as the top of Mount Olympus, from whence they "rul'd the middle Air" [*PL*, 1.516]. Above this was the region of upper air, a temperate domain of perpetual spring, the traditional locale of the earthly paradise. This is where the Garden of Eden is in Dante, where the Gardens of Adonis are in Spenser, and where the Attendant Spirit in *Comus* has his home, a home also associated with the Gardens of Adonis. Eden in *Paradise Lost*, though thought of as on a mountain "above all Hills" [*PL*, 5.261], does not need to be so high up physically. But now that the freezing sphere of middle air has come into human life, that is where it is symbolically. An early sketch of *Paradise Lost* was to have begun with Moses explaining how this upper region has disappeared from human view since the fall.

The four elements are the four possible combinations of the four principles—hot, cold, moist, and dry—which in chaos keep forming chance combinations, for chance combinations are at the bottom of Milton's world just as they are at the bottom of the quantum-theory cosmologies of today. Chaos is an ambiguous world, and its moral quality is no exception. Matter, Milton explicitly says, is intrinsically good: there is nothing to be said for the Manichean view that the material is the evil. Evil must come from a perversion of intelligence, and though a corruption of nature, it cannot be an original part of nature. But of course chaos has no power to resist evil, and, not being part of the creation, it exhibits a curious affinity with the evil which conquers it, an affinity symbolized by Satan's pact with Chaos. The fall of the natural order which succeeds the fall of Adam is essentially an entrance of chaos into creation. And just as there is at least an analogy between God's creation and the human power of making things, so there is at least an analogy between chaos and the superstitions produced by ignorance and fantasy. In trying to grasp the shadows of the chaotic world we can never tell where personification stops and abstract nouns begin:

> *Orcus* and *Ades*, and the dreaded name
> Of *Demogorgon*; *Rumor* next and *Chance*,
> And *Tumult* and *Confusion* all imbroild,
> And *Discord* with a thousand various mouths. [*PL*, 2.964–7]

The poetic effect of such description is, This is chaos; you can make what you like of it. Milton says that nothing once created can be annihilated, but anything formed by chance in chaos is annihilated by the next chance.

The will of God executes the decrees in the mind of God, and all creatures apprehend that mind in their own way. The angels are carefully educated by God himself in the ways of God: he explains the meaning of events to them, even allows them to eavesdrop on what sound like arguments with himself. The faculty addressed by God in man, both before and after the fall, is the reason, a faculty not essentially different from what the angels have, but slower in the speed of its apprehension: discursive rather than intuitive, as Milton says. Below reason is the instinct which appears in the migratory birds who are "intelligent of seasons" [*PL*, 7.427]. The order of physical nature is a "self ballanc't" mechanism [*PL*, 7.242], and its emblem is the emblem of justice and equality, the balancing scales which appear at the end of book 4 to indicate, in the appropriate context, that God permits Satan's journey to

Eden. I say appropriate context, because the same fact could only be expressed in chaos by chance or accident. We are told that at one point in chaos Satan goes into what would now be called "free fall," and that he would have been falling yet if unluckily he had not happened to strike a solid cloud and bounce back up. There is still more in this deliberately grotesque image, as we shall see in a moment.

The activity of God, of which the central form is creation, is regularly symbolized in Milton by music, though music in Milton has its larger Platonic meaning which includes poetry. We may think of creation as the restraining of chaos by order: this aspect of creation is represented by the musical metaphor of "harmony," in the sense of a stable relationship of parts to a whole. There is "harmony" in heaven, symbolized by the songs of the angels, and when Christ moves into chaos and creates order the angelic music accompanies the act. Creation itself takes the form of spheres, harmoniously moving with a music that Adam could hear before his fall, and the connection between the harmony of the spheres and that of the songs and dances of angels is indicated by Raphael when he speaks of

> Mystical dance, which yonder starrie Spheare
> Of Planets and of fixt in all her Wheeles
> Resembles nearest. [*PL*, 5.620–2]

In the *Nativity Ode* also the song of the angels and the music of the spheres are in counterpoint to one another, and at the Incarnation this music is heard for an instant in the fallen world. The chaste soul, like the Lady in *Comus*, achieves a harmony which is attuned to these harmonies of the cosmos, and the elder brother's "divine Philosophy" [l. 475] is largely concerned with the attempt to set forth the order, at once musical, poetic, and mathematical, which can "keep unsteddy Nature to her law," in the words of *Arcades*. Poetry and music, the "Sphear-born harmonious Sisters, Voice, and Vers" [*At a Solemn Music*], impose an order on experience which helps us to make this act of understanding. In the earlier poems particularly, Milton seldom refers to music without associating it with the original creative power of the Word of God, a power that still works, partly through the musical arts, to recreate harmony in the soul of man. As he says in his epigram on the singer Leonora, some divine mind teaches harmony to man through her singing, and her song is the speaking word of that divinity:

Aut Deus, aut vacui certe mens tertia caeli
  Per tua secreto guttura serpit agens;
Serpit agens, facilisque docet mortalia corda
  Sensim immortali assuescere posse sono.
Quod si cuncta quidem Deus est, per cunctaque fusus,
  In te una loquitur, caetera mutus habet.[23]

Such a symbolism would most readily be focused on the figure of Orpheus, who haunts so many of Milton's early poems. The art of Orpheus recreated the sympathy between man and nature which existed in Eden, hence Orpheus represents everything that a human being can do to redeem a soul from death. Eurydice was only "half regain'd" [*L'Allegro*], but we have the wistful hope that a poet who had been taught a greater song than Orpheus knew, singing "With other notes then to th' *Orphean* Lyre" [*PL*, 3.17], might succeed better with human souls, if not with animals and trees. The art of Orpheus suggests magic, and magic suggests the control of elemental spirits:

those Daemons that are found
In fire, air, flood, or under ground,
Whose power hath a true consent
With Planet, or with Element. [*Il Penseroso*]

Whatever one thinks of magic, a soul as pure as the Lady in *Comus* might be able to commune with a harmony in the sublunary world as well as with the spherical one. The Lady's virtue is protected by an attendant spirit, also a musician, descending from the upper air, and by Sabrina, a water-spirit. In fact all the characters in *Comus* are elemental spirits except the Lady and her brothers. Comus and his followers are not what they claim to be, but what they do claim to be is precisely similar: elemental spirits whose power has a true consent with the planets:

We that are of purer fire
Imitate the Starry Quire,
Who in their nightly watchfull Sphears,
Lead in swift round the Months and Years. [ll. 111–14]

Such a conception of "harmony" is more philosophical than genuinely musical: it is harmony in the sense of stable and unchanging relationships, which in terms of music is "perfect Diapason" [*At a Solemn Music*], an everlasting sounding of something like a C major chord. Music itself may disclose "harmony" as a total form, but in listening to it we are listening to intricate and energetic movement:

> Untwisting all the chains that ty
> The hidden soul of harmony. [*L'Allegro*]

This suggests that we ought to revise our conception of creation: it is not so much imposing form on chaos as incorporating energy in form. It would be wrong to overlook Milton's sense of the "enormous bliss" of nature [*PL*, 5.297], the rushing and joyous power that he had celebrated as early as his *Fifth Elegy* on the coming of spring. The frenzied Bacchantes may have been inspired by the wrong god, but at least they were responding to the energy that the true God brought out of nature by creating it, and this kind of enthusiasm, in the conclusion of *Epitaphium Damonis*, finds its place in heaven, again in counterpoint to the more decorous songs of Zion:

> Cantus ubi, choreisque furit lyra mista beatis,
> Festa Sionaeo bacchantur & Orgia Thyrso.[24]

The lion in book 7, pawing to get his hinder parts free, is an eloquent emblem of creation as the emancipating of energy by form, the same power that reappears in human life as liberty, the ability to act which is possible only in a state of internal discipline.

There is demonic music, of course. The song of Comus, imitating the starry choir, is a demonic parody of the Lady's Echo Song, which symbolizes a much more genuine kinship with nature; the "rout that made the hideous roar" in *Lycidas* is a parody of Orpheus's own songs; the devils in book 1 moving "In perfect *Phalanx* to the *Dorian* mood" [*PL*, 1.550] parody the faithful angels moving

> In silence thir bright Legions, to the sound
> Of instrumental Harmonie that breath'd
> Heroic Ardor to advent'rous deeds. [*PL*, 6.64–6]

But the general rhythm of the world that God created is clear enough. The Creator moves downward to his creatures, in a power symbolized by music and poetry and called in the Bible the Word, releasing energy by creating form. The creature moves upward toward its Creator by obeying the inner law of its own being, its *telos* or chief end which is always and at all levels the glorifying of God.

It follows that there must be an upward and a downward demonic movement. The upward one is simple enough: the destructive explosion from below associated in Milton's mind from earliest days with the Gunpowder Plot. We have already noted that the discovery of gunpowder on the part of the rebel angels was not an accident, but the result of turning from their divine original to the originals of nature. When Satan's foot slips in chaos he is saved by falling on a substance of this nature: "instinct with Fire and Nitre" [*PL*, 2.937]. In the background is the myth of Antaeus, the giant son of Earth who was strengthened by his mother whenever he fell back on her: the strategic place of this myth in *Paradise Regained* will meet us later. The Limbo of Vanities, the explosion of deluded souls trying to take heaven by storm, repeats the same movement. One of Milton's epigrams on the Gunpowder Plot establishes the link in imagery, and explains why the account of the Limbo of Vanities in *Paradise Lost* suddenly turns into an anti-Catholic tirade. He says that if those in the unreformed church were to throw their cowls and local gods into the sky instead of gunpowder they would have a better chance of reaching heaven:

> Sic potius foedos in caelum pelle cucullos,
> Et quot habet brutos Roma profana Deos,
> Namque hac aut alia nisi quemque adiuveris arte,
> Crede mihi caeli vix bene scandet iter.[25]

The downward demonic movement is the one expressed in Virgil's phrase "facilis descensus Averno":[26] the movement which the devils when they first were driven into hell felt to be so contrary to their nature, but which now, as the inertia of original sin, drags all life downward to the grave. Creation began by segregating the principles of chaos into distinct elements or orders, in which like was attracted to like and remained aloof from the unlike. In the creation, particles of earth seek the sphere of earth, and so with the other elements: bubbles of air rise in water; springs of water rise in earth; fires go up; heavy objects in air fall to earth. This is still true, but after the fall Milton's personified Sin discovers a new kind of attraction of particles, a sort of moral gravitation:

> Or sympathie, or som connatural force
> Powerful at greatest distance to unite
> With secret amity things of like kinde
> By secretest conveyance. [*PL*, 10.246–9]

We have been looking at some of the details of the vast symmetrical pattern in *Paradise Lost* in which evil parodies good. Some features in this pattern are very conspicuous: there is a council in hell in book 2 and a council in heaven in book 3, each leading up to a volunteer: Christ journeys into chaos to create the world and Satan journeys into chaos to destroy it; Mammon builds Pandemonium in emulation of the City of God, and so on. Others are more difficult for the modern reader to see, especially those derived from the typological way of reading the Bible that Milton assumes to be second nature to his reader. The opening lines of the poem, with their reference to Moses' account of creation, lead us to expect that this is to be yet another creation poem like that of du Bartas, but instead the real creation is postponed until the beginning of the second half of the poem, and what we get immediately is a demonic parody of the creative process, as the devils in the deep begin to assume some order and coherence on relatively firm land. A demonic parody of the flood is included in the imagery, creation and flood being much the same phenomenon in the demonic world.

The same technique of dialectical parody comes into the four great stages of redemption covered in Michael's summary of the Bible. These, we remember, are the restoring of the natural order with the end of the flood, the restoring of the human order with the giving of the law to Israel, the Incarnation and the giving of the gospel to all mankind, and the final apocalypse. The new creation of the world after the flood had been anticipated in Christ's victory in heaven. The angels, like twentieth-century man, carried their warfare to a point at which the destruction of their world seemed imminent, but Christ goes out to battle with the emblem of the rainbow, the promise of indefinitely sustained life:

> Over thir heads a chrystal Firmament,
> Whereon a Saphir Throne, inlaid with pure
> Amber, and colours of the showrie Arch. [*PL*, 6.757–9]

And before long the order of nature is recreated in heaven as it is later to be on earth:

> At his command the uprooted Hills retir'd
> Each to his place, they heard his voice and went
> Obsequious, Heav'n his wonted face renewd,
> And with fresh Flourets Hill and Valley smil'd. [*PL*, 6.781–4]

On earth, the end of the flood is represented by the ark resting on top of Ararat: this is immediately followed by the corresponding demonic image, the Tower of Babel. The ark is "smeard round with Pitch" [*PL*, 11.731], but the similar material of the Tower of Babel is more explicitly associated with the gunpowder-plot imagery attached to the devils, as much of it comes from

> The Plain, wherein a black bituminous gurge
> Boiles out from under ground, the mouth of Hell. [*PL*, 12.41–2]

This dialectic is carried on in the Hebrew period, with such symbols as the "opprobrious Hill" [*PL*, 1.403] over against the temple of Solomon. The Hebrews made their unique contribution to history, as is the wont of human nature, through their least amiable characteristic: it was not the belief that their God was true but that all other gods were false which proved decisive for mankind. The conception "false god," hardly intelligible to a Greek or a Roman, is the conception that underlies Milton's wonderfully skilful counterpoint of Biblical and Classical myth. With the coming of the gospel, however, the worship of the true God is no longer attached to a chosen nation, a holy land, a sacred city or temple, or anything locatable in time or space. The dialectic therefore sharpens into a kingdom not of this world, an invisible kingdom within the mind of man, as against the outward and visible kingdoms of this world, which are in Satan's keeping. The absoluteness of this dialectic is still, according to Milton, not always understood within the Christian church itself:

> That Church that from the name of a distinct place takes autority to set up a distinct Faith or Goverment, is a Scism and Faction, not a Church.[27]

The most important event of the flood, as far as the imagery of *Paradise Lost* is concerned, is the washing away of Eden, the reason for which is, as Michael explains:

> To teach thee that God attributes to place
> No sanctitie, if none be thither brought
> By Men who there frequent, or therein dwell. [*PL*, 11.836–8]

But if Eden disappears as an outward environment, it revives as an inner state of mind, the "paradise within thee, happier farr" [*PL*, 12.587] that Michael promises Adam. One of the first things that Satan is compared to in the poem is the leviathan who looks like an island, but who would be likely to disappear into the water and drown the unlucky fisherman who landed on him. Eden disappears in the same way, but not so deceitfully. It is no good looking for paradise anywhere on earth, but there is a garden inside the human mind, walled up and guarded by angels still, yet a place that the Word of God can open.

We are now perhaps in a position to see why Raphael's doubtful answer to Adam's questions takes up so much space in book 8. To assume that Milton is expressing an irritable obscurantism of his own through Raphael is the kind of assumption that it is never safe to make about Milton. When early critics expressed doubts whether the speeches of Satan were "blasphemous" or not, the answer is in the Renaissance conception of decorum, or appropriateness of the thing said to the character saying it. Of course they are blasphemous, and of course they ought to be. When Raphael blasphemes against our notion of the sacredness of free and unlimited intellectual enquiry, we ought to look first to see whether some principle of decorum is involved before ascribing the blasphemy to Milton himself.

If there is a personal aspect of Milton involved, it is of a very different kind. Milton has little sense of losing himself in an "O altitudo!" like Browne:[28] mysteries, whether of faith or of reason, puzzle and bother him. For instance: the Genesis story speaks only of a serpent in Eden. It does not say that the serpent was a disguise for Satan: Milton got that interpretation from the New Testament. The cursing of the serpent is intelligible in the Genesis story, where the serpent himself is the agent of evil, but it is difficult to see why a harmless and helpless disguise should be cursed. Yet the cursing of the serpent is an unavoidable part of Milton's source, and must be dealt with somehow:

> Which when the Lord God heard, without delay
> To Judgement he proceeded on th' accus'd
> Serpent though brute, unable to transferre

The Guilt on him who made him instrument
Of mischief, and polluted from the end
Of his Creation; justly then accurst,
As vitiated in Nature: more to know
Concern'd not Man (since he no further knew)
Nor alter'd his offence; yet God at last
To Satan first in sin his doom apply'd,
Though in mysterious terms, judg'd as then best:
And on the Serpent thus his curse let fall. [*PL*, 10.163–74]

Milton does not know why the serpent was cursed, and it is characteristic of a curious flat-footed honesty in Milton's mind that he should spread so obvious a bewilderment over a dozen lines of blank verse. It would be quite reasonable to assume that a similar bewilderment about what then seemed the paradoxes of the new Copernican astronomers should be reflected in Raphael's speech.

Adam has really two questions in his mind, though he does not get around to putting them both. First, is the universe geocentric? Second, if not, are there conscious beings in other heavenly bodies? For the earth is a heavenly body, seen from the higher Heaven as "Not unconformed to other shining Globes" [*PL*, 5.259]. What Raphael is saying is not that these questions are unanswerable, but that Adam should refrain from asking them. In front of him is a crucial test of his fidelity: in preparing for it he should concentrate on the Word of God within him and not on the works of God outside him. Whether the universe is geocentric or not in the eyes of God, there is no doubt that Adam's universe is for Adam. This is why Milton deliberately adopts a Ptolemaic onion-shaped cosmos for his poem, though, in contrast to Dante, he puts heaven and hell outside it. Adam already knows that there are other beings in other worlds—the angels in heaven—and the information has no bearing on the essential awareness he needs to prevent his being taken by surprise. His essential knowledge should be human-centred, practical, engaged knowledge. Adam may explore his world, but the most important thing for him to know is how to defend it. In *Areopagitica* Milton speaks of the high courage of those who will dispute of philosophical questions with the enemy at their very gates; but if they forgot the supreme duty of beating off the enemy, they could no longer be called courageous.

So with Adam. If he persists in obedience, nothing he wants to know is likely to be concealed from him; if he fails, there will be nothing in the whole universe outside him to help him. When Michael comes to earth in book 11, his descent is associated, in the last Classical allusion in *Paradise Lost*, with Hermes putting Argus to sleep with his "opiate Rod" [*PL*, 11.133]. The image of the hundred eyes closing down as Adam settles into his new perception of time and space gives us some notion of how extensive a paradise he has lost. We can understand, in passing, why Milton was attracted to the doctrine of mortalism, that human souls sleep until the Last Judgment. Not until history has ended can there be a new paradisal place.

There is only one historical figure outside the Bible who is explicitly and repeatedly alluded to in *Paradise Lost*, and that is Galileo. Such prominence is an impressive tribute to Milton's sense of his importance, and, perhaps, to Milton's own insight in grasping that importance. The references to Galileo are by no means hostile, and it is clear from the use made of him in the argument of *Areopagitica* that in Milton's ideal state he would be a highly respected citizen. But if they are not hostile they are curiously deprecatory. Milton seems to regard Galileo, most inaccurately, as concerned primarily with the question of whether the heavenly bodies, more particularly the moon, are habitable—as a pioneer of science fiction rather than of science. As Satan hoists his great shield, the shield, in a glancing parody of the shield of Achilles which depicted mainly a world at peace, is associated with Galileo peering through his telescope at the moon:

> to descry new Lands,
> Rivers or Mountains in her spotty Globe. [*PL*, 1.290–1]

Galileo thus appears to symbolize, for Milton, the gaze outward on physical nature, as opposed to the concentration inward on human nature, the speculative reason that searches for new places, rather than the moral reason that tries to create a new state of mind.

The symbolic Galileo in Milton thus resembles the later symbolic Newton in Blake: he stands for a philosophical vision that, in Marx's famous phrase, thinks it more important to study the world than to change it. For fallen man, rooted in the demonic perception of the universe, the form of God's creation has been entirely replaced by space, and while he may hope, like Satan, that space may produce or disclose new worlds, there is nothing divine in space that man can *now* see, nothing to afford him a model of the new world he must construct within himself. Of course he will find reason and design in the world, but no further than the rational power with which he perceives it. The Galileo vision in Milton sees man as a spectator of a theatrical nature, and such a vision is opposed to the vision of human liberty. It is not idolatrous in itself, but the demonic basis of it is. The vision of liberty pulls away from the world and attaches itself to the total human body within, the Word that reveals the Eden in the redeemable human soul, and so releases the power that leads to a new heaven and a new earth.

III Children of God and Nature

In the soul of man, as God originally created it, there is a hierarchy. This hierarchy has three main levels: the reason, which is in control of the soul; the will, the agent carrying out the decrees of the reason, and the appetite. Reason and will, the decree and the act, are related in man much as the Father and the Son are related in the Godhead. The will is never free in the sense of being autonomous or detached from some other aspect of the soul, but when reason is in charge of the soul the will is free because it participates in the freedom of the reason. In one of his academic Prolusions Milton says, as an axiom generally accepted: "the human intellect, as head and ruler, surpasses in splendor the other faculties of the mind, it governs and illuminates with its splendor the will itself, otherwise blind and dark, that like the moon shines with another's light" [*Works*, 12:261].

The appetite is subordinate to both, and is controlled by the will from the reason. Of the appetites two are of central importance: the appetite for food and the sexual appetite. Both of these are part of the divine creation, and are therefore good. Even so, it is curious how emphatic Milton is about food as an element of both paradisal and heavenly life. In the unfallen world eating has something sacramental about it: Raphael explains how it is part of the upward movement in nature back toward its Creator, and even the form in which food is provided indicates the "providence" behind it:

> The savourie pulp they chew, and in the rinde
> Still as they thirsted scoop the brimming stream. [*PL*, 4.335–6]

The angels also eat and drink "in communion sweet" [*PL*, 5.637], and Milton insists that, whatever the theologians may say, Raphael really ate the fruit salad provided for him by Eve. Not only does he eat it but he explains how he ate it. He appears to have no excretory organs except the pores of his skin—if angels have skin—but at any rate the upper end of his food pipe has been implanted in him by the Deity.

Milton also insists, again referring to objecting theologians, that sexual intercourse existed between Adam and Eve before the fall. There remains of course only the fourth question, the sexual life of angels, the subject of some curious speculations later on by Swedenborg. We are told that spirits can assume either sex, which seems to imply that sex has some point even in a spiritual nature. Adam's natural curiosity, combined with other elements we shall look at in a moment, prompts him to ask Raphael a direct question on this point. The question, not unnaturally, is not directly answered, but when it is asked Raphael blushes, mutters something about having just remembered another appointment, and bustles off. He does not leave however until he has given Adam a very strong hint what the answer is:

> Let it suffice thee that thou know'st
> Us happie, and without Love no happiness.
> Whatever pure thou in the body enjoy'st
> (And pure thou wert created) we enjoy
> In eminence, and obstacle find none
> Of membrane, joynt, or limb, exclusive barrs. [*PL*, 8.620–5]

Or, as Blake was to say in a tone more ribald than either Milton's or Swedenborg's, in Eternity

> Embraces are Cominglings from the Head even to the Feet,
> And not a pompous High Priest entering by a Secret Place.
> [*Jerusalem*, 69.43–4 (K708/E223)]

There is a rough but useful correspondence between the hierarchy of reason, will, and appetite in the individual and the social hierarchy of men, women, and children that would have developed in Eden if Adam had not fallen. In this analogy the man would correspond to the level of the reason, the woman to that of the will united to the reason, and the child to that of the appetite, subordinate to both but still protected and cherished. We cannot prove this directly, as no unfallen society ever developed, but it seems implicit in Milton's argument. We are told that even in heaven there is such a thing as seniority, and when Satan disguises himself as a stripling cherub he makes all the deference to seniority toward Uriel that a young cherub ought to make, though how there could be young and old cherubim in eternity is not explained. The supremacy of husband over wife is taken for granted by Milton because he found it in the New Testament. When Milton says of Adam and Eve, "Hee for God only, shee for God in him" [*PL*, 4.299], he is merely putting a Pauline doctrine into pentameter verse. The correspondence of reason and will with man and woman is marked in the beginning of book 9, when Eve wants to go and work by herself and Adam allows her to go. Adam is right in doing so because he is leaving her will free, while retaining the natural supremacy of his own reason. He goes wrong only in accepting her (by then perverted) advice in connection with his own decision.

As far as the present world is concerned, we should remember something that many readers of Milton are apt to forget, that the authority of husband over wife is spiritual authority only. No man, except a man living entirely by the light of the gospel, would have the kind of integrity of which such an authority would be a by-product, nor could a woman who did not have a corresponding integrity be capable of responding to it. A bullying or dictatorial attitude toward one's wife would be merely one more example of what Milton calls man's effeminate slackness. Many theologians have asserted that the wife ought to be in subjection to her husband because woman brought sin into the world, but this is arguing directly from the unfallen to the fallen state, something Milton never does. Milton does say in *The Christian Doctrine* that the authority of the husband was increased after the fall, but this is an empirical observation on the patriarchal narratives in the Old Testament, not a deduction from the Eden story.

It is understandable however that Milton should see in the cult of courtly love, of *Frauendienst* or worship of women in the literary conventions of his time, one of the most direct and eloquent symbolic results of the fall of man. For this reason, Milton places the supremacy of Eve over Adam at the central point of the fall itself. "Was shee thy God?" the real God asks Adam [*PL*, 10.145]. As soon as Eve has eaten of the apple she becomes jealous of Adam, that is, her love for Adam is immediately perverted into jealousy, and jealousy is essentially a feeling of possessiveness. She feels that unless she can preserve some kind of power over Adam she will not be his equal, or "perhaps"

> A thing not undesirable, somtime
> Superior; for inferior who is free? [*PL*, 9.824–5]

echoing as she says this the argument of Satan himself, who can only understand ruling and serving, and prefers reigning in hell to serving in heaven. So Eve brings about Adam's fall by making him feel that he cannot live without her and that he must remain with her even at the price of dying with her or of being under her sway indefinitely.

We may understand in the light of this principle of perverted female supremacy one of the puzzling episodes in the dialogue between Raphael and Adam. At the end of book 8, Adam attempts to explain to Raphael something of the feeling which Eve has inspired in him, and he speaks of these feelings as a kind of adoration or awe. He feels that there is something about Eve that creates a mystery, and hints at a kind of reality beyond what his own reason shows him:

> Greatness of mind and nobleness thir seat
> Build in her loveliest, and create an awe
> About her, as a guard Angelic plac't. [*PL*, 8.557–9]

Raphael does not know that Adam has just used, by ironic anticipation, the image of paradise after he has been excluded from it. But he does know that something is very wrong, and in his anxiety to put it right he goes too far. He rebukes Adam in a way that Adam finds baffling, and his speech ends with what Adam must have found, in the context, an insensitively coarse remark:

> Not sunk in carnal pleasure, for which cause
> Among the Beasts no Mate for thee was found. [*PL*, 8.593–4]

Adam is said to be "half" abashed by this; he is, as nearly as anyone can be in an unfallen state, shocked and angered. Yet what Raphael has been too anxious to correct does in fact turn out to be the cause of Adam's fall. The supremacy of Adam over Eve is the free and human relation; the supremacy of Eve could soon become a road leading to intellectual enslavement.

Milton's argument for divorce is really an argument for annulment, that is, an argument that if the relations between man and woman are intolerable, no marriage, in the gospel sense, has really taken place. The marriage Jesus describes as indissoluble is a lifetime companionship that can be consummated, or finished, only by the death of one of the partners. The union of Adam and Eve in Eden is the pattern of such a marriage, but not every legalized sex act in the fallen world achieves that pattern. But the argument for annulment really resolves itself into an argument against idolatry. The man has the right to divorce his wife (or the wife the husband) if she is a threat to his spiritual integrity, and she cannot be that without representing something of what idolatry means to Milton. When Eve, after her fall, comes to Adam and urges him to fall with her, that is the point at which Adam should have "divorced" Eve, hence the argument for divorce comes into the very act of the fall itself.

Few can have read *Paradise Lost* without being struck by the curiously domesticated nature of the life of Adam and Eve in Eden before the fall. Adam and Eve are suburbanites in the nude, and like other suburbanites they are preoccupied with gardening, with their own sexual relations, and with the details of their rudimentary housekeeping. Even what many would now regard as the horrors of suburban life are only delights to Adam and Eve. They do not mind that they are constantly under inspection by angelic neighbours, or by God himself, for, says Milton, "they thought no ill" [*PL*, 4.320]. Such extraordinary trustfulness is a natural part of the state of innocence. There's an angel up in the sky. So there is: how nice; perhaps he'll stay to lunch. And when Eve serves the meal, goes away, and leaves the men to their masculine conversation, we feel that we are as close as paradise can get to port and cigars. Commentators on Milton, at least since Taine a century ago, have said everything on this point that needs to be said. But the prevailing assumption has been that all this represents unconscious humour on the part of a humourless poet, and this assumption is quite wrong.

It is essential to Milton's argument to present Adam and Eve in this way. For it is Milton's belief that the original state of man was civilized, and that it was far closer to the average life of a seventeenth-century Englishman than it was to that of a noble savage. Savagery and primitivism came later, and were never intended by God to be part of man's life. Further, it would be a mistake to imagine, as the hasty reader often does, that because Adam and Eve are unfallen and sinless they must necessarily be insipid. They are not insipid at all, but lively, even explosive personalities. Adam has not been in the world five minutes before he is arguing with his Maker and pointing out to him the deficiencies of a life in which there is no other human being. This amuses his Creator, but it pleases him too to feel that there is so instant a response from the reason which he has planted in Adam's mind. When Raphael rebukes Adam, as Adam feels, unjustly, Adam makes a shrewd flanking attack by way of his question about Raphael's sex life, and on the way mentions in a parenthesis that he is sticking to his own views and is not allowing any angel to bully him out of them:

> Though higher of the genial Bed by far,
> And with mysterious reverence I deem [*PL*, 8.598–9]

Let us return to the episode in book 9 in which we are told that Eve has suddenly taken it into her head to go and do her pruning by herself. Adam makes a long speech, in impeccable blank verse, pointing out that, as they are about to be assailed by a clever and ruthless enemy, it might be better for them to stay together and not separate. Eve says that that is very true, and that she would like to go off and prune by herself. Adam makes another long speech, in equally impeccable blank verse, making the same point with elaborations. Eve says that all that is very true, and that she will now go off and prune by herself. At this point Adam attempts the manœuvre which so many husbands have attempted, of trying to get the last word by telling her to go and do as she likes:

> Go in thy native innocence, relie
> On what thou hast of vertue, summon all,
> For God towards thee hath done his part, do thine.
>   So spake the Patriarch of Mankinde, but *Eve*
> Persisted, yet submiss, though last, repli'd. [*PL*, 9.373–7]

This unfallen spat indicates that there is room for explosive personalities in paradise, because there is no malice in their explosion. Similarly with the liveliness of intellect that they display. When Eve has a troubling dream, and does not understand its meaning, Adam, who is several hours older, explains to her the origin of dreams, how they operate, and what their machinery is. The speech is intended to convey the sense of the freshness of discovery, not of the staleness of opinion.

The same applies to the kind of language they use, the language which has often puzzled readers and been ridiculed by them. Adam and Eve use the kind of stylized hierarchic language which indicates their exuberance in the possession of language as a new and fresh form of intellectual energy. The formality of their speeches is verbal play, and reflects the exuberance with which Milton himself, in addressing his own language in his early *Vacation Exercise* poem, described the appropriate epic diction:

> Such as may make thee search thy coffers round,
> Before thou cloath my fancy in fit sound.

Such formal rhetoric is at the opposite pole of human life from the dialogue in a Hemingway novel, which is equally appropriate to its purpose because it represents a weariness with human speech. Such communication, where nothing really needs to be said, is a parody of the kind of communication which according to Raphael the angels have, and which is intuitive rather than discursive. Adam and Eve are simply enjoying the possession of the power of discursive communication.

After the fall, the hierarchy implanted by God in the human soul is not merely upset, but reversed. Appetite now moves into the top place in the human soul, and by doing so it ceases to be appetite and is transformed into passion, the drive toward death. The appetites are a part of the creation, and like every other part of the creation they are an energy which seeks its fulfilment in form. Hunger is specifically satisfied with food, and the sexual desire by sexual intercourse. When appetite is perverted into passion, the drives of sex and hunger are perverted into lust and greed. Passion operates in the mind as though it were an external force, compelling the soul to obey against its own best interests, and the passions of greed and lust have two qualities that the appetites do not have: excess and mechanical energy. Hunger can be satisfied by food, but greed cannot be satisfied by anything: it seeks an excess of food, and when it runs out of food, it will seek to acquire other things out of mechanical habit. Eve is hungry before she eats the forbidden fruit, greedy immediately afterward, and her greed runs on into a desire to possess Adam.

After Adam has fallen with her, sexual intercourse between them is resumed, but this time its basis is entirely different. It is not the expression of the love of Adam for Eve, but rather the generalized and mechanical expression of the lust of a man for a woman, the woman being Eve because she is the only woman within reach. The will is now the agent of passion instead of reason, for the will must be the agent of one or the other. The behaviour of mankind takes on that mechanical and amorphous quality which Milton describes in chaos: he speaks elsewhere of the futility of efforts to define sin, "to put a girdle about that *Chaos*."[29] This inversion of the human mind, with passion on top and will its agent, reduces reason to the lowest point in the soul, where it is normally a helpless critic of what the passion is doing, able to point out the correct course, but, in the passion-driven mind, powerless to affect its decisions for long.

What happens in the human individual happens by analogy in fallen human society. Passion acts as though it were an external force, a tyrant of the mind, and a society made up of passionate individuals becomes a tyranny, in which the tyrant is the embodiment of the self-enslavement of his victims, as Michael explains to Adam:

> Reason in man obscur'd, or not obeyd,
> Immediately inordinate desires
> And upstart Passions catch the Government
> From Reason, and to servitude reduce
> Man till then free. Therefore since hee permits
> Within himself unworthie Powers to reign
> Over free Reason, God in Judgement just
> Subjects him from without to violent Lords;
> Who oft as undeservedly enthrall
> His outward freedom. [*PL*, 12.86–95]

Usually we have a secular tyrant and a spiritual tyrant or priest. The latter, in Christianity, is what Milton means by a prelate, a person who exerts temporal power in what ought to be the area of spiritual authority. Under the tyrant and the priest and their followers come the victims, the general public, and under them again come the few people equipped with enough reason to protest against what is happening and to try to rouse the conscience of the very small number who can be persuaded to agree and act with them. This is the situation of which the archetype is Abdiel among the rebel angels, which is also, as explained, the archetype of human heroism.

The distinction between lust and greed is that lust is a vice turned outward and affecting other people; greed is a vice that turns inward and affects oneself. These two forms of tyranny produce what for Milton are the two infallible signs of a perverted church: inquisition and indulgence, the desire to suppress freedom of thought and the tendency to provide easy formulas for the less dangerous vices. The former develops the censor who is attacked in *Areopagitica*; the latter develops what Milton calls the "hireling." Among the pamphlets written on the eve of the Restoration, the first two deal with these two forms of religious perversion. *A Treatise of Civil Power in Ecclesiastical Causes* is concerned mainly with the separation of spiritual and temporal authority necessary to avoid what Milton calls in *Areopagitica* "the lazines of a licencing Church" [*Works*, 4:336]; *The Likeliest Means to Remove Hirelings* is concerned with the complementary problem.

If we look at the visions which Michael shows Adam in book 11, between the murder of Abel and the flood, we may be puzzled to find that some of them are not Biblical. The story of Cain and Abel is naturally the first vision, and this story centres on one of Milton's central emblems, the altar of acceptable sacrifice, along with its demonic parody. This is followed by a vision of a lazar-house, the victims of which are said to have brought many of their evils on themselves by intemperance in eating and drinking, in other words by greed. We get a somewhat prosaic homily on the virtue of temperance at this point, yet the reason for it is clear: Milton is trying to define the origin of greed in the human body and its excessive appetite. The vision of the lazar-house is followed by another based on those mysterious verses in Genesis about the sons of God who discovered that the daughters of women were fair. The sons of God, according to Milton, were virtuous men and the daughters of women were daughters of women. The gigantic results of their union illustrate the physical origin of lust in the human body. These two visions are followed by two others, one of a cattle raid and one of a scene of riotous and drunken festivity. These two scenes are war and peace as they are usually understood in human life, war as a direct product of human greed, and "peace," that is, luxury, as a direct product of human lust. These four antediluvian scenes thus make up a vision of greed and lust spilling excessively and mechanically over all human life in a moral flood of which the physical one seems the only possible outcome.

On the demonic level, lust and greed become the two forms of vice which have traditionally been classified as force and fraud, the ethical basis on which Dante divides sins in his *Inferno*. Force and fraud are the outstanding characteristics of the devils as they are revealed in the council in book 2. First we have Moloch speaking in favour of a renewed assault on heaven. We note again the perverted qualities of appetite, excess, and mechanical repetition. Moloch appears to be someone of considerable courage—at any rate he has more of it than most of the other devils have—but if there is anything to be said for Plato's conception of courage as the knowledge of what is formidable, then Moloch, lacking any such knowledge, does not have genuine courage. What he has would better be described as ferocity. He is followed by Belial, who has the astuteness and wiliness that Moloch lacks, and who tries to persuade the devils to caution. Just as Moloch appears to have courage, so Belial appears to have prudence; but what he really has is sloth or indolence: again he has no knowledge of what is formidable, only of what is inconvenient. The force of Moloch is lust in action, an outward-directed destructive power; the fraud of Belial is an inward-directed slothfulness, greedily clutching its "intellectual being" [*PL*, 2.147].

Moloch and Belial are followed by Mammon, who represents evil in the aspect that we have already met so often in Milton, as a parody of good. It is Mammon who sets up in hell a close parody of the City of God, which is golden like that city, though a different kind of gold. Mammon corresponds in the human society to Nimrod, who sets up both the Tower of Babel and a systematic tyranny as a part of human life, and who succeeds to the ferocity and indolence of antediluvian life. Mammon is followed by Beelzebub, and Beelzebub suggests the consolidation of all three preceding views of evil, in the form of an attack on heaven which falls just short of heaven. Satan undertakes the voyage through chaos to realize this combination of force, fraud, and parody of good; and when he gets to the slippery edge of nothing, the outer shell of the primum mobile, just beside the gate of heaven, Milton treats us to a curious digression. There is nothing here at this point, but later on, in human history, this area is that of the Limbo of Vanities, where a number of characters whom he itemizes in some detail find themselves sprawling after death. The people who arrive in the Limbo of Vanities are of two kinds: they are the people who have tried to take the kingdom of heaven either by force or by fraud. The former are those who have committed suicide in order to reach heaven; the latter are hypocrites who have tried to disguise themselves. It is poetically right that, when Satan is in prospect of the end of his journey, he should meet there what is symbolically the goal of the human beings who are coming up from the opposite direction: again an attack on heaven that falls just short of heaven.

The hierarchy in the soul of man is, however, more complicated than this threefold structure of reason, will, and appetite. Reason is subordinate to a higher principle than itself: revelation, coming directly from the Word of God, which emancipates and fulfils the reason and gives it a basis to work on which the reason could not achieve by itself. The point at which revelation impinges on reason is the point at which discursive understanding begins to be intuitive: the point of the emblematic vision or parable, which is the normal unit in the teaching of Jesus. The story of the fall of Satan is a parable to Adam, giving him the kind of knowledge he needs in the only form appropriate to a free man. We are speaking here of knowledge as received: for the poet, who has brought his poetic gifts into line with revelation, the same point would be the point of inspiration. Milton does not have exactly the later Romantic conception of imagination, but Keats was right in seeing in Adam's dream the corresponding conception, a mental image that becomes a reality:[30]

> Each Tree
> Load'n with fairest Fruit that hung to the Eye
> Tempting, stirr'd in me sudden appetite
> To pluck and eate; whereat I wak'd, and found
> Before mine Eyes all real, as the dream
> Had lively shadowd. [*PL*, 8.306–11]

Here the dream is of food in its sacramental form, the provision of God of which the forbidden fruit is, once again, the demonic parody.

Below the appetite, similarly, there is the parody of revelation, the fancy or fantasy, the aspect of the mind that is expressed in dreams, including daydreams, and which has the quality of illuminating the appetite from below, as revelation illuminates the reason from above. This fancy is represented by the corresponding dream of Eve. The occasion of her dream was Satan whispering in her ear; but the dream itself, in its manifest content, was a Freudian wish-fulfilment dream. She finds herself in front of the forbidden tree and eating its fruit, thereby gratifying her hunger; the modern reader cannot help noticing that the dream involves flying, and so is a sexual dream as well. The explanation of the dream given her by Adam, at least the explanation of it as a physical process, is based on the conception of three levels of "spirits," vegetative, cordial, and intellectual, the spirits in the body being the point at which the physical substance is transmuted into a spiritual one. Dreams are produced by a premature uprush of vegetative spirits from the lower parts of the body, which is their natural habitat, into the brain. This process in Eve is thus a microscopic example of the upward demonic explosive movement, from chaos into order, dealt with previously.

When the soul of man is reversed in the fall, this fantasy is now on top, illuminating the passion. In this perverted situation it is the force which Milton always associates with idolatry, the demonic emblematic vision. Idolatry in *Paradise Lost* is specifically associated with the forbidden tree. As soon as Eve has eaten the forbidden fruit, she bows to the tree and does it homage: that act is the beginning and end of all idolatry in the human mind. Idolatry in human history is of course the work of the devils, but the devils are involved in idolatry too, and we are told that every so often, in hell, they are compelled to climb up the branches of a tree which Milton describes as an "illusion" [*PL*, 10.571], and eat the fruit of that tree, fruit which, like the apples of Sodom, is fair outside but dust and ashes inside. The devils cannot inspire idolatry without becoming idols themselves: once again we have the Biblical judgment on idols: "They that make them are like unto them" [Psalms 115:8; 135:18]. This identification with the evil that one creates is also symbolized by the variety of disguises that Satan assumes. Milton speaks of him as "Squat like a Toad, close at the eare of *Eve*" [*PL*, 4.800], as perching on the tree of life "like a Cormorant" [*PL*, 4.196], as moving through the garden "like a black mist" [*PL*, 9.180]. He is not saying that Satan actually took these forms: he merely wants the reader to visualize them in connection with Satan. Similarly, when Satan tries on various animals for size before settling on the serpent, including the lion and the tiger, he is anticipating the later fallen forms of these animals, when they become beasts of prey.

In the genuine fallen human mind, where reason lies at the bottom, a helpless critic of the passion above it, reason, in those who trust to it, may also be illuminated from below in a genuine way, by the power of prophecy, by the revelation which is transmitted to mankind through the scriptures and other agents of divine revelation. Here again Adam and Eve, after their fall, represent complementary forms of such illumination: Adam receives the prophecy of Michael later fulfilled in the scriptures; Eve is visited by unitemized but clearly consoling dreams.

We notice that Eve from the beginning is a more remote and withdrawn character than Adam: in a fallen state, therefore, Eve is more susceptible to greed, and Adam to lust, taking these words in the expanded sense that we have been using them in, as introverted and extroverted vice respectively. The first time we meet Eve, in the chronological sequence, she is looking at her reflection in the water, an image which would suggest to the contemporary reader of Milton the story of Narcissus, interpreted in the mythological handbooks as an emblem of pride and as the Classical equivalent of the story of the fall of man. However, Eve is not narcissistic at this point: she merely feels that her own reflection in the water is very pleasant, and when Adam comes along her first feeling about him is that he is not quite up to her own standard of attractiveness. Her state of mind is not pride but the kind of vanity that we find amusing and disarming, and so innocent. This is the basis in her mind on which Satan is able to work. After her dream, she remains quiet and reserved through the next day, and we notice her action in slipping away unobtrusively from the company of Adam and Raphael. The next morning the same feeling persists in her unaccountable desire to be by herself. Satan then comes to her, disguised as a talking snake, and holds her attention by the fact that he can talk. She does not hear a word he is saying, beyond a general notion that she is being flattered, nor does he intend her to. He wants only to keep her fascinated by the image of the talking snake, while everything he says gets past the guard of her consciousness and falls into the depths of what we should now call her subconscious. What he says thereby instils in her the notion of her own individuality, somebody in her own right, herself and not merely an appendage to Adam or to God. When he leads her to the tree of knowledge and she hesitates before it, she searches her own mind to see what her state of mind is. What she finds there, of course, is Satan's speech, which has got into her mind without her noticing it, and she repeats Satan's arguments as though they were her own.

As soon as she has eaten of the forbidden tree, heaven, which has previously been inside her, part of the community she is attached to, then separates from her and goes up into the sky, becoming something remote and external. She is immediately possessed by the idea of secrecy which is a part of shame: "And I perhaps am secret; Heav'n is high" [*PL*, 9.811]. With the sense of secrecy comes the sense of resentment, because God is no longer inside her as part of her own conscience, but somewhere outside her watching her with a censorious eye: "Our great Forbidder, safe with all his Spies" [*PL*, 9.815]. Thus her love for Adam, turning as it does into jealousy, becomes a desire to have Adam as an appendage to herself:

This may be well: but what if God have seen,
And Death ensue? then I shall be no more,
And *Adam* wedded to another *Eve,*
Shall live with her enjoying, I extinct;
A death to think. [*PL*, 9.826–30]

This is as sombre a depth of irony as Milton reaches in the entire poem. Eve does not so much mind dying: the real death is the thought of Adam surviving with another woman. This is the state into which Adam also falls, and there follow consequently the psychological changes of the fall in his mind too. This ends in a vicious quarrel between the two, all the more terrifying because so petty, and the last line of book 9 is: "And of their vain contest appeared no end." With the words "no end," suddenly the sense of the fate of the devils in hell opens out and one glimpses the possibility of Adam and Eve snarling at each other to all eternity, which of course is what they would do if there were no redemption in the world.

At the same time, Adam is motivated by his desire to live with Eve and his feeling that he cannot live without her. Conceptually and theologically, he is entirely wrong, and we have explained how he should have "divorced" Eve at the moment of her fall. But again, the conceptual and theological situation is not the dramatic one. Adam's decision to die with Eve rather than live without her impresses us, in our fallen state, as a heroic decision. We feel a certain nobility in what Adam does: Eve also feels this and expresses it. When Adam falls, he falls, as Milton says, "Against his better knowledge, not deceav'd" [*PL*, 9.998], but he also attracts some sympathy from a reader who feels that if Adam had actually gone back to God accusing Eve of mortal sin and demanding to be released from his contract with her he would have forfeited that sympathy. The reader feels that, whether or not this is the right thing for Adam to do, this is what he himself might well have done if he had been in Adam's place. And that, of course, is exactly Milton's point.

This sense of a contrast between the dramatic and the conceptual aspects of a situation is there because it fits the Christian myth, yet it follows Classical precedent too. In Homer, Odysseus gets our sympathy by preferring his mortal wife Penelope to the immortality promised him by Calypso. Much closer to Milton, however, is the account of Dido in Virgil. Virgil is a Roman poet writing for Roman readers, and certainly both Virgil and his readers recognized the call of a higher destiny for

Aeneas. Obviously he had to get away from the Carthaginian Dido to Italy and found Rome. Yet, when Aeneas meets Dido in the lower world, Dido walks off with all the dramatic honours of the situation. What poor Aeneas gets is not only an annihilating snub, but the deadliest insult that any woman can give her faithless lover, as she turns contemptuously away and goes off to look for her husband.

The Dido episode in Virgil is a romantic episode, and the sense of the romantic in the relations of Adam and Eve after their fall is centrally important. We are aware at once of the inscrutability of the fallen soul, the sense of the self-enclosed ego or individual remote and cut off from every other form of individual. Along with this goes the sense of melancholy. Book 9 of *Paradise Lost* is, as already suggested, among other things a wonderful cultural anticipation of the eighteenth-century cult of the noble savage. As soon as Adam falls, he loses his sense of humour, a fact indicated by his speech to Eve, which is full of puns, like the speeches of the devils after they have discovered artillery. The reason why Milton associates punning with a sinful nature will be discussed in the last chapter. In any case, the sense of melancholy and of a somewhat precarious dignity, the wrong kind of dignity that cannot survive the first banana-peeling, so to speak, is the psychological basis of the tyrannical and perverted form of human society that is going to become established in the place where Eden was. These are also products of shame, the feeling of being withdrawn from the city of light, of which Adam is a member because he lives in one of its greenest suburbs. He is now plunged into a sense of human life as something that begins anew with each individual, where each individual is the centre of his own universe, removed from everyone else and communicating only with the greatest difficulty, aware of the existence of other people only because reluctantly forced to be. This is the quality of melancholy which seems to Milton characteristic of primitive life, its root the kind of pathos that results from being cut off from one's community. Romanticism continues into the tenth book, where Adam and Eve go through a *Liebestod* stage of a suicide pact, then outgrow the longing to die with each other and advance into the stage of longing to die for each other. This is the point at which the human race becomes, from God's point of view, something worth redeeming.

The human fall parallels the previously described demonic one. When Satan rebels against God, he loses his status in his community. He is therefore like a hand cut off from the body, which has no purpose or usefulness or life in itself once it has become severed from the organism of which it forms part. So Satan's discovery of his own separated ego, which at the first moment of this discovery was so exhilarating, very soon becomes a psychological imprisonment. He finds himself walled in by the jail of his individuality, so that, as he points out, he would create a hell even if he were replaced in heaven. We notice that the devils, unlike man, cannot die. Man is excluded from paradise after he has eaten of the tree of knowledge in order to prevent him from reaching for the tree of life. God fears his doing this, not because he is jealous for his own privileges, although the Genesis wording seems to suggest this and Milton echoes it, but to prevent man from living forever in a fallen world. The latter is the fate of the devils: the devils cannot die because they cannot make the act of surrender involved in death: hence what they have is a kind of parody of immortality. They are not really immortal; they are merely undying. And although Milton was compelled to keep the doctrine of eternal punishment for sinful human beings in his theological structure, *Paradise Lost* is a poem with no relish of damnation in it: this theme is, as nearly as possible, eliminated.

It has been said that a great portrait gives us the feeling that the back of the head has been as solidly realized as the visible parts. If we knew nothing of Milton except *Paradise Lost*, we should still be aware that the structure was supported by a powerful and coherent skeleton of ideas: when we turn to the prose writings these ideas come more clearly into view. Some of them may be called commonplaces, except that when they become integral to Milton's outlook they cease to be commonplaces. And while there are certainly major changes of emphasis between *Areopagitica* and *Paradise Lost*, there is nothing in *Paradise Lost* which is really a denying or a going back on the great issues he had fought for. In any case these issues, so far as the student of Milton is interested in them, are not prefabricated ones: they are issues articulated by Milton himself, as part of that encyclopedic range of ideas which the epic expresses.

One of the main constructs elaborated from the Bible in later Christian thought is that of the different levels of civilization, as we have it in St. Augustine's conception of the City of God and its relations with the church on earth, the Roman power, and the *civitas terrena*. In Milton, where so much of the action takes place before human history begins, much of the symbolism has to be anticipatory. The significant acts of the Son of God prefigure his acts in the Incarnation: the expulsion of the devils prefigures the cleansing of the temple, and the silencing of chaos his command of the Sea of Galilee. Similarly, the devils in book 1 are associated by anticipation with the two aspects of civilization that they later introduce to human life, tyranny and anarchy. Tyranny is represented in the Bible more particularly by Egypt and Babylon, and in book 1 the imagery links the devils with the plagues of Egypt, the drowning of "*Busiris* and his *Memphian* Chivalry" [*PL*, 1.307], and the gorgeous temples in "Babylon and great Alcairo."[31] Anarchy Milton associates with the *Völkerwanderung* at the fall of the Roman Empire, and in later books with the nomadic tribes of Scythia and Great Tartary, a movement repeating that of the flood spilling over human life. The entry of Sin and Death into fallen nature is linked to the great host of Xerxes, attempting "the Libertie of *Greece* to yoke" [*PL*, 10.307], when Xerxes scourged the sea (which ought to have been his ally, being a symbol of chaos) as a traitor to his cause.

Above tyranny is the condition of law, represented by the Hebrews and, in a different context, by the brief periods of "ancient liberty" in Greece and Rome. Tyranny is an externally imposed discipline, and in law there is a principle of inward discipline. The law in itself is concerned only with the outward consequences of actions: as far as the law is concerned, anyone not actually convicted of stealing is an honest man. Hence the primary function of the law is to define the thief, to "discover sin," as Michael says [*PL*, 12.290]. To the criminal, society becomes tyrannical: justice is the internal condition of the just man, but the external antagonist of the criminal, and so acts as an externally compelling force on him. But that very fact indicates that the honest man must have a higher standard of morality than the mere fear of getting caught, and while the law cannot define honesty as it can define theft, the honest man still knows what it is. What the law cannot do is to make people honest. Yet there is a principle of order and stability, and consequently of freedom, in law, and a morally sound society, whether within Christianity or outside it, is capable of achieving freedom, though never for long enough to make the gospel unnecessary.

The Mosaic code provides a complete moral law, yet Milton does not associate it, as he does the republics of Greece and Rome, with liberty: he thinks of it in Pauline terms as a bondage from which the gospel has released us. Mosaic law is partly ceremonial, and so more constraining than moral law alone would be, yet it is a higher gift than moral law, because it prevents morality from becoming an end in itself. Its meaning is typological, the acts it enjoins being symbols of the spiritual truths of the gospel. Hence it corresponds in society to what we have called the emblematic vision in the individual, the point at which reason begins to comprehend revelation. As a series of acts, arbitrary in themselves but deriving their meaning from a higher kind of truth, the ceremonial law sets up a force in society that might be called counter-idolatry. The prohibition not to make gods in the image of man, or nature, may lead, if only as "types and shadows," to understanding that man is the image of God. Hence the gospel can succeed the Mosaic law, as its inevitable fulfilment, in a way that it cannot fulfil the enlightened virtue of the heathen.

The gospel sets one free from the law, but of course one does not become free of the law by breaking the law, only more tangled up with it than ever. What the gospel does is to internalize the law, to remove every aspect of it that acts as an external compulsion. Liberty is thus the same thing as inner necessity. If an artist painting a picture knows exactly what he is doing, every brush stroke is compelled because it is free. If someone learning to play the piano is still hesitating and exercising his freedom of will about playing the right notes, he is not playing very well. He can only set himself free to play the piano when he has compelled himself to play automatically the right notes. Similarly with the ethical nature: the person who is free is simply incapable of stealing or lying. The gospel's moral demands in fact are so rigorous that the law, which is far more tolerant, is compelled to remain where it is: it would produce the most fantastic tyranny to try to make a new law out of the gospel. Milton was attracted by the topic of divorce because for him the legal obstacles to divorce had been derived from the teachings of Jesus, and the law has to be in accord with Moses, not with Jesus. In society the gospel exerts spiritual authority, the power of persuasion inspired by good example. It has no soldiers and no magistrates. The law is represented by temporal authority, which does have soldiers and magistrates, and ought to realize the limitations of what such apparatus can do.

Liberty for Milton is not something that starts with man: it starts with God. It is not something that man naturally wants for himself, but something that God is determined he shall have; man cannot want it unless he is in a regenerate state, prepared to accept the inner discipline and responsibility that go with it. Hence, as Milton says, none can love freedom but good men; the rest want not freedom but licence. When a "licentious" man says he wants liberty, what he really wants is mastery, or lust. If he cannot get mastery, he will give the name liberty to greed, to the querulous desire to be left alone with his pleasanter vices. If he cannot achieve that, he will identify liberty with its demonic parody, a glad acceptance of slavery, proceeding from the influence of Moloch and Belial to that of Mammon.

The knowledge of good and evil which Adam acquired in his fall is knowledge in which evil is primary and good a secondary derivation from evil. Mercy and peace, in this world, are goods which mean that someone has already been cruel or that a war has stopped. This is why temporal authority can never be an end in itself, and why its agents cannot deal with the gospel. Moral law can only define the lawbreaker: it cannot distinguish what is above the law from what is below it, the prophet from the criminal, Jesus from Barabbas. This is the position of the censor as attacked in *Areopagitica*, who finds the prophet as subversive as the genuine traitor. Revelation comes from an infinite mind to a finite one; there can be no definitive human understanding of revelation, and consequently revelation is always addressed to a fundamentally unwilling and resisting audience. The desire to persecute has its origin, not in zeal, but in the deification of some human form of understanding: its root is not "You must believe in God," but "You must believe in what I mean by God."

The society produced by the gospel is the church, and the church is a community whose members have all been made free and equal by their faith. The natural image for this community is the square or cube, probably the shape of the City of God, and certainly that of the militant church as represented by the fighting faithful angels, who "In Cubic Phalanx firm advanc't entire" [*PL*, 6.399]. The natural shape of fallen society is pyramidal, tending upward to a supreme earthly ruler. The church thus works in society as an emancipating and equalizing force: it transforms "ruling" in the sense of applying temporal force to "ruling" in Ezekiel's sense of measuring the temple of God.[32] It accepts whatever temporal authority it finds in society, giving to Caesar what is Caesar's, and resisting Caesar only when he demands the things that are God's. When that happens, conscience is violated and the church may take up arms. The church does not, for Milton, transform society into anything that we should call a democracy, but it does work toward assimilating the people into the people of God, who are free because the gospel has made them free, and equal because God is no respecter of persons.

The freedom the gospel brings is a good but not a moral good: it is a more abundant life, and is not the opposite of evil so much as a greater power of fighting it. The next stage upward in man's evolution, or salvation as Milton would think of it, is the apocalypse, when the life represented by the gospel is finally separated from death. This ultimate separation is eloquently expressed in *Comus*, where the expression is all the more striking because *Comus* is not explicitly Christian in its symbolism:

> But evil on it self shall back recoyl,
> And mix no more with goodness, when at last
> Gather'd like scum, and settl'd to it self
> It shall be in eternal restless change
> Self-fed, and self-consum'd, if this fail,
> The pillar'd firmament is rott'nness,
> And earths base built on stubble. [ll. 592–8]

At this point man realizes that he has not been deprived of the tree of life after all, that it has been steadily growing inside him all through history, and that, when he separates himself from the communion with nature represented by the forbidden tree and attaches himself to the opposite communion, he will find himself, no less than the devils in hell, becoming what he has beheld.[33]

IV The Garden Within

On the top level of the arts we often meet a particular kind of temperament that may be called the conservative temperament. Many great creators have become great primarily by perfecting the forms they have inherited from their traditions. They are usually artists who live entirely for their art, and have little energy left over for any kind of personal expression that is not absorbed into the art itself. When they experiment with new forms and techniques, they normally do so as a means of arriving at certain congenial conventions: they do not value experiment for its own sake, but for the sake of the direction it points out. They are deeply impersonal as a rule: we usually know little about their lives that seems directly relevant to what they produce, and their total body of work, from tentative beginning to disciplined end, reflects the organic evolution of the forms they use. In English literature, Spenser seems to be a poet of this conservative kind: he begins with experiment but moves toward the single convention of the Spenserian stanza, and his work unfolds logically from the allegorical emblems contributed in his nonage to van der Noodt's *Theatre* to the great pageants of *The Faerie Queene*. Shakespeare, though always impossible to classify, has an obviously conservative strain in his temperament: nobody knows what his religious or political or social opinions were, and his personality seems so eerily self-effacing that he has irritated some people into a frenzy of trying to prove that he never existed.

There is a radical or revolutionary temperament, however, also found among the greatest creators, and which contrasts with the conservative one: the kind of contrast that is bound to impress us when we compare, say, Beethoven with Mozart or Bach, Michelangelo with Raphael, Victor Hugo with Flaubert, Turner with Constable, Byron or Shelley with Keats. To make such comparisons in detail might be of limited value and lead to considerable oversimplifying, but the contrast is there, a contrast between creative temperaments roughly parallel to the contrast of sublime and beautiful established by eighteenth-century critics in the arts themselves. It is clear that Milton belongs essentially to the radical group of artists, and many of his virtues and limitations become easier to understand when we keep this distinction in mind. If we do not keep it in mind, we may tend to sink into an unconscious preference for revolutionary or for conservative artists in general, and this may lead, as it has often led in the past, either to admiring Milton uncritically or disliking him uncritically.

The radical or revolutionary artist impresses us, first of all, as a tremendous personal force, a great man who happened to be an artist in one particular field but who would still have been a remarkable man whatever he had gone into. His art has in consequence a kind of oratorical relation to him: his creative *persona* reveals his personality instead of concealing it. He does not enter into the forms of his art like an indwelling spirit, but approaches them analytically and externally, tearing them to pieces and putting them together again in a way which expresses his genius and not theirs. In listening to the Kyrie of the Bach B Minor Mass we feel what amazing things the fugue can do; in listening to the finale of Beethoven's Opus 106, we feel what amazing things can be done with the fugue. This latter is the feeling we have about *Comus* as a masque, for example, when we come to it from Jonson or Campion. Because the art of the revolutionary artist follows a rhythm of personal development external to itself, it goes through a series of metamorphoses: the revolutionary artist plunges into one "period" after another, marking his career off into separate divisions. The Beethoven of the last quartets is a different composer from the Beethoven of the earliest trios, and the Milton of *Paradise Regained* a different poet from the author of the *Nativity Ode*: but when we compare the Mozart of *The Magic Flute* with the infant prodigy of the 1760s we are more impressed by the continuity, and not only because Mozart died young.

The revolutionary aspect of Milton also comes out in that curious mania for doing everything himself which led him to produce his own treatise on theology, his own national history, his own dictionary and grammar, his own art of logic. In the only one of his published works that might conceivably be called an edition of somebody else, *The Judgment of Martin Bucer concerning Divorce*, he says impatiently that he is "a speaker of what God made mine own, and not a translator" [*Works*, 4:60]. Both kinds of genius may seek for an art that transcends art, a poetry or music that goes beyond poetry or music. But the conservative artist finds—if this metaphor conveys anything intelligible to the reader—his greatest profundities at the centre of his art; the radical artist finds them on the frontier. Spenser develops toward the formal elaborations of Spenserian stanza and allegory; Bach toward the formal elaborations of the *Kunst der Fuge* and the *Musikalisches Opfer*. Milton, like Beethoven, is continually exploring the boundaries of his art, getting more experimental and radical as he goes on, moving away from the complex stanza form of the *Nativity Ode* toward the free-verse recitatives of *Samson Agonistes*. And just as the work of the radical artist is iconoclastic in its attitude to tradition, so it is destructive in its effect on tradition. Gide's remark that the greatest French poet was "Victor Hugo, alas," is not, properly interpreted, a glib sneer but an accurate estimate of the place of such a poet in literary history. If there had been no Shakespeare, we should have to say "Milton, alas," to the parallel question about English poetry, and to the same question about Renaissance art there is no answer but "Michelangelo, alas."

The revolutionary artist does not have to be a social and political revolutionary as well, but he often is if he lives in a revolutionary time, though he is usually more of a nuisance than an asset to the causes he espouses. Every social revolution has the problem of establishing continuity with what it overturns, continuity of authority, of administration, of habits of life. For the revolutionary artist, it is precisely the continuity in tradition that he rejects in his art, and hence he tends to see his political situations also vertically, as a break with continuity. Since Burke, we have become familiar with the conception of the continuum of dead, living, and unborn as the one unbreakable social contract, as something that will go on no matter how great the changes in society. In Burke this is a conservative and antirevolutionary theory, and his heavy emphasis on precedent, custom, prudence, even prejudice, and on the gradualness of all well-founded reform, belongs in that context. But the sense of a tradition of liberty, of social conflicts working toward a legal settlement with guarantees for both parties, of society modifying and adjusting its structure instead of attempting a new creation: this is a liberalizing sense for most of us, and the kernel of reality in the theory of progress.

In Milton's prose the lack of this sense of continuity, or more accurately the rejection of the values that go with it, is obvious and striking. In the preface to *The Doctrine and Discipline of Divorce* Milton associates custom with error, and the association is habitual in his mind. *The Tenure of Kings and Magistrates* is a work of astonishing originality in its attempt to give some connected and coherent account of revolution as a force in history. But such an account demands documentation: documentation, in a work justifying a revolution, amounts to an appeal to precedent, and Milton will appeal to precedent only with the greatest reluctance:

> But because it is the vulgar folly of men to desert thir own reason, and shutting thir eyes to think they see best with other mens, I shall show by such examples as ought to have most waight with us, what hath bin don in this case heretofore. [*Works*, 5:19]

Even in Milton's day there were books on how to win friends and influence people, but Milton was clearly not a student of them. Milton does not, however, think that arguments based on precedent and custom are good only for reassuring fools, otherwise he could hardly embark on them with such easy mastery as he does here and elsewhere. He feels rather that there is a greater and a lesser revolution to be achieved in his time. The greater one is religious, and is of apocalyptic proportions; the lesser one is political, and all arguments about custom and precedent and gradualness belong to it. If Milton thinks that the people of England are in danger of losing their sense of religious strategy by being confused about their political tactics, he can be very specific in discussing the latter, but he always sees them as contained within a larger context to which no short-run counsels of prudence apply. "In state," Milton remarks in *The Reason of Church Government*, "many things at first are crude and hard to digest, which only time and deliberation can supple, and concoct. But in religion wherein is no immaturity, nothing out of season, it goes farre otherwise" [*Works*, 3:225].

We spoke in the previous chapter of Milton's conception of liberty as the condition in which genuine action is possible: the condition, therefore, in which man acts as an instrument of the will of God. The state of liberty is attainable only by good men; it entails responsibility and rigorous discipline; it confers authority; it is always in accord with nature and with reason; it is the sole source of human dignity. The New Testament presents God as determined to set man free despite man's efforts to resist his own liberty, and this element in Christianity shows its contrast with all other religions: with, for example, the Homeric religion, which tells us that only the gods are free.[34]

In Milton's day, the word "liberty" was also used in a technical and restricted sense as meaning spontaneity in the worship of God, particularly in a church service. Thus Richard Baxter says he once thought that a set form of liturgy had "nothing which should make the use of it, in the ordinary public worship, to be unlawful to them that have not liberty to do better."[35] In most Nonconformist conceptions of worship, it is the Word of God that is recreated rather than his substantial presence, and hence the decisive event of the service of worship tends to be the sermon rather than the Eucharist, the substantial change in the elements of the Eucharist being denied. The preacher is not, in theory, ambitious to speak for himself, but only in the name of God, as the original prophets did, hence he tries to follow the gospel precepts about avoiding vain repetitions and being over-anxious about his own personal impact, and hopes to reach an utterance which will seem spontaneous to him and his hearers and yet will be guided by the Spirit he invokes. However narrow such a conception of Christian liberty may seem to us, it is the core of Milton's conception of it, and he is careful to ascribe a similar kind of spontaneity to the worship of Adam and Eve before their fall.

Of course a Protestant who also happens to be a major poet and a great prose writer as well cannot confine this conception of prophetic liberty of utterance to the pulpit: it spills over into the marketplace, into Parliament, and into literature, as *Areopagitica* shows. But the fact that liberty for Milton is always essentially verbal liberty, the power to know and utter, means that liberty for him has a specific focus which is not strictly that of either thought or action. We are all familiar with the famous phrase "reason is but choosing" in *Areopagitica*, which Milton himself thought so well of that he makes God the Father repeat it in *Paradise Lost*

("Reason also is choice" [*PL*, 3.108]). To choose means to act in the light of a certain vision of action, and reason in this sense is practical, as distinct from merely speculative, reason. I say merely speculative, because Milton has a low opinion of the kind of reason that finds no outlet in action: this is the reason Belial has, with his "thoughts that wander through Eternity" [*PL*, 2.148]. Liberty for Milton is a release of energy through revelation, just as, to use the example of the previous chapter, we can set free our musical energies only through the study of music. There is a parallel distinction between rational action and action which has no vision to guide it. The latter is mindless, habitual, mechanical action, the action based on tradition, precedent, custom, the doing of what has been done before because it has been done before.

It follows that everything Milton associates with liberty is discontinuous with ordinary life. When he says in *Areopagitica*, "there be delights, there be recreations and jolly pastimes that will fetch the day about from sun to sun, and rock the tedious year as in a delightfull dream" [*Works*, 4:334], he is not objecting to pastime, but pointing out the delusory nature of the happiness that merely rides on nature's cyclical roller coaster. The source of liberty is revelation: why liberty is good for man and why God wants him to have it cannot be understood apart from Christianity. Its product is reason, and reason of course is not confined to Christianity. But the effect of both revelation and reason is to arrest the current of mechanical habit. Revelation is a dialectical view of reality: it sees God as confronting the world, in the present moment, in an apocalyptic contrast of good and evil, life and death, freedom and bondage. Reason is less drastic, but its perspective is also dialectical and vertical. The consciousness withdraws from action and asks: is what we have been doing, without thinking about it, really worth doing? What would happen if we stopped doing it?

In this conception of reason as the withdrawing of consciousness from mechanical habit there is no sharp boundary line between it and what we should now call the imagination, nor between it and what we should call common sense, the inductive or empirical observation of what is really there. But there is the sharpest possible distinction between what Milton means by reason and what we should now mean by rationalization, the attempt to enlist reason in the service of passion. Rationalizing is always labyrinthine, like the attempts of the devils to work out a theology to justify their own revolt, which "found no end, in wandring mazes lost" [*PL*, 2.561], or the arguments of Satan in the serpent, whose symbolic wrigglings "made intricate seem strait" [*PL*, 9.632]. What revelation sees is grace: what reason sees is nature, and both of these are simplifying visions, visions of order and coherence.

Rationalizing always leads back to the same major premise: it is good to go on doing what we are accustomed to do. It is not the reason that Milton identifies with choice, but the perverted reason that is designed to prevent us from making a choice and continue the perpetual-motion machine of unthinking action. Reason can only halt unthinking action when it presents a genuinely new vision. And where are we to obtain such a vision? Not from the nature outside us, because, as we saw in discussing Milton's conception of idolatry, the fall of man was the fall of Narcissus, and what we see in nature is like ourselves. It can only come from something inside us which is also totally different from us. That something is ultimately revelation, and the kernel of revelation is paradise, the feeling that man's home is not in this world, but in another world (though occupying the same time and space) that makes more human sense. But such revelation has to be a personal force as well as a vision, for reason may see a better course of action without giving one the power to embark on it. And if genuine wisdom does not come from what is outside us in space, neither can it come from time, from experience or history or the knowledge of precedents and traditions that in our day inspire liberals and conservatives alike.

It follows that what man can do to achieve his own salvation, or even to achieve the social goals of reason and revelation, is largely negative. More precisely, it is, once more, iconoclastic. Man can demonstrate his willingness to be set free by knocking down his idols, but if he takes no advantage of the help then offered him, he will simply have to set new idols up, except that they will of course be the same old ones, error and custom. The prototype of all such efforts is that of Samson, who pulled down the Philistine temple and allowed the Israelite slaves to escape, but did not, by this act, save or redeem Israel. In his political attitude, it is somewhat disconcerting to realize that for Milton the most important symbol of the civil wars of his time was simply King Charles's head. The monarchy had become the English people's golden calf, and until it was pulled down, and the consequences of pulling it down faced, nothing else could be done.

We have spoken of the similarity of the structure of the first three books of *Paradise Lost* to that of the Jonsonian masque, a murky disorganized antimasque being followed by a vision of splendour and glory. But the Jonsonian masque normally leads to compliments and praises of the person in whose honour the masque is being held, and that person never speaks himself: if he did the spell would be broken and the masque would vanish into its elements, an illusion of tinsel and candlelight. In Milton, God the Father, in flagrant defiance of Milton's own theology, which tells us that we can know nothing about the Father except through the human incarnation of the Son, does speak, and with disastrous consequences. The rest of the poem hardly recovers from his speech, and there are few difficulties in the appreciation of *Paradise Lost* that are not directly connected with it. Further, he keeps on speaking at intervals, and whenever he opens his ambrosial mouth the sensitive reader shudders. Nowhere else in Milton is the contrast between the conceptual and the dramatic aspects of a situation, already glanced at, so grotesque: between recognizing that God is the source of all goodness and introducing God as a character saying, "I am the source of all goodness." The Father observes the improved behaviour of Adam after the fall and parenthetically remarks, "my motions in him" [*PL*, 11.91]. Theologically, nothing could be more correct: dramatically, nothing is better calculated to give the impression of a smirking hypocrite.

The speech the Father makes in book 3 has perhaps been modelled on the speech of Zeus at the opening of the *Odyssey*. But that speech is in perfect dramatic propriety. Zeus is merely saying that men often blame the gods for disasters they bring upon themselves, and gives an example, the death of Aegisthus, which has already occurred. What God does in Milton is to embark on a profoundly unconvincing argument purporting to show that Adam is responsible for his own fall, although God, being omniscient, foreknew it. But if God had foreknowledge he must have known in the instant of creating Adam that he was creating a being who would fall. And even if the argument held together, the *qui s'excuse s'accuse* tone in which it is delivered would still make it emotionally unconvincing.

Nor are the Father's other words and actions any more reassuring. They often do not seem very sharply distinguished from those of Satan. He professes a great concern for his creation ("thou know'st how dear, / To me are all my works," he says to the Son [*PL*, 3.276–7]), yet when the news is brought him that one-third of his angelic creation has revolted against him he merely smiles. And although the Son is a considerably more attractive figure than the Father, he too has caught the contagion of unconcern: he is a "gracious Judge, without revile" [*PL*, 10.118], but there is nothing in him of Blake's Holy Word—

> Calling the lapsed Soul,
> And weeping in the evening dew[36]

—weeping such tears as even Satan has the grace to shed for his woebegone followers. Satan interprets his one-third as nearly half, and God the Father speaks of his two-thirds as "farr the greater part" [*PL*, 7.145], but there is little moral difference between the two communiqués. Satan is never shown sending his followers on pointless errands, though the Father, according to Raphael, frequently does so.

We understand Milton very well when he shows us Satan accommodating himself to his actions with "necessitie, / The Tyrants plea" [*PL*, 4.393–4], but the Father seems equally caught in the trap of his own pseudo-logic:

> I else must change
> Thir nature, and revoke the high Decree
> Unchangeable, Eternal [*PL*, 3.125–7]

We understand very well also the fact that Satan, in the council in hell, volunteers to journey to the earth a split second too quickly, because he will have to go anyway and there is no point in letting a minor devil get the credit for volunteering. The insidious corruption of power could hardly have found a better image. But it is difficult to see why the Father should be teasing the angels for a volunteer, considering that they have just proved their courage by an entirely unnecessary display of it. It seems, to sum this up, very strange that the main "argument," in the more limited sense of the doctrinal coherence of the poem, should be so largely entrusted to the one character who is conspicuously no good at argument; and I find that the objections of students and many critics to the poem usually reduce themselves to a single one: Why is everything rational in *Paradise Lost* so profoundly unreasonable?

I am concerned with the twentieth-century reader, and for him there is no answer in what may be called the Great Historical Bromide: the assertion that such problems would not exist for the seventeenth-century reader, who could not possibly have felt such resentment against a character clearly labelled "God," and talking like a seventeenth-century clergyman. Even so, some of these questions can be answered at once if we adopt the view, mentioned earlier, that the angels are undergoing a spiritual education as well as Adam. The sentry duty that Raphael and others are assigned, "to enure / Our prompt obedience" [*PL*, 8.239–40], may be only a military metaphor for such education. Similarly with the calling for volunteers: it is not lack of courage but lack of understanding that holds the angels back—for one thing, they do not know how to die. The dramatizing of the Atonement is a greater mystery than anything they have encountered before, and is necessary if they are to watch the working out of that drama with any comprehension. But still two questions keep revolving around Milton's portrayal of the Father. First, why is he there, in defiance of all poetic tact? Second, what has happened to the great Promethean rebel who steered his way through four revolutions and then, in his crowning masterpiece, associates rebellion with Satan and goodness and virtue with this grinning reactionary mask? I shall try to answer these questions separately, and then see if I can combine the answers in a way that may give us some useful insight into the poem.

First, then, the fact that the Father in book 3 claims foreknowledge but disclaims foreordination is to be related to our earlier principle that liberty, for Milton, arrests the current of habit and of the cause–effect mechanism. We are not to read the great cycle of events in *Paradise Lost* cyclically: if we do we shall be reading it fatalistically. For inscrutable reasons the Father begets the Son; that inevitably causes the jealousy and revolt of Satan; that inevitably causes Satan's defeat and expulsion; that inevitably causes his attempt to assault the virtue of Adam and Eve, and so on through the whole dreary sequence. If we think of human life in time as a horizontal line, the Father is telling us that he is not to be found at the beginning of that line, as a First Cause from which everything inevitably proceeds. He is above the line, travelling along with human life like the moon on a journey. The great events in *Paradise Lost* should be read rather as a discontinuous series of crises, in each of which there is an opportunity to break the whole chain. We see these crises forming when Satan argues himself out of the possibility of submission to God, and when Adam (with the aid of some arm-twisting on the part of the poet) absolves God from any responsibility for his own sin. The failures, like the two great falls, look inevitable because they are failures, but the crucial victory, Christ's victory recorded in *Paradise Regained*, is not inevitable at all, at least from any point of view that we can take. At each crisis of life the important factor is not the consequences of previous actions, but the confrontation, across a vast apocalyptic gulf, with the source of deliverance. So whatever one thinks of the Father's argument, some argument separating present knowledge and past causation is essential to Milton's conception of the poem.

It seems to me—I have no evidence that this is Milton's view—that what God is saying in *Paradise Lost* is similar in many respects to what God is saying in the Book of Job. After the dialogue with the three friends and Elihu has reached a deadlock, God enters the argument himself with a series of rhetorical questions asking Job if he knows as much as God does about the creation. He seems to be trying to bully Job into submission by convicting him of ignorance of the divine ways. But perhaps his meaning can be taken differently. Perhaps he is merely discouraging Job from looking horizontally along a cause–effect sequence until he reaches a First Cause at the creation. Job is not even given the explanation that has been given the reader in the story of Satan's wager. It is not how he got into his calamity but how he can get out of it that is important, and this latter involves a direct and vertical relation between God and Job in the present tense.

There remains the question of what has happened to the political revolutionary in *Paradise Lost*. When he first seriously considered possible epic subjects, around the later 1630s, Milton tells us, he thought of Arthur as his hero. It is interesting to speculate about what Milton might have done with Arthur, as compared, say, with his two great predecessors Malory and Spenser. In Malory there is a graded series of knights, each knight being better than any other knight he can knock off his horse. Lancelot by this standard is the best knight in the world, "but if it were Sir Tristram";[37] the pagan knight Palomides is third, and Gawain and Gareth follow. Arthur, though an able knight and treated with respect as king, is by no means at the top of this list of seeded players, and if he goes into a tournament disguised and comes up against Lancelot or Tristram, down he goes over his horse's crupper. Malory reflects the society of the fifteenth-century baronial wars, where the king, though he may struggle into ascendancy for a time, may well be less permanently powerful than a great noble like the Earl of Warwick. In Spenser, Arthur is qualitatively different in strength and courage from all the knights of the Faerie Queene's court, who are related to him somewhat as the apostles are to Christ—the analogy is strained, but, considering the allegory, not pointless. Spenser is reflecting the mystique of the Tudor monarchy, and the skill with which its propaganda transformed a bastard Welsh ancestry into a myth of a reborn British Messiah. The Round Table, symbol of a feudal king's role as merely *primus inter pares*, is of no use to Spenser. But how could Arthur have been made, as he surely would have been made had Milton written an Arthurian epic before 1645, a symbol of the reformed church and Parliament triumphant over the encroachments of the king? For Arthur is a king, or prince, and any symbolism attached to him would have to reflect the fact.

Such a poem would have to make an extensive use of myth, and be closer in technique to *Comus* than to *Paradise Lost*. The more we think of Arthur historically, the more he tends to vanish into a period much like that of Milton's own time as Milton eventually came to conceive it, when the Britons, after throwing off the tyranny of Rome, collapsed under the tyranny of the English. There is not much left of Arthur in the *History of Britain*, and the place he might have had is occupied by a gloomy "digression" on how a nation may be led to rid itself of its masters and still not be capable of a rational freedom, in Gibbon's phrase. In *The Reason of Church Government* Milton speaks of looking for a hero "before the conquest" [*Works*, 3:237], restricting himself to that period for many reasons, one of which may have been that the Crusades began immediately afterwards, and he wanted neither competition nor association with Tasso's theme.

Of this mythical Arthur we have only a tantalizing allusion in *Mansus* to an Arthur making wars beneath the earth ("Arturumque etiam sub terris bella moventem" [l. 81]), indicating that Milton may have been thinking of Arthur as a figure like Blake's Orc, a revolutionary power hidden among the people, regarded as evil by his enemies, yet able to emerge and break the Saxon phalanxes in war. We also have that amazing poem *De Idea Platonica quemadmodum Aristoteles intellexit*, a poem in which the unborn embryos of Blake's Albion, Shelley's Prometheus, and Dylan Thomas's "long world's gentleman"[38] can be seen faintly stirring, where we meet an "archetypal giant" (*archetypus gigas*) who is not Adam but an eternal and incorruptible image of man, at once single and universal (*unusque et universus*). To these we may add the remark in *Of Reformation*, the earliest of the anti-Episcopal pamphlets: "a Commonwealth ought to be but as one huge Christian personage, one mighty growth, and stature of an honest man" [*Works*, 3:38]. These vague hints of a subterranean warrior and of a single human body who is both social and individual in form are not enough to base any theory on: they merely indicate the kind of imagery that might have attached itself to a revolutionary hero at this period of Milton's development.

The conception of society in *Paradise Lost* is quite as revolutionary as it is in the earlier prose. When Milton says of the Star Chamber that it has now "fall'n from the Starres with *Lucifer*,"[39] or that "*Lucifer* before *Adam* was the first prelat Angel,"[40] he is suggesting what the opening books of *Paradise Lost* make clear: that hell is the model for perverted orders of society, whether in state or church. There can be no objection to monarchy as such, for Milton, only to monarchy as a possible focus for idolatry, but the tendency for a king to acquire the same kind of "false glitter" [*PL*, 10.452] that Satan still has in hell is endemic in monarchy. The temporal authority represented by Nimrod in book 12 derives its structure from the demonic warrior aristocracy, and this authority, however inevitable, is still a usurpation:

> And from Rebellion shall derive his name,
> Though of Rebellion others he accuse. [*PL*, 12.36–7]

What is harder to understand is, first, why the imagery of dictatorial power is attached to heaven as well as hell, and, second, what has happened to the conception of a revolutionary hero.

There is such a figure in Milton, but we have to look for it in his Samson rather than in his Satan. Samson in the Book of Judges is a typical boaster or trickster hero, whose strength reminds us of Hercules, but who never does anything good-natured or unselfish, as Hercules often does. He is given rather to practical jokes in extremely doubtful taste, such as setting fire to the tails of foxes and turning them into the fields of Philistine farmers to burn up their crops. Milton's skill in transforming this overgrown juvenile delinquent into a figure of such dignity and power is extraordinary, but even so there could hardly be a greater contrast between his shaggy ferocity and the demure suburban gravity of Adam. Adam is what leaders of men were intended to be, peaceful patriarchs; Samson is what the ascendancy of Nimrod and the later Philistines has forced human leaders to become. The difference in context is emphasized by the role of the heroine. We saw that Eve is human, not demonic, although permanently entrapped by something demonic after her fall, just as Cleopatra is permanently entrapped by Egypt. Delilah, however, is purely a tentacle of a Philistine society, and as such perhaps the nearest thing to a real siren in all English drama: a dry, crepitating, whispering evil, audible and tangible but not visible, full of the unbearable pathos of the cast off and forsaken, able, like Dido in hell, to unsettle her former lover's self-respect, yet never quite becoming human.

From the Philistine point of view it is Samson who is the sinister and demonic figure, an "ev'ning Dragon" descending on the roosts of the "villatic Fowl" [*SA*, ll. 1692–5]. We saw earlier that in Milton's view the church should accept whatever temporal authority is provided for it, but that if the Christian conscience is violated the church may become a revolutionary force. Samson's life in Gaza is similarly based on a rigid separation of spiritual from temporal authority: as soon as his religious integrity is touched by his having to appear in the temple of Dagon, that is the end of the temple of Dagon. But his tragedy is similar in many respects to the tragedy of Coriolanus in Shakespeare. Like Coriolanus, "his heart's his mouth" [3.1.256]: he has nothing of the astuteness or the sense of obstacles that a leader must have if he is to crystallize a society around his leadership. Samson, as a leader, can only smash Philistines with his own hands: he cannot build an Israelite society, and is so loosely attached to his own people that he takes no responsibility for the fact that "*Israel* still serves with all his Sons" [*SA*, l. 240]. True, the chorus of Danites, standing around uttering timid complacencies in teeth-loosening doggerel, are not a very reassuring social object; but they are what they are largely because Samson is no David. In his battles and final martyrdom Samson is an Old Testament prototype of Christ, but the aspect of the Messiah he typifies is the terrible blood-soaked figure of Isaiah who has trodden the winepress alone.

I have not spoken of the individual aspect of Milton's Samson because I am not concerned here with *Samson Agonistes* as such, only with Milton's view of the nature and function of the revolutionary hero in a revolutionary situation. Milton naturally had a good deal of respect for the political wisdom that dwells with prudence, that tacks and veers and catches the wind and makes the best of the confused mixture of good and evil which is human life. In the notebook in which he considers subjects for epic and tragedy, he does not mention Arthur, but he does pause at the name of Alfred the Great, "whose actions are wel like those of Ulysses" [*Works*, 18:243]. He is willing to consider Oliver Cromwell as an emergency leader, like the judges of Israel to whom Samson belonged, but is at pains to point out that peace is not merely the end of a war, but a qualitatively different human condition from war, and one that requires far more complex qualities than the army commander as such possesses.

In a Catholic poet—Dante is the obvious example—the separation of divine and demonic worlds would be something that man sees or participates in through a process of sacramental discipline, which continues in the next world in the form of purgatory. But for Milton such revelation cannot come from anything continuous, however important habit and discipline may be in themselves. The place of sacrament and purgatory in his work is taken by the temptation, the agon or contest which is the theme of all four of his major poems. Each of these crises presents continuous and habitual life with an interruption, in which reality is split vertically into two opposed orders. The Lady in *Comus*, Christ in *Paradise Regained*, and Samson in *Samson Agonistes*, all adhere steadily to the divine vision, and as they do so the demonic world becomes more and more obviously demonic. But the victory over temptation leads to an exhaustion of power, and in the moment of victory power flows in from a source that is both identical with and different from the victor. Sabrina restores to the Lady her own power of movement; Christ is sustained on the pinnacle of the temple by the Father whose "Godhead" he carries; Samson changes his mind about going to the temple of Dagon in a way that shows that his mind has been changed for him.

The theme of the externalizing of the demonic and the internalizing of the divine runs through every aspect of Milton's writing. We have seen how the law is a tyranny to a criminal, for whom it is external, and how it is irksome and frustrating to us as long as we think of it as command rather than condition. The Word of God is a collection of dark sayings and hard names as long as it is a book in front of us, but swallowed by us, so to speak, as Ezekiel swallowed his roll [Ezekiel 3:1–3], it becomes the charter of human dignity. We see this process of going from the book to the internal scripture dramatized in the summary of the Bible that Michael gives to Adam, which begins as a series of visions and then, after Abraham's act of faith in leaving Chaldea, is simply narrated. Milton appears to mean by the Holy Spirit what God gives to his creatures, which may be anything from life itself to a specific talent for writing poetry. It is this Spirit that understands the Bible, and that acts as the "Umpire *Conscience*" [*PL*, 3.195] in the mind. The degeneracy of language, which has reduced "charity" to patronizing the indigent, has also reduced "conscience" to a subjective hunch derived from an infantile dependence on parents, which is not quite what Milton means by conscience. What he does mean is rather the power of living a free life. The Holy Spirit, which makes this possible, comes from God, and therefore tries to return to him, bringing us along in the process. But because it is the God within, it is where all liberty starts.

In *Paradise Lost*, of course, it is paradise itself that is internalized, transformed from an outward place to an inner state of mind. We saw that Eden is finally washed away in the flood, in order to show that for God there is no longer anything sacred which can be located either in outward space or in past time. The world we fell from we can return to only by attaining the kind of freedom to which all education, as Milton defines it, leads, and it is this freedom that is said by Michael to be a happier paradise than that of the original garden [*PL*, 12.586–7].

Applying this principle of internalizing and spiritual discernment to the reading of *Paradise Lost* itself, we find in that poem a father-figure who seems harsh, arbitrary, inscrutable, and more given to rationalization than to reason. There is nothing to be done with this objectionable creature except swallow him. The heaven of *Paradise Lost*, with God the supreme sovereign and the angels in a state of unquestioning obedience to his will, can only be set up on earth inside the individual's mind. The free man's mind is a dictatorship of reason obeyed by the will without argument: we go wrong only when we take these conceptions of kingship and service of freedom as *social* models. Absolute monarchs and their flunkeys on earth always follow the model of hell, not of heaven. The cleavage between the conceptual and the dramatic aspects of the Father clears up when we realize that the one is the opposite of the other. The reason why kingship on earth is so apt to become idolatrous is precisely that it is the external projection of the inner sovereignty of God. This projection will eventually disappear even in heaven itself, as God tells us:

> For regal Scepter then no more shall need,
> God shall be All in All. [*PL*, 3.340–1]

God's sovereignty, therefore, has its earthly model in the mind of the Enoch or Noah or Samson who refuses to compromise with evil, refuses to admit any of the arguments that evil advances in favour of compromise, and who, faced with the supreme test, can produce out of some unknown depth the power to suffer and die. This power suffers alone: Christ renounced the help of legions of angels when captured in the garden, just as he went out alone to win the war in heaven after the legions of angels had done their best, and just as Adam is told by Raphael that, whether there are other beings in other worlds or not, he must, like Beowulf, fight his dragon alone. Something of this lonely fight comes into Milton's personal statements in *Paradise Lost*: the cold climate, the late age, blindness, the loss of touch with literary fashions evidenced in the old-style blank verse, the religious and therefore conventionally unheroic subject, all suggest a kind of last-ditch desperateness. The lonely fight in the life of Christ is the theme of *Paradise Regained*, the subject of our last chapter.

We seem to find in Milton, then, a revolutionary who became disillusioned with the failure of the English people to achieve a free commonwealth, and was finally compelled to find the true revolution within the individual. Reactionaries and obscurantists of all kinds are always delighted with this solution, because they know of no conception of the individual except the opaque ego and Satan's defiant "here at least / We shall be free" [*PL*, 1.258–9] in a world far removed from any threat to the status quo. Of course it is true that Milton turned from social to individual and poetic activity after 1660: the personal reasons are obvious enough, but it is hard to think of *Paradise Lost* as some kind of consolation prize. An original purchaser, standing at a bookstall with the surge and thunder of the mighty poem breaking over him, might well have asked, But this is a blind, defeated, disillusioned, gouty old man: where did he get all this energy? It is a fair question, even if it may not have an answer.

We have got far enough with *Paradise Lost* to see that we have to turn its universe inside out, with God sitting within the human soul at the centre and Satan on a remote periphery plotting against our freedom. From this perspective, perhaps, we can see what Blake meant when he said that Milton was a true poet and of the devil's (i.e., the revolutionary) party without knowing it.[41] The more we study the poem, the more doubtful we become of the last three words, yet they do say something that is true. In dealing with Satan, Milton moves with superb confidence, because Satan is his poetic creature: he knows what he means by Satan and he knows how to realize a Satanic personality. The weak spots of the poem, such as God's speech in book 3 and Raphael's doubtful answer to Adam in book 8, are not so well realized poetically, because what Milton wants the reader to grasp is something existential, something beyond poetry. The better we know the poem, the more important become these passages that we cannot fully understand without possessing the poem.

All revolutionary myths are sleeping-beauty myths: what the revolution attacks is a usurpation, and what it replaces it with is historically, or at least morally, prior to the usurpation. The Protestant in Milton fought for the restoration of the primitive church of the Gospels, against the usurpation of tradition, or custom and error. The humanist in him fought for the ancient liberty of the Greek and Roman republics against the usurpation of kings and priests. The Parliamentarian in him fought for the liberties of the lords and commons against the usurpations of Star Chamber and royal prerogative. All these are causes rooted in history, models of the past to be recreated in the future. There is no evidence that Milton ceased to believe in any of these causes, but he was driven by a deeper logic than that of disillusionment to study the primal pattern, the ultimate myth of the gate of origin, the definitive insight into how things came to be, which Raphael gives Adam as the essence of his message and which Satan cuts off from himself. Milton's source told him that although heaven is a city and a society, the pattern established for man on earth by God was not social but individual, and not a city but a garden.

The ultimate precedent, therefore, in which all other precedents are rooted, is not Utopian but Arcadian, not historical but pastoral, not a social construct but an individual state of mind. In the Old Testament, Moses, the law, comes to the border of the Promised Land which only Joshua, who has the same name as Jesus, can conquer. But in the Old Testament the Promised Land becomes the society of Israel, whereas in Milton, when Jesus defeats Satan in the desert, it is "Eden" that he raises in the wilderness, and his mission is not to restore any "earthly *Canaan*," but to bring back

> Through the worlds wilderness long wanderd man
> Safe to eternal Paradise of rest. [*PL*, 12.313–14]

Social and political revolution, to be of any use, has to be related to the vision of what it is to achieve. And we find that the goal of man's quest for liberty is individualization: there is no social model or ideal state in the human mind. Social relations are always in the sphere of the law. Even the church is a by-product of the individuals composing it who possess the higher or internal form of scripture in their minds: the church is not, beyond a certain point, the teacher of these individuals, but the product of their dialogue with one another. Milton divides the cause of liberty into civil, domestic, and religious spheres, and he fought with courage and high intelligence for the civil and religious causes as he understood them. But it is domestic liberty that is really Milton's own sphere: the cause of education and free speech, and a conception of marriage which finds its model in Adam and Eve alone in Eden. And while civil and religious liberty are the concern of skilful and subtle dialecticians, domestic liberty, the goal of human development itself, takes us from dialectic to the emblematic vision or parable, and requires a poet.

Many critics of Milton tell us that Milton's style is oppressively brocaded and ornate, a kind of Anglicized Latin, sonorous and lofty but never direct or simple. There are two groups of such critics, the ignorant and the perverse: one group is numerous and the other influential, and those whose notions of Milton were formed in youth by the first book of *Paradise Lost* have little power of resistance to them. It seems a curious view of a poet who distinguished poetic from discursive writing as more simple, sensuous, and passionate. Simplicity of language is a deep moral principle to Milton: whenever he is attacking the tyranny of tradition it is always the humanist's contempt for the "knotty Africanisms"[42] and gabbling abstractions of theological lawyers that is foremost in the attack. The complex historical issues and formidable titles of such works as *Tetrachordon*, *Eikonoklastes*, or *Animadversions upon the Remonstrant's Defence* often prevent us from discovering that they are brilliant polemical writings, crackling with wit and epigram and the free play of an exuberant and, granted the polemical context, good-humoured mind. Milton was, so far as I know, the first great English writer to fight for semantic sanity, to urge his readers not to react automatically to smear or bogey words like "heretic" or "blasphemer," but to look at such words and see what, if anything, they really mean. He can show amazing insight in defining the mythical complexes that organize the processes of confused and panic-stricken minds:

> So that we who by Gods speciall grace have shak'n off the servitude of a great male Tyrant, our pretended Father the Pope, should now, if we be not betimes aware of these wily teachers, sink under the slavery of a Female notion, the cloudy conception of a demy-island mother.[43]

In handling scriptural quotations, particularly in the divorce tracts, he is a precise and delicate stylist in his constant feeling for the context and decorum of the passages he deals with, and he is a stylist too in his contempt for the trumpery show of logic by which malice can always score a point over charity. He is never tired of defending vigorous and outspoken language—to such an extent, in fact, that it seems strange that there should be no passage needing such defence in the whole of his poetry, and few if any in his prose. He constantly dwells on the simplicity and plainness of the Gospels, and his own poetic style, however erudite, is seldom ambiguous, even in the proper critical sense of that term. He employs ambiguity only for very special contexts, such as the word "fruit" in the first line of *Paradise Lost* and the word "solitary" in the last. Wherever we turn in Milton, we find his awareness of the fact that oratory and rhetoric cannot function properly unless they can achieve the kind of simplicity that means what it says, and that they cannot attain this simplicity unless they are employed in the service of human liberty. Hence a decline in style and literary sensitivity is one of the first signs of general decline:

> Therefore when the esteem of Science, and liberal study waxes low in the Common-wealth, wee may presume that also there all civil Vertue, and worthy action is grown as low to a decline: and then Eloquence, as it were consorted in the same destiny, with the decrease and fall of vertue corrupts also and fades.[44]

Or, even more explicitly:

> While it is Plato's opinion that by a change in the manner and habit of dressing serious commotions and mutations are portended in a commonwealth, I, for my part, would rather believe that the fall of that city and its low and obscure condition were consequent on the general vitiation of its usage in the matter of speech.[45]

Paradise Lost, in the final period of Milton's career, represents not only an intensification but a colossal simplifying of his thought and vision. The story of Adam, in his day, was, as poetic material, the dreariest commonplace: Milton reached it by cutting through all the complex religious and political issues of his day until he got down to the myth that generated them, the myth that creates in us, whether we always know it or not, the unshakeable conviction that the real form of human life is a form of leisure and peace and freedom, the conviction that is both the light of intelligence and the heat of courage. Because he reached it the hard way, the story of Adam in Milton has the simplicity that is so like the commonplace, and yet so different, the simplicity that keeps us in the centre of human experience. As commonplace, the story of Adam is rationalized superstition, asserting that for mysterious reasons in a dim past man is forever prevented from getting anything he really wants. Reached the way Milton reached it, it becomes the counterpart in history to what the music of the spheres is in nature: a glimpse of a central point of order which absorbs both hope and disillusionment into serenity.

V Revolt in the Desert

Among the least fully realized parts of *Paradise Lost* is what seems a hurried and perfunctory summary of the Bible in the latter part of Michael's revelation. The reason is that such events as the Incarnation and the Last Judgment cannot be given their full poetic resonance at that point in the *Paradise Lost* scheme, otherwise the conclusion would become top-heavy. They must either be dramatized separately or assumed to have their importance already understood by the reader. *Paradise Regained* dramatizes the third of four epiphanies in which Christ confronts Satan: it refers back to the original war in heaven as recounted in *Paradise Lost*, and forward to the final binding of Satan prophesied in the Book of Revelation [20:1–3].[46] The defeat of Satan as tempter fulfils the prophecy in Genesis that the seed of Adam shall "bruise the serpent's head" [Genesis 3:15], which Satan refers to so light-heartedly in *Paradise Lost*.

This imagery suggests the romance theme of a knight-errant killing a dragon, and is one of several such images in the Bible. Besides the serpent in Eden, the Old Testament speaks of a dragon or sea monster, called "Leviathan," or "Rahab," who was defeated once at the creation and is to be destroyed, or, in the metaphor of the sea serpent, hooked and landed, on the day of judgment. A comparison of Satan to the Leviathan appears early in *Paradise Lost*. Isaiah refers both to the previous and to the future victories over this Leviathan, and Ezekiel and Isaiah appear to identify him with Egypt as the symbolic land of bondage. In the Book of Revelation this figure becomes a dragon with seven heads and ten horns, whose tail draws a third of the stars from heaven, the basis of Milton's account of Satan's fall. The connection of this dragon with Egypt in Milton is indicated in Michael's references to the Nile's seven mouths and to the plagues of Egypt as the ten wounds of the river dragon [*PL*,

12.157–9, 190–1]. In the symbolism of Revelation, again, the Satan of Job and the Gospels, the serpent of the Eden story, and the leviathan of the prophecies, are all explicitly identified.

From this is derived the conventional symbol of Christ as a dragon-killer, such as we have in medieval sculptures portraying him with a dragon or basilisk under his feet. In the first book of *The Faerie Queene*, the story of St. George and the dragon is used as an allegory of the imitation of Christ by the church. St. George's dragon in Spenser is identified with the Satan-serpent-leviathan complex in the Bible, and as a result of St. George's victory the parents of his lady Una, who are Adam and Eve, are restored to their inheritance, the Garden of Eden, which is also the unfallen world. In *The Reason of Church Government* Milton refers to the allegory of St. George and "the Kings daughter the Church" [*Works*, 3:275]. Michael explains to Adam, however, that the contest of Christ and Satan will be not a physical but a spiritual and intellectual fight, the cutting weapons used being those of dialectic, and the true dragon being a spiritual enemy [*PL*, 12.386–435].

I mentioned earlier the passage in *The Reason of Church Government* in which Milton speaks of the literary genre of the "brief epic."[47] As *Paradise Regained* is clearly Milton's essay in the brief epic, and as the model for that genre is stated by Milton to be the Book of Job, we should expect *Paradise Regained* to have a particularly close relation to that drama. In Job the contest of God and Satan takes the form of a wager on Job's virtue, and the scheme of *Paradise Regained* is not greatly different, with Christ occupying the place of Job. Satan, we notice, soon disappears from the action of Job, and when Job's mind is finally enlightened by God, God's speech consists very largely of discourses on two monsters, Behemoth and Leviathan, the latter of whom, the more important, is finally said to be "king over all the children of pride" [Job 41:34]. These monsters seem to represent an order of nature over which Satan is permitted some control, but, in a larger perspective, they are seen to be creatures of God. By pointing these beasts out to Job, God has, so to speak, put them under Job's feet, and taken Job into his own protection. Thus the victory of Job is, in terms of this symbolism, a dialectical victory over both Satan and Leviathan, Satan and Leviathan being much the same thing from different points of view.

In more traditional views of the Incarnation the central point of the contest of Christ and Satan is located between Christ's death on the cross and his Resurrection. It is then that he descends to hell, harrows hell, and achieves his final victory over hell and death. In medieval paintings of the harrowing of hell, hell is usually represented as Leviathan, a huge open-mouthed monster into which, or whom, Christ descends, like the Jonah whom Christ accepted as a prototype of his own Passion. For Milton, however, the scriptural evidence for the descent into hell was weak, and besides, Milton believed that the whole of Christ's human nature died on the cross, with no soul or spirit able to survive and visit hell. In the synoptic Gospels, the temptation immediately follows the Baptism. Milton's view of baptism is an exception to his generally antisacramental attitude to Biblical symbolism: he is willing to see in it a symbol of the three-day crisis of Christian redemption, death, burial, and resurrection. So the temptation is what becomes for Milton the scripturally authorized version of the descent into hell, the passing into the domain of Satan, and the reconquest of everything in it that is redeemable. Certain features, such as the bewilderment of the forsaken disciples and the elegiac complaint of the Virgin Mary at the beginning of the second book, might seem more natural if Milton had followed medieval tradition in making *Paradise Regained* the harrowing of hell.[48] In any case Christ's withdrawal from the world at this point is the opposite of a "fugitive and cloister'd vertue"[49] as he is being led directly into the jaws of hell itself, and not yet as a conqueror.

The Bible gives us two parallel versions of the fall and redemption of man. The first is the *Paradise Lost* version. Adam falls from the garden into a wilderness, losing the tree of life and the water of life. Christ, the second Adam, wins back the garden ("*Eden* rais'd in the wast Wilderness" [*PR*, 1.7]) and restores to man the tree and river of life. This version is elaborated by Spenser as well as Milton, for in Spenser the fight between St. George and the dragon takes place at the boundary of Eden, and St. George is refreshed by the paradisal well of life and tree of life, which continue in the church as the sacraments of baptism and communion. As the natural home of Christ on earth is a fertile garden, the Eden in which he walked in the cool of the day, so the natural home of devils is the wilderness, "A pathless Desert, dusk with horrid shades" [*PR*, 1.296], a blasted land like the country traversed in *The City of Dreadful Night* or by Browning's Childe Roland, the sort of scene one instinctively calls "God-forsaken," where the panic inspired by hunger, lost direction, and loneliness would have unsettled the reason of most people in much less than forty days.

Inside the story of Adam comes the second version, the story of Israel, who falls from the Promised Land into the bondage of Egypt and Babylon.

Besides being a second Adam, Christ is a second Israel, who wins back, in a spiritual form, the Promised Land and its capital city of Jerusalem. In this capacity the story of the Exodus, or deliverance of Israel from Egypt, prefigures his life in the Gospels. Israel is led to Egypt through a Joseph; Christ is taken to Egypt by a Joseph. Christ is saved from a wicked king who orders a massacre of infants; Israel is saved from the slaughter of Egyptian firstborn. Moses organizes Israel into twelve tribes and separates it from Egypt at the crossing of the Red Sea; Christ gathers twelve followers and is marked out as the Redeemer at his Baptism in the Jordan, which the Israelites also later cross. Israel wanders forty years in the wilderness; Christ forty days. The Israelites receive the law from Mount Sinai; the Gospel is preached in the Sermon on the Mount, which in its structure is largely a commentary on the Decalogue. The Israelites are plagued by serpents and are redeemed by placing a brazen serpent on a pole. This, like the story of Jonah, is also accepted as a prototype of the Crucifixion by Christ himself [John 3:14; Matthew 12:40].[50] The Israelites conquer the Promised Land under Joshua, who has the same name as Jesus, corresponding to Christ's victory over death and hell, as, in the church's calendar, Easter immediately follows the commemorating of the temptation in Lent. Thus when the Angel Gabriel tells the Virgin Mary to call her child's name Jesus, or Joshua, the meaning is that the reign of the law is now over and the assault on the Promised Land has begun.

The death of Moses just outside the Promised Land represents the inability of the law alone to redeem mankind, as Milton emphasizes both in *Paradise Lost* and in *The Christian Doctrine*.[51] The difficulty of the temptation for Christ, as *Paradise Regained* presents it, is complicated by the fact that Christ is still, at this stage of his career, within the law. His temptation is part of a much subtler process of separating, in his own mind, the law which is to be annihilated from the law which is to be fulfilled and internalized. Milton explicitly says that Christ in the wilderness "into himself descended" [*PR*, 2.111], and employed his time in clarifying his own mind about the nature of his Messianic mission. We see little of what is actually passing in Christ's mind, but as his refusal of one after another of Satan's temptations drives Satan on to display his resources in a steadily rising scale of comprehensiveness and intensity, the poetic effect is that of negatively clarifying Christ's own thoughts. The climax of the temptation corresponds to the death of Moses: it is the point at which Jesus passes from obedience to the law to works of faith, from the last Hebrew prophet to the founder of Christianity.

The typical Old Testament figures who represent the law and the prophets, respectively, are Moses and Elijah, who accompany Jesus in the Transfiguration and are the two "witnesses" to his teaching in the Book of Revelation. Both of them prefigured the forty-day retirement and fast of Jesus in their own lives. The Old Testament says that Elijah will come again before the Messiah, a prophecy fulfilled by John the Baptist, but in a sense Moses has to be reborn too, as the law is fulfilled in the gospel. The Bible suggests the possibility that Moses did not die but was, like Elijah, transported directly to paradise. An early version of *Paradise Lost* was to have begun with some speculations on this point.[52]

Christ has fasted for forty days, and, as Luke remarks with some restraint, "he afterward hungered" [4.2]. He has a Freudian wish-fulfilment dream, like Eve in *Paradise Lost*, in which memories of Old Testament stories of prophets are mingled with food. Still, he is not hungry until after the first temptation to turn stones to bread, which consequently has nothing to do with hunger but is superficially an appeal to his charity, corresponding to the miraculous provision of manna in the Exodus. Jesus' answer that man shall not live by bread alone is a quotation from a passage in Deuteronomy that refers to the giving of manna [8.3; cf. *PR*, 1.349–50]. A contrast is involved between the material bread of the law and the bread of life in the gospel. This contrast distinguishes the gospel from what, for Milton, was the sacramental fallacy, the tendency to translate the Jewish ceremonial code into Christian terms, the fallacy that produced the doctrine of transubstantiation, which Milton characterizes as a banquet of cannibals. Milton's interest in this first temptation, however, is less in the temptation as such than in the tactical manœuvre which Satan makes after his disguise is penetrated.

Milton's most obvious source for *Paradise Regained*, apart from the Bible itself, was Giles Fletcher's poem *Christ's Victory and Triumph*, of which the temptation forms an episode. In Fletcher, the first temptation is primarily a temptation of despair, and hence closely follows the episode of Despair in the first book of *The Faerie Queene*. Milton's Christ uses only the term "distrust," but still Milton is here the poetic grandson of Spenser.[53] Despair's argument in Spenser is based on the logic of law without gospel, i.e., sin is inevitable, and the longer one lives the more one sins. The emotional overtones are those of the indolence and passivity which is at the heart of all passion, and some of them are echoed in the argument of Comus to the Lady:

> Refreshment after toil, ease after pain [l. 686]

Satan's argument in *Paradise Regained* is a refinement of Despair's. Good and evil are inseparable in the fallen world, and, in a world where all instruments are corrupted, one must either use corrupt instruments or not act at all. The use of evil or Satanic means being inevitable, Satan himself must be a reluctant agent of the will of God, as long as we can preserve a belief in the will of God. In terms of the law alone, which can discover but not remove sin, this argument is more difficult to refute than it looks—in fact it could be a clever parody of the central argument of *Areopagitica*. Christ's answer, leading up as it does to a prophecy of the cessation of oracles and the coming of the Word of God to the human heart, is based on the gospel or spiritual view of Scripture. Satan has never met this view before, and is sufficiently baffled to retire and consult with his colleagues before going further.

The conflict in *Paradise Regained* is ultimately a spiritual one, but the basis of the human spirit is the physical body, and the body is the battlefield of the spirit. Milton is clear that the soul is the form of the body, and that there are not two essences in man. Another allegorical poem between *The Faerie Queene* and *Paradise Regained*, *The Purple Island*, by Giles Fletcher's brother Phineas, begins with a detailed allegory of the physical body and then expands into a psychomachia, in which the principals are Christ and the Dragon. This allegory is based on the defence of the House of Alma in the second book of *The Faerie Queene*, which presents the quest of Guyon, the knight of temperance or continence, the physical integrity which is not so much virtue as the prerequisite of virtue. The crucial ordeals of Guyon are the temptation of money in the cave of Mammon, mentioned by Milton in a famous passage in *Areopagitica*, and the Bower of Bliss, where the tempting agent is female and the temptation itself primarily erotic. In Giles Fletcher's version of the temptation of Christ the final[54] temptation is modelled on the Bower of Bliss. Satan's rejection of Belial's proposal to tempt Christ with women indicates Milton's deliberate departure from Fletcher's precedent. Milton had already dealt with such themes in *Comus*. *Comus*, which leads up to Sabrina's deliverance of the Lady by sprinkling her with water, an act with some analogies to baptism, presents, so to speak, the temptation of innocence, where the assault on sexual continence is naturally central. *Paradise Regained* follows baptism, and presents the temptation of experience.[55]

The sequence of temptations, which now proceeds unbroken to the end of the poem, begins, then, with an attack on the physical basis of Jesus' humanity. There are two of these temptations—a banquet and an offer of money; neither is in the Gospels, and it is clear that the temptations of "Beauty and money" in the second book of *The Faerie Queene* are mainly responsible for them. They take place in a pleasant grove, and one line is a vestigial survival of the Bower of Bliss, with its triumph of artifice over nature:

> Natures own work it seem'd (Nature taught Art). [*PR*, 2.295]

Attacks on temperance could be resisted by any genuine prophet or saint, or even by a virtuous heathen. Satan is an imaginative Oriental bargainer, and one has the feeling that although of course he would like to gain Christ as cheaply as possible, he is reconciled to seeing these temptations fail. His strategy, as we shall see, is cumulative, and individual temptations are expendable. The temptations of food and money continue the argument of the first temptation, in that they urge the necessary use of doubtful means for good ends. Their rejection establishes the principle, which is also in Spenser, that the moral status of the instrument depends on the mental attitude toward it. If the initial attitude is one of passive dependence, the instrument will become an illusory end in itself. It is not immediately apparent, however, why Satan has so much higher an opinion of food than of women as a temptation, even granting that there is really only one temptation of food.

We should be careful not to take anything in Satan's reply to Belial, such as his remark that beauty stands "In the admiration only of weak minds" [*PR*, 2.221], at its face value. Nothing that Satan says in the poem is as trustworthy as that. He is, of course, right in thinking that Christ cannot be tempted to sins which are foreign to his nature; he can be tempted only to be some form of Antichrist, some physical or material counterpart of himself. But he is right for the wrong reasons.

If we look back at our earlier discussion of lust and greed, we can see that the initial attacks on Jesus are based on greed, and that lust, in its primitive sexual form, is what is sacrificed in Satan's gambit. The reason is that Satan assumes Christ to be a hero of some kind, in view of what was said of him at the Baptism. If he is designed to redeem Adam, he must be strong at Adam's weak point of susceptibility to "Femal charm" [*PL*, 9.999].[56] For Satan, heroic action means his own type of aggressive and destructive parody-heroism, which is a form of lust. His assumption that the Messiah's heroism will be in some way of this type, or can be easily diverted to it, is genuine, and he is consequently willing to give

Jesus credit for a heroic contempt of "effeminate slackness" [*PL*, 11.634], besides being unwilling to put him prematurely on his guard by presenting him with a relatively crude form of lust. Satan's own contempt for the kind of heroism that Christ seems to prefer is also genuine, and for anyone else this would be itself a major temptation, a form of shame. Faithful in Bunyan, for example, remarks that shame, in the sense of worldly contempt, was his worst enemy. Satan, the accuser of Israel, is what, since Milton's day, we have learned to call a Philistine. Both Satan and Christ divide the world into the material and the spiritual, but for Satan the material is real and the spiritual is imaginary, or, as he says, "Allegoric" [*PR*, 4.390]. It is only from Christ's point of view that he is an Archimago or master of illusion: from ours he is consistently a realist.

Hence, just as Comus puns on the word "nature," so all the elements of the dialectical conflict are attached to a material context by Satan and to a spiritual one by Christ. By rejecting everything that Satan offers in Satan's sense, Christ gets it again in its true or spiritual form, just as Adam, if he had successfully resisted his temptation, would still have become as the gods (i.e., the true gods or angels), knowing good, and evil as the possible negation of good. In *The Christian Doctrine* Milton speaks of the virtue of urbanity and its opposing vice of obscenity, which, he says, consists of taking words in a double sense. In this context he means what we mean by the *double entendre*: still, Christ is the source of urbanity and Satan of obscenity, and something of the *double entendre*, the great words "the kingdom, the power and the glory" profaned to their worldly opposites, runs all through Satan's speeches. As in the previous conflict, Satan is "scoffing in ambiguous words" [*PL*, 6.568].

The opening colloquy between Satan and Christ in the first book is already a clash of oracular powers. Satan's dialectical instrument is the evasive or quibbling oracle, which cheats its hearer, as it did Macbeth, by double meanings that would be bad jokes if their serious consequences did not make them obscene. Christ speaks throughout with the simplicity and plainness that, as we saw, Milton emphasizes so much in the Gospels. The climax of *Paradise Regained*, when Satan falls from the pinnacle and Christ stands on it, is marked by two very carefully placed Classical allusions, almost the only mythological ones in the poem. One is to Hercules and Antaeus, of which more later; the other is to Oedipus and the Sphinx. Christ has not only overcome temptation, but, as the Word of God, he has solved the verbal riddle of human life, putting all the words which are properly attributes of God into their rightful context.

The temptations which follow are temptations to false heroic action, and fall into three parts: the temptation of Parthia, or false power; the temptation of Rome, or false justice; and the temptation of Athens, or false wisdom. One problem of interpretation is raised by Milton's curious proportioning of emphasis. The temptation of Parthia seems much the crudest of the three: it is not easy to think of Jesus as some kind of Genghis Khan. Yet it takes up the entire third book, while the other two are huddled with the third temptation into the fourth.

In Jesus' day, with the memory of the Maccabees still vivid, the question of armed rebellion against Roman power was very insistent; it was the course that most Jews expected the Messiah to take, and had already been in the mind of the youthful Christ:

> victorious deeds
> Flam'd in my heart, heroic acts, one while
> To rescue *Israel* from the *Roman* yoke [*PR*, 1.215–17]

And, though even then Christ thought of putting down violence rather than of using violence, still Satan's arguments on this point are unanswerable: to defeat Roman power by arms requires princely virtues, and princely virtues, as Machiavelli demonstrated, are not moral virtues, far less spiritual ones: they are martial courage and cunning, both demonic gifts. What Satan unwittingly does for Christ in the temptations of Parthia and Rome is to dramatize the nature of that aspect of law that is to be annihilated by the gospel—law as a compelling external force in which spiritual authority is subject to and administered by temporal authority.

Satan is shrewd enough to throw in the suggestion that, by gaining the power of Parthia, Christ will be able to realize the patriotic dream of reuniting the lost ten tribes with the Jewish remnant. In rejecting this, Christ rejects also the legal conception of Israel as a chosen people and is ready to usher in the new Christian conception of Israel as the body of believers. But there seems also to be some personal reference, however indirect, to the great blighted hope of Milton's political life.[57]

The final binding of Satan, the last phase of the total cycle, is prophesied in the Book of Revelation, where, in the twelfth chapter, we have again a wilderness, a symbolic female figure representing the church, and a threatening dragon beaten off by Michael, the angelic champion of Israel, in a repetition of the first encounter. Milton, like everyone else, took the Book of Revelation to be in part a prophecy of the troubles the church was to suffer after the apostolic period. In *The Reason of Church Government* he attacks the supporters of tradition because they do not understand that the Book of Revelation foretells an apostasy of the church and "the Churches flight into the wildernes" [*Works,* 3:246]. Several times in the prose pamphlets Milton refers to the rebellion against Charles I in terms of the Exodus from Egypt, and expresses a hope that England will be a new chosen people, chosen this time for the gospel instead of the law, the rescued apocalyptic church coming out of the wilderness with Michael into a new Promised Land. In this role the English nation would represent the returning lost tribes, a new Israel taking up the cross that the Jews had rejected. By the time he wrote *Paradise Regained,* the English had chosen, in the terrible phrase of *The Ready and Easy Way,* "a captain back for *Egypt*" [*Works,* 6:149]. Yet even Milton cannot allow Christ to dismiss the unfaithful tribes, who have lost their birthright rather than their home, without adding a few wistful cadences in another key, too gentle in tone to be a direct reply to Satan, and at most only overheard by him:

> Yet he at length, time to himself best known,
> Remembring *Abraham* by some wond'rous call
> May bring them back repentant and sincere,
> And at their passing cleave the *Assyrian* flood,
> While to their native land with joy they hast,
> As the Red Sea and *Jordan* once he cleft,
> When to the promis'd land thir Fathers pass'd;
> To his due time and providence I leave them. [*PR,* 3.433–40]

The temptation of Parthia, to ally the Messiah with an anti-Roman power in order to overthrow Rome, had thus been a temptation of Milton as well as of Milton's Christ. It is clear from what we have said in the previous chapter that if Milton had written an epic around the time he wrote *The Reason of Church Government,* it would have been more closely affiliated to the epic-romance convention established by Boiardo, Ariosto, and Spenser, in which Arthur would have represented a crusader or Christian warrior and some heroine an aspect of "the Kings daughter the Church" [*Works,* 3:275], like Spenser's Una. But the female figure over whom physical wars are fought is likely to be closer to the erotic conventions "inductive mainly to the sin of *Eve*" [*PL,* 11.519], to courtly love, uxoriousness, and lust. The rejected romance tradition appears in Milton's reference to "The fairest of her Sex *Angelica*" [*PR*, 3.341], where we might expect the more familiar Helen of Troy or Guinevere. The shadowy and insubstantial landscape of Boiardo may be Milton's reason for choosing it rather than a more concretely historical theme.

In *Paradise Regained* Satan displays all his kingdom: consequently Christ must refuse all of it, including much that in other contexts he might handle fearlessly. Later in his career he shows no hesitation in providing miraculous food, sitting at table with sinners, or accepting money and other gifts. But he has not yet entered on his ministry: the teaching and healing Christ that we know, with his compassion and courtesy, his love of children, and his sense of humour, has no place in Satan's kingdom. The haughtiness and aloofness of Christ mean that, before Christ can work in the world, he must recognize and repudiate all worldliness. In *Paradise Regained* Christ is looking at the world as it is under the wrath, as the domain of Satan. Wrath is the reaction of goodness contemplating badness; it is disinterested and impersonal, and is the opposite of anger or irritation. If God is capable of wrath, he must be incapable of irritation. This is the real reason for the difficulty we stumbled over earlier,[58] the Father's being such a monster of indifference to his creation in *Paradise Lost* that he merely smiles when he observes that a third of his angels have revolted. The word "unmoved," so often applied to Christ in *Paradise Regained*, refers to his emotions as well as his intellect: Satan is condemned but not railed at. Christ cannot exercise mercy until he has separated it from sentimentality, and his comments on the misery of man under wrath are part of this separation. This means that once more we are faced with a contrast between the dramatic and the conceptual aspects of the situation. Dramatically, Christ becomes an increasingly unsympathetic figure, a pusillanimous quietist in the temptation of Parthia, an inhuman snob in the temptation of Rome, a peevish obscurantist in the temptation of Athens.

We said that when Adam decides to die with Eve rather than live without her, we are expected to feel some sympathy for Adam, to the point at least of feeling that we might well have done the same thing in his place, as, of course, we would. Conversely, one may almost say that the point at which the reader loses sympathy with Jesus in *Paradise Regained* is the point at which he himself would have collapsed under the temptation. All of us are, like Christ, in the world, and, unlike him, partly of it. Whatever in us is of the world is bound to condemn Christ's rejection of the world at some point or other. This aspect of the temptation story is the theme of the other great literary treatment of it, the Grand Inquisitor episode in *The Brothers Karamazov*,[59] but it is present in Milton too.[60]

Paradise Regained thus illustrates to the full the contrast between the dramatic and conceptual aspects of a situation that we have seen to be characteristic of Milton's temptation scenes.[61] One might think that Milton had selected the temptation of Christ because it is, with the possible exception of the agony in the garden (on which Milton also meditated a "Christus patiens" [*Works*, 18:240]), the only episode in which suspense and the feeling of the possible awful consequences of failure are consistently present. Christ's immediate discerning of Satan under his initial disguise, and his ability to reply "Why art *thou* solicitous?" to every temptation, destroy all opportunity for narrative suspense. Of course Christ, like Adam, must be "sufficient to have stood, though free to fall" [*PL*, 3.99], and he can hardly be sufficient to have stood if, like Eve, he can be deceived by a disguise, or if, like Uriel, he is too simple to understand hypocrisy. In any case dramatic propriety is on the side of clear vision: the more objective one is, the more easily one may see the subjective motivations in others, and anyone with Christ's purity of motivation would know the thoughts of others, as in the Gospels he is said to do. Narrative suspense and dramatic sympathy go together: we can have them in *Samson Agonistes*, but they must be renounced here.

The reader may feel that the effect is to make both Christ and Satan seem bored with their roles, and that such boredom is infectious. Of course in long poems there are two areas of criticism, the structure or design and the poetic realization of details, and value judgments established in one area are not transferable to the other. It is quite possible for a poem to be, as *Paradise Regained* may be, a magnificent success in its structure and yet often tired and perfunctory in its execution. In structure, however, *Paradise Regained* is not only a success but a technical experiment that is practically *sui generis*. None of the ordinary literary categories apply to it; its poetic predecessors are nothing like it and it has left no descendants. If it is a "brief epic," it has little resemblance to the epyllion; its closest affinities are with the debate and with the dialectical colloquy of Plato and Boethius, to which most of the Book of Job also belongs. But these forms usually either incorporate one argument into another dialectically or build up two different cases rhetorically; Milton's feat of constructing a double argument on the same words, each highly plausible and yet as different as light from darkness, is, so far as I know, unique in English literature. It is the supreme poetic statement of the dialectician in Milton, the poet who defended the freedom of the press on the ground that "this permission of free writing, were there no good else in it . . . is such an unripping, such an Anatomie of the shiest, and tenderest particular truths, as makes not only the whole Nation in many points the wiser, but also presents, and carries home to Princes, and men most remote from vulgar concourse, such a full insight of every lurking evil."[62]

The rejecting of the temptation of Rome forces Satan to relinquish one of his trump cards, which is the appeal to opportunity, the panic inspired by the ticking clock. The aspect of temptation which suggests the temporal also has a connection with Milton's own life and the collision of impulses to complete and postpone his masterpiece already referred to. This problem, in itself peculiar to Milton as a poet, was for him also a special case of the general principle that the Christian must learn to will to relax the will, to perform real acts in God's time and not pseudo-acts in his own. In the temptations of Adam and Samson the same theme recurs of an action not so much wrong in itself as wrong at that time, a hasty snatching of a chance before the real time has fulfilled itself. Christ is older than Milton was at twenty-three when he wrote his famous sonnet, and Satan is constantly urging him, from the first temptation on, to be his own providence, to release some of his own latent energies. The discipline of waiting is not only more difficult and inglorious, but constantly subject to the danger of passing insensibly into procrastination.

The subtlest thing that Satan says in the poem is his remark that

each act is rightliest done,
Not when it must, but when it may be best. [*PR*, 4.475–6]

The demonic hero judges the present by an intuitive sense of the immediate future. He is distinguished from other men by his capacity to take thought for the morrow, to be in short a diviner. Thus Satan is a spokesman for that dark and forbidden future knowledge which we have spoken of as in the Classical epics gained from the gods below and not the gods above.[63] We are not surprised to find that Satan's oracular powers in *Paradise Regained* include a knowledge of Christ's future "fate" gained by astrology. Christ's main scriptural ally in rejecting this temptation is Ecclesiastes, with its doctrine that there is a time for all things, but the sense of strain in waiting for God's time comes out in several places in the poem, from the reference to the lost tribes, already quoted, to the strain of the forty days' fast itself.

The temptation of Athens has, as its Antichrist core, the Stoic ideal, the "apathy" of the invulnerable individual who feels that the wise man in a bad world can only do the best he can for himself. This is the simple giving up of social action for individual improvement, which, as we saw in the previous chapter, was not the real meaning of the impact of the Restoration on Milton. In rejecting this temptation, Christ also rejects the contemplative life as an end: Christ's aim is to redeem the world, not to live a morally sinless life, which he might conceivably have done as a philosopher. In the temptation of Athens the clash of the two oracular traditions, the prophetic and the demonic, reaches its climax. Here again it is Greek philosophy in its context as part of Satan's kingdom that is being rejected. A Christian working outward from his faith might find the study of Plato and Aristotle profitable enough; but if he were to *exchange* the direct tradition of revelation for their doctrines, which is what Christ is being tempted to do, he would find in them only the fine flower of a great speculative tree, with its roots in the demonic metaphysics and theology described in the second book of *Paradise Lost*.

The third temptation begins with a night of storm, not in itself a temptation but an indispensable preliminary to one. Its object is to impress Christ with Satan's power as prince of an indifferent and mindless order of nature, to suggest that his Father has either forsaken him or is unable to reach him in a fallen world. It is, in short, another suggestion of despair or distrust, but with the specific aim of making Christ feel lonely and deserted, hence isolated, hence the self-contained ego which is the form of pride. It demonstrates the fact that in a world of death and mutability the light of nature is surrounded by the darkness of nature; but as Christ has already rejected all arguments based on the analogy of natural and revealed wisdom, this fact comes as no great surprise. The placing of Christ on the pinnacle of the temple follows and is, as Satan makes clear, a temptation of Jesus purely in his capacity as Son of God, an ordeal that no simple human nature would be able to survive. Here, for once, we can cautiously accept what Satan says, although of course his motive in saying it is to drop a suggestion of arrogance into Christ's mind.

The temptation of the pinnacle is equally a bodily and a mental assault. Christ has been weakened by forty days of fasting and by the night of storm. We saw that Satan won over Eve by instilling thoughts into her mind while her consciousness was preoccupied with the wonder of a talking snake, so that Eve, when she came to search her own mind, found Satan's thoughts there and took them for her own. Christ is far more astute, but still the sequence of blinding visions of earthly glory may have left in his mind some faint trace of attachment, some unconscious sense of exaltation. If so, he will feel dizzy on the pinnacle. Mentally, then, Christ is being tested for *hubris,* or pride of mind. He is in the position of a tragic hero, on top of the wheel of fortune, subject to the fatal instant of distraction that will bring him down.

Physically, Christ is being tested for exhaustion, for a slight yielding to pressure that will make him stagger out of sheer weariness. Satan quotes the Psalms to show that the Messiah could fall, trusting in the support of angels; but Christ, though led by the Spirit into the wilderness, is not being led by the Spirit to fall off the pinnacle. That would be his own act, and the Antichrist core of it would be a trust not in angels but in his own fortune, or luck, and trusting to luck is the same thing as trusting Satan. It would perhaps be a reasonable definition of cowardice to say that a coward is a man whose instinct it is, in a crisis, to do what his enemy wants him to do. Christ's ordeal is one of fortitude as well as wisdom, and he has proved himself no coward; but even brave men have had traitors lurking within them, something that cooperated with an outward attack. If there is the smallest trace either of pride in Christ's mind or what we should now call the death impulse in his body—the impulse that would make any other man accept the vinegar sponge on the cross—this final test will reveal it. If not, Christ is ready to be God's sacrificial victim, a martyr who, so far from being, like many martyrs, half in love with easeful death, dies as the implacable enemy of death.

Christ has thus far been tempted *quasi homo,* purely as man. For Milton, Christ, having resisted the whole of Satan's world, has done what man can do: he has come to the end of the negative and iconoclastic effort which is all that man as such can accomplish in aid of his own salvation. The only possible next step is for God to indicate acceptance of what has been done.[64] Thus the fact that Christ successfully stands on the pinnacle is miraculous, but not a miracle drawn from his own divine nature, not an ace hidden up his sleeve, which is what Satan is looking for. It means that his human will has been taken over by the omnipotent divine will at the necessary point, and prefigures the commending of his spirit to the Father at the instant of his death on the cross.

Christ's answer, "Tempt not the Lord thy God" [*PR,* 4.561] is the only remark Christ makes in the poem which employs ambiguity.[65] Primarily, it means "Do not put the Father to unnecessary tests," the meaning of the passage in Deuteronomy which Jesus is quoting [6:16]. But here the Son carries the name and nature of the Father, and the statement bears the secondary meaning "Do not continue the temptation of the Son of God." At this point, perhaps, Satan for the first time recognizes in Jesus his old antagonist of the war in heaven. Earlier in the poem he had spoken of Christ as an opaque cloud which might be a cooling or shading screen between himself and the wrath of the Father. This is, not surprisingly, the direct opposite of Christ's true nature

> In whose conspicuous count'nance, without cloud
> Made visible, th' Almighty Father shines [*PL*, 3.385–6]

So far from screening the fire of the Father, the Son is focusing it like a burning glass, the two natures of the Godhead united as closely as Milton's Christology will permit. And just as this last temptation was of Christ in his specific role as Son of God, so with his victory Satan is defeated in his own headquarters, the lower heaven or element of air which is the spatial limit of his conquest at the fall. That is why Christ's victory is immediately followed by a reference to the struggle of Hercules and Antaeus, in which Hercules (a prototype of Christ also in the *Nativity Ode* and elsewhere) overcame the monstrous son of earth in the air.

There is a hidden irony in Satan's quotation from the ninety-first Psalm. He quotes the eleventh and twelfth verses; the thirteenth reads: "Thou shalt tread upon the lion and adder: the young lion and the dragon shalt thou trample under feet." In his fall Satan assumes the position of the dragon under Christ's feet, the only place for him after his failure to gain entrance to Christ's body or mind. At this point a new centre of gravity is established in the world, as the gospel is finally separated from the law. Judaism joins Classical wisdom as part of the demonic illusion, as the centre of religion passes from the temple Christ is standing on into the Christian temple, the body of Christ above it. The destruction of the Garden of Eden at the flood showed that God "attributes to place / No sanctitie" [*PL*, 11.836–7], and the later destruction of the temple, prefigured at this point, illustrates the same principle. Christ's casting the devils out of heaven prefigured the cleansing of the temple, with which, according to John, his ministry began. Here, with the end of the temptation, Christ has chased the devils out of the temple of his own body and mind and is ready to repeat the process for each human soul.

The temptation of the pinnacle corresponds to the point in *Samson Agonistes* at which Samson, after beating off Manoah, Delilah, and Harapha, refuses to go to the Philistine festival. He is right in refusing, but he has come to the end of his own will. At that point he appears to change his mind, but what has happened is that God has accepted his efforts and taken over his will.[66] In *Samson Agonistes*, which is a tragedy, this point is the "peripety": Samson is now certain to die, though also certain of redemption. Jesus has also made it impossible for himself to avoid death, as his prototypes Elijah and perhaps Moses did; but *Paradise Regained* is not a tragedy, but an episode in the divine comedy, and we need another term for the crucial point of the action.

We have already met Milton's distinction between the literal and what he calls the metaphorical generation of the Son by the Father. The latter, we said, was epiphany, the manifesting of Christ in his divine capacity to others, and it is this epiphany and not literal generation that is taking place in the first chronological event of *Paradise Lost*. The same distinction recurs in the Incarnation. Two of the Gospels, Matthew and Luke, the two which give us the account of the temptation, are nativity Gospels: they begin with Christ's infancy or physical generation in the world. The other two, Mark and John, are epiphanic Gospels, and begin with the Baptism, where Jesus is pointed out to man as the Son of God. (In the Western churches epiphany means particularly the showing of the infant Christ to the Magi, but in the Eastern churches it means particularly the Baptism.) Epiphany is the theological equivalent of what in literature is called *anagnorisis* or "recognition." The Father recognizes Jesus as the Son at the Baptism: Satan recognizes him on the pinnacle in a different, yet closely related, sense. The action of *Paradise Regained* begins with the Baptism, an epiphany which Satan sees but does not understand, and ends with an epiphany to Satan alone, the nature of which he can hardly fail to understand.

With the end of the temptation, Christ's work is essentially accomplished. The Passion itself, and more particularly the Crucifixion, is also epiphanic, an exhibition to mankind of what Christ is and what he has done. The two poles of Christ's career on earth are the Baptism and the Crucifixion, both public events. And just as the Crucifixion was followed by the Resurrection, which was esoteric, shown only to Christ's followers, so the Baptism is followed by a hidden event in which Christ disappears from the sight of mankind and then "Home to his Mothers house private return'd" [*PR*, 4.639], the fate of the world having been changed in the meantime. *Paradise Regained* is the definitive statement in Milton of the dialectical separation of heaven from hell that reason based on revelation makes, and the individual nature of every act of freedom. To use terms which are not Milton's but express something of his attitude, the central myth of mankind is the myth of lost identity: the goal of all reason, courage, and vision is the regaining of identity. The recovery of identity is not the feeling that I am myself and not another, but the realization that there is only one man, one mind, and one world, and that all walls of partition have been broken down forever.[67]

4

The Revelation to Eve

1969

From StS, *135–59. Originally published in* Paradise Lost: A Tercentenary Tribute, *ed. Balachandra Rajan (Toronto: University of Toronto Press, 1969), 18–47. There are typescripts in NFF, 1988, box 2, files cc–ff.*

Dreams are of great importance in the Classical epics, where they may be true or deceitful, and may descend through the gate of ivory or of horn. An epic designed to justify the ways of God to men would have to be especially careful in its treatment of dreams: in Homer Zeus himself may send a deceiving dream as well as a true one, but in *Paradise Lost* the two gates must be as wide apart as the gates of heaven and hell themselves.

The creation of Adam is associated with two dreams: first a dream of the trees of Paradise, then a dream of Eve. In both cases Adam awakes to find the dream true. Keats was later to see in these dreams a symbol of the imagination of the poet,[1] which tries to realize a world that others can understand and live in, and is therefore a fully creative and not merely a subjective or fantastic power. Milton's meaning is different but not wholly dissimilar. Adam's dreams are prompted by appetite in its two main forms of food and sexual love. In the unfallen state appetite is good, being a part of God's creation, and what Adam calls "mimic Fansie" [*PL*, 5.110] is aligned with reason. What Adam wants, in short, is what Adam has: desire in the unfallen state is completely satisfied by the appropriate object. Eve's dreams, like Adam's, are very close to her waking experience, and help to bind together her sense of time in a world too happy to have much history: "Works of day pass't, or morrows next designe" (*PL*, 5.33). The Satan-inspired dream of Eve, on the other hand, uses the kind of symbolism that we now think of as typical of a dream. Because she is unfallen, such a dream can only come from outside her, though, like Bunyan's Christian in the Valley of the Shadow, she is troubled to think that it may have proceeded from her own mind. She is right by anticipation: since the fall, inner desires which are excessive by nature and can never be satisfied have taken root in us, and produce the wish-fulfilment fantasies of lust and greed, which are the two appetites in their fallen form. They are the reflection in us of what Satan describes as

> fierce desire,
> Among our other torments not the least,
> Still unfulfill'd (*PL*, 4.509–11)

After the fall, Adam, fully awake and conscious, receives from Michael his second revelation, the tremendous Biblical vision of the future, stretching from Cain to the Last Judgment, with which the great poem reaches its close. From the previous revelation of Raphael Eve had absented herself, in order to hear it later from Adam alone. But now Adam is less trustworthy as a medium of revelation: while he wakes to hear the revelation, Eve is put to sleep, as Adam was when she was created, the little symmetry in the design being called to our attention (*PL*, 11.369). Eve is given dreams which are inspired this time by God instead of by Satan, and which constitute a revelation that is distinctively hers. We are told very little about these dreams, except that their central subject is the defeat of the serpent by a redeemer descended from her.

The famous, or notorious, line in *Paradise Lost* (4.299) about the relations of Adam and Eve, "Hee for God only, shee for God in him," illustrates a central problem in reading the poem. This is the problem of the language of analogy. The statement is made of the unfallen Adam and Eve, and so is not literally true of men and women as we know them. Fallen life shows an analogy to unfallen life, and the analogy accounts for the social supremacy of men over women that we find assumed in the Bible, from the account of the fall itself in Genesis (3:16; *PL*, 10.195–6) to St. Paul's directives for the primitive church. But obviously no fallen son of Adam can represent God in the way that the unfallen Adam could. The example of the unfallen Adam merely puts a heavier responsibility on his male descendants to be worthy of what ought to be a purely spiritual authority. Similarly, monogamous marriage arises in the world as a fallen analogy of the divinely sanctioned union of Adam and Eve, and a prejudice in favour of the permanence of all marriages is therefore justifiable. But, for Milton, to prohibit divorce altogether is to ignore the fact that the relation of ordinary to paradisal marriage is analogous only, and that the realities of unfallen life are ideals, not always attainable ones, in this world.

The analogy also extends in the other direction. The relation of man to woman symbolizes, or dramatizes, the relation of creator to creature. God speaks of himself as male, and his revelation uses the terms Father and Son, although in most contexts, apart from the Incarnation, we can hardly ascribe literal sex to the Deity. We think of God as male primarily because he is the Creator: we think of Nature as female, not merely as a mother from whose body we are born, but as a creature of God. Human souls, including male souls, are symbolically female when thought of as creatures: the redeemed souls of men and women, who are aware of their status as creatures, make up a female church or Bride of Christ. Among spirits, whether fallen or unfallen, sex is not functional: spirits can be of what sex they please (*PL*, 1.423–44). But in human life the sexes represent the polarizing of man's existence between God and Nature, creation and creature. Man is set above woman to remind him of the rightful places that God and Nature respectively should hold in his life. Adam's substance, so to speak, is in the God who created him: in himself, apart from God, he is only the shadow of himself. Similarly Eve's substance is in Adam, as her formation from his rib indicates.

Being cut off or "alienated" (*PL*, 9.9) from God puts one into the state of pride. This state is subjective, and needs an object, which is normally an idol, idolatry being the worshipping of something created instead of the creator. For Adam, once turned away from God, the most immediate idol is the fallen Eve, the fairest of creatures, and for his descendants idolatry becomes a debased form of woman-worship, or taking woman, along with the Mother Nature to which in this context she belongs, to be numinous instead of a creation ranking below man on the chain of being. For Eve, on the other hand, the root of idolatry is self-worship. There is nothing wrong with her admiring her own image in the water, but the episode suggests, again by anticipation, the story of Narcissus, who fell in love with his image—that is, exchanged his real or divine self for his own subjective shadow. The direction of the fallen Narcissus is also Satan's, as his "daughter" Sin indicates when she says to him:

> Thy self in me thy perfect image viewing
> Becam'st enamour'd. (*PL*, 2.764–5)

But the fact that man is capable of idolatry is connected with the peculiar role of sex in human life. The devils are not, strictly speaking, idolaters: they are atheists or fatalists. They assert that they were not created by God, and originated directly from nature, but they have no occasion to associate nature with anything feminine.

In Classical mythology there is a pervasive sexual symbolism which points to a blurred memory on the part of fallen man of the relation of God to his creation. The chief of gods in this mythology is a male sky-god, Jupiter, who, where the context is appropriate, may be spoken of by a Christian poet in terms recalling the Christian God without violation of decorum. But the fact that Jupiter has a consort who is also his sister—*et soror et coniunx*, as Virgil says[2]—shows that the original Jupiter is, like Juno, a deified spirit of nature, not a creator qualitatively distinct from his creation. Classical myth, vaguely aware that a spirit of nature, when deified, is a devil, also said that his rule was a usurpation, and that before him there was a Golden Age of Saturn and Rhea, when, as Milton ingeniously suggests in *Il Penseroso* (ll. 23–6), incestuous unions might have been innocent. The myth of the Golden Age takes us one step nearer to the authentic revelation of the original state of man. One very brief passage in the *Argonautica* picked up by Milton (*PL*, 10.580–4) hints that Saturn and Rhea in their turn succeeded a still more primitive pair, Ophion and Eurynome. The word Ophion, serpent, indicates that we here are very close to a genuine memory of the real beginnings of idolatry. Eurynome means wide-ruling: Milton's gloss, "the wide- / encroaching Eve perhaps," is somewhat puzzling, but it seems to say that the memory of the fallen Eve is the source, for the heathen, of the myth of a great mother-goddess from whom all deified principles in nature have ultimately descended, even though their fathers are the fallen angels.

Classical mythology does not clearly separate creator and creature, but it does contain a sexual symbolism which, as we should expect, puts the male above and the female below. Milton himself uses this symbolism in both Classical and Christian contexts. The male principle in nature is associated with the sky, the sun, the wind, or the rain. The specifically female part of nature is the earth, and the imagery of caves, labyrinths, and waters issuing from underground recall the process of birth from a womb. Trees and shady spots generally, and more particularly flowers, are also feminine, and so is the moon, the lowest heavenly body. The imagery of the labyrinth or maze is associated sometimes with meandering rivers, sometimes with a tangle of shrubs or trees. A forest so dense that the (male) sky is shut out, as in the "branching Elm Star-proof" of *Arcades*, may be a symbol of natural virginity, the abode of Diana. The sexual union of sun and earth is celebrated with great exuberance and power in Milton's *Fifth Elegy*, on the coming of spring. In *Paradise Lost* Adam smiles on Eve

> as *Jupiter*
> On *Juno* smiles, when he impregns the Clouds
> That shed *May* Flowers (*PL*, 4.499–501),

an allusion which places Jupiter and Juno definitely in the category of deified nature-spirits. Similarly Adam's voice calls to Eve "Milde, as when *Zephyrus* on *Flora* breathes" (*PL*, 5.16).

In Biblical symbolism, too, the earth or fertile land is often in a feminine relation to its ruler or owner, representing what Milton calls "the holy Cov'nant of Union, and Marriage betweene the King and his Realme,"[3] meaning in this context Charles I, though he was later to ridicule the same king for thinking of his parliament as "but a Female."[4] The land of Israel is called "married" (Beulah) by Isaiah [62:4], and the "black but comely" bride of the Song of Songs [1:5] is also associated with the fertile land ruled by King Solomon. When Adam awakens Eve in book 5 he addresses her in language prefiguring (or, for the reader, recalling) the aubade of the bride in the Song of Songs. It is also the Song of Songs that introduces the image of the female body as an enclosed garden (*hortus conclusus*) which had an extensive religious and poetic later life. We are not surprised to find the garden of Eden in *Paradise Lost* described in feminine imagery, with its river rising from underground and running "With mazie error under pendant shades" (*PL*, 4.239), and where a vine "gently creeps," in an image later associated with Eve's hair. The newly created Eve awakens "Under a shade {i.e., tree} of flours," and the first thing she sees is her own reflection in a lake "Of waters issu'd from a Cave" (*PL*, 4.450–4). The contrast with Adam awakening in the sunlight and inspecting first of all his own body is clearly deliberate.

The fallen forms of the two human appetites are lust and greed: in a more demonic context they become force and fraud, the two weapons of Satan. Satan finds that he is unable to destroy the world by force. God displays the scales, the symbol of created order, in a significant place in the sky, between the Virgin of divine justice and the scorpion, and Satan, then as later in *Paradise Regained* able to read the future in the "Starry Rubric" (*PR*, 4.393), does not try to fight. The scales prefigure the later rainbow, which guarantees the permanence of the natural order after the deluge. Satan's only effective weapon, then, is fraud, and fraud creates an evil analogy to the good. The greatest good for Eve is knowledge of God through Adam: Satan presents her with a dream of attaining knowledge, and eventually godhead, for herself, under the image of suddenly rising from the earth into the air, where she is just as suddenly abandoned. The sexual sensations of flying and falling, and the orgasm rhythm of the whole dream, show that Satan's symbolism is as eloquent as his rhetoric. This demonic surge upward to the sky suggests two other images: the Gunpowder Plot and the struggles of rebellious Titans bound under exploding volcanoes, both of which enter the imagery of *Paradise Lost*. We have also the Limbo of Vanities, the upward sweep of those who try to take heaven by force or fraud. After the flood, when man settles down systematically to idolatry, a more solid image of demonic pride, the Tower of Babel, is set up.

Eve rises into the air, where she sees "The Earth outstretcht immense, a prospect wide" (*PL*, 5.88). The air is, later, Satan's headquarters, as Satan appears to realize already ("in the Air, as wee," he says [*PL*, 5.79]). From there, it is further suggested, she may rise to heaven if she likes, and see what the gods are doing. She seems to be symbolically at the point, usually represented by a mountain-top under the moon, which is the boundary between terrestrial and celestial worlds in Dante's *Purgatorio*, Spenser's *Mutabilitie Cantos*, several poems of Yeats, and elsewhere, and would also have been the top of the Tower of Babel if that point had ever been reached. The imagery of Eve's dream of ascent is echoed in the later elevation of Adam, who is taken to a hill

> Of Paradise the highest, from whose top
> The Hemisphere of Earth in cleerest Ken
> Stretcht out to amplest reach of prospect lay (*PL*, 11.378–80)

where Michael's vision is displayed to him. Eve at this time is placed on a much lower level to receive her dreams—another example of the curious antithetical symmetry which pervades the poem. The elevation of Adam in its turn is explicitly compared to Satan's placing of Christ on a mountain-top during the temptation (though in *Paradise Regained* the climactic temptation was shifted to the pinnacle of the temple, following Luke's order). We can understand the link between Satan's temptation of Eve and his temptation of Christ, but why should God's purely benevolent design of imparting prophetic knowledge to Adam be included in the same complex of imagery?

The reason is that Satan is not the only one who can construct analogies. God constantly frustrates Satan by turning to good what Satan intended to be evil. Adam's new knowledge of good and evil, "that is to say of knowing good by evill,"[5] is placed in its proper context of the revelation of God to man which is later recorded in the Bible. Even outside Christianity the same principle operates. The word "fall" is a spatial metaphor: we are now "down," and any effort to better ourselves must take us "up." Leaving Christianity out of account for the moment, there are both good and bad men in the world; both wish to go "up," and both have to start from the same point. The bad man recognizes no God except what he considers to be his own good, and his life is a structure of pride like the Tower of Babel. The good man—let us say a virtuous heathen—recognizes the existence of a good that is not himself, and attempts to seek for it. One conspicuous result of such imaginative virtue is the structure of Classical poetry and philosophy, a natural and reasonable human analogy of revelation—not itself revelation, of course, or possessing any final authority, but an impressive monument, nonetheless, of the wisdom which still remains implanted by God in the human mind. This structure is a kind of virtuous Tower of Babel: there is a considerable confusion of tongues in it, but it represents man dreaming of his Creator, and following the impulse to return to his Creator which is an original part of his nature. We may call it the anabasis of Eros. Love awakes in the soul, is attracted first by objects of sense, and then by more abstract and conceptual elements until it begins to draw nearer to God. Once Christianity appears in the world, this analogical structure of love is not abolished but becomes a supplement to its revelation. As such it forms the basis for the imagery of a good deal of Milton's own poetry, including the bulk of his earlier poetry. A pedagogical version of it is the model for Milton's ideal curriculum of education.

The lower part of this analogical structure is composed of Classical mythology. Classical myths, the fables of the heathen, are almost literally dreams, blurred and distorted versions, created partly by memory and partly by fancy, of what the Bible presents, in Milton's view, so much more simply and plainly. They are dreams of man as a child of Eve rather than of Adam, and are dominated by female images and personalities.

Mother Nature and, more particularly, Mother Earth, appear as the great *diva triformis*, the goddess of the moon, the forest, and the lower world, all symbolically female regions, or as Venus, the goddess of sexual love who personates the "God" (*PL*, 10.145) that Eve became to Adam at the moment of his fall. Venus has two male figures subordinated to her, Eros and Adonis, the gods of love and death, the poles of Mother Nature's cycle. The Spenserian image of the Gardens of Adonis, with Venus presiding over her wounded lover, appears at the end of *Comus*, a kind of erotic Pietà, as Venus with the infant God of Love is a kind of erotic Nativity. The dying-god flowers, the anemone and the hyacinth particularly, appear in the Latin elegies, and again in *Naturam non pati senium*, as ornaments of the Earth. Tammuz (Adonis) himself, in both the *Nativity Ode* and *Paradise Lost*, is introduced as the object of a female cult. The image of a mother hiding or shrouding a male child, as the Earth hides the seeds of new life, is associated with the Garden of Eden, with the references to Amalthea hiding her "Florid Son" Dionysus, and to the Abyssinian princes in their prison-Paradise (*PL*, 4.275–80). The feminine images of labyrinth, cave, flowers, shade, thicket, and moonlit night partake of the darkness, mystery, lost direction, and concealment characteristic of religions of nature without the daylight of revelation.

It is within this shrouding and enclosing female Nature that the imagination of the poet awakens. In *Ad patrem* Milton speaks of his poetry as dreams in a secluded cave. The poet at this stage is psychologically close to the lover, and what he loves, at first, is simply the sensuous beauty and delight of nature in general, like the narrator of the first and seventh *Elegies* admiring all the pretty girls he sees on the streets. The minor poet may remain at this stage of uncommitted, or temporarily committed, attraction, sporting with Amaryllis in the shade or with the tangles of Neaera's hair—again we notice the thematic feminine words "shade" and "tangles." If the poet-lover becomes more serious he may go in either a right or a wrong direction. The wrong direction is that of the courtly love convention of unquestioning obedience to a mistress and the acceptance of the frustration that her whims and coyness may cause. Milton shows a consistent dislike of this convention and a reluctance to write within it: for him it is the purest expression of "Mans effeminate slackness" (*PL*, 11.634) which allows a woman, and hence the created nature which she represents, to have rule over him. The right direction, of course, is marriage, the wedded love which in *Paradise Lost* is contrasted with the frustration of "the starv'd Lover" and the jealousy which is "the injur'd Lovers Hell" (*PL*, 4.769; 5.450). This is a rational state in which the man is normally the superior, and its prototype in Classical mythology is the union of love and the soul represented by the Cupid and Psyche story in Apuleius.

It is conventional in courtly love poetry for the poet to abandon sensuous love at a certain point and turn to ideal, philosophical, or religious forms of love. Milton is unusual, however, in the promptness with which he makes the break. For him, as man continues to ascend the scale of his own nature, the Adam within him awakes, and progressively dominates the element of Eve. Man's attitude to the world around him then becomes less sensuous and more rational. He begins to think of nature less as a mother or mistress and more as an intelligently designed and created order. Nature is coming to represent less herself and more the wisdom of God which the virtuous man is seeking. On the upper levels of natural religion, one tends to become a Platonist, thinking in terms of a lower world of the body and a higher world of the soul, which may become released from the lower world as from a prison. In Milton's earlier poems we meet flights in the air which may be purely demonic like Eve's dream, as notably in *In quintum Novembris*; or the symbolism may be that of the soul escaping from the body and seeking its natural element in a higher world, as in the elegy on the Bishop of Ely.

The lower part of the analogy of Eros is the world of sense, where nature, the objective world, appears mainly in feminine images to the perceiver. There are thus two levels of nature, though there are also different ways of conceiving these two levels. One way is that of the simple physical contrast of winter and summer. Nature in this context exists as a cyclical movement between life and death. The earth rises to pour out her treasures of life in the spring as the sun awakens her, and sinks back to sleep in the winter. The image of Proserpine, spending half the year below the ground with her secret lover, and rising above the ground for the other half, appears in *Paradise Lost* as a poignant anticipation of Eve, driven from her natural habitat of Eden to the cursed wilderness below. Arethusa, the nymph of the underground river who rises with her lover Alpheus in Proserpine's land of Sicily, is a similar image, appearing in both *Arcades* and *Lycidas*. In the *Nativity Ode* Nature has stopped her sexual activities partly out of respect for her Creator and partly because it is too cold, or rather because the sun is, and reposes in a sterility which assumes innocence.

These two levels of nature modulate into a more conceptual relation in

Paradise Lost as a lower level of chaos or the abyss, "The Womb of nature and perhaps her Grave" (*PL*, 2.911), and an upper level of cosmos or creation proper, which comes into being after the abyss has been made pregnant by a male Spirit of God, who in natural imagery would be associated with birds or the wind. The difference in this perception of the two levels of nature is connected with the difference between two views of death. Sensibly and objectively, death is annihilation, a return to the underworld of chaos; rationally, it is the separation from the sensible body that enables one's immortal soul to live in the world appropriate to it.

As we rise to a still more penetrating vision of nature, its two levels take on the Platonic aspect just mentioned. Here we have a lower physical and sensible aspect and a higher intellectual one: nature as attractive object and nature as designed object or creature. The imagery of these two levels might be called the "allegro" and the "penseroso" imagery. The former is that of the earthly paradise, as expressed in the fables of the Elysian fields and the gardens of the Hesperides; the latter is that of the music of the spheres, the sense of harmonious design that conveys to us the intuition that nature is not just there, as a mother is just there to a small child, but has been intelligently and purposefully put there by a power superior to her.

The poet in nature is thus placed in a far more comprehensive situation than singing the praises of pretty girls would ever reveal to him. Even in his most sensuous poetry, the poet feels links drawing him, not merely to nature, but to the hidden powers of nature, to whatever it is that can "keep unsteddy Nature to her law," in the words of *Arcades*. In the poem to Salzilli,[6] Milton speaks of the poet's song as having the power to prevent floods: this is the image of the poet as a benevolent magician controlling nature by the "sweet compulsion" of his song, of which the archetype is Orpheus. This image frequently appears in Shakespeare, especially in *A Midsummer Night's Dream* and *The Tempest*, which one suspects were the favourite plays of L'Allegro. In these two comedies the spirits of the elements represent powers of nature which are linked to human activity. Milton does not, like the later Romantics, make much of the metaphor of the poet as "creator," participating in the creative activity of God by producing poems, but he could certainly have understood what Coleridge meant by calling the poet a tamer of chaos.[7] The poet identifies himself with the created order, with the law of unsteady nature against the annihilation into which by herself nature would plunge. The Salzilli image, with its affinities to magic and the figure of Orpheus, is thus connected with the imagery of the permanence of the created order which was reaffirmed after the flood, and confirmed by the emblem of the rainbow.

The poet, if he is following rightly his innate impulse to rise from nature to God, will not look in nature for anything numinous: the so-called gods of nature are devils. The elemental spirit, like Shakespeare's Puck or Ariel, is a more accurate image because such a spirit is, even when mischievous or unwilling, amenable to rational control. The Christian poet finds his identity with nature, not by looking for gods in it, but through a feeling of protection and security in nature which is ultimately a sense of the providence of God as revealed through nature. The symbol of this hidden beneficent design is the Genius, whether of the wood, as in *Arcades*, or of the shore, as in *Lycidas*. The Attendant Spirit and Sabrina in *Comus* are elemental spirits who take on this role of good Genius or guiding daemon in the lower world. The image of the Genius is Virgilian, but Milton indicates a larger background for it in the *Apology for Smectymnuus* when he speaks of "having read of heathen Philosophers, some to have taught, that whosoever would but use his eare to listen, might heare the voice of his guiding *Genius* ever before him, calling and as it were pointing to that way which is his part to follow" [*Works*, 3:318]. The Lady's "Echo" song in *Comus* helps to bring out this identity of human and physical nature as common creatures of God.

The poet's art is a musical one, in the Platonic sense: verse is closely allied to voice, and poems are generally described in musical metaphors as sung or played on a reed. The music that we know is a subordinate art to the verbal music of poetry, as Milton indicates in a parenthesis in *Paradise Lost*: "For Eloquence the Soul, Song charms the Sense" (*PL*, 2.556). The curious context of this remark—he is speaking of the arts of the devils in hell—reminds us that the analogy of Eros is, outside Christianity, pervaded by demonic inspiration, and rooted in it. The greater human art is, however, the more obviously it becomes the praise of God, and as praise of God it forms a part of the response to the Creator by the creature which is what is meant, symbolically, by "harmony." Harmony includes both the music of the spheres in nature and "That undisturbed Song of pure concent" in heaven referred to in *At a Solemn Music*.

As the poet gains in the understanding of the meaning of his own art, he realizes that his art is on the side, not merely of order as against chaos, but of life as against death. The supreme effort of Orpheus as poet was not to charm the trees, but to raise Eurydice from the lower world, his failure representing the inadequacy of unaided human art (cf. *PL*, 3.17 ff.). Prospero in Shakespeare claims that his magic was able to raise the dead, and the poet's music is at least "consent" with a life-giving power: "Dead things with inbreath'd sense able to pierce."[8] The metaphors here extend into medicine: in the Shakespearean romance of *Pericles* a doctor raises the dead (or what amounts to that) by music, and Asclepius as well as Orpheus haunts Milton's Latin elegies (especially, of course, the one on the death of the Vice-Chancellor, who was a doctor). In the *Apology for Smectymnuus*, again, Milton speaks of what Comus carries in his glass as "a thick intoxicating potion which a certaine Sorceresse the abuser of loves name carries about" [*Works*, 3:305]. The antidote for this, a healing drug or herb which leads one to knowledge and virtue, is mentioned in the *Second Elegy* and enters *Comus* as the mysterious "haemony," which is compared to the Homeric moly. The Biblical archetypes of the narcotic potion and haemony are, of course, the fruits of the trees of knowledge and life respectively.

If we may associate the Attendant Spirit with the musician Henry Lawes, it may be reasonable to associate his shepherd friend with the poet Milton, and see in this haemony something closely connected with the poet's art. Haemony is a dark inconspicuous plant which bears a flower in "another Countrey" (*Comus*, ll. 630–2), and in *Lycidas* the image of a plant that does not grow here but bears its flower in another world is associated specifically with the poet's desire for fame. It is explained in *Lycidas* that fame, the love of which is an impetus powerful enough to make a poet "scorn delights, and live laborious dayes," has nothing to do with Virgil's *fama* or rumour, but is a secular counterpart of what in Christian revelation is the hope of immortality. In *Paradise Lost* this image of the exotic flower appears as the amaranth (*PL*, 3.353), which represents the genuine form of immortality, and originally bloomed beside the Tree of Life.

In writing within the analogy of Eros, the poet is elaborating and articulating a dream of man which is neither the dream that Satan gave Eve, nor the dream that God gave her later, but something in between: a dream about God based on the fallen knowledge of good and evil, in which, though the knowledge of evil may be primary, there is a great deal of good, and in the good a great deal of genuine pleasure. The pleasure is at its most eloquent, of course, in *L'Allegro* and *Il Penseroso*. The tone of *L'Allegro* is pastoral, the pastoral being the expression of the heightened pleasure that comes from simplifying one's wants and moderating one's desires, so that lust and greed subside into something more like their proper forms, "unreproved pleasures free." As night falls we encounter an expected series of images: elemental spirits recalling Puck and Queen Mab; Hymen, the spirit of wedded love; an erotic (Lydian) music expressly described as a maze or labyrinth, and finally an Elysian world. This is a world of

> Such sights as youthful Poets dream
> On Summer eeves by haunted stream. (ll. 129–30)

The word "haunted," in a context like this, has usually in it a sense of the gentler presences that impel us to associate Nature with feminine pronouns.

The imagery of *Il Penseroso* is even more explicitly feminine, from the "secret shades" where the goddess of Melancholy is born, to the moon wandering in the maze of the sky. Here also the poet is a Platonist, speculating about the world inhabited by the soul when freed from the body, and about the spirits

> Whose power hath a true consent
> With Planet, or with Element. (ll. 95–6)

"Consent" is again the musical metaphor, linked to the music sent by the "Genius of the Wood" to the poet hiding from "Day's garish eie" and sleeping in the lap of nature. The analogy of Eros stretches (at least in the poetic convention assumed) far back beyond Plato to the ancient teaching of the "thrice great *Hermes*," and continues through the magical imagery of medieval and Renaissance romance—the modern reader can see it continuing in Shelley and Yeats. Religious images also form a part of the "penseroso" dream: we notice, first, that they are images of "high church" practice—cloisters, stained glass, organ music, Gothic architecture—and, secondly, that they are appreciated on purely aesthetic grounds. The Nonconformist poet sees these tendencies in Christianity as a part of the analogy of Eros, to be enjoyed and appreciated in some contexts and condemned in others. Melancholy herself is a nun, not a Christian nun, of course, but a vestal virgin, being a daughter of Vesta.

Both she and Mirth take their poet to the upper limits of their dreaming analogy world. Mirth leads him to the earthly paradise, an Elysium where Orpheus lies dreaming, and where he might be awakened, by the music the poet hears, to complete the redemption of Eurydice. The poem of melancholy, mentioning Orpheus in passing, leads to a hermitage where the poet learns the secrets of the inner harmony of nature, and comes "To something like Prophetic strain" (l. 174)—that is, to an aesthetic analogy of religious experience. In these poems we are in substantially the same cosmos that the poet outlines in the *Vacation Exercise* poem, where, in language oddly anticipating Eve's first dream, he can "look in" to the world of the gods, and comes to rest in the palace of Alcinous, whose gardens are another type of the earthly Paradise, and where music or poetry once again is an erotic maze of "willing chains and sweet captivitie" (ll. 35–52).

Of course, one does not move upward effortlessly in this ascent of Eros. Every man, within Christianity or outside it, is faced in the world with a moral challenge. He cannot simply live on the unmoral level of plants and animals: he must either go downwards to sin or upwards to virtue. Mother Nature must ultimately become either the evil enchantress Circe or Hecate, or turn into some kind of *ewigweibliche*[9] inspiration like the Muse Urania or the Queen in *Arcades*. The first line of defence against Circe is reason, for the alliance of nature and reason is the key to the fact that Nature is a designed order, a fellow creature of God. As Milton says, "they expresse nature best, who in their lives least wander from her safe leading, which may be call'd regenerate reason."[10] But reason in this world is a limited monarchy, and the great leap from the sensible to the intellectual world can result only from a moral revolution in the soul. Just as Eden was the home of man only as long as man remained unfallen, so nature in its purity, as the order God created and saw to be good, is perceptible only to the pure, the perception being symbolized by hearing the music of the spheres. Hence a need for purity in the major poet, a principle with an obvious personal application to Milton himself, which anyone but Milton might have found embarrassing. Even in that very light-hearted poem the *First Elegy*, there is a reference to the moly which may preserve the young poet from the enchantments of Circe, and in the *Sixth Elegy* there is a much more solemn statement of the contrast between the poet who remains on the sensuous level, celebrating wine and women in his song, and the poet who becomes what is described, still in Classical imagery, as the augur or priest of the gods. For the latter a rigid chastity is prescribed—chastity less as a virtue than as a necessary kind of discipline, like an athlete's training. We see that the impulse we have called Eros can develop away from the love of the sensuous toward the love of God so that nothing of the sexually "erotic" is left in it. This is not a paradox to any student of Plato, as Milton well understood, though Milton's fullest exposition of Plato's Eros, in *The Doctrine and Discipline of Divorce*, applies it mainly to wedded love.

The Lady in *Comus* has reached the pinnacle of the ascent of Eros, and has gone as far as natural virtue can go. Her chastity is virginity as well—an identification which is traditional in magic and romance, but in Milton indicates the non-Christian setting of the imagery. In an explicitly Christian poem chastity would not exclude marriage. In any case the Lady's chastity draws her away from the sensible world toward the world of the angels, who

> in cleer dream, and solemn vision
> Tell her of things that no gross ear can hear,
> Till oft convers with heav'nly habitants
> Begin to cast a beam on th' outward shape,
> The unpolluted temple of the mind,
> And turns it by degrees to the souls essence,
> Till all be made immortal. (ll. 456–62)

Immortality here is spoken of in Platonic terms as natural, the essence of the soul as distinct from the mortal body. Such a conception of it is, for Milton, not actually Christian but part of the "divine Philosophy" of the brothers, which has hermetic, Platonic, and Neoplatonic affinities. Of course Milton in *Comus* is dealing with the conventions of poetry, not with the doctrines of religion or the facts of life, but even so the upper levels of virtue are not reached by the Lady entirely through her own efforts, hence the providential guidance given her by the Attendant Spirit. The further up one goes toward one's Creator, the more clearly the demonic element in Nature, its pollution by Sin and Death, becomes revealed. We are no longer, in *Comus*, within the world of "unreproved pleasures free," where Bacchus has begotten Mirth on Venus, but in a world of "grots, and caverns shag'ed with horrid shades," where Bacchus has begotten Comus on Circe. The feminine images of darkness, the forest, the labyrinth, the moon, the charm, the entanglement, are here all connected with Hecate and Circe and the kind of sensual degradation symbolized by Circe's beasts and the sexual emblems borne by Comus, the enchanting rod and the cup or glass.

The conflict in *Comus* is, like all of Milton's temptations, a dialectical one in which the genuine and perverted versions of the same ideas are separated. Comus and his followers claim to "imitate the Starry Quire" [l. 112], and therefore among other things to represent the genuine design of nature. The Lady is tempted by the suggestion that innocence is both amoral and natural, as the sex life of animals proves. The Lady's resistance separates the humanly natural and innocent from its opposite. There is a structural parallel with *The Tempest*, where Prospero creates a humanly natural society out of what is thrown on his island. His agent is Ariel, a spirit natural but not human: there is no place for Ariel in the new society, and he has to be set free in his own element. The Lady has, without realizing it, been making use of the Attendant Spirit, an elemental spirit of the upper air, as her protector, and when she is freed, the Attendant Spirit, like Ariel, returns to his own world. That world is nature in its pure or original form, symbolized, not by the "penseroso" heavenly spheres to which the Lady is attuned, but by the "allegro" earthly-Paradise figures of Cupid and Psyche, their offspring Youth and Joy, and the Gardens of Adonis. Again, it is a central point in Milton's ethic that when man has done all he can, God accepts what he does and strengthens man's power. After Jesus has, *quasi homo*, done all he can, God's power enables him miraculously to stand on the pinnacle of the temple: after Samson has done all he can, God's power takes over his will and sends him to the Philistine temple for his triumphant martyrdom. Sabrina represents a similar extra power granted to the Lady, and the poem closes with the inevitably accurate lines:

> Or if Vertue feeble were,
> Heav'n it self would stoop to her. (ll. 1021–2)

An explicitly Christian poem, like the *Nativity Ode*, would naturally have a different direction of imagery. The *Nativity Ode* deals, not with the anabasis of Eros, but with the katabasis of Agape, with the descent of divine love to man.[11] Consequently, the images of *Comus* appear in roughly the reverse order. First comes the music of the spheres, in counterpoint to the song of the angels, unconscious and explicit praises of God respectively, then a vision of Nature in her original creation before the fall. The true gods, that is, the angels and the personified virtues, are a part of this vision, as is the reference to the "age of gold." Astraea, the goddess of justice, returns to the earth "Orb'd in a Rain-bow," the rainbow, like the scales which are also an emblem of justice, being a recurrent image of the permanence in the order of nature. Fallen nature is now, of course, full of false gods, most of whom traditionally assume male forms. But we notice feminine imagery reappearing whenever there is any feeling of regret or nostalgia for the passing of the older order. Nobody regrets the passing of Moloch, but we feel differently about the nymphs who "in twilight shade of tangled thickets mourn" (the two thematic words again), about the Genius driven out of "haunted spring, and dale," about the fairies obliged to leave, in the last phrase associated with the gods and spirits of nature, their "Moon-lov'd maze." Finally we reach the Mother and Son in their genuine forms, while the feminine "youngest teemed Star" has overtones partly of Psyche, the bride of Eros, and partly of the wise virgins of the Bridegroom's wedding. Here as elsewhere we notice how the fact that Milton is unaccustomed to the word "its" (although it does occur once in this poem), and substitutes "his" or "her" instead, gives grammatical gender, and hence a trace of sexual feeling, to the imagery. Thus hell is referred to as "her," which perhaps indicates that hell is to Satan what the church is to Christ, the society he leads and the environment he lives in.

It is obvious that in Milton, as in most Christian poets, the same images can be used in innocent or demonic contexts, and that the tone depends a good deal on whether the theme is implicitly or explicitly Christian. We have already met this principle in *Il Penseroso* and in the Genius, who may be part of the apotheosis of Lycidas or part of the retinue of false gods in the *Nativity Ode*. The fairy world, again, suggests the free play of the imagination in *L'Allegro* and the illusions of Satanic evil at the end of the first book of *Paradise Lost* and in *Comus*. Another Virgilian and magical image of the enchantress charming the moon may be used in a demonic context in *Paradise Lost*, where the labouring moon eclipses at the night-hag's charms, or it may be used playfully, in the context of the poetic Eros convention, as it is in one of the Italian sonnets:

> E'l cantar che di mezzo l'hemispero
> Traviar ben puo la faticosa Luna. (*Diodati, e te'l dirò*, ll. 11–12)[12]

In this context the image is an analogy of the conception of harmony descending into chaos and forming a creation out of it, so central to Milton's view of creation, the creation being the primary example of what we have called the katabasis of Agape. It is also in connection with a singer that Milton makes a use, very rare for him, of this descending Agape image in a secular context. The singer Leonora, it is suggested, sings with the voice of the descending Spirit of God, which pervades all things, and which teaches us through her to become accustomed to the more rarefied music of immortality.

Comus depicts the victory of innocence, and the help of Sabrina shows that the Lady's innocence has been recognized by "Heaven." The analogy between Sabrina's sprinkling of the Lady and the rite of baptism, the introduction to revelation, is clear enough. *Paradise Regained* is a song of experience, beginning after baptism and recognition, and, in terms of the sexual symbolism, it is a man's vision of the powers behind nature, not a woman's dream of them. God made nature and is the real power behind it, but the visible part of nature, the part that corresponds to our dying bodies, has been usurped by Satan. Christ is, in our terms, the incarnation of Agape, to whom Satan exhibits the analogy of Eros as his domain. For the whole chain of being so far as we can see it, from chaos to man, and including the spirits of the elements, is Satan's, or so he claims:

> What both from Men and Angels I receive,
> Tetrarchs of fire, air, flood, and on the earth
> Nations besides from all the quarter'd winds,
> God of this world invok't and world beneath. (*PR*, 4.200–3)

The claim is considerably oversimplified, but it is true that the analogy of Eros is pervaded with a demonic element, and that it is Christ's task to recognize and reject that element. In *Paradise Regained* Christ descends, like Spenser's Guyon in the cave of Mammon, to a lower world, nature in its aspect as Satan's visible world displayed, where, unlike Proserpine, he refuses to eat so much as a pomegranate seed, rejecting every iota of it and making a complete break with it in order to ground himself wholly on the prophetic Hebrew tradition. Because he did this, we may say, speaking from Milton's point of view, the author of *L'Allegro* and *Il Penseroso* is able to be the most liberal and humane of poets, and the analogy of Eros is now safeguarded, not only by the providence of God, as in *Comus*, but by the gospel as well.

We first enter the wilderness of Satan's kingdom, much the same world as the demonic forest of *Comus*, being a "woody maze" [*PR*, 2.246] and "A pathless Desert dusk with horrid shades" [*PR*, 1.296], parts of it being also

> to a Superstitious eye the haunt
> Of Wood-Gods and Wood-Nymphs. (*PR*, 2.296–7)

The suppression of explicit sexual imagery is connected with the fact that Satan realizes the uselessness of a sexual temptation of Jesus, as urged by Belial in a scrambled echo of the Song of Songs:

> Virgin majesty with mild
> And sweet allay'd, yet terrible to approach,
> Skill'd to retire, and in retiring draw
> Hearts after them tangl'd in Amorous Nets. (*PR*, 2.159–62)

Satan is always lying, even when talking to other devils or to himself, and his rejection of Belial's suggestion means that he is really adopting it, but in disguised and sublimated forms. His first major attack, after the failure of the first temptation, is on the two appetites, for food and for sexual experience. The emphasis is on food for obvious reasons, but the banquet he summons up is served by beautiful nymphs recalling the "Fairy Damsels met in Forest wide" [*PR*, 2.359] of medieval romance. As Christ refuses one temptation after another, Satan is compelled to go further and further up the ladder of Eros, and in the temptations of Parthia and Rome he moves from passive to active sensuality. The forces of Parthia remind the poet again of the faery damsels of romance, specifically the Angelica of Boiardo and Ariosto, and the vision of the Emperor Tiberius hints at more elementary delights than purely administrative ones. Jesus' answer, with its echo of the "gold cup" of the Great Whore, who is the symbol of the persecuting Roman Emperors, indicates how clearly he sees the sexual cup of Comus in what Satan is offering:

> (For I have also heard, perhaps have read)
> Their wines of *Setia*, *Cales*, and *Falerne*,
> *Chios* and *Creet*, and how they quaff in Gold,
> Crystal and Myrrhine cups imboss'd with Gems
> And studs of Pearl. (*PR*, 4.116–20)

Satan gradually realizes, with increasing contempt, that Jesus does not want the sublimated eroticism of power. What he must want, then, Satan assumes, is the kind of wisdom that Yeats calls the property of the dead, a wisdom involving a retreat from the world, or what we should now think of as a kind of return to the womb. Such a desire could be readily satisfied in the city which is under the patronage of the virgin goddess of wisdom:

Athens the eye of *Greece*, Mother of Arts
And Eloquence, native to famous wits
Or hospitable, in her sweet recess,
City or Suburban, studious walks and shades;
See there the Olive Grove of *Academe*,
Plato's retirement, where the *Attic* Bird
Trills her thick-warbl'd notes the summer long,
There flowrie hill *Hymettus* with the sound
Of Bees industrious murmur oft invites
To studious musing; there *Ilissus* rouls
His whispering stream. (*PR*, 4.240–50)

The overtones of a shrouding female *hortus conclusus* are unmistakable, and the whole passage reads like a feeble parody of *Il Penseroso*. Satan, as usual, has the right explanation of Jesus' attitude in a perverted form. In the temptation, Jesus fulfils the law in the wilderness and becomes the true Joshua, or conqueror of the Promised Land, which is also the feminine garden of Eden (*PR*, 1.7). In the Passion and Resurrection, Christ fulfils the prophecy made to Adam; by overcoming the temptation he fulfils the dream of Eve. The Virgin Mary, the "second *Eve*" [*PL*, 5.387], is very prominent in the poem, and the typology of the whole temptation is summed up, from our present point of view, in the final line: "Home to his Mothers house private return'd."

We may notice in passing how Satan perverts even the genuine elements of the civilization he displays. What was really impressive about Greek culture, for Milton, was "the Libertie of *Greece*" (*PL*, 10.307) that Xerxes tried to yoke. The philosophy of Plato and Socrates was a product of liberty, not, as Satan presents it, an escape from the world or a means of getting entangled in sophisticated arguments. "The Mountain Nymph, sweet Liberty" which appears in *L'Allegro* is certainly liberty in a different context, but it is not a wholly different kind of liberty. Satan's temptation of Athens ends "These rules will render thee a King compleat" [*PR*, 4.283], and Christ's answer ends "These only with our Law best form a King" [*PR*, 4.364]. Two conceptions of cyropaedia, of education as the training of a prince, are colliding here.[13] One leads to the conception of the king as a temporal ruler, who, if not a tyrant, would be the philosopher-king of Plato's "ayrie Burgomasters,"[14] in Milton's phrase. The other is the institute of a Christian prince, leading to the king who is a spiritual ruler or prophet, a herald of freedom. A social and political aspect of Milton's analogical and sexual imagery is implied, and one which is set out in the prose works.

Jesus returns to his mother's house at the end of the temptation, but leaves it again to be about his father's business when he starts on his ministry, or work in the world proper. Here the female principle complementing Jesus is not the mother but the redeemed Bride or Church. Consequently it is semantically dangerous for Christians to think in terms of a Mother Church: it implies a regression to the law. "But marke Readers," says Milton, "the crafty scope of these Prelates, they endeavour to impresse deeply into weak, and superstitious fancies the awfull notion of a mother, that hereby they might cheat them into a blind and implicite obedience to whatsoever they shall decree, or think fit."[15] Christians should think of their church as a bride, a young virgin, still under tutelage. "For of any age or sex, most unfitly may a virgin be left to an uncertaine and arbitrary education. . . . In like manner the Church bearing the same resemblance, it were not reason to think she should be left destitute of that care which is as necessary, and proper to her, as instruction."[16] This last means that the relation of Christ and the church ought to be precisely the relation of Adam to Eve in the unfallen state. The conception is Pauline, but the interpretation of Paul involved is, of course, a left-wing Protestant one. The Word, the male principle, should have "absolute rule" [*PL*, 4.301]; the church has only to murmur "unargu'd I obey" [*PL*, 4.636]. The autonomous church, who claims the authority to teach the Word herself, is in the position of the unfaithful bride or harlot identified with Israel and frequently denounced by the prophets, or else a man-made counterfeit of the church, "like that aire-born *Helena* in the fables."[17]

Similarly society is in a female relationship to the prophet, the speaker of the Word, the possessor of Adam's spiritual authority. Delilah, like Job's wife, represents the threat of the forces of social inertia and habit to the voice of genuine leadership, or prophecy. There are two degrees of female recalcitrance in the Bible: there is Israel as the disobedient harlot of Hosea and Ezekiel, who is eventually forgiven and brought back to repentance, and who is represented in Christian tradition by the story of Mary Magdalene, and there is the Great Whore, the consolidated form of social apostasy, Delilah as Philistine. They correspond respectively to the fallen Eve and her demonic shadow in nature, the aspect of her that tempted Adam to fall too. Here we see the relevance of the theme of divorce in Milton to his sexual imagery. Milton's arguments for divorce do not concern us here; but behind these arguments is a larger symbolic structure in which the intolerable wife is the symbol of the custom and error that entangles the prophet. Adam could have prevented his fall only by "divorcing" Eve after she had fallen, and before Jesus can return to his mother's house he has to complete a parallel divorce from the entire fallen human society, which of course for Adam consisted only of Eve. This divorce of Christ, being a recreation of man, repeats the original creation, "when by his divorcing command the world first rose out of Chaos, nor can be renewed again out of confusion but by the separating of unmeet consorts."[18]

A secular counterpart to the symbolism of Word and church also appears in the prose. Thus we read of "men inchanted with the *Circaean* cup of servitude,"[19] and mazes and labyrinths and coverts, whether of argument or of action, often have a latent suggestion of some enchantress hampering the freedom of a warfaring Christian. On the other hand, Truth in the prose is often personified in terms recalling the innocent and naked Eve. Truth and Justice, so closely associated in the *Nativity Ode*, are explicitly identified in *Eikonoklastes*. Truth for Milton is existential, being ultimately a person and not a principle or rational vision: hence Truth is also the Astraea represented by the Virgin of the zodiac, already mentioned, who is flanked with the scales symbolizing justice within its context of God's creative and ordering power. The vision of Truth in *Areopagitica* and elsewhere is thus closely associated with the insight into the harmony of created nature in *Comus* and *At a Solemn Music*. Both aspects of Truth take us upward to the Wisdom personified in the Bible as the daughter of the Creator, playing before him[20] when the world was ordered, and the exact opposite of Athene, the virgin mother of Athens whom Jesus has to abandon before he can return to the home of the genuine virgin mother. If he had not abandoned her, she would eventually have turned into Sin, the daughter who was born of Satan much as Athene is said to have been born of Zeus. Sin is described as serpentine, like the Gorgon's head on Athene's shield: it seems strange that this image can represent a genuine ideal in the context of *Comus*, but so it is.

What we have been looking at in Milton's imagery is a particular way of relating the two great mythological structures on which the literature of our own Near Eastern and Western traditions has been founded. One structure is dominated by a male father-god, stresses the rational order of nature, and thinks of nature as an artefact, something designed and constructed. The other centres on a mother-goddess, perennially renewing the mystery of birth in the act of love. The father-god myth subordinates the female principle, making it a daughter-figure of Truth or Wisdom; the mother-goddess myth subordinates the male principle, making it the son-lover-victim figure of the dying god. The male mythology was dominant from the beginning of the Christian era down to the Romantic movement. In the medieval and Renaissance period its rival was incorporated in the Venus–Eros cult of the courtly love convention. After the Romantic movement began, the mother-centred myth gained ground. The father-myth is an inherently conservative one; the other is more naturally revolutionary, and the revolutionary emphasis in Milton shows how near he is to the mythology of Romanticism and its later by-products, the revolutionary erotic, Promethean, and Dionysian myths of Freud, Marx, and Nietzsche. The artefact myth has declined during the last two centuries partly because so many of its central elements came to be regarded as fictions, and again it is interesting to see how these elements in Milton are represented by symbols either known to be fictions, like the music of the spheres, or presented as possible fictions, like the Ptolemaic cosmos.

Milton, of course, accepted the artefact myth as primary along with the traditional ideas about how the sexual myth was to be subordinated to it. But he was also a poet who understood the claims of both on the imagination. The father-god myth has a moral principle built into it: it assumes a creator with an intelligent and purposeful Plan A for man's creation, who after Adam's defection falls back on an equally well designed Plan B for his salvation. The mother-goddess myth has only very ambiguous moral principles: it expresses an unconditioned desire which, either as that or in its frustrated form of resentment, may go in any direction and take any form. Theoretically, as we said, Eve's dream is fulfilled in the moment that Christ is raised, as she was, to a high eminence by Satan, then left to fall, and is sustained by the power of God as Satan falls instead. But Eve had shown, even in the unfallen state, a disconcerting capacity to have her own thoughts, her own desires, her own resentments even, to arrive at her own conclusions independently of Adam's superior reason. This tendency had led her to separate herself from Adam and fall under Satan's influence. God, who made her as she was, nevertheless had her separated again, and perhaps let her dream more or less in her own way: Michael suggests that he is only establishing the general atmosphere—

> Her also I with gentle Dreams have calm'd
> Portending good (*PL*, 12.595–6)

—and Eve's own account is even vaguer. It is significant that the revelation to Adam is so full and explicit, extending through most of two whole books, and the revelation to Eve so briefly, even evasively, referred to. The awakened father of mankind follows the master plan of God's salvation as it is unrolled scene by scene, and agrees to the justice, wisdom, and reason incorporated into it. We are expected to be similarly convicted and convinced, but, if the clear light of reason is ever dimmed by a passion or emotion that is not quite so sure of its objects, we may remember that, far below this rarefied pinnacle of rational vision, there lies a humiliated mother dreaming of the vengeance of her mighty son.

5

Agon and *Logos*

1973

From SM, *201–27. Originally published in slightly shorter form in* The Prison and the Pinnacle, *ed. Balachandra Rajan (Toronto: University of Toronto Press, 1973), 135–63. There are two copies of a typescript with the title "Agon and Logos: Revolution and Revelation," dated 1971, among the Frye papers (NFF, 1988, box 3, files ck and cl).*

Milton intended *Paradise Lost* to be a Christian conquest of the Classical epic genre, and similarly *Samson Agonistes* is a Christian conquest of the Classical genre of dramatic tragedy. In Classical literature, as in Classical life and culture generally, there are, as Milton sees it, two elements. One is a development of natural human ability, or what we now call creative imagination, outside the Christian revelation, and therefore possessing, not the truth of that revelation, but an analogy of or parallel to that truth. Although the poetry of the Bible, according to *The Reason of Church Government*, is better as poetry than Classical poetry, the latter is a safer model for poets not sure of receiving the highest kind of inspiration. But Classical culture is not simply a human development, unfortunately: man without revelation cannot avoid accepting some demonic version, which means parody, of that revelation. Hence such forms as the Homeric epic and the Sophoclean tragedy are genuine models of style, decorum, and "ancient liberty";[1] at the same time they are also connected with something ultimately demonic, a pseudo-revelation from fallen angels. The use of Classical genres by a Christian poet should show in what respects they are humanly analogous to the forms of Christian revelation, and in what respects they are demonic parodies of them.

In *Paradise Regained*, a brief epic for which Milton mentions no Classical model, the sense of parody is at its sharpest. Christ can overcome the temptations of Satan because he can clearly see the demonic taproot of everything Satan offers. I have never understood why Christ's rejection of Classical culture in that poem should be such a puzzle to critics: it seems so obvious that in that context Christ has to reject every syllable of it. It does not mean that *Milton* is rejecting it: it is only because Christ does reject it that Milton can accept so much of it. The rejection of the English dramatic tradition in the Preface to *Samson Agonistes* is much harder to understand. The theme of *Paradise Regained* is, appropriately, a parody of a dragon-killing romance, or, more accurately, it presents the reality of which the dragon-killing romance is a parody. For Milton there is no strength except spiritual strength, and no conflict except mental conflict, hence the prophecy that the Messiah will defeat the serpent can only be fulfilled by a dramatic dialogue.

In *Paradise Lost* too, so far as we can think of it as an epic modelled on Homer and Virgil, the sense of parody is much sharper than the sense of analogy. The Classical epic is a poem of heroic action, of *klea andrōn*, brave deeds of men. Christianity has a completely opposed notion of what a hero is: a Christian hero is one who imitates or approximates the heroism of Christ, which consisted in suffering, endurance, and compassion. The sense of opposition doubtless greatly intensified in Milton's mind between his discussion of Christian heroism in *The Reason of Church Government* and the writing of *Paradise Lost*. In the latter poem, in any case, the conventional heroics of the Classical epic are mainly transferred to Satan and the other devils. There is, it is true, a great war in heaven in which the faithful angels perform prodigies of valour, but when on the third day the Son of God disposes of the entire rebel host single-handed, the sense of parody is strongly reinforced. The whole war in heaven is something of a joke to God, for whom any strength apart from his will does not exist. The same sense of the identity of strength and divine will, along with the unreality of any strength apart from it, recurs in *Comus*, where the elder brother explains how the Lady's chastity is an invincible strength, and in the Samson story itself, where Samson kills a thousand Philistines "with what trivial weapon came to hand," the jawbone of an ass (*SA*, l. 142).

Paradise Lost, as I have said elsewhere, restates in Christian terms, reversing the pagan ones, not only what a hero is but what an act is. For Milton the only genuine act is an act performed according to the will of God. Adam's eating of the tree of knowledge was therefore not an act, but the pseudo-act of disobedience; the revolt of Satan was the parody-act of rebellion. The only genuine actions in *Paradise Lost* are those performed by the Son of God, the acts of creation and redemption. The same principle, applied to *Samson Agonistes*, will help to explain Milton's conception of tragic action. Nothing really happens anywhere except the accomplishing of the will of God. In the world of the angels above man this will can be clearly seen as a benign providence; in the world of animals below man it can be seen in a kind of reflecting mirror, as the automatic accuracy of instinct. As the working of God's will is relatively uncomplicated in these worlds, there is no possibility of anything like tragic action, as Milton conceives it, among either angels (faithful angels, of course) or animals.

In human life too it is still true that nothing really happens except the accomplishing of God's will, or what we call providence. But there—or here—the will of God is much harder to see, because it is concealed by the powerful current of pseudo-acts released by human passion and demonic instigation. God's providence can be seen by the human reason, but the reason, being normally a submerged and suppressed critic of a dictatorial passion, is seldom attended to. The three levels of reality are indicated by the Messenger when he says:

> But providence or instinct of nature seems,
> Or reason though disturb'd, and scarse consulted
> To have guided me aright, I know not how. (*SA*, ll. 1545–7)

They also appear in one of the choral odes, where God is told that in relation to man he

> Temperst thy providence through his short course,
> Not evenly, as thou rul'st
> The Angelic orders and inferiour creatures mute,
> Irrational and brute. (*SA*, ll. 670–3)

Human life sets up a kind of perpetual Saturnalia or inversion of the providential order, in which the wicked flourish and the good are persecuted or ridiculed. For the most part we have to wait for a judgment after the end of life, whether of an individual life or of human history itself, in order to see good vindicated and evil confounded. But every once in a while the wicked do meet with appalling disasters in a form which makes it clear to the eye of reason that the disaster is the consequence of previous folly or arrogance. The good, merely because they are good, are in for a rough time in human society: their normal fate is, at best, ridicule or neglect, at worst martyrdom. The good man, or prophet as he usually is, is an agent of a counter-counter-movement in human life, of God's will working against human evil, and his life may well be tragic in relation to that evil, which often claims him as its victim. Yet the good may occasionally be recognized as having been right even through the torrent of lies and illusions which is the normal course of history.

We have tragedy when it is possible for the human reason, in contemplating the fall of Belshazzar or the justification of Job, to catch a glimpse of the working of God's will in human life against the power of human passion or evil. Tragedy is thus, for Milton, the recognition of God's will by human reason in the form of justice or law. As justice or law is an equalizing or balancing principle, its emblem being the scales, the tragic vision has the equalizing effect that Aristotle calls catharsis. According to the explanation of catharsis given by Milton in his Preface to *Samson Agonistes*, the consequences of human passion cannot be seen as tragic by human passion, but only by human reason, which casts passion out of itself by seeing a greater passion before it, on the principle of like curing like in homeopathic medicine. That is, in the soul passion normally dominates reason; in tragedy passion is externalized, in a position where only reason can recognize it; the effect of catharsis is thus to revolutionize the soul, restoring reason to its ascendancy and casting out passion by passion.

There are, as is obvious, at least two levels of tragic action. The lower level, in which disaster appears to be the inevitable consequence of folly or wrongdoing, is what is expressed by the word "nemesis" in Greek tragedy. This kind of nemesis tragedy has already happened to Samson before *Samson Agonistes* begins: it belongs to a play that Milton gave a title to but did not write, *Samson Hybristes*. In the play that we have, this nemesis action is the tragic action so far as it affects the Philistines. Samson himself goes through a redemption in which he is accepted once again as an agent of God's will and a champion of Israel. Hence, though he is inevitably involved in a tragic death, it is not a death to which the conception of nemesis is any longer relevant.

The tragedies of the Philistines and of Samson are, respectively, the elements of demonic parody and of analogy in the tragic action. What happens to the Philistines is the same kind of thing that happens to such figures as Ajax in Sophocles or Heracles in Euripides, where the causes of catastrophe are, ultimately, devils. Samson, on the other hand, is a human analogy of Christ, of whose death his death is a prototype. It follows that the central area of tragic action, for Milton, is the Old Testament, where the Christian reader or audience may see the higher kind of tragedy in its true perspective, as part of the analogy of the law.

This conception of two levels of tragic action, however, recurs in Greek tragedy, most explicitly at the end of the *Oresteia*. Here there is a nemesis movement represented by the Furies, who are not capable of distinguishing the elements of equity in a tragic situation, such as the amount and kind of provocation given by the victim, but are the unleashing of an essentially automatic force, the righting of a disturbed balance in nature. This nemesis movement is overruled by a legal decision in which gods and men are included, and which is the higher tragic vision of the whole action, ending in the acquittal of Orestes. Similarly in the two Oedipus plays of Sophocles. In the first one, *Oedipus Tyrannos*, Oedipus tears out his eyes in a kind of reflex revulsion of horror, without stopping to consider that his own unconsciousness of the guilt he has been involved in is a point of some ethical relevance. The action of *Oedipus Tyrannos* goes through a self-discovery which moves backwards in time and ends in blindness; *Samson Agonistes* goes in the opposite direction, through a progressive and forward-moving self-discovery away from blindness. It therefore runs parallel (to a very limited degree) with the action of the second Oedipus play, *Oedipus at Colonus*.

We first see Samson in the throes of nemesis, tormented by the mechanical furies of his own conscience. Christian ethics has always distinguished remorse from repentance (*metanoia*), and although there is genuine repentance in Samson, the sterile brooding, the self-chewing which is what "remorse" literally means, is more prominent at first. Just as Samson's body is infested by vermin, so all the mental vermin engendered by the lord of flies (the devil Beelzebub, invoked by Harapha) are infesting his mind, producing there what at times suggests an allegorical reading on Milton's part of the torments of Prometheus:

> Thoughts my Tormenters arm'd with deadly stings
> Mangle my apprehensive tenderest parts. (*SA*, ll. 623–4)

Samson has been tempted and has lost, and the result of losing a temptation is demonic possession. The Chorus is puzzled by the fact that Samson is so much worse off than they are: there seems to be a kind of manic-depressive rhythm in nemesis which ensures that the bigger they are, the harder they fall. This is closely linked with the wheel-of-fortune rhythm in tragedy that so fascinated medieval writers:

> Nor only dost degrade them, or remit
> To life obscur'd, which were a fair dismission,
> But throw'st them lower then thou didst exalt them high,
> Unseemly falls in human eie,
> Too grievous for the trespass or omission. (*SA*, ll. 687–91)

The overtones of this last line would take us a long way—into the Book of Job, for example. But to the main point the answer, or part of the answer, is that those elected by God are capable of sin in a way that ordinary people, or what the Chorus calls the "common rout" (*SA*, l. 674), are not. This is *a fortiori* true of Adam in Eden, for whom the most trivial of trespasses, by ordinary human standards, was also the greatest possible sin. Yet even Adam could not fall as low as the devils, who fell from a greater height. The same principle applies in reverse to the Philistines. The divine vengeance on them extends primarily to their lords and priests: in the destruction of their temple "The vulgar only scap'd who stood without" (*SA*, l. 1659). The wheel-of-fortune rhythm for them may be heard in the two off-stage noises, the shout of triumph and the death-groan, which we hear as the wheel turns a half-circle.

The nemesis of Samson takes the form of "captivity and loss of eyes" [*SA*, l. 1744], and the action of the play, we said, so far as it affects Samson, moves away from nemesis. Manoa has elaborate plans to free Samson from captivity, and he also expresses the hope that God will restore Samson's eyesight along with his strength. Much of this is only the facile hopefulness of a rather weak man, but it is true that symbolically Samson's freedom and vision are both restored. They are restored within the realities of his situation, which means that the process is full of tragic ironies, starting with the reversal of Manoa's picture of how the restoration might take place. But it does take place nonetheless. At the beginning of the play Samson is a slave in both external and internal bondage: besides being "at the Mill with slaves," he is in a "Prison within Prison," and is, as the Chorus says, "the Dungeon of thy self" (*SA*, ll. 41, 153–6). Yet he asserts his spiritual freedom, negatively, by refusing to take part in a Philistine festival, and then positively by accepting the dispensation that God gives him to go, of which more later. At the temple itself he performs various feats in obedience to commands, but the crucial act he performs "of my own accord" [*SA*, l. 1643], as a free man. Similarly, although in his blindness he possesses an internal light, such as Milton claims for himself in the *Second Defence* and elsewhere, he is well aware that, as the Chorus says, it "puts forth no visual beam" (*SA*, l. 163). But in his final enterprise he is, according to the Semichorus, "with inward eyes illuminated" (*SA*, l. 1689).

In the Book of Judges Samson's final prayer is "let me die with the Philistines" [16:30]. Milton does not quote this directly, though it is the theme of Samson's speech to Manoa, but he does ascribe to Samson a most eloquent longing for death. This longing in itself is despair, but God transmutes it to a heroic achievement ending in death. God is thus acting in accordance with the same homeopathic principle, of casting out salt humours by salt and the like, which is part of the catharsis of tragedy. And in proportion as Samson is released from nemesis, the whole nemesis machinery is transferred to the Philistines. It is they who acquire the hybris or "spirit of phrenzie" [*SA*, l. 1675] which is the normal condition of the Greek tragic hero. With the last line of the first Semichorus, "And with blindness internal struck" (*SA*, l. 1686), the transfer is completed.

The "spirit of phrenzie" is associated with drunkenness, the "jocund and sublime" Philistines [*SA*, l. 1669] being a contrast in this respect to the water-drinking Samson. It is still morning, but, as Milton remarks in the Commonplace Book, people who are habitually drunk can get drunk without the aid of wine. This drunkenness however is a Dionysian drunkenness, an enthusiasm or possession by a god, or what they consider a god. The Bible says of Samson that his hair began to grow again when he was in the Philistine prison-house. There are few concessions to probability in folk tales, yet we may perhaps ask the question, Once the Philistines had learned the secret of Samson's strength, why did they allow his hair to grow again? Two answers are suggested by Milton. One, the mill owners were making a good deal of money by exploiting his labour, "The work of many hands," as Samson calls it [*SA*, l. 1260]. Two, the Philistines really believed in the power of Dagon, and therefore believed that Samson's strength could be contained within limits convenient to them. It was this belief in particular that was their "spirit of phrenzie."

The King James Bible says that Samson was commanded to make sport for the Philistines, and, as the schoolboy added, he brought down the house. The New English Bible makes it clear that what Samson had to do was fight, like a gladiator. The two translations are not inconsistent: elsewhere in the Old Testament (as Huizinga points out in *Homo Ludens*) to "play" or "make sport" can mean to fight to the death.[2] But gladiatorial fighting would not have suited Milton's conception. Dramatically, Samson would not want to spoil his climax by killing individual Philistines. More important, Milton says more than once that when Samson had his genuine strength, no single person dared oppose him. Hence the behaviour of Harapha. The model for Harapha's character is his son Goliath, and while Goliath is certainly a boaster—it was conventional for warriors of his type to begin battles with boasts—there is no indication that he is a coward. He expects King Saul to come out to meet him, the Saul who was said to be head and shoulders over every man in Israel, and when David turns up with his slingshot he is genuinely disappointed as well as contemptuous. During the colloquy with Harapha Samson suddenly asserts his role once again as a champion of Jehovah, and Harapha does not dare pursue the matter further. He may, of course, have been a coward all along, but it may be that something more than simple cowardice is breaking him down.

It is essential to Milton's dramatic purpose, then, that Samson in the temple is purely an entertainer, almost the buffoon, of a Philistine carnival, an *agonistes* in the sense of a performer or actor—hardly as a contestant in games, for he is not competing with anyone. At the same time he is a tragic hero, a defeated champion, and an *agonistes* in that sense, to his Danite followers. The action moves quickly through what Yeats would call a double gyre, as the tragedy becomes a triumph and the carnival a shambles. It is this aspect of Samson's situation in particular that makes him a dramatic prototype of Christ, for Christ is also a tragic hero to his followers as well as a mocked and ridiculed figure of a carnival to his enemies, and the same reversal of action occurs there.

In *Samson Agonistes* the reversal is expressed in a complex imagery of light and darkness. Milton knew too much Hebrew not to pick up the overtones of *shemesh*, the Hebrew word for sun, in Samson's name, and perhaps he saw something of a solar-shaped myth in the story of the long-haired hero who fell into the dark prison of the west. The play opens at sunrise with Samson physically in the open air, but, like other Titans, including Prometheus at the end of Aeschylus's play, he seems to be symbolically in a kind of subterranean prison or "interlunar cave" [*SA*, l. 89], and the very rare Classical allusions in the play link him with Atlas and Ixion. It is almost as though Samson, or a power guiding

Samson, were moving under the world like the sun at night, back to the place of its rising. The action ends abruptly at noon, with the zenith of the Philistine triumph suddenly blown to pieces by the explosion of a dark hidden fire rising like the phoenix from its ashes. From the Israelite point of view, this means that the "total Eclipse" Samson complains of has lifted and that although "he seems to hide his face," the true sun-god has unexpectedly returned [*SA*, ll. 81, 1749].

Samson Agonistes is a real play, with a real plot and real characters, and it could be acted with success, I should think, in front of any audience ready to accept its conventions. Yet Milton said that it was not intended for the stage, a statement often connected with the prejudice against stage plays among extreme Puritans in England. The prejudice itself is not very interesting nor particularly relevant to Milton, but the traditions behind it are more so.

What Milton would call paganism is a religious development focused on visual symbols. Polytheism is impossible without pictures or statues to distinguish one god from another. As a pagan society becomes more centralized, it converges on a capital city, such as Gaza is described as being, and the visual worship of gods is supplemented by various forms of spectacle, including a strong concentration on the supreme ruler or king as a visible symbol. Hebrew religion is founded on revelation, which means revelation through the ear. In the theophanies of the Old Testament, God speaks and man listens, but the status of what is visible is much more doubtful. Even where the vision is expressly said to be of God, the description is always of something or someone else, variously described as an angel, a spirit, or simply a man. Much of the vagueness in Milton's conception of the Holy Spirit is simply the result of his accepting literally the ambiguities in such passages. God is, in himself, invisible, and hence, as the first two commandments enjoin, no permanent image of him should ever be made. Thus in the story of the burning bush, the visual object, the burning bush itself, is there only to catch Moses' attention: what is significant is what is said. We are told that God spoke, but that the angel of the Lord appeared; that Moses had no trouble listening to God, but could not look at him.

The shift of metaphors from eye to ear, in other words, introduces into religion the conception of idolatry, and this in turn is the source of two characteristics which separate the Biblical tradition from the pagan one. These are the dialectical and the revolutionary. Polytheism, even when it takes the form, as it did with the Philistines, of concentrating on a single national deity, has the kind of tolerance that is the result of intellectual vagueness, because the conception "false god" is very difficult for it to assimilate. At the same time it is also conservative and authoritarian, because its religion is ultimately the authority of the state. The Philistines have both lords and priests, but it is clear that the lords have supreme power. The Bible was produced by a subject nation never lucky at the game of empire, and it looks forward to a future in which the great powers of the earth, along with their gods, will be overthrown. The visual metaphors are transferred to this future state: the "day of Jehovah" in Judaism, the second coming in Christianity, are occasions that will be openly visible to the faithful. Hence the objections of early Christians, including Tertullian and Lactantius, to the games and contests of the Roman circus, which, apart from their brutality, focused attention on the power of the secular state and its heathen cults. It was essentially the visual stimulation in them that was dangerous, and the title of Tertullian's attack has a visual emphasis: *De Spectaculis*. Tertullian urges his readers to avoid all such entertainments and concentrate on the better spectacles afforded by Christianity, the future second coming of Christ and the Last Judgment. Milton refers to this passage in his Commonplace Book in a way which makes it quite clear that he has no use for the blinkered bigotry that lumped in the plays of Sophocles with gladiatorial fights as equally "stage shows" [cf. *Works*, 18:102]. But of course the fundamental Christian emphases are also his.

The visual image is centripetal: it holds the body immobile in a pose of static obedience, and sets the sign of authority before it. The revelation by the Word is centrifugal: it is primarily a command, the starting point of a course of action. In the Biblical view everything we can see is a creature of God, and a secondary repetition of the primary Word of God: "let there be light, and there was light." Adam was surrounded with a visible paradise, but what the forbidden tree primarily forbids is idolatry, the taking of the visible object to be the source of creative power, as Eve does when after her fall she bows in homage to the tree. Since the fall, paradise has been an invisible and embryonic inner state, to be brought into being by the revelation through the Word. The Word not only causes all images of gods to shrivel into nothingness, but continues to operate in society as an iconoclastic force, in other words a revolutionary force, demolishing everything to which man is tempted to offer false homage. To revert to the burning bush story, God there tells Moses that he is entering history, giving himself a Hebrew name and a specific and highly partisan political role, the role of delivering an oppressed class from the constituted authority of their oppressors. Further, God defines himself existentially as "I am," not essentially as He Who is, so that there is no possibility of Hebrew religion ever depersonalizing its supreme God, as Classical religion tended to do in Stoicism and elsewhere.

As Christianity became a social institution, the Tertullian prejudice against visual stimulation relaxed somewhat, and in medieval Christianity there is again a strong emphasis on the visual symbols which are the normal sign of a secure and confident society. This emphasis on the visibility of the church was followed in its turn, in some areas of Protestantism, by an iconoclastic reaction which condemned the use of images, the decoration of stained glass and sculpture, and the visual focus of the elevated host, and therefore, of course, revived the old condemnation of spectacles in theatres. Milton was no William Prynne,[3] but he was a revolutionary iconoclast whose instinct, in attacking the government of Charles I, was to centre his attack on the visual image of royalty, and on the dangers of that image as a potential source of idolatry. Hence he could hardly avoid reflecting some of the same antivisual tendencies that were present in his cultural milieu.

In this world the essential conflict between good and evil takes the aural form of a conflict between the Word and the oracle, true and false rhetoric. Yet the ultimate object of all false rhetoric is a visual image commanding obedience to something other than God. Thus in *Paradise Regained* Jesus enters a desert, with no visual features to distract him, to engage in a mortal combat with the false word, the accuser. But Satan can only operate by summoning up a series of visual hallucinations. If Christ were to accept any one of these, he would instantly have become identified with it, according to the Psalmist's axiom about idols (Psalm 115): "They that make them are like unto them," which is echoed in *Paradise Lost* in the passage about the metamorphoses of the devils:

what they saw
They felt themselvs now changing. (*PL*, 10.540–1)[4]

Samson Agonistes exhibits a parallel conflict between the Word of God within Samson, the ultimate source of his strength, and the temptations of the accuser, which take the form of a sequence of dialogues. The importance of this aspect of the conflict is one of the things that Samson's blindness symbolizes. Samson lives in a kind of seance-world of disembodied voices, between the mill with its slaves and the temple with its lords: as he says of the Chorus:

> I hear the sound of words, thir sense the air
> Dissolves unjointed e're it reach my ear. (*SA*, ll. 176–7)

Everyone who speaks to Samson, including Manoa and the Chorus, has something to add in the way of reproach, something to suggest distrust or uncertainty, something of Eliot's "loud lament of the disconsolate chimera" heard by the Word in the desert.[5] Even Samson's hearing has to be mortified: he can only break from Dalila by, so to speak, putting out his ears. Greek tragedies of course also concentrate on dialogue and have catastrophes reported by messengers, but still a Greek play, with its masks and amphitheatre setting, is a very intense visual experience, as the etymology of the word "theatre" reminds us. The action of Milton's play, like that of the Book of Job, forms a kind of visual anti-play. In this respect it anticipates some of the techniques of a later dramatist who has also often been called a Puritan, Bernard Shaw. Superficially it seems like a discussion of past and future events without any action at all except what is offstage. More closely examined, the action is there all right, but it is a curious kind of internalized action: the important events are going on invisibly in Samson's mind.

Meanwhile, the Philistines are preparing their festival of Dagon. I have been calling the building that Samson destroys a temple, because that is symbolically what it is, a place for the celebration of the Dagon cult. But of course it is also a theatre, as the Messenger calls it, a very un-Athenian theatre where the entertainment is like that of a Roman circus. The Philistine program committee, like so many of its kind, has not engaged its chief attraction until the last moment, which explains, if it does not excuse, the frantic mixture of bluster and promises in the Officer's message. So Samson is removed from an action of which his mind is the circumference to a theatre in which, blind and unable to stare back, he is the visual focus for the whole Philistine society, the gaze of Gaza, so to speak. But by that time he is once again an agent of God, and it is very dangerous for a Philistine society to make a visual focus out of that.

We remember that Tertullian urged his readers to withdraw from actual spectacles and feast their minds on the tremendous show promised in the Book of Revelation, when all their enemies would be seen burning in the lake of fire. In the famous passage about literary genres in

The Reason of Church Government [*Works*, 3:238], the Scriptural model for tragedy is said to be the Book of Revelation ("intermingling her solemn Scenes and Acts with a sevenfold *Chorus*"). Nothing could be less like the Book of Revelation than *Samson Agonistes*, and yet *Samson Agonistes*, with its seven great choral odes (it has seven characters also, counting the Chorus as one), has for its subject a prototype of the underside, so to speak, of the vision of the Book of Revelation. This is the aspect of it that comes to a climax in the elegy over the fall of Babylon in chapter 18. The identification there of the city of Babylon with the Great Whore who says "I am a queen, and no widow,"[6] and the emphasis on merchandise and shipping, perhaps indicates a larger significance for the role of Dalila and the elaborate ship imagery attached to her in *Samson Agonistes*. This larger significance is anticipated in *Paradise Lost*, with its comparison of the fallen Adam and Eve to Samson and "Philistean Dalilah" [*PL*, 9.1061].

The visual emphasis that Milton distrusts as potential idolatry exists in time as well as space. In time it takes the form of an anxiety of continuity, which produces the doctrine of apostolic succession in the church and the principle of hereditary succession in the state. The belief that all matrimonial contracts have to be treated as unbreakable is a by-product of the same anxiety. Apostolic succession replaces the spiritual succession of those called by God with the mechanical continuity of a human office; hereditary succession similarly destroys the divine principle of the leadership of the elect. The genuine king, like the genuine prophet, emerges when God calls him. The succession of leaders and prophets is discontinuous in human terms, and no human devices will safeguard it. Thus, according to the opening of the Gospel of Matthew, Jesus was legitimately descended from Abraham and David through his father Joseph, and yet Jesus was not the son of Joseph. Samson was one of a line of heroes called by God when his people turned again to God after a period of apostasy. The calling is represented by a very beautiful annunciation story in the Book of Judges, which ends with the angel returning to heaven in the fire on an altar. This image, twice referred to in *Samson Agonistes*, modulates into the image of the phoenix, the image of divine succession, a unique power of renewal through total self-sacrifice which cannot be programmed, so to speak, by any human institution.

One play that I often think of in connection with *Samson Agonistes* is Racine's *Athalie*, another great seventeenth-century tragedy on an Old Testament subject. The connection is largely one of contrast, *Athalie* being a spectacular play with crowds of characters: like Byron later, in a very different way, Racine thinks of the Old Testament not as the desert of the law but as a source of Oriental glamour. We notice too how *Athalie* turns on the issue of hereditary succession through the youthful prince Joash, who is in the Davidic line leading to Christ. In this, if in nothing else, Racine resembles Shakespeare, whose histories in particular so strongly emphasize the crucial importance of a clear line of succession. I suspect that the prominence of this theme in Shakespeare is one reason why Shakespeare has so little influence on the tragic drama of Milton.

The Biblical narrator remarks of the age of anarchy following Samson, "In those days there was no king in Israel; every man did that which was right in his own eyes" [Judges 17:6, 21:25]. The Old Testament never quite makes up its mind whether hereditary kingship was a good thing for Israel or not, but still the glories of the reigns of David and Solomon are made much of, and it is easy for a Christian reader to see in these royal figures the prototypes of Christ as the world's only really legitimate monarch. Certainly the distinction between the person and the office, which Milton makes so much of in the regicide pamphlets, is derived from the Old Testament's attitude to kings. In *The Reason of Church Government* there is a long allegorical passage describing the king as an unfallen Samson,[7] an image about his long hair being echoed in *Samson Agonistes*.[8] The inference seems clear that Samson, so long as he was a leader chosen by God, was not merely a legitimate king but may at one time have had the power to set up the kingdom of God on earth, there being no limits to the divine strength which was the source of his. One of the remarks about Samson made by the Chorus brings out this larger dimension of his significance:

> But thee whose strength, while vertue was her mate,
> Might have subdu'd the Earth,
> Universally crown'd with highest praises. (*SA*, ll. 173–5)

However,[9] Samson did not redeem the world: his achievement has to be paralleled and contrasted with that of Christ. *Paradise Lost* tells the story of how man lost the garden that was all about him, and of how he is enabled to regain this garden as an inner state. In *Paradise Regained*, Christ, by successfully resisting the temptation, symbolically transforms the desert he is in into the Garden of Eden again, as the poem's seventh line tells us. But the garden imagery is combined with that of the temple, the central image of the Jewish law that Christ both obeys and transcends in the action of the poem. Milton followed Luke's account of the temptation, where placing Jesus on the pinnacle of the temple is Satan's final act, accompanied by a quotation from Psalm 91:11–12, designed to suggest that if he falls off no harm will come to him. Christ remains motionless on the pinnacle, which means that the true temple of God passes into his own body, becoming a temple which can be raised again after it is destroyed, in contrast to Herod's temple below him, which was permanently destroyed a few years later. The two temples represent the two aspects of the law, which for Christianity is simultaneously abolished and fulfilled by the gospel.

Paradise Regained was a natural sequel to *Paradise Lost*, and one can see how, typologically, Milton was attracted to the story of Samson as the Old Testament counterpart of the same theme. As an Old Testament prototype of Christ, Samson, in destroying the demonic temple, illustrates the kind of thing that, according to Milton, man by himself can do in self-redemption. Man cannot transform himself into a superior being, or redeem himself; but he can express a willingness to be redeemed by knocking down the idols that surround him. What is achieved by this may be negative and iconoclastic, but it is by no means futile: it indicates the mental separation from nature that man has to make before he can be joined to God. In a sense it is really Samson who fulfils the prophecy in Psalm 91 quoted by Satan, for although he does fall under the temple and is crushed in the fall, his achievement, in its proper context, is providentially sustained.

If *Samson Agonistes* did not exist, we could say with some confidence that Milton could never have chosen Samson for a hero, because Samson is the only important Old Testament figure who simply will not fit into Milton's conception of the Old Testament. The statement remains essentially true even after we see how Milton has transmuted his hero. The stories about Samson in the Book of Judges are savage and primitive even for that very savage and primitive context. The Chorus does the best it can with Samson's chief and not very amiable virtue of total abstinence from wine, but it can only celebrate his feat of tearing up the gates of Gaza by suppressing the reason for his spending the night there. In nearly all the folk tales related to the Samson and Dalila motif, the part of Samson is played by an ogre or cannibal giant whom everyone is glad to be rid of, and the vicious and lethal practical jokes that Samson plays on the Philistines clearly roused a reserved admiration in Milton, even though he shared the bias of the Biblical narrative. Milton tells us that Samson, as he gropes for the pillars of the temple

> stood, as one who pray'd,
> Or some great matter in his mind revolv'd. (*SA*, ll. 1637–8)

We know from the Book of Judges that the subject of his meditations is a plea for private revenge, "only this once" [16:28]. This also has to be suppressed, as no catastrophe involving the will of God, for Milton, can take place without manifesting the axiom "Vengeance is mine," which belongs to a higher morality than the Biblical Samson can reach.

For Milton the Old Testament is the book of the law, and it is extraordinary to see how the wild berserker of the Book of Judges has been so tamed by Milton that he can find his way through a surprising amount of casuistry. The nicest legal points of the limits of civil obedience to a spiritually hostile power, of the obligations of a wife to a husband of a different nation and religion, of the relation of a deliberate action necessarily involving death to wilful suicide, of the distinction between command and constraint, are raised and debated with great skill in the play, most of them by Samson himself. Another set of associations of the Greek word *agon* is with law cases, where *agonistes* means advocate. This aspect of Samson connects with the legal metaphor in the Bible by which the conception of a redeemer developed out of words meaning an ally in a lawsuit or trial.

Samson has to work his way from bondage to liberty through the law, and hence to some extent he recapitulates Milton's own program for the people of England. Questions of religious, domestic, and civil liberty are the main issues raised in his colloquies with Manoa, Dalila, and the Philistine Officer. From the beginning Samson is marked out in contrast to his followers, who prefer "Bondage with ease then strenuous liberty" [*SA*, l. 271]. In worldly terms it is the maddest paradox that Samson, being worked to death as a slave in a Philistine mill, is actually closer to freedom than he would be living at ease in retirement at home, but as God conceives of liberty this is none the less true. Thus Manoa's proposal, made out of the most genuine love for Samson, is still a very subtle and dangerous temptation, as is more obvious when it is repeated, in a more sinister context, by Dalila. Dalila, of course, represents the threat to domestic liberty in its crucial form of marriage to an idolater. The Bible does not call Dalila Samson's wife, but in Milton she must be a wife to absorb his divorce arguments. The Officer's summons brings the whole dialectic of liberty in an ungodly world into a dramatic focus. So far as the Philistines are Samson's secular overlords, they have a right to his obedience; so far as he is being ordered to join in an act of worship to Dagon, they have none. Samson decides that what he is being summoned to is a religious event, and refuses to take part in it.

In *Paradise Regained*, after Christ has refused all of Satan's temptations, Satan sets him on the pinnacle of the temple, where he remains miraculously poised. Miraculously, because he has done all he can; what he has done has been accepted by the Father, and the Father moves in to sustain him at the crucial point. On a smaller scale, the Lady in *Comus*, still paralysed after repudiating Comus, is miraculously saved by Sabrina, according to the promise of the last two lines of the masque:

> Or if Vertue feeble were,
> Heav'n it self would stoop to her. [ll. 1021–2]

Samson has also done what he can and has also come to the end of his own will. As noted previously, during the encounter with Harapha Samson reasserts himself as a champion of Jehovah, and Harapha slinks off, perhaps because he was a coward anyway, but more likely because Samson's claim has been accepted. Samson is, like Jesus in *Paradise Regained*, a man under the law, to an exceptional degree because of his Nazarite vow. The nearest that any Old Testament character can get to the freedom of the gospel is a dispensation, when God transcends his own law, and moves his elect to do the same. Samson's first marriage to the woman of Timnah was such a dispensation. We are not told, either by Milton or the Bible, that his marriage to Dalila was one too, but if it were, the dispensation to Samson parallels the dispensation to Hosea, made for very different purposes, who was ordered first to marry a "wife of whoredoms" and then to "go again" and love an adulteress. The fact that God has fully accepted Samson once again is marked by another dispensation, when God's will takes over Samson's will and changes his mind about going to the festival. Of course, this moment also makes it certain that Samson will die, just as the moment of Christ's triumph over Satan in *Paradise Regained* makes the Crucifixion certain. Hence it is not only the crisis of the action, but the peripeteia or turning point of the tragedy. Samson says:

If I obey them,
I do it freely; venturing to displease
God for the fear of Man, and Man prefer,
Set God behind: which, in his jealousie
Shall never, unrepented, find forgiveness.
Yet that he may dispense with me or thee
Present in Temples at Idolatrous Rites
For some important cause, thou needst not doubt. (*SA*, ll. 1372–9)

The word "yet" may well be the most precisely marked peripeteia in the whole range of drama.

A second major change that Milton makes in Samson's character is in his relation to society. In heroic literature there is often a narrative tension, and sometimes a moral tension as well, between the themes of war and of quest. There is, let us say, a central war going on which it is the duty of heroes to engage in, but the crucial hero, whose presence is necessary for success, has withdrawn from the action or is on some private venture of his own. The role of Achilles in the *Iliad* comes readily to mind; much closer to the general tone of the Samson stories in the Bible is the situation in Ariosto. Here the heroes who are supposed to be fighting in a crusade, defending Paris against the infidels, keep wandering off and rescuing attractive heroines in remote quarters of the earth, and the climactic action, reminding the modern reader of the American crusade against Communism, is a trip to the moon to recollect some scattered heroic wits. In *Paradise Regained* the crusade and the lonely quest are united in the person of Christ, because for Milton Christ is the only figure in history in whom they could have been united.

Samson in the Bible is a pure quest figure: he lounges about the Philistine countryside killing and destroying and burning crops and sleeping with their women, but with no hint of any organization behind him. The final sentence in the Book of Judges, "He judged Israel twenty years,"[10] comes as a considerable shock: that Samson has never shown the slightest capacity to judge anything, much less lead a nation. But in Milton all Samson's exploits are carefully integrated into a consistent crusade for God's people against God's enemies. To the Chorus's reproach, "Yet *Israel* still serves with all his Sons," Samson responds, "That fault I take not on me" (*SA*, ll. 240–1), and goes on to show that the failure of his people to follow him was as crucial as his own failure. The same awareness of his social surroundings comes out even in details. When the timid Chorus expresses uneasiness after Harapha's departure, and again after the first exit of the Officer, Samson quiets their fears very unobtrusively, but in a way which shows the born leader under all the rags and filth and chains.

Samson's role as leader makes clear many things about *Samson Agonistes*, beginning with its date, which some people have tried to put earlier than 1660. The death of Samson, though tragic, points to a world above tragedy; the destruction of the Gaza aristocracy, though tragic, or at least "sad," as Manoa says [*SA*, l. 1560], points to a world below it. In between is the tragic failure of Israel to live up to its role as God's people. In many tragedies there is a nontragic point of escape indicated in the action, a moment of opportunity, of taking the tide of fortune at the flood, and the missing of this point is part of the parabola shape of tragedy, the point from which the "catastrophe," which means the downward turn, begins. Near the end of the play Manoa says that Samson

> To *Israel*
> Honour hath left, and freedom, let but them
> Find courage to lay hold on this occasion. (*SA*, ll. 1714–16)

But the Bible tells us that in a few years the Philistines were stronger than ever. As they occupied territory assigned to Dan in the conquest of Canaan, Dan moved out and went north. In the Book of Judges, the account of Samson is immediately followed by another story about the Danites in which, after appearing in a most contemptible light as idolaters, thieves, and murderers, they vanish from history. In Jacob's prophecy of the twelve tribes at the end of Genesis, Dan is described as a treacherous "serpent by the way" [49:17], and in the list of the twelve tribes in the Book of Revelation the name of Dan is omitted. For Milton this would practically mean being erased from the book of life.

The tragedy of Israel, and of Dan in particular, is an allegory of the tragedy of the English people, choosing a "captain back for *Egypt*," as Milton says in the *Ready and Easy Way* [*Works*, 6:149], and deliberately renouncing their great destiny. The self-identification of the blind Milton, living in retirement after the Restoration, with the blind Samson is impossible to miss: it is there in the complaints about poverty and disease, its furthest reach being perhaps the curious parenthesis about fair-weather friends: "of the most / I would be understood" (*SA*, ll. 190–1). But there may be some identification also with the hopeful and bitterly disappointed Manoa, if we think of the great image in *Areopagitica*: "Methinks

I see in my mind a noble and puissant Nation rousing herself like a strong man after sleep, and shaking her invincible locks" [*Works*, 4:344]. This is precisely Manoa's picture of Samson miraculously restored to his strength as though the blinding and captivity had been only a bad dream. In *Samson Agonistes* we are sombrely reminded not only of the original story of Samson, but of the fact that it was so brief and so ineffectual an episode in the history of Israel. Within a generation after the death of Dan's great champion, Dan had effectively ceased to exist as a tribe. No once-favoured group of people, whether Danites in Israel or Puritans in England, is likely to get a second chance to renounce its destiny.

In the criticism of Shakespeare we notice how much of what is written really amounts to a rationalizing of the acting. What is said about characters, repetition of imagery, or the mood and emotional tone of the play, is very often potentially a set of suggestions for some producer or group of actors to consider for a possible performance. The ontological status of such criticism is a matter of some interest, especially to those who believe that there is such a subject as hermeneutics. For *Samson Agonistes* the critical situation is considerably altered by the presence of a chorus. A chorus in the play is primarily a stylizing of the audience. The Danites in *Samson Agonistes*, like Job's friends, represent a kind of moral norm. They are on the right side and are carried along by the action to genuine profundity and eloquence at the end, but, like so many of Jesus' disciples, they never fully understand the meaning of the events they are involved in. They function as eyes for Samson, but they do not see what he sees. Some of the verse given them to speak seems to me to be doggerel, or, if that is too violent a word, an indication that the highest kind of spiritual insight is not being expressed.

From the point of view of the Chorus, the action of the play is a melodrama with Jehovah as hero and Dagon as villain. Jehovah is the true God: somehow or other the Philistines ought to know this; somehow or other they ought to accept, as a valid argument, Samson's explanation of his attack on them:

> I was no private but a person rais'd
> With strength sufficient and command from Heav'n
> To free my Countrey. (*SA*, ll. 1211–13)

Samson's act is cited by Milton in his *First Defence* as a precedent for the Parliamentary revolution. When God himself is a partisan actor in history, it is not difficult to hear in the background the tedious self-righteous cry: whatever we do is right because we're we, and they, after all, are only they.

Against this is the creative imagination of the poet working out his play, and giving to every aspect of that play its own realization. It is particularly in the last speech of Dalila that we can understand how Milton is a true poet, and of Dalila's party without knowing it, at least as long as he is speaking with her voice. The Chorus says smugly, "a manifest Serpent by her sting" (*SA*, l. 997), but we are bound to have some dramatic sympathy, if not moral sympathy, with Dalila in her desperate attempt to restore her self-respect, after Samson's bitter and contemptuous rejection of her, by building up a fantasy about her future fame. However we see her, we can understand that she sees herself as a kind of Antigone, damned whether she does or doesn't. When she designs a memorial for herself in language anticipating Manoa's design for Samson's tomb, we concur in the imaginative symmetry, just as we do in *Paradise Lost* when Moloch persuades Solomon to build him a temple opposite Zion. When she compares herself to Jael,[11] we can agree that Jael's act was also treacherous, if less cold-blooded than hers. Above all, when she appeals to Fame to justify her, we can see, at least for the moment, that although Fame seems the most arbitrary and whimsical of all gods, still there is a rough justice in his (or her) dispositions, and that he averages out to a more fair-minded god than a jealous Jehovah.

Then we come back with a shock to realize how much of Milton himself is standing in the *choros gerontōn*,[12] agreeing with them that God's ways are just and justifiable. For most modern readers, I should think, Milton's creative imagination is always right and his justifying apparatus always wrong: the imagination is that of a poet who is for all time; the apparatus comes from seventeenth-century anxieties which, at least on their political side, were as dead as mutton even before *Samson Agonistes* was written, to say nothing of three centuries later. Yet the imagination would probably never have conceived a line without the driving force of the anxieties. What is our final role as readers? Do we simply try to deliver the immortal poet from the "prison within prison" of the anxieties of his age and class, or can we find a place for them too in our response?

The answer begins with the fact that we have our own anxieties too, and that they are unlikely to meet the test of time any better than his. The task of criticism is neither to leave such a work as *Samson Agonistes* sitting in the seventeenth century, ignoring all the reasons for its appeal to us, nor to annex it to our own age, ignoring its original assumptions. The two points of 1671 and 1971 form the base of a triangle of which *Samson Agonistes* itself is the apex, in a world above both, though related to both.

Milton describes the action of *Paradise Lost*, at the beginning, as "this great Argument," and the action of Samson Agonistes, at the end, as "this great event." The question whether Christianity and tragedy are compatible has often been raised; the real question, however, is not that, but the relation of tragedy to a revolutionary attitude. I have tried to indicate very briefly the revolutionary qualities of the Biblical tradition which were followed so closely by Milton: its conception of God as having a historical role in delivering a subject nation from its overlords; its iconoclasm; its insistence on right belief; and its utter repudiation of all gods except its own. *Paradise Regained* and *Samson Agonistes* are both, in different ways, set within the human situation, and they therefore express the central revolutionary attitude, in both religious and social context, that Milton held and expressed in his prose writings.

The revolutionary mind does not reject tragedy, but it prefers to think of it as explicable, as something with a cause, and therefore, if possible, a cure. It is apt to get impatient with the contemplating of a tragic situation as an ultimate mystery at the heart of things. *Paradise Lost* is among other things an attempt to account for the origin of tragedy: it deals, rather more coherently than Nietzsche was later to do, with the birth of tragedy from the spirit of music. In the third book, however, Milton shifts the scene to the angelic order, above tragedy, where God explains the human situation from that perspective. Here Milton deserts the revolutionary point of view of his own religion, which means that, not being an angel, he is compelled to adopt the rival perspective of the pagan world. The model for the God of book 3 is Zeus in the *Odyssey*: nowhere in the Bible does God speak in such a tone. Still, the effort to gain a larger perspective on tragedy in *Paradise Lost* is deeply significant.

The supreme Greek god, from Homer to the Stoics, is, we said, an essential God, He Who is; the God of the burning bush is an existential I am. We may perhaps suggest, however simplistic it may sound, that when God is conceived as essential, tragedy becomes existential, and vice versa. In Greek literature tragedy is inherent in the human situation, and it is that partly because in the long run the gods can shrug it off and detach themselves from it. For Milton, no tragic action can take place without the will of God being directly involved, and therefore tragedy, for Milton, is ultimately explicable in terms of God's revelation. Writers who elude this antithesis, notably Shakespeare, cannot have a decisive influence on Milton's tragic form: Shakespeare's tragedies are not religious in so specific a sense.

So when the Chorus describes itself at the end of the play as being equipped

> with new acquist
> Of true experience from this great event (*SA*, ll. 1755–6)

it is possible that, once again, the Chorus does not fully understand what it is saying. It is seeing the death of Samson much as a Greek audience might see the end of *Oedipus at Colonus*, as a deep and awful mystery, something to be contemplated as a vision. It sees the hand of God in it, of course, but in a way that deepens the sense of mystery. The Danites see only as far as the old dispensation allows them to see. For Milton, and ideally for us, the words "new" and "true" carry a heavier weight of meaning: true experience is something that leads to renewed action, as the experience of losing Lycidas led his friend "Tomorrow to fresh Woods, and Pastures new." As the blinded Samson says to the sighted Harapha, in a line with a dozen kinds of irony in it, "The way to know were not to see but taste" (*SA*, l. 1091). Like the Chorus, we are led to "calm of mind all passion spent" [*SA*, l. 1758], but we are not necessarily old and tired and blinkered by the law. When catharsis dissipates, for an instant, the clouds of passions and prejudice and anxiety and special pleading, some of us may also catch a glimpse of a boundless energy which, however destructive to social establishments, is always there, always confronting us, and always the same, and yet has always the power to create all things anew.

6

Tribute to Balachandra Rajan

1985

From the typescript in NFF, 1991, box 40, file 2. This was written for a Festschrift in honour of Balachandra Rajan that was never published; Frye refers to and quotes from several of the unpublished papers intended for the Festschrift. Contributors included prominent Milton scholars, such as C.A. Patrides, as well as writers and scholars of Canadian literature (William Davison Butt, Hugh Hood, George Woodcock). The file also contains a preliminary typescript with holograph corrections.

The presence of Balachandra Rajan in the Canadian academic community has been a pure bonus: something that could never have been expected or deserved. In contrast to so many of the authors in Mr. Butt's brilliant survey, Canadians who dash around the world but set up the same stage sets and props wherever they get off the plane, Rajan is an Indian who has found Western intellectual patterns, Western languages, Western culture-heroes, congenial to him and has settled down with them. He is a most effective speaker at academic conferences, but his effectiveness is not itself simply academic: sincerity and authority have their own body language which is intelligible in itself. He is the kind of colleague who inspires a sense of security even in those in other universities who hardly ever see him: they still know that, in his office or classroom at least, the job is being done right.

However, this *Festschrift* is about a good deal more than that. It is rather about Rajan's "inconclusiveness," in the sense given the word by Mr. Patrides, where it has nothing to do with being tentative or unfinished, but refers to a necessary quality of any academic discipline dealing with an inexhaustible subject. After several hundred books and perhaps several thousand articles have appeared on one major writer, we may begin to feel, not that the writer is exhaustible, but that the assumptions on which the criticism of him are based in any given period may well be. Hence the present popularity of critical theory, which springs from a recognition that a genuine breakthrough in the assumptions of criticism would revitalize the critical treatment of the major classics. Many of the breakthroughs, naturally, turn out in practice to be merely hernias; many of them, on the other hand, are not so much new discoveries as rehabilitations of existing but neglected principles.

For example: anyone who talks about "the" style of *Paradise Lost* is wasting his reader's time. Milton has a great number of styles, each of them, in his word, "answerable" to its particular context [cf. *PL*, 9.20]. Beelzebub and Eve obviously cannot talk in the same "style": we should take this for granted, and not be deceived by the fact that they are both in a single poem written in iambic pentameter throughout. Rajan's chapter on the "Providence of Style" in *Paradise Lost*[1] starts at this point, and thereby rehabilitates the old word "decorum": the appropriateness of the style to the context or the person speaking. But he goes much further. All the different styles in the poem, he points out, are interconnected, "a web of involvement and relationship,"[2] which makes Satan's professions of independence doubly ironic. Every passage, even every line, resonates against the entire work: the result is artificial in the old and good sense of the word. "No other style could bear witness so powerfully to the nature of Providence . . . the order in which all things are justified and settled."[3] To which one can add only that Rajan's own lapidary style is also "providentially" related to his subject.

Again, if we look at the critical opinions on *Comus* summarized in the Variorum Milton,[4] we find page after page telling us that Milton was a poet, and therefore pagan and sensuous; but he was also a Puritan, which he shouldn't have been, because Puritanism is antipoetic, and therefore aesthetic and didactic elements in the same poem must be at odds with each other. Gradually but inexorably this assumption goes out of date, and so of course does all the criticism based on it. The progress from information to garbage is slower with criticism than with newspapers, but equally sure if a critic talks not about Milton as he was, but about what the critic himself would have been if he had been Milton. Rajan once again begins by rehabilitating the neglected principle that the more solidly a poet is planted in his own time, the clearer his communication to later ages will be. And once again he goes a great deal further, reaching the luminous conclusion, "Religious significances press in upon the world of *Comus* particularly in its central confrontation; but they do not transgress its decorum since the purpose of that decorum is to suggest how an action shaped in terms of a classical fable invokes and opens out into a Christian meaning."[5] Rajan avoids the "either/or" fallacy, but he does much more than avoid it: he reverses it into a positive elucidation of the poem's structure.

For Rajan the identity of a work of literature has two aspects: an aspect of unity, which is synchronic and structural, and an aspect of process, which is diachronic and open-ended. Hugh Hood's admirably clear essay explores Rajan's debts to Eliot and Yeats in building up his own critical view: Eliot, for example, not only laid down the essential critical principles in "Tradition and the Individual Talent," but wrote the *Quartets* serially during the war, thereby both completing the total form of his work and also showing how, according to Eliot's own axiom, each Quartet altered the direction of the process. In Yeats, Mr. Hood explains, we have a more dramatic form of dialectical conflict, with development and destruction working on each other, which has doubtless played an important role in Rajan's growing interest in the "form of the unfinished."[6]

Rajan has never attempted to make an overwhelming answer to the poet's overwhelming question, to "cover" the whole subject in some definitive and monumental way. Most efforts at this kind of response are ideologically inspired, and are concerned with social and political implications rather than strictly literary ones. Rajan is not a politically-minded critic, but of course his work has also its social aspect, and various elements in that aspect are studied by Mr. Hood, Mr. Woodcock, and Mr. Patrides. The last named points to the two novels, more particularly *The Dark Dancer*,[7] as being concerned with the conflicts of Eastern and Western social attitudes during a revolutionary time. It is clear that the revolutionary ferment in India has played some role in focusing Rajan's awareness of and sympathy with the revolutionary career of Milton, along with the opposed responses in Eliot and Yeats. This *Festschrift* is a remarkable tribute to a most remarkable man, whose quiet books, articles, edited books, and novels cannot be overlooked in the general noise of publication, because they create their own silence around them.

Essays on Blake

7

Blake on Trial Again

January 1947

Review of Mark Schorer, William Blake: The Politics of Vision *(New York: Henry Holt, 1946) and* The Portable Blake, *ed. Alfred Kazin (New York: Viking, 1946). From* Poetry: A Magazine of Verse, *69 (January 1947): 223–8. Reprinted in RW, 160–3.*

There has always been a tendency among critics of Blake to interpret him in terms of the critic's own time. Swinburne[1] dressed him in the tight sadistic corsets and exuberant rhetorical crinolines of the Victorian romantics; Symons[2] posed him among the bourgeois-baiters and *poètes maudits* of the turn of the century; and Middleton Murry[3] made him express the common postwar view that the gospel of Jesus might work if it were shot in one arm with a practical application of D.H. Lawrence and in the other with a theoretical approval of Marx. Bronowski's book[4] perhaps reflects the uneasy social conscience of a slightly later period, expressed in the dictum that poetry must be either tendentious or unreal. This dictum has been largely abandoned, and Blake now appears with such names as Rimbaud, Rilke, Kafka, Kierkegaard, Joyce, Yeats, and Henry James in the foreground of fashionable culture. Dr. Schorer, however, though he displays the pantheon of the *Partisan Review* with some prominence, agrees with Bronowski in regarding Blake's attitude to social questions as the key to his present modernity.

Modern criticism appears to be moving towards a showdown with the claim, advanced by many artists since the Romantic period at least, that the arts represent an autonomous and authoritative prophetic tradition which is as significant for religion as for culture. The controversy at present seems to revolve elliptically around two foci: the angelic Rilke, who stands for a complete and selfless acceptance of the artist's prophetic role, and the demonic Rimbaud, who stands for the total rejection of it. Blake appears to Dr. Schorer more or less as a poet who tried to be Rilke and Rimbaud at once and failed to be either. He accepted the prophetic role of the artist, identified art and religion, and devoted his own life utterly to art, but, Dr. Schorer says, "demanded too much of art because he hoped for so much from life."[5] For instead of waiting quietly as Rilke did for the word to form itself, he took the impatient Rimbaud path, and plunged into Rimbaud's "long, immense et raisonné dérèglement de tous les sens."[6] The result was a Rilke who became steadily less, instead of more, articulate, a Rimbaud who destroyed the unity of his vision but refused to shut up. The reason for Blake's course was, says Dr. Schorer, his entanglement in another dichotomy, the contrast between pure and applied poetry, the palace of art and the marketplace of society. Blake had a deep interest in the revolutionary movements of his time, wrote several revolutionary poems and came in touch with a group of prominent radicals. Yet he found their type of rationalism poetically indigestible, and when he turned his wonderful lyrical gifts to the expression of revolutionary ideas, he had to evolve a poetic language which would communicate conceptions of a kind fundamentally antagonistic to his type of genius. Hence the enormous development of myth and symbol in his "Prophecies," which, as it continued to complicate itself, became a malignant and cancerous growth on his poetry.

Dr. Schorer intends his approach to be sympathetic and not hostile, and (in spite of a garrulous discursiveness which spoils the shape of the book)[7] his study has many virtues. He has an erudite knowledge of Blake's background which enables him to relate Blake to his time instead of isolating him like a cultural leper, as is customary; and he has cut out all the traditional verbiage about the lonely and enraptured mystic who looked upon the face of God. But in ending as he does with a sigh and a shake of the head, he has really put the old charge of madness into twentieth-century euphemisms. For though he certainly does not regard the term madness as having any meaning, he yet applies to the Prophecies the same opinion that many of Blake's contemporaries expressed about his painting: that he could have been the greatest genius of his age had it not been for a curious mental perversity.

But if Blake was a failure he was an amazingly confident one. "Mark well my words! they are of your eternal salvation," he says,[8] and he never conceded any validity to the adverse criticisms of his poems with which he was fully and painfully familiar. He was hurt by neglect, of course, especially when it took the form of insult and abuse; but he continued placidly to live in paradise, as his wife said,[9] and he obviously succeeded in getting something well worth having, whether we can follow his explanation of what it was or not. The mind that conceived the transparent clarity of the *Songs of Innocence* also conceived *Jerusalem*, and the odds that Blake was right even about his Prophecies have gone steadily up with the gradual rise of his reputation since his death. One scholar after another has informed the English public that in singing the hymn wrongly called "Jerusalem" they are endorsing the Anglo-Israelite superstition, but the public knows better, and obstinately keeps on singing it. The issues raised by Dr. Schorer are real issues, and the verdict of so grave and thoughtful a scholar must be treated with respect; but the best way to approach Blake is to surrender unconditionally to Blake's own terms.

This addition of *The Portable Blake* to a well-known series gives us the lyrics and minor Prophecies (including the *Gates of Paradise* engravings) fairly complete, snippets from the longer Prophecies, selections from the prose (some letters, and the bulk of the *Descriptive Catalogue*, the Rossetti MS material, and the marginalia), the Job engravings, and the extracts from Crabb Robinson's diary relating to Blake. Except for the last two, all this is in (and apparently reprinted from) Keynes's one-volume edition, *The Poetry and Prose of William Blake*, now in print again in England, which contains everything Blake ever wrote, and, it is perhaps ill-natured to add, is also a quite portable volume. It is unfortunate that so few of the marginalia are accompanied by the portions of the text on which they comment, so that such a remark as, "Well Said Enough!" [K464/E652] in the marginalia to Reynolds's *Discourses* is simply left in the air. The brilliant and amusing *Island in the Moon* is omitted, though it might well have replaced the fragments of the longer Prophecies.

Mr. Kazin's Introduction follows Dr. Schorer's general line of approach, and is often sensitive and eloquent in dealing with the lyrical poems. On the deeper aspects of Blake's thought as represented in the Prophecies he is, again like Dr. Schorer, simply not good enough. It is curious that he refers to Foster Damon's study,[10] quite correctly, as "one of the great landmarks in Blake scholarship," and yet does not see how that study, by demonstrating at least something of the powerful articulation of ideas in the Prophecies, has already disproved so many of his own assertions. To say that a large part of Blake's writing is rant is hopelessly dated criticism. In general, it may be said of Mr. Kazin, as to a lesser extent of Dr. Schorer, that his desire to explain Blake to the reader has not proved equal to his desire to have the reader overhear him making learned and acute comments about Blake, with the result that the reader gets a much clearer impression of the sagacity of the critic than of the genius of the subject. Neither writer, of course, has intended to produce such an impression, which is really the result of a defective method, a reluctance to come to grips with the whole Blake because of a fear that Blake is not intelligent enough to withstand exhaustive scrutiny, that he will let the reader down who looks long and deeply into his obscurities in the hope of some reward. But if one quality in Blake is clear it is his honesty, and honest poets do not let their readers down.

8

Review of *The Portable Blake*

October 1947

Review of The Portable Blake, *ed. Alfred Kazin (New York: Viking, 1946). From* University of Toronto Quarterly, *17 (October 1947): 107.*

The Portable Blake gives all the best lyrics, the "minor" or shorter Prophecies almost complete, good extracts from the letters and miscellaneous writings, and extracts from the three long Prophecies. In addition there are the Job engravings and the passages relating to Blake from Crabb Robinson's diary, besides the editorial comment. One curious blunder is the printing of the marginalia without the original passages to which they refer even when the comment (for example, "Well Said Enough!" or "Damned Fool!" [K464, 467/E652, 656]) does not stand alone. The Job series also carries only the leading Biblical quotations underneath, and hardly suggests the conception of Job as an epitome of Biblical symbolism which the variety of quotation in the original is designed to suggest. The extracts from the long Prophecies are skilfully made, though from a purple-passage attitude towards them which I find unacceptable. The brilliant satire *An Island in the Moon,* which shows a unique side of Blake's genius, is the most conspicuous omission. The introduction attempts with fair success to give a sympathetic impression of Blake's personality, though it follows the enraptured-crank stereotype too closely, and avoids the deeper aspects of his thought altogether. The book can be recommended as a classroom text, as it is considerably cheaper than the complete one-volume *Poetry and Prose* edited by Keynes, from which its text is taken, and which presumably the serious student would prefer having.

9

Blake's Treatment of the Archetype

1950

From English Institute Essays, 1950, *ed. Alan S. Downer (New York: Columbia University Press, 1951), 170–96. Reprinted in* Discussions of William Blake, *ed. John E. Grant (Boston: Heath, 1961), 6–16;* Critics on Blake, *ed. Judith O'Neill (Coral Gables: University of Florida Press, 1970), 47–61; and* Blake's Poetry and Designs, *ed. Mary Lynn Johnson and John E. Grant (New York: Norton, 1979), 510–25.*

The reader of Blake soon becomes familiar with the words "innocence" and "experience." The world of experience is the world that adults live in while they are awake. It is a very big world, and a lot of it seems to be dead, but still it makes its own kind of sense. When we stare at it, it stares unwinkingly back, and the changes that occur in it are, on the whole, orderly and predictable changes. This quality in the world that reassures us we call law. Sitting in the middle of the lawful world is the society of awakened adults. This society consists of individuals who apparently have agreed to put certain restraints on themselves. So we say that human society is also controlled by law. Law, then, is the basis both of reason and of society: without it there is no happiness, and our philosophers tell us that they really do not know which is more splendid, the law of the starry heavens outside us, or the moral law within.[1] True, there was a time when we were children and took a different view of life. In childhood happiness seemed to be based, not on law and reason, but on love, protection, and peace. But we can see now that such a view of life was an illusion derived from an excess of economic security. As Isaac Watts says, in a song of innocence which is thought to have inspired Blake:

> Sleep, my babe; thy food and raiment,
>   House and home, thy friends provide;
> All without thy care or payment:
>   All thy wants are well supplied.[2]

And after all, from the adult point of view, the child is not so innocent as he looks. He is actually a little bundle of anarchic will, whose desires take no account of either the social or the natural order. As he grows up and enters the world of law, his illegal desires can no longer be tolerated even by himself, and so they are driven underground into the world of the dream, to be joined there by new desires, mainly sexual in origin. In the dream, a blind, unreasoning, childish will is still at work revenging itself on experience and rearranging it in terms of desire. It is a great comfort to know that this world, in which we are compelled to spend about a third of our time, is unreal, and can never displace the world of experience in which reason predominates over passion, order over chaos, Classical values over Romantic ones, the solid over the gaseous, and the cool over the hot.

The world of law, stretching from the starry heavens to the moral conscience, is the domain of Urizen in Blake's symbolism. It sits on a volcano in which the rebellious Titan Orc, the spirit of passion, lies bound, writhing and struggling to get free. Each of these spirits is Satanic or devilish to the other. While we dream, Urizen, the principle of reality, is the censor, or, as Blake calls him, the accuser, a smug and grinning hypocrite, an impotent old man, the caricature that the child in us makes out of the adult world that thwarts him. But as long as we are awake, Orc, the lawless pleasure principle, is an evil dragon bound under the conscious world in chains, and we all hope he will stay there.

The dream world is, however, not quite securely bound: every so often it breaks loose and projects itself on society in the form of war. It seems odd that we should keep plunging with great relief into moral holidays of aggression in which robbery and murder become virtues instead of crimes. It almost suggests that keeping our desires in leash and seeing that others do likewise is a heavy and sooner or later an intolerable strain. On a still closer view, even the difference between war and law begins to blur. The social contract, which from a distance seems a reasonable effort of cooperation, looks closer up like an armed truce founded on passion, in which the real purpose of law is to defend by force what has been snatched in self-will. Plainly, we cannot settle the conflict of Orc and Urizen by siding with one against the other, still less by pretending that either of them is an illusion. We must look for a third factor in human life, one which meets the requirements of both the dream and the reality.

This third factor, called Los by Blake, might provisionally be called work, or constructive activity. All such work operates in the world of experience: it takes account of law and of our waking ideas of reality. Work takes the energy which is wasted in war or thwarted in dreams and sets it free to act in experience. And as work cultivates land and makes farms and gardens out of jungle and wilderness, as it domesticates animals and builds cities, it becomes increasingly obvious that work is the realization of a dream and that this dream is descended from the child's lost vision of a world where the environment is the home.

The worker, then, does not call the world of experience real because he perceives it out of a habit acquired from his ancestors: it is real to him only as the material cause of his work. And the world of dreams is not unreal, but the formal cause: it dictates the desirable human shape which the work assumes. Work, therefore, by realizing in experience the child's and the dreamer's worlds, indicates what there is about each that is genuinely innocent. When we say that a child is in the state of innocence, we do not mean that he is sinless or harmless, but that he is able to assume a coherence, a simplicity, and a kindliness in the world that adults have lost and wish they could regain. When we dream, we are, whatever we put into the dream, revolting against experience and creating another world, usually one we like better. Whatever in childhood or the dream is delivered and realized by work is innocent; whatever is suppressed or distorted by experience becomes selfish or vicious. "He who desires but acts not, breeds pestilence" [K151/E35].

Work begins by imposing a human form on nature, for "Where man is not, nature is barren" [K152/E38]. But in society work collides with the cycle of law and war. A few seize all its benefits and become idlers, the work of the rest is wasted in supporting them, and so work is perverted into drudgery. "God made Man happy & Rich, but the Subtil made the innocent, Poor."[3] Neither idleness nor drudgery can be work: real work is the creative act of a free man, and wherever real work is going on it is humanizing society as well as nature. The work that, projected on nature, forms civilization, becomes, when projected on society, prophecy, a vision of complete human freedom and equality. Such a vision is a revolutionary force in human life, destroying all the social barriers founded on idleness and all the intellectual ones founded on ignorance.

So far we have spoken only of what seems naturally and humanly possible, of what can be accomplished by human nature. But if we confine the conception of work to what now seems possible, we are still judging the dream by the canons of waking reality. In other words, we have quite failed to distinguish work from law, Los from Urizen, and are back where we started. The real driving power of civilization and prophecy is not the mature mind's sophisticated and cautious adaptations of the child's or the dreamer's desires: it comes from the original and innocent form of those desires, with all their reckless disregard of the lessons of experience.

The creative root of civilization and prophecy can only be art, which deals not only with the possible, but with "probable impossibilities"—it is interesting to see Blake quoting Aristotle's phrase in one of his marginalia.[4] And just as the controlling idea of civilization is the humanizing of nature, and the controlling idea of prophecy the emancipation of man, so the controlling idea of art, the source of them both, must be the simultaneous vision of both. This is apocalypse, the complete transformation of both nature and human nature into the same form. "Less than All cannot satisfy Man" [K97/E2]; the child in us who cries for the moon will never stop crying until the moon is his plaything, until we are delivered from the tyranny of time, space, and death, from the remoteness of a gigantic nature, and from our own weakness and selfishness. Man cannot be free until he is everywhere: at the centre of the universe, like the child, and at the circumference of the universe, like the dreamer. Such an apocalypse is entirely impossible under the conditions of experience that we know, and could only take place in the eternal and infinite context that is given it by religion. In fact, Blake's view of art could almost be defined as the attempt to realize the religious vision in human society. Such religion has to be sharply distinguished from all forms of religion which have been kidnapped by the cycle of law and war, and have become capable only of reinforcing the social contract or of inspiring crusades.

When we say that the goal of human work can only be accomplished in eternity, many people would infer that this involves renouncing all practicable improvement of human status in favour of something which by hypothesis remains forever out of man's reach. We make this inference because we confuse the eternal with the indefinite: we are so possessed by the categories of time and space that we can hardly think of eternity and infinity except as endless time and space, respectively. But the home of time, so to speak, the only part of time that man can live in, is now; and the home of space is here. In the world of experience there is no such time as now; the present never quite exists, but is hidden somewhere between a past that no longer exists and a future that does not yet exist. The mature man does not know where "here" is: he can draw a circle around himself and say that "here" is inside it, but he cannot locate anything except a "there." In both time and space man is being continually excluded from his own home. The dreamer, whose space is inside his mind, has a better notion of where "here" is, and the child, who is not yet fully conscious of the iron chain of memory that binds his ego to time and space, still has some capacity for living in the present. It is to this perspective that man returns when his conception of "reality" begins to acquire some human meaning.

> The Sky is an immortal Tent built by the Sons of Los:
> And every Space that a Man views around his dwelling-place
> Standing on his own roof or in his garden on a mount
> Of twenty-five cubits in height, such space is his Universe:
> And on its verge the Sun rises & sets, the Clouds bow
> To meet the flat Earth & the Sea in such an order'd Space:
> The Starry heavens reach no further, but here bend and set
> On all sides, & the two Poles turn on their Valves of gold . . .
>
> [*M*, 29.4–11; K516/E127]

If the vision of innocence is taken out of its eternal and infinite context, the real here and now, and put inside time, it becomes either a myth of a golden age or a paradise lost in the past, or a hope which is yet to be attained in the future, or both. If it is put inside space, it must be somewhere else, presumably in the sky. It is only these temporal and spatial perversions of the innocent vision that really do snatch it out of man's grasp. Because the innocent vision is so deep down in human consciousness and is subject to so much distortion, repression, and censorship, we naturally tend, when we project it on the outer world, to put it as far off in time and space as we can get it. But what the artist has to reveal, as a guide for the work of civilization and prophecy, is the form of the world as it would be if we could live in it here and now.

Innocence and experience are the middle two of four possible states. The state of experience Blake calls Generation, and the state of innocence, the potentially creative world of dreams and childhood, Beulah. Beyond Beulah is Eden, the world of the apocalypse in which innocence and experience have become the same thing, and below Generation is Ulro, the world as it is when no work is being done, the world where dreams are impotent and waking life haphazard. Eden and Ulro are, respectively, Blake's heaven or unfallen world and his hell or fallen world. Eden is the world of the creator and the creature, Beulah the world of the lover and the beloved, Generation the world of the subject and the object, and Ulro the world of the ego and the enemy, or the obstacle. This is, of course, one world, looked at in four different ways. The four ways represent the four moods or states in which art is created: the apocalyptic mood of Eden, the idyllic mood of Beulah, the elegiac mood of Generation, and the satiric mood of Ulro. These four moods are the tonalities of Blake's expression; every poem of his regularly resolves on one of them.

For Blake the function of art is to reveal the human or intelligible form of the world, and it sees the other three states in relation to that form. This fact is the key to Blake's conception of imagery, the pattern of which I have tried to simplify by a table.

EXPERIENCE		CATEGORY	INNOCENCE	
Individual Form	*Collective Form*		*Collective Form*	*Individual Form*
sky-god (Nobodaddy)	aristocracy of gods	(1) Divine	human powers	incarnate God (Jesus)
a) leader and high priest (Caiaphas)	tyrants and victims	(2) Human	community	a) one man (Albion)
b) harlot (Rahab)				b) bride (Jerusalem)
dragon (Covering Cherub)	beasts of prey (tiger, leviathan)	(3) Animal	flock of sheep	one lamb (Bowlahoola)
tree of mystery	forest, wilderness (Entuthon Benython)	(4) Vegetable	garden or park (Allamanda)	tree of life
a) opaque furnace or brick kilns	a) city of destruction (Sodom, Babylon, Egypt)	(5) Mineral	city, temple (Golgonooza)	living stone
b) "Stone of Night"	b) ruins, caves			
(not given)	salt lake or dead sea (Udan Adan)	(6) Chaotic	fourfold river of life	"Globule of Blood"

Let us take the word "image" in its vulgar sense, which is good enough just now, of a verbal or pictorial replica of a physical object. For Blake the real form of the object is what he calls its "human form." In Ulro, the world with no human work in it, the mineral kingdom consists mainly of shapeless rocks lying around at random. When man comes into the world, he tries to make cities, buildings, roads, and sculptures out of this mineral kingdom. Such human artefacts therefore constitute the intelligible form of the mineral world, the mineral world as human desire would like to see it. Similarly, the "natural" or unworked form of the vegetable world is a forest, a heath, or a wilderness; its human and intelligible form is that of the garden, the grove, or the park, the last being the original meaning of the word "paradise." The natural form of the animal world consists of beasts of prey: its human form is a society of domesticated animals of which the flock of sheep is the most commonly employed symbol. The city, the garden, and the sheepfold are thus the human forms of the mineral, vegetable, and animal kingdoms, respectively. Blake calls these archetypes Golgonooza, Allamanda, and Bowlahoola, and identifies them with the head, heart, and bowels of the total human form. Below the world of solid substance is a chaotic or liquid world, and the human form of that is the river or circulating body of fresh water.

Each of these human forms has a contrasting counterpart in Ulro, the world of undeveloped nature and regressive humanity. To the city which is the home of the soul or City of God, the fallen world opposes the city of destruction which is doomed through the breakdown of work described by Ezekiel in a passage quoted by Blake as "pride, fullness of bread, & abundance of Idleness" [Ezekiel 16:49].[5] Against the image of the sheep in the pasture, we have the image of the forest inhabited by menacing beasts like the famous tiger, the blasted heath or waste land full of monsters, or the desert with its fiery serpents. To the river which is the water of life the fallen world opposes the image of the devouring sea and the dragons and leviathans in its depths. Blake usually calls the fallen city Babylon, the forest Entuthon Benython, and the dead sea or salt lake Udan Adan. Labyrinths and mazes are the only patterns of Ulro; images of highways and paths made straight belong to the world informed with intelligence.

The essential principle of the fallen world appears to be discreteness or opacity. Whatever we see in it we see as a self-enclosed entity, unlike all others. When we say that two things are identical, we mean that they are very similar; in other words "identity" is a meaningless word in ordinary experience. Hence in Ulro, and even in Generation, all classes or societies are aggregates of similar but separate individuals. But when man builds houses out of stones, and cities out of houses, it becomes clear that the real or intelligible form of a thing includes its relation to its environment as well as its self-contained existence. This environment is its own larger "human form." The stones that make a city do not cease to be stones, but they cease to be separate stones: their purpose, shape, and function is identical with that of the city as a whole. In the human world, as in the work of art, the individual thing is there, and the total form which gives it meaning is there: what has vanished is the shapeless collection or mass of similar things. This is what Blake means when he says that in the apocalypse all human forms are "identified" [*J*, 99.1–2; K747/E258]. The same is true of the effect of work on human society. In a completely human society man would not lose his individuality, but he would lose his separate and isolated ego, what Blake calls his Selfhood. The prophetic vision of freedom and equality thus cannot stop at the Generation level of a Utopia, which means an orderly molecular aggregate of individuals existing in some future time. Such a vision does not capture, though it may adumbrate, the real form of society, which can only be a larger human body. This means literally the body of one man, though not of a separate man.

Everywhere in the human world we find that the Ulro distinction between the singular and the plural has broken down. The real form of human society is the body of one man; the flock of sheep is the body of one lamb; the garden is the body of one tree, the so-called tree of life. The city is the body of one building or temple, a house of many mansions, and the building itself is the body of one stone, a glowing and fiery precious stone, the unfallen stone of alchemy which assimilates everything else to itself, Blake's grain of sand which contains the world.

The second great principle of Ulro is the principle of hierarchy or degree which produces the great chain of being. In the human world there is no chain of being: all aspects of existence are equal as well as identical. The one man is also the one lamb, and the body and blood of the animal form are the bread and wine which are the human forms of the vegetable world. The tree of life is the upright vertebrate form of man; the living stone, the glowing transparent furnace, is the furnace of heart and lungs and bowels in the animal body. The river of life is the blood that circulates within that body. Eden, which according to Blake was a city as well as a garden, had a fourfold river, but no sea, for the river remained inside paradise, which was the body of one man. England is an island in the sea, like St. John's Patmos; the human form of England is Atlantis, the island which has replaced the sea. Again, where there is no longer any difference between society and the individual, there can hardly be any difference between society and marriage or between a home and a wife or child. Hence Jerusalem in Blake is "A City, yet a Woman,"[6] and at the same time the vision of innocent human society.

On the analogy of the chain of being, it is natural for man to invent an imaginary category of gods above him, and he usually locates them in what is above him in space, that is, the sky. The more developed society is, the more clearly man realizes that a society of gods would have to be, like the society of man, the body of one God. Eventually he realizes that the intelligible forms of man and of whatever is above man on the chain of being must be identical. The identity of God and man is for Blake the whole of Christianity: the adoration of a superhuman God he calls natural religion, because the source of it is remote and unconquered nature. In other words, the superhuman God is the deified accuser or censor of waking experience, whose function it is to discourage further work. Blake calls this God Nobodaddy, and curses and reviles him so much that some have inferred that he was inspired by an obscure psychological compulsion to attack the Fatherhood of God. Blake is doing nothing of the kind, as a glance at the last plate of *Jerusalem* will soon show: he is merely insisting that man cannot approach the superhuman aspect of God except through Christ, the God who is Man. If man attempts to approach the Father directly, as Milton, for instance, does in a few unlucky passages in *Paradise Lost*, all he will ever get is Nobodaddy. Theologically, the only unusual feature of Blake is not his attitude to the person of the Father, but his use of what is technically known as pre-existence: the doctrine that the humanity of Christ is coeternal with his divinity.

There is nothing in the Ulro world corresponding to the identity of the individual and the total form in the unfallen one. But natural religion, being a parody of real religion, often develops a set of individual symbols corresponding to the lamb, the tree of life, the glowing stone, and the rest. This consolidation of Ulro symbols Blake calls Druidism. Man progresses toward a free and equal community, and regresses toward tyranny; and as the human form of the community is Christ, the one God who is one Man, so the human form of tyranny is the isolated hero or inscrutable leader with his back to an aggregate of followers, or the priest of a veiled temple with an imaginary sky-god supposed to be behind the veil. The Biblical prototypes of this leader and priest are Moses and Aaron. Against the tree of life we have what Blake calls the tree of mystery, the barren fig tree, the dead tree of the cross, Adam's tree of knowledge, with its forbidden fruit corresponding to the fruits of healing on the tree of life. Against the fiery precious stone, the bodily form in which John saw God "like a jasper and a sardine stone" [Revelation 4:3], we have the furnace, the prison of heat without light which is the form of the opaque warm-blooded body in the world of frustration, or the stone of Druidical sacrifice like the one that Hardy associates with Tess. Against the animal body of the lamb, we have the figure that Blake calls, after Ezekiel, the Covering Cherub, who represents a great many things, the unreal world of gods, human tyranny and exploitation, and the remoteness of the sky, but whose animal form is that of the serpent or dragon wrapped around the forbidden tree. The dragon, being both monstrous and fictitious, is the best animal representative of the bogies inspired by human inertia: the Book of Revelation calls it "the beast that was, and is not, and yet is" [17:8].

Once we have understood Blake's scheme of imagery, we have broken the back of one of the main obstacles to reading the Prophecies: the difficulty in grasping their narrative structure. Narrative is normally the first thing we look for in trying to read a long poem, but Blake's poems are presented as a series of engraved plates, and the mental process of following a narrative sequence is, especially in the later poems, subordinated to a process of comprehending an interrelated pattern of images and ideas. The plate in Blake's epics has a function rather similar to that of the stanza with its final alexandrine in *The Faerie Queene*: it brings the narrative to a full stop and forces the reader to try to build up from the narrative his own reconstruction of the author's meaning. Blake thinks almost entirely in terms of two narrative structures. One of these is the narrative of history, the cycle of law and war, the conflict of Orc and Urizen, which in itself has no end and no point and may be called the tragic or historical vision of life. The other is the comic vision of the apocalypse or work of Los, the clarification of the mind which enables one to grasp the human form of the world. But the latter is not concerned with temporal sequence and is consequently not so much a real narrative as a dialectic.

The tragic narrative is the story of how the dream world escapes into experience and is gradually imprisoned by experience. This is the main theme of heroic or romantic poetry and is represented in Blake by Orc.

Orc is first shown us, in the *Preludium* to *America*, as the libido of the dream, a boy lusting for a dim maternal figure and bitterly hating an old man who keeps him in chains. Then we see him as the conquering hero of romance, killing dragons and sea monsters, ridding the barren land of its impotent aged kings, freeing imprisoned women, and giving new hope to men. Finally we see him subside into the world of darkness again from whence he emerged, as the world of law slowly recovers its balance. His rise and decline has the rotary movement of the solar and seasonal cycles, and like them is a part of the legal machinery of nature.

Blake has a strong moral objection to all heroic poetry that does not see heroism in its proper tragic context, and even when it does, he is suspicious of it. For him the whole conception of *κλέα ἀνδρῶν*[7] as being in itself, without regard to the larger consequences of brave deeds, a legitimate theme for poetry, has been completely outmoded. It has been outmoded, for one thing, by Christianity, which has brought to the theme of the heroic act a radically new conception of what a hero is and what an act is. The true hero is the man who, whether as thinker, fighter, artist, martyr, or ordinary worker, helps in achieving the apocalyptic vision of art; and an act is anything that has a real relation to that achievement. Events such as the battle of Agincourt or the retreat from Moscow are not really heroic, because they are not really acts: they are part of the purposeless warfare of the state of nature and are not progressing towards a better kind of humanity. So Blake is interested in Orc only when his heroism appears to coincide with something of potentially apocalyptic importance, like the French or American revolutions.

For the rest, he keeps Orc strictly subordinated to his main theme of the progressive work of Los, the source of which is found in prophetic scriptures, especially, of course, the Bible. Comprehensive as his view of art is, Blake does not exactly say that the Bible is a work of art: he says "The Old & New Testaments are the Great Code of Art" [K777/E274]. The Bible tells the artist what the function of art is and what his creative powers are trying to accomplish. Apart from its historical and political applications, Blake's symbolism is almost entirely Biblical in origin, and the subordination of the heroic Orc theme to the apocalyptic Los theme follows the Biblical pattern.

The tragic vision of life has the rhythm of the individual's organic cycle: it rises in the middle and declines at the end. The apocalyptic theme turns the tragic vision inside out. The tragedy comes in the middle, with the eclipse of the innocent vision, and the story ends with the re-establishment of the vision. Blake's major myth thus breaks into two parts, a Genesis and an Exodus. The first part accounts for the existence of the world of experience in terms of the myths of creation and fall. Blake sees no difference between creation and fall, between establishing the Ulro world and placing man in it. How man fell out of a city and garden is told twice in Genesis, once of Adam and once of Israel—Israel, who corresponds to Albion in Blake's symbolism, being both a community and a single man. The Book of Genesis ends with Israel in Egypt, the city of destruction. In the Book of Exodus we find the state of experience described in a comprehensive body of Ulro symbols. There is the fallen civilization of Egypt, destroyed by the plagues which its own tyranny has raised, the devouring sea, the desert with its fiery serpents, the leader and the priest, the invisible sky-god who confirms their despotic power, and the labyrinthine wanderings of a people who have nothing but law and are unable to work. Society has been reduced to a frightened rabble following a leader who obviously has no notion of where he is going. In front of it is the Promised Land with its milk and honey, but all the people can see are enemies, giants, and mysterious terrors. From there on the story splits in two. The histories go on with the Orc or heroic narrative of how the Israelites conquered Canaan and proceeded to run through another cycle from bondage in Egypt to bondage in Babylon. But in the prophecies, as they advance from social criticism to apocalyptic, the Promised Land is the city and garden that all human effort is trying to reach, and its conqueror can only be the Messiah or true form of man.

The New Testament has the same structure as the Old. In the life of Jesus the story of the Exodus is repeated. Jesus is carried off to Egypt by a father whose name is Joseph, Herod corresponds to Pharaoh, and the massacre of the innocents to the attempts to exterminate the Hebrew children. The organizing of Christianity around twelve disciples corresponds to the organizing of the religion of Israel among twelve tribes, the forty days wandering of Jesus in the desert to the forty years of Israel, the Crucifixion to the lifting of the brazen serpent on the pole, and the Resurrection to the invasion of Canaan by Joshua, who has the same name as Jesus. From there on the New Testament splits into a historical section describing the beginning of a new Christian cycle, which is reaching its Babylonian phase in Blake's own time, and a prophetic section, the Book of Revelation, which deals with what it describes, in a phrase which has fascinated so many apocalyptic thinkers from Joachim of Fiore to

Blake, as the "everlasting gospel," the story of Jesus told not historically as an event in the past, but visually as a real presence.

The characters of Blake's poems—Orc, Los, Urizen, Vala, and the rest—take shape in accordance with Blake's idea of the real act. No word in the language contains a greater etymological lie than the word "individual." The so-called undivided man is a battleground of conflicting forces, and the appearance of consistency in his behaviour derives from the force that usually takes the lead. To get at the real elements of human character, one needs to get past the individual into the dramatis personae that make up his behaviour. Blake's analysis of the individual shows a good many parallels with more recent analyses, especially those of Freud and Jung. The scheme of the Four Zoas is strikingly Freudian, and the contrast of the Orc and Los themes in Blake is very like the contrast between Jung's early book on the libido and his later study of the symbols of individuation.[8] Jung's anima and persona are closely analogous to Blake's emanation and spectre, and his counsellor and shadow seem to have some relation to Blake's Los and Spectre of Urthona.

But a therapeutic approach will still relate any such analysis primarily to the individual. In Blake anything that is a significant act of individual behaviour is also a significant act of social behaviour. Orc, the libido, produces revolution in society: Vala, the elusive anima, produces the social code of *Frauendienst;*[9] Urizen, the moral censor, produces the religion of the externalized God. "We who dwell on Earth can do nothing of ourselves," says Blake: "every thing is conducted by Spirits" [*J*, pl. 3; K621/E145]. Man performs no act as an individual: all his acts are determined by an inner force which is also a social and historical force, and they derive their significance from their relation to the total human act, restoration of the innocent world. John Doe does nothing as John Doe: he eats and sleeps in the spirit of Orc the Polypus: he obeys laws in the spirit of Urizen the conscience; he loses his temper in the spirit of Tharmas the destroyer; and he dies in the spirit of Satan the death impulse.

Furthermore, as the goal of life is the humanization of nature, there is a profound similarity between human and natural behaviour, which in the apocalypse becomes identity. It is a glimmering of this fact that has produced the god, the personalized aspect of nature, and a belief in gods gradually builds the sense of an omnipotent personal community out of nature. As long as these gods remain on the other side of nature, they are merely the shadows of superstition: when they are seen to be the real elements of human life as well, we have discovered the key to all symbolism in art. Blake's Tharmas, the "id" of the individual and the stampeding mob of society, is also the god of the sea, Poseidon the earth-shaker. His connection with the sea is not founded on resemblance or association, but, like the storm scene in *King Lear*, on an ultimate identity of human rage and natural tempest.

In the opening plates of *Jerusalem* Blake has left us a poignant account of one such struggle of contending forces within himself, between his creative powers and his egocentric will. He saw the Industrial Revolution and the great political and cultural changes that came with it, and he realized that something profoundly new and disquieting was coming into the world, something with unlimited possibilities for good or for evil, which it would tax all his powers to interpret. And so his natural desire to make his living as an engraver and a figure in society collided with an overwhelming impulse to tell the whole poetic truth about what he saw. The latter force won, and dictated its terms accordingly. He was not allowed to worry about his audience. He revised, but was not allowed to decorate or stylize, only to say what had to be said. He was not allowed the double talk of the sophisticated poet, who can address several levels of readers at once by using familiar conceptions ambiguously. Nothing was allowed him but a terrifying concentration of his powers of utterance.

What finally emerged, out of one of the hottest poetic crucibles of modern times, was a poetry which consisted almost entirely in the articulation of archetypes. By an archetype I mean an element in a work of literature, whether a character, an image, a narrative formula, or an idea, which can be assimilated to a larger unifying category. The existence of such a category depends on the existence of a unified conception of art. Blake began his Prophecies with a powerfully integrated theory of the nature, structure, function, and meaning of art, and all the symbolic units of his poetry, his moods, his images, his narratives, and his characters, form archetypes of that theory. Given his premises about art, everything he does logically follows. His premises may be wrong, but there are two things which may make us hesitate to call them absurd. One is their comprehensiveness and consistency: if the Bible is the code of art, Blake seems to provide something of a code of modern art, both in his structure of symbols and in his range of ideas. The other is their relationship to earlier traditions of criticism. Theories of poetry and of archetypes seem to belong to criticism rather than to poetry itself, and when I speak of

Blake's treatment of the archetype I imply that Blake is a poet of unique interest to critics like ourselves. The Biblical origin of his symbolism and his apocalyptic theory of perception have a great deal in common with the theory of anagogy which underlies the poetry of Dante, the main structure of which survived through the Renaissance at least as late as Milton. Blake had the same creative powers as other great poets, but he made a very unusual effort to drag them up to consciousness, and to do deliberately what most poets prefer to do instinctively. It is possible that what impelled him to do this was the breakdown of a tradition of criticism which could have answered a very important question. Blake did not need the answer, but we do.

The question relates to the application of Blake's archetypes to the criticism of poetry as a whole. The papers delivered to this body of scholars are supposed to deal with general issues of criticism rather than with pure research. Now pure research is, up to a point, a coordinated and systematic form of study, and the question arises whether general criticism could also acquire a systematic form. In other words, is criticism a mere aggregate of research and comment and generalization, or is it, considered as a whole, an intelligible structure of knowledge? If the latter, there must be a quality in literature which enables it to be so, an order of words corresponding to the order of nature which makes the natural sciences intelligible. If criticism is more than aggregated commentary, literature must be somewhat more than an aggregate of poems and plays and novels: it must possess some kind of total form which criticism can in some measure grasp and expound.

It is on this question that the possibility of literary archetypes depends. If there is no total structure of literature, and no intelligible form to criticism as a whole, then there is no such thing as an archetype. The only organizing principle so far discovered in literature is chronology, and consequently all our larger critical categories are concerned with sources and direct transmission. But every student of literature has, whether consciously or not, picked up thousands of resemblances, analogies, and parallels in his reading where there is no question of direct transmission. If there are no archetypes, then these must be merely private associations, and the connections among them must be arbitrary and fanciful. But if criticism makes sense, and literature makes sense, then the mental processes of the cultivated reader may be found to make sense too.

The difficulty of a "private mythology" is not peculiar to Blake: every poet has a private mythology, his own formation of symbols. His mythology is a cross-section of his life, and the critic, like the biographer, has the job of making sure that what was private to the poet shall be public to everyone else. But, having no theory of archetypes, we do not know how to proceed. Blake supplies us with a few leading principles which may guide us in analysing the symbolic formation of poets and isolating the archetypal elements in them. Out of such a study the structure of literature may slowly begin to emerge, and criticism, in interpreting that structure, may take its rightful place among the major disciplines of modern thought. There is, of course, the possibility that the study of Blake is a long and tortuous blind alley, but those who are able to use Blake's symbols as a calculus for all their criticism will not be much inclined to consider it.

The question that we have just tried to answer, however, is not the one that the student of Blake most frequently meets. The latter question runs in effect: you may show that Blake had one of the most powerful minds in the modern world, that his thought is staggeringly comprehensive and consistent, that his insight was profound, his mood exalted, and his usefulness to critics unlimited. But surely all this profits a poet nothing if he does not preserve the hieratic decorum of conventional poetic utterance. And how are we to evaluate an utterance which is now lucid epigram and now a mere clashing of symbols, now disciplined and lovely verse and now a rush of prosy gabble? Whatever it is, is it really poetry or really great and good poetry? Well, probably not, in terms of what criticism now knows, or thinks it knows, about the canons of beauty and the form of literary expression.

Othello was merely a bloody farce in terms of what the learned and acute Thomas Rymer knew about drama.[10] Rymer was perfectly right in his own terms; he is like the people who say that Blake was mad. One cannot refute them; one merely loses interest in their conception of sanity. And critics may be as right about Blake as Rymer was about Shakespeare, and still be just as wrong. We do not yet know whether literature and criticism are forms or aggregates: we know almost nothing about archetypes or about any of the great critical problems connected with them. In Dante's day critics did know something about the symbols of the Bible, but we have made little effort to recover that knowledge. We do not know very much even about genres: we do not know whether Blake's "Prophecy" form is a real genre or not, and we certainly do not know how to treat it if it is. I leave the question of Blake's language in more competent hands, but after all, even the poets are only beginning to assimilate contemporary speech, and when the speech of *Jerusalem* becomes so blunt and colloquial that Blake himself calls it prosaic, do critics really know whether it is too prosaic to be poetic, or even whether such an antithesis exists at all? I may be speaking only of myself, for criticism today is full of confident value judgments, on Blake and on everyone else, implying a complete understanding of all such mysteries. But I wonder if these are really critical judgments, or if they are merely the aberrations of the history of taste. I suspect that a long course of patient and detailed study lies ahead of us before we really know much about the critical problems which the study of Blake raises, and which have to be reckoned with in making any value judgment on him. Then we shall understand the poets, including Blake, much better, and I am not concerned with what the results of that better understanding will be.

10

J.G. Davies' *The Theology of William Blake*

1950

Review of J.G. Davies, The Theology of William Blake *(Oxford: Clarendon Press, 1948). From* The Review of English Studies, *n.s. 1 (1950), 77–8.*

Mr. Davies is a careful and vigilant reader of Blake, and sticks to his subject with a restraint unusual in Blake's critics. He leaves the symbolism alone, very sensibly, and all other aspects of Blake which are not his concern. Sometimes this is carried to excess—Blake's identification of Christianity with art, for instance, is mentioned only in passing—but on the whole his book gains from its omissions. He first relates Blake to the Church of his day, and does so with great clarity, though he is reluctant to press the point that Blake regarded corruption as inseparable from a visible and corporeal church. He then studies Blake's relation to and divergence from Swedenborg, in the most coherent study of this important question I know, in which he makes several points, such as the connection of *The Book of Thel* with Swedenborg's doctrine of function, of great help to Blake's students. This is followed by a general consideration of Blake's mysticism, in which it is regrettable that he did not make more use of, say, Otto's *Mysticism East and West,*[1] which deals with Blake's kind of mysticism more directly than von Hügel[2] or Underhill[3] do. On the other hand, he quotes very aptly from Berdyaev.[4]

In dealing with Blake's cyclic myth, the author says, "theology must always start, not from God nor from man, but from the God-man" (89). One wishes that he had started his commentary at the same point, and not written a chapter on an alleged 'Doctrine of God' in Blake. The remaining chapters, dealing respectively with the fall and creation myths, the redemption of man by Christ, Blake's doctrine of man, and his ethical ideas, are on far more solid ground. An interesting note on Blake's use of dialectic and a clear and accurate explanation of the relation of law to gospel in Blake's thought are among the best things here. On the debit side, the assertion that Blake thought of unfallen man as androgynous seems to me untenable in view of Blake's use of the term "hermaphroditic" to describe Satan. I feel, too, that Blake had more concrete ideas about the resurrection of the body than Mr. Davies attributes to him.

Mr. Davies writes throughout from the standpoint of a liberal and catholic churchman who finds Blake essentially though on some points dubiously orthodox. This is quite justifiable, yet some of the inner vitality of Blake is lost by so external an approach. He regrets that "Blake was not a more obedient son of the Church" (30), but if he had been he would not have been Blake. On the other hand, those who know best how bad some critics of Blake can be on the subject of theology will be most grateful to Mr. Davies for not falsifying Blake's meaning. It is possible to find critics who will deny that Blake believed in original sin, or who will treat him as an antinomian on one page, as a pietist on another, and as a Gnostic on a third. Mr. Davies' incisive study makes it unnecessary for the bewildered reader of Blake to trust to such blind guides.

11

Bernard Blackstone's *English Blake*

January 1951

Review of Bernard Blackstone, English Blake *(Cambridge: Cambridge University Press, 1949). From* Modern Language Notes, *66 (January 1951): 55–7.*

The first half of this book is a rapid review of Blake's poems in chronological order. The commentary is too brief to go very deeply into the subject at any point, but it makes a good reference guide. This is held together by a skeleton of biography, which repeats the old Gilchrist[1] chestnuts rather uncritically: some of Gilchrist's anecdotes, one feels, belong less to a life of Blake than to a Theophrastan[2] Character of the Eccentric Artist. For those with a special interest in Blake, the best thing in these two hundred pages is a good concise account of the background of *An Island in the Moon*. Mr. Blackstone dips a cautious toe into the symbolism, but decides, no doubt with most readers' sympathy, not to plunge too far below the surface. Only in a few trivial cases does one wish for more careful study of it: thus Blake's outline of history is divided into six ages on page 71, and three on page 203, but Blake's own directive consistently gives seven.

The second part consists of essays on different aspects of Blake's thought. The discussion of Blake's social and ethical views is rather oppressed by some heavy irony directed against both eighteenth-century and modern hypocrisies, but it presents the essential humanity of Blake with great sympathy and clarity. Mr. Blackstone takes Blake seriously, and never patronizes him or pretends to have reached a more balanced outlook himself, like many of Blake's critics. (In passing, I cannot believe Mr. Blackstone's suggestion that Blake resented his own monogamy or found his marriage unsatisfying: in Catherine Blake's pictures there is a humorous twist to her mouth which suggests that for all her simplicity—or because of it—she understood Blake far better than we do.) He is also quite sound on Blake's attitude to religion and art, though he deals with Blake's general emotional reaction rather than with the specific details of his thought. Thus the final chapter on "Art" mentions all the things that Blake hated, but says nothing about his conception of outline. The chief aspect of Blake neglected is his relation to English literature. His immense debt to eighteenth-century poetry is greatly underestimated, and the discussions of Milton and of Pope's *Essay on Man* are among the least satisfactory parts of the book.

The most distinctive feature of Mr. Blackstone's approach, as compared with other critics, is his sense of Blake's close relation to English philosophy. Working from Blake's express statement that he had carefully read *The Advancement of Learning* and the *Essay concerning Human Understanding*, Mr. Blackstone goes through Bacon, Newton, and Locke and shows how deeply the design of their thought was etched in reverse on Blake's mind. Blake's hostility to them implies a corresponding affinity with Berkeley, and Mr. Blackstone illustrates some of these affinities in detail. Blake's reading of Berkeley cannot be definitely proved except for the *Siris*, which proves very little, but the assumption that he knew the *Principles* at least is reasonable enough. In any case the passages in Berkeley which Mr. Blackstone considers to be sources for passages in Blake would do just as well as analogues. Blake, says Mr. Blackstone, "repudiated the doctrine that Nature works by secondary causes, that time and space are real and are the theatre of motion in which only primary qualities are concerned, and that secondary qualities are less 'real' than primary ones."[3] All of this is quite true, and he shows very ably how for Blake the refusal to believe that secondary qualities are secondary opens the mind to a great rush of "minute particulars" of colours and sounds and perfumes.

The quality of the writing improves steadily in vigour and point as the book goes on. Mr. Blackstone is at his best when expounding Blake and speaking from Blake's point of view, and he quotes very well. In the earlier part of the book there are too many vague generalizations about the history of European thought, and he is too easily satisfied with the sort of cliché which is not sharply enough focused in meaning to be either true or false (for example, page 141, "Protestantism bows to the authority of the Bible; but the Bible is to be interpreted by each believer according to his own inner light"). Even in dealing with Blake himself, he shows some awkwardness in handling philosophical statements. He says on page 241, "We may say that the greater part of his writing is an attempt to express what is ultimately inexpressible." We may say nothing of the kind: Blake had no more concern with the inexpressible than a logician has with the unknowable. On page 69, "Blake was primarily interested not in poetry but in truth." No such antithesis was capable of entering Blake's mind on any terms, as Mr. Blackstone must know. On page 237 Blake is said to attack "the futility of scientific research, which seeks to discover causes of phenomena in the phenomenal multiverse itself and not in the noumenal world which lies behind." Blake knows nothing of any noumenal world lying, like Milton's Paradise of Fools, "o'er the backside of the World far off" [*PL*, 3.494]: he is no post-Kantian Romantic, nor is he interested in acquiring any such sophisticated equivalent of a Polynesian's *mana*. Mr. Blackstone seems more at home with the Oriental mystics, and his comments on them are all too brief.

Such lapses are not inherent in the author's thinking; they seem to result chiefly from the prolixity of the book, which is much too long. Mr. Blackstone seems unaware that a great deal of what he says has been said before; perhaps, as he gives very few signs of having read any critic of Blake later than Gilchrist, he actually is unaware of it. But scholarly work on Blake is too well organized by now for such primitivism to be any longer a virtue. Nevertheless, his book can be recommended as a good all-round introduction to Blake for the general reader. Reduced to two-thirds or less of its present bulk, it would make an admirable one.

12

Poetry and Design in William Blake

September 1951

From Journal of Aesthetics and Art Criticism, *10 (September 1951): 35–42.*

The ability to paint and the ability to write have often belonged to the same person; but it is rare to find them equally developed. Most people so gifted have been either writers who have made a hobby of painting, like D.H. Lawrence, or painters who have made a hobby of writing, like Wyndham Lewis. When the two are combined, one usually predominates. It is not uncommon for poets who can draw to illustrate their poems, like Edward Lear; nor is it uncommon for painters who can write to provide inscriptions to their paintings, like Rossetti. In a world as specialized as ours, concentration on one gift and a rigorous subordination of all others is practically a moral principle. Mr. Eliot uses the word "schizophrenia" even about the attempt to write both poetry and philosophy.[1] Blake, it is clear, had a different attitude, and the reasons for his different attitude are of some interest.

Besides being a poet and painter, Blake was a professional engraver and a tireless and versatile experimenter in a great variety of media. He was an artisan or craftsman who was an expert in an important minor art as well as two major ones. His political sympathies were anarchist and revolutionary. The combination of talents and outlook reminds us of William Morris, and as the French Revolution wore on into Napoleonic imperialism, Blake came more and more to anticipate Morris in his view of the social function of art. Like Morris, he felt that revolutionary action would only go from one kind of slavery to another unless it were directed toward the goal of a free and equal working society. Like Morris, he believed that real work and creative activity were the same thing, and that as long as society supported a class of parasites, work for the great majority of people would be perverted into drudgery. And so, like Morris, he came to feel that the essential revolutionary act was in the revolt of the creative artist who is also a manufacturer, in the original sense of one who works with his hands instead of with automata. And as the tendency of a class-ridden society is to produce expensive luxuries for the rich and shoddy ugliness for the poor, the true manufacturer should present his work as cheaply and as independently of commerce and patronage alike as possible.

The creative producer, then, has to imitate, on a necessarily limited scale, the mass-producing methods of commerce. Also, a revolutionary break with both patronage and commercial exploitation is only possible if some revolutionary new method of production is discovered. Blake made at least three attempts to develop his own means of production. First, and most important to students of literature, was his discovery of the engraving process which he used for most of his poems. It is clear that Blake expected this process to be more efficient and less laborious than it was: he expected, in short, that it would make him independent of publishers as well as of patrons, so that he could achieve personal independence as both poet and painter at a single blow. A character in his early satire, *An Island in the Moon*, speaks of printing off two thousand copies of engraved works in three volumes folio, and selling them for £100 apiece. Next came an attempt at large-scale reproduction of prints by means of a millboard, but the millboard proved too fragile for more than a few copies, and the variety of results it produced was too unpredictable. He was still dependent on patrons and connoisseurs to do the work he wanted to do, and on publishers' commissions to keep himself alive the rest of the time. Finally Blake turned to another idea on a much bigger scale: he thought he might gain government support for the arts if he could start a revival of fresco-painting on the walls of public buildings. The chief commercial disadvantage of fresco, Blake thought, was that the original painting had to remain as long as the wall it was painted on did, and he proposed that frescoes should be painted, not directly on the plaster, but on canvas stretched over the plaster, so that they could be taken off and changed. After he had worked out what he thought was a practicable method of painting such "portable frescoes," he held the one exhibition of his life in 1809, to introduce it to the public. The fate of this exhibition is well known, though it is seldom realized that its primary object was to advertise, not Blake, but a new instrument of production that would initiate a social revolution.

It is natural that Blake, whose main source of income was illustrating books, should at first think of his own poems as constructed on the same principle as the illustrated book, an alternation of text and design. In the passage from *An Island in the Moon* already quoted, he speaks of making every other plate a high finished print. An early Prophecy called *Tiriel* survives in a manuscript and a group of twelve separate illustrations, about the same number of plates that would be needed for the text. Fortunately for us, however, Blake began his experiments with aphorisms and lyrics which took only a single plate apiece, and so hit very early on a form in which text and design are simultaneously present and contrapuntally related. From the start Blake avoids all devices that would tend to obscure either text or design at the expense of the other. In illuminated books we often find what we may call the tradition of hieroglyphic, in which the verbal sign itself becomes a picture, such as the ornamented capitals of medieval manuscripts or the tortuous decorations of the Book of Kells. There is nothing of this in Blake: occasionally the shoots and tendrils of the design are entangled with the longer letters of the text, but that is all. The words are left alone to do their own work. The only exception I can think of is the heading to *The Book of Los*, where Urizen is shown wrapped up in a net inside the letter O of "Los," and even this is intended as a joke.

More surprising than the independence of the words from the design is the independence of the design from the words. Blake's age, after all, was the age of the pictorial Slough of Despond known as "historical painting," in which the painter was praised for his grasp of archaeology and the history of costume and for the number of literary points he could make. Again, the *Songs of Innocence and Experience* are in the direct tradition of the emblem books: they are by far the finest emblem books in English literature. But the typical emblem is a literary idea to begin with: its design takes its form, not from pictorial laws, but from the demands of the verbal commentary, and it is allegorical in a way that Blake's lyrics never are. In Blake the poem does not point to the picture, as it regularly does in the emblem. On the other hand, the design is not, like most illustrations, an attempt to simplify the verbal meaning. The *Songs of Innocence* are not difficult poems to read, and one might expect them to be made even easier, at least for children, by being put into a picture book. Perhaps even Blake expected this. But when we contemplate the great spiral sweep that encircles *The Divine Image*, or the passionate red flower that explodes over *Infant Joy*, or the marching horizontal lines of *Holy Thursday*, we can see that, so far from simplifying the text, the design has added a new dimension of subtlety and power.

In the earliest Prophecies, *The Book of Thel* and *Visions of the Daughters of Albion*, text and design approach one another rather tentatively. In *Thel* the design is always at the bottom or the top of the page, but in the *Visions* the text is occasionally broken in the middle, and an important step has been taken toward the free interpenetration of the two which belongs to Blake's mature period. In the early Prophecies there is often an unequal balance between the amount Blake has to say in each of the two arts. Thus *The Marriage of Heaven and Hell* is in literature one of Blake's best-known and most explicit works, but for that very reason it is less successful pictorially. The text predominates too much, and what design there is follows the text closely and obviously. So much so, in fact, that some of the marginal decorations become a rather irritating form of punctuation. Thus on plate 11 the words "whatever their enlarged & numerous senses could percieve" are followed by a little drawing of a bird; the words "thus began Priesthood" are followed by a black serpentine spiral, and the words "at length they pronounc'd that the Gods had order'd such things" are followed by tiny kneeling figures. On the other hand, *The Book of Urizen* is pictorially one of Blake's greatest works: here there is no plate without a major design on it, and there are ten plates without text. Blake here seems to be trying to forget about the poem, which with its short lines sits awkwardly on the plate in double column. It is clear that there were pictorial as well as poetic reasons for the long seven-beat line of Blake's Prophecies.

The finest of the earlier Prophecies, as far as the balance between verbal and pictorial elements is concerned, are undoubtedly the "continent" poems, *America*, *Europe*, and *The Song of Los*, the last of these divided into two parts called *Africa* and *Asia*. After 1795 Blake began to meditate a Prophecy of epic proportions, and between then and 1800 he undertook two colossal projects which enabled him to work out the archetypes of his verbal and pictorial systems respectively, on an epic scale. Each of these was a dream of nine nights: one was the great unfinished poem, *The Four Zoas*, which never reached the engraving process, but was left in a manuscript full of extraordinary sketches; the other was his illustrated edition of Young's *Night Thoughts*. The fascination that Young's poem clearly had for Blake was not due to Young so much as to the fact that Young's poem was based, like Blake's own symbolism, on the Bible. Throughout Blake's illustrations we can see how he infallibly goes to the Biblical archetype which gives what point and direction there is to Young's narrative. It was from his work on Young that Blake gained a coordinated vision of the Leviathan, the four "Zoas" of Ezekiel, the Great Whore with her beast, and the other essential elements of his later symbolism. The final fruits of his effort were the two great poems *Milton* and *Jerusalem,* in fifty and one hundred plates respectively, after which Blake turned his main attention away from poetry.

It is difficult to convey adequately the sense of the uniqueness of Blake's achievement in these engraved poems. In the Preface to *Jerusalem* Blake speaks with pride of having developed a free and unfettered verse, but he hardly seems to notice that he had at the same time perfected a far more difficult and radical form of mixed art, for which there is hardly a parallel in the history of modern culture. The union of musical and poetic ideas in a Wagner opera is a remote analogy; but the poetry is not independent of the music in Wagner as it is of the painting in Blake. Blake seems to have worked on his text and his pictorial ideas simultaneously: this is clear from the manuscript of *The Four Zoas,* where the pencil sketches in the margins indicate that Blake did not think in terms of a poem to be written first and decorated afterward, but, from the beginning, in terms of a narrative sequence of plates.

Blake felt that his conception of outline was one which held all the arts together, and his engraving technique does a great deal to prove his case. The stamped designs produced by a relief etching on metal, in which the details stand out from surrounding blank space, give us something of the three-dimensional quality of sculpture. On the other hand, the tremendous energy of Blake's drawings with their swirling human figures makes them of particular interest to dancers and students of ballet, even if more sedentary observers merely find them out of drawing. About the colour it is more difficult to speak. After reading what Blake has to say about the subordinating of colour to outline in painting, we are not surprised to find that there is no fixed colour symbolism in the designs: every copy is coloured differently. At the same time, as he developed confidence and scope, he began to move toward the luminous splendours of the golden city that was the end of his vision. "A word fitly spoken," says the Book of Proverbs, "is like apples of gold in pictures of silver" [25:11]. Such ideas were entirely unbefitting to Blake's station in life. The text of the only surviving coloured copy of *Jerusalem* is in a strong orange which looks like a poor man's substitute for the golden letters he doubtless dreamed of.

The designs play a great variety of roles in relation to the words, besides that of direct illustration. The natural symbols lend themselves admirably to pictorial metamorphosis, and the process is simplified by the fact that the symbols of experience are often direct parodies of those of innocence. Vines with grapes, ears of wheat, and a profusion of green leaves sprout from the tree of life; brambles, thorns, thistles, dead trees, and tangles of roots belong to the tree of mystery. In plate 75 of *Jerusalem* a row of angels, with haloes around their bodies, make a line of intersecting circles, the "wheels within wheels" of Ezekiel's vision. At the bottom of the page the same rhythm is picked up and parodied by a picture of Rahab and Tirzah caught in the rolling coils of serpents.

I have spoken of the analogy between Wagner and Blake, and some of Blake's pictorial symbols incorporate ideas in a way that reminds one of Wagner's technique of the leitmotif. Thus it is one of Blake's doctrines that we see the sky as a huge concave vault because we see it with eyes that are imprisoned in a concave vault of bone.[2] The title page of *The Book of Urizen* depicts Urizen himself, the fallen reason of man, and it therefore endeavours to give a concentrated impression of befuddled stupidity. The picture is built up in a series of rounded arches. Urizen sits crouching in the foetus posture that Blake regularly uses for mental cowardice, and two great knees loom out of the foreground. His skull and bushy eyebrows are above; behind his head are the two tables of the law,[3] each with a rounded top; behind them is the arch of a cave, the traditional symbol since Plato of blinded vision, and over the cave droops a dismal willow branch, an imp of the tree of mystery.

Occasionally, though rarely, the design comments ironically on the text, if an ironic touch in the text permits it. Thus the seventh plate of *America* contains the speech of the terrified reactionary angel of Albion denouncing the rebellious Orc as "Blasphemous Demon, Antichrist, hater of Dignities," and so on. The design shows a graceful spreading tree with birds of paradise sitting on its branches; underneath is a ram and some children asleep, sunk in the profound peace of the state of innocence. A much more frequent type of comment, and one which also is sometimes ironic, is a pictorial reference or quotation, generally to the Bible. *The Marriage of Heaven and Hell* concludes with a portrait of Nebuchadnezzar going on all fours. Nebuchadnezzar is not mentioned in the text, but the Prophecy deals with the overthrow of senile tyranny, and Nebuchadnezzar, the tyrant of Babylon who becomes a monstrous animal, first cousin to Behemoth and Leviathan, is for Blake a central symbol of the kind of thing he is attacking. The great picture of Albion before the cross of Christ, which concludes the third part of *Jerusalem*, is a more familiar example. It is more common, however, to have the designs focus and sharpen the verbal symbolism. Thus the poem *Europe*, if we had only the text, would seem an almost perversely intellectualized treatment of the theme of tyranny and superstition. It is when we look at the plates depicting famine, war, and pestilence that we realize how acutely aware of human misery Blake always is.

In the longer poems there is, of course, a good deal of syncopation between design and narrative. At the bottom of plate 8 of *Jerusalem* is a female figure harnessed to the moon: the symbol is not mentioned in the text until plate 63. The effect of such devices is to bind the whole poem together tightly in a single unit of meaning. And here, perhaps, we come closest to the centre of the aesthetic problem that Blake's achievement raises. The words of a poem form rhythms which approach those of music at one boundary of literature, and form patterns which approach those of painting at the other boundary. To the rhythmical movement of poetry we may give the general name of narrative; the pattern we may call the meaning or significance. The Renaissance maxim *ut pictura poesis* thus refers primarily to the integrity of meaning which is built up in a poem out of a pattern of interlocking images. When Spenser begins the last canto of the Legend of Temperance with the words "Now gins this goodly frame of Temperance / Fairely to rise,"[4] he means that, in addition to the narrative, a unified structure of meaning has been built up which can be apprehended simultaneously, like a painting, or, to follow Spenser's image, like a building. Such a passage shows the principle of *ut pictura poesis* in action.

When we think of "meaning" we usually think of something to be expressed in general propositions. But the units of poetry are images rather than ideas, and a poem's total meaning is therefore a total image, a single visualizable picture. Not many rhetorical critics pursue their image-linking to this ultimate point. They usually remain close to the texture of the poem, engaged in the detailed study of the poetic equivalents of the technique of brush and palette knife. The critic who can only express meaning in terms of propositions has to stop his interpretation of the poem at the point of fitting it into the background of a history of ideas.

But it is possible to go farther, and it is only when literary critics stand back far enough to see the imagery as one pattern that they are in a position to solve the problems of structure, of genre, and of archetype. The meaning of, for instance, Spenser's *Mutabilitie Cantos* is not the conflict of being and becoming, which is only an aspect of its content. Its meaning is the total structure of its imagery, and this structure is a spherical, luminous, ordered background with a dark mass thrusting up defiantly in the central foreground: the same structural archetype that we find at the opening of the Book of Job. The propositional content of Blake's *Europe* could be expressed somewhat as follows: the root of evil and suffering is the fallen nature of man; this fallen nature is a part of physical nature; hence the basis of superstition and tyranny is the deification of physical nature; this deification has polluted Western culture from the sky-gods of Greece and Rome to the gravitational universe of Newton. But its poetic meaning, its total image, is given us by Blake himself in his frontispiece to the poem, the famous picture of the Ancient of Days, the bearded god whose sharp cruel compasses etch the circumference of the human skull and of the spherical universe which is its objective shadow.

Blake's Prophecies are in the tradition of the Christian epic, and the meaning or total image of the Christian epic is the apocalypse, the vision of reality separated into its eternal constituents of heaven and hell. At the time that he was completing his epic Prophecies, Blake was preoccupied by the pictorial vision of the Last Judgment. He has left us the magnificent picture reproduced as plate 4 of Darrell Figgis's book on Blake's paintings, and an elaborate commentary for a still larger design of which nothing else remains.[5] After this, Blake tended to make the picture the unit of a new kind of nonverbal narrative, and so turned from poetry to the sequences of his Milton, Bunyan, Dante, and Job illustrations.

The only complete edition of Blake's engraved poems is in the third volume of *The Works of William Blake* edited by Ellis and Yeats and published by Bernard Quaritch in 1893. This edition was a heroic publishing effort, and it showed the true spirit of scholarship, as it must have lost a great deal of money. But it is increasingly difficult to obtain, and the reproductions, which are in black and white and done from lithographs, a rather greasy medium that failed to interest Blake himself, are not very satisfactory, to put it mildly. There are passable colour reproductions of the lyrics and a few of the shorter Prophecies, but so far as I know there has been no good edition, with or without colour, of *America, Europe, Milton,* or *Jerusalem.* There are even editions of the lyrics which have been illustrated by other people. For one reason or another, many literary students of Blake have only the vaguest notion of what sort of pictorial basis underlies his poetry. A good many foolish ideas about Blake have resulted from staring at the naked text. The notion that he was an automatic writer is perhaps the most absurd of these; the notion that his Prophecies offer only the dry bones of a vision that died within him runs it a close second. We spoke at the beginning of the specialized nature of modern culture; and a man who possesses so much interest for students of religion, philosophy, history, politics, poetry, and painting will be chopped by his critics into as many pieces as Osiris. It is all the more necessary to correct the tendency to identify blinkered vision with directed vision by trying to expose oneself to the whole impact of Blake at once.

13

Introduction to *Selected Poetry and Prose of William Blake*

1953

Introduction to Selected Poetry and Prose of William Blake, *ed. Northrop Frye (New York: Random House, 1953), xiii–xxviii.*

William Blake was born in 1757, the second of five children in the family of a London shopkeeper, a retail hosier. In the days before photography, illustrations to books had to be engraved by hand, and it was possible for an artist without influence or income to make a fairly steady living as an engraver. When Blake showed a talent for drawing, therefore, he was promptly apprenticed to that trade, as the shortest way of making him self-supporting. He was thus committed in his early teens to a life of constant association with books and the pictorial arts. His master was James Basire, from whom he absorbed the love for "Gothic" that was then in fashion, and who held some curious views about the antiquity and traditions of Druids which probably left their mark on Blake's symbolism.

After serving his apprenticeship, Blake spent the remainder of his life as a London engraver, dependent on publishers' commissions, and, when they failed, on private patrons. He could manage his financial affairs well enough, but he had no aptitude for the fierce competition in his crowded trade, and he complained of living in a "City of Assassinations."[1] He had little sense either of the pictorial clichés and conventions that the public were used to, and when he tried to follow them, he unconsciously caricatured them. Without two or three patrons—Thomas Butts, who bought his work steadily for over twenty years, William Hayley, John Linnell—it is difficult to see how he could have survived, much less produced so much work of his own.

The poem *How sweet I roam'd* is said on good contemporary authority to have been written at about the age of fourteen, and all the early poems in *Poetical Sketches* were completed by his twenty-first year. *Poetical Sketches* was printed in 1783, through the good offices of a clergyman named Henry Mathew,[2] who was the centre of a group to which Blake was attached for a time, and which included two women writers of some fame, Anna Letitia Barbauld (a possible influence on Blake's lyrics) and Hannah More. Mathew contributed a preface to *Poetical Sketches* stating that Blake had not bothered to revise the poems because he was abandoning poetry for his profession—i.e., engraving. It was the first and last book of Blake's to appear in a conventional form during his life. Five years later Blake had worked out a method of engraving which would enable him to print words and design illustrations at the same time. It is clear from the references to this process in *An Island in the Moon* that Blake expected it to be far less expensive and cumbersome than it proved to be. He must at one time, in fact, have hoped that it would make him independent of publishers, and enable him to become his own publisher on a uniquely lavish scale. His disappointment, if there was one, did not prevent him from sticking to the process for at least twenty years, and employing it for all his poetry except what he left in manuscript.

The years between 1788 and 1795, when Blake was living at Lambeth in South London, are a period of extraordinary creative energy. Besides a wonderful series of what he called "colour printed drawings"—*The Elohim Creating Adam, Satan Exulting over Eve, Elijah in the Chariot of Fire*,[3] and others equally famous—he produced nearly all his shorter poems. Two volumes, *Songs of Innocence* and *Songs of Experience*, contained the lyrics; the other poems were in a new genre which has generally been called "Prophecies," the name that Blake himself gave to two of them (*America* and *Europe*) and which is as appropriate as any other. All were engraved except *The French Revolution*, which he evidently tried to publish in the regular way—the one surviving copy appears to be a proof—and *Tiriel* (not given here), which he left in manuscript. A set of illustrations for *Tiriel* exists, indicating that Blake at first thought of illustrated rather than illuminated books, keeping text and design separate. But very shortly he had launched into his wonderful new art form, a sequence of plates with a free interpenetration of text and design, so that a plate may be a picture, or all text, or a text marginally decorated, or a design with a few lines of text in the centre, or any other proportion of words and pictures. The engraved poems of Blake are one of the few successful combinations of two arts by one master in the world, and one of the most startlingly and radically original productions of modern culture.

After 1795 Blake became preoccupied with the task of consolidating his essential ideas, both poetic and pictorial, into some kind of vast synthesis, with the Bible as its model. Some years later he wrote that he had at this time "recollected all my scatter'd thoughts on Art & resumed my primitive & original ways of Execution in both painting & engraving."[4] Similarly, his next poetic efforts were directed toward an epic or "major" Prophecy that would follow the pattern of the Bible and present a visionary narrative of the life of man between creation and apocalypse. First of all, he plunged into an extravagant but superb scheme of illustrating Young's *Night Thoughts*, for which he made over five hundred designs. Blake, like Housman's God, creates a world his poet never made,[5] and as we see Young's meditative verse placidly ambling, like a middle-aged Alice, through a wonderland of Oriental splendours and demonic terrors, it becomes very clear that what Blake is really illustrating is the Bible. His greatest pictures almost always illustrate Biblical allusions in Young's text. The next step for Blake was to write a Biblical poem of his own for which illustration on this level would be more appropriate. For an undetermined time—perhaps seven years—he worked at his epic, a poem which, like Young's, was a "dream of nine nights" ending in a Last Judgment, and which bore the titles *Vala* and *The Four Zoas*. Several recensions of it failed to satisfy him, and he left it in manuscript—a manuscript full of sketches showing that he worked on text and design simultaneously, and thought from the beginning in terms of a sequence of plates.

His work during this period was interrupted by a three-year sojourn (1800–3) at Felpham in Sussex, where he came under the patronage of the poet William Hayley and attempted, unsuccessfully, to execute the sort of commissions he got through Hayley. At Felpham he went through two crucial experiences, one intellectual and artistic, the other physical and social, in the course of which his vision of life took final shape, and by doing so consolidated the form of everything opposed to that vision.

The first experience was the temptation presented by Hayley and the kind of Augustan culture he stood for. This culture had its own standards of beauty and good taste, which were backed by the whole Classical tradition and had been dominant in France and England for over a century. In addition, it had the moral virtues that belonged to it, including tact and generosity. Blake had nothing to meet this with but the ungracious defiance of his own tradition, the line of prophets crying in the wilderness. This experience forms the basis of the poem *Milton,* in which Blake presents himself as a battlefield over which the prophetic tradition, headed by Milton, defeats the powers of Satan, the spirit of compromise, prudence, and hypocrisy. Satan is formidable only when he is disguised—transformed into an angel of light, as the Bible says—as a reasonable and cultivated man who is a sincere personal friend. Blake is not interested in the moral problem of what he did or should have done: he is interested in tracing out the ramifications of the prophetic and worldly attitudes until they reach their apocalyptic limits. These limits are represented by the story of Michael and Satan fighting over the body of Moses—i.e., man in this world.

Blake's second experience was his trial for treason as a result of a quarrel with the soldier Schofield. Blake found Schofield trespassing in his garden and threw him out, whereupon Schofield went to a magistrate and swore that Blake had damned the king and said that he hoped and expected to see Napoleon win the war. Schofield had, fortunately for Blake, overestimated the extent of judicial hysteria in wartime. But Blake had glimpsed for a moment the lethal malignity in human nature which makes the Crucifixion the central event of history. This experience forms the autobiographical core of *Jerusalem,* which, like *Milton,* expands from an event in Blake's life to the apocalyptic form of the same event, the salvation of the world by God contrasted with what Blake calls "Druidism," or the attempt of man by searching to find out God, with the object of torturing and killing him. *Milton* and *Jerusalem* consist of fifty and one hundred plates respectively. It is probable that, besides *The Four Zoas,* there were earlier and much longer versions of these poems, though the story of a great holocaust of Blake's writings after his death is not now generally accepted.

Blake was, in literature, more of an amateur than any other English poet of his rank; and with *Jerusalem,* which has the date 1804 on its title page, and was probably complete by 1808 except for minor revisions, he considered that he had said all he had to say as a poet. Until his death in 1827, he contented himself with re-engraving his old poems and writing a few occasional verses, notably *The Everlasting Gospel.* In 1808 he writes that his time "in future must alone be devoted to Designing & Painting."[6] By 1809 he was full of a new project: to decorate public buildings with paintings in a new kind of fresco, which would be applied, not directly to the plaster on the wall, but to canvas stretched over the plaster, so that they could be taken off and changed at pleasure. The only exhibition of his life, in 1809, was designed to advertise, not his paintings, but a practicable method of producing "portable frescoes," and it was for this exhibition that he wrote his *Descriptive Catalogue*. Only one reviewer noticed the exhibition, Robert Hunt of the *Examiner*, brother of Leigh Hunt, who had already made one attack on Blake which has left its traces in *Jerusalem*. Hunt said this time that Blake was a harmless lunatic who would have to be shut up if he insisted on making a nuisance of himself by publicly exhibiting his pictures. Hunt's review in itself was merely typical of the nineteenth-century conception of criticism as a moral steam roller, and, except for labouring the charge of insanity, is not very different in tone from the *Quarterly* on Keats or Ruskin on Whistler.[7] But it does help to explain why the next few years of Blake's life were quiet ones. No longer particularly interested in writing poetry, and with no encouragement to continue with frescoes, he turned for his last period to the illustrating of other poets, beginning with Bunyan and Milton.

Basire had taught Blake a great respect for clear outline, and for making figure drawing and landscape depend on pictorial and not on representative considerations. To Blake a painting was a coloured drawing, and he even regarded oil painting as an illegitimate art, because, unlike water colour and fresco, it seemed to emphasize colour at the expense of outline. To "firm, determinate outline," as he went on, he attached enormous importance.[8] The Roman (or Florentine) school of Raphael and Michelangelo (whom Blake knew chiefly by prints), and the German school of Dürer were, Blake felt, of his mind in this matter. The Venetians, especially Titian and Correggio, the Dutch, especially Rembrandt and Rubens, and of course Reynolds were against him. He was accustomed to hearing his type of art described as hard, stiff, angular, and awkward, but, as with Hayley, opposition merely consolidated his own views. For some years before his exhibition, Blake's isolation had been embittered by a series of disappointments and misunderstandings, and Stothard's rival illustration of Chaucer, which Blake ridicules in his catalogue, had been painted as a result of some sharp practice, not far removed from swindling, by a print-seller named Cromek. The *Descriptive Catalogue* is in part an appeal to the public over the heads of what Blake considered a conspiratorial monopoly of bad artists. The only contemporary painter with whom Blake felt anything in common was Fuseli,[9] who shared some of his reputation for eccentricity. A somewhat quixotic admiration for the painter James Barry,[10] from whom he may have derived his idea of "portable frescoes," was the only other exception Blake made to his condemnation of contemporary art.

His meeting with John Linnell in 1818 was one of the great events of Blake's life. Linnell brought friends, money, sympathy, and recognition to Blake, who, at the age of sixty, found himself at last talking to other artists who did not think of him as someone to be cheated or ridiculed. Disciples gathered around him—Linnell himself, Samuel Palmer, Edward Calvert, George Richmond—and the extent to which Blake mellowed, both as a painter and as a man, shows how forced and unnatural his sectarian pose had been for him all along. One of the group, John Varley, had occult interests, and for him Blake turned a painfully acquired skill in drawing from direct visualization, without models, into a social asset. The result was the series of "Visionary Heads," drawings of Solomon, Saul, Richard III, the man who built the pyramids, the ghost of a flea—anything his friends asked for or might be interested in. More important results were the two astounding series of illustrations to Dante and to the Book of Job, which were the work of his last years, and with which he was still occupied when he died in 1827.

His life, then, was on the whole a lonely one; but it was very far from being miserable. There was his wife Catherine, who signed her marriage register with a cross, but learned to read, write, and help in the preparing and colouring of prints. Blake's life, even without children, seems almost excessively domesticated. The pictures of his "sweet Shadow of Delight" [K534/E143] show an unexpectedly strong face, with a twist to the mouth full of a tough and resilient humour—the face of a woman well designed by nature to live with William Blake. One of the few anecdotes about Blake that I believe tells how she annihilated a visitor who wondered where the soap was with, "Mr. Blake's skin don't dirt!" And there was London. Whatever his ancestry—Yeats's struggles to add Blake to the roster of great Irishmen are not very convincing[11]—Blake was as rooted in London as the dome of St. Paul's. He would not often have agreed with Samuel Johnson, but Johnson's remark that the full tide of human existence was to be found at Charing Cross[12] expresses a feeling that was deep in Blake as well.

> The fields from Islington to Marybone,
> To Primrose Hill and Saint John's Wood,
> Were builded over with pillars of gold,
> And there Jerusalem's pillars stood. [*J*, pl. 27; K649/E171]

He loved London, and he never left it, except for his three dismal years on the Sussex coast, a good fifty miles from the full tide of human existence. It was partly, of course, war and poverty that kept him so confined: a pathetic letter, written at the time of the six-months' peace of Amiens with Napoleon, says, "Now I hope to see the Great Works of Art, as they are so near to Felpham."[13] But still he is temperamentally the complete opposite of the poets of savage pilgrimage, like Byron or D.H. Lawrence, who use a variety of scenes and places to intensify a subjective attitude. Blake is one of the wise typified by Wordsworth's skylark, who soar but never roam.[14] That is, he had a markedly introverted temperament, but he did not identify introversion with profundity; and by staying where he was, he intensified the reality, for himself, of everything he meant by "Albion": the cities, countries, people, and buildings that make up the structure of human society.

Blake was systematically taught only in the trade of engraving, if we except a few rebellious months at the Royal Academy in 1779–80. In all other fields he was essentially self-educated. He read, or at least looked through, the books he had to illustrate or engrave illustrations for, and we have to allow for a large amount of desultory and miscellaneous reading in his background that we cannot now recapture. Otherwise he read what he liked—or what he disliked: the vitriolic wit of his marginalia had more scope with books that he found only just short of being beneath contempt. He was not an industrious reader, or even a persistent one. Some of the books surviving from his library are uncut; his marginalia, even the exhaustive annotations to Reynolds, often fail to follow a book through to the end; and he read in the light, or darkness, of some violent prejudices. He divided the world of culture into an Armageddon between the imaginative and the malignant, and, once he had decided that Plato or Virgil or Titian or Locke belonged on the wrong side, he never slackened in the intensity with which he misunderstood them.

Much of his intolerance was merely the result of his isolation, but one would not have had him different: anyone can be "fair" to Francis Bacon, but only Blake could have said "King James was Bacon's Primum Mobile."[15] And one should not underestimate Blake's grasp even of what he disliked. Among Classical poets, his friend and biographer Tatham tells us that "he was very fond of Ovid, especially the *Fasti*"[16]—though I think this must be a slip for the *Metamorphoses*. He knew the Platonist Thomas Taylor, and not only read but used Taylor's translations from Plato and the Neoplatonists. He knew Aristotle's *Poetics*; he had read Voltaire and

Rousseau, probably in French, and he tells us that he had read and annotated Locke's *Essay on the Human Understanding*, Burke's *Treatise on the Sublime and Beautiful*, and Bacon's *Advancement of Learning*—all books he loathed. He learned enough Greek and Hebrew to read his Bible in the original, but does not seem otherwise to have been greatly interested in other languages.

Even more than Bunyan, Blake was a poet of the Bible. The Bible accounts for, I should guess, at least nine-tenths of the literary echoes and allusions in his work. The number of these echoes cannot be estimated by casual reading. Such a line as this from *The Four Zoas*:

> Man began
> To wake upon the Couch of Death; he sneezed seven times;

does not look like an explicit reference to a miracle of Elisha, but it is;[17] and the striking image:

> That line of blood that stretch'd across the windows of the morning,

from the same poem, does not immediately impress one as being connected with the story of Rahab in Joshua, though the connection is clear enough if one knows what Rahab means in Blake's symbolism.[18] Even so apparently spontaneous a line as "O Earth, O Earth, return!" in the *Introduction* to the *Songs of Experience*, is quoted from Jeremiah [22:29], perhaps by way of the conclusion of Milton's *Ready and Easy Way*.[19] Blake seems in general to have admired other literature in proportion as it resembled the Bible. This is the chief reason why he knew Hesiod and Ovid, with their creation myths and theogonies, so much better than Homer and Virgil; and why the Icelandic *Eddas*, especially the *Prose Edda*, which, like the Bible, is a narrative stretching from creation to apocalypse, are so important an influence on his work. Again, Milton had a far greater hold on his imagination than any other English poet, but for Shakespeare he seems not to have had much deep affection. We should perhaps not have guessed that Chaucer was a favourite of his without the *Descriptive Catalogue*, but his affinity to Spenser and Bunyan is clear enough.

Blake regarded the "Augustan" period of English literature between Dryden and Johnson as an unqualified disaster, but still he was very much a poet of his own age. Literary critics, however, have remained obstinately confused about what that age was. Blake's formative period was the period of Gray, Cowper, Collins, Smart, Chatterton, Ossian, the Wartons, and Percy's *Reliques*—roughly the English equivalent of *Sturm und Drang*. Admiration for the Gothic, for Druids and ancient bards, for Spenser and Milton as opposed to Dryden and Pope, for enthusiasm, fancy, imagination, and political liberty, for the primitive, the sublime, and the apocalyptic: every one of these values becomes an influence on Blake. In prose, Blake's period is the age of "sensibility," of the influence of Richardson, whom Blake apparently liked, and of Sterne, whom he seems to imitate to some extent in *An Island in the Moon*. We open *The Vicar of Wakefield* and find "the tame correct paintings of the Flemish school" contrasted with "the erroneous, but sublime animations of the Roman pencil,"[20] a contrast which, though Blake would not have accepted "correct" or "erroneous," clearly belongs in his cultural milieu. The age of Blake is not the Augustan age, not a mere reaction against it, not the Romantic age, and above all not "pre-Romantic." It is a perfectly definable cultural entity, and much of our difficulty in understanding Blake begins with our difficulty in understanding Ossian, Chatterton, and Smart's *Jubilate Agno*.

The *Lyrical Ballads*, with its manifesto of Romanticism, appeared when Blake was forty, had written half his own poetry and formed all his attitudes. Later, he came into personal contact with some of the Romantics. He appears in Crabb Robinson's useful diary as an artist who met with some appreciation along with much misunderstanding. He met Southey and Wordsworth, who dismissed him as mad; Lamb was deeply impressed by *The Tyger* and by his Chaucer criticism, and Coleridge made some kindly if rather episcopal comments on his lyrics. He kept in touch with Romantic poetry; he read Wordsworth with great but not uncritical admiration, and his late *Ghost of Abel* is partly an answer to Byron's *Cain*. But there is a dogged loyalty to his own age in the marginal note on Wordsworth written at the very end of his life: "I own myself an admirer of Ossian equally with any other Poet whatever, Rowley & Chatterton also."[21]

His intellectual interests are also of his age. The great religious force in Blake's day was Swedenborg, and Blake appears to have joined the Swedenborgian Church of the New Jerusalem in London for a time (the statement that Blake's *father* was Swedenborgian is very dubious).[22] The apocalyptic tone of Swedenborg, his emphasis on open vision, his doctrine of "correspondence" between physical and spiritual worlds which underlies much of Blake's technique of symbolism, his conception of a Christianity based on the unity of God and Man in Christ instead of on the duality of a divine and a human nature, were some of his teachings that interested Blake. The attacks on Swedenborg in *The Marriage of Heaven and Hell* imply a strong sense of his importance. In the rather schematic quality of Swedenborg's thinking there is much to remind us that Swedenborg was a converted scientist. This comes out again in his tendency to treat his own visions of the spiritual world not imaginatively, as Blake does, but existentially, as experiences to be described in the same way that a scientist describes what he sees in nature. Consequently orthodox Swedenborgians could regard their master's religious teachings as fulfilling rather than contradicting his earlier scientific work.

Blake's view of science was very different. Just as he distinguished between art and the art of Pope and Reynolds, so he at least tried to distinguish between science and Newtonian science, which latter he thought was superstitious nonsense. On this point it was very difficult for him to make himself understood, as there was nothing in the science, philosophy, or even religion of his own time to appeal to. It was one thing for Blake to explain in his poetry, by means of a complicated theory of vortices, that the earth is really "one infinite plane" [*M*, 15.32; K497/E109]: it was quite another to find himself asserting to a good-humoured Crabb Robinson that the earth was flat. "But when I urged the circumnavigation," said Robinson, "dinner was announced."[23] Blake could make no sense out of a scientific world view which regarded matter as a congealed mass of solid particles, which regarded space as containing matter in the same way that a bag of beans contains beans, which regarded time as having no real connection with space, and which nevertheless thought of both time and space as endless extension. But there were as yet no objections to these views from any reputable quarter, and all Blake could say was that he would rather be mad with Cowper than sane with Newton and Locke.[24]

He reached a similar deadlock in his political thinking. After dropping out of the Mathew circle, he became acquainted with the publisher Joseph Johnson, who was the medium for a good deal of liberal and radical opinion. The people Blake met or may have met in Johnson's company included Godwin, with his wife Mary Wollstonecraft, Thomas Paine, Joseph Priestley (who may be "Inflammable Gass the Wind-finder" in *An Island in the Moon*), Thomas Holcroft, and the clergyman Richard Price, who had defended the American and French revolutions—quite a representative group of contemporary radicals. Blake's own sympathy with the two revolutions is clear enough from his poetry, and his contempt for all forms of worldly greatness, whether military or civilian, is written all over his work. On the outbreak of war with France, a censorship was clamped down in England. Paine escaped to France, as a result, it is said, of a warning by Blake. It is pleasant to think of so materialistic a thinker owing his life to someone's second sight, but Paine was jailed and nearly guillotined in France, so apparently even second sight cannot see everything. Paine's publisher, however (not Johnson, though Johnson was fined and imprisoned some years later), was imprisoned for blasphemy.

Blake retired into obscurity, muttering and growling. "To defend the Bible in this year 1798 would cost a man his life," he wrote on the margin of Bishop Watson's complacent attack on Paine's *Age of Reason*.[25] His later Prophecies are full of allusions to political events—to an extent that students of these works are only just beginning to realize. But if he remained quiescent, it was not wholly from prudence, a virtue which he defined as "a rich, ugly old maid courted by Incapacity" [*MHH*, pl. 7; K151/E35]. It was partly through a profound disbelief in the intellectual basis of the revolutionary creed, which he called "Deism." First Louis XIV and his successors, then Voltaire (who, as Blake points out, was not a radical but the flatterer of Frederick the Great), then a Reason-worshipping Robespierre, then Napoleon. There was for Blake no progress in liberty there, so he confined his attention to the poetry and art in which be could believe.

Much of Blake's poetry is for the common reader, and will not mislead him. The lyrics speak for themselves: they may contain great riches of meaning, but still what the attentive and sympathetic reader thinks they mean is basically what they do mean. It is otherwise with the "Prophecies," where commentaries can save one a good deal of time. The statements originally made about these poems, that they are a hopeless jumble of private associations and the like, have been thoroughly disproved years ago, and no critic now makes them who has any notion of what he is talking about. The Prophecies are based on a rigorously consistent body of ideas; they have been most carefully constructed and revised, and they are difficult because it was impossible to make them simpler. The few genuine obscurities arising from unfinished revision or from veiled references to Blake's life or political events do not affect the main arguments. Without making any promises to supply a "key" to Blake's thought, a few suggestions about the leading ideas of the Prophecies may be useful.

The central conception in Blake's thought might be expressed somewhat as follows: the imagination turns nature inside out. "Where man is not, nature is barren," said Blake [*MHH*, pl. 10; K152/E38], and by "nature" he meant the world as, say, it would have appeared to a single intelligence at the beginning of human life. Such an intelligence would be a tiny centre of a universe stretching away from him in all directions, a universe with plenty of resources for killing him, and full of force and will to survive, but with nothing in it to respond to his intelligence. The "natural man" stares helplessly at nature, minimizing his own intelligence and fascinated by its mysterious remoteness and stupid power. He builds his own societies on the analogy of nature, giving the primary place to force and cunning, so that the "natural society" which was so widely discussed in Blake's day is, for Blake, identical with tyranny, class distinctions, and economic injustice. The natural man builds his religions on the assumption that some "god" must lurk behind nature, combining its mystery with something analogous to intelligence. Religion of this kind—natural religion as Blake calls it—begins by personifying the forces of nature, then goes on to erect, on the analogy of human society, a ruling class of Olympian aristocrats, and finally arrives at its masterpiece, a whiskery old man up in the sky, with an uncertain temper and reactionary political views, whom Blake calls Nobodaddy, and, in the Prophecies, Urizen or Satan. Whatever the name of God may be, whether Jehovah or Jesus, there are always some who will think of him in terms of this Nobodaddy.

Or, varying the psychological symbols, we may say that an isolated intelligence wholly surrounded by nature is, in a sense, unborn. The body of Mother Nature surrounds us like an embryo. Hence our sexual desires, as long as they are directed toward something outside us, are really desires for a mother, and in the final analysis are desires for a death which is complete identification with Mother Nature. Blake's lyrics are full of symbols—crystal cabinets, golden chapels and nets, cups of gold, and others—which represent both Nature and the womb. We note that Nobodaddy's habitation in the Old Testament, first in the ark of the covenant and then in the Temple, had a feminine touch—curtains. Natural religion, then, leads to a mother as well as to a father. Blake calls this mother, as Queen of Heaven, Enitharmon or space; as vegetable nature, Vala; as the maternal principle, Tirzah; as the harlot—not the harlot of commercial exploitation but the symbol of the mocking, coy, elusive, and remote outside world—Rahab.

Can human beings do any better than this? They can, and they do whenever they are engaged in real work, i.e., not making war or feeding parasites. When they are working, men are building cities and planting gardens, that is, making nature into the form of human life. Work is man's response to his own desire, and this desire can only be called a desire to see the world in a human form. Such desire is not need, for an animal may need food without planting a garden to get it, nor is it want, or desire *for* something in particular. Cities and gardens reverse the "natural" perspective: here man is surrounding nature. Works of art are, if we like, "imitated" from nature: but their function is not to reproduce nature at second hand, but to give nature the form of civilized human intelligence.

We think of the child as more "natural" than the adult, but the precise opposite is true. The child is born civilized: he assumes that the world he is born into has a human shape and meaning, and was probably made for his own benefit. This is known as the "state of innocence": only after years of exposure to nature is he resigned to accepting the vast, mysterious, unconscious world of "experience," with all the human cruelties and stupidities that result from the view that man is a helpless captive of nature. The child's innocence, however, is not extinguished: it is only driven underground into his subconscious, where it becomes a world of suppressed and smoldering desire, joined by other outlawed desires of largely sexual origin. Creative artists can release this power, but in most people it remains stifled, emerging spasmodically in wars and revolutions. The buried power of human desire, symbolized in mythology by stories of Titans imprisoned under volcanoes, is called Orc in Blake's symbolism; the power which liberates it by creating the world of civilization and art ("Golgonooza") is called Los. The world of experience that sits grimly on top of Orc is the domain of Urizen. This word is of Greek origin, and is from the same root as "horizon"—the sense of a bound or limit to human effort.

"The marriage of heaven and hell" means that some day man's "hell," or buried furnace of desire, will explode and burn up "heaven," or the remote and mocking sky. It has been said that *The Marriage of Heaven and Hell* contains all Freud, but this is true only of its psychological aspect: on its social and political side it could be said in the same sense to contain all Marx. (Assuming, that is, that "all" means essential: Blake would have regarded both Freud and Marx as heathen idolaters and high priests of Nobodaddy.) Ordinarily, however, a revolutionary upheaval settles into the form of what has preceded it, just as the child grows into an adult like his father. This cycle of the growth of Orc into Urizen and the rebirth of Orc is traced in *The Mental Traveller*, where the symbolism has both psychological and social aspects.

As long as human life is an antithesis of desire and reason, it will be full of chaos and anarchy. Reason tries to control or suppress desire, in the name of order, and desire periodically retaliates by smashing the order. Man in a state of mere desire or mere reason is called by Blake a "Spectre." Intellectually, the Spectre works with abstractions, trying to understand nature by patterns and diagrams. These have no power to order life, but the Spectre cannot realize that, and keeps trying to fit human life to nature by imitating nature's regularity, or law. The result of this is morality, the futile attempt to make the reasonable desirable. Emotionally and sexually, the Spectre is a "ravening devouring lust,"[26] looking outside himself for gratification, instead of understanding that everything he can love is his "Emanation," loved by virtue of his capacity to love. Only creative work, which never attempts either to destroy or to suppress, can resolve the deadlock. Creation releases desire, and so provides the real form of desire, which is desire for freedom, equality, love, and innocence. Creation puts reason to work, and so provides the real form of reason, the constructive and unified shape of human intelligence, for true reason is "the bound or outward circumference of Energy" [*MHH*, pl. 4; K149/E34].

There are thus four levels of human existence. There is the savage and lonely world of unworked nature, Blake's Ulro or hell, where life is, in Hobbes's phrase, nasty, brutish, and short. This world of "Single Vision & Newton's sleep" [K818/E722] has retreated to the stars, but is still watching us, and waiting its chance to return. Above this is ordinary life trying to struggle out of savagery, which Blake calls Generation or experience. Above this again is the life of expanded and released desire which we all have some glimpses of in inspired moments, but which is most commonly the world of children and lovers. Blake calls this state Beulah or innocence. Finally, there is the "fourfold vision" of a life in which creation dominates reason, the life of "Wisdom, Art and Science" [*J*, pl. 3; K621/E146] which Blake calls Eden.

We cannot, by ourselves, get outside nature. However splendid our natural cities and gardens, they will only be little hollowings on the surface of the earth. But suppose we could think away the external or nonhuman world: what would the shape of things be like then? Clearly the whole universe would then have the shape of a single infinite human body. Everything that we call "real" in nature would then be inside the body and mind of this human being, just as in the dream the world of suppressed desire is all inside the mind of the dreamer. There would no longer be any difference, except one of perspective, between the group and the individual, as all individuals would be members of one human body. Everything in the world, including the sun, moon, and stars, would be part of this human body, and everything would be identical with everything else. This does not mean that all things would be separate and similar, like peas in a pod or "identical" twins: it means identical in the sense in which a grown man feels identical with himself at the age of seven, though he is identifying himself with another human being, quite different in time, space, matter, form, and personality.

For Blake, Christianity is the religion which teaches that this is in fact the real shape of things, and that the only God is universal and perfect Man, the risen Jesus. It is man, not of course natural man, but man as a creator, struggling to achieve his real human form, that God is interested in. The Bible speaks of an apocalypse or revelation of a world transformed into an infinite city, garden, and human body, as the state from which man fell, and to which he has again to be restored. The Bible calls this redeemed man Adam or Israel; Blake, being an Englishman, calls him Albion. What Albion is looking for is Jerusalem, "a City, yet a Woman,"[27] the human form that is at once his bride and his own home. The world of the apocalypse is not a future ideal, for ideals are, like the natural stars, always out of reach. It is a real presence, the authentic form of what exists here and now, and is not something to be promised to the dead, but something to be manifested to the living.

Everything that Blake means by "art" is the attempt of the trained and disciplined human mind to present this concrete, simple, and outrageously anthropomorphic view of reality. "Jesus & his Apostles & Disciples were all Artists," Blake says.[28] Such a statement will seem nonsense as long as we think of art in conventional terms, according to which Reynolds and Blake are both eighteenth-century English painters. Blake means that the reason alone, no matter in how rarefied a way it may be conceived, cannot comprehend the human shape of reality, for reason sooner or later will come to terms with the persisting appearance of a subhuman nature, and start suppressing desire. The desire which rebels against reason cannot comprehend it either, as, whether it takes the form of a lusting individual or of a revolutionary society, it is looking for something in the external world to gratify it. Only the effort of a mind in which intelligence and love are equally awake, a mind in the creative state that Blake calls imagination, can know what it means to

> Hold Infinity in the palm of your hand
> And Eternity in an hour.[29]

14

David Erdman's *Blake: Prophet against Empire*

July 1955

Review of David Erdman, Blake: Prophet against Empire: A Poet's Interpretation of the History of His Own Times *(Princeton: Princeton University Press, 1954); from* Philological Quarterly, *34 (July 1955): 273–4. Frye's review was part of the Blake section of "English Literature, 1660–1800: A Current Bibliography."*

There have been several studies of Blake's social and political interests and of his awareness of, and involvement with, the historical events of his time. Mr. Erdman's book, however, is the first in this tradition to employ consistently a full knowledge of the meaning of Blake's Prophecies and an ability to recognize the historical allusions made in them. It is also the first to make a consistent use of the *primary* sources of historical scholarship. The author carefully sifts fact from legend in Blake's biography, and replaces the often rather vague statements of previous critics about the social conditions of Blake's age with precise and fully documented annotations. He employs throughout the heuristic principle that Blake himself is (as his statements about art indicate that he naturally would be) not vague but exact, not abstract or generalized but concrete and particular. The result is that Blake emerges from Mr. Erdman's treatment as a poet who has, like Spenser before him, a detailed and coherent "historical allegory."

Mr. Erdman's book is almost a social history of England between 1760 and 1820, as seen from Blake's point of view. It begins with the short peaceful interlude of the 1760s, which the author regards as having impressed Blake in his childhood with his sense of an underlying state of innocence, then goes through the American Revolution, the Gordon riots, and the radicalism that gathered around Wilkes, to the French Revolution, the long war with France, the repressive measures of the Pitt government, the madness of George III, the misery and famine in England, and so on to the end of the Napoleonic era. All these events and many smaller ones are shown to be reflected in Blake's symbols. Blake's attitude to Paine, Voltaire, Rousseau, Lafayette, Marie Antoinette, George III, and others is worked out from a close study of both the engraved and the manuscript poems, sometimes from almost illegible scrawls in the Rossetti MS. The paintings and engravings are studied with a thoroughness unique in Blake commentary, and the result is often to reinterpret a whole poem: thus the engravings Blake did for Stedman's book on Surinam throw a flood of light on *Visions of the Daughters of Albion*. Even when dealing with allusions which are unmistakable or long recognized, such as the allusion to Chancellor Thurlow in *Europe*, he adds much concrete detail.

Blake's relation to and opinion of other artists, and in particular his keen sense of the social relevance of art, is also more fully treated than in any previous study. Angelica Kauffmann, Gillray, William Sharp, Mortimer, to say nothing of Barry, Flaxman, and Fuseli, take on a new significance in this connection, especially Gillray, whose caricatures are shown to have influenced Blake's designs. Similarly with the poets: the Hartford wit Joel Barlow is shown to have influenced *America*, and the clergyman Richard Warner to be alluded to in the second part of *Jerusalem*. One of the most admirable features of the book is the correcting of the glib interpretation of Blake's "dark Satanic mills" and similar phrases as covering the Industrial Revolution in toto. Mr. Erdman shows accurately just what mechanical and industrial phenomena, both military and civilian, actually did, from the evidence of the text, catch Blake's eye and got recorded in his symbolism.

In its totality the book may, perhaps, be criticized as exaggerating Blake's domestic radicalism and underestimating his hatred and distrust of what he called "Deism," which made him dislike French imperialism quite as much as the English variety. But the host of new facts and the clarification of both text and context which Mr. Erdman's study has brought are of a value quite independent of this.

15

Notes for a Commentary on *Milton*

1957

From The Divine Vision: Studies in the Poetry and Art of William Blake, *ed. Vivian de Sola Pinto (London: Gollancz, 1957), 99–137. In a memorandum regarding a possible third collection of essays (27 January 1975), Frye noted that he would not want to reprint this without revisions. The collection did not materialize at this time, and the "Notes" were not reprinted.*

A footnote by Frye at the beginning of the essay indicates that all references to Milton *are accompanied by the plate and line numbers given in Keynes,* Poetry and Prose of William Blake *(1927; rpt. 1956). "Of the four copies of* Milton,*" Frye writes, "the Keynes text adopts the order of the latest and most complete (Copy 'D' in the Keynes-Wolf Census), adding the Preface from the earlier copies. As there is no point in repeating what I have said elsewhere about* Milton, *the reader is respectfully referred, for aspects of the poem not discussed here but falling within my general approach to it, to my* Fearful Symmetry *(Princeton, 1947), especially chapter 10." Frye's references to the 1927 edition, which are very complete, are retained here because this edition includes in its numbering seven illustrated plates excluded from the numbering in the later Keynes editions (1957, 1966) and in Erdman (although for the content of the illustrated plates Frye would have had to rely on other sources). For the convenience of readers, references to Keynes,* The Complete Writings of William Blake *(1966), used throughout the remainder of the present volume, have been added in square brackets where applicable. With a very few exceptions, indicated in the notes, these also correspond to the plate numbering used in Erdman,* The Complete Poetry and Prose of William Blake *(rev. ed., 1982).*

I Introduction

Blake is a poet of the Bible, and from early life he saw in the Bible the outlines of an epic narrative. This narrative begins with myths of creation, fall, and deluge (which are all the same event in Blake) and goes on to the history of Israel, presented as a sequence of revolutions and captivities. This sequence is interrupted, though not terminated, by the Incarnation, and, after a period of undetermined length, an apocalypse and Last Judgment put an end to history and return us to the world as it was before the fall. It is natural, then, that Blake's poetic ambitions should have moved steadily in the direction of writing a Christian epic poem that would reshape this narrative and so in its own context justify the ways of God to men—the Miltonic phrase is on the title page of *Milton*.

Many of Blake's shorter "Prophecies" can be read as episodes from such an epic. *America* and *The Marriage of Heaven and Hell* (1793) deal with the last phase, the French and American revolutions being regarded as signs of an imminent apocalypse. *Europe* (1794) begins with the Incarnation, covering the New Testament part of the myth. *The (First) Book of Urizen* (1794) begins a series of prophetic essays at the other end, of creation and fall. In 1795 came an extraordinary burst of pictorial activity climaxed by over five hundred designs for Young's *Night Thoughts*. In Young's poem, nine "nights" of vision of which the ninth is a Last Judgment, Blake got a hint for a larger epic scheme of his own. *Vala*, much of which is written on the backs of proofs for the Young designs, has also nine "nights," the first four dealing with the creation–fall–deluge complex, the next four with four generalized phases of a cycle of history from revolution to decline under tyranny. The last night of this sequence, the eighth, covers, like *Europe*, the period from the Incarnation to Blake's time. The ninth night is an apocalypse, as in Young. This poem was still in manuscript when Blake moved to Felpham and the company of Hayley in 1800, by which time its name had been changed to *The Four Zoas*.

The Four Zoas illustrates a good deal of interest and reading in epic literature. Its original form of a sybil's prophecy shows the influence of the Icelandic *Eddas*, and possibly of the sixth book of the *Aeneid*, which Blake certainly knew, although he seems more interested in the second: the Laocoön story always fascinated him, and some aspects of his "Covering Cherub" may be derived from Virgil's Pyrrhus.[1] The names of the first two characters in *The Four Zoas*, Tharmas and Enion, are probably taken from the Thaumas and Eione of Hesiod. Of English epic poets, Blake knew Chaucer and Spenser, and would have found in Chaucer's *House of Fame*, for all its irony, many points of contact with his own

Golgonooza. A Chaucerian synonym for fame, *los* or *loos*, may be the source of the name of Blake's great hero.[2]

But Milton, whom he had known and loved from childhood, was always for Blake his primary master both for the Christian epic and for his understanding of the Bible. It was Blake's habit to record his differences rather than his agreements, but even when he is most critical of Milton he shows how closely he is following him. It seems almost incredible, for instance, that the incisive comment on Milton's view of the Trinity in *The Marriage of Heaven and Hell* could have been made by a reader who did not know the *Christian Doctrine*.[3] Besides, in every age Milton has been a political symbol as well as a poet. To the Tory Samuel Johnson Milton was "an acrimonious and surly republican,"[4] a view which brought a violent reaction from the mildly liberal Cowper. To anyone as far left of centre as Blake, Milton was not only the last of England's major poets, but England's one major prophet as well. Blake's poem, based on his conviction that Milton not only should be "living at this hour" but actually was, is a vision of Milton as the deliverer of his people, like Milton's own Samson, or, perhaps a closer analogy, as a guardian angel, like Michael in Israel (and, according to *Lycidas*, in England as well). The notion that Blake was primarily concerned to "correct" Milton's theological and domestic difficulties rests on a story of Crabb Robinson's which is much better ignored.[5]

The immediate effect of Hayley on Blake was to sharpen his sense and increase his knowledge of the epic tradition. Hayley had written a poem about epic poetry, with erudite notes, and even his redoubtable soap opera in heroic couplets, *The Triumphs of Temper*, links itself in a preface with the heroi-comical branch of epic. Besides the usual Classical training of his day (Blake began reading Greek with Hayley), Hayley had a wider knowledge of modern European literatures than was common at that time. Of the few important commissions that Blake got out of Hayley, one of the first was the series of heads of poets, most of them epic poets, done as a frieze for Hayley's library. A man of Blake's intellectual curiosity was unlikely to draw a head of Ercilla without inquiring who Ercilla was,[6] and his education must have rapidly expanded in many directions. Nor was Milton neglected. Hayley, a liberal like Cowper, had written a life of Milton also, and Cowper, when he came to Felpham in 1792, brought with him an unfinished Milton project, of which the central part was his translations of Milton's Latin and Italian poems. This was eventually published by Hayley in 1808, with some assistance from Blake, though both the designing and the engraving commissions were eventually taken away from him.

Blake came to Felpham practically determined to make his stay there a period of definitive vision, and it is not surprising that the immediate result of it should be a poem in the epic tradition with a particular relationship to Milton. Sir Geoffrey Keynes is definite that the "2 Books" of the title page originally read "12 Books," and the original *Milton* would undoubtedly have followed the narrative of the scriptural epic as preserved in *The Four Zoas*. After dealing with creation, deluge, the fall of Satan and Adam, and the various phases of the cycle of history, it would have shown the apocalypse consolidating from the wars and tyrannies of the eighteenth century through some crucial act of poetic vision in Blake's own life. The poem referred to in letters to Butts of April and July, 1803, is clearly much longer than the present *Milton*, though there is no evidence that it introduced Milton himself as a character.

When the poem was cut down to two books, only the act of vision remained, and the remainder survives vestigially. The cycle of history is represented by the Bard's Song, which also makes some attempt to work in the Blakean story of the beginning of things. Plate 3, carrying over the account of the creation of the physical world out of Urizen by Los from two earlier Prophecies, is a later plate, connected with the Bard's Song by the opening line of plate 11 [10] (also a later plate), identifying Urizen with the Satan of the Bard's story. The apocalypse appears only in the distance at the end of the poem. Thus the poem as we now have it is, in Milton's language, not a "diffuse" but a "brief" epic, not a Blakean *Paradise Lost* but a Blakean *Paradise Regained*. The theme of Blake's poem is a struggle with Satan in which Milton occupies the place that Christ occupies in *Paradise Regained*, and hence it might be described, without a comma, as "Paradise Regained by John Milton."

The personal references in *Milton* are to a time when Blake was getting bored with Felpham and distrustful of Hayley's influence on him—say the earlier months of 1803, before the Schofield fracas of August. *Milton* as we have it is clearly pre-Schofield in its general setting, though Schofield and his accompanying symbols are mentioned once (*M*, 21.59 [19.59]) in an obviously later insertion. The date 1804 on the title page probably means that by then the writing had been essentially completed and the engraving begun. The serenity of tone makes the end of 1805 practically a *terminus ad quem* for the writing. On December 11 of that year Blake wrote what shows every sign of being intended as the last letter to

Hayley. After that came Cromek, the Stothard quarrel, the first Hunt attack, and the "despair" entry of January 20, 1807.[7] Still later come the bitter epigrams on Hayley, when Blake was recreating in his mind some black thoughts that had passed through it at the time of the Schofield affair. His reference in the "Public Address" to a poem about his Felpham sojourn which will expose a "nest of villains" [K592/E572] is not to the *Milton* we have, and perhaps indicates that he thought of rewriting it to fit his more neurotic later mood. Fortunately he never did so, and in fact seems to have revised the poem in the same serene spirit in which he wrote it. Plates 3, 4, and 5, which are later, stress the universal rather than the personal aspect of the Satan-Hayley myth with which the poem begins, and the noisy preface disappears from the later copies, in spite of the fact that it contains one of Blake's greatest lyrics. The *engraving* of *Milton* is a by-product of intense concentration on the illustrating of Milton's poems, an activity which extended over a great part of Blake's life, and is remarkably consistent in its iconography. For instance, the "sixfold emanation" of the poem, illustrated on plates 19 [17] and 48 [41], reappears as the six spirits surrounding Milton, noted in the description to an illustration to *Il Penseroso* (no. 11), written in 1816.

II Structure of the Symbolism: Eden

Milton is based on the conception of four levels of vision expounded in a poem written by Blake in the summer of 1801 and sent in a letter to Butts of November 1802. In the highest or paradisal view of reality (Eden), man is one with God, and everything else is part of a divine, and therefore a human, creation. Imagination attempts to recreate the world in the form in which man originally possessed it. In the next highest view, which is sexual rather than fully human (*M*, 4.5), the view of the lower Paradise or Beulah, the relation of creator and creature becomes the relation of lover and beloved, and the created world becomes an "emanation" or responsive bride, like Shelley's epipsyche. This view survives in our world as the child's innocent vision, the sense of reality as a protected home. Below this is the world of Generation or experience, which is split into a subjective and an objective aspect. Here the emanation becomes a remote and tantalizing "female will," and the perceiver is transformed into a "Spectre" or "Selfhood," "a Male Form howling in Jealousy" (*M*, 3.36), who, in the poem "My Spectre around me," written about the same time as *Milton* and referred to in it (*M*, 35.5 [32.5]), is depicted as tracking through the snow a disappearing mistress who is actually inside him. Below this again is Ulro or hell, the world of "Single vision & Newton's sleep" [K818/E722], divided between an ego and a vast menacing form of "nature," which to the imagination wavers uncertainly between a paternal and a maternal figure, both equally stupid and cruel.

In ordinary life this hierarchy of worlds is reversed. At the apex of experience is the inscrutable and unthinkably remote world of the stars, the ultimate inspiration for all our belief in fate. Next comes the world we work in, sitting on top of the child's innocent vision, which with the advance of maturity is driven underground into the subconscious. But deeper than the buried child Orc, the terrible boy who bursts out in revolution, there is the buried unfallen humanity Los, the patient smith who forges the golden city (cf. Isaiah 54:16), but who also keeps the world of Generation going as a defence against the ultimate horror of Ulro.

In the "natural" or commonsense view of reality, as expounded, according to Blake, by Locke, each subject is a separate centre of perception, and each object is a separate thing, things being classified for convenience by their similarities or general resemblances. This process leads from sensation to reflection, from the concrete to the abstract, "Within labouring, beholding Without, from Particulars to Generals" (*M*, 3.37). The imaginative view turns the natural one inside out. Here the subject is not at the centre but at the circumference of reality, hence all perceivers are one perceiver, who is the totality of humanity (Albion) and, because totally human, divine as well (Jesus). Rilke is close to Blake when he speaks of the poet's perspective as that of an angel containing all time and space, but blind and looking into himself.[8] From this point of view, space is no longer extension (Enitharmon controlled by the fallen Urizen), but form (Enitharmon controlled by Los); time is no longer duration (Spectre of Urthona) but creative life (Los). In plates 30–1 [28–9] we learn that the view of space and time as indefinite extensions receding from us is a projection caused by the cramped quarters of our present bodies.

The commonsense view perceives separation and similarity; the imaginative view perceives two kinds of identity. Blake speaks of "Identities or Things" [K470/E656]: a thing may be identified *as* itself, yet it cannot be identified except as an individual of a class. The class is its "living form," not its abstract essence, and form in Blake is a synonym for image, or experienced reality (thus the "Forms Eternal" of *M*, 35.38

[32.38] are opposed to what Blake thought of as Platonic forms). All Blake's images and mythical figures are "minute particulars"[9] or individuals identified with their total forms. Hence they are "States, Combinations of Individuals" (*M*, 35.10 [32.10]), and can be seen in either singular or collective aspects. Ololon is the sixfold emanation of Milton because Milton had three wives and three daughters, yet also a mighty host descending to the earth and a single virgin in Blake's garden. Blake refers impartially to Ololon as "she" or "they."

Further, all things are identical *with* each other. A man feels identical with himself at the age of seven, although between the man and the child there is little that is similar in regard to form, matter, time, space, or personality. And as in the imaginative view all things are within the life of a single eternal and infinite God-Man, all aspects, forms, or images of that body are identical. This is a view of things which can only be expressed poetically, through metaphor. The metaphor, in its radical form, is a statement of identification: the hero is a lion; this is that; A is B. When the hero is metaphorically a lion he remains a hero and the lion remains a lion. Hence a world where everything is identical with everything else is not a world of monotonous uniformity, as a world where everything was *like* everything else would be. In the imaginative world everything is one in essence, but infinitely varied in identity, as Blake remarks in a note on Swedenborg.[10] We sometimes use the word "identical" to mean very similar, as in the phrase "identical twins," but if twins were really identical they would be the same person, and hence could be different in form, like a tree and a dryad.

The language of religion is instinctively metaphorical: Christ *is* God and Man; in the Trinity three *is* one; the body and blood *are* the bread and wine, and so on. In the Bible, especially in the Book of Revelation, we find a world of total identification, the individual identified with the class, "all Human Forms identified," as Blake says at the end of his own *Jerusalem*. Hence it is a world in which all things have attained a human instead of a merely natural form. If we ask what the human forms of things are, we have only to took at what man tries to do with them. Man tries to build cities out of stones, and to develop farms and gardens out of plants; hence the city and garden are the human forms of the mineral and vegetable worlds respectively. In the apocalypse, then, all aspects of reality are seen in their human forms; each individual is identical with its class or living form, and all living forms are identical with, and therefore eternally different from, one another. To illustrate in a table:

1. The *divine* world is a world in which all "gods," or aspects of infinite and eternal humanity, are One God. There are four such aspects in Blake, the four "Zoas" or living creatures who in Ezekiel's vision make up the spiritual body of the Word. Some knowledge of them is assumed by Blake, and for reasons of space has to be assumed here also. Albion fell, like Milton's Adam, through idolatrous adoration of his female principle, though, unlike Adam, he could create her out of his own body. The result was that Luvah or Orc, the sexual (ὄρχις) aspect of him, assumed control in place of the intellectual one (*M*, 21.21 [19.21]; *M*, 38.39 [34.39]), and plunged us all into a world dominated by a sense of sexual shame (represented by the accusing eagle who watches the sleeping Albion on plate 42).

2. The *spiritual* or angelic world is a world in which all spirits or angels are One Spirit. The fact that this world is out of physical reach is expressed by associating it with fire, in which fallen man cannot live, and with the heavenly bodies. Angels have traditionally been the spirits of sun, moon, and stars; the imagination, as Blake says in a famous passage in the Rossetti MS, sees the sun as a company of angels, and the One Spirit descends to man as a single, though infinitely varied, tongue of flame. In Blake there are seven of these "Angels of the Divine Presence" [K521/E131] or "Eyes of God" [K686/E205], and they appear in human history as seven progressive conceptions of God, ending with Jesus. They are listed on plate 14 [13] and instruct Milton in the doctrine of identity on plate 35 [32]. The Second Coming of Jesus, which ends history, introduces an eighth (Albion or redeemed man): hence Ololon, the heroine of *Milton* whose appearance prefigures the apocalypse, is associated with a "Starry Eight" [K525/E135].

3. The *human* world is a world in which all men are One Man, or expressed in terms of sexual rather than social love, a world in which a Bridegroom and a Bride are one flesh. This human world extends over the whole of what we ordinarily think of as nonhuman nature (*M*, 27.41 [25.41]), for, as the universe is a divine creation, it is also a human creation when God and Man are one.

4. The *animal* world is a world of domesticated animals, of which the sheep has a conventional priority in the Bible, for a world in which the lion lies down with the lamb is clearly conceived from the lamb's point of view. Hence the imaginative or human animal world is a world in which all animals are a single sheepfold, and all sheep One Lamb.

5. The *vegetable* world is a world in which all plants are a garden or farm, the Eden and Promised Land of the Bible. All trees in the garden are One Tree of Life; all plants on the farm are a single harvest and vintage, the bread and wine of which are identical with the body and blood of the One Lamb of the animal world.

6. The *mineral* world is a city of streets and highways, a city in which all buildings are One Temple, a house of many mansions, and that temple One (precious) Stone, the cornerstone of Zion.

7. The *chaotic* world, represented by the sea, disappears in the apocalypse (Revelation 21:1), its place being taken by a circulating river of fresh water ("the deeps shrink to their fountains," as Blake says in *America* [8.8; K199/E54]). This river is the water of life restored to man, and as it is identical with the circulating blood of man's risen body all water is a single "Globule of [Man's] Blood," as Blake calls it.

In Blake, as in the Bible, Jesus is the unifying principle which identifies all these images with one another. Jesus *is* God and Man; he *is* the bread and wine, the body and blood, the tree, bread and water of life, the vine of which we are branches, the cornerstone of the city, and his body *is* the temple. In the apocalypse the Globule of Blood is the sun (*M*, 31.23 [29.23]), for sun, moon, and stars are inside the risen body of Christ, and are hence identical with the gold and gems of which the City of God is composed. Further, as risen man can live in fire, all the above images may be thought of as burning: the tree is a burning tree, like a candlestick or the bush of the Exodus; the stones burn with a gem-like flame, and the Jehovah of the Bible is "no other than he who dwells in flaming fire" [*MHH*, pl. 6; K150/E35]. A note scribbled on the back of a sketch for the last plate of *Milton* speaks of returning "from flames of fire tried & pure & white" [K535/E674]. The poet who sees the world in a grain of sand and heaven in a wild flower, and who identifies earth and heaven in vision, has the same conception of identity as that of the famous Buddhist prayer to the jewel in the lotus.[11]

Two other identifications are of importance. In the opening stanza of the *Introduction* to the *Songs of Experience*, we are told a good deal about Blake's view of the poet. The poet is one "Who Present, Past, & Future, sees": in vision all times are one. But if all times are one, all spaces are one too: if all time is an eternal present, all space is an infinite presence. The poet is of the tradition of the Hebrew prophets deriving from the Word of God that walked in the Garden of Eden and discovered the fall of man; yet he also calls himself, as he does in *Milton*, a "Bard," a word with its roots in the British tradition. The imaginative form of Israel, the Garden of Eden or Promised Land, is the same place as the imaginative form of Britain, usually called Atlantis, and the famous hymn "And did those feet in ancient time," which begins *Milton*, identifies the two.

In the ritual of the Eucharist man eats the bread and wine which "is" the body and blood of a God-Man. The ritual dramatizes the fall: the true sacrament for Blake is the formation of a true human society, which is an apocalyptic process separating the individual from the ego or Selfhood, clod-love from pebble-love. This apocalyptic sacrament is to be conceived more as God eating man than as man eating God: a "harvest and vintage" in which the imaginative form of man is identified with all other forms, and the chaff and lees of the Selfhood are thrown away. The wars of Blake's time are interpreted as the treading of an apocalyptic winepress, following Isaiah; the growth of science (*M*, 27.18 [25.18]) as the gathering of an apocalyptic harvest. In the earlier *Europe* these signs are the French Revolution and Newton respectively. At the beginning of the poem, on plate 2, we see wheat and grapes lit up by a huge star or comet representing the descent of Milton; at the end, on plate 50 [43], the naked female figure in the centre appears to represent the identification of vegetable and human forms.

III Structure of the Symbolism: Ulro

This world of total and realized metaphor is heaven: its opposite is hell, the pure state of nature of which Blake took so low a view. Ulro is the world as it would appear to humanity at the beginning of the fall, without a single image of human desire, or form of human work, yet established in it—no habitations, no cultivation, nothing but suggestions of indifference, mystery, inscrutable fate, a relentless fight to survive, and loneliness. The demonic vision of reality is an elaborate parody of the apocalyptic vision. Error disappears only when recognized as error, and error can be recognized only as the opposite of truth. Blake came increasingly to think of the apocalypse in negative terms as a growing consolidation of the natural vision. Hence the central figure of the demonic outlook, Satan, is the youngest son of Los, brought forth "Refusing Form in vain" (*M*, 3.41) and "permitted to imitate" (*M*, 44.25–6 [39.25–6]) the unfallen state. Here is the form of the demonic imitation:

1. The *divine* world begins in the perception of a nonhuman power and will in nature, "The Fairies, Nymphs, Gnomes & Genii of the Four Elements" (*M*, 34.20 [31.20]). These spirits, with the advance of natural science, move further away, chiefly into the stars, and become gods. Such gods are conceived, on the analogy of the demonic human society, as inscrutable tyrants, jealous of their privileges, and while they do not exist, the results of believing in them do. One of them is usually in supreme control, asserting that he is "God alone" and that "There is no other" (*M*, 9.25–6). In the demonic vision everything is hierarchic, leading up to an ego at the top, in contrast to the Christ who is a total form, and so self-evidently one. This solitary super-ego, or old man of the sky, Newton's Pantocrator (*M*, 4.11), Blake calls "Nobodaddy" in the Rossetti MS, "Urizen" (fallen) in the earlier Prophecies, and "Satan" in *Milton* and *Jerusalem*. The essential attribute of Blake's Satan is death, and he works within man as what we should now call the death impulse, the inner traitor of the soul who, like Judas Iscariot, eventually goes to his own place (*M*, 11.12 [10.12]; cf. *M*, 28.41–2 [26.41–2]).

2. The *spiritual* world is a society of self-righteous demons, who take possession of man to destroy him. They originate of course from the star-gods of a fatalistic view of divinity, and are usually represented in *Jerusalem* by the twelve sons of Albion, the number being zodiacal. As the true spirits are all One Spirit or tongue of flame, so evil spirits are all one "False Tongue," or Satan as accuser of sin (*M*, 2.10; cf. James 3:6). This false tongue is called by Blake the "Covering Cherub," who is to Satan what the Holy Spirit is to Jesus. The Covering Cherub is the serpent of Eden who is identified with the visionary Prince of Tyre, the archetypal tyrant, in Ezekiel 28, a chapter which underlies Blake's description of the fall of Satan in plate 9.

3. The *human* world is a society of tyrants and victims, with a supreme tyrant usually in control. Such societies in the Bible are typified by Egypt and Babylon, and the tyrants by Pharaoh and Nebuchadnezzar. The individual in such a society is a Selfhood who creates the cruel and lazy sky-gods in his own image. Corresponding to the Bride, the demonic vision has a harlot, the Whore of Babylon whose name is Mystery, the opposite of revelation or apocalypse.

4. The *animal* world is a society of tyrants and victims also, and its symbols in Blake are either beasts of prey or parasites, many of them listed on plate 29 [27]. "Every Thing has its Vermin," Blake says

[K620/E144], and among the beasts of prey are the serpent of Eden and the two monsters who appear at the end of Job, Behemoth and Leviathan. These are associated by Blake with the military and naval warfare of his own time, and in his 1809 Exhibition he saw them in charge of Pitt and Nelson respectively. In the Bible Leviathan is identified with Pharaoh (Ezekiel 29:3), and Nebuchadnezzar turns into a variety of behemoth [Daniel 4:32–3].

5. The *vegetable* world is a heath, forest, or wilderness, called Entuthon Benython (the second part of which may be connected with the Greek βένθος, depth). Its individual form is the Tree of Mystery, the self-enrooting banyan of "The Human Abstract," which is also the oak worshipped by the Druids, and, in the Bible, the tree of moral knowledge, the Cross and the barren fig tree.

6. The *mineral* world, or demonic city, is featured by hierarchically-shaped buildings like the pyramid or tower of Babel, servile architecture as Ruskin would call them, and by structures which, like the furnace, the winepress, and the mill, imprison fire or disintegrate form (*M*, 43.16 ff. [38.16 ff.]).

7. The *chaotic* world is the sea (or snow or desert), the sea which as the "Red" Sea recalls the spilt blood of fallen man (*M*, 31.63 [29.63]) [cf. *J*, 89.49; K735/E249]. As the Dead Sea or salt lake it is called Udan Adan (*M*, 25.60 [23.60]), and as the Atlantic Ocean it is the "Sea of Time and Space" which separates England and America and conceals the Atlantis which is the imaginative form of both.

All demonic images may be also identified with one another, in fact must be if *Milton* is to be read with any comprehension. The entire universe of nature is the "dark Satanic mills" of a cyclical labyrinth (*M*, 14.43 [13.43]), and this universe is, in relation to the real world, both underground and (adopting the deluge version of the fall) underwater. It is an embryonic world, described by Blake as the Mundane Shell (*M*, 19.21 ff. [17.21 ff.]), and within it is the vast interrelated mass of spawning generative life which Blake calls the "Polypus" and identifies with Orc or Luvah, the natural body of which we are members (*M*, 31.31 [29.31]; *M*, 38.24 [34.24]). The Covering Cherub may be seen in the stars who mark the circumference of the single vision, for Satan is above all a sky-god or lord of the natural heaven, a dragon whose tail drew down a third of the stars (*M*, 13.26 [12.26]). As his journey in *Paradise Lost* shows, his empire extends over both chaos and what we call the cosmos. As

Leviathan, Satan is not only a sea-monster but the sea itself, the sea that covers Atlantis, Sodom, Pharaoh's Egyptians, and, according to Milton, the Garden of Eden after the flood. To find Atlantis again we have only to drain the sea, not the Atlantic Ocean, but the "Sea of Time and Space" on top of our imaginations (*M*, 17.36 ff. [15.36 ff.]).

Another feature of the Ulro vision requiring comment is the "female will," the separated objective world that confronts us in the fallen perspective [K661/E176–7]. The outer world of nature is a "Female Space" (*M*, 11.6 [10.6]) because, like a "harlot coy" [K168/E471] increasing her price by pretending to be a virgin, it continually retreats from the perceiver. The perceiver is a human being, who may be a man or a woman—in other words Blake's "female will" has nothing to do with human women except when women dramatize it in their sexual rituals, as they do, for instance, in the Courtly Love convention. The relation of humanity to external nature is shown as a cycle of four phases in *The Mental Traveller*, a poem dating from the Felpham period, where nature is a female figure appearing first as a mother to an infant, then as a wife to an adult, then as a daughter to an old man, and then as a mirage to a ghost. None of these relations is quite true: the mother is actually an old nurse, the wife a temporary mistress, the daughter a changeling, and the mirage an outward reflection of the "emanation," which is inside the mind. Thus in every phase nature is both virgin and harlot, unpossessed and mocking. In the first phase her Blakean name is Tirzah, in the second Vala, in the third Rahab, in the fourth the Shadowy Female. All four names are important in *Milton*. The Shadowy Female is associated with the Lilith of Isaiah in *M*, 20.43 [18.43]. Rahab is identified with Egypt and Leviathan in the Bible, and by Blake with the apocalyptic Whore (*M*, 46.22 [40.22]). Tirzah in the Exodus story is one of five sisters, daughters of Zelopehad (*M*, 31.58 [29.58]), who demand a separate female inheritance: these five are the five fallen senses in Blake, the five foolish virgins without light. Their names are given in *M*, 19.11 [17.11] and elsewhere.

"Natural religion" is called an "impossible absurdity" (*M*, 46.13 [40.13]), but it is not a mere intellectual error: it is rather the working of the death-wish in human life. All human work, art, and prophecy go to build up the city and garden of a free, happy, and equal human civilization, but all such work implies the predominance of a human over a subhuman vision of life. Natural religion operates in three stages: natural law, the admiration for the automatism of external nature; moral law, the attempt to imitate this automatism in human life; and finally "accusation of sin," or attempts to enforce conformity as a supreme virtue. At each state the underlying form of natural religion, a deep distrust in the worth of human life itself, becomes more clearly revealed. Human sacrifice is the purest form of this, but war and slavery are also products of shame, the contempt for life that springs from the thwarting of the sexual drive. For war is always treated by Blake, with a psychological insight which would be startling to those who do not know him, as a sexual perversion, ending in "Glory & Victory a Phallic Whip."[12] This is how war is visualized in plate 29 [27].

As for Blake's condemnation of Newton, even that shows how deeply Miltonic a poet Blake was. In *Paradise Lost* Raphael refuses to answer Adam's questions about cosmology: he does not mean that Adam's descendants should not study astronomy, but that in preparing for a crucial ordeal in his own life Adam should be concentrating on the Word of God within him and not on the works of God without. Blake's view of Newtonian science is similar: it is not its truth but the mental attitude to it that is in question. If the beauty of nature's mathematical order can encourage men to think that the miseries they perpetrate in their own society are inevitable or of little importance, its study can be a pernicious narcotic. We tend to think of the eighteenth century rather sentimentally as an age of common sense and enlightenment: Blake thought of it as an age of imperialistic war and slavery which finally erupted in the senseless hysteria of the Napoleonic wars and in the ruthless extermination of culture "Where Human Thought is crush'd beneath the iron hand of Power" (*M*, 27.5 [25.5]).

IV Structure of the Symbolism: Generation

The world that we ordinarily live in is not heaven, but neither is it quite hell. It is the world of experience, a world not under the wrath but under the law. Heaven and hell, Eden and Ulro, form a great antithesis of eternal life and eternal death, and the whole effort of imagination and art is directed toward separating them. The rhythm of existence in this world, where the presiding genius is Orc or Luvah, Blake's Eros, is cyclical, following the movements of the heavenly bodies. History shows a series of cycles: seven major ones, or "Eyes of God," since the beginning of time, and twenty-seven minor ones, or "Churches," from Adam's time to our own. Each major cycle begins with a revolt against tyranny, and gradually ages into a new tyranny as the pressure of natural religion gets stronger.

First of all, in Blake's version of history, were the Druids, the survivors of Atlantis, who developed a culture of megalithic temples, tree and serpent worship, and finally expired in a frenzy of human sacrifice, burning victims in wicker cages (*M*, 41.11 [37.11]). Druid architecture is illustrated in the early part of the poem, in plates 4 and 6. The Druids were giants, but their culture established the pattern followed after men collapsed into their present human forms. They belonged to the second "Eye" of Moloch; with the third, Elohim, human life began as we know it. Adam represents the "limit of contraction" (*M*, 14.21 [13.21]), or the nadir of the fall of man's body, hence nature, the objective counterpart of that body, "is a Vision of the Science of the Elohim" (*M*, 31.65 [29.65]). The story of Adam is also associated with trees and serpents. The sixth "Eye," Jehovah, was Hebrew civilization, which went through the four stages summarized in *The Four Zoas*, of revolt (birth of Orc), study of natural law (Urizen exploring his dens), moral law (crucifixion of Orc), and a final blood-bath of mass murder. This last stage is symbolized by a flood, out of which an "ark," or historical womb, preserves the embryo of new life.[13]

The Exodus story tells how a revolt against Egyptian tyranny was gradually "perverted to ten commands," as Blake says in *America* [8.3; K198/E54]. The Israelites were trying to reach a new Jerusalem and a Promised Land identical with the Garden of Eden. The Exodus story says that Moses, the spirit of the law, died at the boundary of the Promised Land, the conquest of which was achieved by Joshua, who has the same name as Jesus. Symbolically, this means that the Israelites never really came out of the wilderness, and the reign of the law did not end, nor was the conquest of the genuine Promised Land begun, until Jesus was given Joshua's name. The four stages of Israelite culture were, first, the revolt against Egypt; second, the wandering in the labyrinthine wilderness; third, the giving of the moral law and the crucifixion of Orc as the brazen serpent on the pole; and finally an entry into "Canaan" accompanied by annihilation wars.

The career of Jesus corresponds closely to the Exodus: he is led into Egypt, wanders in the desert, preaches the gospel from a mountain, gathers twelve followers, is crucified like the brazen serpent, and conquers the true Promised Land. But the cycle of civilization he started, the seventh "Eye," symbolized in Blake by Lazarus (*M*, 26.26 [24.26]) and by Theotormon (*M*, 24.38 [22.38]), also had its core of natural religion, inherited partly from Jewish and partly from Classical culture. The progress of the Christian cycle is traced in *Europe*, which begins with an echo of the *Nativity Ode* (echoed again in *Milton* when the great "Vision of beatitude" begins, *M*, 27.71 [25.71]).[14] The *Nativity Ode*, like most of Milton's earlier poems, has two levels of nature. One is the fallen or corrupt nature trying to "hide her guilty front with innocent snow," Blake's Leutha; the other is a divinely sanctioned order symbolized by the harmony of the spheres. It is part of the argument of *Europe* (and of *Milton*) that this divinely sanctioned order is in fact the very world of the false gods that Jesus came to drive away. By Newton's time it has disappeared entirely into an invisible world of "primary qualities," and the period after Newton begins its death agonies as a new cycle rises in America.

The world of Generation has a structure of symbolism parallel to Eden and Ulro, most of the symbols being derived from the Exodus narrative. Thus:

1. The *divine* world is a world of moral gods, like the jealous Jehovah of the ten commandments. Such gods are stupid and priggish, caring nothing about art or imagination but only about the proper ritual for themselves and for a morality of mediocrity, but they are not actively vicious unless cornered or threatened. The helpless *dieu fainéant* who appears in the early Job plates, unable to prevent Satan doing as he likes, represents this aspect of Jehovah, whose destruction by Milton is depicted in plate 18 [16].

2. The *spiritual* (always in Blake a synonym of mental or intellectual) world is a world of generalizations or abstract ideas, hazy reflections derived as a residue from sense experience, which are called, like the individual who holds them, "spectres." They originate in natural law, and they develop moralism because they are conceived in panic (we speak of grasping or seizing such ideas) and express themselves in aggression. Precepts and arguments, unlike the concrete examples of art and experience, can be used only as weapons: they must refute or be refuted, and hence, as described on plate 30 [28], they are either cowards or bullies until liberalized by being made into the images of art.

3. The *human* world is a society of the respectable people of the law and the subrespectable, the latter including both geniuses and criminals, for morality cannot distinguish "tygers of wrath" [K152, 281/E37, 314] from ordinary beasts of prey. In a true human society all men are brothers, and the parental relation is subordinated to the fraternal

one. In Generation the chief symbols of society are parental, implying that as many as possible are to be kept in leading strings. In Blake the "priest" is sinister and the "monk" benevolent because the former is called father and the latter brother, and religion dominated by father and mother symbols is a religion that has fallen under the law.

4. The *animal* world, not important in *Milton*, is the exact counterpart of the human one, a society of respectable animal slaves, "horses of instruction" [K152, 211/E37, 314] or sheep designed to be fleeced, along with outlaws like the tiger and the wolf.

5. The *garden* of the ordinary world is symbolized by Blake as "Canaan," i.e., the land possessed by a people who have given up the real Promised Land and settled down under the Mosaic law and the Levitical priesthood. Canaan of course includes eighteenth-century Europe, its counterpart in the next cycle. Israel has twelve tribes because society's pattern is that of the zodiacal cycle of nature, and the forty-eight cities assigned to the Levites (Joshua 21:41; *M*, 43.1 [38.1]) correspond to the remaining constellations (*M*, 41.54 [37.54]). We are told that the Israelites were frightened away from the Promised Land by "giants" or "ghosts" ("Rephaim," *M*, 31.57 [29.57]), and hence in Canaan would be still under the domain of the same giants, who are actually the constellations marking the limits of the gigantic world perceived by the dwarfed eye, which "shrinks the Organs / Of Life till they become Finite & Itself seems Infinite" (*M*, 11.6–7 [10.6–7]). Of these giants, who in the aggregate make up the Covering Cherub, the most important are Og, Sihon, and Anak. They are politically the tyrants of Canaan, such as William Pitt and Napoleon, intellectually the ideas derived from a world under the stars (*M*, 41.50 [37.50]), and psychologically the moral censors who keep us from using our imaginations (*M*, 22.35 [20.35]).

6. The *city* of the world of experience is the earthly Jerusalem, with the temple at the centre. The shape of this temple—an outer court for Gentiles, an inner court for the people of the law, and an inmost Holy of Holies with nothing there, suggests the hierarchic structure of a moral society and the structure of the generalizing mind, which moves from sensation to reflection to unreality. The symbolism of Jewish ritual has been traditionally regarded by Christians as a concealed allegory of what is revealed in the New Testament, and for Blake the Book of Revelation in particular is an imaginative translation of the Book of Exodus. Aaron's breastplate has twelve precious stones sym

bolizing the remoteness of Israel from the zodiac;[15] the City of God has twelve precious stones identifying the stars with the body of risen man. The lament of the Shadowy Female on plate 20 [18] contains several allusions to Aaron's costume, and illustrates once more the fact that priests always worship a female will. That is why both the ark with its curtains and the temple with its veil over a "secret place" (destroyed by Jesus) bear a marked resemblance to the female genitalia (cf. *M*, 41.40 [37.40]; *M*, 43.25 ff. [38.25 ff.]).

7. The *watery* world includes, first, the Jordan, and second, the four fallen rivers of Eden. Three of these, the Nile, Euphrates, and Tigris, are now the rivers of Egypt, Babylon, and Assyria: the fourth is identified with the Arnon, which flows westward into the Dead Sea. The Arnon marked the boundary of the empire of Moloch (*PL*, 1.399), to whom parents sacrificed their children. Hence the Arnon symbolizes what Blake calls "Storgous Appetite" [K308/E341] (cf. *M*, 38.30 [34.30]), or the process of ensuring that the next generation will be exactly like its predecessor. The significance of the Jordan and the Arnon will become clearer later.

Christianity has always seen in the law an aspect that is fulfilled by the gospel, and another aspect that is annihilated by it. For Blake this means that Generation is the battlefield of the imaginative and natural visions, and that there is a dialectic forming within the natural cycle, which eventually will separate Eden from Ulro and stop the cycle from turning. On one side are the world's unacknowledged legislators, the artists and prophets, generally ridiculed or persecuted in their time, and hence called by Blake the "Reprobate" [*M*, 7.3].[16] They do not form a social class, for "Every honest man is a Prophet,"[17] and every Christian is an artist; but genius and sanctity are at their centre. On the other side are the "Elect" [*M*, 7.2], the rulers and teachers (kings and priests) who support the natural or demonic vision. Everything in their world that makes it better than a hell on earth (Ulro) has been the work of previous artists and prophets: the Elect do not improve anything, but are "Created continually" (*M*, 5.11) by the perpetual-motion machine of ritual and morality. Between them come the great mass of humanity, who are victims of tyranny yet civilized by the imagination, and whom Blake calls the "Redeemed."

Reprobate and Redeemed form imaginative contraries in this world, and as "Without Contraries is no progression" [*MHH*, pl. 3; K149/E34], the dialectic of their "Mental Fight" gradually pulls the honest and well-meaning away from superstition towards vision, the ultimate goal being expressed by the verse "Would to God that all the Lord's people were Prophets," which Blake adopts as the motto of *Milton*, probably because Milton had used it in an unusually apocalyptic passage in *Areopagitica*.[18] The Elect are something to be separated from, not something to be fought with: they represent a "Negation," not a contrary (*M*, 33 [30], design), and when the struggle is complete the Negation disappears (*M*, 46.32 ff. [40.32 ff.]). They cannot be fought with because they cannot understand a conflict of "States," but only a conflict of individuals (*M*, 35.22 [32.22]), based on the illusory contraries of moral good and evil. In Satan's world, "where the Contraries of Beulah War beneath Negation's Banner" (*M*, 38.23 [34.23]) we have the parody-conflicts of war and hunting as we know them (*M*, 39.2 ff. [35.2 ff.]), where we pretend that we are good and the enemy bad.

V Structure of the Symbolism: Beulah

The child lives in the state of innocence, not because he is morally good, but because he accepts the world as his home, and assumes that friendly animals, benevolent guardians, a green and pleasant land, and a life of spontaneous enjoyment are his birthright. He then grows up into the less intelligible world of experience, and the innocent vision is driven into the subconscious, to become a perversion of sexual energy. Here we have the world gingerly explored by modern psychology, the furnace of frustrated desire underneath consciousness, the human volcano with the bound Orc, that will some day, Blake prophesies, explode and burn up the sky-world of experience sitting on top of it. Hence Beulah, for all its association with "the weak & weary" (*M*, 34.1 [31.1]), is also a potentially destructive force. We read of "the wind of Beulah that unroots the rocks & hills" (*M*, 7.33), and it is the source of the terror as well as the beauty of art, the inspiration of which comes from Beulah (*M*, 2.1).

But an explosion by itself will do nothing: human desire must fulfil itself as an achieved vision. Blake's conception of vision includes *telos*: the oak tree is the unconscious vision of the acorn; the eternal city and garden are the conscious vision of man, the reason or bounding outline of his desire. Although Orc appears to be smothered under the world of Urizen, the real power that keeps him chained is Los, who has the task of articulating human vision, and so of restoring the Golden Age, as Blake says of his own art. Such an achieved vision, the total form of art, prophecy, and imagination in this world, is the central aspect of Blake's Beulah, which has also a symbolic structure parallel to the others:

1. The *divine* world is the world of Los, the spirit of art and prophecy, the power working in man to create the human form of the world. He is also time, a mental category which we may perceive in either of two ways. In the natural vision time continually falls away from a beginning, and in this vision everything seems to be lost and to disappear in time. In the imaginative vision time continually moves forward to an end or final cause, and in this vision everything is preserved, until time becomes timeless (*M*, 24.18 ff. [22.18 ff.]).

2. The *spiritual* or mental world is the world of Enitharmon or space, in its imaginative sense of form, in contrast to the fallen sense of extension given in *Europe*. Blake calls it Cathedron, and it is a world where in mental life the truculent and panic-stricken spectres of polemic are brought out of the dark cave of "speculation" into the realized imagery of art, and where in physical life the powers of a nonhuman nature, the spirits of the elements, become living forms or "woven bodies."

3. The *human* world is the world of the sons of Los, who are not the spirits of the arts so much as the imaginative attitudes which produce all genuine work (cf. *M*, 30.14 [28.14]). Of the sons of Los, seven are particularly mentioned in *Milton*: five of them appeared in *Europe* in their perverted forms.[19]

4, 5, 6. The *animal* and *vegetable* worlds constitute the "Cultivated land" (*M*, 29.42 [27.42]) of true work, or imaginative commerce, which Blake calls Allamanda, and the *city* of the imagination is the palace of art, or Golgonooza, the central gate of which is called Luban.

7. The world of experience is "under" the law: moral virtue and the predictability of nature are its ceiling, the "vault of paved heaven," as it appears to the lunatic of the "Mad Song." But the top of the moral world is the bottom of the imagination. Morality and science are the minimum basis of the imaginative life, or what is called in the *Introduction* to the *Songs of Experience* its "starry floor." The genuine science of law that works in the basement of the imagination is called Bowlahoola. *Milton* is pervaded by Blake's later feeling that the fallen world is providentially protected by Los as a defence against chaos or nonexist-

ence, symbolized by the sea (*M*, 43.14 [38.14]; hence Bowlahoola is founded by Tharmas the sea-god as his own boundary, *M*, 26.48 [24.48]). The building of the Mundane Shell and "Mathematic power," associated with Urizen in *The Four Zoas*, are transferred to Los in *Milton* (*M*, 38.31 [34.31]; *M*, 31.38 [29.38]), though the emphasis is thrown on the "continual" building of a barrier which, as Blake says elsewhere, is burned up as soon as men cease to behold it (cf. *M*, 29.60 [27.61]).

In Beulah the amorphous society of man begins to assume the shape of the single human body of the awakened Albion, hence these last three worlds—commerce, art, and law—may be seen as the emerging forms of the circulatory, cerebral, and unconscious digestive systems of an infinite Man. Correspondingly, nature begins to take on its proper form of a female "emanation," a form loved because created. Christianity preserves this symbolism when it speaks of the Church as the Bride of Christ; but in Blake the creature in Eternity is female and the creator male, and human beings are not creatures in the resurrection. In the imaginative view Enitharmon with her "looms" that weave bodies is a benevolent mother, not a vacuous "fate"; the city of Jerusalem becomes a bride; the sun and moon appear as the emanations, Ocalythron and Elynittria, of the spirits of prophecy and art, Rintrah and Palamabron. The garden becomes the fruitful land, the black but comely bride of the Song of Songs, the liberated Earth of the first two poems in the *Songs of Experience*, the land which is "married" (the meaning of the word Beulah; see Isaiah 62:4). The river becomes the genuine "milky way" (*M*, 39.50 ff. [35.50 ff.]), the nourishing stream which, in the form of Ololon (*M*, 23.15 [21.15]), is the heroine of *Milton*.[20]

A human being "has no Body distinct from his Soul" [*MHH*, pl. 4; K149/E34]: he has either a spiritual body or a natural body, depending on which world he lives in. The things he creates are "souls" to which he gives bodily form (*M*, 28.13 ff. [26.13 ff.]). Beulah, Blake's Gardens of Adonis, is the place from which "souls" come and to which they return, and as described here (plates 33–4 [30–1]) and in *The Book of Thel*, most of its inhabitants are wistful and timid desires seeking embodiment. It is not a place where "Mental Fight" can be carried on (*M*, 33.3 [30.3]), but a resting place after the results of the fight have been achieved. We need this point to understand Blake's treatment of its predominant moods of pity and love.

VI Conclusion: Structure of the Narrative

At this point a full commentary on *Milton* could begin: here we must be content with summary. After Preface and Invocation, we have first a "Bard's Song," the theme of which is the cyclical movement of an "Eye" of history from revolt to collapse, an expanded form of the version given in the Argument to *The Marriage of Heaven and Hell*. Rintrah in Blake is the spirit of prophecy who has the "Science of Wrath": that is, he is the spirit in man capable of complete imaginative detachment from worldliness. Wrath is the disinterested and impersonal vision of life contemplating death, and is the opposite of anger or irritation. Rintrah is the spirit of Elijah and John the Baptist, the fiery prophet of the desert, and in art he survives as the spirit of the sublime, the vision of a Milton or a Michelangelo which is as far away as art can get from the mundane. Palamabron is the more delicate and refined spirit of the beautiful which appears in high civilizations. Rintrah is the imaginative pioneer breaking the Mundane Shell with the "plough": Palamabron follows cultivating it with the "harrow." In this world all such effort is temporary, and sooner or later Satan, the dusty "Miller of Eternity," appears, like the button-moulder of *Peer Gynt*, to grind everything down again.

Palamabron, unlike Rintrah, is in the world: he has the "Science of Pity," and is so close to the world that sooner or later Satan begins producing imitations of him, or vice versa. When this happens, culture becomes decadent or barbaric, and the cycle must begin over again in the prophetic wrath of Rintrah. Rintrah as Elijah was reborn once as John the Baptist, and it is time for him to be reborn again. The crucial phase of the cycle is always the collision between Palamabron and Satan, when Palamabron must remember that he is Rintrah's brother, with the same power of detaching himself wholly from the world, and not Satan's brother, regardless of his sympathy for Satan's victims. Blake himself experienced such a collision at Felpham, where the role of Palamabron was played by himself, that of Satan by Hayley, and that of Rintrah by Blake's real brother Robert, dead but still alive.[21]

Rintrah and Palamabron are the two "Witnesses" of Revelation 11 (*M*, 24.59 [22.59] refers to Revelation 11:8), who are Moses and Elijah, the law and the prophets, Rintrah being the "Reprobate" Elijah figure. The two aspects of annihilation and fulfilment in the conception of Moses or the law are symbolized by the story of the struggle of Michael and Satan over the body of Moses, which Blake adapts for *Milton*. Satan is, of course, "Elect," and Palamabron, separated from Satan and joined to Rintrah, is of the "Redeemed" class. As Blake is Palamabron, this means that Blake is redeemed by the return of Milton. The conception of three classes seems to have come from the "Goon" of the *Bhagavadgita,* as they are called in the Wilkins translation Blake read.[22] Blake returns to them in the *Descriptive Catalogue,* where he speaks of a strong or sublime man, a man of beauty or pathos, and an ugly man who represents both "the human reason" and "the incapability of intellect"—a typically Blakean equation. According to the newly discovered inscription on the gate in the frontispiece to *Jerusalem,*[23] the Druidic trilithon represents a geometrical or abstract form of the perversion of the relations of the three classes, the "Sublime & Pathos" [K620/E144] being the uprights and the fallen reason covering them.

The Bard's Song concludes with the lament of Leutha, who is the emanation or imaginative world of Satan. Thus she is the hell he lives in, and, as a deliberate echo from *Paradise Lost* informs us, she corresponds to Milton's Sin, the keeper of hell's gate.[24] Her particular sin is "dark secret love" [K213/E23], the associating of love with possession which causes Satan to think he loves Palamabron, and hence to want to take over his work. Leutha corresponds to the repentant harlot of Biblical symbolism: sin is redeemable, and hence Leutha's world, the matrix of our own, is providentially protected until the Last Judgment.

The moral of the Bard's Song is, first, that the culture Milton belonged to is in a desperate state: Palamabron still preserves his integrity, like Job, but is fighting for his life, and those for whom he works are increasingly pulled under the self-righteousness and callous indifference of Satan. Second, that Palamabron's pity and love, which lead him to make social friends of his spiritual enemies, are not strong enough to hold out. The three classes belong to the sexual threefold world of Beulah, not the human fourfold world of Eden, and hence are involved in the fallen world. Ololon gives what is intended to be a key to the argument when she says (referring to the fact that the fall began in Beulah):

> Altho' our Human Power can sustain the severe contentions
> Of Friendship, our Sexual cannot, but flies into the Ulro.
> Hence arose all our terrors in Eternity. [*M*, 41.32–4]

The Bard's Song shocks those who recognize that it associates pity and love with guilt (*M*, 14.48–9 [13.48–9]), but Milton understands. Milton had portrayed Christ as rejecting Classical wisdom in *Paradise Regained*, on the ground that if Christ were to exchange the prophetic tradition for it, he would get only a development of the kind of natural religion which exists in hell. Yet Milton, according to Blake's Preface, had not successfully resisted this temptation himself. In heaven he is still "pond'ring the intricate mazes of Providence" (*M*, 2.17). The sinister image of the maze, and the deliberate recall of *PL*, 2.561, indicates that Milton is still sufficiently in the grip of natural religion to be without his emanation, which is partly his influence after death (*M*, 46.10 [40.9–11]), for the world still worships false gods (*M*, 15.14–15 [14.14–15]), and the results of doing so are painfully evident. So Milton resolves to return to the world in human form to bring about a dialectical opposition between imagination and nature, and stop the cycle of nature from turning. There is no question of "reincarnation," as Milton enters the body of a full-grown poet with a highly developed personality of his own, but Blake is adapting, whether he knew it or not, the Oriental myth of the Bodhisattva, the saint who voluntarily re-enters the world to help liberate it.

The process of return sends Milton into a "vortex," the void outside existence which becomes a womb when entered (*M*, 48.37 ff. [41.37 ff.]).[25] The sons of Los are terrified at his approach, because Milton is journeying through chaos like his own Satan, and they assume that he is Satan. The chaos is simultaneously the chaos of the moral law, the labyrinthine desert, and the chaos of the natural law, the labyrinthine Newtonian universe. From the latter point of view Milton is a falling star or comet, the comet being here, as in *America* and *Europe*, the symbol of a new "Eye" or phase of human fortunes, like the new star at the birth of Christ, which with fear of change perplexes monarchs. From the former point of view he is a pillar of fire, described in *America* as "The fiery joy, that Urizen perverted to ten commands" [8.3; K198/E54].

Milton is repeating the journey of Moses in the wilderness, and the journey of Christ in *Paradise Regained*. Negatively, he must preserve the "wrath" of Rintrah, the total detachment that will split him off from Satan's world. Hence he must resist the temptation to cross the Jordan and enter "Canaan" instead of the Promised Land, thereby turning the wheel of time around once more instead of stopping it. Positively, he must preserve the other side of wrath, the mercy (*M*, 25.34 [23.34]) or forgiveness of sins which withdraws completely from the movement of attack and revenge in history. He could easily become a new force in history, like Luther before him, another king of the wood who will last until destroyed by the next one (*M*, 43.29 ff. [38.29 ff.]), but, like Shelley's Prometheus, he can redeem man only by renouncing all desire for revenge.

Again, he must recapitulate the struggle of the three classes, retaining his own form of a prophet while consolidating and destroying the Negation of the moral law (*M*, 22.20 ff. [20.20 ff.]). Also he must repeat the Incarnation, in the sense of achieving an Adamic body, or a fallen human perspective, without falling prey to the Urizenic abstract vision. This is symbolized by the contest of Milton and Urizen on the banks of the sinister river Arnon, in which Milton kneads a shape of red clay (the meaning of the word "Adam" in Hebrew, and more or less of the word "Milton" in Greek) on icy water. The episode suggests Jacob's wrestling with the angel and Christ's healing the blind man with clay and spittle [Genesis 32:24–6; John 9:6]. We are not told just what relation this body has to the body of William Blake, but the process going on between the desert and the Promised Land is simultaneously going on between the sea and the Sussex coast, the mountains of the one (*M*, 19.16 [17.16]) being identical with the "Rocks of Bognor" (*M*, 44.49 [39.49]) on the other.

The moral act which begins in wrath and ends in forgiveness is also an intellectual act. Besides the Adam, Noah, and Israel accounts of the fall and redemption of man, there is a fourth, the story told in the Book of Job, which Blake had begun to read in Hebrew.[26] The story of Job is the story of man, who suffers undeservedly because he falls into Satan's world. Satan cannot touch his real life (cf. *M*, 44.18 ff. [39.18 ff.]) or imagination, but he is capable of arranging the conditions of a fallen world, and, like Jesus judging Adam in *Paradise Lost*, of compelling him to live in it. "In the Book of Job," Blake had said, "Milton's Messiah is call'd Satan" [*MHH*, pl. 5; K150/E34]. Eventually Job is enlightened by God, who points out to him the two vast monsters, Behemoth and Leviathan, the giant forms of fallen nature, and clearly identical with Satan, who in the meantime has disappeared from the action. The fourteenth and fifteenth plates of the Job series represent the difference between the "Redeemed" and the full "Reprobate" vision. In the former, Job and his wife are separated from the unfallen world, the frieze of angels, by a demiurge controlling the movements of the sun and the moon, while the acts of creation proceed around the margin. In the latter, Behemoth and Leviathan take up the lower part of the plate, and Job and his wife are above them. One is a threefold vision with the providentially protected cycle of nature in the middle; the other is the final contrast of Eden and Ulro. These two visions correspond roughly to the visions in *Milton* at the end of the first and of the second book respectively.

Milton finds in the world he returns to a crisis in history with the Napoleonic wars, a crisis in religion with the collapse of Swedenborg and the failure of anyone to make a genuinely imaginative development out of the challenge of the Methodist movement, a crisis in philosophy with the dogmatic formulation of natural religion in contemporary Deism, and a crisis in art with the domination of "the tame high finisher of paltry Blots" (*M*, 48.9 [41.9]). All these crises are negative signs of an imminent awakening, and have to be turned inside out by the imagination. Thus when Blake describes war as the treading of a winepress, he is not closing his eyes to its horror: he is seeing the wars of human life as the literal Word of God (*M*, 49.14 [42.14]), its natural or demonic parody, which in its inside-out or "adverse" form (*M*, 29.8 ff. [27.8 ff.]) becomes apocalyptic. The vision of Milton-Blake begins with the "Wine-press on the Rhine" (*M*, 27.3 [25.3]), expands to the vision of art and science on plate 30 [28], and finally achieves the vision of time and space as the home, tent,[27] or tabernacle of man. At the end of book 1, the whole objective world is seen as a creation of Los, and is thereby transformed into a responsive emanation, the Beulah described at the opening of book 2, from whence Ololon the milky way descends, like the angels descending Jacob's ladder (*M*, 39.35 [35.35]). The emanation retreats from anyone who seeks her in the outside world, but appears when the natural perspective is reversed; hence the paradox that although the object of Milton's journey is to seek Ololon, Ololon in fact seeks him.

Her journey differs from Milton's in that she traverses the created rather than the creating states, or the four emanation worlds. The first of these is Beulah, the emanation of Eden; the next is called Alla, the "Night of Beulah" [*M*, 39.32] or world of dreams freed from what we should call a censor (*M*, 25.39 ff. [23.39 ff.]). The third is the projection of our own world, single vision and Newton's sleep; the fourth is the nightmare or delirium world which can always be found below the third one, and inspires its constant panic and cruelty. Both are forms of Ulro, distinguished as Al-Ulro and Or-Ulro (*M*, 38.12 ff. [34.12 ff.]). Or-Ulro is the world from which Thel ran shrieking: Ololon has more courage, as well as the support of numbers.

As she comes down to "Blake's Cottage at Felpham" (so labelled on plate 40 [36; K527]), the moment of vision is accomplished, the moment neither in time nor out of time which contains the whole of time, the "Pulsation of the Artery" in which "the Poet's Work is Done" (*M*, 31.1 ff. [29.1 ff.]). As Satan splits off from Milton, and the female will from Ololon, we hear in the distance the "Cry of the Poor Man" (*M*, 49.34 [42.34]), and the preparations for a greater awakening of humanity (cf. *M*, 4.21 ff.). In this expectant hush the poem ends, as quietly as *Paradise Regained* ends with the return of Christ to his mother, and one of the most gigantic imaginative achievements in English poetry comes to a controlled close.

16

William Blake (I)

1957

From The English Romantic Poets and Essayists: A Review of Research and Criticism, *ed. Carol W. and Lawrence H. Houtchens (New York: Modern Language Association of America, 1957), 1–31. Frye's essay was revised in 1966 by Martin Nurmi. This is Frye's 1957 version.*

I Bibliographies

The literary works of William Blake consist, with unimportant exceptions, of: (a) the juvenile *Poetical Sketches*, published in 1783, (b) *The French Revolution*, one of seven announced books, of which the only surviving copy is a proof, (c) the *Descriptive Catalogue* printed to accompany the 1809 exhibition, (d) marginalia to a number of books, (e) the engraved (or more strictly, etched) works, (f) manuscript material. The engraved works, or illuminated books, form the central canon of Blake's literary production. When the textual unit is an aphorism or a lyric poem, it normally goes on a single plate, with an accompanying design; when it is a longer work, or "Prophecy," it forms part of a series of plates, in which a plate may be all text, all design, or any proportion of the two. An important bibliographical aid of a type peculiar to Blake study is supplied by Geoffrey Keynes and E. Wolf, *William Blake's Illuminated Books: A Census* (1953). It is obvious that each original copy of the engraved works is a separate bibliographical item. The manuscript material includes letters, a few unpublished works in foul draft (*Tiriel*, *An Island in the Moon*, *The Four Zoas*), a set of lyrics in a fair draft known as the Pickering MS, and the notebook that Blake kept by him for a great part of his life, now known as the Rossetti MS, into which he huddled an extraordinary amount of both literary and pictorial material.

Geoffrey Keynes's *A Bibliography of William Blake* (1921) is practically definitive up to the date of its appearance, for both primary and secondary sources, and is an indispensable guide to the student of Blake at every stage. A second bibliography by B. Jugaku (Kobe, Japan, 1929) is often listed in books on Blake, but is said by Ruthven Todd, in his edition of Gilchrist in Everyman's Library (1942), not to be independent of Keynes. After 1921 the student will be dependent on the usual aids, the most important being the annual bibliography in *Philological Quarterly*. (Many of the more recent critical notes in this bibliography have been supplied by D.V. Erdman, whose advice has been of great help to me in preparing this essay.) The Blake section of *The Cambridge Bibliography of English Literature* (1940) was also contributed by Keynes. If the Keynes bibliography is unavailable, there is a convenient shorter bibliography of earlier criticism up to 1914 in *William Blake: Poet and Mystic* (1914), the English translation of P. Berger, *William Blake, mysticisme et poésie* (1907). For the beginner there is an introductory bibliography in Kathleen Raine, *William Blake* (1951), a British Council pamphlet in the Bibliographical Series of Supplements to "British Book News," and a fuller though less up to date one in the edition of Gilchrist by Todd just referred to. I am greatly obliged to Mr. Charles Moore, of London, Ontario, for lending his excellent unpublished bibliography, *La poésie de William Blake en France*.

II Editions

Editions which are reproductions of the engraved plates will be considered below in a separate section. The first major editors of Blake's text were the Rossetti brothers, Dante Gabriel and William, who owned the notebook which has been called the Rossetti MS after them. (One may speak of them both as owning it, as the ten shillings that Dante Gabriel paid for it was borrowed from William.) Dante Gabriel edited a selection of Blake's poems for the second volume of Gilchrist's life (1863), and William produced *The Poetical Works of William Blake*, with an appreciative essay, in 1874. Dante Gabriel especially followed the bad tradition of trying to improve Blake's text. *The Works of William Blake, Poetic, Symbolic and Critical*, by Edwin J. Ellis and William Butler Yeats, appeared in three volumes in 1893. This edition has its importance, as we shall see, but from the point of view of textual criticism the less said about it the better. The first genuinely critical edition of large scope was the Oxford edition of the lyrical poems, by John Sampson, which later included excerpts from the Prophecies (1905; rev. 1913). It was supplemented by the edition of *Jerusalem* by E.R.D. Maclagan and A.G.B. Russell in 1904, and of *Milton* in 1907. The standard edition however is *The Writings of William Blake* (3 vols., 1925) by Geoffrey Keynes, which provides a clean, complete, and reliable text, also well illustrated, and arranged chronologically, of the whole of Blake's literary output. A little, but not much, has turned up since then, chiefly a letter or two and the original copy, now in Sir Geoffrey's possession, of the marginal annotations to Bacon's *Essays*, much more extensive than the Gilchrist transcription on which the 1925 edition had to depend.

The Oxford edition by Sampson had not included the complete prophetic books: these were edited by D.J. Sloss and J.P.R. Wallis in two volumes in 1926. The textual criticism of this edition is very painstaking, though the extensive commentary on Blake's meaning and thought is practically a total loss. The Keynes edition was presented in a condensed form, omitting variora, in *The Poetry and Prose of William Blake*, the first edition of which appeared in 1927, and the fourth, which unfortunately changed the pagination, in 1939. It is the indispensable text for all serious study of Blake, in graduate seminars or elsewhere: it is somewhat overpunctuated, but one's chief objection to it is that it is not kept in print constantly enough. Not many poets go into a single volume as compactly and as completely as Blake does.

Of current popular editions, the text in Everyman's Library is well edited by Max Plowman, and what it has is complete, though it omits some important things, including *The Four Zoas*. The Viking Portable and Modern Library editions, with introductions by Alfred Kazin and by me respectively, use the Keynes text, and have only selections from the longer Prophecies. A Modern Library Giant contains the complete poetic works of Blake and Donne, and will be useful to anyone who wants to have Blake and Donne bound up together.

For Blake's engraved poems the engraving process itself helps to establish a definitive text. The differences that exist among the various copies are seldom strictly textual differences: a passage may appear in one copy and be missing or deleted from another, but variant readings are rare. But with Blake's untidy, often illegible manuscripts, with their bewildering variety of insertions, revisions, sketches, and overwritings, the most exhaustive editor can seldom be quite sure that every scribble and erasure has been deciphered or accounted for. The Rossetti MS has been edited with a facsimile by Geoffrey Keynes, *The Note Book of William*

Blake Called the Rossetti Manuscript (1935). The study of it by B. Jugaku, *A Bibliographical Study of William Blake's Note-Book* (1953), leaves many problems still unsolved, editorial and otherwise. One of the most intricate and yet central of these is the establishing of the layers of revision of the *Songs of Experience*, the drafts of which belong to this notebook, in their chronological order. Studies of this are now in progress: see Martin K. Nurmi, "Blake's Revisions of *The Tyger*" (*PMLA*, 1956). New editions of *An Island in the Moon* by Palmer Brown, and of *The Four Zoas* (originally called *Vala*) by H.M. Margoliouth and G.E. Bentley, Jr., are in progress, and textual improvements in both are promised. The numerous sketches in the manuscript of *The Four Zoas* are of particular importance, as they show that Blake thought from the beginning in terms of a series of designed plates, not of writing a poem and then illustrating it. A facsimile of the complete poem is perhaps the greatest editorial need of Blake criticism at present. As this goes to press, the edition of *Vala* (i.e., the original poem), by H.M. Margoliouth, has appeared, and takes its place at once as an essential critical text.

III Biographies

The more important biographical primary sources are available in two volumes. *The Letters of William Blake together with a Life by Frederick Tatham*, edited by Archibald G.B. Russell (1906), contains what the title says it contains, and the remainder are assembled in the back of Arthur Symons, *William Blake* (1907). The most important for the development of the Blake legend are the diary and reminiscences of Crabb Robinson, the sketch by J.T. Smith in the second volume of *Nollekens and his Times* (1828), and the account in Alan Cunningham, *Lives of the Most Eminent British Painters, Sculptors, and Architects* (1830). The memoirs of the younger painters who came into contact with Blake in his later years are also of importance, especially A.H. Palmer, *The Life and Letters of Samuel Palmer* (1892), Alfred T. Story, *The Life of John Linnell* (1892), and *A Memoir of Edward Calvert*, "by his third son," Samuel Calvert (1893).

Blake's letters practically begin with his removal to Felpham at the age of forty-three, and the above memoirs come almost entirely from the last period of his life. In this last period Blake had, in the Linnell circle, a few friends he trusted, but for those outside this circle, half a century of derision and neglect had developed in him a kind of intellectual deafness, not unlike the physical deafness of Beethoven in some of its social results. The main interest of these memoirs is anecdotal, and the impression they give of Blake is in the strictest sense of the word a caricature: the features are striking, the points they make may be accurate, but our impression of Blake's personality is gained from their treatment of him and not from Blake himself. It is clear too that, though among his real friends Blake may have been "a man without a mask," elsewhere he was always ready to caricature himself, to assume whatever mask seemed to be called for; and he has confused biographers in consequence more than so intensely personal a writer would normally be expected to do. The cranky but shrewd Tatham observes that "many of his Eccentric speeches, were thrown forth more as a piece of sarcasm, upon the Enquirer, than from his real opinion."[1] The early attaching of the word "mystic" to Blake helped to suggest an earnestly oracular temperament, an innocent who could write songs of innocence, but one to be smiled at sympathetically, like a solemn child. A glance at a picture of Blake's life mask should be enough to disturb this conception of him. A highly unofficial but attractive little sketch of Blake's personality may be found in a poem in Jacques Prévert's *Paroles* (1943).

The Life of William Blake, Pictor Ignotus, by Alexander Gilchrist, appeared in 1863, two years after its author's death: his wife and the Rossettis were responsible for finishing it and for issuing the revised and enlarged edition of 1880. The second volume of the 1880 edition is an extraordinary (and still very useful) grab bag containing D.G. Rossetti's edition, lists of engravings and drawings, reproductions, and a fine "Essay on Blake," a review of the first edition, by James Smetham. The reprint of the first volume in Everyman's Library, with an introduction, notes, and bibliography by Ruthven Todd, makes a handbook practically indispensable for the Blake student. Gilchrist's is technically a most superior biography, which makes a real effort to arrange both the poetic and pictorial works in chronological order—if Blake ever has a definitive biographer, he will follow Gilchrist's method. Further, his life is a sprightly and charming narrative: it is permeated with a deep sympathy for Blake, and it could never have clouded up Blake in the way that, for instance, Dowden clouded up Shelley.[2] But of course it transmitted and expanded the anecdotal interest of Gilchrist's predecessors, and hence unconsciously helped to popularize Blake as a kind of Theophrastan character type:[3] a lovable, absent-minded, enthusiastic artist, heroic in the sense of doing his work cheerfully and obstinately in the face of neglect, and preserving the peculiarly Victorian and English sense of the right of genius to harmless eccentricities.

The biographical part of almost every general book on Blake since then has been mainly potted Gilchrist, and the biographical interest in Blake has been oppressively anecdotal. The consequences for Blake criticism have been disastrous, for the biographical picture thus dubiously highlighted becomes the basis for criticism. That is, the critic makes his value judgments on Blake's poetry in terms of what his biographical stereotype might have been expected to produce. Even as late a study as Bernard Blackstone's *English Blake* (1949) follows the same procedure, if with more sympathy than usual. Gilchrist's own conception of the relation of biographical to critical study is, in contrast to most of his successors, very well balanced, which is one reason why his biography is so good as a biography.

The Ellis and Yeats edition of 1893, already mentioned, included a memoir, the only new feature of which was Yeats's attempt to provide Blake with an Irish ancestry. Hazard Adams's *Blake and Yeats: The Contrary Vision* (1955) disposes briefly of what was left of the evidence for this, which was never impressive. Ellis carried on by himself in *The Real Blake* (1907), a biography whose chief resemblance to the real Blake is in a certain facility for drawing without the model.

Harold Bruce's *William Blake in This World* (1925) was the first real attempt since Gilchrist to sift fact from legend, and provide a solid chronological framework. It was followed in 1927 by Mona Wilson, *The Life of William Blake* (reissued with additions, 1948). This is a clearly written presentation of the biographical knowledge of Blake up to 1927, which means that it is still essentially a revision of Gilchrist. Its chief disadvantage is its highly selective treatment of Blake's total output: there are, for example, many useful clues to Blake's life and thought in his work as illustrator and engraver that still await investigation. Thomas Wright's *The Life of William Blake* (2 vols., 1929) has more data on this point. The tone of Wright's book is that of the enthusiastic antiquarian, and there are a few lapses in judgment (such as his sponsoring of the notion of a romantic attachment between Blake and Mary Wollstonecraft, a legend which may have been transferred to Blake from Fuseli), but he writes with much pungency and first-hand insight. Wright was the chief promoter of the Blake Society, whose papers also contain some scattered biographical information; he had previously written a life of Cowper and used the special knowledge of the Hayley circle gained from it to good advantage. On this last the student may also consult Morchard Bishop, *Blake's Hayley* (1951).

More recent biographical scholarship has been fragmentary. Geoffrey Keynes's *Blake Studies* (1949) is a series of essays, mainly biographical, dealing with such topics as the Rossetti MS, the corrections in the *Poetical Sketches*, some of the lesser-known engraving commissions in Blake's later life, and the disentangling of its subject from another contemporary engraver with the same name. The material in these studies will be indispensable to the next biographer, and so will the new material being brought forward in a number of biographical research articles, including several by D.V. Erdman: one may note especially his "William Blake's Exactness in Dates" (*Philological Quarterly*, 1949) and "Blake's Early Swedenborgianism" (*Comparative Literature*, 1953), which gets rid of one of Ellis's red herrings. Among other recent biographical articles, G.E. Bentley, Jr., "William Blake and 'Johnny of Norfolk'" (*Studies in Philology*, 1956) may be mentioned. The books of Schorer and Erdman, mentioned below under "Criticism," provide a great deal of historical and potentially biographical information about Blake's surprisingly numerous social contacts.

But Erdman was able to remark in 1953 that "Blake biography is still in a pre-scientific state." The first step, for any approach to definitiveness in biography, is a *catalogue raisonné* of all Blake's work in both literature and the graphic arts, dated as carefully as possible, and including of course the complex problems of dating raised by the manuscripts. The most competent person to undertake such a work, Sir Geoffrey Keynes, has listed it in *Blake Studies* as in progress. Blake's life was quiet, verging on humdrum, for all his reputation for eccentricity, and the rewards of biographical research are unlikely to be picturesque: the Annette Vallons and Harriet Westbrooks of Blake's life appear to have been confined to his imagination.[4] It is probable, for instance, that we know so little of the period between the failure of his exhibition in 1809 and his meeting with Linnell in 1818 because there is really not much to be known. But for so remarkable a personality facts are surely better than anecdote or impressionism. The question of Blake's "madness," of course, is now recognized to be not a question of fact at all, but a pseudo-problem.

IV Criticism

The reputation of Blake as a poet has followed much the same curve as the reputation of Shelley. He is presented at first as a natural genius in exquisite and spontaneous lyric, a naive intelligence who could only react emotionally, his more didactic Prophecies illustrating a tendency to squirt ink like a cuttlefish at anything that annoyed him. Gradually, the inconsistency of this with the real character of the poet who defined poetry as "Allegory address'd to the Intellectual powers" [K825/E730] forces critics to approach, however gingerly, the more intricate involutions of the longer poems containing the substance of Blake's thought. At first, of course, the tendency is not to read them but to write them off or argue about them, on the ground that they are schizophrenic, heretical, not "real poetry," too private in symbolism to be understood, and so on and so on. Such judgments are contemporary with the biographical pictures of Blake as deficient in a sense of reality. But, as Blake has slowly established his authority in one field after another, it becomes clear that his critic, like the critic of Shelley, must simply stop arguing and come to grips with the real strength, complexity, and normality of his subject's mind.

In engraving his poetry, one of Blake's aims was undoubtedly to make himself independent of publishers, but by a curious irony he produced the exact opposite of what his own conception of art was. That is, what he produced were *objets d'art* for well-to-do connoisseurs. This fact has both delayed and isolated Blake's reputation. He was a professional engraver, but more of an amateur poet than any other poet of his rank; consequently he was known for many years after his death chiefly as a pictorial artist. Even now, the variety of his appeal makes it peculiarly difficult to assess his creative personality, so to speak, as a unit. The advance of Blake scholarship, even the scholarship of interpretation, has been substantial enough to discourage some of those who, to paraphrase Thomas Wright, rush into print to announce that the prophetic books are unintelligible; yet it has had its own disadvantages. The responsible student of English literature, even the eighteenth-century or Romantic specialist, confronted with the weighty commentaries that are still essential, is likely to feel that Blake is a special interest, to be taken up like chess by those who fancy it. Hence a good deal of Blake criticism falls into the hands of the irresponsible student, who contributes nothing to Blake scholarship but simply makes value judgments on the poetry, the basis of the judgments being usually the fact that he does not know what five sixths of the poetry means. Some simplification of genuine Blake scholarship is in order, now that there is less risk of distorting its subject, and in what follows I shall attempt to indicate the direction that such a simplification might take.

Swinburne's brilliant and generous essay, *William Blake*, appeared in 1868 as a critical pendant to the Gilchrist life, and established Blake once for all as an important poet. The virtues of this essay speak eloquently for themselves; its limitations are unfortunately the main concern of the historian of Blake scholarship, however ungrateful the task. In the first place, Swinburne, on the authority less of Gilchrist than of his own temperament, strongly emphasized the social isolation of Blake, and passed over Blake's radical, even revolutionary, political views, dismissing *The French Revolution*, for instance, as "mere wind and splutter."[5] The stereotype that he took from Gilchrist was rather that of the rebellion of the artist against society, and it was this aspect of Blake that was stressed in later Victorian criticism of him. Blake thus became a prophet of the aesthetic radicals, whose enemies were the Philistine and the Puritan rather than the tyrant and the usurer. Yeats, for instance, speaks of Blake as having begun the practice of "preaching against the Philistine."[6]

In the second place, Blake became, for Swinburne, an exponent of the "romantic agony," maintaining that conventional or moral good was evil and that the salvation and freedom of man lay in the recrudescence of long-suppressed instincts. The chief document used in this presentation of Blake was *The Marriage of Heaven and Hell*, apparently the most explicit of the Prophecies, but actually, because of its highly ambiguous irony, one of the most elusive. (It is in fact Blake's second prose satire, and it is significant that his first, *An Island in the Moon*, was unknown to Swinburne and despised by Symons.) Swinburne interprets this work as a document falling within his own conception of the sadist tradition—Swinburne refers to Sade, though not by name, in a long footnote. The influence of this sadist or diabolist Blake is visible in Bernard Shaw, who seems to have made some use of Blake for *The Devil's Disciple*, and in André Gide. The same view of Blake was evidently accepted by Mario Praz in his influential *Romantic Agony* (1933), and it is still doing duty, though largely for schematic reasons, in D.G. James, *The Romantic Comedy* (1948). It would be convenient enough to have a genuine example of what Swinburne calls a "dysangel," if only as a clay pigeon, in the ultra-respectable English tradition, but criticism is reluctantly forced to say that this conception of Blake could hardly be more mistaken.

Blake's lyrical gifts, his anticonventional views, and his unification of poetry and painting made him a considerable influence on the late pre-Raphaelite developments around the turn of the century. The two fine essays of Yeats in *Ideas of Good and Evil* (1903) did much to establish Blake as a prophet of English *symbolisme*. The second volume of the Ellis and Yeats edition is an exposition of Blake's symbolism, which assimilates Blake to occult, Gnostic, and theosophical writers. Some genuine interpretation is present and some interesting parallels, especially with Boehme, are established, but the charts and diagrams rely heavily on forced symmetries and manipulated evidence (such as the identification of two quite different characters, Tiriel and Thiriel). It is curious that a critic who was also a very great poet should have treated Blake's prophetic books not as poems to be read but as code messages to be deciphered, especially when he also shows such incisive understanding of Blake's theory of imagination. This commentary must, if anything, have increased the prevalence of the notion that any interpretation of Blake is as good as any other.

Arthur Symons's *William Blake* (1907) gives us a less sadistic but even more aesthetic Blake than Swinburne's, a Blake whose defence of the more energetic virtues was now seen to have affinities with the *Herrenmoral* of Nietzsche.[7] In the same year Pierre Berger produced *William Blake, mysticisme et poésie*, translated by D.H. Conner as *William Blake: Poet and Mystic* (1914). Berger's book was among other things the first really thoughtful and systematic study yet made of the prophetic books. It demonstrated a coherent and controlling mind at work in them; the commentary provides much new and specific information about Blake's meaning—something that Swinburne and Symons hardly provide at all outside *The Marriage of Heaven and Hell*—and it marks the beginning of the critical effort to clear up these poems for the common reader. Also, as one might have expected from his nationality, Berger's view of *The French Revolution*, and of the political and social reference of Blake's outlook generally, was better balanced than Swinburne's.

Of minor critics in this early period, a place of honour should be reserved for Garth Wilkinson, a Swedenborgian who referred to Blake several times in his works and produced an indifferent edition of the *Songs of Innocence and Experience* in 1839. It was Wilkinson who first attracted James Thomson (B.V.) to Blake; Thomson appended an essay on Blake to his poem *Shelley* in 1884. Other early studies of Blake, stimulated by Swinburne and Yeats, include those of Alfred T. Story (1893), Richard Garnett (1895), Irene Langridge (1904), François Benoît (1906), and Elizabeth Cary (1907). All of these had their insights; some, especially Garnett, helped to develop Blake scholarship, and they were as well illustrated as the methods of reproduction of sixty years ago allowed. But with the passing of time they take on an increasingly historical importance. To these we may add Paul Elmer More, *Shelburne Essays*, Fourth Series (1906), a review of the Sampson edition.

After 1907 there follows something of an interregnum in Blake scholarship, in which the information and apparatus provided by the earlier critics was absorbed into the academic tradition by a steady though often reluctant osmosis. Basil de Selincourt's *William Blake* (1909) follows the older tradition in maintaining a balance between the literary and pictorial aspects of Blake criticism, which now tended increasingly to concentrate on purely literary aspects. G.K. Chesterton's *William Blake* (1910) is a breezy little book, doubtless of interest to admirers of Chesterton. Charles Gardner's *Vision and Vesture: Blake and Modern Thought* (1916) makes, as its subtitle indicates, an interesting attempt to align Blake with other nineteenth-century currents of thought. His second book, *William Blake the Man* (1919), is less distinctive, but has some good passages on the relation of Blake to Swedenborg. Perhaps the chapter on Blake in Oliver Elton's *A Survey of English Literature, 1780–1830* (1920) may be taken as summing up this transitional period.

The decade of the 1920s, with the centenary year falling in 1927, was the time when the study of Blake came to full maturity, what with the appearance of the Keynes bibliography and standard edition, already mentioned. In interpretation the great landmark is S. Foster Damon's *William Blake: His Philosophy and Symbols* (1924). This was the first, and in many respects still the best, effort to attempt commentary as well as comment, to pursue Blake's meaning into the texture of his poetry and the details of his symbolism. For the special student of Blake it is the commentary, the second half of the book, which is of greatest value, although there is much in the first half too that is unique. Not only was Damon's sheer erudition of formidable range, but his general literary culture was broader and richer than that of any previous critic of Blake since Swinburne. His commentary is based largely on a translation of Blake's characters into personifications, and the result, if not exhaustive of Blake's meaning, at any rate does give a meaning, and a coherent and consistent one. In his commentary on the designs he is unsurpassed, and there are several smaller areas of Blake criticism, such as the question of the purely poetic merits of the Prophecies, upon which he is still the only critic to have made much headway.

Of minor studies during this decade, Max Plowman's *An Introduction to the Study of Blake* (1927) is just that, a lucid and unpretentious book.

Osbert Burdett's *William Blake* (1926) is the volume in the English Men of Letters series, and a good, if now somewhat dated, general study. Jack Lindsay's *William Blake: Creative Will and the Poetic Image* (1927) is a lively appreciative essay, and Philippe Soupault's *William Blake* (1928), translated by Lewis May in the same year, is more sophisticated, almost a minor classic of Blake criticism, with some illuminating suggestions about Blake's pictorial affinities. The studies by Allardyce Nicoll (1922), Herbert Jenkins (1925), Ernest Short (1925), C.H. Herford (1928), and Alan Clutton-Brock (1933) are expendable. With the growing specialization of Blake scholarship, the general essay has become a somewhat obsolete genre: a belated example is Stanley Gardner's *Infinity on the Anvil* (1954). For the contemporary student looking for a handbook to serve as a general introduction to Blake, H.M. Margoliouth's *William Blake* (1950), a volume in the Home University Library, is up to date and admirably concise.

But while Blake scholarship and criticism advanced immeasurably in the 1920s, Blake himself lost the place of honour with the avant-garde that he had held ever since his original discovery. In the shifting and regrouping of critical values which took place around Eliot and Pound, Blake was one of the poets, along with Milton and Shelley, who fell under the disapproval of the Romantic in literature, the radical in politics, and the Protestant in religion. The remarks about Blake in Irving Babbitt's *Rousseau and Romanticism* (1919), ill-informed as they are, may have helped to popularize the conception of Blake as an apocryphal writer in a new canon of orthodoxy. Eliot's influential essay on Blake in *The Sacred Wood* (1920) identified him as an intellectual Robinson Crusoe, weakening his poetic energies in an effort to construct a philosophy out of the bits and pieces of his self-educated reading, instead of working within a more central cultural tradition, deriving his thought from professional thinkers, in the manner of Dante. Blake accordingly became a major interest chiefly among poets and critics holding to the more old-fashioned Romantic and liberal sympathies, and to the unification of art and thought within the creative personality.

Among these was Middleton Murry, whose *William Blake* (1933) is best classified, on the whole, as a general introduction to Blake, though more elaborate than Plowman's. It presents Blake in the light of its author's preoccupation with a personal version of the Christian tradition liberalized by some insights of Marx in economics and of D.H. Lawrence in psychology—that is, it is to some extent a self-projecting study. But it does not really distort Blake or manipulate his thought in some other interest. It seldom comes to grips with the details of the symbolism, but in the area of general comment, and particularly in dealing with such critical issues as the revisions of *The Four Zoas*, it remains one of the best and closest studies of Blake's poetry and thought. An essay in the same author's *Mystery of Keats* (1949) compares Keats with Blake.

The study of Blake since 1933 may be divided into two main parts, dealing respectively with what in the criticism of Spenser would be called the moral and the historical allegory. We begin with the former, the books dealing primarily with Blake's "thought" as a system of ideas and its relation to certain intellectual traditions in religion and philosophy.

It has been increasingly recognized that the kind of scholarly problem represented by such words as "mysticism" and "occultism" is of less importance in the study of Blake than used to be assumed. Damon's book, it is true, did accept Blake as a mystic, and interpreted much of his symbolism in mystical terms. Some errors of interpretation resulted—*The Mental Traveller*, for example, was interpreted as a poem of a "mystic way," although its imagery is obviously closer to Freud's *Interpretation of Dreams* than to *The Cloud of Unknowing*. (On this poem see also John H. Sutherland, "Blake's 'Mental Traveller,'" *English Literary History*, 1955.) This was the only point on which Damon's conception of Blake was seriously questioned. Helen White's *The Mysticism of William Blake* (1927) comes to the conclusion that Blake does not fit very well into the tradition ordinarily called "mystical," the tradition in which, say, the Spanish saints of the Counter-Reformation would have a central place; and on the whole she must be regarded as having made her point. The result has been a tendency to deprecate or ignore the term "mystic" in connection with Blake, a tendency marked in Schorer, in my attempts to distinguish a "mystic" from a "visionary," in Erdman, and others.

Yet it is still possible to rehabilitate the term for Blake if some other conception of it, less ethical and more speculative and aesthetic, is taken as a norm. For instance, if one begins by reading the *Bhagavadgita*, preferably in the Wilkins translation that Blake used,[8] then learns from such traditions as those of Zen Buddhism how mysticism and art may be associated, then cautiously makes his way to the Western world by way of the Christianized Platonism of the Renaissance, he will come much closer to the kind of associations with the term which fit Blake. Suggestions about the affinities between Blake and Oriental thought are made from time to time: the affinities are remarkable, but probably few would care to follow them up in a field where almost nothing but pure analogy can be established. A more solid link is afforded by Blake's very probable knowledge of some of Thomas Taylor's translations from Plato and the Neoplatonists. This study is still fragmentary, and perhaps Blake's rare and crotchety references to Plato indicate the limitations of its value. The interested reader may consult, with caution, articles by F.E. Pierce, especially "Blake and Thomas Taylor" (*PMLA*, 1928), several recent articles by George M. Harper (e.g., "The Neo-Platonic Concept of Time in Blake's Prophetic Books," also in *PMLA*, 1954), and John E. Brown, "Neo-Platonism in the Poetry of William Blake" (*Journal of Aesthetics and Art Criticism*, 1951). The value of all such work depends on the accuracy of its reading of Blake, and there is certainly room for a good analogical study of Blake's relation to Oriental and Platonic traditions. One by P.F. Fisher of the Royal Military College (Canada) is in progress.

Other studies of Blake's mysticism, which in my opinion do not upset the views advanced above, are Adeline Butterworth's *William Blake, Mystic* (1911), a somewhat rhapsodic essay notable for bringing some of the designs to Young's *Night Thoughts* to attention; Maung Ba-Han's *William Blake: His Mysticism* (1924); Jacomina Korteling's *Mysticism in Blake and Wordsworth* (1928); Waldemar Bagdasarianz's *William Blake: Versuch einer Entwicklungsgeschichte des Mystikers* (1935). A readable popular account of Blake as a mystic is in Sheldon Cheney's *Men Who Have Walked with God* (1946).

The linking of Blake with various occult traditions stems from the conviction that a "dysangel" who talks so much and so fervently about Jesus must be some kind of Christian heretic. It goes without saying that Blake's religious views have been persistently misinterpreted, usually through a desire to make him bizarre in some way or other, the resulting muddle of inconsistencies being promptly attached to Blake's mind instead of the critic's. Actually (for the fact is as well established as any other in Blake scholarship) Blake is a Bible-soaked middle-class English Protestant: all his theological conceptions are quite consistent with this position, most of his symbolism, especially in *Milton* and *Jerusalem*, is elementary Biblical typology, and the bulk of his mysterious and esoteric doctrines come straight out of the New Testament. It is clear that he was interested in Boehme and Swedenborg, for example, not as occultists but as Christian visionaries. Any attempt to locate a major source for Blake's *beliefs* (as distinct from whatever symbols or concepts he might have absorbed into his iconography) outside the general Christian tradition as it came to him is sure to result in, at best, a negative thesis, in which his divergences will be of far greater significance than his resemblances.

The word "pantheist" was attached to Blake by Swinburne, but is a most unlucky guess for the author of the *Songs of Experience*. Attempts to connect Blake with the Gnostic tradition have always had a curious fascination for his critics, but have not yet been established on any basis that does not do violence to Blake's meaning. Some of the Gnostics interpreted the Bible as a straightforward antithesis of law and gospel, with everything in the New Testament contradicting and cancelling out everything in the Old, but it is quite wrong to ascribe such views to Blake, as is done in John Henry Clarke's *William Blake on the Lord's Prayer* (1927). A persistent exaggeration of the esoteric elements in Blake's thought vitiates much of the work of Denis Saurat on Blake, not least his recent *William Blake* (Paris, 1954), and has apparently extended elsewhere. (Cf. Kathleen Raine, "Who Made the Tyger?" *Encounter*, 1954). Blake's relation to Boehme and Swedenborg is a subject for careful investigation, because Blake may have got some of his Biblical typology from Swedenborg's doctrine of correspondence (instead of getting it, as a modern poet would do, from Dante or some other sacramental symbolist). However, the usual tendency is to compare Swedenborg's visions with Blake's legendary powers of visualization and second sight, a tendency marked in Jacques Roos's *Aspects littéraires du mysticisme philosophique . . .* (1951). The conception of Blake as an intellectual Robinson Crusoe might not have arisen if studies of his thought had not been so peripheral in their emphasis.

Some attempt at clearing up the doctrinal confusion is made in J.G. Davies's *The Theology of William Blake* (1948), which, besides having a good chapter on Swedenborg, quotes Blake accurately and brings out certain points, such as his belief in original sin, that are central to any serious study of his religious thought. Its standard however is a somewhat pedestrian conception of orthodoxy which leaves little room for paradox in statement, and some curious misconceptions greatly weaken it, such as its view of the status of the doctrine of the resurrection of the body in the Prophecies, a doctrine as central to them as the Incarnation is to the *Quartets*. The chapter on Blake in H.N. Fairchild's *Religious Trends in English Poetry* (1949) is a competent piece of scholarly writing, but very far from being a systematic presentation of Blake's religious position. M. Bottrall's *The Divine Image: A Study of Blake's Interpretation of Christianity* (1950) is on the whole the most satisfactory treatment to date of its theme, and suggests some interesting parallels with William Law.

The student interested in Blake's religious views should first get what few contemporary critics have, a coherent idea of Protestantism, and then investigate the doctrine technically known as pre-existence: the doctrine that Christ's humanity is co-eternal with his divinity. This doctrine is not strictly a heresy, in the sense of being a doctrine inconsistent with the Christian tradition (in Blake's day it was held by Isaac Watts), but it is the only unusual feature of Blake's religious beliefs, granted his Protestant premises.

As for Blake's philosophical views, it is becoming more obvious that he got them chiefly from a negative reaction to the English philosophers of the Enlightenment: he not only refers frequently to Bacon, Newton, and Locke, but says explicitly that he had read at least Bacon and Locke with some care. Some parallelism between his thought and that of other critics of Locke, especially Berkeley, would be expected, though Blake's reading of Berkeley cannot be definitely proved except for *Siris*, which proves very little. The eighteenth-century context of Blake's epistemology is dealt with by me, and, independently and with more documentation, by Bernard Blackstone in *English Blake* (1949). The study of Blake's antagonism to Locke and similarity to Berkeley is the most distinctive contribution made by Blackstone's book to Blake scholarship, the rest of it being for the most part repetitive of biographical and historical data available elsewhere. It is especially Blake's knowledge and conception of Newton that needs further clarification at present, and a study of this by Martin Nurmi is due to appear soon.[9]

At the same time Blake's use of certain occult sources is undeniable: Damon has shown how he used Agrippa for *Tiriel* and Porphyry's allegory of Homer's cave of the nymphs for *The Book of Thel*. Some explicit statements, too, such as his identification of Arthur with the constellation Boötes in the *Descriptive Catalogue*, show his interest in the contemporary astrologizing of myth. M.O. Percival's *William Blake's Circle of Destiny* (1938) is a remarkable essay in this field, the main achievement of which is to establish a number of analogous patterns between Blake's symbolism and the symbols of astrology, alchemy, and Kabbalism. The disadvantage of the book for the Blake student is that in establishing analogues to such symbols as the "Seven Eyes" the author frequently fails to lay the primary emphasis on the (usually Biblical) source. But, with this reservation, Percival's book is a study that will become steadily more useful and enlightening as Blake's own argument becomes more clearly understood, and as the morphology of occult systems of thought becomes better established.

This last has already been investigated, on a psychological basis, by Jung and his school. In Blake criticism there are at least two "Jungian" approaches to Blake: L.A.D. Johnstone's *A Psychological Study of William Blake* (1945) and W.P. Witcutt's *Blake: A Psychological Study* (1946). The former is brief and the latter is not very reliable in its interpretation of Blake, besides leaving out some aspects which should be central to any psychological study, such as the Oedipus situation in the *Preludium* to *America*. However, its identification of Jung's four faculties with the four Zoas seems sound enough.

It has long been the dream of students of occultism, mythology, and comparative religion that some day a key to a universal language of symbolism will be discovered. Works which seem to move in the direction of establishing a theory or grammar of symbolism have also always attracted poets; there were many such works in Blake's day, and Blake used them just as Spenser used Natalis Comes and as modern poets use Frazer and Frobenius.[10] The study of Blake's handling of such material is obviously indispensable. Denis Saurat's *Blake and Modern Thought* (1929) is the pioneer study in this field: the second chapter, much the most valuable part of the book, stresses the importance of Davies' *Celtic Researches*,[11] which Blake certainly read, of Bryant's *Ancient Mythology*,[12] which he certainly illustrated, and of contemporary theories about the antiquity and survival of the "Druids." Further information on this subject may be found in the essays on Blake in E.B. Hungerford's *Shores of Darkness* (1940) and in Ruthven Todd's *Tracks in the Snow* (1946). The latter stresses also the influence of Stukeley[13] and Owen Pughe.[14] More work in this direction, especially on the Welsh sources, needs to be done, although it should be done without value judgments. The poetic merits of Blake's Prophecies, whatever they may be, no more depend on the scholarly merits of Davies or Bryant than the poetic merits of *The Waste Land* depend on the view that Arthurian scholars take of *From Ritual to Romance*.

The same hope of finding some sort of grammar of symbolism has led a few of Blake's critics to look for it in Blake. The Ellis-Yeats commentary, which shows the influence of Blavatskian theosophy, belongs to this tradition to some extent, and so perhaps does Emily Hamblen's *On the Minor Prophecies of William Blake* (1930), where we return to etymological speculation, of the kind that so attracted Bryant. My study, *Fearful Symmetry* (1947), the most sustained attempt at a critical translation of Blake's moral allegory, locates this grammar of symbolism within literature itself: in other words, as a result of trying to solve a specific problem in literary criticism, the argument of Blake's Prophecies, this book became unconsciously an example of contemporary mythical or archetypal criticism. Thus Orc is Blake's example of the literary and mythical dying god, Urizen Blake's example of the literary and mythical father-god, and so on. There are mistakes in the book, but it seems to have been useful to those who have used it, and I have not changed my mind about any of my renderings of Blake's meaning.

If this literature-based approach to Blake's symbolism is sound, more investigation is clearly needed of Blake's relations, conscious and unconscious, with literature in general and English literature in particular. The studies of Platonic influence have no counterpart in any study of Blake's surprisingly extensive knowledge of Classical literature, which included much of Ovid, Virgil, Homer, Hesiod, and Apuleius, besides lesser authors. Blake's view of Classical imagination as comparatively debased did not prevent him from using a good deal of it. In English literature the chief influence on Blake was Milton, an influence not satisfactorily studied in Denis Saurat's *Blake and Milton* (1920; rev. ed. 1935), or in Raymond D. Havens's *The Influence of Milton on English Poetry* (1922). The latter is obsolete and the former, even in the revised edition, makes some reckless statements (e.g., "Blake never calls the Redeemer to help him in his struggles")[15] which are not simply slips but indicate a wrong conception of Blake—and, one may parenthetically add, of Milton. Blake's literary relation to his own time is a still more important subject, yet a sadly neglected one. Margaret Ruth Lowery's *Windows of the Morning* (1940) is a study of Blake's early *Poetical Sketches*, which makes a real effort to relate Blake to the other poets of the later eighteenth century. In spite of some controversial points, such as her view of the influence of Chatterton on Blake, the study is of considerable importance. I have frequently expressed the view that a more coherent conception of Blake's cultural period, avoiding the false teleologies of "post-Augustan" and "pre-Romantic," would do much to make sense of the problem of Blake's place in English literature.

The rhetorical or "new" critics have not been much attracted by Blake, though a steady series of notes on the lyrics has appeared in the *Explicator*. The best essay on Blake's poetic vocabulary is Josephine Miles's "The Language of William Blake," published in the volume *English Institute Essays, 1950* (1951), a volume which also contains essays on the archetypal and historical approaches to Blake by me and by Erdman respectively. There are brief but perceptive comments about Blake's versification in Lytton Strachey's *Books and Characters* (1922), in Edith Sitwell's *The Pleasures of Poetry*, Second Series (1931), and some close explication of the lyrics in Stanley Gardner's *Infinity on the Anvil*, mentioned above.

Turning now to the "historical allegory," there are three books that lay particular stress on the social context of Blake's work. Jacob Bronowski's *A Man without a Mask* (1943), the title of which is a phrase used about Blake by Samuel Palmer, is a crisp and incisive study which sketches in the historical background of Blake's time and sets Blake against it. It had always been obvious that Blake's poetry was in part a poetry of social protest, but Bronowski's study was the first to show in detail how wide open Blake's eyes were and how much of the life around him he absorbed and recorded. This book has been reprinted in Pelican Books under the not unusual title of *William Blake*.

Mark Schorer's *William Blake: The Politics of Vision* (1946) is a longer study with the same general emphasis, though independent of Bronowski and more varied in range. It has more allusions to twentieth-century poetry and criticism than any other book on Blake, and hence is one in which the modern reader may feel particularly at home, Blake's affinities with the modern world being more frequently asserted than documented. It lays stress on Blake as an intellectual revolutionary, as one who was in contact, through the publisher Johnson, with a good deal of English radical sentiment. The book has a clear grasp of the central problem of all historical study of Blake, the peculiarly English combination of the political radical and the religious evangelical, a combination which made the intellectual basis of the French Revolution as intolerable to him as the misery of the London poor. Schorer sees in the impossible demands which this attitude made on life the key to what for him is the essential characteristic of the Prophecies: a powerful energy of expression which never finds its appropriate form.

David V. Erdman's *Blake: Prophet against Empire* (1954) does for the two previous studies more or less what Damon did for the criticism before his time: that is, it pursues the social reference of Blake's poetry into its texture and details. The book is based on a clear and accurate reading of the whole of Blake's poetry, including the Prophecies, besides keeping in view the total range of his work as illustrator and engraver, which often throws unexpected light on the symbolism. Many traditional errors and vague notions, parroted from one writer to another, are corrected or cleared up, and an exhaustive program of research not only explains an extraordinary number of obscure points and problems, but builds up a logical biographical narrative as it goes on. For it is obvious that the historical study of Blake is, in contrast to the philosophical approach, much more closely involved with questions of biography, and anyone who wishes to follow this line of scholarship must become something of a biographer. The historical background too has been studied in its primary sources: instead of generalizations about the dark Satanic mills, we are told just what social phenomena, from exploitation to the new machinery, did catch Blake's eye and got recorded in the poems and designs.

Studies of Blake's influence on later poets will not detain us long. The influence of Blake on Yeats is dealt with in Margaret Rudd's *Divided Image* (1953), in Virginia Moore's *The Unicorn* (1954), and in Hazard Adams's *Blake and Yeats: The Contrary Vision* (1955). The last named is the only satisfactory study of the Blake side. There are also several studies of Blake and Dante Gabriel Rossetti, the fullest being Kerrison Preston's *Blake and Rossetti* (1944). Irving Fiske's *Bernard Shaw's Debt to William Blake* (1951) is a Shaw Society pamphlet enthusiastically endorsed by Shaw himself. In the *Joyce Review* (1957) I have set out the chief parallels between the myths of the Prophecies and of *Finnegans Wake*, without committing myself on the question of how far Joyce was aware of them.[16] The influence of Blake on Dylan Thomas still awaits study.

V Blake as a Graphic Artist

Of Blake's work as painter, engraver, and illustrator, there has been little criticism of much freshness or distinctiveness. Blake, as D.H. Lawrence said, "dares handle the human body,"[17] but he was far more daring than that, and his dizzy foreshortenings and swirling calligraphic rhythms still await competent exposition. There is a good historical account of Blake in R.H. Wilenski's *English Painting* (1933); there is an essay in Sturge Moore's *Art and Life* (1910), and a more important one in Roger Fry's *Vision and Design* (1920). The relation of Blake's theories of painting to eighteenth-century aesthetic theory and taste has been little explored, beyond some incidental information in Erdman's book and a useful chapter on Blake in Stephen A. Larrabee's *English Bards and Grecian Marbles* (1943), which, as its title indicates, deals with what for Blake was the negative side of it.

On Blake's iconography the pioneer work, one of the major efforts of

Blake scholarship, is Joseph H. Wicksteed's *Blake's Vision of the Book of Job*, a brilliant commentary on the Job engravings which was first published in 1910, but did not make its full impact on Blake criticism until the revised edition of 1924. It established once for all the existence of a coherent iconography in one of Blake's greatest works of art, especially in the significance given to right and left hands, to Gothic and "Druid" buildings, and the like. Albert S. Roe's *Blake's Illustrations to the Divine Comedy* (1953) does for the Dante drawings and engravings what Wicksteed did for the Job series. The book, beautifully produced by the Princeton University Press, contains the hundred Dante drawings and an able commentary, which shows very deftly how Blake managed to illustrate Dante's poem and his own reading of that poem at the same time.

Some of Blake's pictures are complicated enough to require separate iconographical treatment. Unfortunately the commentaries on *The River of Life* by Joseph Wicksteed, and on *The Spiritual Condition of Man* and *The Sea of Time and Space* by Kerrison Preston, are not readily available; one would like to see such commentaries gathered together in book form. More accessible, and equally useful, is Piloo Nanavutty's "A Title-Page in Blake's Genesis Manuscript" (*Journal of the Warburg and Courtauld Institutes*, 1947). The study of the sources of Blake's iconography begins, and so far practically ends, with two important articles—Collins Baker's "The Sources of Blake's Pictorial Expression" (*Huntington Library Quarterly*, 1940–41) and Anthony Blunt's "Blake's Pictorial Imagination" (*Journal of the Warburg and Courtauld Institutes*, 1943)—and a few other articles of more restricted interest in the latter journal. A rare example of Blake's pictorial relation to a contemporary is studied in D.V. Erdman's "William Blake's Debt to James Gillray" (*Art Quarterly*, 1949). Finally, the only really serious study to date of the mystery of Blake's engraving process has been made by Ruthven Todd in "The Techniques of William Blake's Illuminated Printing" (*Print*, 1948). The defunct Canadian magazine *Here and Now* carried in its first issue (1948) reproductions of poems of Todd illustrated by Joan Miró, his collaborator in working out the process, exemplifying it in practice.

Two well-produced collections of Blake's graphic work appeared in the 1920s. Darrell Figgis's *The Paintings of William Blake* (1925) is a fine anthology of Blake's most famous paintings, mostly in black and white, with a few in colour. The companion volume is Laurence Binyon's *The Engraved Designs of William Blake* (1926). These two books are essential to any serious study of this side of Blake. Geoffrey Keynes's *The Pencil*

Drawings of William Blake (1927) contains the Visionary Heads and some wonderful sketches—a new edition of this work is promised. The finest set of Blake's woodcuts, the illustrations made to Thornton's edition of Virgil's *Georgics*, was issued by Geoffrey Keynes, also in 1927. No attempt can be made here to list everything that comes into the general category of miscellaneous "picture books," catalogues of exhibitions, and the like. Adrian van Sinderen's *Blake: The Mystic Genius* (1949), Geoffrey Keynes's *William Blake's Engravings* (1950), and the descriptive catalogue of an exhibition assembled from American collections by the Philadelphia Museum of Art in 1939 may be mentioned, more or less at random, for their general variety of interest. The van Sinderen book contains colour reproductions of the twelve illustrations to Milton's *L'Allegro* and *Il Penseroso*.

A complete set of the paintings, drawings, and engravings of the Job series was issued by Laurence Binyon and Geoffrey Keynes in 1935, except for the more recently discovered "New Zealand" set, which appeared with a note by Philip Hofer in 1937. *William Blake's Designs for Gray's Poems* (1922), with a note by H.J.C. Grierson, is a fine example of one of Blake's most interesting series. There is as yet, not unnaturally, no complete edition of the five hundred–odd illustrations to Young's *Night Thoughts*, but a selection, with some of the most gorgeous designs Blake ever made reproduced in colour, was issued by Geoffrey Keynes in 1927. It was also Geoffrey Keynes who was responsible for reproducing the illustrations to *The Pilgrim's Progress* in 1941 and for most of the editions of Blake's illustrations to Milton's poems, nearly all of which have now been reproduced. Another edition of a *Paradise Lost* set was published by the Heritage Press in 1941.

It is hardly necessary to labour the point that Blake's engraved poems cannot be safely studied from the text alone. Many misled and misleading interpretations of Blake might never have been proposed if this had been kept in mind. Further, text and designs in a long poem form different aspects of it. The design may sometimes illustrate the text on the same plate, but it by no means invariably does so. It is curious how little literary criticism of Blake appears to have been based on the designs equally with the text. Damon's book, which covers more of Blake's output in both arts than any other single commentary, is a mine of information about the designs accompanying the engraved poems, where the characters and themes are identified with great skill and accuracy. Joseph Wicksteed, *Blake's Innocence and Experience* (1928), also pays close attention to the iconography of the designs, as one would expect from the author of the Job commentary. Erdman's commentary and mine make a consistent use of the designs, though mine gives little direct evidence of the fact: my article, "Poetry and Design in William Blake" (*Journal of Aesthetics and Art Criticism*, 1951) [no. 12 in this volume], is intended to be a general introduction to this aspect of Blake criticism. Blake's *Gates of Paradise*, the only one of the engraved poems which is completely unintelligible without the designs, has been studied by Chauncey B. Tinker in *Painter and Poet* (1938).

All the engraved poems have been reproduced in some form or other. The third volume of the Ellis and Yeats edition contains a practically complete set of reproductions of the prophetic books, in black and white lithograph. The unique *Book of Ahania* has not to my knowledge been reproduced since. One's admiration for this heroic early effort should not interfere with one's opinion of the quality of the reproductions, which look rather as though the originals had been stamped on highly absorbent blotting paper. Since then, a number of reproductions of the engraved poems, of varying merit, in both colour and black and white, have appeared from time to time. Nearly all of them have been reproduced by the Blake Press (William Muir, Edmonton, England) at various dates from 1884 on; the edition of *Europe* is particularly successful. Finally, the Blake Trust in England has begun to issue a series of colour reproductions in expensive and limited editions, using the whole resources of modern methods of reproduction, printed by the Trianon Press. A superb *Jerusalem* appeared in 1952, along with a black and white reproduction of the Rinder copy of the same poem in a second volume, and a commentary by Joseph Wicksteed in a third. *Songs of Innocence and Experience* followed in 1955. I understand that *The Book of Urizen*, pictorially one of the most splendid of them all, is planned for the near future, and one hopes that the series will eventually embrace the whole canon.

The present essay, though it has tried to record everything of permanent value for the contemporary student of English literature interested in Blake, has still given only a selection from the vast spate of comment which, in less than a century, has followed Gilchrist's discovery of his "pictor ignotus." Two things should be said in conclusion. First, Blake scholarship today moves ahead fairly fast. This essay will be out of date in some respects before it appears: new studies are springing up on all sides, even those that I happen to have heard of forming an impressive list. Ignoring this scholarship will assuredly result in ignoring many essential facts. Second, the days of looking into one's heart to write about Blake are over. It is now possible to say with some authority that some approaches to Blake are fruitful and that others are blind alleys; that some readings of Blake are right and others wrong; and that the right reading is increasingly a matter of fact, not of guesswork. The permanently valuable critics of Blake are those who have realized that Blake will repay any amount of time and patience expended on him, and that nothing in him is to be glibly dismissed or rejected. The permanently valuable critics of the future will be those who follow in this tradition.

Postscript

To bring this chronicle down to the end of 1956 and the beginning of the bicentenary year, which will see some important new publications, the new edition of the pencil sketches by Geoffrey Keynes, mentioned above, has appeared, and the same editor has also issued *The Letters of William Blake*, a definitive (so far as present knowledge extends) edition of Blake's letters and other personal documents, such as receipts and the Schofield memoranda, with a full bibliographical register. Two new monographs also appeared at the end of the year. William Gaunt's *Arrows of Desire* fills the need for a "background" biographical narrative which deals less with Blake than with figures who came into contact, personal or intellectual, with him, ranging from Ossian and Chatterton to Linnell and Gilchrist. It is a useful supplement to such an introduction to Blake as that of H.M. Margoliouth, mentioned above. Margaret Rudd's *Organiz'd Innocence* is a commentary on the major Prophecies (*The Four Zoas*, *Milton*, *Jerusalem*) which has a quasi-biographical slant, taking off from the postulate that a feeling of doubt or ambivalence on Blake's part towards his work and his marriage "is certainly what the prophetic books are *about*" (author's italics).[18]

It is beginning to look, from the evidence brought forward in H.M. Margoliouth's edition of *Vala*, mentioned above, and from some investigations of G.E. Bentley, Jr.—see especially "The Date of Blake's *Vala* or *The Four Zoas*" (*Modern Language Notes*, 1956)—that *The Four Zoas* was written mainly during the Felpham period (1800–3), or later, which presumably means that Blake must have worked on his three long poems simultaneously rather than serially.

17

Blake after Two Centuries

October 1957

From FI, *138–50. Originally published in* University of Toronto Quarterly, *27 (October 1957): 10–21.*

I

The value of centenaries and similar observances is that they call attention, not simply to great men, but to what we do with our great men. The anniversary punctuates, so to speak, the scholarly and critical absorption of its subject into society. From this point of view, a centenary date might well be more impressive for those interested in William Blake than his birth on November 28, 1757. The year 1857 would bring us to a transitional point in the life of Alexander Gilchrist, who had recently got a life of Etty off his hands, married, moved to Chelsea to be near his idol Carlyle, was busy winding up some family business, and was preparing to start in earnest on *The Life of William Blake, Pictor Ignotus*. This last was no empty phrase. Scattered notices of Blake had appeared in collections of artists' biographies, but nothing like a full volume had been devoted to Blake in the thirty years since his death. Blake was fortunate in his first posthumous group of admirers. Gilchrist was a remarkable person, his wife Anne equally so, and Rossetti and Swinburne, if not exactly emancipated spirits, were at least sufficiently free of the more lethal Victorian virtues to admire Blake without undue inhibitions. They make an instructive contrast to whoever it was (apparently not Ruskin, who has been accused of it) that cut up one of the two coloured copies of *Jerusalem*,[1] the anonymous worthy who apparently destroyed the great *Vision of the Last Judgement*, and the member of the Linnell family who erased the genitalia from the drawings on the *Four Zoas* manuscript.

Gilchrist died in 1861 with his masterpiece unfinished: Anne Gilchrist brought it out in 1863 in two volumes. The first volume was Gilchrist's biography: no better biography has been written since, for all our advance in understanding. The main part of the second volume was Rossetti's edition of the lyrics, where Blake, however expurgated and improved in his metres, still did achieve something like a representative showing as a poet. Swinburne's critical essay appeared in 1868, and soon afterwards there began, a slow trickle at first, then a flood still in full spate, of critical studies, biographies, editions, illustrated editions, collections of paintings and engravings, handbooks, catalogues, appreciations, research articles, chapters in other books, and specialized studies pouring out of the presses of at least twenty countries. Max Beerbohm's Enoch Soames sold his soul to the devil in exchange for a glance at the future British Museum catalogue of critical work on him, only to discover that posterity took the same view of him that his contemporaries had done.[2] Such irony is not for Blake, who in his lifetime was something of an Enoch Soames too, but an Enoch Soames who was right.

Much more than a Cinderella success story is involved here. In her little British Council bibliography, Miss Kathleen Raine remarks on the spontaneous personal affection shown in the public response to the recent discovery of a large and rather confused allegorical picture by Blake in a house in Devon.[3] A new Michelangelo would have been more important, but it would not have aroused that specific reaction of affectionate pride. Blake's deep love of England is clearly not an unrequited love, nor is the sense that he is one of us confined to Englishmen. People get attracted to him through feeling that he is for them a personal discovery and something of a private possession. I constantly hear of doctors, housewives, clergymen, teachers, manual workers, shopkeepers, who are, in the most frequent phrase used, "frightfully keen on Blake," who have bought every book on him they could afford, and kept him around like an amiable household god. I have taught Blake to Jesuits and I have taught him to Communist organizers; I have taught him to deans of women and I have taught him to ferocious young poets of unpredictable rhythms and unprintable (or at least privately printed) diction. His admirers have nothing in common except the feeling that Blake says something to them that no one else can say: that whatever their standards and values may be, Blake has the charity to include them, not as part of a general principle of benevolence, which Blake himself would have despised, but uniquely as individuals.

Undergraduates, too, have fewer barriers against Blake than against most poets: besides the absence of unfamiliar conventions or a special poetic language, he lacks the two qualities that undergraduates are most afraid of, sentimentality and irony. Again, some poets travel better than others, and just as Byron and Poe in the nineteenth century proved to be more readily exportable than Wordsworth or Hawthorne, so in the twentieth century Blake seems the easiest of all our poets to export to India or Japan. He can hardly ever lack admirers among the fellow countrymen of Rouault and of Gérard de Nerval, or of Hölderlin and of Novalis. Within ninety years after the first critical study of him was published, Blake appears to be headed for what at one time seemed his least likely fate: a genuine, permanent, and international popularity.

This popularity has been achieved in spite of Blake's reputation for being difficult and esoteric, someone not to be understood without preliminary study of a dozen occult systems of thought and several thousand pages of commentary. I have written one of the thickest of the commentaries myself, and I certainly meant all I said, but I quite realize how often the popular estimate of Blake is sounder in perspective than the scholarly one. Scholars will assert that the famous *Jerusalem* hymn is crypto-Anglo-Israelitism or what not; but when it was sung in front of Transport House at the Labour victory of 1945 the singers showed that they understood it far better than such scholars did. Scholars will assert that the question in *The Tyger*, "Did he who made the lamb make thee?" is to be answered with a confident yes or no: yes if Blake is believed to be a pantheist, no if he is believed to be a Gnostic. Most of those who love the poem are content to leave it a question, and they are right. "You say," wrote Blake to the Rev. Dr. Trusler, author of *The Way to be Rich and Respectable*, "that I want somebody to Elucidate my Ideas. But you ought to know that What is Grand is necessarily obscure to Weak men. That which can be made Explicit to the Idiot is not worth my care." Having thus brought his correspondent into focus, he goes on: "But I am happy to find a Great Majority of Fellow Mortals who can Elucidate My Visions, & Particularly they have been Elucidated by Children, who have taken a greater delight in contemplating my Pictures than I even hoped" [K793–4/E702–3]. Children have always found Blake easier than the Truslers have done.

II

Clearly, if Blake can be popular we need a new definition of popularity. Several very different things are included under the term popular, and the simple conception "What the public wants" will not do. Best-seller popularity depends more on news value than on any aesthetic qualities, whether good or bad. But there is another sense in which the term popular may be used, as referring to the art which affords a key to imaginative experience for the untrained. The centre of gravity of popular fiction in this sense is the folk tale, and in American culture, for instance, it would be represented by *Huckleberry Finn*, *Rip van Winkle*, some tales of Poe, of Uncle Remus, and the various cycles of native humour like the Western tall tale. Much that is popular even in this context is still rubbish, and some of it may be quite unpopular in the best-seller meaning of the word. The popular in the second sense is the contemporary primitive, and it tends to become primitive with the passing of time. Such primitive and popular elements recur in great art, even very difficult and complex art. One thinks of Shakespeare's late romances, with their archaic nature myths and their improbable coincidences turning up "like an old tale" [*The Winter's Tale* 5.3.117]. One thinks more particularly of the Bible, which is one long folk tale from beginning to end, and the most primitive and popular book in the world.

The two senses of popular seem to be, up to a point, connected with the distinction of content and form. "What the public wants," as the first word suggests, relates primarily to content: certain conventional choices of subject—domestic, sentimental, heroic, sexually provocative—come into vogue by turns. Certain story types, on the other hand, which remain fairly constant from ancient myth to contemporary comic strip, are isolated in the art which is popular in the second sense. Like the corresponding primitive and popular forms in the plastic arts, they are abstract and stylized, and have a curiously archaic look about them whenever they appear. The generic term for such story types is myth, because myths are stories about divine beings which are abstract and stylized stories in the sense that they are unaffected by canons of realism or probability.

Blake's only fictions are in his prophetic books, and although they are certainly mythical enough, there are other aspects of popular literature in its formal sense more obviously relevant to him. The conceptual element in poetry is also a part of its content, and conceptual thinking in poetry is more or less assimilated to another kind of thinking which organizes the poetic structure. The unit of this formally poetic thinking is the metaphor, and the metaphor is inherently illogical, an identification of two or more things which could never be identified except by a lunatic, a lover, or a poet—one may perhaps add an extremely primitive savage. We are educated in conceptual thinking, and so usually find poetry which comes to terms with it easier to read, like Wordsworth's. Poetry which is popular in the sense of having a vogue is popular by reason of having such a conceptual content: it talks about the Deity in the eighteenth century, or Duty in the nineteenth, or it speaks to the eternal bourgeois in the heart of man, like Kipling's *If*, Longfellow's *Psalm of Life*, or Burns's *A Man's a Man for a' That*. Poetry which concentrates on metaphor to the point of appearing to exclude conceptual thought altogether, like surrealist poetry, impresses most readers as wilfully crazy, or, if they are compelled to take it seriously, as incredibly difficult and esoteric.

Yet greater experience with literature soon shows that it is metaphor which is direct and primitive, and conceptual thought which is sophisticated. Hence there is a body of verse that can be called popular in the sense of providing the direct, primitive, metaphorical key to poetic experience for educated and uneducated alike. Most good teaching anthologies are largely composed of such verse, and in such anthologies the lyrics of Blake leap into the foreground with a vividness that almost exaggerates Blake's relative importance as a poet:

> O Rose, thou art sick!
> The invisible worm
> That flies in the night,
> In the howling storm,
>
> Has found out thy bed
> Of crimson joy:
> And his dark secret love
> Does thy life destroy. [K213/E23]

I say exaggerates, because there are many fine poets who do not have this specific kind of directness. One may always meet a poem with a set of questions designed to avoid its impact: What does it mean? Why is it considered a good poem? Is it morally beneficial? Does it say profound things about life? and so forth. But such a poem as *The Sick Rose* has a peculiar power of brushing them aside, of speaking with the unanswerable authority of poetry itself. Blake's lyrics, with many of those of Herrick, Burns, and Donne, the sonnets of Shakespeare, Wordsworth's Lucy poems, and a few of the great ballads, are popular poetry in the sense that they are a practically foolproof introduction to poetic experience.

Metaphor, then, is a formal principle of poetry, and myth of fiction. We begin to see how Blake hangs together: his Prophecies are so intensely mythical because his lyrics are so intensely metaphorical. At present his Prophecies seem to have little to do with popular literature in any sense of the word, but opinion will have changed on this point long before the tercentenary rolls around. It will then be generally understood that just as Blake's lyrics are among the best possible introductions to poetic experience, so his Prophecies are among the best possible introductions to the grammar and structure of literary mythology. His practice again is consistent with his theory, which lays an almost exclusive emphasis on the imagination or forming power. However, there comes a point at which our distinction of form and content breaks down, and we have to raise the question of what kind of content formal art has.

"The Nature of my Work is Visionary or Imaginative," said Blake: "it is an Endeavour to Restore what the Ancients call'd the Golden Age."[4] By vision he meant the view of the world, not as it might be, still less as it ordinarily appears, but as it really is when it is seen by human consciousness at its greatest height and intensity. It is the artist's business to attain this heightened or transfigured view of things, and show us what kind of world is actually in front of us, with all its glowing splendours and horrifying evils. It is only the direct, metaphorical, and mythical perceptions, which work without compromise with unimaginative notions of reality, that can clearly render the forms of such a world. Such psychological experiments as those recorded in Mr. Aldous Huxley's *The Doors of Perception* (the title of which comes from Blake [K154/E39], although taking mescalin is not precisely what Blake meant by "cleansing" the doors of perception) seem to show that the formal principles of this heightened vision are constantly latent in the mind, which perhaps explains the communicability of such visions. For Blake, however, the Bible provides the key to the relation between the two worlds. The ordinary world is "fallen," the manifestation of man's own sin and ignorance; the true world is the apocalypse presented at the end of the Bible and the paradise presented at the beginning of it: the true city and garden that is man's home, and which all existing cities and gardens struggle to make manifest in the lower world.

The apocalypse of the Bible is a world in which all human forms are identified, as Blake says at the end of his *Jerusalem*. That is, all forms are identified as human. Cities and gardens, sun moon and stars, rivers and stones, trees and human bodies—all are equally alive, equally parts of the same infinite body which is at once the body of God and of risen man. In this world "Each Identity is Eternal," for "In Eternity one Thing never Changes into another Thing."[5] It is a world of forms like Plato's except that in Blake these forms are images of pure being seen by a spiritual body, not ideas of pure essence seen by a soul, a conception which would rule out the artist as a revealer of reality. To Blake this vision of apocalypse and resurrection was the grammar of poetry and painting alike, and it was also the source of the formal principles of art. He lived in a way that brought him into the most constant contact with this world, for we notice that isolation, solitude, and a certain amount of mental stress or disturbance have a tendency to light up this vision in the mind. When Christopher Smart is shut into a madhouse with no company except his cat Jeoffry, the cat leaps into the same apocalyptic limelight as Blake's tiger:

> For he keeps the Lord's watch in the night against the adversary.
> For he counteracts the powers of darkness by his electrical skin and
>   glaring eyes . . .
> For he is of the tribe of Tiger.
> For the Cherub Cat is a term of the Angel Tiger . . .
> For by stroaking of him I have found out electricity.
> For I perceived God's light about him both wax and fire.
> For the Electrical fire is the spiritual substance, which God sends from
>   heaven to sustain the bodies both of man and beast.[6]

Similarly when John Clare is confined to an asylum and is in the depths of schizophrenia, the luminous fragility of Blake's *Book of Thel*, along with the glowing lights and gemmed trees of Mr. Huxley's adventures in heaven and hell, appear in his vision:

> The birds sing on the clouds in that eternal land,
> Jewels and siller are they a', and gouden is the sand.
> The sun is one vast world of fire that burneth a' to-day,
> And nights wi' hells of darkness for ever keeps away.
> And dearly I love the queen o' that bright land,
> The lily flowers o' woman that meeteth no decay.[7]

Blake's attitude to art makes no psychological distinctions among the arts, and the same imagination that the poet uses appears in Blake's theory of painting as "outline," which again is an intense concentration on the formal principles of the art. The abstract school of painting today assumes that the formal principles of painting are quasi-geometrical, but Blake, with the faded white ghosts of eighteenth-century Classicism in front of him, warned sharply against the preference of "mathematic form" to "living form."[8] Blake despised everything that was amorphous or vague in art: the imagination for him could express itself only as rigorous and exactly ordered form. But by living form he meant a vitalized Classicism, where the outline is held in the tight grip of imaginative intensity, a Classicism that would have more in common with Van Gogh than with Flaxman or David. Blake's painting, though strongly formalized, is not abstract in tendency, but what one might call hieroglyphic in tendency. It presents the same world that his poetry presents; yet (except in lapses) it is not literary painting. The tense stylized figures of the Byzantines with their staring eyes and weightless bodies; medieval primitives with their glittering gold haloes and childlike sense of primary colour; Eastern "mandalas" that communicate the sense of powerful spiritual discipline in repose; the calligraphic distortions of Klee: these all belong in different ways to the hieroglyphic tradition in painting, and are allied to the vision that Blake evolved from his study of Renaissance prints.

III

The conception of formally popular art which underlies the present argument is still an unexplored subject in criticism, and many aspects of it can be only suggested here. It has been neglected partly because the original proponents of it, notably Herder, confused it by mixing it up with a pseudohistorical myth of the Golden Age family. Formally popular art was supposed to have been derived from a "folk" whose art was rural and spontaneous and communal and unspecialized and a number of other things that no art can be. When we remove this notion of a "folk," we are left with a third conception of popular art as the art which is central to a specific cultural tradition. There is no question here of looking for *the* centre or isolating an imaginary essence of a tradition, but only of seeing what some of its prevailing and recurrent rhythms have been. The sources of a cultural tradition are, of course, its religious and social context as well as its own earlier products. In English culture we notice at once a strong and constant affinity with art which is popular in the formal sense, in striking contrast to, say, French culture, which has much more the character of something deliberately imposed.

One characteristic of the English tradition has obviously been affected by Protestantism. This is the tendency to anchor the apocalyptic vision in a direct individual experience, as the product, not of sacramental discipline, but of imaginative experiment. The experience may be as forced as *Grace Abounding* or as relaxed as Keats's speculations about a vale of soul-making, but it tends to be autonomous, to make the experience its own authority.[9] The 1611 Bible is not a "monument of English prose," but the exact opposite of what a monument is: it is a translation with a unique power of making the Bible a personal possession of its reader, and to this its enormous popularity as well as its importance in English culture is due. It has also fostered, of course, the kind of Biblical culture that has made *The Pilgrim's Progress* one of the most popular books in the language, that has given *Paradise Lost* its central place in English literature, and that has instigated some very inadequate performances of Handel's *Messiah* (a work with a unique power of catching this quality of direct vision in music) in Midland towns. Such Biblical culture, absorbed as part of a poet's own imaginative experience, was inspiring visions of revelation and resurrection at least as early as the *Pearl* poet, and had lost nothing of its intensity when Dylan Thomas was shattering the sedate trumpet of the BBC with the same tones:

> Though they be mad and dead as nails,
> Heads of the characters hammer through daisies;
> Break in the sun till the sun breaks down,
> And death shall have no dominion.[10]

Blake, who was brought up on the Bible and on Milton, is unusually close to this simple and naive Biblism even for an English poet. The occult and esoteric elements in his thought have been grossly exaggerated by critics who, as Johnson said of Hume, have not read the New Testament with attention.[11] What is so obviously true of most of his paintings is true also of his poetry: it is the work of a man whose Bible was his textbook. The Prophecies recreate the Bible in English symbolism, just as the 1611 translation recreates it in the English language, and, no less than *Paradise Lost* or *The Pilgrim's Progress*, they record a direct search for the New Jerusalem which exists here and now in England's green and pleasant land.

A second characteristic of the English tradition is of social origin, and is derived from an apparently permanent English tendency to political resistance. This tendency has taken different forms in different ages—Roundhead, Whig, radical, liberal, socialist—but is so constant that it may be actually a kind of anarchism, or what in a play of Bernard Shaw's is called an obstinate refusal to be governed at all.[12] From Milton's defence of the liberty of prophesying to Mill's defence of the right to be eccentric, it is pervaded by a sense that the final cause of society is the free individual. This sense distinguishes it sharply from such revolutionary traditions as those of America or Russia, where a fundamental social pattern is established *a priori* by the revolution, and other patterns are rejected as un-American or counter-revolutionary.

In Blake's political outlook one finds a radicalism of a common English type, which includes a strong individual protest against all institutional radicalism. Blake was brought up in the centre of English social resistance, the city of London, in the period of Wilkes and the Gordon riots. His sympathy first with the American and then with the French Revolution placed him as far to the left as he could go and still continue to function as an artist. Yet his denunciation of what he called the "Deism" of the French revolutionaries, and of the ideology of Voltaire and Rousseau, is nearly as strong as Burke's. At the same time his poems point directly towards the English society of his time: even his most complex Prophecies have far more in common with Dickens than they have with Plotinus. And though he said "Houses of Commons & Houses of Lords appear to me to be fools; they seem to me to be something Else besides Human Life,"[13] this expresses, not a withdrawal from society, but a sense of the inadequacy of everything that falls short of the apocalyptic vision itself. Blake's is the same impossible vision that caused Milton to break with four kinds of revolt in England, and which still earlier had inspired the dream of John Ball, a dream based, like *Areopagitica* and *The Marriage of Heaven and Hell*, on a sense of ironic contrast between the fallen and unfallen worlds:

When Adam delved and Eve span,
Who was then the gentleman?

In breaking with all forms of social organization, however, Blake is merely following the logic of art itself, whose myths and visions are at once the cause and the clarified form of social developments. Every society is the embodiment of a myth, and as the artist is the shaper of myth, there is a sense in which he holds in his hand the thunderbolts that destroy one society and create another. Another busy and versatile English radical, William Morris, not a mythopoeic poet himself but a mere collector of myths, nevertheless portrayed those myths in *The Earthly Paradise* as a group of old men who had outgrown the desire to be made kings or gods. In this cycle they are ineffectual exiles, but in Morris's later work they return as revolutionary dreams, though of a kind that, again, rejects all existing types of revolutionary organization.

The possibility is raised in passing that formally popular art has a perennially subversive quality about it, whereas art that has a vogue popularity remains subservient to society. We note that Russian Communism denounced "Formalism" as the essence of the bourgeois in art, and turned to vogue popularity instead, a vogue artificially sustained by political control, as part of its general policy of perverting revolutionary values. This tendency follows the example set by Tolstoy, who, though a greater artist than Morris, was also more confused about the nature of popular art.

Blake formed his creative habits in the age immediately preceding Romanticism: still, his characteristics are Romantic in the expanded sense of giving a primary place to imagination and individual feeling. Like the Romantics, Blake thought of the "Augustan" period from 1660 to 1760 as an interruption of the normal native tradition. This sense of belonging to and restoring the native tradition helps to distinguish Romanticism in England from Romanticism on the Continent, especially in France. It also enabled the English Romantic writers—in their fertile periods at any rate—to lean less heavily on religious and political conservatism in their search for a tradition.

The great achievement of English Romanticism was its grasp of the principle of creative autonomy, its declaration of artistic independence. The thing that is new in Wordsworth's *Prelude*, in Coleridge's criticism, in Keats's letters, is the sense, not that the poet is superior or inferior to others, but simply that he has an authority, as distinct from a social function, of his own. He does not need to claim any extraneous authority, and still less need he take refuge in any withdrawal from society. The creative process is an end in itself, not to be judged by its power to illustrate something else, however true or good. Some Romantics, especially Coleridge, wobble on this point, but Blake, like Keats and Shelley, is firm, and consistent when he says, "I will not Reason & Compare: my business is to Create" [*J*, 10.21; K629/E153]. The difficulties revealed by such poems as Shelley's *Triumph of Life* or Keats's *Fall of Hyperion* are concerned with the content of the poetic vision, not with any doubts about the validity of that vision as a mean between subjective dream and objective action. "The poet and the dreamer are distinct," says Keats's Moneta,[14] and Rousseau in Shelley's poem is typically the bastard poet whose work spilled over into action instead of remaining creative.

Hence the English Romantic tradition has close affinities with the individualism of the Protestant and the radical traditions. In all three the tendency is to take the individual as the primary field or area of operations instead of the interests of society, a tendency which is not necessarily egocentric, any more than its opposite is necessarily altruistic. English Romanticism is greatly aided in its feeling of being central to the tradition of English literature by the example of Shakespeare, who was in proportion to his abilities the most unpretentious poet who ever lived, a poet of whom one can predicate nothing except that he wrote plays, and stuck to his own business as a poet. He is the great poetic example of an inductive and practical approach to experience in English culture which is another aspect of its individualism.

I have no thought of trying to prefer one kind of English culture to another, and I regard all value judgments that inhibit one's sympathies with anything outside a given tradition as dismally uncritical. I say only that this combination of Protestant, radical, and Romantic qualities is frequent enough in English culture to account for the popularity, in every sense, of the products of it described above. There have been no lack of Catholic, Tory, and Classical elements too, but the tradition dealt with here has been popular enough to give these latter elements something of the quality of a consciously intellectual reaction. During the twenties of the present century, after the shock of the First World War, this intellectual reaction gathered strength. Its most articulate supporters were cultural evangelists who came from places like Missouri and Idaho, and who had a clear sense of the shape of the true English tradition, from its beginnings in Provence and medieval Italy to its later developments in France. Mr. Eliot's version of this tradition was finally announced as Classical, royalist, and Anglo-Catholic,[15] implying that whatever was Protestant, radical, and Romantic would have to go into the intellectual doghouse.

Many others who did not have the specific motivations of Mr. Eliot or of Mr. Pound joined in the chorus of denigration of Miltonic, Romantic, liberal, and allied values. Critics still know too little of the real principles of criticism to have any defence against such fashions, when well organized; hence although the fashion itself is on its way out, the prejudices set up by it still remain. Blake must of course be seen in the context of the tradition he belonged to, unless he is to be unnaturally isolated from it, and when the fashionable judgments on his tradition consist so largely of pseudocritical hokum, one's understanding of Blake inevitably suffers. We come back again to the reason for anniversaries. There may be others in the English tradition as great as Blake, but there can hardly be many as urgently great, looming over the dither of our situation with a more inescapable clarity, full of answers to questions that we have hardly learned how to formulate. Whatever other qualities Blake may have had or lacked, he certainly had courage and simplicity. Whatever other qualities our own age may have or lack, it is certainly an age of fearfulness and complexity. And every age learns most from those who most directly confront it.

18

Blake's Introduction to Experience

November 1957

From Huntington Library Quarterly, *21 (November 1957), 57–67. Reprinted in* Blake: A Collection of Critical Essays, *ed. Northrop Frye (Englewood Cliffs, N.J.: Prentice-Hall, 1966), 23–31.*

Students of literature often think of Blake as the author of a number of lyrical poems of the most transparent simplicity, and of a number of "Prophecies" of the most impenetrable complexity. The Prophecies are the subject of some bulky commentaries, including one by the present writer, which seem to suggest that they are a special interest, and may not even be primarily a literary one. The ordinary reader is thus apt to make a sharp distinction between the lyrical poems and the Prophecies, often with a hazy and quite erroneous notion in his mind that the Prophecies are later than the lyrics, and represent some kind of mental breakdown.

Actually Blake, however versatile, is rigorously consistent in both his theory and practice as an artist. The *Poetical Sketches*, written mostly in his teens, contain early lyrics and early Prophecies in about equal proportions. While he was working on the *Songs of Innocence and of Experience*, he was also working on their prophetic counterparts. While he was working at Felpham on his three most elaborate Prophecies, he was also writing the poems in the Pickering MS, which include such pellucid lyrics as *Mary*, *William Bond*, and *The Smile*. The extent to which the Prophecies themselves are permeated by a warm and simple lyrical feeling may be appreciated by any reader who does not shy at the proper names. Hence the method, adopted in some critical studies, including my own *Fearful Symmetry*, of concentrating on the Prophecies and nc glecting the lyrics on the ground that they can be understood without commentary, may have the long-run disadvantage of compromising with a thoroughly mistaken view of Blake.

What I propose to do here is to examine one of Blake's shortest and best-known poems in such a way as to make it an introduction to some of the main principles of Blake's thought. The poem selected is the *Introduction* to the *Songs of Experience*, which for many reasons is as logical a place as any to begin the study of Blake. I do not claim that the way of reading it set forth here is necessary for all readers, but only that for those interested in further study of Blake it is a valid reading.

> Hear the voice of the Bard!
> Who Present, Past, & Future, sees;
> Whose ears have heard
> The Holy Word
> That walk'd among the ancient trees . . . [K210/E18]

This stanza tells us a great deal about Blake's view of the place and function of the poet. The second line, repeated many years later in *Jerusalem* ("I see the Past, Present & Future existing all at once / Before me" [15.8–9; K635/E159]), establishes at once the principle that the imagination unifies time by making the present moment real. In our ordinary experience of time we are aware only of three unrealities: a vanished past, an unborn future, and a present that never quite comes into existence. The centre of time is now, yet there never seems to be such a time as now. In the ordinary world we can bind experience together only through the memory, which Blake declares has nothing to do with imagination. There is no contact with any other points of time except those that have apparently disappeared in the past. As Proust says, in such a world our only paradises can be the paradises that we have lost.[1] For Blake, as for Eliot in the *Quartets*, there must also be another dimension of experience, a vertical timeless axis crossing the horizontal flow of time at every moment, providing in that moment a still point of a turning world, a moment neither in nor out of time, a moment that Blake in the Prophecies calls the moment in each day that Satan cannot find [*M*, 39.42; K526/E136].

The worst theological error we can make, for Blake, is the "Deist" one of putting God at the beginning of the temporal sequence, as a First Cause. Such a view leads logically to an absolute fatalism, though its devotees are seldom so logical. The only God worth worshipping is a God who, though in his essence timeless, continually enters and redeems time, in other words an incarnate God, a God who is also Man. There is a Trinity in Blake of Father, Son, and Spirit, but Blake takes very seriously the Christian doctrines that the Spirit proceeds from the Son and that no man can know the Father except through the Son, the humanity of God. Attempts to approach the Father directly produce what Blake calls "Nobodaddy," whom we shall meet again in the next poem, *Earth's Answer*, and who is the ill-tempered old man in the sky that results from our efforts to visualize a First Cause. Attempts to approach the Spirit directly produce the vague millennialism of the revolutionaries of Blake's time, where human nature as it exists is assumed to be perfectible at some time in the future. What Blake thinks of this he has expressed in the prose introduction to the third part of *Jerusalem*. For Blake there is no God but Jesus, who is also man, and who exists neither in the past like the historical Jesus, nor in the future like the Jewish Messiah, but now in a real present, in which the real past and the real future are contained. The word "eternity" in Blake means the reality of the present moment, not the indefinite extension of the temporal sequence.

The modern poet or "Bard" thus finds himself in the tradition of the Hebrew prophets, who derive their inspiration from Christ as Word of God, and whose life is a listening for and speaking with that Word. In the Christian view, as recorded in *Paradise Lost*, it was not the Father but Jesus who created the unfallen world, placed man in Eden, and discovered man's fall while "walking in the garden in the cool of the day" (Genesis 3:8), the passage alluded to in the last line of the stanza.

> Calling the lapsèd Soul,
> And weeping in the evening dew;
> That might controll
> The starry pole,
> And fallen, fallen light renew!

"Calling" refers primarily to Christ, the Holy Word calling Adam in the garden, and the "lapsèd Soul" is presumably Adam, though the epithet seems curious, as Blake did not believe in a soul, but only in a spiritual body, as far as individual man is concerned. The word "weeping" also refers primarily to Christ. Neither in the Biblical story nor in *Paradise Lost*, where we might expect it, do we get much sense of Christ as deeply moved by man's fate, except in theory. Blake is making a much more definite identification than Milton does of Adam's "gracious judge, without revile" [*PL*, 10.118] with the Jesus of the Gospels who wept over the death of man as typified in Lazarus. Both the calling and the weeping, of course, are repeated by the Bard; the denunciations of the prophet and the elegiac vision of the poet of experience derive from God's concern over fallen man.

In the last three lines the grammatical antecedent of "That" is "Soul"; hence we seem to be told that man, if he had not fallen, would have had the powers as well as the destiny of a god. He would not now be subject to an involuntary subordination to a "nature" that alternately freezes and roasts him. On a second look, however, we see that Blake is not saying "might have controlled," but "might controll": the conquest of nature is now within man's powers, and is a conquest to which the poets and prophets are summoning him with the voice of the Word of God. We are very close here to Blake's central doctrine of art, and the reason for his insistence that "Jesus & his Apostles & Disciples were all Artists."[2]

The ordinary world that we see is a mindless chaos held together by automatic order: an impressive ruin, but a "slumberous mass," and not the world man wants to live in. What kind of world man wants to live in is indicated by the kind of world he keeps trying to create: a city and a garden. But his cities and gardens, unlike the New Jerusalem and Eden of the Biblical revelation, are not eternal or infinite, nor are they identical with the body of God. By "Artist" Blake means something more like charitable man or man of visible love. He is the man who lives now in the true world which is man's home, and tries to make that world visible to others. "Let every Christian," urges Blake, "engage himself openly & publicly before all the World in some Mental pursuit for the Building up of Jerusalem" [*J*, pl. 77; K717/E232].

The second stanza particularly illustrates the fact that what is true of time must be equally true of space. Just as the real form of time is "A vision of the Eternal Now" [K77/E592], so the real form of space is "here." Again, in ordinary experience of space, the centre of space, which is "here," cannot be located, except vaguely as within a certain area: all experienced space is "there," which is why, when we invent such gods as Nobodaddy, we place them "up there," in the sky and out of sight. But as "eternal" means really present, so "infinite" means really here. Christ is a real presence in space as well as a real present in time, and the poet's imagination has the function of bringing into ordinary experience what is really here and now, the bodily presence of God. Just as there is no God except a God who is also Man, so there is no real man except Jesus, man who is also God. Thus the imagination of the poet, by making concrete and visible a hidden creative power, repeats the Incarnation.

If all times are now in the imagination, all spaces are here. Adam before his fall lived in a paradisal garden, a garden which is to be one day restored to him, but which since his fall has existed, as Jesus taught, within us, no longer a place but a state of mind. Thus Blake begins *Milton* by speaking of his own brain as a part of the Garden of Eden, which his art attempts to realize in the world. In the Bible the Garden of Eden is the imaginative form of what existed in history as the tyrannies of Egypt and Babylon. Similarly the Promised Land, flowing with milk and honey, is the imaginative form of what existed historically as the theocracy of Israel. England, along with America, is also the historical form of what in the imagination is the kingdom of Atlantis, which included both, but now lies under the "Sea of Time and Space" flooding the fallen mind. We begin at this point to see the connection between our present poem and the famous lyric, written much later as a preface to *Milton*, "And did those feet in ancient time." As all imaginative places are the same place, Atlantis, Eden, and the Promised Land are the same place; hence when Christ walked in the Garden of Eden in the cool of the day he was also walking on the spiritual form of England's mountains green, among the "Druid" oaks. We note that Blake speaks in the first line of his poem not of a poet or a prophet but of a "Bard," in his day an almost technical term for a tradition of *British* poets going back to the dawn of history. "All had originally one language, and one religion: this was the religion of Jesus, the everlasting Gospel."[3]

> O Earth, O Earth, return!
> Arise from out the dewy grass;
> Night is worn,
> And the morn
> Rises from the slumberous mass.

The first words spoken by Jesus through the mouth of his "Bard" are, appropriately enough, quoted from the Hebrew prophets. The first line refers partly to the desperate cry of Jeremiah faced with the invincible stupidity of his king: "O earth, earth, earth, hear the word of the Lord!" (Jeremiah 22:29). A century earlier Milton, after twenty years spent in defending the liberty of the English people, helplessly watching them choose "a captain back for Egypt" [*Works*, 6:149], could express himself only in the same terms, in a passage at the end of *The Ready and Easy Way* that may have focused Blake's attention on his source:

> Thus much I should perhaps have said though I were sure I should have spoken only to trees and stones; and had none to cry to, but with the Prophet, *O earth, earth, earth!* to tell the very soil it self, what her perverse inhabitants are deaf to. [*Works*, 6:148]

There is also an echo in the same line from Isaiah (21:11–12):

> He calleth to me out of Seir, Watchman, what of the night? Watchman, what of the night? The watchman said, The morning cometh, and also the night: if ye will enquire, enquire ye: return, come.

Both in the Hebrew language and in Blake's, "cometh" could also be rendered by "has come": the light and the darkness are simultaneously with us, one being "here" and the other "there," one trying to shine from within, the other surrounding us. Hence a third Biblical allusion appears dimly but firmly attached to the other two (John 1:5): "And the light shineth in darkness; and the darkness comprehended it not." The "fallen light," therefore, is the alternating light and darkness of the world we know; the unfallen light would be the eternal light of the City of God, where there is no longer need for sun or moon, and where we can finally see, as Blake explains in the Prophecies, that no creative act of man has, in fact, really disappeared in time.

We notice in this stanza that the "Soul" is now identified, not as Adam, but as "Earth," a being who, as we can see by a glance at the next poem, is female. Thus the "Soul" is a kind of *anima mundi*; she includes not only the individual man and the "Church" but the totality of life, the whole creation that, as Paul says, groaneth and travaileth in pain together until now [Romans 8:22]. She is also Nature red in tooth and claw,[4] the struggle for existence in the animal world, of which man, in his fallen aspect, forms part. The prophet sees in every dawn the image of a resurrection that will lift the world into another state of being altogether. He is always prepared to say "the time is at hand." But every dawn in the world "out there" declines into sunset, as the spinning earth turns away into darkness.

Turn away no more;
Why wilt thou turn away?
The starry floor,
The wat'ry shore,
Is giv'n thee till the break of day.

There are two ways of looking at the "fallen" world: as fallen, and as a protection against worse things. Man might conceivably have fallen into total chaos, or nonexistence, or, like Tithonus or Swift's Struldbrugs, he might have been forced to live without the hope of death. This world is pervaded by a force that we call natural law, and natural law, however mindless and automatic, at any rate affords a solid bottom to life: it provides a sense of the predictable and trustworthy on which the imagination may build. The role of natural law (called Bowlahoola in the Prophecies) as the basis of imaginative effort is what Blake has in mind when he calls creation "an act of Mercy";[5] the providential aspect of time, in sweeping everything away into an apparent nonexistence, is brought out in his observation that "Time is the mercy of Eternity" [*M*, 24.72; K510/E121]. In the Bible a similar sense of the created world as a protection against chaos, usually symbolized in the Bible by the sea, as a firmament in the midst of the waters, comes out in the verse in Job (38:11): "Hitherto shalt thou come, but no further: and here shall thy proud waves be stayed." It is this verse that Blake has in mind when he speaks of the "wat'ry shore" as given to Earth until the Last Judgment; it is the same guarantee that God gave to Noah in the figure of the rainbow. Similarly the automatic accuracy of the heavenly bodies, of which Earth of course is one, affords a minimum basis for imaginative effort. Newtonian science is quite acceptable to Blake as long as it deals with the automatism of nature as the "floor" and not the ceiling of experience.

In Blake's Prophecies there are two perspectives, so to speak, on human life. One is a tragic and ironic vision; the other sees life as part of a redemptive divine comedy. The usual form taken by the tragic vision is that of a cyclical narrative, seen at its fullest and clearest in *The Mental Traveller* and *The Gates of Paradise*. Here there are two main characters, a male figure, the narrator in *The Gates of Paradise* and the "Boy" of *The Mental Traveller*, and a female figure who, in the latter poem, grows younger as the male grows older and vice versa, and who in *The Gates of Paradise* is described as "Wife, Sister, Daughter, to the Tomb" [K771/E269].

The "Boy" of *The Mental Traveller* is struggling humanity, called Orc in the Prophecies. The female figure is nature, which human culture partially but never completely subdues in a series of historical cycles. The relations between them are roughly those of mother and son, wife and husband, daughter and father. Very roughly, for none of these relations is quite accurate: the mother is an old nurse, the wife merely a temporary possession, and the daughter a changeling. The "Female will," as Blake calls it, has no necessary connection with human women, who are part of humanity, except when a woman wants to make a career of being a "harlot coy," or acting as nature does. The female will is rather the elusive, retreating, mysterious remoteness of the external world.

The *Introduction* to the *Songs of Experience*, despite its deeply serious tone, takes on the whole the redemptive or providential view. Hence the relation of the two figures is reversed, or rather, as they are not the same figures, the relation of a male and a female figure is used to symbolize the redemption of man instead of his bondage. The two characters correspond to the Bridegroom and Bride of Biblical symbolism. The male character is primarily Christ or the Word of God, which extends to take in the prophets and poets, and is ultimately Christ as the creative power in the whole of humanity. The "Bard" is called Los in the Prophecies, the Holy Spirit who proceeds from the Son. The female character Earth embraces everything that Christ is trying to redeem, the forgiven harlot of the Old Testament prophets who keeps turning away from forgiveness. She has no name, as such, in the Prophecies, though her different aspects have different names, the most important being Ahania and Enion. She is in general what Blake calls the "emanation," the total form of what man, or rather God in man, is trying to create. This total form, a city, a garden, a home, and a bed of love, or as Blake says "a City, yet a Woman,"[6] is Jerusalem. But just as the female will is not necessarily human women, so Earth, the Bride of Christ, includes men, as in the more conventional symbol of the church.

In her *Answer* Earth rejects with bitterness and some contempt the optimistic tone of the Bard's final words. She does not feel protected; she feels imprisoned, in the situation dramatized in Blake's poem *Visions of the Daughters of Albion*. She recalls Io, guarded by the myriad-eyed Argus, or Andromeda, chained on the seashore and constantly devoured by a possessive jealousy. Earth is not saying, as some critics accuse her of saying, that all would be well if lovers would only learn to copulate in the daytime. She is saying that nearly all of man's creative life remains embryonic, shrouded in darkness, on the level of wish, hope, dream, and private fantasy. Man is summoned by the Bard to love the world and let his love shine before men, but his natural tendency, as a child of fallen nature, is the miser's tendency to associate love with some private and secret possession of his own. This "dark secret love" [K213/E23], or rather perversion of love, is what Blake means by jealousy.

The "Selfish father of men" [K211/E18] who keeps Earth imprisoned is not God the Father, of course, but the false father that man visualizes as soon as he takes his mind off the Incarnation. To make God a Father is to make ourselves children: if we do this in the light of the Gospels, we see the world in the light of the state of innocence. But if we take the point of view of the child of ordinary experience, our God becomes a protection of ordinary childishness, a vision of undeveloped humanity. If we think of God as sulky, capricious, irritable, and mindlessly cruel, like Dante's primal love who made hell, or tied in knots of legal quibbles, like Milton's father-god, we may have a very awful divinity, but we have not got a very presentable human being. There is no excuse for keeping such a creature around when we have a clear revelation of God's human nature in the Gospels.

The source of this scarecrow is fallen nature: man makes a gigantic idol out of the dark world and is so impressed by its stupidity, cruelty, empty spaces, and automatism that he tries to live in accordance with the dreary ideals it suggests. He naturally assumes that his god is jealous of everything he clings to with secret longing and wants it surrendered to him; hence he develops a religion of sacrifice. There are two other reasons for Earth's calling her tormentor the "Father of the ancient men" [K211/E18]. In the first place, he is the ghost of what in the New Testament would be called the first Adam. In the second place, he is the god to whom the "Druids" sacrificed human beings in droves, as an eloquent symbol of their belief, quite true in itself, that their god hated human life. This false father still exists as the shadow thrown by Newtonian science into the stars, or what Blake calls the "Spectre." He is the genius of discouragement, trying to impress us with the reality of the world of experience and the utter unreality of anything better. His chief weapons are moral conformity, sexual shame, and the kind of rationality that always turns out to be anti-intellectual. If we could only get rid of him, "every thing would appear to man as it is, infinite" [*MHH*, pl. 14; K154/E39].

In the three characters of these two poems we have the three generating forces, so to speak, of all Blake's symbolism. First is the Bard, representative of the whole class that Blake in *Milton* calls "Reprobate," personified by Los, and including all genuine prophets and artists. They are given this name because their normal social role is that of a persecuted and ridiculed minority. Earth includes the total class of the "Redeemed," or those capable of responding to the Reprobate. In the later Prophecies Blake tends to use the masculine and purely human symbol of "Albion" as representing what the prophet tries to redeem. We can see part of the reason for this change in the poems we are studying: the Bard appeals to Earth, but Earth reminds him that man is responsible for his own evils, and that he should talk only to man if he is to do anything to help her.

The father of the ancient men is what in *Milton* is called the "Elect," because the idolatry of fallen nature incarnates itself in all natural societies; that is, the tyrannies of warriors and priests. In *Milton* too the Reprobate and Redeemed are called "Contraries," because the conflict between them is the "Mental fight" in which every man is obligated to engage. The Elect constitutes a "Negation": he is the aspect of the law that the gospel annihilates, as distinct from the "starry floor," or basis of imaginative order which it fulfils.

19

Preface to Peter Fisher's *The Valley of Vision*

1961

Editor's preface to Peter F. Fisher's The Valley of Vision: Blake as Prophet and Revolutionary *(Toronto: University of Toronto Press, 1961), v–viii. Fisher completed his dissertation on "The Doctrine of William Blake in the Background of the Eighteenth Century" with Frye at the University of Toronto in 1949.*

When Peter Francis Fisher was drowned in a sailing accident on September 2, 1958, at the age of forty, Canada lost one of its most brilliant and versatile scholars. A soldier with a fine military record, he had a keen interest in the theory of strategy, wrote papers on the campaigns of Alexander the Great, and was ready to discuss any aspect of military theory from Sun-Tzu Wu to Clausewitz. He took a doctor's degree in English literature, and his contributions to literary scholarship include articles on *Beowulf*, on *A Midsummer Night's Dream*, on *Heart of Midlothian*, and on Milton's logic and theodicy, besides two articles on Blake, "Blake and the Druids," and "Blake's Attacks on the Classical Tradition," and the present volume.[1] But he was always more than anything else a philosopher, and while head of the English department at the Royal Military College of Canada he expanded the curriculum there to include logic and the history of philosophy, in which he did most of his teaching. In philosophy too his interests showed the same breadth. Thoreau remarks that the adventurous student will always study the classics, in whatever languages they may be written,[2] and in that sense I have never known a more adventurous student than Peter Fisher.

Blake had always been a central interest of his, and the year after his graduation he walked into my office and announced that he wanted to do an M.A. thesis on "Blake's method, in the Cartesian sense." He nearly walked out again when he discovered that I had not read the *Bhagavadgita* in Sanskrit, which he took for granted that any serious student of Blake would have done as a matter of course. Up to that time, misled by bad translations, I had been assuming that most Oriental philosophy represented an extreme form of the type of abstraction that Blake most abhorred. In that respect I learned far more than I taught, and our conversations thereafter took the form of a kind of symbolic shorthand in which terms from Blake and from Mahayana Buddhism were apt to be used interchangeably.[3]

Fisher's careful self-teaching in Oriental philosophy focused his attention on the philosophy-producing mechanism in the human mind that throws up one construct after another. Towards the constructs themselves he was detached and tolerant: he treated them all with respect, and none with servility. He had arrived by his own route at the strongly "existential" view, the sense of the priority of the philosopher to whatever philosophizing he does, that Blake himself had. His interest in Eastern thought he reinforced by a close study of Plato and the Neoplatonists, in the course of which he developed a good deal of admiration for Thomas Taylor, often regarded as the main source of Blake's knowledge of this tradition, as an interpreter of Plato.[4] Needless to say, he had an unusual sympathy with such mavericks in Western thought as Paracelsus, though he did not exaggerate their importance. In short, he was well equipped to be an interpreter of Blake, who was able to make equally selective use of Swedenborg and of Thomas Paine, of Cornelius Agrippa on magic and of Voltaire on history.

Fisher's book is not a study of Blake's sources but of his context. He is trying to answer the question, Given Blake's general point of view, why does he make the specific judgments he does make, judgments which so often seem merely glib or petulant or perverse? Blake himself, in explaining a painting which included the figures of Moses and Abraham, remarked, "It ought to be understood that the Persons, Moses & Abraham, are not here meant, but the States Signified by those Names."[5] Fisher explains what Blake meant by "States," and shows that such names as Plato, Bacon, or Newton, or such terms as "priest" or "Deist" in Blake's writings, refer not to individuals but to cultural forces in Western civilization, the influence of which accounted for the social conditions that Blake attacked. The attack itself, as Fisher shows, was based on a revolutionary dialectic, a sense of the underlying opposition between reactionaries committed to obscurantism and social injustice, the "Elect" as Blake calls them, and the prophets committed to a greater vision (the "Reprobate"), with the mass of the public (the "Redeemed") in between. It is only in a crisis that such opposition clearly reveals itself, but it is the duty of the "Reprobate" to keep provoking an intellectual and imaginative crisis.

The papers that came to me after Fisher's death indicate that he had planned a book in twelve chapters, the last three dealing respectively with Blake's three long poems, *The Four Zoas*, *Milton*, and *Jerusalem*. Chapters 2 to 10 were in revised form, and I have been able to add a Preface, an opening chapter, and the beginning of an eleventh chapter from an unrevised manuscript. Thus his book is virtually complete except for the last chapter on *Jerusalem*, of which nothing remains except a note or two. It is clear that even the revised manuscript was due to be revised again, that the dry Aristotelian style was to be given more warmth and colour, that the sentences were to be tightened up and more examples given, and, perhaps, that less knowledge of Blake on the reader's part would be assumed. Even as it stands, however, *The Valley of Vision* is not simply a contribution to our understanding of Blake, but, as an interpretation of one of the great creative minds of Western culture by a critical mind of singular erudition and power, a lasting contribution to human intelligence.

20

The Road of Excess

1963

From StS, *160–74. Originally published in* Myth and Symbol: Critical Approaches and Applications, *ed. Bernice Slote (Lincoln: University of Nebraska Press, 1963), 3–20.*

It will be easiest for me to begin with a personal reference. My first sustained effort in scholarship was an attempt to work out a unified commentary on the prophetic books of Blake. These poems are mythical in shape: I had to learn something about myth to write about them, and so I discovered, after the book was published, that I was a member of a school of "myth criticism" of which I had not previously heard. My second effort, completed ten years later, was an attempt to work out a unified commentary on the theory of literary criticism, in which again myth had a prominent place. To me, the progress from one interest to the other was inevitable, and it was obvious to anyone who read both books that my critical ideas had been derived from Blake. How completely the second book was contained in embryo in the first, however, was something I did not realize myself until I recently read through *Fearful Symmetry*, for the first time in fifteen years, in order to write a preface to a new paperback edition. It seems perhaps worthwhile to examine what has been so far a mere assumption, the actual connecting links between my study of Blake and my study of the theory of criticism. At least the question is interesting to me, and so provides the only genuine motive yet discovered for undertaking any research.

Blake is one of the poets who believe that, as Wallace Stevens says, the only subject of poetry is poetry itself,[1] and that the writing of a poem is itself a theory of poetry.[2] He interests a critic because he removes the barriers between poetry and criticism. He defines the greatest poetry as "Allegory address'd to the Intellectual powers,"[3] and defends the practice of not being too explicit on the ground that it "rouzes the faculties to act."[4] His language in his later Prophecies is almost deliberately colloquial and "unpoetic," as though he intended his poetry to be also a work of criticism, just as he expected the critic's response to be also a creative one. He understood, in his own way, the principle later stated by Arnold that poetry is a criticism of life,[5] and it was an uncompromising way. For him, the artist demonstrates a certain way of life: his aim is not to be appreciated or admired, but to transfer to others the imaginative habit and energy of his mind. The main work of criticism is teaching, and teaching for Blake cannot be separated from creation.

Blake's statements about art are extreme enough to make it clear that he is demanding some kind of mental adjustment to take them in. One of the Laocoön Aphorisms reads: "A Poet, a Painter, a Musician, an Architect: the Man Or Woman who is not one of these is not a Christian" [K776/E274]. If we respond to this in terms of what we ordinarily associate with the words used, the aphorism will sound, as Blake intended it to sound, like someone in the last stages of paranoia. Blake has an unusual faculty for putting his central beliefs in this mock-paranoid form, and in consequence has deliberately misled all readers who would rather believe that he was mad than that their own use of language could be inadequate. Thus when a Devil says in *The Marriage of Heaven and Hell*, "those who envy or calumniate great men hate God; for there is no other God" [K158/E43], our habitual understanding of the phrase "great men" turns the remark into something that makes Carlyle at his worst sound by comparison like a wise and prudent thinker. When we read in the *Descriptive Catalogue*, however, that Chaucer's Parson is "according to Christ's definition, the greatest of his age" [K570/E535], we begin to wonder if this paradoxical Devil has really so sulphurous a smell. Similarly, Blake's equating of the arts with Christianity implies, first, that his conception of art includes much more than we usually associate with it, and, second, that it excludes most of what we do associate with it. Blake is calling a work of art what a more conventional terminology would call a charitable act, while at the same time the painting of, say, Reynolds is for him not bad painting but anti-painting. Whether we agree or sympathize with Blake's attitude, what he says does involve a whole theory of criticism, and this theory we should examine.

One feature of Blake's Prophecies which strikes every reader is the gradual elimination, especially in the two later poems *Milton* and *Jerusalem* that form the climax of this part of his work, of anything resembling narrative movement. The following passage occurs in plate 71 of *Jerusalem*:

> What is Above is Within, for every-thing in Eternity is translucent:
> The Circumference is Within, Without is formed the Selfish Center,
> And the Circumference still expands going forward to Eternity,
> And the Center has Eternal States; these States we now explore.
> [K709/E225]

I still have the copy of Blake that I used as an undergraduate, and I see that in the margin beside this passage I have written the words "Something moves, anyhow."[6] But even that was more of an expression of hope than of considered critical judgment. This plotless type of writing has been discussed a good deal by other critics, notably Hugh Kenner and Marshall McLuhan, who call it "mental landscape," and ascribe its invention to the French *symbolistes*. But in Blake we not only have the technique already complete, but an even more thoroughgoing way of presenting it.

If we read *Milton* and *Jerusalem* as Blake intended them to be read, we are not reading them in any conventional sense at all: we are staring at a sequence of plates, most of them with designs. We can see, of course, that a sequence of illustrated plates would be an intolerably cumbersome and inappropriate method of presenting a long poem in which narrative was the main interest. The long poems of other poets that Blake illustrated, such as Young's *Night Thoughts* and Blair's *Grave*, are meditative poems where, even without Blake's assistance, the reader's attention is expected to drop out of the text every so often and soar, or plunge, whichever metaphor is appropriate, although perhaps wander is even more accurate. No doubt the development of Blake's engraving technique had much to do with the plotlessness of the engraved poems. We notice that the three poems of Blake in which the sense of narrative movement is strongest—*Tiriel, The French Revolution, The Four Zoas*—were never engraved. We notice, too, that the illustration on a plate often does not illustrate the text on the same plate, and that in one copy of *Jerusalem* the sequence of plates in part 2 is slightly different. The elimination of narrative movement is clearly central to the structure of these poems, and the device of a sequence of plates is consistent with the whole scheme, not a mere accident.

The theme of *Milton* is an instant of illumination in the mind of the poet, an instant which, like the moments of recognition in Proust, links him with a series of previous moments stretching back to the creation of the world. Proust was led to see men as giants in time,[7] but for Blake there is only one giant, Albion, whose dream is time. For Blake in *Milton*, as for Eliot in *Little Gidding*, history is a pattern of timeless moments. What is said, so to speak, in the text of *Milton* is designed to present the context of the illuminated moment as a single simultaneous pattern of apprehension. Hence it does not form a narrative, but recedes spatially, as it were, from that moment. *Jerusalem* is conceived like a painting of the Last Judgment, stretching from heaven to hell and crowded with figures and allusions. Again, everything said in the text is intended to fit somewhere into this simultaneous conceptual pattern, not to form a linear narrative. If I ever get a big enough office, I shall have the hundred plates of my *Jerusalem* reproduction framed and hung around the walls, so that the frontispiece will have the second plate on one side and the last plate on the other. This will be *Jerusalem* presented as Blake thought of it, symbolizing the state of mind in which the poet himself could say, "I see the Past, Present & Future existing all at once / Before me" [15.8–9; K635/E159]. In the still later Job engravings the technique of placing the words within a pictorial unit is of course much more obvious.

Many forms of literature, including the drama, fiction, and epic and narrative poetry, depend on narrative movement in a specific way. That is, they depend for their appeal on the participation of the reader or listener in the narrative as it moves along in time. It is continuity that keeps us turning the pages of a novel, or sitting in a theatre. But there is always something of a summoned-up illusion about such continuity. We may keep reading a novel or attending to a play "to see how it turns out." But once we know how it turns out, and the spell ceases to bind us, we tend to forget the continuity, the very element in the play or novel that enabled us to participate in it. Remembering the plot of anything seems to be unusually difficult. Every member of this audience is familiar with many literary narratives, could even lecture on them with very little notice, and yet could not give a consecutive account of what happened in them, just as all the evangelical zeal of the hero of *The Way of All Flesh* was not equal to remembering the story of the resurrection of Christ in the Gospel of John. Nor does this seem particularly regrettable. Just as the pun is the lowest form of wit, so it is generally agreed, among knowledgeable people like ourselves, that summarizing a plot is the lowest form of criticism.

I have dealt with this question elsewhere, and can only give the main point here. Narrative in literature may also be seen as theme, and theme *is* narrative, but narrative seen as a simultaneous unity. At a certain point in the narrative, the point which Aristotle calls *anagnorisis* or recognition, the sense of linear continuity or participation in the action changes perspective, and what we now see is a total design or unifying structure in the narrative. In detective stories, when we find out who done it, or in certain types of comedy or romance that depend on what are now called "gimmicks," such as Jonson's *Epicoene*, the point of *anagnorisis* is the revelation of something which has previously been a mystery. In such works Aristotle's word *anagnorisis* is best translated "discovery." But in most serious works of literature, and more particularly in epics and tragedies, the better translation is "recognition." The reader already knows what is going to happen, but wishes to see, or rather to participate in, the completion of the design.

Thus the end of reading or listening is the beginning of critical understanding, and nothing that we call criticism can begin until the whole of what it is striving to comprehend has been presented to it. Participation in the continuity of narrative leads to the discovery or recognition of the theme, which *is* the narrative seen as total design. This theme is what, as we say, the story has been all about, the point of telling it. What we reach at the end of participation becomes the centre of our critical attention. The elements in the narrative thereupon regroup themselves in a new way. Certain unusually vivid bits of characterization or scenes of exceptional intensity move up near the centre of our memory. This reconstructing and regrouping of elements in our critical response to a narrative goes on more or less unconsciously, but the fact that it goes on is what makes remembering plot so difficult.

Thus there are two kinds of response to a work of literature, especially one that tells a story. The first kind is a participating response in time, moving in measure like a dancer with the rhythm of continuity. It is typically an uncritical, or more accurately a precritical response. We cannot begin criticism, strictly speaking, until we have heard the author out, unless he is a bore, when the critical response starts prematurely and, as we say, we can't get into the book. The second kind of response is thematic, detached, fully conscious, and one which sees and is capable of examining the work as a simultaneous whole. It may be an act of understanding, or it may be a value judgment, or it may be both. Naturally these two types of response overlap more in practice than I suggest here, but the distinction between them is clear enough, and fundamental in the theory of criticism. Some critics, including Professors Wimsatt and Beardsley in *The Verbal Icon*, stress the deficiencies of "holism" as a critical theory; but we should distinguish between "holism" as a critical theory and as a heuristic principle.

There are, of course, great differences of emphasis within literature itself, according to which kind of response the author is more interested in. At one pole of fiction we have the pure story-teller, whose sole interest is in suspense and the pacing of narrative, and who could not care less what the larger meaning of his story was, or what a critic would find in it afterwards. The attitude of such a story-teller is expressed in the well-known preface to *Huckleberry Finn*: "Persons attempting to find a motive in this narrative will be prosecuted; persons attempting to find a moral in it will be banished; persons attempting to find a plot in it will be shot." Motive and moral and plot certainly are in *Huckleberry Finn*, but the author, or so he says, doesn't want to hear about them. All the story-teller wants to do is to keep the attention of his audience to the end: once the end is reached, he has no further interest in his audience. He may even be hostile to criticism or anti-intellectual in his attitude to literature, afraid that criticism will spoil the simple entertainment that he designed. The lyrical poet concerned with expressing certain feelings or emotions in the lyrical conventions of his day often takes a similar attitude, because it is natural for him to identify his conventional literary emotions with his "real" personal emotions. He therefore feels that if the critic finds any meaning or significance in his work beyond the intensity of those emotions, it must be only what the critic wants to say instead. Anticritical statements are usually designed only to keep the critic in his place, but the attitude they represent, when genuine, is objective, thrown outward into the designing of the continuity. It is the attitude that Schiller, in his essay on *Naive and Sentimental Poetry*, means by naive, and which includes what we mean in English by naive. Naive writers' *obiter dicta* are often repeated, for consolation, by the kind of critic who is beginning to suspect that literary criticism is a more difficult discipline than he realized when he entered into it. But it is not possible for any reader today to respond to a work of literature with complete or genuine *naïveté*. Response is what Schiller calls sentimental by its very nature, and is hence to some degree involved with criticism.

If we compare, let us say, Malory with Spenser, we can see that Malory's chief interest is in telling the stories in the "French book" he is using. He seems to know that some of them, especially the Grail stories, have overtones in them that the reader will linger with long after he has finished reading. But Malory makes no explicit reference to this, nor does one feel that Malory himself, preoccupied as he was with a nervous habit of robbing churches, would have been much interested in a purely critical reaction to his book. But for Spenser it is clear that the romance form, the quest of the knight journeying into a dark forest in search of some sinister villain who can be forced to release some suppliant female, is merely a projection of what Spenser really wants to say. When he says at the end of book 2 of *The Faerie Queene*

> Now gins this goodly frame of Temperaunce
> Fayrely to rise [canto 7, stanza 1]

it is clear that his interest is thematic, in the emergence of a fully articulated view of the virtue of Temperance which the reader can contemplate, as it were, like a statue, seeing all of its parts at once. This simultaneous vision extends over the entire poem, for Temperance is only one of the virtues surrounding the ideal Prince, and the emergence of the total form of that Prince is the thematic mould into which the enormous narrative is finally poured. The stanza in Spenser, especially the final alexandrine, has a role rather similar to the engraved design in Blake: it deliberately arrests the narrative and forces the reader to concentrate on something else.

In our day the prevailing attitude to fiction is overwhelmingly thematic. Even as early as Dickens we often feel that the plot, when it is a matter of unplausible mysteries unconvincingly revealed, is something superimposed on the real narrative, which is more like a procession of characters. In our day the born story-teller is even rather peripheral to fiction, at best a borderline case like Somerset Maugham, and the serious novelist is as a rule the novelist who writes not because he has a story to tell but because he has a theme to illustrate. One reason for this present preference of the thematic is that the ironic tone is central to modern literature. It is the function of irony, typically in Greek tragedy, to give the audience a clearer view of the total design than the actors themselves are aware of. Irony thus sets up a thematic detachment as soon as possible in the work, and provides an additional clue to the total meaning.

There may be, then, and there usually is, a kind of empathic communion set up in the reader or audience of a work of literature, which follows the work continuously to the end. The sense of empathy may be established by a story, where we read on to see what happens. Or by a pulsating rhythm, such as the dactylic hexameter in Homer, which has a surge and sweep that can carry us through even the longueurs referred to by Horace.[8] We notice the effectiveness of rhythm in continuity more clearly in music, and most clearly in fast movements. I recall a cartoon of a tired man at a concert consulting his program and saying, "Well, the next movement is *prestissimo molto ed appassionato*, thank God." Or by the fluctuating intensity of a mood or emotion, again most clearly in music and in lyrical poetry. Or by a continuous sense of lifelikeness in realistic fiction, a sense which can extend itself even to realistic painting, as the eye darts from one detail to another. All these empathic responses are "naive," or essentially precritical.

Certain forms of art are also designed to give us the strongest possible emphasis on the continuous process of creation. The sketch, for example, is often more prized than the finished painting because of the greater sense of process in it. *Tachisme*[9] and action painting, spontaneous improvisation in swing, jazz, or more recently electronic music, and the kind of action poetry, often read to jazz, which evokes the ghosts of those primeval jam sessions postulated by early critics of the ballad, are more complete examples. All forms of art which lay great stress on continuous spontaneity seem to have a good deal of resistance to criticism, even to the education which is the natural context of criticism. We are told in Professor Lord's *Singer of Tales* that the most continuous form of poetry ever devised, the formulaic epic, demands illiteracy for success on the part of the poet, and there seems to be an inevitable affinity between the continuous and the unreflecting.

It is this continuity which is particularly Aristotle's imitation of an action. One's attention is completely absorbed in it: no other work of art is demanding attention at the same time, hence one has the sense of a unique and novel experience, at least as an ideal (for of course one may be rereading a book or seeing a familiar play). But, as in the world of action itself, one cannot participate and be a spectator at the same time. At best one is what Wyndham Lewis calls a "dithyrambic spectator."[10] Lewis's disapproval of the dithyrambic spectator indicates an opposed emphasis on the detached contemplation of the entire work of art, and one so extreme that it talks of eliminating the sense of linear participating movement in the arts altogether. It would not clarify our argument to examine Lewis's very muddled polemics at this point, but they have some interest as documents in a tradition which strongly emphasized a visual and contemplative approach to art. Blake's plotless Prophecies are, somewhat unexpectedly, in a similar (though by no means identical) tradition.

Just as the sense of participation in the movement of literature is absorbed, unique and novel, isolated from everything else, so the contemplative sense of its simultaneous wholeness tends to put the work of literature in some kind of framework or context. There are several such contexts, some of them indicated already. One of them is the allegorical context, where the total meaning or significance of the literary work is seen in relation to other forms of significance, such as moral ideas or historical events. A few works of literature, such as *The Pilgrim's Progress*, are technically allegories, which means that this explicit relation to external meaning is also a part of its continuity. Most literary works are not allegorical in this technical sense, but they bear a relation to historical events and moral ideas which is brought out in the kind of criticism usually called commentary. As I have explained elsewhere, commentary allegorizes the works it comments on.[11]

We notice that Blake is somewhat ambiguous in his use of the term "allegory." He says in a letter to Butts, "Allegory address'd to the Intellectual powers . . . is My Definition of the Most Sublime Poetry" [K825/E730]. But in commenting on one of his paintings of the Last Judgment, he says: "The Last Judgment is not Fable or Allegory, but Vision. Fable or Allegory are a totally distinct & inferior kind of Poetry" [K604/E554]. The first use of the term recognizes the fact that "the most sublime poetry," including his own Prophecies, will demand commentary. The second use indicates that his own poems and pictures are not allegorical in the Spenserian or continuous sense, nor are they allegorical in a much more obvious and central way. They do not subordinate their literary qualities to the ideas they convey, on the assumption that the latter are more important. In the second passage quoted above Blake goes on to say with great precision: "Fable is Allegory, but what Critics call The Fable, is Vision itself." Fable is here taken in its eighteenth-century critical sense of fiction or literary structure. Aristotle's word for intellectual content, *dianoia*, "thought," can be understood in two ways, as a moral attached to a fable, or as the structure of the fable itself. The latter, according to Blake, contains its own moral significances by implication, and it destroys its imaginative quality to assume that some external moral attached to it can be a definitive translation of its "thought."

We touch here on a central dilemma of literature. If literature is didactic, it tends to injure its own integrity; if it ceases wholly to be didactic, it tends to injure its own seriousness. "Didactic poetry is my abhorrence," said Shelley,[12] but it is clear that if the main body of Shelley's work had not been directly concerned with social, moral, religious, philosophical, political issues he would have lost most of his self-respect as a poet. Nobody wants to be an ineffectual angel, and Bernard Shaw, one of Shelley's most direct descendants in English literature, insisted that art should never be anything but didactic. This dilemma is partly solved by giving an ironic resolution to a work of fiction. The ironic resolution is the negative pole of the allegorical one. Irony presents a human conflict which, unlike a comedy, a romance, or even a tragedy, is unsatisfactory and incomplete unless we see in it a significance beyond itself, something typical of the human situation as a whole. What that significance is, irony does not say: it leaves that question up to the reader or audience. Irony preserves the seriousness of literature by demanding an expanded perspective on the action it presents, but it preserves the integrity of literature by not limiting or prescribing for that perspective.

Blake is clearly not an ironic writer, however, any more than he is an allegorist, and we must look for some other element in his thematic emphasis. A third context to which the theme of a literary work may be attached is its context in literature itself, or what we may call its archetypal framework. Just as continuous empathy is naive and absorbed in a unique and novel experience, so the contemplation of a unified work is self-conscious, educated, and one which tends to classify its object. We cannot in practice study a literary work without remembering that we have encountered many similar ones previously. Hence after following a narrative through to the end, our critical response includes the establishing of its categories, which are chiefly its convention and its genre. In this perspective the particular story is seen as a *projection* of the theme, as one of an infinite number of possible ways of getting to the theme. What we have just experienced we now see to be a comedy, a tragedy, a courtly love lyrical complaint, or one of innumerable treatments of the Tristan or Endymion or Faust story.

Further, just as some works of literature are explicitly or continuously allegorical, so some works are continuously, or at least explicitly, allusive, calling the reader's attention to their relation to previous works. If we try to consider *Lycidas* in isolation from the tradition of the pastoral elegy established by Theocritus and Virgil, or *Ash-Wednesday* in isolation from its relation to Dante's *Purgatorio*, we are simply reading these works out of context, which is as bad a critical procedure as quoting a passage out of context. If we read an Elizabethan sonnet sequence without taking account of the conventional nature of every feature in it, including the poet's protests that he is not following convention and is really in love with a real person, we shall merely substitute the wrong context for the right one. That is, the sonnet sequence will become a biographical allegory, as the sonnets of Shakespeare do when, with Oscar Wilde, we reach the conclusion that the profoundest understanding of these sonnets, the deepest appreciation of all their eloquence and passion and power, comes when we identify the "man in hue" of Sonnet 20 with an unknown Elizabethan pansy named Willie Hughes.[13]

Blake's Prophecies are intensely allusive, though nine-tenths of the allusions are to the Bible. "The Old & New Testaments are the Great Code of Art," Blake says,[14] and he thinks of the framework of the Bible, stretching from Creation to Last Judgement and surveying the whole of human history in between, as indicating the framework of the whole of literary experience, and establishing the ultimate context for all works of literature whatever. If the Bible did not exist, at least as a form, it would be necessary for literary critics to invent the same kind of total and definitive verbal structure out of the fragmentary myths and legends and folk tales we have outside it. Such a structure is the first and most indispensable of critical conceptions, the embodiment of the whole of literature as an order of words, as a potentially unified imaginative experience. But although its relation to the Bible takes us well on toward a solution of the thematic emphasis in Blake's illuminated poetry, it does not in itself fully explain that emphasis. If it did, the Prophecies would simply be, in the last analysis, Biblical commentaries, and this they are far from being.

Blake's uniqueness as a poet has much to do with his ability to sense the historical significance of his own time. Up to that time, literature and the arts had much the same educational and cultural value that they have now, but they competed with religion, philosophy, and law on what were at best equal and more usually subordinate terms. Consequently when, for example, Renaissance critics spoke of the profundity of poetry, they tended to locate that profundity in its allegorical meaning, the relations that could be established between poetry and ideas, more particularly moral and religious ideas. In the Romantic period, on the other hand, many poets and critics were ready to claim an authority and importance for poetry and the imaginative arts prior to that of other disciplines. When Shelley quotes Tasso on the similarity of the creative work of the poet to the creative work of God, he carries the idea a great deal further than Tasso did.[15] The fact of this change in the Romantic period is familiar, but the trends that made it possible are still not identified with assurance.

My own guess is that the change had something to do with a growing feeling that the origin of human civilization was human too. In traditional Christianity it was not: God planted the Garden of Eden and suggested the models for the law, rituals, even the architecture of human civilization. Hence a rational understanding of "nature," which included the understanding of the divine as well as the physical origin of human nature, took precedence over the poetic imagination and supplied a criterion for it. The essential moral ideas fitted into a divine scheme for the redemption of man; we understand the revelation of this scheme rationally; literature forms a series of more indirect parables or emblems of it. Thus poetry could be the companion of camps, as Sidney says:[16] it could kindle an enthusiasm for virtue by providing examples for precepts. The sense of excitement in participating in the action of the heroic narrative of, say, the *Iliad* was heightened by thinking of the theme or total meaning of the *Iliad* as an allegory of heroism. Thus, paradoxically, the Renaissance insistence on the allegorical nature of major poetry preserved the *naïveté* of the participating response. We see this principle at work wherever poet and audience are completely in agreement about the moral implications of a poetic theme, as they are, at least theoretically, in a hiss-the-villain melodrama.

Blake was the first and the most radical of the Romantics who identified the creative imagination of the poet with the creative power of God. For Blake God was not a superhuman lawgiver or the mathematical architect of the stars; God was the inspired suffering humanity of Jesus. Everything we call "nature," the physical world around us, is submoral, subhuman, subimaginative; every act worth performing has as its object the redeeming of this nature into something with a genuinely human, and therefore divine, shape. Hence Blake's poetry is not allegorical but mythopoeic, not obliquely related to a rational understanding of the human situation, the resolution of which is out of human hands, but a product of the creative energy that alone can redeem that situation. Blake forces the reader to concentrate on the meaning of his work, but not didactically in the ordinary sense, because his meaning is his theme, the total simultaneous shape of his poem. The context into which the theme or meaning of the individual poem fits is not the received ideas of our cultural tradition, of which it is or should be an allegory. It is not, or not only, the entire structure of literature as an order of words, as represented by the Bible. It is rather the expanded vision that he calls apocalypse or Last Judgment: the vision of the end and goal of human civilization as the entire universe in the form that human desire wants to see it, as a heaven eternally separated from a hell. What Blake did was closely related to the Romantic movement, and Shelley and Keats at least are mythopoeic poets for reasons not far removed from Blake's.

Since the Romantic movement, there has been a more conservative tendency to deprecate the central place it gave to the creative imagination and to return, or attempt to return, to the older hierarchy. T.S. Eliot is both a familiar and a coherent exponent of this tendency, and he has been followed by Auden, with his Kierkegaardian reinforcements. According to Eliot, it is the function of art, by imposing an order on life, to give us the sense of an order in life, and so to lead us into a state of serenity and reconciliation preparatory to another and superior kind of experience, where "that guide" can lead us no further. The implication is that there is a spiritually existential world above that of art, a world of action and behaviour, of which the most direct imitation in this world is not art but the sacramental act. This latter is a form of uncritical or precritical religious participation that leads to a genuinely religious contemplation, which for Eliot is a state of heightened consciousness with strong affinities to mysticism. Mysticism is a word which has been applied both to Blake and to St. John of the Cross: in other words it has been rather loosely applied, because these two poets have little in common. It is clear that Eliot's mystical affinities are of the St. John of the Cross type. The function of art, for Eliot, is again of the subordinated or allegorical kind. Its order represents a higher existential order, hence its greatest ambition should be to get beyond itself, pointing to its superior reality with such urgency and clarity that it disappears in that reality. This, however, only happens either in the greatest or the most explicitly religious art: nine-tenths of our literary experience is on the subordinate plane where we are seeing an order in life without worrying too much about the significance of that order. On this plane the naive precritical direct experience of participation can still be maintained, as it is in Renaissance critical theory. The Romantics, according to this view, spoil both the form and the fun of poetry by insisting so much on the profundity of the imaginative experience as to make it a kind of portentous *ersatz* religion.

This leads us back to the aphorism of Blake with which we began, where the artist is identified with the Christian. Elsewhere he speaks of "Religion, or Civilized Life such as it is in the Christian Church," and says that poetry, painting, and music are "the three Powers in Man of conversing with Paradise, which the flood did not Sweep away."[17] For Blake art is not a substitute for religion, though a great deal of religion as ordinarily conceived is a substitute for art, in that it abuses the mythopoeic faculty by creating fantasies about another world or rationalizing the evils of this one instead of working toward genuine human life. If we describe Blake's conception of art independently of the traditional myth of fall and apocalypse that embodies it, we may say that the poetic activity is fundamentally one of identifying the human with the nonhuman world. This identity is what the poetic metaphor expresses, and the end of the poetic vision is the humanization of reality, "All Human Forms identified," as Blake says at the end of *Jerusalem* [K747/E258]. Here we have the basis for a critical theory which puts such central conceptions as myth and metaphor into their proper central place. So far from usurping the function of religion, it keeps literature in the context of human civilization, yet without limiting the infinite variety and range of the poetic imagination. The criteria it suggests are not moral ones, nor are they collections of imposing abstractions like Unity, but the interests, in the widest sense, of mankind itself, or himself, as Blake would prefer to say.

In this conception of art the productive or creative effort is inseparable from the awareness of what it is doing. It is this unity of energy and consciousness that Blake attempts to express by the word "vision." In Blake there is no either/or dialectic where one must be either a detached spectator or a preoccupied actor. Hence there is no division, though there may be a distinction, between the creative power of shaping the form and the critical power of seeing the world it belongs to. Any division instantly makes art barbaric and the knowledge of it pedantic—a bound Orc and a bewildered Urizen, to use Blake's symbols. The vision inspires the act, and the act realizes the vision. This is the most thoroughgoing view of the partnership of creation and criticism in literature I know, but for me, though other views may seem more reasonable and more plausible for a time, it is in the long run the only one that will hold.

21

Introduction to *Blake: A Collection of Critical Essays*

1966

Introduction to Blake: A Collection of Critical Essays, *ed. Northrop Frye (Englewood Cliffs, N.J.: Prentice-Hall, 1966), 1–7. The volume contains the following essays: Robert F. Gleckner, "Point of View and Context in Blake's Songs"; Martin K. Nurmi, "Fact and Symbol in 'The Chimney Sweeper' of Blake's* Songs of Innocence*"; Northrop Frye, "Blake's Introduction to Experience"; John E. Grant, "Interpreting Blake's 'The Fly'"; William J. Keith, "The Complexities of Blake's 'Sunflower': An Archetypal Speculation"; Irene H. Chayes, "Little Girls Lost: Problems of a Romantic Archetype"; Hazard Adams, "'The Crystal Cabinet' and 'The Golden Net'"; David V. Erdman, "Blake's Vision of Slavery"; Harold Bloom, "States of Being:* The Four Zoas*"; Northrop Frye, "Poetry and Design in William Blake"; Anthony Blunt, "The First Illuminated Books"; Jean H. Hagstrum, "William Blake Rejects the Enlightenment"; Peter F. Fisher, "Blake and the Druids." The book includes a dedication "To the memory of Peter F. Fisher" with the epigraph*

> *The starry floor,*
> *The wat'ry shore,*
> *Is giv'n thee till the break of day.*

This book offers what it is hoped is a representative collection of contemporary critical essays on Blake. I have found it very difficult to make, and I still feel like apologizing to the reader, not for anything I have included, but for what I have been compelled to leave out. Apart from restrictions of space, what I have left out that I might have included was left out mainly in the interest of trying to get some distribution over the whole of Blake's output and outlook, while avoiding topics too impossibly specialized. Some of the best and most important criticism on Blake today is editorial and bibliographical, and such things as G.E. Bentley's recent edition of *The Four Zoas*, Foster Damon's *Blake Dictionary*, or David V. Erdman's reconstruction of obliterated passages in *Jerusalem*, however brilliant in themselves and fascinating as well as necessary to the Blake expert, do not lend themselves to a collection of critical essays for the general reader. On the other hand, Blake's total range of interests is so enormous that nobody can cover more than a small corner of it: there will never be any such person as the world's greatest authority on Blake. The kind of general comment represented by T.S. Eliot's essay in *The Sacred Wood* (1920) already belongs to a vanished world. All Blake criticism today that is worth reading is specialized to some degree, and in the nature of things has to be.

In this situation the best I can do is to give the sense of a busy and widespread body of criticism *in process*. Blake criticism today is moving ahead rapidly after a very slow start; new editions, bibliographies, reproductions of the illuminated books, are providing the apparatus his students need. The lack of such apparatus forty years ago makes Foster Damon's great pioneering study, *William Blake: His Philosophy and Symbols* (1924), almost unbelievable. But a good deal of dust has still to settle. One of the contributors to this book remarked to me in a letter that in his opinion such a collection was premature: that it would be another twenty years at least before the full impact of Blake had consolidated and clarified itself. He is also one of half a dozen contributors who, even since I made the selection, have done more and, as they consider, better work on Blake. Again, the reader will notice that all the essays in this book are by academic scholars. Blake makes an immense appeal to a great variety of people outside the academic profession: poets, novelists, painters, philosophers, psychologists, theologians, students of everything from mathematics to ballet. But there is little written on Blake outside the academic world: there is still too great a gap between the private possession of Blake and the public declaration of that possession. The main reason for this, of course, is the one just glanced at: the great variety of things Blake could do and the complexity of what he did.

The largest single section of this book is concerned with commentary on some of the well-known lyrics from *Songs of Innocence* and *Songs of Experience*. These explicatory essays deal with poems which make a vivid impact on the reader at once, and it is only after we turn to the secondary matter of trying to understand what they "say" that complications arise.

Mr. Gleckner and Mr. Grant, in particular, deal with these. There are two main elements of complication. One is context: most of Blake's best-known lyrics are expressions either of what he called innocence or of what he called experience, and as these are "two contrary states of the soul," one should know which of these contraries any given poem represents. The other is what Mr. Gleckner calls point of view and what some critics call *persona*: just who is speaking in the poem? "Blake himself" is an answer that tells us nothing: a poet speaks in many moods and states of mind. Blake in particular thought of the individual as a bundle of these moods or states which are far more articulate than he is, and over which he has only the most limited control. The longer poems or "Prophecies" are full of monologues by such states—in the standard edition of Sir Geoffrey Keynes these monologues are put in quotation marks, but Blake himself rarely provides any helpful punctuation, and in the lyrics it is often an intricate matter to decide just what should be thought of as the "point of view." In Mr. Grant's article one may see something of the critical disagreements provoked by what looks at first sight one of the world's least complicated poems.

Mr. Nurmi and Mr. Erdman are concerned with a different type of interpretation, showing how Blake's poems recorded the life of his time as Blake saw it. They show too how concrete and specific his reactions were, and how little truth there is in the popular picture of him as a mystic with his gaze fixed on eternity and turned away from his neighbour. In reading about child labour and slavery in Blake's time (or their equivalents in our time) we hardly know which is more detestable: the cruelty involved or the complacency with which that cruelty was rationalized in pamphlets, parliamentary debates, newspapers, and sermons. Blake was struck with this too, and never failed to see the rationalizing of evil as an essential part of the evil itself, if not its actual essence. That is why he gave so much attention to what he thought of as intellectual errors, to abstraction and Deism and natural religion, which he violently attacked, not because he thought they were bad arguments, but because he thought they were arguments designed to defend bad things. That is, abstraction and the like are states of mind resulting from what we should now call anxiety, and anxiety is the state of mind that contemplates the horror of war or the suppression of freedom and says, "Oh yes, but ...." Blake does not react in this way, and so he can establish a direct human contact with readers however remote in time or space from his world.

Mrs. Chayes and Mr. Keith follow up a third critical approach, the one now called archetypal. Blake's use of imagery and symbolism, in the lyrics at least, is simple but haunting, drawing many of the reader's previous literary associations together into a focus. This is because Blake himself was an intensive rather than an extensive reader. He studied the Bible and Ovid's *Metamorphoses* with great concentration, and struck his roots directly into the central mythical heritage of our culture. His lyrics are in the tradition of the "emblem books" which used a great deal of mythological and allegorical material from Christian and Classical sources. Blake's technique, without being allegorical, nevertheless unobtrusively stirs echoes in our mind of Narcissus, of Persephone, of Eve, of the sky-god Jupiter, and of the kind of significance that modern psychologists and anthropologists help us attach to such myths. For the same reason Blake can, unexpectedly, throw light on the imagery of other poets who came after him and did not know him or thought of him as mad. An increasing number of scholars in English Romanticism find that Blake, simply because of the concentration and accuracy of his imagery, enlightens their understanding of Wordsworth, Coleridge, Shelley, Keats, in spite of his lack of influence in his own time.

Many readers of Blake know only the lyrics, and are unaware, or only vaguely aware, that Blake also wrote a number of longer poems, usually called "Prophecies," the title he occasionally gave them himself. One of the shorter and clearer Prophecies, *Visions of the Daughters of Albion*, is the subject of Mr. Erdman's commentary, already referred to. To the general reader the later Prophecies are apt to look formidable at first, but to anyone who will approach them without prejudice they can be an inexhaustible source of profit and delight. My article on the *Introduction* to the *Songs of Experience* attempts to show how one may proceed from the simpler to the more complex poetry of Blake. I have strictly limited the amount of commentary on the Prophecies for this book, as most of it belongs in critical studies that need to be read by themselves. Some of the later lyrics, very simple in language but very difficult in thought, form a transition from lyric to Prophecy, and are studied by Mr. Adams. For the longer Prophecies I have selected Mr. Bloom's brief but extremely lucid guide to *The Four Zoas*. This poem was left in manuscript, exists in several layers of revision, and is divided into nine sections, called "Nights," there being two complete versions of the seventh Night. Which one is closer to Blake's final intentions about the poem (though of course even the phrase "final intentions" is special pleading) is still disputed. But the reader will, with Mr. Bloom's help, find it an extremely lovely and profound poem for all its incompleteness.

Mr. Adams's essay indicates that there is a tough skeleton of ideas behind Blake's lyrics which criticism could, to some extent, reconstruct even if we did not have the Prophecies. The Prophecies themselves are not merely mythical poems: they are guides to the process of poetical myth-making, and can be used as a key to poetic mythology just as the lyrics can be used as a key to Romanticism.

For all his greatness as a poet, Blake was an amateur in literature: what he was professional in was painting and engraving. His poetry is unique in English literature in that it was not (except for a volume of early lyrics) published, but was etched on copper plate with accompanying designs, stamped on paper, and coloured by hand. Blake was one of England's greatest painters as well as poets, and his poetry was produced in a form which combined the two arts. My second article is an attempt to introduce the reader to this combination of the two arts in his work. The complicated engraving process he invented has been reconstructed, as summarized by Sir Anthony Blunt. (None of Blake's original plates survives except one small corner of a plate of the poem *America*.) Sir Anthony also deals with some of the paintings that, as much as the poetry, tell us about Blake's thought and attitudes. Mr. Grant's essay on *The Fly*, already referred to, also deals to some extent with the pictorial impression the poem makes and with some problems in Blake's iconography.

In spite of the specialization of scholarship that Blake's versatility makes necessary, certain aspects of it have become simpler. Formerly, allusions to Blake often used to assume that he was a timeless mystic who was dazed all his life by having been born in a definite place at a definite time; that he influenced no one and that no one influenced him; that his interests were occult and esoteric, with few parallels west of India. Gradually this notion is giving place to a figure who is a much more credible product of eighteenth-century, middle-class, Nonconformist England, whose religious views were Christian, whose philosophical views were derived from a negative reaction to Bacon, Newton, and Locke, whose political and social views were close to a large body of contemporary liberal opinion, and whose poetry and painting were strongly influenced by his own cultural environment.

The two final articles in the book deal with some of Blake's intellectual reactions to his milieu. Blake belongs, not to the half of the eighteenth century that we characterize by the daytime metaphor of "Enlightenment," but to the darker, *Sturm-und-Drang* half, to the enthusiasm for the sublime and the "Gothic," for graveyard meditations and evangelical enthusiasm, to the emphasis on feeling and sensibility, the cult of the primitive, and allied developments that had gathered strength by mid-century and had modulated to "Romanticism" by 1800. Mr. Hagstrum deals with the critical, negative aspect of Blake's intellectual position, with his repudiation of the more "Augustan" and "Neo-Classical" values that we attach, with some oversimplification, to the names of Pope and Samuel Johnson. Mr. Fisher explores Blake's interest in the extraordinary eighteenth-century myth of the "Druids." The books about the Druids were, at their best, primitive attempts at essays in comparative religion and the language of symbolism. As such, they would naturally interest a poet—poets of all ages, including our own, have used such books. They are generally written by cranks, but that does not detract from their value to poets, most cranks of this type being essentially frustrated poets. Blake made a surprisingly restrained and sensible use of such material—surprisingly in view of what seems his uninhibited tendency to myth-making and of his popular reputation for off-beat thinking. One hopes that some younger scholar will carry on Mr. Fisher's work, especially in Blake's reading of British historians and antiquarians: Rapin, Holinshed, and, above all, Camden's *Britannia*.

The reader will notice that the contributors to this book read Blake as they would read any other poet. There are disagreements over how a given poem is to be read, as there are with all poets, but there is general agreement on Blake's general meaning, and a common feeling that some readings of him are obviously right and others obviously wrong. This simple fact represents a considerable critical achievement. There have been many books asserting that Blake was mad, that his Prophecies were unintelligible, that what he said was too private or emotionally coloured to have any meaning except what the reader chose to give it. Such sentiments are supported by others who wish to find that Blake was a precocious discoverer of their own views, or who wish to believe in something chaotic or elusive at the centre of creative power that will make criticism look foolish. The real reason for this resistance to the normality of Blake's mind is hard to express, because it is a phenomenon unknown (I think) to psychology and only vaguely understood even by critics.

What I am referring to is the sense of panic engendered by lucidity. It is a well-known principle in science and philosophy that the simplest questions are those that only great genius can answer, because it takes great genius to become aware of them as questions. The situation is much the same in literature. The great poets, who say something definitive about the human situation, are resisted for a long time as mad, obscure, obscene, or what not, until their revelation seems less dazzling. I said that this phenomenon is unknown to psychology: it is, of course, the central psychological principle of resistance, but the area in which it operates is unexplored. The instinct to call Blake mad was the same instinct that insisted, for well over a century, that Shakespeare was a wild and undisciplined genius with no knowledge of the "rules" of dramatic structure. Similarly, Dickens and D.H. Lawrence were long regarded as flawed and imperfect novelists compared to Thackeray or Galsworthy; torrents of scorn were heaped on Swift in the nineteenth century and on Milton in the twentieth. Our own time has become more cautious: it has happened too often that the thundering denouncer of one generation has sounded like a noisy fool in the next. There are still various devices, such as inventing literary "isms" or selecting a central tradition, that will rationalize our resistance to literature, or to most of it. But a really definitive poet, such as Blake was, makes his way in spite of all resistance.

It is the peculiar quality of a definitive poet that he always seems to have a special relevance to the preoccupations of one's own age, whatever they are. Blake's early critics found him especially eloquent on the sense of the infinity of experience, which they found more fully expressed in Whitman. *Symbolisme* filtered in from France, and Blake's lyrics became poems that presented more than they said. When Nietzsche was better understood, Blake's doctrine that reality is what man creates and not what he studies was better understood too. Freud became a part of our understanding of life, and *The Marriage of Heaven and Hell*, with such aphorisms as "He who desires but acts not, breeds pestilence" [K151/E35] took on a new meaning. Frazer joined Freud and the symbolism of "Druidism" in *Jerusalem* became clarified; revolutionary doctrines began to trouble the West and the character of Orc in the Prophecies seemed charged with an immediate significance. At present, one may notice that the character in *Jerusalem* called the Spectre of Urthona is a pure existentialist, and a very articulate one. And whatever the cultural interests of the year 2000 may be, it will be discovered in that year that Blake had them particularly in mind, and wrote his poems primarily to illustrate them. In the nature of poetry it cannot be otherwise: poets who are for all time are also for all ages. Naturally, anything that assists the reader to understand such poets is to be welcomed, and it is hoped that the present book will therefore be welcomed too.

22

The Keys to the Gates

1966

From StS, *175–99. Originally published in* Some British Romantics: A Collection of Essays, *ed. James V. Logan, John E. Jordan, and Northrop Frye (Columbus: Ohio State University Press, 1966), 1–40. Reprinted in* Romanticism and Consciousness: Essays in Criticism, *ed. Harold Bloom (New York: Norton, 1970), 233–54.*

The criticism of Blake, especially of Blake's Prophecies, has developed in direct proportion to the theory of criticism itself. The complaints that Blake was "mad" are no longer of any importance, not because anybody has proved him sane, but because critical theory has realized that madness, like obscenity, is a word with no critical meaning. There are critical standards of coherence and incoherence, but if a poem is coherent in itself the sanity of its author is a matter of interest only to the more naive type of biographer. Those who have assumed that the Prophecies are incoherent because they have found them difficult often use the phrase "private symbolism." This is also now a matter of no importance, because in critical theory there is no such thing as private symbolism. There may be allegorical allusions to a poet's private life that can only be interpreted by biographical research, but no set of such allusions can ever form a poetic structure. They can only be isolated signposts, like the allusions to the prototypes of the beautiful youth, dark lady, and rival poet which historians and other speculative critics are persuaded that they see in the Shakespeare sonnets.

When I first embarked on an intensive study of Blake's Prophecies, I assumed that my task was to follow the trail blazed by Foster Damon's great book,[1] and take further steps to demonstrate the coherence of those poems. My primary interests, like Damon's, were literary, not occult or philosophical or religious. Many other writers had asserted that while the Prophecies were doubtless coherent enough intellectually, they would turn out to depend for their coherence on some extrapoetic system of ideas. A student interested in Blake's Prophecies as poems would have to begin by rejecting this hypothesis, which contradicts all Blake's views about the primacy of art and the cultural disaster of substituting abstractions for art. But as I went on, I was puzzled and annoyed by a schematic quality in these Prophecies that refused to dissolve into what I then regarded as properly literary forms. There were even diagrams in Blake's own designs which suggested that he himself attached a good deal of value to schematism, and such statements as "I must Create a System" [*J*, 10.20; K629/E153]. Perhaps, then, these critics I had begun by rejecting were right after all: perhaps Blake was not opposed to abstraction but only to other people's abstractions, and was really interested merely in expounding some conceptual system or other in an oblique and allegorical way. In any event, the schematic, diagrammatic quality of Blake's thought was there, and would not go away or turn into anything else. Yeats had recognized it; Damon had recognized it; I had to recognize it. Like Shelley, Blake expressed an abhorrence of didactic poetry but continued to write it.

This problem began to solve itself as soon as I realized that poetic thought is inherently and necessarily schematic. Blake soon led me, in my search for poetic analogues, to Dante and Milton, and it was clear that the schematic cosmologies of Dante and Milton, however they got into Dante and Milton, were, once they got there, poetic constructs, examples of the way poets think, and not foreign bodies of knowledge. If the Prophecies are normal poems, or at least a normal expression of poetic genius, and if Blake nevertheless meant to teach some system by them, that system could only be something connected with the principles of poetic thought. Blake's "message," then, is not simply *his* message, nor is it an extraliterary message. What he is trying to say is what he thinks poetry is trying to say: the imaginative content implied by the existence of an imaginative form of language. I finished my book in the full conviction that learning to read Blake was a step, and for me a necessary step, in learning to read poetry, and to write criticism. For if poetic thought is inherently schematic, criticism must be so too. I began to notice that as soon as a critic confined himself to talking seriously about literature, his criticism tightened up and took on a systematic, even a schematic, form.

The nature of poetic "truth" was discussed by Aristotle in connection with action. As compared with the historian, the poet makes no specific or particular statements: he gives the typical, recurring, or universal event, and is not to be judged by the standards of truth that we apply to specific statements. Poetry, then, does not state historical truth, but contains it: it sets forth what we may call the *myth* of history, the kind of thing that happens [*Poetics*, sec. 9]. History itself is designed to record events, or, as we may say, to provide a primary verbal imitation of events. But it also, unconsciously perhaps, illustrates and provides examples for the poetic vision. Hence we feel that *Lear* or *Macbeth* or *Oedipus Rex*, although they deal almost entirely with legend rather than actual history, contain infinite reserves of historical wisdom and insight. Thus poetry is "something more philosophical" than history.

This last observation of Aristotle's has been of little use to critics except as a means of annoying historians, and it is difficult to see in what sense Anacreon is more philosophical than Thucydides. The statement is best interpreted, as it was by Renaissance critics, schematically, following a diagram in which poetry is intermediate between history and philosophy, pure example and pure precept. It follows that poetry must have a relation to thought paralleling its relation to action. The poet does not think in the sense of producing concepts, ideas, or propositions, which are specific predications to be judged by their truth or falsehood. As he produces the mythical structures of history, so he produces the mythical structures of thought, the conceptual frameworks that enter into and inform the philosophies contemporary with him. And just as we feel that the great tragedy, if not historical, yet contains an infinity of the kind of meaning that actual history illustrates, so we feel that great "philosophical" poetry, if not actually philosophical, contains an infinity of the kind of meaning that discursive writing illustrates. This sense of the infinite treasures of thought latent in poetry is eloquently expressed by several Elizabethan critics, and there is perhaps no modern poet who suggests the same kind of intellectual richness so immediately as Blake does.

Blake, in fact, gives us so good an introduction to the nature and structure of poetic thought that, if one has any interest in the subject at all, one can hardly avoid exploiting him. There are at least three reasons why he is uniquely useful for this purpose. One is that his Prophecies are works of philosophical poetry which give us practically nothing at all unless we are willing to grapple with the kind of poetic thought that they express. Another is that Blake also wrote such haunting and lucid lyrics, of which we can at first say little except that they seem to belong in the centre of our literary experience. We may not know why they are in the centre, and some readers would rather not know; but for the saving remnant who do want to know, there are the Prophecies to help us understand. The third reason is Blake's quality as an illustrator of other poets. If a person of considerable literary experience is reading a poem he is familiar with, it is easy for him to fall—in fact it is very difficult for him not to fall—into a passive habit of not really reading the poem, but merely of spotting the critical clichés he is accustomed to associate with it. Thus, if he is reading Gray's *Ode on the Death of a Favourite Cat*, and sees the goldfish described as "angel forms," "genii of the stream," and with "scaly armour," his stock response will start murmuring: "Gray means fish, of course, but he is saying so in terms of eighteenth-century personification, Augustan artificiality, his own peculiar demure humour," and the like. Such a reading entirely obliterates Gray's actual processes of poetic thought and substitutes something in its place that, whatever it is, is certainly not poetry or philosophy, any more than it is history. But if he is reading the poem in the context of Blake's illustrations, Blake will compel him to see the angel forms, the genii of the stream, and the warriors in scaly armour, as well as the fish, in such a way as to make the unvisualized clichés of professional reading impossible, and to bring the metaphorical structure of the poem clearly into view.

I am suggesting that no one can read Blake seriously and sympathetically without feeling that the keys to poetic thought are in him, and what follows attempts to explain how a documentation of such a feeling would proceed. I make no claim that I am saying anything here that I have not said before, though I may be saying it in less compass.

Eastern Gate: Twofold Vision

The structure of metaphors and imagery that informed poetry, through the Middle Ages and the Renaissance, arranged reality on four levels. On top was heaven, the place of the presence of God; below it was the proper level of human nature, represented by the stories of the Garden of Eden and the Golden Age; below that was the physical world, theologically fallen, which man is in but not of; and at the bottom was the world of sin, death, and corruption. This was a deeply conservative view of reality in which man, in fallen nature, was confronted with a moral dialectic that either lowered him into sin or raised him to his proper level. The raising media included education, virtue, and obedience to law. In the Middle Ages, this construct was closely linked with similar constructs in theology and science. These links weakened after the sixteenth century and eventually disappeared, leaving the construct to survive only in poetry, and, even there, increasingly by inertia. It is still present in Pope's *Essay on Man*, but accompanied with a growing emphasis on the limitation of poetic objectives. This limitation means, among other things, that mythopoeic literature, which demands a clear and explicit framework of imagery, is in the age of Pope and Swift largely confined to parody.

As the eighteenth century proceeded, the imaginative climate began to change, and we can see poets trying to move toward a less conservative structure of imagery. This became a crucial problem when the French Revolution confronted the Romantic poets. No major poet in the past had been really challenged by a revolutionary situation except Milton, and even Milton had reverted to the traditional structure for *Paradise Lost*. Blake was not only older than Wordsworth and Coleridge, but more consistently revolutionary in his attitude: again, unlike most English writers of the period, he saw the American Revolution as an event of the same kind as its French successor. He was, therefore, the first English poet to work out the revolutionary structure of imagery that continues through Romantic poetry and thought to our own time.

At the centre of Blake's thought are the two conceptions of innocence and experience, "the two contrary states of the human soul." Innocence is characteristic of the child, experience of the adult. In innocence, there are two factors. One is an assumption that the world was made for the benefit of human beings, has a human shape and a human meaning, and is a world in which providence, protection, communication with other beings, including animals, and, in general, "mercy, pity, peace and love," have a genuine function. The other is ignorance of the fact that the world is not like this. As the child grows up, his conscious mind accepts "experience," or reality without any human shape or meaning, and his childhood innocent vision, having nowhere else to go, is driven underground into what we should call the subconscious, where it takes an essentially sexual form. The original innocent vision becomes a melancholy dream of how man once possessed a happy garden, but lost it forever, though he may regain it after he dies. The following diagram illustrates the process as well as the interconnection of *Songs of Innocence and of Experience*, *The Marriage of Heaven and Hell*, and the early political Prophecies *The French Revolution* and *America* in Blake's thought:

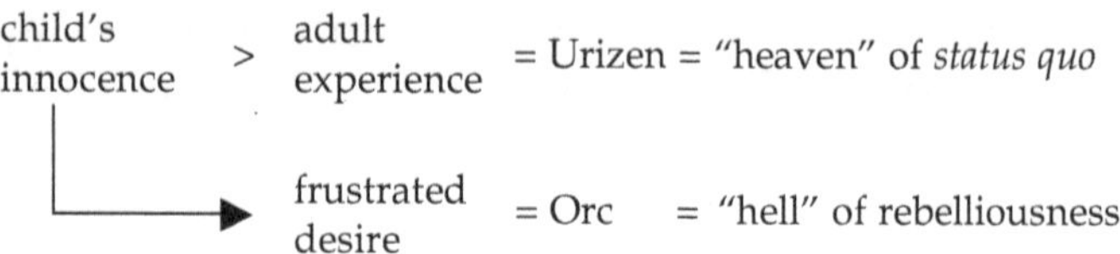

In place of the old construct, therefore, in which man regains his happy garden home by doing his duty and obeying the law, we have an uneasy revolutionary conception of conscious values and standards of reality sitting on top of a volcano of thwarted and mainly sexual energy. This construct has two aspects, individual or psychological, and social or political. Politically, it represents an ascendant class threatened by the growing body of those excluded from social benefits, until the latter are strong enough to overturn society. Psychologically, it represents a conscious ego threatened by a sexually-rooted desire. Thus the mythical structure that informs both the psychology of Freud and the political doctrines of Marx is present in *The Marriage of Heaven and Hell*, which gives us both aspects of the Romantic movement: the reaction to political revolution and the manifesto of feeling and desire as opposed to the domination of reason.

In the associations that Blake makes with Urizen and Orc, Urizen is an old man and Orc a youth: Urizen has the counter-revolutionary colour white and Orc is a revolutionary red. Urizen is therefore associated with sterile winter, bleaching bones, and clouds; Orc with summer, blood, and the sun. The colours white and red suggest the bread and wine of a final harvest and vintage, prophesied in the fourteenth chapter of Revelation. Orc is "underneath" Urizen, and underneath the white cliffs of Albion on the map are the "vineyards of red France" in the throes of revolution [K245/E66]. In a map of Palestine, the kingdom of Israel, whose other name, Jacob, means usurper, sits on top of Edom, the kingdom of the red and hairy Esau, the rightful heir. Isaiah's vision of a Messiah appearing in Edom with his body soaked in blood from "treading the winepress" of war, haunts nearly all Blake's Prophecies. There are many other associations; perhaps we may derive the most important from the following passage in *America:*

> The terror answerd: I am Orc, wreath'd round the accursed tree:
> The times are ended: shadows pass the morning gins to break;
> The fiery joy, that Urizen perverted to ten commands,

What night he led the starry hosts thro' the wide wilderness:
That stony law I stamp to dust: and scatter religion abroad
To the four winds as a torn book, & none shall gather the leaves:
But they shall rot on desart sands, & consume in bottomless deeps:
To make the desarts blossom, & the deeps shrink to their fountains,
And to renew the fiery joy, and burst the stony roof.
That pale religious letchery, seeking Virginity,
May find it in a harlot, and in coarse-clad honesty
The undefil'd tho' ravish'd in her cradle night and morn:
For every thing that lives is holy, life delights in life:
Because the soul of sweet delight can never be defil'd.
Fires inwrap the earthly globe, yet man is not consumd:
Amidst the lustful fires he walks: his feet become like brass,
His knees and thighs like silver, & his breast and head like gold.[2]

At various times in history, there has been a political revolution symbolized by the birth or rebirth of Orc, the "terrible boy": each one, however, has eventually subsided into the same Urizenic form as its predecessor. Orc is the human protest of energy and desire, the impulse to freedom and to sexual love. Urizen is the "reality principle," the belief that knowledge of what is real comes from outside the human body. If we believe that reality is what we bring into existence through an act of creation, then we are free to build up our own civilization and abolish the anomalies and injustices that hamper its growth; but if we believe that reality is primarily what is "out there," then we are condemned, in Marx's phrase, to study the world and never to change it. And the world that we study in this way we are compelled to see in the distorted perspective of the human body with its five cramped senses, not our powers of perception as they are developed and expanded by the arts. Man in his present state is so constructed that all he can see outside him is the world under the law. He may believe that gods or angels or devils or fairies or ghosts are also "out there," but he cannot see these things: he can see only the human and the subhuman, moving in established and predictable patterns. The basis of this vision of reality is the world of the heavenly bodies, circling around automatically and out of reach.

One early Orc rebellion was the Exodus from Egypt, where Orc is represented by a pillar of fire (the "fiery joy") and Urizen by a pillar of cloud, or what *Finnegans Wake* calls "Delude of Isreal."[3] Orc was a human society of twelve (actually thirteen) tribes; Urizen, a legal mechanism symbolized by the twelvefold Zodiac with its captive sun, which is why Urizen is said to have "led the starry hosts" through the wilderness [K198/E54]. The eventual victory of Urizen was marked by the establishing of Aaron's priesthood (the twelve stones in his breastplate symbolized the Zodiac as well as the tribes, according to Josephus), and by the negative moral law of the Decalogue, the moral law being the human imitation of the automatism of natural law. The final triumph of Urizen was symbolized by the hanging of the brazen serpent (Orc) on the pole, a form of the "accursed tree" [K198/E54], and recalling the earlier association of tree and serpent with the exile of Adam and Eve into a wilderness, as well as anticipating the Crucifixion.

Jesus was another Orc figure, gathering twelve followers and starting a new civilization. Christian civilization, like its predecessors, assumed the Urizenic form that it presented so clearly in Blake's own time. This historical perversion of Christianity is studied in *Europe,* where Enitharmon, the Queen of Heaven, summons up twelve starry children, along with Orc as the captive sun, to reimpose the cult of external reality, or what Blake calls natural religion, on Christendom. With the Resurrection, traditionally symbolized by a red cross on a white ground, Jesus made a definitive step into reality: the revolutionary apocalypse Blake hopes for in his day is a Second Coming or mass resurrection, which is why resurrection imagery is prominently displayed in *America*. Now, at the end of European civilization, comes another rebellion of Orc in America, bearing on its various banners a tree, a serpent, and thirteen red and white stripes. The spread of this rebellion to Europe itself is a sign that bigger things are on the way.

The Israelites ended their revolt in the desert of the moral law: now it is time to reverse the movement, to enter the Promised Land, the original Eden, which is to Israel what Atlantis is to Britain and America. The Promised Land is not a different place from the desert, but the desert itself transformed (Blake's imagery comes partly from Isaiah 35, a chapter he alludes to in *The Marriage of Heaven and Hell*). The "deeps shrink to their fountains" because in the apocalypse there is no more sea: dead water is transformed to living water (as in Ezekiel's vision, Ezekiel 47:8). The spiritual body of risen man is sexually free, an aspect symbolized by the "lustful fires" [K199/E54] in which he walks. Man under the law is sexually in a prison of heat without light, a volcano: in the resurrection he is unhurt by flames, like the three Hebrews in Nebuchadnezzar's furnace who were seen walking with the son of God

[Daniel 3:21–5]. According to *The Marriage of Heaven and Hell*, Jesus became Jehovah after his death, and Jehovah, not Satan, is the one who dwells in flaming fire. The risen man, then, is the genuine form of the metallic statue of Nebuchadnezzar's dream [Daniel 2:31–5], without the feet of clay that made that statue an image of tyranny and the cycle of history.

The Resurrection rolled the stone away covering the tomb ("burst the stony roof" [K199/E54]). The stone that covers the tomb of man under the law is the vast arch of the sky, which we see as a concave "vault of paved heaven" (a phrase in the early *Mad Song* [K9/E415]) because we are looking at it from under the "stony roof" of the skull. The risen body would be more like the shape of one of Blake's Last Judgment paintings, with an "opened centre" or radiance of light on top, in the place which is the true location of heaven. Finally, the entire Bible or revelation of the divine in and to man can be read either as the charter of human freedom or as a code of restrictive and negative moral commands. Orc proposes to use Urizen's version of the holy book as fertilizer to help make the desert blossom: what he would do, in other words, is to internalize the law, transform it from arbitrary commands to the inner discipline of the free spirit.

Northern Gate: Single Vision

The optimistic revolutionary construct set up in Blake's early Prophecies is found again in Shelley, whose Prometheus and Jupiter correspond to Orc and Urizen. But in later Romanticism, it quickly turns pessimistic and once more conservative, notably in Schopenhauer, where the world as idea, the world of genuine humanity, sits on top of a dark, threatening, and immensely powerful world as will. A similar construct is in Darwin and Huxley, where the ethical creation of human society maintains itself precariously against the evolutionary force below it. In Freud, civilization is essentially an anxiety structure, where the "reality principle," Blake's Urizen, must maintain its ascendancy somehow over the nihilistic upthrusts of desire. It may permit a certain amount of expression to the "pleasure principle," but not to the extent of being taken over by it. And in Blake, if every revolt of Orc in history has been "perverted to ten commands" [K198/E54], the inference seems to be that history exhibits only a gloomy series of cycles, beginning in hope and inevitably ending in renewed tyranny. In Blake's later Prophecies, we do find this

Spenglerian view of history, with a good many of Spengler's symbols attached to it.

The cyclical movement of history is summarized by Blake in four stages. The first stage is the revolutionary birth of Orc; the second, the transfer of power from Orc to Urizen at the height of Orc's powers, accompanied by the binding or imprisoning of Orc; the third, the consolidating of "natural religion" or the sense of reality as out there, symbolized by Urizen exploring his dens; the fourth, a collapse and chaos symbolized by the crucifixion of Orc, the hanging of the serpent on the dead tree. This fourth stage is the one that Blake sees his own age entering, after the triumph of natural religion or "Deism" in the decades following Newton and Locke. It is an age characterized by mass wars (Isaiah's treading of the wine-press), by technology and complex machinery, by tyranny and "empire" (imperialism being the demonic enemy of culture), and by unimaginative art, especially in architecture. The central symbol of this final phase is the labyrinthine desert in which the Mosaic exodus ended. Jesus spent forty days in the desert, according to Mark, "with the wild beasts" [1:13]: the passage from empire to ruin, from the phase of the tyrant to the phase of the wild beast, is symbolized in the story of Nebuchadnezzar [Daniel 4:28–33], whose metamorphosis is illustrated at the end of *The Marriage of Heaven and Hell*. The figure of Ijim in *Tiriel* has a parallel significance.

As Blake's symbolism becomes more concentrated, he tends to generalize the whole cycle in the conception of "Druidism." The Druids, according to Blake's authorities, worshipped the tree and the serpent, the Druid temple of Avebury, illustrated on the last plate of *Jerusalem*, being serpent-shaped; and they went in for orgies of human sacrifice which illustrate, even more clearly than warfare, the fact that the suppression or perversion of the sexual impulse ends in a death wish (I am not reading modern conceptions into Blake here, but following Blake's own symbolism). This "Druid" imagery is illustrated in the following passage from *Europe*, describing the reaction of the tyrannical "King" or guardian angel of the reactionary Albion and his councillors to the American revolution and kindred portents of apocalyptic disaffection:

> In thoughts perturb'd, they rose from the bright ruins silent following
> The fiery King, who sought his ancient temple serpent-form'd
> That stretches out its shady length along the Island white.
> Round him roll'd his clouds of war; silent the Angel went,
> Along the infinite shores of Thames to golden Verulam.

There stand the venerable porches that high-towering rear
Their oak-surrounded pillars, form'd of massy stones, uncut
With tool; stones precious; such eternal in the heavens,
Of colours twelve, few known on earth, give light in the opake,
Plac'd in the order of the stars, when the five senses whelm'd
In deluge o'er the earth-born man: then turn'd the fluxile eyes
Into two stationary orbs, concentrating all things.
The ever-varying spiral ascents to the heavens of heavens
Were bended downward; and the nostrils golden gates shut
Turn'd outward, barr'd and petrify'd against the infinite . . . .

Now arriv'd the ancient Guardian at the southern porch,
That planted thick with trees of blackest leaf, & in a vale
Obscure, inclos'd the Stone of Night; oblique it stood, o'erhung
With purple flowers and berries red; image of that sweet south,
Once open to the heavens and elevated on the human neck,
Now overgrown with hair and coverd with a stony roof,
Downward 'tis sunk beneath th' attractive north, that round the feet
A raging whirlpool draws the dizzy enquirer to his grave.[4]

It is an intricate passage, but it all makes sense. The serpent temple of Avebury is identified with the white-cliffed Albion in its final Druid phase. It is centred at Verulam, which, as the site of a Roman camp, a "Gothic" cathedral, and the baronial title of Bacon, takes in the whole cycle of British civilization. As we approach the temple, it appears to be a Stonehenge-like circle of twelve precious stones, "plac'd in the order of the stars," or symbolizing the Zodiac. The imagery recalls the similar decadence of Israel in the desert: the twelve Zodiacal gems of Aaron's breastplate have been mentioned, and the Israelites also built megalithic monuments on which they were forbidden to use iron (Joshua 8:31), hence "uncut with tool," iron being in Blake the symbol of Los the blacksmith, the builder of the true city of gems (Isaiah 54:16).

The central form of Druid architecture is the trilithic cromlech or dolmen, the arch of three stones. According to Blake, the two uprights of this arch symbolize the two aspects of creative power, strength and beauty, or sublimity and pathos, as he calls them in the *Descriptive Catalogue*, the horizontal stone being the dominant Urizenic reason. Human society presents this arch in the form of an "Elect" class tyrannizing over the "Reprobate," the unfashionable artists and prophets who embody human sublimity, and the "Redeemed," the gentler souls who are in the company of the beautiful and pathetic. This trilithic structure reappears in such later militaristic monuments as the Arch of Titus: in its "Druid" form, it is illustrated with great power in *Milton*, plate 6, and *Jerusalem*, plate 70. In the former, the balancing rock in front may represent the "Stone of Night" in the above passage. To pass under this arch is to be subjugated, in a fairly literal sense, to what is, according to the *Descriptive Catalogue*, both the human reason and the "incapability of intellect" [K580/E545], as intellect in Blake is always associated with the creative and imaginative. Another form of tyrannical architecture characteristic of a degenerate civilization is the pyramid,[5] representing the volcano or imprisoning mountain under which Orc lies. Blake connects the pyramids with the servitude of the Israelites among the brick-kilns and the epithet "furnace of iron" (1 Kings 8:51) applied to Egypt in the Bible. The association of pyramids and fire is as old as Plato's pun on the word *πύρ*.

The temple of Verulam is a monument to the fall of man, in Blake the same event as the deluge and the creation of the world in its present "out there" form. This form is that of the law, the basis of which is revolution in its mechanical sense of revolving wheels, the symbol of which is the *ouroboros*, the serpent with its tail in its mouth (indicated in a passage omitted above). We see the world from individual "opake" centres, instead of being identified with a universal Man who is also God, who created what we see as alien to us, and who would consequently see his world from the circumference instead of the centre, the perspective reinstated in man by the arts. Such a God-Man would be "full of eyes," like the creatures of Ezekiel's vision, and by an unexpected but quite logical extension of the symbolism, Blake makes him full of noses too. Burning meat to gods on altars, after all, does assume that gods have circumferential noses.

The "Stone of Night," the opposite of the "lively stones" (1 Peter 2:5) of the genuine temple, is an image of the human head, the phrase "stony roof" being repeated from the passage in *America* quoted above. It is in the south because the south is the zenith, the place of the sun in full strength in Blake's symbolism. Now it is covered with purple flowers and red berries, probably of the nightshade: the colours are those of the dying god, which is what Orc (usually Luvah in this context) comes to be in Blake's later poems. The Stone of Night has fallen like a meteor through the bottom or nadir of existence, represented by the north, and now has the same relation to its original that a gravestone has to a living body. We may compare the "grave plot" that Thel reached when she passed under the "northern bar" [K130/E6], and the black coffin which is the body of the chimney sweep (and the enslaved Negro, who also belongs in the "southern clime").[6] Blake's imagery of the north combines the magnetic needle and the legend of the northern maelstrom, the latter supplying a demonic parody of the ascending spiral image on the altar.

From the perspective of single vision, then, our original diagram of buried innocence trying to push its way into experience has to be completed by the death in which all life, individual or historical, ends. Death in Blake's symbolism is Satan, the "Limit of Opacity" [K304/E338], reduction to inorganic matter, who operates in the living man as a death wish or "accuser" of sin. His source in the outer world is the sky, Satan being the starry dragon of Revelation 12:4. Blake identifies this dragon with the Covering Cherub of Ezekiel 28, and the Covering Cherub again with the angel trying to keep us out of the Garden of Eden. Thus the sky is, first, the outward illusion of reality that keeps us out of our proper home; second, the macrocosmic Stone of Night, the rock on top of man's tomb designed to prevent his resurrection; and third, the circumference of what Blake calls the "Mundane Shell," the world as it appears to the embryonic and unborn imagination. Thus:

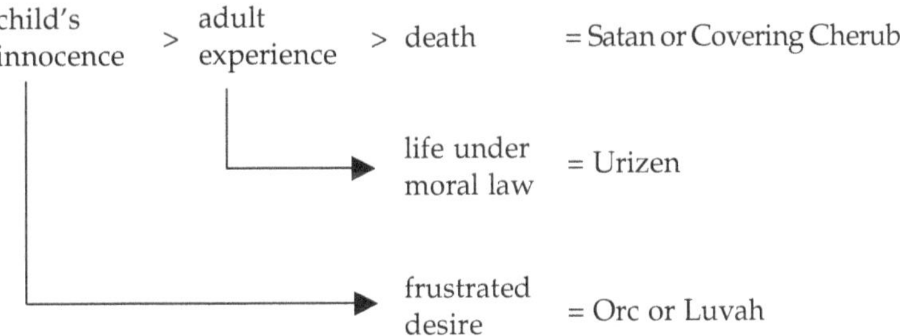

Ordinary human life, symbolized in Blake first by "Adam" and later by "Reuben," oscillates between the two submerged states.

The conception of Druidism in Blake, then, is a conception of human energy and desire continuously martyred by the tyranny of human reason, or superstition. The phrase "dying god" that we have used for Luvah suggests Frazer, and Blake's Druid symbolism has some remarkable anticipations of Frazer's *Golden Bough* complex, including the mistletoe and the oak. The anticipations even extend to Frazer's own unconscious symbolism: the colours of the three states above are, reading up, red, white, and black; and Frazer's book ends with the remark that the web of human thought has been woven of these three colours, though the status of the white or scientific one in Blake is very different. The following passage from *Jerusalem*, plate 66, illustrates Blake's handling of sacrificial symbolism:

> The Daughters of Albion clothed in garments of needle work
> Strip them off from their shoulders and bosoms, they lay aside
> Their garments; they sit naked upon the Stone of trial.
> The Knife of flint passes over the howling Victim: his blood
> Gushes & stains the fair side of the fair Daughters of Albion.
> They put aside his curls; they divide his seven locks upon
> His forehead: they bind his forehead with thorns of iron
> They put into his hand a reed, they mock: Saying: Behold
> The King of Canaan whose are seven hundred chariots of iron!
> They take off his vesture whole with their Knives of flint:
> But they cut asunder his inner garments: searching with
> Their cruel fingers for his heart, & there they enter in pomp,
> In many tears; & there they erect a temple & an altar:
> They pour cold water on his brain in front, to cause
> Lids to grow over his eyes in veils of tears: and caverns
> To freeze over his nostrils, while they feed his tongue from cups
> And dishes of painted clay. [*J*, 66.17–33; K702/E218]

The imagery combines the mockery and passion of Jesus with features from Aztec sacrifices, as Blake realizes that the two widely separated rituals mean essentially the same thing. In the Mexican rites, the "vesture whole" is the skin, not the garment, and the heart is extracted from the body, not merely pierced by a spear as in the Passion. As the passage goes on, the victim expands from an individual body into a country: that is, he is beginning to embody not merely the dying god, but the original universal Man, Albion, whose present dead body is England. The veils and caverns are religious images derived from analogies between the human body and the landscape. Serpent worship is for Blake a perennial feature of this kind of superstition, and the victim is fed from dishes of clay partly because, as Blake says in *The Everlasting Gospel*, "dust & Clay is the Serpent's meat" [K755/E523]. An early Biblical dying-god figure is that of Sisera, the King of Canaan, whose murder at the hands of Jael suggests the nailing down of Jesus and Prometheus; and the reference to "needle work" in the first line also comes from Deborah's war song [Judges 4:18–21; 5:30]. The role given to the Daughters of Albion shows how clearly Blake associates the ritual of sacrifice, many features of which are repeated in judicial executions, with a perversion of the erotic instinct; and, in fact, Blake is clearer than Frazer about the role of the "white goddess" in the dying-god cult, the Cybele who decrees the death of Attis.

Southern Gate: Threefold Vision

The conception of a cycle common to individual and to historical life is the basis of the symbolism of several modern poets, including Yeats, Joyce in *Finnegans Wake*, and Graves in *The White Goddess*. In its modern forms, it usually revolves around a female figure. *The Marriage of Heaven and Hell* prophesies that eventually the bound Orc will be set free and will destroy the present world in a "consummation," which means both burning up and the climax of a marriage. When the marriage is accomplished "by an improvement of sensual enjoyment" [K154/E39], the world of form and reason will be their "bound or outward circumference" [K149/E34] instead of a separate and therefore tyrannizing principle. One would think then that a female figure would be more appropriate for the symbolism of the world of form than the aged and male Urizen.

In traditional Christian symbolism, God the Creator is symbolically male, and all human souls, whether of men or of women, are creatures, and therefore symbolically female. In Blake, the real man is creating man; hence all human beings, men or women, are symbolically male. The symbolic female in Blake is what we call nature, and has four relations to humanity, depending on the quality of the vision. In the world of death, or Satan, which Blake calls Ulro, the human body is completely absorbed in the body of nature—a "dark Hermaphrodite," as Blake says in *The Gates of Paradise* [K770/E268]. In the ordinary world of experience, which Blake calls Generation, the relation of humanity to nature is that of subject to object. In the usually frustrated and suppressed world of sexual desire, which Blake calls Beulah, the relation is that of lover to beloved, and in the purely imaginative or creative state, called Eden, the relation is that of creator to creature. In the first two worlds, nature is a remote and tantalizing "female will"; in the last two she is an "emanation." Human women are associated with this female nature only when in their behaviour they dramatize its characteristics. The relations between man and nature in the individual and historical cycle are different, and are summarized in *The Mental Traveller*, a poem as closely related to the cyclical symbolism of twentieth-century poetry as Keats's *La Belle Dame Sans Merci* is to pre-Raphaelite poetry.

The Mental Traveller traces the life of a "Boy" from infancy through manhood to death and rebirth. This Boy represents humanity, and consequently the cycle he goes through can be read either individually and psychologically, or socially and historically. The latter reading is easier, and closer to the centre of gravity of what Blake is talking about. The poem traces a cycle, but the cycle differs from that of the single vision in that the emphasis is thrown on rebirth and return instead of on death. A female principle, nature, cycles in contrary motion against the Boy, growing young as he grows old and vice versa, and producing four phases that we may call son and mother, husband and wife, father and daughter, ghost (Blake's "spectre") and ghostly bride (Blake's "emanation"). Having set them down, we next observe that not one of these relations is genuine: the mother is not really a mother, nor the daughter really a daughter, and similarly with the other states. The "Woman Old," the nurse who takes charge of the Boy, is Mother Nature, whom Blake calls Tirzah, and who ensures that everyone enters this world in the mutilated and imprisoned form of the physical body. The sacrifice of the dying god repeats this symbolism, which is why the birth of the Boy also contains the symbols of the Passion (we should compare this part of *The Mental Traveller* with the end of *Jerusalem*, plate 67).

As the Boy grows up, he subdues a part of nature to his will, which thereupon becomes his mistress: a stage represented elsewhere in the *Preludium* to *America*. As the cycle completes what Yeats would call its first gyre, we reach the opposite pole of a "Female Babe" whom, like the newborn Boy, no one dares touch. This female represents the "emanation" or accumulated form of what the Boy has created in his life. If she were a real daughter and not a changeling, she would be the Boy's own permanent creation, as Jerusalem is the daughter of Albion, "a City, yet a Woman";[7] and with the appearance of such a permanent creation, the cycle of nature would come to an end. But in this world all creative achievements are inherited by someone else and are lost to their creator. This failure to take possession of one's own deepest experience is the theme of *The Crystal Cabinet* (by comparing the imagery of this latter poem with *Jerusalem*, plate 70, we discover that the Female Babe's name, in this context, is Rahab). The Boy, now an old man at the point of death, acquires, like the aged king David, another "maiden" to keep his body warm on his deathbed. He is now in the desert or wilderness, which symbolizes the end of a cycle, and his maiden is Lilith, the bride of the desert, whom Blake elsewhere calls the Shadowy Female. The Boy as an old man is in an "alastor" relation to her: he ought to be still making the kind of creative effort that produced the Female Babe, but instead he keeps seeking his "emanation" or created form outside himself, until eventually the desert is partially renewed by his efforts, he comes again into the place of seed, and the cycle starts once more.

A greatly abbreviated account of the same cycle, in a more purely historical context, is in the *Argument* of *The Marriage of Heaven and Hell*. Here we start with Rintrah, the prophet in the desert, the Moses or Elijah or John the Baptist who announces a new era of history; then we follow the historical cycle as it makes the desert blossom and produces the honey of the Promised Land. We notice how, as in the time of Moses, water springs up in the desert and how Orc's "red clay" puts life on the white bones of Urizen. Eventually the new society becomes decadent and tyrannical, forcing the prophet out into the desert once more to begin another cycle.

The poem called *The Gates of Paradise*, based on a series of illustrations reproduced in the standard editions of Blake, describes the same cycle in slightly different and more individualized terms. Here conception in the womb, the mutilation of birth which produces the "mother's grief," is symbolized by the caterpillar and by the mandrake. The mandrake is traditionally an aphrodisiac, a plant with male and female forms, an opiate, the seed of hanged men, a "man-dragon" that shrieks when uprooted (i.e., born), and recalls the frustrated sunflower of the *Songs of Experience*. The association of the mandrake with the mother in Genesis 30:14 is the main reason why Blake uses "Reuben" instead of "Adam" as the symbol of ordinary man in *Jerusalem*. The embryo then takes on the substance of the four elements and the four humours that traditionally correspond to them, of which "Earth's Melancholy" is the dominant one. Then the infant is born and grows into an aggressive adolescent, like the Boy in *The Mental Traveller* binding nature down for his delight. This attitude divides nature into a part that is possessed and a part that eludes, and the separation indicates that the boy in this poem also is bound to the cyclical movement. The youth then collides with Urizen, the spear in the revolutionary left hand being opposed to the sword of established order in the right. The caption of this emblem, "My Son! my Son!" refers to Absalom's revolt against David [2 Samuel 18:33]. Orc is not the son of Urizen, but Absalom, hung on a tree (traditionally by his golden hair, like the mistletoe: cf. *The Book of Ahania*, II, 9 [K251/E86]), is another dying god or Druid victim.

The other plates are not difficult to interpret: they represent the frustration of desire, the reaction into despair, and the growing of the youthful and rebellious Orc into a wing-clipping Urizen again. Finally the hero, like the early Tiriel and like the Boy of *The Mental Traveller* in his old age, becomes a wandering pilgrim making his way, like the old man in the *Pardoner's Tale*, toward his own death. He enters "Death's Door," the lower half of a design from Blair's *Grave* omitting the resurrection theme in the upper half, and is once more identified with Mother Nature, with a caption quoted from Job 17:14. The Prologue asks us why we worship this dreary womb-to-tomb treadmill as God—that is, why we think of God as a sky-god of automatic order, when this sky-god is really Satan, the corpse of God. The Epilogue returns to the same attack, and concludes by calling Satan "The lost Traveller's Dream under the Hill" [K771/E269]. Apart from the general theme of the dreaming traveller which is common to this poem and to *The Mental Traveller* (where the "mental" travelling is done by the poet and reader, not the hero), there is a more specific allusion to the passage in *The Pilgrim's Progress* where Christian, after falling asleep under Hill Difficulty and losing his roll, is forced to retrace his steps like the Israelites in the desert, to whom Bunyan explicitly refers.

The passage from death to rebirth is represented in Blake's symbolism by Tharmas, the power of renewing life. The ability of the individual to renew his life is resurrection, and the resurrection is a break with the cycle, but in ordinary life such a renewal takes place only in the group or species, and within the cycle. Tharmas is symbolized by the sea, the end and the beginning of life. As the original fall of man was also the deluge, we are in this world symbolically under water, our true home being Atlantis, or the Red Sea, which the Israelites found to be dry land. Tharmas and Orc are the strength and beauty, the sublime and the pathetic, the uprights of the Druid trilithon already mentioned, with Urizen, the anti-intellectual "reason," connecting them. Thus:

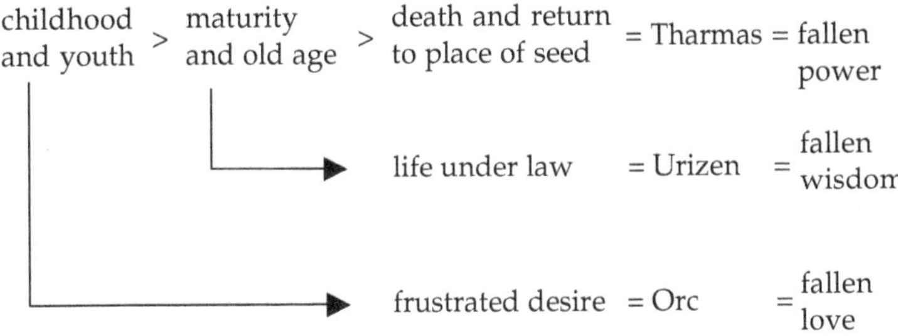

Western Gate: Fourfold Vision

In *The Marriage of Heaven and Hell,* Blake presents the revolutionary vision of man as a self-centred anxious ego sitting on top of a rebellious desire, and he associates the emancipating of desire with the end of the world as we know it. The Proverbs of Hell say, "He who desires but acts not, breeds pestilence" [K151/E35]. Putting desire into action does not lead to anarchy, for the fires of Orc are "thought-creating": what it does lead to is an apocalypse in which "the whole creation will be consumed and appear infinite and holy, whereas it now appears finite & corrupt" [K154/E39]. But when we read other works of Blake, we begin to wonder if this "Voice of the Devil" tells the whole story. Blake certainly means what he says in *The Marriage of Heaven and Hell,* but that work is a satire, deriving its norms from other conceptions. As we read further in Blake, it becomes clear that the emancipating of desire, for him, is not the cause but the effect of the purging of reality. There was some political disillusionment as Blake proceeded—the perversion of the French Revolution into Napoleonic imperialism, the strength of the reactionary power in Britain, the continued ascendancy of the slave-owners in America, and a growing feeling that Voltaire and Rousseau were reactionaries and not revolutionaries were the main elements in it—but although this leads to some changes in emphasis in later poems, there is no evidence that he was ever really confused about the difference between the apocalyptic and the historical versions of reality.

Blake dislikes any terminology which implies that there are two perceivers in man, such as a soul and a body, which perceive different worlds. There is only one world, but there are two kinds of things to be done with it. There is, first, what Blake calls the natural vision, which assumes that the objective world is essentially independent of man. This vision becomes increasingly hypnotized by the automatic order and tantalizing remoteness of nature, creates gods in the image of its mindless mechanism, and rationalizes all evils and injustices of existence under some such formula as "Whatever is, is right." In extreme forms, this alienating vision becomes the reflection of the death wish in the soul, and develops annihilation wars like those of Blake's own time. Then there is the human vision, which takes the objective world to be the "starry floor," the bottom of reality, its permanence being important only as a stable basis for human creation. The goal of the human vision is "Religion, or Civilized Life such as it is in the Christian Church."[8] This is a life of pure creation, such as is ascribed in Christianity to God, and which for Blake would participate in the infinite and eternal perspective of God. We note that Blake, like Kierkegaard, leads us toward an "either/or" dilemma, but that his terms are the reverse of Kierkegaard's. It is the aesthetic element for Blake which moves in the sphere of existential freedom; it is the ethical element which is the spectator, under the bondage of the law and the knowledge of good and evil.

We begin, then, with the view of an orthodox or moral "good," founded on an acceptance of the world out there, contrasted with the submerged "evil" desires of man to live in a world that makes more human sense. This vision of life turns out to be, when examined, a cyclical vision, completed by the more elaborate cycles just examined. But in addition to the cyclical vision there is also a dialectic, a separating out of the two opposing human and natural visions. The categories of these visions are not moral good and evil, but life and death, one producing the real heaven of creation and the other the real hell of torture and tyranny. We have met one pole of this dialectic already in the conception of Satan, or death, as the only possible goal of all human effort from one point of view. The other pole is the impulse to transform the world into a human and imaginative form, the impulse that creates all art, all genuine religion, all culture and civilization. This impulse is personified by Blake as Los, the spirit of prophecy and creativity, and it is Los, not Orc, who is the hero of Blake's Prophecies. Los derives, not from the suppressed desires of the individual child, but from a deeper creative impulse alluded to in Biblical myths about the unfallen state. These myths tell us that man's original state was not primitive, or derived from nature at all, but civilized, in the environment of a garden and a city. This unfallen state is, so to speak, the previous tree of which contemporary man is the seed, and the form he is attempting to recreate. Thus:

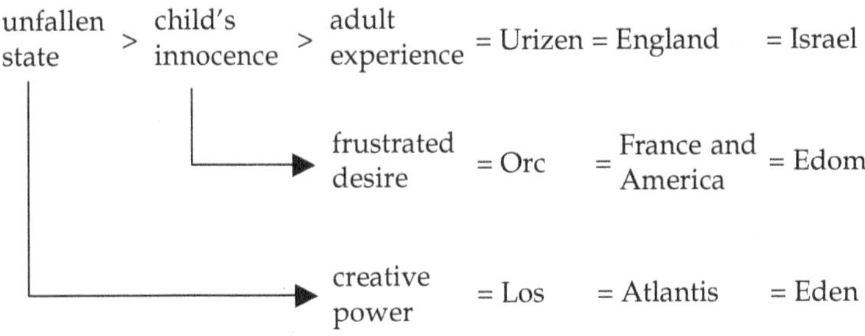

It seems curious that, especially in the earlier Prophecies, Los appears to play a more reactionary and sinister role than Urizen himself. We discover that it is Los, not Urizen, who is the father of Orc; Los, not Urizen, who actively restrains Orc, tying him down under Mount Atlas with the "Chain of Jealousy"; and Los who is the object of Orc's bitter Oedipal resentments. In the *Preludium* to *America*, he is referred to by his alternative name of Urthona, and there it is he and not Urizen who rivets Orc's "tenfold chains." These chains evidently include an incest taboo, for Orc is copulating with his sister in this *Preludium*. Evidently, as Blake conceives it, there is a deeply conservative element in the creative spirit that seems to help perpetuate the reign of Urizen. In fact, certain functions given to Urizen in earlier Prophecies are transferred to Los in later ones. According to William Morris, the joy that the medieval craftsman took in his work was so complete that he was able to accept the tyranny of medieval society: similarly, Blake is able to live in the age of Pitt and Nelson and yet be absorbed in building his palace of art on the "Great Atlantic Mountains" [K558/E481], which will be here after the "Sea of Time and Space" above it is no more.

This principle that effective social action is to be found in the creation of art and not in revolution is, of course, common to many Romantics in Blake's period. It should not, however—certainly not in Blake—be regarded as a mere neurotic or wish-fulfilment substitute for the failure of revolution. Apart from the fact that the creation of art is a highly social act, Blake's conception of art is very different from the dictionary's. It is based on what we call the arts, because of his doctrine that human reality is created and not observed. But it includes much that we do not think of as art, and excludes much that we do, such as the paintings of Reynolds.

We notice that in *The Gates of Paradise* cycle there is one point at which there is a break from the cycle, the plate captioned "Fear & Hope are—

Vision" [K768/E266], and described in the commentary as a glimpse of "The Immortal Man that cannot Die" [K771/E269]. The corresponding point in *The Mental Traveller* comes in describing the form ("emanation") of the life that the Boy has been constructing, just before it takes shape as the elusive "Female Babe":

> And these are the gems of the Human Soul,
> The rubies & pearls of a lovesick eye,
> The countless gold of the akeing heart,
> The martyr's groan & the lover's sigh. [K425/E484]

The curiously wooden allegory is not characteristic of Blake, but it recurs in *Jerusalem*, plate 12, where the same theme is under discussion. Evidently, Blake means by "art" a creative life rooted in the arts, but including what more traditional language calls charity. Every act man performs is either creative or destructive. Both kinds seem to disappear in time, but in fact it is only the destructive act, the act of war or slavery or parasitism or hatred, that is really lost.

Los is not simply creative power, but the spirit of time: more accurately, he is the power that constructs in time the palace of art (Golgonooza), which is timeless. As Blake says in a grammatically violent aphorism, the ruins of time build mansions in eternity.[9] The products of self-sacrifice and martyrdom and endurance of injustice still exist, in an invisible but permanent world created out of time by the imagination. This world is the genuine Atlantis or Eden that we actually live in. As soon as we realize that we do live in it, we enter into what Blake means by the Last Judgment. Most people do not make this act of realization, and those who do make it have the responsibility of being evangelists for it. According to Blake, most of what the enlightened can do for the unenlightened is negative: their task is to sharpen the dialectic of the human and natural visions by showing that there are only the alternatives of apocalypse and annihilation.

Blake obviously hopes for a very considerable social response to vision in or soon after his lifetime. But even if everybody responded completely and at once, the City of God would not become immediately visible: if it did, it would simply be one more objective environment. The real "heaven" is not a glittering city, but the power of bringing such cities into existence. In the poem *My Spectre around me*, Blake depicts a figure like the Boy of *The Mental Traveller* in old age, searching vainly for his "emanation," the total body of what he can love and create, outside himself instead of inside. The natural tendency of desire (Orc) in itself is to find its object. Hence the effect of the creative impulse on desire is bound to be restrictive until the release of desire becomes the inevitable by-product of creation.

The real world, being the source of a human vision, is human and not natural (which means indefinite) in shape. It does not stretch away forever into the stars, but has the form of a single giant man's body, the parts of which are arranged thus:

Urizen	=	head	=	city
Tharmas	=	body	=	garden
Orc	=	loins	=	soil or bed of love
Urthona (Los)	=	legs	=	underworld of dream and repose

Except that it is unfallen, the four levels of this world correspond very closely to the four traditional levels that we find in medieval and Renaissance poetry. The present physical world, by the "improvement of sensual enjoyment" [K154/E39], would become an integral part of nature, and so Comus's attempt to seduce the Lady by an appeal to "nature" would no longer be a seduction or a specious argument. But the really important distinction is that for earlier poets the two upper levels, the city and the garden, were divine and not human in origin, whereas for Blake they are both divine and human, and their recovery depends on the creative power in man as well as in God.

The difference between the traditional and the Blakean versions of reality corresponds to the difference between the first and the last plates of the Job illustrations. In the first plate, Job and his family are in the state of innocence (Beulah), in a peaceful pastoral repose like that of the twenty-third Psalm. They preserve this state in the traditional way, by obeying a divine Providence that has arranged it, and hence are imaginatively children. There is nothing in the picture that suggests anything inadequate except that, in a recall of a very different Psalm (137), there are musical instruments hung on the tree above. In the last plate, things are much as they were before, but Job's family have taken the instruments down from the tree and are playing them. In Blake, we recover our original state, not by returning to it, but by recreating it. The act of creation, in its turn, is not producing something out of nothing, but the act of setting free what we already possess.

23

William Blake (II)

1967

From The Encyclopedia of Philosophy, *ed. Paul Edwards (New York: Macmillan, 1967), 1:319–20.*

BLAKE, WILLIAM (1757–1827), English poet, painter, and engraver. Blake was born in London, the second of five children in the family of a retail hosier. His social status precluded university education, and he was apprenticed to an engraver. Apart from that training and a few months at the Royal Academy, Blake was self-educated. Most of his pictorial work took the form of illustrations for books, Biblical subjects forming the largest group. His painting and engraving were thus primarily related to literature, and the interdependence of poetry and painting is a central principle of all his work. He lived in London nearly all his life, very frugally, sometimes in poverty, and constantly dependent on patrons. He met Wordsworth, Coleridge, and Lamb, and was admired by the last two; but he died practically unknown as a poet, although he had been writing poetry since the age of twelve. After one volume of juvenile verse (*Poetical Sketches*, 1783) was published through the efforts of friends, Blake determined to produce his poetry by engraving the text himself and accompanying it with illustrations. Practically all his later poetry, except what was left in manuscript, took the form of a text and designs etched on copper, stamped on paper, and then coloured by hand. Most of his lyrics are in two collections: *Songs of Innocence* (first engraved in 1789) and *Songs of Experience* (1794). Others are longer poems, generally called Prophecies, which are sequences of plates. The "Prophecies" include *The Book of Thel* (1789), *The Marriage of Heaven and Hell* (1793), *America* (1793), *Europe* (1794), *Milton* (about 1808, in 50 plates) and *Jerusalem* (about 1818, in 100 plates).

Thought

The Prophecies are symbolic poems in which the characters are states or attitudes of human life. This means that these poems embody religious and philosophical concepts as well as poetic imagery. These concepts are mainly concerned with Blake's sense of the relevance and importance of the arts and of the creative faculty of man, and seem to have been derived mainly from a negative reaction to the British empirical tradition of thought. He tells us that he had read Locke and Bacon in his youth and had decided that they mocked inspiration and vision. Blake's attitude would be better understood if it were thought of as anti-Cartesian, although he is unlikely to have read Descartes, and his attitude embodies many elements that would now be called existential.

Imagination

According to Blake, man is a working or constructing imagination—the creative artist is normative man. In this context there is no difference between human essence and human existence, for the imagination is the human existence itself and is also essential human nature. Works of art are neither intellectual nor emotional, motivated neither by desire nor by reason, neither free nor compelled: all such antitheses become unities in them. Even more important, the imagination destroys the antithesis of subject and object. Man starts out as an isolated intelligence in an alien nature, but the imagination creates a world in its own image, the world of cities and gardens and human communities and domesticated animals.

Interpretation of the Bible

For Blake, the Bible is a definitive parable of human existence, as it tells how man finds himself in an unsatisfactory world and tries to build a better one—one which eventually takes the form of a splendid golden city, the symbol of the imaginative and creative human community. God in Blake's work is the creative power in man (here Blake shows the influence of Swedenborg, with his emphasis on the unity of divine and human natures in Jesus), and human power is divine because it is infinite and eternal. These two words do not mean endless in time and space; they mean the genuine experience of the central points of time and space, the now and the here. Many features of Blake's anti-Lockean position remind us of Berkeley, especially his insistence that "mental things are alone real";[1] but this doctrine of God takes Blake far beyond the subjective idealism and nominalism of Berkeley.

In Blake's reading of the Bible, "the creation"—the alien and stupid nature that man now lives in—is part of "the fall" and is the world man struggles to transcend. The objective world is the anti-creation, the enemy to be destroyed. Blake says that man has no body distinct from his soul. He does oppose mind and body, but as contrasting attitudes to nature, not as separate essential principles. The "corporeal understanding," or perverted human activity, contemplates nature as it is (as a vast, objective, subhuman body) and tries to overcome the alienation of the subject by identifying the subject with nature as it sees nature. Nature is controlled, apparently, by automatic laws like the law of gravitation and by a struggle to survive in which force and cunning are more important than love or intelligence. Perverted human life imitates nature by continually waging war and by maintaining a parasitic class. Perverted religion, or natural religion, as Blake calls it, invents harsh and tyrannical gods on the analogy of nature. Perverted thought exposes itself passively to impressions from the external world and then evolves abstract principles out of these impressions which attempt to formulate the general laws of nature. These are the operations known as sensation and reflection in Locke. The abstracting tendency is perverted because it is not a genuine effort to understand nature, but is a step toward imitating the automatism of nature by imposing a conforming morality on human life. The principle of this conformity is the acceptance of injustice and exploitation as inescapable elements of existence. The end of this perverted process is hatred and contempt of life, as expressed in the deliberate efforts at self-annihilation which Blake saw as beginning with the Napoleonic wars in his own time.

Prophetic Books

The action in Blake's Prophecies is concerned with the conflict of these creative and perverted states in human life. The sense of conservatism, of accepting things as they are, is symbolized by Urizen, who is associated with old age and the sky. When conservatism deepens into hatred of life itself, Urizen is replaced by Satan. The force that struggles against Urizen is the revolutionary impulse in man, called Orc or Luvah, who is associated with youth and sexual desire. Orc cannot achieve a permanent deliverance from Urizen; that is possible only for the creative power itself, called Los. The central theme of the Prophecies is the effort of humanity, called Albion, to achieve through Los the kind of civilization which is symbolized in the Bible as Jerusalem and thus to reach the integration of human and divine powers represented in Christianity by Jesus.

Bibliography

The most convenient edition of Blake's literary work is the one-volume *The Poetry and Prose of William Blake*, ed. Geoffrey Keynes (London and New York, 1927).

Works on Blake include Bernard Blackstone, *English Blake* (London, 1949); S. Foster Damon, *William Blake: His Philosophy and Symbols* (Boston and New York, 1924); David V. Erdman, *Blake: Prophet against Empire* (Princeton, 1954); Northrop Frye, *Fearful Symmetry: A Study of William Blake* (Princeton, 1947); and Mark Schorer, *William Blake: The Politics of Vision* (New York, 1946).

24

Comment on *Adam and Eve and the Angel Raphael*

1967

Descriptive entry in the catalogue of the International Art Exhibition at Expo '67 in Montreal, Man and His World, *14. This art exhibition, which ran from 28 April to 27 October 1967, consisted of 170 works of art from different parts of the world covering a period of about five thousand years; they were arranged in sections such as "Urban Man" and "Man and His Conflicts." Frye's entry pertains to a Blake pen and watercolour painting of 1808, on loan from the Museum of Fine Arts, Boston, which appeared in the section "Man and Love" and was reproduced in the catalogue. The text also appeared in French.*

The illustration, now entitled The Archangel Raphael with Adam and Eve, *is reproduced as the frontispiece to the present volume.*

William Blake was born in London in 1757, and died there in 1827. As his family was not well off, he was early apprenticed to an engraver, and made his living partly by engraving illustrations to books, often his own or others' designs, and partly by selling his paintings. His paintings were in watercolour and were almost invariably illustrations to literary works. His favourite book was the Bible, and the bulk of his illustrations are directly or indirectly Biblical in theme, including a famous series on the Book of Job done near the end of his life. He also illustrated Dante, Blair's *Grave,* Young's *Night Thoughts,* the poems of Gray, and more particularly Milton, who was clearly his favourite poet. All of Milton's major poems were illustrated by him, sometimes more than once. *Adam and Eve and the Angel Raphael* is from one of the sets of illustrations to *Paradise Lost.*

Blake was also a great poet as well as a painter. He believed that the creative life, of which the artist is the symbol, was the highest life possible to man. The opposite of the creative life is the uniform or predictable life, encouraged by most moral codes and most religious and political authority, where life becomes so automatic that it is essentially a mere waiting for death. The creative life is also a life of love, both sexual and nonsexual, a love which respects the liberty of both lover and beloved. The opposite of love is what Blake calls "jealousy," by which he means both possessive love and the tantalizing or frustrating of love. For Blake the loss of love and creativity, and the plunging of man into jealousy and uniformity, is what is meant by the Biblical story of the fall of man, as expanded and reinterpreted by Milton. In this picture Adam and Eve are portrayed in their original "unfallen" state of innocent love and spontaneous life, and the angel Raphael is urging them to persist in it. In the background is the forbidden tree, symbolizing the "knowledge of good and evil," that is, the sense of guilt and shame in sexual love, along with the notion that passive and automatic behaviour is "good" and independent and vigorous life "evil," because it threatens authority. The self-consciousness that makes us analyse and judge our actions instead of acting freely is symbolized by the serpent who is coiled around the tree. As Blake says in one of his own poems:

> Serpent reasonings us entice
> Of good and evil, virtue and vice.[1]

He hopes that eventually man will throw off the tyranny of guilt and shame and return to the state of innocence symbolized here by Adam and Eve, and says:

> The cherub with his flaming sword is hereby commanded to leave his guard at (the) tree of life; and when he does, the whole creation will be consumed and appear infinite and holy, whereas it now appears finite and corrupt. This will come to pass by an improvement of sensual enjoyment. [*MHH*, pl. 14; K154/E39]

25

Blake's Reading of the Book of Job (I)

1969

From William Blake: Essays for S. Foster Damon, *ed. Alvin H. Rosenfeld (Providence: Brown University Press, 1969), 221–34. A rewritten version was published in* SM, *228–44 (see headnote to no. 27 in the present volume).*

Blake's Job engravings and paintings have often been commented on, and never more lucidly than by the subject of this *Festschrift*.[1] But one aspect of Blake's great work could perhaps be discussed a little more fully. Everyone realizes that Blake recreated the Book of Job in his engravings and was not simply illustrating it. At the same time he appears to be following the book with some fidelity, and his attitude toward it, in striking contrast to his attitude toward Dante's *Commedia*, seems to be on the whole an attitude of critical acceptance. He remarked, apropos of Homer, that "Every Poem must necessarily be a perfect Unity," but the rest of the sentence suggests that the *Iliad* is not "peculiarly so" [K778/E269]: in other words, the perfect unity is only potential in the poem itself, and is really achieved by the reader. The extraordinary sense of unity that one feels about the Job engravings, considered as a series, indicates that Blake succeeded in creating this unity out of his reading of the Book of Job. Hence it may be worth attempting some conjectural reconstruction of the reader's "vision" of Job that preceded the final recreation in the engravings.

In the first place, the Bible as a whole was to Blake an epic of the fall and redemption of man: man loses his paradisal garden with its trees and water of life early in Genesis and gets it back at the end of Revelation. One thing that Blake clearly saw in the story of Job was a microcosm of the whole Biblical story. This was the chief reason for the relatively few definite changes that he makes from what is in the text, the most obvious of which is his altering of the character of Job's wife. In the Book of Job the wife is a Delilah figure, a temptress who suggests that Job renounce his integrity, and this is how Blake depicted her in earlier illustrations of the book. But when the Book of Job is thought of as a miniature Bible, Job occupies the place of Adam or Israel or Blake's own Albion, the symbolic figure of humanity, and Job's wife thus becomes the Eve or Rachel who must form a part of his redemption. In *Jerusalem* Albion's wife, Brittannia, is a very shadowy character: the main theme is the restoration to Albion of his daughter Jerusalem. This emphasis on the restored daughter (apart from the link with King Lear, whose three daughters are among the daughters of Albion) was doubtless derived from a parallel emphasis in the Book of Job, as illustrated in Blake's twentieth plate. Similarly, the three friends are almost wholly demonic in Blake's illustrations, assimilated to the threefold accuser figure who runs through all Blake's work from the *Accusers of Theft, Adultery and Murder*[2] to Hand in *Jerusalem*, and who is identified with the three accusers of Socrates (*J*, pl. 93)[3] and, probably, the three witnesses against Faithful in *The Pilgrim's Progress*. It is said of the friends, in a verse quoted on Blake's plate 8, that "they sat down with him upon the ground seven days and seven nights, and none spake a word unto him: for they saw that his grief was very great" (Job 2:13). Seven days of silent sympathy from friends who are at least not fair-weather friends, and have nothing to gain from visiting Job in his destitution, are surely on the credit side of any moral ledger. But when we think of Job as continuously martyred humanity, it is hardly possible to see in the friends anything but representatives of the continuous social anxiety, the Theotormon complex, so to speak, that makes human misery constant by trying to rationalize and explain it away in every crisis.

The Book of Job has a formidable literary reputation, but it is not easy to make sense of it as it stands. It begins with the astonishing scenes of Satan in the court of God, where Satan has the role, always central to his nature, of the accuser of mankind. He suggests that God has set things up in such a way that he can't lose: if he rewards obedience, he gives man so powerful a motive for being obedient that service of God becomes merely a conditioned reflex. What Satan is really raising is the issue of man's free will. Under the conventional view of the law, as accepted by Job's friends, in which God sends rain and sunshine on the just and storms and drought on the unjust, man has no real power of moral choice, and God has not yet succeeded in creating anything more than an automaton. The friends' view of providence is easily refuted by experience, but there are two equally easy ways of countering this. One is to say that God's ways are inscrutable when they appear to be merely insane on such premises; the other is to assume that this providence will manifest itself in another world, from which no evidence ever leaks out. Hence for Blake the religion of Job's friends is socially as strongly established as it ever was, except that its basis has tended to shift somewhat from "Honesty is the best policy" to "Maybe it doesn't seem so now, but you just wait." Satan may be the accuser of mankind, but if he had not stated his case so sharply in the opening of the Book of Job it is a question how either Judaism or Christianity could ever have developed. The latter is centred on a martyred God and the former on a chosen people which is also a homeless and frequently persecuted people, hence both are radically opposed to the kind of wish-thinking that Job's friends represent, however much of it they accept or compromise with in practice.

Job's friends are better poets, and have more flexible minds, than one would imagine from Blake's pictures, but it is true that they keep revolving around the central point in their whole system of values: somehow or other it must be a crime to be unfortunate, otherwise God is not a just God. The suppressed premise here is that God administers both the human moral law and the physical natural law, but it never occurs to them to doubt this. Hence in all their gropings after some explanation for Job's plight that will make imaginative, if not rational, sense in their terms, the one explanation that they are too pious even to speculate about is the one that has already been given to the reader. The account of God's having left Job to fight alone in order to win a wager with Satan hangs sardonically over all their debate.

The three friends, we are told, ceased to answer Job "because he was righteous in his own eyes" (32:1). But Job is not really righteous in his own eyes: he is merely convinced that there is far too great a disproportion between what has happened to him and anything he could conceivably have done, when considered as a crime and punishment situation. Better a God wholly indifferent to moral values than so insufferably stupid a God as the one the friends are forced to appeal to. Job's friends cannot shake his convictions without beginning to disturb their own, so the discussion comes to a deadlock. Elihu then breaks in impatiently to overwhelm Job with the eloquence of what he has to say "on God's behalf" (36:2), but although his powers of eloquence are considerable, he succeeds only in restating the earlier arguments. Then God himself answers Job out of the whirlwind and asks, "Who is this that darkeneth counsel by words without knowledge?" (38:2), meaning apparently Elihu, and we wait for the definitive revelation to which the whole drama seems to have been leading up.

God is also quite a good poet, if not as good as Elihu, whom he paraphrases extensively, but nonetheless we feel uncomfortable about the way in which he triumphantly displays a number of trump cards that seem to belong to a different game. He begins by asking Job a long series of rhetorical questions which have a hectoring and bullying sound to them. The general theme is: Were you around when I made the world, or do you understand all about how it was made? No? Well, then, why are you raising doubts about my administrative competence? This is followed by poems on two beasts, Behemoth and Leviathan, which appear to be hyperbolic descriptions of a hippopotamus and a crocodile. They are remarkable poems, but we wonder about their relevance to Job's boils and murdered children. Job replies meekly that he has "uttered that I understood not; things too wonderful for me, which I knew not. . . . Wherefore I abhor myself, and repent in dust and ashes" (42:3, 6). God then appears to say, in effect, "Well, that's better," and forthwith restores him to prosperity. Nothing further is said about Satan, so that Job, unlike us, learns nothing about the original compact. No wonder that Bernard Shaw should speak of the ignoble and impertinent retort of God at the end of the Book of Job,[4] or that Shaw's black girl, on her way to seek God, should find the God of Job one of the lowest possible forms of religious experience.[5]

The Book of Job starts with much the same problem as that of Plato's *Republic* [592b]. In Plato also justice is related to the extreme case of one who suffers nothing but misery and humiliation by persisting in justice. Like Plato, too, the author of Job uses the dramatic form of dialogue. Socrates builds up dialectically, step by step, a picture of a just human community, asks whether such a community does or is likely to exist, is told probably not, and then remarks that the wise man will live according to the laws of this ideal human community regardless of the kind of world he actually does live in. His superb and brilliant performance is, in the broadest sense, a comedy: this is the comic vision of human life, where we are led up to, and by implication inspired by, a glimpse of a community in which everyone lives happily ever after, even if we do not leave the theatre in exactly the same condition. The myth of the Christian

Bible, ending as it does in apocalyptic vision, is comic in the same sense. In the Book of Job we recognize at first a tragic and existential counterpart to Plato, a discussion following out the irony of the human situation until it reaches the point that we now call the metaphysical absurd. The Book of Job is technically a comedy by virtue of Job's restoration in the last few verses, but the comic conclusion seems so wrenched and arbitrary that it is hard to think of it as anything but a wantonly spoiled tragedy.

The simplest answer is to suppose that the Book of Job, begun by a colossal poetic genius, then fell into the hands of a superstitious editor whose own attitude was a cruder version of that of Job's friends, and who twisted one of the world's profoundest poems into an obscurantist tirade against the use of the questioning intelligence in matters of religion. Something like this could have happened: there are signs of nervous editing, as in so many parts of the Bible, and it is impossible to say how far they have gone. But such a hypothesis is of little practical use to anyone, least of all Blake. The version we have is the only one that exists, and the only one that has influenced later literature and religion. Even Blake could hardly have reconstructed an Ur-Job, and anyone faced with Blake's task clearly has to make more sense of the total structure of the poem as we have it than this account of it has so far made.

In the first place, of course, the comic conclusion, the restoration of Job to prosperity, would not seem arbitrary to Blake, or for that matter to anyone who was thinking of the story of Job as an epitome of the story of the Bible as a whole. In the total story Adam loses his garden and is led back to a restored garden which is also a city: this means, according to Milton, that he loses paradise as a physical environment and regains it as an inner state of mind, the latter being "happier far." Similarly Job, as Blake sees him, begins in the state of Beulah, the pastoral repose of plate 1, and ends in the apocalyptic Eden of plate 21, where the musical instruments have been taken down from the trees and the sheep are waking up. Through suffering Job passes from obedience to law to the service of freedom. The former is symbolized by the sacrificial altar in front of plates 1 and 21, with its significant inscriptions about the importance of outgrowing the moral and ritual aspect of religion which sacrifice represents. The genuine form of sacrifice, called in Blake the annihilation of the Selfhood, is the real subject of plate 18. But for the Christian myth that Blake, like Milton, is using, Job's restoration is possible only as a result of a redemptive act, the Incarnation of God as Man.

Clearly there must have been, for Blake, something in the final revelation to Job that we have missed, something with an effective redemptive force.

We said earlier that the assumption underlying the religion of the three friends was that moral and natural laws are administered by the same God. For Blake, of course, this was "natural religion," and nonsense. Nature to him was the state of experience, indifferent to human values and exhibiting no sense of design or purpose beyond an automatic and mechanical one. Anyone who associates human and natural law is trying to make the latter the model of the former, eliminating everything unpredictable from human behaviour and with it everything that makes for a free and creative human community. Persistently through history man has projected his gods, thrown shadows of himself into the objective, which in this context means the alienated, world. He continually tries to invent a God who is a philosophical first cause, a personal guarantor of the mindless order of nature, who will be some variant of the old man with the compasses lowering over *Europe* as the idol of all the eighteen centuries of "Christian" tyranny. As long as an obedient moral life is associated with a comfortable physical one, this deity may look providential and benignant. But when the crunch comes he turns into Satan, the sense of littleness and futility that makes us accept any kind of misery as somehow ultimately just, or, at least, inevitable. Thus for Blake Satan and the God he consults with at the opening of the book are two aspects of the same God. Satan is clearly younger than God, and they seem to be related much as Father and Son are in *Paradise Lost*, God being the weak, sick *dieu fainéant* of plates 2 and 5 resigning his power to his own demonic Messiah. Many years earlier Blake had remarked in *The Marriage of Heaven and Hell* that "in the Book of Job, Milton's Messiah is call'd Satan" [K150/E34]. Blake here was thinking partly of the Son's activity in spoiling his own creation in book 10 of *Paradise Lost* (technically Sin and Death spoil it, but the Creator cannot abdicate responsibility so easily), and then destroying it altogether in the flood.

This pattern of age followed by youth is repeated later when Elihu takes over from his three elders. By turning dialogue into monologue he is trying to consolidate their confused and variable notions of natural religion into a single closed system of fatalism. This of course is why he is shown pointing to twelve stars, representing the cycle of the zodiac, with his left or sinister hand in plate 12. Elihu here has much the same role as that of Newton in *Europe*: he is a spokesman of natural religion so fully articulate that he overreaches himself and blows his whole system, in more than one sense, sky-high.

If this analysis is so far sound, it throws a very different light on God's speech to Job at the end. Perhaps all the rhetorical questions about the creation are designed, not to bully Job into an uncritical submission, but to warn him off from looking in the wrong direction for his redeeming power. Job's instinctive tendency is to search for the *cause* of his calamities. There may be something in his previous history, or in that of his family (cf. 1:5), which was a fatal but unconscious sin, like the sin of Oedipus. As Job refuses to believe in any such cause, the friends give up and Elihu takes over. Under Elihu's influence Job is carried back to the conception of a transcendent power from which everything good or bad proceeds. Elihu is of course also preoccupied with the perennial theological chess problem of how to account for evil without involving God in it. But still the argument runs: if God does seem to be the author of evil, his power is too great to be questioned; which, if true, is still the impotent and unredeeming truth that does not satisfy Job. Two opposed attitudes, however, have been developing through the drama. Elihu, pointing to the stars in plate 12, insists: "Look upon the heavens & behold the clouds which are higher than thou" (cf. Job 35:5). But in the hymn to wisdom which forms part of Job's speech in chapter 28, it is said: "Neither is {wisdom} found in the land of the living. The depth saith, It is not in me: and the sea saith, It is not with me" [28:13–14]. God comes down on the side of Job and not Elihu. The implication of what he says is, in effect: don't look into the objective world to find me: I'm not there. Even if you carried your search to the mainsprings of creation, you would find no help there. The answer to the question of how you can get out of your calamities is not concealed in the question of how you got into them. This last point brings the Book of Job closer to Blake's view of the fall than even the story of Adam in Eden, where the fall results from a breach of contract, reassuring to theological lawyers but something of an obstacle to poets, including even Milton. We notice that Blake's later accounts of the fall, notably the one in *Jerusalem* 29, echo Job rather than Genesis.

If we are right, it looks as though Blake's vision of Job was a pretty drastic overhaul of the original, for this seems to imply that the God of the opening scenes with Satan and the God who answers Job out of the whirlwind are opposed principles, whereas the text clearly regards them as the same God. And yet in Blake they are really the same God too. The true God for Blake is the creative imagination of man, the eternal Jesus whose religion is the Everlasting Gospel, and all false gods are the shadows projected by this imagination into the outer world. Job's progress, as Blake sees it, is from a God projected into the sky, an amiable Providence who cannot survive the first disasters of experience, to the recovery or resurrection of this God in Job's own mind. The metaphor of a lawsuit hangs over the entire book: Job keeps trying to identify his prosecutor and to call on his advocate (the word translated "redeemer" in 19:25). He eventually finds that the former is the ghost of the latter.

For Blake the God who is man's mind and the narcissistic reflection of this God in nature have faced each other in every age of history. The tendencies in man to be "idolatrous to his own shadow"[6] and yet continually to recover his own creative powers alternate like the pillar of cloud and the pillar of fire in the Exodus story. In *A Vision of the Last Judgment* Blake speaks of "That Angel of the Divine Presence mention'd in Exodus, xiv c., 19 v. & in other Places; this Angel is frequently call'd by the Name of Jehovah Elohim, The 'I am' of the Oaks of Albion" [K610/E559]. The Angel of the Divine Presence is the existential reality, or "I am," of God, who when projected into the outer world becomes the deified order of nature. In the latter situation two characters in Blake are identified with this Angel: Laocoön, strangled by the serpents of reasoning, and the God of Job in plate 2, about to resign in favour of Satan. The verse in Exodus that Blake refers to reads, "And the angel of God, which went before the camp of Israel, removed and went behind them; and the pillar of the cloud went from before their face, and stood behind them" [Exodus 14:19]. This suggests the Angel coming the other way, from the outer world into the human consciousness, and thereby making possible, for Israel, the great feat of crossing the Red Sea, escaping from Egypt, and achieving its identity as a community.

The "whirlwind" out of which God answers Job is thus, for Blake, closely akin to, perhaps identical with, the "vortex" in *Milton* which takes Milton from "Heaven" to earth, earth being of course the only place where "Heaven" can be actualized. Milton enters Blake's left foot, but ordinarily, when the projected God becomes the real one, the Word of human imagination, what he enters is the ear, which is also a kind of vortex, called "labyrinthine" in *Jerusalem*, and described in *The Book of Thel*, in a very different context, as a "whirlpool fierce to draw creations in" [K130/E6]. In the margin of plate 12, the lowest point of the series, marking the consolidation of error which is necessary before it can be thrown off, we see the sleeping Albion with his emanations rising into the sky and becoming the withdrawn and alienated universe of Satan. In the margin of plate 13 we see the "Eyes" of God forming a single gigantic "whirlwind" in which the God speaking to Job is Job's contemporary, so to speak. In Blake's symbolism there are seven Eyes, of whom Jehovah and Jesus are the sixth and seventh, but actually every "Eye" is Jesus, the divine and human Logos, when imaginatively used. In the parallel between the Job engravings and the tarot trumps suggested by Professor Damon (*Blake Dictionary*, s.v. "Job"), the thirteenth occupies the position of Christ the Hanged Man, the archetypal martyr whose ordeal eventually turns into triumph. In plate 17 the God whom Job finally sees is clearly Christ, and the verses from the Gospel of John quoted at the bottom indicate that the only possible visualized form of God is the Son of Man.

In both the poem itself and in Blake a strong emphasis is thrown on the destroyed and reintegrated *community* of Job. This is essential for that aspect of the symbolism in which Job represents not simply *a* man but mankind as a whole. And yet Job has to be an individual too, for Satan's assault on him is part of a struggle between alienation and identity in which the former carries its conquests up to the very last stronghold of the latter, which is the individual consciousness. Everything Job has, as distinct from what he is, disappears into the illusory satanic world of time. He is alienated from his own body by his boils, and from society by the accusing or "Elect" friends, leaving Job himself in the isolated position of the "Reprobate" prophet, the scapegoat driven like Elijah into the wilderness, with only his wife to represent the "Redeemed." Finally Elihu, pointing to the stars so far above him, alienates him from his earlier view of God, who is now wholly replaced by the accuser. With the turning point of plate 13 the community starts rebuilding again, extending to a risen God in plate 16, the friends in plate 18, and a still larger community in plate 19.

This ambiguity between Job as individual and Job as social being or patriarch is of a kind central to all mythical structures of this descent-and-return shape. The suffering Job, we said, must be an individual, but when we think of the restored Job as an individual continuous with his previous sufferings, difficulties arise. The origin of the Book of Job appears to have been an ancient folk tale preserved in the prose beginning and ending of the book we now have, and in such a folk tale the restoration of Job as an individual can be accepted without question. But for a work so profound as the existing book, restoration could only be the arbitrary act of a deity quite separate from Job, and a somewhat vulgar act at that. That is, the restored Job would have to lose his memory to feel that three new daughters could "make up for" the murdering of the previous daughters. To give the restoration any point, we must allegorize the individual Job, as all commentary, including this one, is obliged to do to some extent. Otherwise, we appear to be assuming that when Job improves his state of mind or his theology, his misery disappears too, which takes us back to the point at which the book began, and makes the book itself pointless. To say that Job is restored in a different world from the world of his sufferings is more logically consistent, but considerably impoverishes the human significance of the story.

The general critical principle involved here is that in a descent-and-return mythical structure the individual descends; the community returns. Temptation, alienation, despair, decisive choice, death itself, are ordeals that only the individual can carry to their limit. But only a re-created society, like the one that crystallizes in the final scene of a comedy around a hero's marriage, can fully experience the sense of a brave new world. In plate 20 Job's arms, outspread over his daughters, show that he with his daughters forms part of a larger human body, so that although the objective order from which his calamities came has been annihilated for Job, the calamities being depicted on the walls "In the shadows of Possibility," as Blake says in *Jerusalem* [92.18; K739/E252], Job's renewed state is not a subjective one. This ambiguity of "human body," which may be an individual or a society, is involved in the contrast between the natural body which dies and the spiritual body which rises again. Job has a "vile body" given over to boils, but it is in his "flesh" (Job 19:26) that he sees God, the subject of plate 17.

The dialectic between the existential and the projected aspects of God which Blake extracts from his text is accompanied by a parallel dialectic between two aspects of Satan. For Blake, Satan does not disappear from the action after the beginning, nor does Job, as we suggested earlier, really fail to learn the truth about the origin of his calamities. Satan returns to the action in the form of the two monsters, Behemoth and Leviathan, whom God points out to Job as the climax of his revelation. The Satan of the opening scenes is the regent of the universe, the prince of the power of the air, the controlling power of nature as nature really is, indifferent to human values, as full of death and disaster as of life, and caring nothing for the individual. Job suffers not because of anything he has done but because he is in this condition, as all of us are. Satan achieved his power through God's permission, or, to come closer to Blake, through the inevitable collapse of all human efforts to unite the vision of innocence, of the world as created and protected, with the "contrary" vision of experience. Such efforts, as we remarked earlier, look plausible only to those who happen to be both moral and prosperous. But this state is purely a matter of temporary luck, and Job's sufferings exemplify a principle often referred to elsewhere in Blake, that if we stay too long in Beulah it turns into Ulro.

Job in his original prosperity is an imaginative child: but his childlike state of innocence turns into experience and his vision of innocence, like the child's, is driven into the depths of his mind, where it becomes a helpless but still defiant part of his "integrity," a bound Orc. Satan's world is a world in which everybody is an object or thing, and the pressure put on Job to make him admit that he is a thing too is very powerful, but not omnipotent. Satan's world, to adapt a phrase of Kierkegaard, *is* but does not *exist*. Job begins to exist, in this sense, when he remains defiant and calls loudly for some explanation of what has happened to him, paying no attention to the frantic expostulations of his friends and Elihu that such an attitude is blasphemous and will only make matters worse. His existence is at first negative: that is, to be a conscious being is to be isolated, separated from everything else. Hence he feels that the satanic order is not simply indifferent but is for some reason actively hostile. This attitude becomes positive with God's speech, and Job begins to feel not separated from everything else but identified, or, as Blake would say, outlined. The turning point comes when Job realizes that the satanic state of experience is not something inevitable or ultimately mysterious but something to be fought, and that the dethroned vision of innocence is something he can fight it with.

Just as the crucial turning point of the action is between plates 12 and 13, so the crucial act of renewed vision is between plates 14 and 15. Plate 14 is the reappearance of the vision of innocence, the Beulah vision, except that it is coming the other way, out of Job's mind and not from his circumstances. There are three levels in this plate: Job and his friends are on earth; above them is a Demiurge or creator-God controlling the order of nature; and above that is the infinite human universe, in which the morning stars and the sons of God are the same thing. The next step is to realize that Satan is the enemy of God, that his rule is not inevitable but is to be fought by God's creative power, and that this creative power exists nowhere at present except in man's creative power. At that point we pass into plate 15, where there are only two levels, God and Job united on top, and below them the cycle of nature inhabited by Behemoth and Leviathan.

These monsters are identical with Satan, except that, being Satan revealed instead of Satan mysterious and disguised as God, they represent, not so much the natural miseries of drought and famine and pestilence, as the social and political miseries symbolized mainly, in the Bible, by Egypt and Babylon, and in the Book of Job itself by the Sabean raiders. Ezekiel (chapter 29) identifies the Leviathan with the Pharaoh of Egypt, and Daniel (chapter 4) tells how Nebuchadnezzar of Babylon turned into Behemoth, the subject of several of Blake's pictures. This political aspect of the monsters is brought out in the phrases emphasized by Blake on plate 15: Behemoth is "chief of the ways of God" and Leviathan is "King over all the Children of Pride" [Job 40:19, 41:34]. As the power in man that makes for tyranny rather than civilization, they can be, if not destroyed, at least brought under some measure of control, like the Blatant Beast in Spenser. At the same time the root of tyranny, for Blake, is still natural religion, the establishing of the order of nature, whether theistically or atheistically regarded, as the circumference of human effort (the original meaning of "Urizen"). Hence we are all born inside the belly of Leviathan, the world of stars and its indefinite space, but those who can see Leviathan for what he is have been placed outside him, like Jonah, and like Job in plate 15. After Job has attained this enlightenment, the prophecy of Jesus is fulfilled and Satan falls from heaven (pl. 16).

Blake's vision of the Book of Job was certainly a work of the creative imagination, but what made it possible was a powerful critical analysis of the book. This criticism performed what we are slowly beginning to realize is the essential critical act: it put the Book of Job into its literary context. That context, the Christian Bible as a whole, lay of course ready to hand. Yet to comprehend the story of Job as a microcosm or epitome of the whole Bible, and to comprehend it as intensely as Blake did, and as the quotations on the engravings show that he did, took a critical mind of first-rate quality. We often tend to associate Blake's criticism with what he rejected, and to find him in consequence somewhat erratic. But when we examine his attitude to what he accepted, and see that he was a great critic too, we can understand how he himself can be sympathetic to his own critics, in the sense of being, however difficult, uniquely rewarding to those who are willing to make an adequate effort. Professor Damon was one of the first of those who made such an effort, and his success, the chief reason for the present book, points up its own moral.

26

William Blake (III)

25 August 1971

From the typescript in NFF, 1988, box 4, file k. Originally presented as a lecture for the Open University, and recorded for the BBC Open University program. Reprinted in RW, *192–201. An earlier typescript with holograph corrections is in NFF, 1988, box 4, file j.*

William Blake was an engraver by profession, and he used an engraving process to produce his poems. The details of the process are still not certain, but the essentials are clear enough. He traced the words of his poems and the designs that accompanied them on a copper plate in some acid-resisting material, then immersed the plate in acid so that it ate away the copper and left the design and text in relief, then stamped the design on paper, and finally coloured the design by hand. He used this method for two kinds of poetry: short lyrics, and longer poems with mythical characters in them, generally called "Prophecies." Most of his better-known lyrics are in two collections called *Songs of Innocence* and *Songs of Experience*. The *Songs of Innocence*, one of his first engraved works, appeared in 1789, the *Songs of Experience* in 1794. But after 1794 Blake always engraved the two series together, with a subtitle connecting them, and reading, "showing the two contrary states of the human soul."

The poems in the two books, then, relate to each other, and Blake intended them to have such a relation. Sometimes the poems are linked by identical titles: there is a *Holy Thursday* and a *Nurse's Song* in both books. Sometimes two poems are linked by contrasting titles. One such contrasting pair is *The Lamb* in the *Songs of Innocence* and *The Tyger* in the *Songs of Experience*. Here is *The Lamb*:

Little Lamb, who made thee?
Dost thou know who made thee?
Gave thee life, & bid thee feed
By the stream & o'er the mead;
Gave thee clothing of delight,
Softest clothing, wooly, bright;
Gave thee such a tender voice,
Making all the vales rejoice?
Little Lamb, who made thee?
Dost thou know who made thee?

Little Lamb, I'll tell thee,
Little Lamb, I'll tell thee:
He is called by thy name,
For he calls himself a Lamb.
He is meek, & he is mild;
He became a little child.
I a child, & thou a lamb,
We are called by his name.
Little Lamb, God bless thee!
Little Lamb, God bless thee! [K115/E8–9]

The *Songs of Innocence* are about the state of innocence, which has always been represented in literature by the child. In Blake the child is innocent not because he is morally good, but because he is born civilized. That is, he makes the civilized assumption that the world has a human shape and a human meaning. He thinks the world was made for his benefit, and that his parents were put there to look after him. In this poem, the child asks the lamb the first question of the catechism that most middle-class children were taught in Blake's day: "Who made you?" The answer is God, which in Christian terms means Jesus Christ. The child is so proud of his knowledge, and so sure of the answer, that he doesn't give the lamb time to bleat; he instantly answers his own question. Both he and the lamb were made by Jesus, and the proof of this is that Jesus himself is called both a child and a lamb.

Here is *The Tyger*:

Tyger! Tyger! burning bright
In the forests of the night,

What immortal hand or eye
Could frame thy fearful symmetry?

In what distant deeps or skies
Burnt the fire of thine eyes?
On what wings dare he aspire?
What the hand dare sieze the fire?

And what shoulder, & what art,
Could twist the sinews of thy heart?
And when thy heart began to beat,
What dread hand? & what dread feet?

What the hammer? what the chain?
In what furnace was thy brain?
What the anvil? what dread grasp
Dare its deadly terrors clasp?

When the stars threw down their spears,
And water'd heaven with their tears,
Did he smile his work to see?
Did he who made the Lamb make thee?

Tyger! Tyger! burning bright
In the forests of the night,
What immortal hand or eye
Dare frame thy fearful symmetry? [K214/E24–5]

We say that if the child thinks the world makes sense, that's only because he doesn't know any better; when he grows up he will find that the world is not at all like this. The child's own life is taken care of by his parents, and it is natural for him to believe that the whole order of nature is similarly taken care of by a paternal or providential God. But the world of experience that the adult lives in is a world of nature, a subhuman, submoral, subintelligent, ruthless, ferocious world. If we think of this world as created by a benevolent Father-God, we can put only lambs into it: tigers don't fit such a world. The official Christian explanation is that God created a pure and innocent world, full of lambs, and pronounced it good, but that man was disobedient and so somehow lamb-eating tigers got into it: we don't know how, but it's all man's fault. Blake is not satisfied with this answer, if it is an answer. The climax of the poem comes in the question, "Did he who made the Lamb make thee?" Some students of Blake have tried to answer this question, either by yes or by no, but they would have been wiser to leave it a question. The argument of *The Lamb* moves from the child and the lamb towards the figure of Jesus, who created both and is both. But the argument of *The Tyger* focuses simply on the tiger himself: his creator is only there in a series of questions. So we begin to wonder whether the conception of "creation" applies at all to the kind of world the tiger is in.

Perhaps there are two kinds of creation. There is what institutional religion calls "the" creation, the physical environment of man. And if we think of "the" creation as something deliberately produced by an omniscient God, and think of it in terms of what man wants and could imagine having, then any child can see that "the" creation is a monstrous bungle, and that any God who made it must be what Housman calls him, a brute and a blackguard.[1] There's another kind of creation, which man is capable of, and which produces the arts among other things. A lot of bungle gets into this too, but the genuine basis of it is the child's simple belief that things ought to make sense, that subjects and objects, children and lambs, ought to be produced by the same kind of creative power.

The moral that Blake draws is a revolutionary one. He watched the American and French Revolutions going on in his day, and felt that they showed where the world was going. When the child grows into an adult, and finds that reality doesn't make any benevolent or providential sense, what happens to his original innocent vision? The answer seems easy enough now, but Blake was the first poet in English literature to give the answer. When the child grows into an adult, his innocent vision is driven underground into what we now call the subconscious, where it becomes a boiling, heaving mass of suppressed desires and energies, very largely sexual in nature as the child matures. This means that humanity, individually and socially, exists on two levels. The individual has, in his conscious and waking world, an ego trying to come to terms with reality as it sees it, trying to believe that obeying law is the only good we can do, because obedience makes life predictable and eliminates uncertainty. Underneath is a squirming Titan of sex and desire, bound under its volcano of suppressed power. Society has, similarly, an uneasy ruling class threatened by revolution. These two levels of mind and society are given symbolic names in Blake's Prophecies. The upper level of experience he calls Urizen, a word of Greek origin from the same root as horizon, meaning a bound or limit. The world of the bound Titan is called Orc, from the Latin Orcus, hell, because hell for Blake is the state of having desires and being unable to gratify them. Urizen and Orc are an old man and a young man; Urizen is associated with snow, clouds, winter, bleaching bones, and the white cliffs of Albion, Orc with summer, fire, sex, and "the vineyards of red France."[2]

Let us look at another poem in the *Songs of Innocence, The Chimney Sweeper*:

> When my mother died I was very young,
> And my Father sold me while yet my tongue
> Could scarcely cry "'weep! 'weep! 'weep! 'weep!"
> So your chimneys I sweep, & in soot I sleep.
>
> There's little Tom Dacre, who cried when his head,
> That curl'd like a lambs back, was shav'd: so I said
> "Hush, Tom! never mind it, for when your head's bare
> "You know that the soot cannot spoil your white hair."
>
> And so he was quiet, & that very night
> As Tom was a-sleeping, he had such a sight!
> That thousands of sweepers, Dick, Joe, Ned, & Jack,
> Were all of them lock'd up in coffins of black.
>
> And by came an Angel who had a bright key,
> And he open'd the coffins & set them all free;
> Then down a green plain leaping, laughing, they run,
> And wash in a river, and shine in the Sun.
>
> Then naked & white, all their bags left behind,
> They rise upon clouds and sport in the wind;
> And the Angel told Tom, if he'd be a good boy,
> He'd have God for his father, & never want joy.
>
> And so Tom awoke; and we rose in the dark,
> And got with our bags & our brushes to work.
> Tho' the morning was cold, Tom was happy & warm;
> So if all do their duty they need not fear harm. [K117–18/E10]

If we read this poem carelessly, we may get the impression that the function of religion is to make the poor and exploited content with their lot; also that if chimney sweepers do what they are told no harm can befall them. One has only to glance at some of the facts about the treatment of chimney sweeps in Blake's day to realize that if this is what the poem means, it is the most intolerably smug poem in English literature. Blake not being at all a smug poet, we must have got it wrong. If we look again at the last line, "So if all do their duty they need not fear harm," we see that "all" can only mean society as a whole. The poem is about the state of innocence, so it ends with children made happy and warm by a dream of the resurrection. But this dream is part of a submerged world of desire which, if it is suppressed long enough, can turn explosive. Away off in the background is the comment that the same dream that keeps children quiet can also blow their exploiters sky-high.

Let us now look at one of the early "Prophecies," *America*, engraved in 1793. In this poem the revolutionary spirit of America is Orc, and he is opposed by the reactionary government of Great Britain, called "The Guardian Prince of Albion." For Blake, the great precedent for revolution was the exodus of Israel from Egypt. The Bible describes how Israel gathered its twelve tribes (there were actually thirteen of them), faced the power of Egypt, crossed the Red Sea, and entered the desert. At that point Israel began to decline as a revolutionary force and became a new tyranny, worshipping the same god of moral law that the Egyptians had symbolized in their pyramids, that is, tombs of dead tyrants. The revolutionary side of Israel, for Blake, is symbolized by the pillar of fire; the reactionary side by the pillar of cloud, the ten commandments, and the rise of the moral law. The thirteen revolutionary tribes became worshippers of the mechanical order of nature symbolized by the twelve signs of the zodiac and the sun. Finally, the complete defeat of the revolutionary spirit is symbolized by the story of the hanging of the serpent of brass on a pole, which Blake identifies with the martyrdom of Orc by Urizen.

The same cycle recurred many centuries later, when Jesus led a revolt against the Jewish moral law. Christianity also declined from a revolutionary religion into an agent of moral law, and had reached the end of its historical cycle with the revolutions of Blake's own day. This Christian cycle is prefigured in the life of Jesus with his twelve disciples, the crucifixion corresponding to the death of Orc at the end of the cycle, and the resurrection to the beginning of a new era. If we look further back in the Bible, we see a dim memory of a previous cycle connected with the story of Adam and Eve, where we again have a serpent and a sinister tree. The champion of *America*, Orc, thus describes himself:

> The Terror answer'd: "I am Orc, wreath'd round the accursed tree:
> "The times are ended; shadows pass, the morning 'gins to break;
> "The fiery joy, that Urizen perverted to ten commands,
> "What night he led the starry hosts thro' the wide wilderness,
> "That stony law I stamp to dust: and scatter religion abroad
> "To the four winds as a torn book, & none shall gather the leaves;
> "But they shall rot on desart sands, & consume in bottomless deeps,
> "To make the desarts blossom, & the deeps shrink to their fountains,
> "And to renew the fiery joy, and burst the stony roof;
> "That pale religious lechery, seeking Virginity,
> "May find it in a harlot, and in coarse-clad honesty
> "The undefil'd, tho' ravish'd in her cradle night and morn;
> "For every thing that lives is holy, life delights in life;
> "Because the soul of sweet delight can never be defil'd.
> "Fires inwrap the earthly globe, yet man is not consum'd;
> "Amidst the lustful fires he walks: his feet become like brass,
> "His knees and thighs like silver, & his breast and head like gold."
>
> [8.1–17; K198–9/E54]

Here Orc describes himself as the revolutionary power which manifested itself at the Exodus and at the time of Christ and is again reappearing. The same symbols recur each time, so we are not surprised to find that early American flags featured serpents, trees, stars, the colours red and white, and a strong emphasis on the number thirteen.

In another poem, *The Marriage of Heaven and Hell*, "heaven" is the moral order, symbolized by the circling stars in the sky, and "hell" is the buried furnace of suppressed human desire that is going to explode and set the heavens on fire. The Bible prophesies a similar show of fireworks at the end of time which is called in theology the last "consummation," but "consummation" means sexual contact as well as burning up. The explosion of "hell" is nothing less than the resurrection of Man freed from the cycles of history. The Bible says that Man was born in paradise, but that a jealous God shut man out of paradise and locked the door. Blake says that in his day man is pounding on that door and will not stop until he has broken it down.

> The ancient tradition that the world will be consumed in fire at the end of six thousand years is true, as I have heard from Hell.
>
> For the cherub with his flaming sword is hereby commanded to leave his guard at [the] tree of life; and when he does, the whole creation will be consumed and appear infinite and holy, whereas it now appears finite & corrupt.
>
> This will come to pass by an improvement of sensual enjoyment.
>
> But first the notion that man has a body distinct from his soul is to be expunged; this I shall do by printing in the infernal method, by corrosives, which in Hell are salutary and medicinal, melting apparent surfaces away, and displaying the infinite which was hid.
>
> If the doors of perception were cleansed every thing would appear to man as it is, infinite.
>
> For man has closed himself up, till he sees all things thro' narrow chinks of his cavern. [pl. 14; K154/E39]

For Blake's great revolutionary predecessor Milton, liberty is something that man does not want, but that God is determined he shall have. For Blake, however, there is no God except the God who works through, and as, man, and the creative imagination of man is the God dwelling in him. This means that the vision of the artist is the vision that defines the goal of man's freedom. The artist's work, unlike the philosopher's, is based on sense experience. What we see and hear is nature, but what we see in painting and hear in music is the humanity buried in nature. Blake's poetry focuses on the final moment of vision, which he calls the Last Judgment, in which the world appears to everybody the way that it now appears in art. To the thinker or reasoner, the body is not important, and established religions are always preaching some theory of evaporating essence. Man's body is going to die, but he has a "soul" which will survive in a disembodied state. But for the artist, the freedom of man can only mean the freedom of the body, so Blake's revolution is a sexual revolution as well, or what he calls "an improvement of sensual enjoyment."

As Blake went on, he tended increasingly to think of the rebellion of Orc against Urizen as merely something that turns the cycle of history. Every Orc turns into a Urizen sooner or later: the Americans kept on owning slaves: the French set up Napoleon as an imperialistic dictator. Only man's creative power can free him, and this power is buried in him even more deeply than the desire that produces revolutions and wish-fulfilment dreams. This deeper creative power Blake calls Los, and Los is the hero of all Blake's later Prophecies, including his tremendous epic *The Four Zoas*. The four "Zoas" are the four elements of the human imagination, Los, Orc, Urizen, and a fourth power associated with strength, called Tharmas. When one of these powers tries to dominate the others, man falls into the slavery of worshipping idols that he has created himself. When they are reintegrated, man finds himself in the world described in the closing lines of the poem:

> The Sun has left his blackness & has found a fresher morning,
> And the mild moon rejoices in the clear & cloudless night,
> And Man walks forth from midst of the fires: the evil is all consum'd.
> His eyes behold the Angelic spheres arising night & day;
> The stars consum'd like a lamp blown out, & in their stead, behold
> The Expanding Eyes of Man behold the depths of wondrous worlds!
> One Earth, one sea beneath; nor Erring Globes wander, but Stars
> Of fire rise up nightly from the Ocean; & one Sun
> Each morning, like a New born Man, issues with songs & joy
> Calling the Plowman to his Labour & the Shepherd to his rest.
> He walks upon the Eternal Mountains, raising his heavenly voice,
> Conversing with the Animal forms of Wisdom night & day,
> That, risen from the Sea of fire, renew'd walk o'er the Earth;
> For Tharmas brought his flocks upon the hills, & in the Vales
> Around the Eternal Man's bright tent, the little Children play
> Among the wooly flocks. The hammer of Urthona sounds
> In the deep caves beneath; his limbs renew'd, his Lions roar
> Around the Furnaces & in Evening sport upon the plains.
> They raise their faces from the Earth, conversing with the Man:
>
> "How is it we have walk'd thro' fires & yet are not consum'd?
> "How is it that all things are chang'd, even as in ancient times?"

[K379/E406–7]

27

Blake's Reading of the Book of Job (II)

1976

From SM, *228–44. Rewritten from the original version (no. 25 in this volume), which was published seven years earlier. Both versions are included in the present volume for the insight they provide into NF's process of revision. The rewritten version is longer, and the argument is significantly rearranged in order to explore the significance of the Job story for Blake's thought.*

For all the discussion that there has been over Blake's illustrations to the Book of Job, much of the best of it contributed by the subject of this *Festschrift*,[1] there is perhaps still room for more consideration of how Blake read the book. Everyone realizes that Blake recreated the book in his engravings, and was not simply illustrating it. At the same time he appears to be following it with considerable fidelity, and his attitude toward it, in striking contrast to his attitude toward the original of the other great work of his last period, the illustrations to Dante's *Commedia*, seems to be on the whole an attitude of critical acceptance. He remarked, apropos of Homer, that "Every Poem must necessarily be a perfect Unity," but that the *Iliad* is not "peculiarly so" [K778/E269], which implies that the perfect unity is potential in the poem itself, and is really achieved by the reader. The sense of unity that one feels about the Job engravings, considered as a series, indicates that Blake extracted a corresponding unity out of his text.

This fact is more complicated than it looks, because despite the Book of Job's formidable literary reputation, it is not easy to see how its argument makes a sense congenial to Blake. It begins with the astonishing scenes of Satan in the court of God, where Satan has the role, always central to his nature for Blake, of the accuser of mankind. He suggests that God has set things up in such a way that he can't lose: if he rewards obedience, he gives man so powerful a motive for being obedient that the service of God becomes a conditioned reflex. He may be raising the issue of man's free will, but not in a way that could ever help man to become free. Later in the poem, Job's three friends keep revolving around the central pseudo-problem of the righteousness of God's ways. Those who do well will be rewarded and those who do evil will be punished; therefore it must be a crime to be unfortunate. If it were not, God would not be a just God. The suppressed premise here is that God administers both the human moral law and the physical natural law, but it never occurs to them to doubt this. Blake doubts it, however: it is the basis of what he repudiates as natural religion.

The friends' view of providence is easily refuted by experience, but when it is, they can give two possible answers. One is to say that God's ways are inscrutable, although they seem to the unprejudiced reader to be merely insane on such premises. The other is to assume that God's providence will manifest itself in another world, from which no evidence ever leaks out. If it appears that "honesty is the best policy" is nonsense, the argument shifts to "maybe it doesn't seem so now, but you just wait."

The arguments of the three friends reach a deadlock, and Elihu takes over, to overwhelm Job with the eloquence of what he has to say "on God's behalf" (36:2), but although his eloquence is genuine enough, he is concerned mostly with restating the earlier arguments. When God himself answers Job out of the whirlwind and asks "Who is this that darkeneth counsel by words without knowledge?" (38:2), apparently meaning Elihu, we expect the definitive revelation to which the whole drama seems to have been leading up. But we feel uncomfortable about the way in which God triumphantly displays a number of trump cards that seem to belong to a different game. He asks Job a series of rhetorical questions which have a hectoring and bullying sound to them. Were you around when I made the world, or do you understand all about how it was made? No? Well, then, why are you raising doubts about my administrative competence? This is followed by poems on the two beasts Behemoth and Leviathan—remarkable poems, but we wonder about their relevance to Job's boils and murdered children. Job replies meekly that he has "uttered that I understood not; things too wonderful for me, which I knew not . . . wherefore I abhor myself, and repent in dust and ashes" (42:3, 6). God then appears to say, in effect, "Well, that's better," and forthwith restores Job to prosperity. Job's friends and their natural religion, apparently, have really been right all along, even though they are said not to be. Somehow it does not sound like the kind of argument that Blake would regard with much favour.

The Book of Job is technically a comedy by virtue of Job's restoration in the last few verses, but the comic conclusion seems so wrenched and arbitrary that it is hard to think of it as anything but a wantonly spoiled tragedy. In all the gropings that Job and the three friends and Elihu all make after some explanation for Job's plight, one explanation that they never speculate about is the one that has already been given to the reader. It never occurs to them that God might have deliberately exposed Job to such an ordeal in order to win a wager with Satan. They are all, including Job himself, far too pious and sincere for such a notion ever to occur to them. The prologue in heaven hangs sardonically over the whole debate, and we wait for God to reveal to Job something of what the reader knows. But not a word is said about Satan at the end of the action, and Job learns nothing about the original compact. The simplest answer is to suppose that the Book of Job, begun by a colossal poetic genius, fell into the hands of a superstitious editor whose attitude was a cruder version of that of Job's friends, and who twisted one of the world's profoundest poems into an obscurantist tirade against the use of the questioning intelligence. Something like this could have happened: there are signs of nervous editing, as in so many parts of the Bible, and it is impossible to say how far expurgation has gone. But such a hypothesis is of no use to us: the version we have is the only one that has influenced later literature and religion, and the only one that Blake read. He must have read it, however, in a way very different from the summary of it just given.

First of all, the comic conclusion, the restoring of Job to prosperity, would not have seemed arbitrary to Blake, but inevitable. The Bible as a whole takes the form of a U-shaped narrative in which Adam loses his garden and is led back, at the end of time, to a restored garden which is also a city. This means, according to Milton, that he loses paradise as a physical environment and regains it as an inner state of mind. The latter, Michael tells Adam in *Paradise Lost*, is "happier far" than the original Eden. Blake would have seen the story of Job as an epitome of the Biblical narrative, in which the final restoration provides a greater happiness than the original state. As Blake sees the story, Job begins in the state of Beulah, the pastoral repose of plate 1, and ends in the apocalyptic state of Eden (in Blake's sense of the term) of plate 21. The contrasts are obvious and have often been noted: the musical instruments have been taken down from the trees in the later plate, suggesting, by way of Psalm 137, that even the original state still had something of alienation and exile about it; the sheep have wakened up, and, in contrast to the first plate, the sun is rising and the moon setting. The sacrificial altar common to the foreground of both plates contains significant inscriptions about the importance of outgrowing the literal and ritual aspects of religion which sacrifice represents. The genuine form of sacrifice, self-sacrifice, or what Blake calls the annihilation of the Selfhood, is the real subject of plate 18.

Job is one of the "wisdom" books, and the primitive conception of wisdom, still clearly visible in the Old Testament, is that of following the tried and tested ways, the ways sanctioned by custom and tradition. This means that wisdom is primarily an attribute of advanced age, when one has had most experience in being conservative. In the Book of Proverbs and elsewhere there is a strong emphasis on bringing up young people in the ways of their seniors, and on being prompt to punish them if they diverge. There are three stages of a conflict of age and youth in the Job plates: the relation of the God of the opening plates to an obviously much younger Satan; the relation of the three friends to the youthful Elihu; and the relation of the God of the closing plates (Jehovah, more or less) to Jesus.

The God of plates 2 and 5 is the weak, sick *dieu fainéant* who is the God projected by Job himself into the natural order. As long as a virtuous moral life can be associated with a comfortable physical one, such a deity may seem providential and benignant. But when the crunch comes he turns into Satan, the author of evil and disaster. This fact is not realized by Job, his three friends, or Elihu, all of whom try to work out some explanation of Job's plight in terms of God alone. But for Blake the God of the opening plates resigns his power to Satan in the same way that God the Father transfers power to his Son in *Paradise Lost*, and similarly demonstrates by doing so the essential link between their natures. Many years earlier Blake had remarked that "in the Book of Job, Milton's Messiah is call'd Satan" [*MHH*, pl. 5; K150/E34].

The identity of the God of plate 2 with Satan is clear in the nightmare of plate 11, where at the bottom of the plate Paul's description of the Antichrist is quoted. The Antichrist is notable for his superficial resemblance to Christ, and similarly, all gods portrayed as old men in the sky are variants of the Satan whom Paul, again, calls the prince of the power of the air. Over the head of God in plate 2 is the inscription *Malak Yahweh,* along with the translation "The Angel of the Divine Presence." This recalls the passage in *A Vision of the Last Judgment* in which Blake speaks of "That Angel of the Divine Presence mention'd in Exodus, xiv c., 19 v. & in other Places; this Angel is frequently call'd by the Name of Jehovah Elohim, The 'I am' of the Oaks of Albion" [K610/E559]. Apparently Blake means that the existential reality or "I am" of God is identical with the human imagination, but when it gets projected into the outer world of nature it is perverted into something evil. Laocoön, strangled by the serpents of reasoning, is also identified by Blake with the perverted form of this Angel. In plate 2 the primary Biblical reference may be to Numbers 22:22, where the *Malak Yahweh* blocks the path of Balaam as his "Satan," or adversary. The verse in Exodus that Blake refers to reads, "And the angel of God, which went before the camp of Israel, removed and went behind them; and the pillar of the cloud went from before their face, and stood behind them" [14:19]. The two tendencies in man to be "idolatrous to his own Shadow"[2] and yet continually to recover his own creative powers alternate like the pillar of cloud and the pillar of fire in the Exodus story. When the Angel comes the other way, from the outer world into the human consciousness, it makes possible, for Israel, the great revolutionary feat of escaping from Egypt and achieving its own identity.

The design on plate 5 takes the form of a vortex or gyre in which an imaginary God turns into a real devil, the order of nature which everything genuine and creative in human life has to fight against. The fall of Job repeats the fall of Adam, and its cause is the same: the pseudo-knowledge of good and evil which first tries to separate them, and ends by realizing that in such knowledge evil is the rule and good an accidental and precarious exception. This vortex is again reversed in plate 13, where it becomes the "whirlwind" out of which God answers Job. We remember the vortex in *Milton* which takes Milton from "Heaven" to earth, earth being the place where "Heaven" has to be realized. Milton enters Blake's left foot, but ordinarily, when the projected God reverses his movement and becomes the real one, the Word of human imagination, what he enters is the ear, which is also a kind of vortex, called "labyrinthine" in *Jerusalem*, and described in *The Book of Thel*, in a very different context, as a "whirlpool fierce to draw creations in" [K130/E6]. But the God of the whirlwind in plate 13 has to be clarified a good deal before he becomes the genuine human imagination: this process is completed in plate 17 with the significant caption from Job 42:5: "I have heard of thee by the hearing of the ear: but now mine eye seeth thee." The only New Testament reference to Job, "Ye have heard of the patience of Job, and have seen the end of the Lord" (James 5:11), quoted by Blake on plate 7, repeats this progress from ear to eye. For Blake, no one can "see" God until God becomes a human being, and even then he is not so much what we see as what we see with. Some Renaissance mythographers saw in the story of Narcissus, who exchanged his identity for that of his objective reflection in water, a counterpart to the Biblical story of the fall of Adam, and Blake, describing the fall of Albion in *Jerusalem* in imagery closely related to the Book of Job, also speaks of Albion as becoming "idolatrous to his own shadow." The recovery by Job of his own imagination is Narcissus coming in the opposite direction, the reflected shadow becoming his own substance.

The fact that Blake saw in the story of Job a microcosm of the entire Biblical story is the reason for the two major changes that he makes from what is in the text: the role of Job's wife and the character of the three friends. In the text Job's wife is a Dalila figure, a temptress who suggests that Job renounce his integrity, and this is how Blake depicted her in earlier illustrations of the book. In *Jerusalem* Albion's wife, "Brittannia," is a very shadowy, not to say unnecessary, character: the main theme is the restoration to Albion of his daughter Jerusalem. This emphasis on the restored daughter (apart from the link with *King Lear*, whose three daughters are also Albion's) was derived from a parallel emphasis in the Book of Job, as illustrated here in plate 20. But still, when the Book of Job is thought of as a miniature Bible, Job occupies the place of Adam or Israel or, again, Albion, the symbolic figure of humanity, and Job's wife thus becomes the Eve or Rachel who must form a part of his redemption.

Similarly, the three friends are almost wholly demonic in Blake's illustrations, and are assimilated to the threefold accuser figure who runs through all Blake's work from the early *Accusers of Theft, Adultery and Murder*[3] to Hand in *Jerusalem*, and who are, or is, identified with the three accusers of Socrates (*Jerusalem*, plate 93)[4] and, probably, the three witnesses against Faithful in *The Pilgrim's Progress*. The three friends have been constantly ridiculed, from the Book of Job itself on, as "miserable comforters" (16:2), and yet it is said of them, in a verse quoted on plate 8, that "they sat down with him upon the ground seven days and seven nights, and none spake a word unto him: for they saw that his grief was very great" (2:13). Seven days of silent sympathy from friends who are at least not fair-weather friends, and have nothing to gain from visiting Job in his destitution, may deserve some sympathy in its turn. But when we think of Job as continuously martyred humanity, it is hardly possible to see in the friends anything but representatives of the continuous social anxiety, the Theotormon complex, so to speak, that makes human misery constant by trying to rationalize and explain it away in every crisis. We may note that a still later treatment of the Job story, MacLeish's *J.B.*, follows Blake both in favouring the wife and in denigrating the friends.

The friends, in any case, try to remain loyal to the *dieu fainéant* of the opening plates, the God of natural religion. Nature for Blake is the state of experience, indifferent to human values, exhibiting no sense of design or purpose beyond an automatic and mechanical one, and caring nothing for the individual. Job suffers not because of anything he has done but because he is in the world of Satan or Nature, like the rest of us. Satan achieved his power through God's "permission," or, to come closer to Blake, through the inevitable collapse of all efforts to unite the vision of innocence, of the world as created and protected, with the contrary vision of experience. Such efforts, we said, look plausible only to those who happen to be both "good" and prosperous. But the prosperity is a matter of luck, and Job's sufferings illustrate a principle often referred to elsewhere in Blake, that if we stay in Beulah it will sooner or later turn into "Ulro," that is, "meer Nature or Hell," as Blake calls it in his notes to Swedenborg [K93/E605]. The God of plates 1 to 5 sooner or later turns into what Blake calls the ghost of the priest and king, the conception that rationalizes tyranny.

And just as the senile God of plate 5 is pushed out of the way by a viciously destructive and younger Satan, so the harangues of the three friends give place to the monologue of the young Elihu, who begins with a perfunctory apology for withholding his wisdom for so long while the old men drivelled. Elihu consolidates the confused and variable notions of natural religion that the three friends propound into a closed system of fatalism. He is shown in plate 12 pointing upwards with his left or sinister hand to a sky with twelve stars in it, representing the cycle of the Zodiac. Like all his kind, he insists on the grandeur of nature and the littleness of mankind: "Look upon the heavens and behold the clouds which are higher than thou" (cf. Job 35:5). If we have been reading the Book of Job along with Blake, we have already been told that wisdom is not there, or anywhere else in nature: "The depth saith, [Wisdom] is not in me: and the sea saith, It is not with me" (28:14). Elihu has thus much the same role as that of Newton in *Europe*: he is a spokesman of natural religion so fully articulate that he overreaches himself and blows his whole system, in more than one sense, sky-high. He is a negative agent of Job's emancipation, as Newton is for Blake's time. The words in plate 12 just quoted are attached to the figure of a sleeping old man at the bottom of creation, whose dreams rise up from his head into the stars. This figure is Blake's Albion, and the design recurs in the account of Albion's fall in *Jerusalem*, plate 19.

The third and decisive conflict of age and youth forms the resolution of the sequence, when God as a projected old man in the sky turns into Christ, God as Man, God as the essence of Job himself, whom Job has stopped projecting into creation and has recovered as his own real nature. In Blake's mythology there are seven "Eyes," seven historical and social visions or conceptions, of God, the sixth and seventh being Jehovah and Jesus [*M*, pl. 13, ll. 17–26; K494/E107]. The third, Elohim, is associated with the creation of Adam, or the human form as we know it; the fourth, Shaddai, is a frequent name of God in the Book of Job. Blake may have thought the Book of Job to be or to conceal a very ancient myth, perhaps older than most of the Old Testament. Reminders of this progression of seven Eyes can be seen in the angels of the title page and the shadowy figures behind the appearance of God in the whirlwind in plate 13. But actually every stage of history has to go through the same struggle of replacing "Jehovah," the projected old man in the sky who is Zeus and Jupiter as well, with Jesus, the divine and human Logos, who is every "Eye" when imaginatively used.

The transformation of Jehovah into Jesus occupies the four plates 14, 15, 16, and 17. Job in his original prosperity is an imaginative child, but his childlike state of innocence turns into experience, and his vision of innocence, like the child's, is driven into the submerged part of his mind, where it becomes a helpless but still defiant part of his "integrity," a bound Orc. Satan's world is a world in which everybody is an object or thing, and the pressure put on Job to make him admit that he is a thing too is very powerful, but not omnipotent. Satan's world, to adapt a phrase of Kierkegaard's, *is* but does not *exist*. Job begins to exist, in this sense, when he remains defiant and calls loudly for some explanation of what has happened to him, paying no attention to the frantic expostulations of his friends and Elihu that such an attitude is blasphemous and will only make matters worse. There is a core of truth in what they say, even in the remark that they considered Job "righteous in his own eyes." The *dieu fainéant* who turned into Satan was a creation of Job's mind, and in a sense Job keeps him in business by resisting him, somewhat as Prometheus in Shelley kept Jupiter in business until he recalled his curse.

So Job's existence is at first negative, the existence of an isolated conscious being. In this position he feels that the Satanic order is not simply indifferent but actively hostile. This attitude becomes positive with God's speech, and Job, though still isolated, begins to feel not separated from everything else but identified, or, as Blake would say, outlined. The turning point comes when he realizes that the Satanic state of experience is not something inevitable or ultimately mysterious but something to be fought, and that his dethroned vision of innocence is something that he can fight it with.

If we look at the series of Old Testament books as Blake did, and as the King James Bible usually presents them, in the Septuagint order with the books of the Apocrypha omitted, we see an order which may be the result of sheer accident, but nonetheless points to a simple and profound analysis of the Old Testament as a whole. The books from Genesis to Esther are concerned with law, history, and ritual; the books from Job to Malachi with prophecy, poetry, and wisdom. In this order Job would occupy the place of a poetic and prophetic version of Genesis, an account of the fall of man which avoids the moralizing and the breach of contract so dear to theological lawyers, and concentrates on the limiting of imaginative range and the mutilation of the physical body. We noticed earlier that the account of the fall in *Jerusalem* echoes Job more than it does Genesis. When Albion goes in for "imputing Sin & Righteousness to Individuals" [*J*, 70.17; K709/E224], including himself, the Zoa Luvah, representing Urizen as well as the bound Orc, takes charge of him, smites him with sore boils, and starts him on the dreary path of misery and persecution symbolized in Blake by the "Druid" symbols of serpent and tree, which we find in the stories of the fall of Adam, the fall of Israel (Numbers 21), and the Crucifixion of Christ. We can see traces of a serpent-wound tree in the background of plate 2.

The crucial act of renewed vision is the one between plates 14 and 15, the vision of the Creation and the vision of Behemoth and Leviathan. Plate 14 is the reappearance of the vision of innocence, the Beulah vision of plate 1, except that it is coming the other way, out of Job's mind and not from his circumstances. There are three levels in this plate: Job and his friends are on earth; above them is a Demiurge or creator-God controlling the order of nature; and above that is the infinite human universe, in which the morning stars and the sons of God have become the same thing. It is still an imperfect vision, because, although it does distinguish the "good" world that God originally made from the bad world that man fell into later, it has not yet detached itself from the world of experience. God's rhetorical questions about the creation, his insistence that Job was not present when the world was made, have for Blake a very different meaning from a mere attempt to shout Job down with the voice of his own superego. God is really saying: "don't look into Nature to find me: I'm not there; there's nothing there but idols and demons. Don't look for a first cause: the important question is how can you get out of your situation, not how you got into it. You are not a participant in the creation: your consciousness or imagination is something wholly detached from it. And because you are not a participant in creation you can be delivered from it." The next step is to realize that Satan is the enemy of God, that his rule is not inevitable but is to be fought by God's creative power, and that this creative power is man's creative power. This takes us into plate 15, where there are only two levels, God and Job united on top, and below them the cycle of nature dominated by Behemoth and Leviathan.

In this plate we can see that, for Blake, Satan does not disappear from the action of the Book of Job after the prologue, nor does Job really fail to learn the truth about the Satanic origin of his calamities. Satan is Leviathan, looked at from the right point of view as the body of fallen nature, and not a mysterious cause of human suffering but a symptom of it to be attacked. If we had seen Job restored to prosperity, with all his brand new daughters and livestock, we might not have seen any daughters or livestock: we might have seen nothing but a beggar on a dunghill. But the beggar would know something we do not know, and would have seen something that we have not seen, which is how Leviathan looks from the outside. Leviathan being Satan revealed instead of Satan mysterious and disguised as God, he represents not only the natural miseries of drought and famine and pestilence and boils, but also the social and political miseries symbolized in the Bible by Egypt and Babylon, and in the Book of Job itself by the Sabean raiders. Ezekiel (29) identifies the leviathan with the Pharaoh of Egypt, and Daniel (4) tells how Nebuchadnezzar of Babylon turned into a variety of behemoth, this latter being a favourite pictorial subject for Blake. The political aspect of the two monsters is brought out in the phrases in the text emphasized by Blake on plate 15: Behemoth is "chief of the ways of God" and Leviathan is "King over all the Children of Pride" [Job 40:19, 41:34]. Their "natural" kernels are the hippopotamus and the crocodile, both Egyptian animals.

At the same time the root of human tyranny, for Blake, is still natural religion, taking the order of nature to be the circumference or horizon of all human effort, the word "horizon" being reflected in the name "Urizen." All of us are born inside the belly of Leviathan, the world of stars and its indefinite space, which is symbolically subterranean, the tomb out of which the Resurrection takes us, and submarine as well, for Leviathan is a sea-monster and Noah's flood has never receded. Those delivered from Leviathan, like Job and Jonah, normally have to be fished for, hence the prominence of fishing imagery in the Gospels. Similarly in Blake the kingdom of the imagination is Atlantis, underneath the "Sea of Time and Space." After Job has attained the enlightenment of plate 15, the prophecy of Jesus is fulfilled and Satan falls from heaven in plate 16, cast out of and separated from the divine nature. The deity in plate 17 is unmistakably Jesus, as the New Testament quotations at the bottom of the plate make clear: if he looks older, it is because he is the divine essence of Job's own mind, and Job is an old man in Blake, if not necessarily so in the Book of Job itself. The casting out of Satan from God's nature in plate 16 is repeated in reverse in the sacrifice scene of plate 18, which is, as said, really a scene of self-sacrifice, and represents Job's casting the demonic principle out of himself.

Job has to be an individual, for Satan's assault on him is part of a struggle between alienation and identity, in which the former carries its conquests up to the very last stronghold of the latter, which is the individual consciousness. Everything Job *has* disappears into the illusory Satanic world of time. He is alienated from his own body by his boils, and from society by the accusing or "Elect" friends, to use the language of Blake's *Milton*, leaving Job himself in the position of the "Reprobate" prophet, the scapegoat driven like Elijah into the wilderness, with only his wife to represent "Redeemed" society. Finally Elihu, pointing to the stars so far above him, alienates him from his earlier view of God, who is now wholly replaced by the accuser. Part of the situation Job is in is one that frequently occurs in tragedy: what are the limits of one's "property," in the Aristotelian sense? That is, how much can a man lose of what he has without losing something of what he is? The implication in God's injunction to Satan that he could take away whatever Job had but not his life, is that Job's identity must remain untouched: the test is whether he will cling to that identity or throw it away. As he is not being punished for anything but tested, the metaphor of a "trial" or lawsuit, held in a court of God with accusers and defendants, hangs over the entire book. Job keeps trying to identify his prosecutor and to call on his advocate (the word translated "redeemer" in 19:25), and he eventually finds that his accuser is the ghost or "Spectre" of his redeemer.

But a trial is a social metaphor, and Job has to represent, not simply an individual, but mankind as a whole. If we think of God as a trinity of power and wisdom and love, it may seem strange that there is so much about God's power and wisdom in the Book of Job and so little about love of any kind. But the implications of the social dimension of love are there in the text, and Blake makes them the main subject of the final three plates. We are told, in a passage quoted on plate 18, that Job's captivity was "turned" when he prayed for his friends; the friends are received into the new community in plate 19, and the family, symbolized by the three daughters, is re-established in plate 20. In plate 1 we see a community of twelve, Job, his wife, his seven sons, and his three daughters, making up a figure of the twelvefold Israel who, in Blake's view of the Exodus, achieved liberation from Egypt only to be enslaved once again by the hypnotizing twelvefold Zodiac of stars over their heads:

> The fiery joy, that Urizen perverted to ten commands,
> What night he led the starry hosts thro' the wide wilderness.[5]

In plate 21 this community of twelve is restored, with the differences from the beginning already noted.

The ambiguity between Job as individual and Job as social being or patriarch is of a kind central to all mythical structures of this descent-and-return shape. The suffering Job must be an individual, but when we think of the restored Job as an individual too, continuous with his previous sufferings, difficulties arise. The origin of the Book of Job appears to have been an ancient folk tale preserved in the prose opening and ending of the book we now have, and in such a folk tale the restoration of Job as an individual can be accepted without question. But for the book we have, restoration of an individual alone could only be an arbitrary act of a deity separate from Job, and a somewhat vulgar act at that, because of its elimination of love. Even in a society as patriarchal as Job's, three new daughters would hardly "make up for" the loss of the previous daughters. We can see the restoring of an individual Job, perhaps, in terms of the analogy of waking up from a dream, where anxiety and humiliation are dealt with simply by abolishing the world in which they exist. But if the restoration of Job is not imaginatively continuous with his misery, what is the point of the poem? If, when Job improves his state of mind or his theology, his misery disappears too, we go back to the point at which the book began, and, in spite of the phrase "twice as much as he had before" (42:10), the book itself becomes meaningless. To say that Job is restored in a different world from the world of his sufferings would be more logically consistent, but it would considerably impoverish the human significance of the story.

The general critical principle involved is that in a descent-and-return mythical structure, as a rule, only the individual descends; only the community returns. Temptation, alienation, despair, decisive choice, death itself, are ordeals that only the individual can carry to their limit. But only a recreated society, like the one that crystallizes in the final scene of a comedy around a hero's marriage, can fully experience the sense of redemption. In plate 20 Job's arms, outspread over his daughters, show that he with his daughters forms part of a larger human body, so that although the objective order from which his calamities came has been annihilated for Job (the calamities being depicted on the walls "In the shadows of Possibility," as Blake says in *Jerusalem* [92.18; K739/E252]), Job's renewed state is not a subjective one. His daughters constitute his "Emanation," the total body of what he loves and creates through love. The ambiguity of the phrase "human body," which may be an individual or a social body, is involved in the contrast between the natural body which dies and the spiritual body which rises again. Job has what Paul calls a "vile body" [Philippians 3:21], given over to boils, but it is in his "flesh" (Job 19:26) that he sees the God who appears in plate 17.

At the beginning of the creation we are told that "the earth was without form, and void; and darkness was upon the face of the deep." Darkness and chaos, the latter being symbolized by the sea, have a twofold role in the Bible. They are, essentially, Satan and the leviathan, and hence Satan and the leviathan may be thought of as eternally enemies of God, totally shut out of the divine nature, reduced to annihilation at the Last Judgment. (In traditional Christianity they go on surviving indefinitely in hell, along with most of the human race, but that doctrine was for Blake a political ploy on the part of the church, and a most contemptible one.) Yet, we are also told, the first act of creation was to separate light from darkness, and the second to separate land from sea. Hence darkness and chaos are also dialectically incorporated into the creation, and therefore Satan and the leviathan could also, in a different context, be regarded as creatures of God, on whom God would look with a by no means unfriendly eye. They are so regarded in the Book of Job, though nowhere else in the Bible.

The question of whether death was also incorporated into the original creation is more difficult. For man, according to Genesis, death came only as a consequence of disobedience. In any case we are now confronted by a nature with death as well as darkness and chaos built into it, and have to realize the influence on our minds of two gods. One, who allowed darkness, chaos, and death into the natural order, is really Satan, the death impulse in us, and the other is Jesus, who escaped from death and is our own essential life. Blake's Laocoön engraving describes the three figures of the sculpture as Jehovah with his two sons Satan and Adam, and around "Jehovah's" head he puts, in addition to the "*Malak Yahweh*" and "Angel of the Divine Presence" already mentioned, the inscription:

> He repented that he had made Adam (of the Female, the Adamah)
> & it grieved him at his heart. [K776/E273]

This last phrase, from Genesis 6:6, is also quoted in the Job illustrations (plate 5), and the rest of it is from the Hebrew text of Genesis 2:7. The total meaning is that the alleged creation of Adam was really the separating of a subjective consciousness from an objective existence, a dying mind from a dead body. The "lapsed Soul" of the *Introduction* to the *Songs of Experience* is not Adam, but the unity of man (*adam*) with the nature and the rest of life (the female *adamah* or "ground"), which are now united only by death.

The traditional creating God, then, is really a destroying God, the flood being another version of the creation of the order of nature at the beginning of the Bible, including man as he now exists. This "creation" is at the opposite pole from the destruction of the world by fire prophesied in the Book of Revelation at the end. Such a destruction would be an utterly pointless firework display if we did not realize that the traditional creation was itself a destruction, and the traditional destruction in the future the real creation and the manifesting again of what was there before the so-called creation. The Book of Job, for Blake, tells the same story as his own *Jerusalem*, whose theme is:

> Of the Sleep of Ulro! and of the passage through
> Eternal Death! and of the awaking to Eternal Life. [K622/E146]

But it also tells the story of the "Bible of Hell," the Bible as Blake read it. The God who saves man is not a God who comes down out of the sky to impose order and authority and obedience, but a God who bursts out of the tomb of death with his face blackened by the soot of hell. This is the drama going on behind the wings of the quiet sequence of visions in the last third of the Job engravings. Blake's vision of the Book of Job was certainly a work of the creative imagination, but what made it possible was a powerful critical analysis of the book, of the whole Bible of which it forms a microcosm, and of the human life which, according to Matthew Arnold, is the theatre in which creation and criticism have become the same thing.

28

Blake's Biblical Illustrations

4 February 1983

From the typescript in NFF, 1988, box 48, file 1 (another copy is in 1991, box 39, file 1). Originally presented as an address at the Blake Symposium at the Art Gallery of Ontario, Toronto, in connection with an exhibit entitled "William Blake: His Art and Times," which ran from 4 December 1982 to 6 February 1983. Published in Northrop Frye Newsletter, *2, no. 2 (Summer 1990): 1–12. Reprinted in* EAC, *62–78.*

It is rare to have an experience that seems to bring one's past life around in a curve, suggesting the closing up of a period of time rather than the usual open continuity. But when I see the name of Blake in letters of such vast size outside the Art Gallery in my own city (I almost said "of my own city," because I am old enough to think of it occasionally as the Art Gallery of Toronto), it does seem to round off an era with a shape to it. I began working on a book on Blake in the '30s of this century, when I was also around the Art Gallery a good deal because my wife was employed there. At that time there was one workable edition of Blake's poetry and prose and a few presentable collections of reproductions, but very little serious criticism of either. My chief aim in my book was to remove the poet Blake from the mystical and occult quarantine that most commentators assigned him and put him in the middle of English literature, which is where he belongs and where he said he belonged.

Since then, Blake scholarship has put increasing emphasis on the pictorial side of Blake, as it naturally would have done, and its progress has been parallel, establishing a social context for Blake as painter, illustrator, and engraver. You may see a very full and authoritative treatment of this in Professor Bindman's catalogue to the present exhibition,[1] and I am assuming some familiarity on your part both with this catalogue and with the exhibition it describes. The literary critic of Blake has continually to stop and remind himself that Blake was almost totally unrecognized as a poet during his lifetime, and did not begin to influence later poets until nearly half a century after his death. But the painting and engraving Blake had real connections with Flaxman, Fuseli, Linnell, Samuel Palmer, and many others, and has a historical dimension that the poet lacks.

Nevertheless, all Blake's pictorial work was closely associated with books: nothing of real importance that he produced is wholly independent of some kind of verbal context. In thinking about his work, therefore, we have to think first of all of the conception of illustration and its place in the pictorial arts. In reading poetry or fiction we internalize the imagery, vividly or vaguely according to temperament: illustration prescribes our visual response in a definite direction. As a rule our own visualizations, however vague, survive all suggested ones, which may be one reason why the elaborately illustrated literary work, a publisher's conception which did so much to help keep Blake alive, has now less of a vogue than it enjoyed in his lifetime. I should imagine that a film version of a favourite novel, or even a performance of a favourite play, seldom permanently displaces the inner vision of it for most people. The chief exception, a significant one in view of the *Songs of Innocence* and Blake's other connections with the genre, is children's books, where, as in the Tenniel illustrations to *Alice in Wonderland*, text and illustration can hardly be separated in our memory.

As is well known, Coleridge makes a distinction between two aspects of creativity, which he called fancy and imagination. What Coleridge meant by this is not our present concern, but in the relation of Blake's pictorial work to literary texts we can see different levels of vision that are roughly parallel. We may call them, tentatively, the levels of illustration and of illumination. Contrary to what we might think at first, Blake is normally respectful of his text: even his most extraordinary flights can be supported by something in it. In illustrating Gray's *Ode on the Death of a Favourite Cat*, for example, Blake demurely illustrates not only Gray's cat and fish, but Gray's poetic epithets as well: the fish are called "genii of the stream" and the cat a "nymph," and we accordingly see very unusual fish and a cat in partly human shape. Such illustrations as these, or those of the fairies in the *Midsummer Night's Dream* illustrations, or the lark and sun and moon of the illustrations of *L'Allegro*, are "fanciful" in a fairly restricted sense, but they are so because the poems they illustrate are also fanciful, or at least are usually read that way.

On this general level of vision there is another and perhaps more serious quality of fancy that operates in the area of the grotesque. In some painters, including Blake, the grotesque verges on the occult. Blake had acquired, partly from his study of Swedenborg, the technique of what some psychologists call a hypnagogic vision, the twilight area of perception which is neither objective, like the walls of a room, nor subjective, like a hallucination. Our senses, Blake says, condense what we see into an objective world, and filter out any perception that disturbs this carefully regulated and predictable vision. But, to use an analogy later than Blake, we could have evolved to see the world in very different ways, and some people can see and converse with other possible modes of being that ordinarily never take definite shape or sound. It is to this world that the "Visionary Heads" belong: these include various historical figures and such creatures as the "Ghost of a Flea."

Blake's friend Varley, we are told, took these visions "seriously": that is, he assumed that they were ghostly but objective, perceived by a kind of X-ray eyesight. For Blake they were among the realities of vision, and no further evidence for their reality was needed beyond the drawing itself. Admittedly we get into something of a block here, because our language instinctively seeks out clear distinctions between objective reality and subjective illusion. For Blake there was a far more important distinction between the passive attitude that stares at the world, and the active or creative one that builds something out of it. The former is what Blake calls "reason," and regards as stupid; the latter, its direct opposite, he calls mental, intellectual, or imaginative. Blake could have given many of his drawings the same title that Goya used: "The sleep of reason produces monsters."[2] But for Blake the word "of" would indicate a different kind of genitive. Goya meant: when reason goes to sleep, monsters are produced in the mind. Blake would have meant: when man falls into the state of sleep he calls reason, monsters inhabit his mind, though only a genuinely creative vision can see that they are monsters.

This kind of fancy, to give it that name again, has run through the whole history of painting: we find it in Hieronymus Bosch and Brueghel, in Blake's contemporary Fuseli, in Redon and the later Surrealist and Dadaist movement, in much of the "magical realism" of our own time. It shows us the infinite variety of what can be seen by a visionary skill that tries to see more than the conventionalizing apparatus of the eye has been conditioned to show us. Such variety of vision, as we saw, may be "fanciful" in the idiom of the innocent make-believes of children, or it may be terrifying, like the nightmares of children. Blake would say that we live in a hell that is shown to be a hell by the wars and plagues and famines and slavery that exist in it, but which we dare not look at steadily in its real form. Those who consistently see it in the forms of these other possibilities are often said to be mad, and may sometimes actually go mad; but this need not affect the quality of their vision if they are artists. Sanity is not a critical but a social judgment, and no society is capable of making such a judgment beyond a very limited degree. What the vision of Blake shows us is the much profounder insanity of the society he lived in. The Reverend Doctor Trusler, for example, after commissioning from Blake a picture illustrating "Malevolence," refused what Blake sent on the ground that he wished to reject all "Fancy" from his work. But as one of his books was called *The Way to Be Rich and Respectable*, it seems clear that neurotic fantasy may disguise itself as its opposite.

Above this pictorial fancy there is the systematic recreation of the visible world into what Blake would call its spiritual or imaginative form. From the Palaeolithic cave drawings of Lascaux and Altamira to our own day, there has always been something of the unborn world about the art of painting. In contrast to sculpture, which is normally linked to biological form, the two-dimensional aspect of painting suggests a recreation of vision by the mind, an objective world transfigured. Even when the underlying cultural impulse is a so-called "realistic" one, we have this in Vermeer in seventeenth-century Holland, in Renoir in French Impressionism, in the later Turner in Victorian England. Another publication of the Art Gallery of Ontario is David Wistow's *Tom Thomson and the Group of Seven*, which deals with a movement in painting utterly remote from Blake in time, place, setting, technique, and objectives. Yet it begins with an epigraph from Emily Carr which would apply with equal accuracy to Blake:

> Oh, these men, this Group of Seven, what have they created?
> —a world stripped of earthiness, shorn of fretting details,
> purged, purified;
> a naked soul, pure and unashamed; lovely spaces filled with
> wonderful serenity.

In Blake's greatest pictorial work, even when the text it accompanies is by someone else, we no longer have the feeling of subordination to a text that the word "illustration" normally suggests. We have rather the sense of turning to an independent art related to the text but no longer "following" it or merely assisting the reader to visualize it. The distinction between illustration and this kind of illumination is roughly parallel to the difference between reciting a poem and setting it to music. In recitation the poem is turned from print to sound, and guides the ear as illustration guides the eye. But when a poem is set to music its rhythm and much of its structure are taken over by the music. It is the same poem, but its setting and context are different. In "illumination," similarly, the context is no longer visual commentary, but an act of creative criticism.

According to Giambattista Vico, writing in Italy at the beginning of the eighteenth century, human culture begins in a mythological and poetic stage, after which it becomes aristocratic and allegorical, then demotic, descriptive, and realistic, and finally goes through a *ricorso* or return back to the mythological. It is a corollary of this conception that much the same structural principles of the arts hold throughout each phase, but are easiest to see in the mythological stage, before they have become adapted to class interest or popular demands for likeness or ordinary experience. Literature that is close to the mythological has an affinity with abstract and conventionalized "primitive" painting, because in myths, where the characters are so often gods, things happen of the kind that happen only in stories, just as highly conventionalized painting presents visual relationships and designs, like a saint's halo, that occur only in pictures. According to Vico, Classical culture had passed through its three stages and then gone in a *ricorso* back to mythology at the beginning of the Christian era, and another such *ricorso* seemed to be taking shape in Vico's own time.

Blake had not read Vico, but he had developed parallel intuitions from contemporary books: he had read about the ancient Druids and their caste of bards in Stukeley,[3] about the morphology of myth in Jacob Bryant,[4] about Biblical typology in Swedenborg, about the legendary history of Britain as transmitted from Geoffrey of Monmouth down to Milton, about the cycles of Norse mythology in translations of the *Old* and *Prose Eddas*. He also regarded his own time as one in which a squalid pseudo-realism was about to be swept away on a whirlwind of new mythology coming in the wake of political revolution. It is when Blake is faced with a fairly representative poet of his own century, such as Edward Young or Gray, that we can see most clearly what the direction of his illuminating activity is. Gray wrote in a domesticated eighteenth-century idiom, but took a keen interest in his more "primitive" Norse and Celtic poetic ancestors, and Blake is at his best and boldest, in illuminating Gray, when he gives us his great vision of Hyperion the sun-god in *The Progress of Poesy*, or the world serpent Midgard and the wolf Fenri of Norse apocalyptic at the end of *The Descent of Odin*. Young's *Night Thoughts*, in nine nights ending with a Last Judgment, are less erudite but more speculative, and as what the poet speculates about is frequently cosmological, Blake's drawings expand accordingly. Finally, after 537 efforts to reconstruct Young's meditations into myths, Blake abandoned Young for his own much less inhibited dream of nine nights, known as *Vala* or *The Four Zoas*.

In Blake's illustrations of Milton, who sticks so closely to his Biblical and mythological sources, illustration becomes much the same thing as illumination, and we may say this also of the Dante series. Blake's dislike of Dante's literal and legalistic biases in the *Inferno* sometimes leads him to taking more liberties with Dante's text than he usually does: Paolo and Francesca [pl. 10], for example, appear to have reached an apotheosis in Blake that Dante does not give them. The picture of the Canterbury pilgrims, on the other hand, is relatively realistic by Blake's standards, and the mythological reconstruction of Chaucer is made only verbally through the *Descriptive Catalogue*, in which we are told, for example, that "The Plowman of Chaucer is Hercules in his supreme eternal state, divested of his spectrous shadow; which is the Miller. . . ." [K571/E536]. Blake's brief comments about the *L'Allegro* and *Il Penseroso* illustrations indicate a similar type of interest in them.

But naturally it is in Blake's own illuminated poems that text and design reach a perfect balance. Only in the early experiment *Tiriel* do we have a text with accompanying illustrations. Everywhere else the text and design interpenetrate in every variety of proportion, ranging from all text, or text with slight marginal decoration, to all picture, or picture surrounding a title or colophon, or design framing a short lyric. With his own work Blake can provide a constant contrapuntal relation between our verbal and our pictorial experience of the poem, so that there is no shift of attention from verbal to pictorial worlds: the two blend together as aspects of a single creative conception.

In his illustrations to the Bible, again, everything in Blake's design can usually be justified by the text. There are dozens of them that are simply Biblical illustrations, and call for no further comment. Such a departure from a specific Biblical reference as the picture of the Virgin hushing the child John the Baptist is rare, and even this belongs to a very traditional type of departure. There is a collection of Blake's Bible illustrations made by the late Sir Geoffrey Keynes,[5] in which the Job designs are omitted, because, the introduction tells us, apart from being readily available elsewhere, they are less illustrations to the book than an imaginative reconstruction of it. I think this is a false antithesis. Blake is not imposing his own meaning on Job except insofar as he is trying to make imaginative sense of the text as he read it. It may not be the same as the sense we make of it, and it is certainly a Christian and apocalyptic reading of the book, but its relation to the text of Job is quite as consistent as its relation to Blake's mind. I also have to omit the Job series, but for different reasons.

But still the influence of the Bible on Blake is so pervasive that it is difficult to know where it stops. His picture of the temptation of Christ on the mountain top is closely related to his picture of the temptation on the pinnacle of the temple in *Paradise Regained*. In the former Jesus stands on an eminent but quite solid and horizontal rock: in the latter his foot touches the pinnacle in a way that shows that his balance is miraculous. This detail results from a very sharp insight into the implications of Milton's text. But sometimes an illustration of Milton is reinforced by Blake's view of the Bible. Thus Michael's prophecy of the Crucifixion in *Paradise Lost* features the typological serpent of the temptation in Eden and of the brazen serpent on a pole in the Book of Numbers. Blake is illustrating Michael's line "But to the cross he nails thy enemies" [*PL*, 12.415], but has done so with the image that had been central in his mind for many years, the dying god as a serpent "wreath'd round the accursed tree" [K198/E54] who had appeared in *America* (1793) and elsewhere. Again, the illustration of Jesus' offer to redeem man (*Paradise Lost*, book 5) shows Jesus standing in front of God the Father, a grotesque creature with his face concealed by long hair, as in the portrait of the senile Urizen in the frontispiece to *The Book of Ahania*. Blake is illustrating *Paradise Lost*, but he is also illustrating his own view of Milton's Father, besides anticipating the whole of the "God is dead" theology of a few years ago. Similarly, the explicitly sexual embrace of Eve by the serpent that we see in Blake gives a dimension to that episode which is not in Milton, though it is by no means unknown to tradition, and reappears in Dylan Thomas's "tree-tailed worm that mounted Eve."[6]

At the end of *The Marriage of Heaven and Hell* Blake tells us that, after converting an "Angel" (conservative) into a "Devil" (radical):

> . . . we often read the Bible together in its infernal or diabolical sense, which the world shall have if they behave well.
>
> I have also The Bible of Hell, which the world shall have whether they will or no. [pl. 24; K158/E44]

The "Bible of Hell" is probably the series of prophetic books that includes *The Book of Urizen* and *The Book of Ahania*, which read very like the Genesis and Exodus of a revised Old Testament. We shall come back to these in a moment. The Bible in its infernal or diabolical sense needs a more long-range perspective for its explanation.

We spoke of Vico and his conception of a sequence of cultural languages, running from the mythological through the allegorical to the demotic and back again, and remarked that for Vico one such sequence began in the early Christian centuries and was nearing its *ricorso* in his own time. In Vico's day there had been no permanently successful example of a democratic culture, and he had no evidence for any essential change in the nature of his cycle. But Blake, with the American, the French, and the beginning of the Industrial Revolutions before him, felt, at least for most of the productive period of his life, that a far-reaching change was taking place in human fortunes, of a kind that the apocalyptic visions in the New Testament finally did seem to be really pointing to.

We have now to invoke a broader principle than anything Vico gives us. No human society lives directly in nature as an animal or insect society might do. Human consciousness invariably creates some kind of transparent envelope out of its own social concerns, and looks at nature through this transparent cultural filter, which in its verbal aspect is a mythology. A cosmology, or systematic view of nature, usually forms part of the more developed mythologies. The culture of Western Europe, at the time of early Christianity, produced such a mythology and cosmology, mainly out of the Bible, later annexing a good deal of Classical myth and philosophy to it. The Bible itself, as I see it, does not set forth a mythological universe of this kind, but it provides any number of hints and suggestions for one, and naturally the construct set up in the Middle Ages, however close to the Bible, was mainly a rationalizing of the social authority of church and state.

This construct was on four main levels. On top was heaven, in the sense of the place of the presence of God. Strictly it was a metaphorical top, as categories of time and space do not apply directly to God, but the metaphors were invariably drawn from "up there," beyond the sky. Below, on the second level, was the model world that God originally created, saw to be good, and intended to be man's home, the paradisal Eden with no sin or death in it. Man fell out of this world into the third level, the "fallen" world he now inhabits, an alien order of nature to which only animals and plants seem relatively well adapted, as they do not sin. The Garden of Eden has disappeared, and only the stars in their courses, with their legendary spherical music, are left to remind us of the perfection of the original creation. Still further below, on a fourth level, is the demonic world.

This structure is a rigid hierarchy, with the initiative for everything that is good for man coming from above in the form of grace. Even the revolutionary Milton never thought of liberty as anything that man wanted or had a right to: it is good only because it is something that God wishes him to have. The main object of man's existence is to recognize that his fallen world presents him with a moral dialectic: he must move upward as close to his proper level (the second) as he can, or else sink down to sin and a death beyond the physical. The second and third levels constitute two aspects of the order of nature: the higher one is specifically the order of human nature, as many things are "natural" to man, such as wearing clothes, being under social discipline, obeying laws, and the like, that are not natural to animals.

Because this mythology was a structure of authority, enforced by authority, it lasted far longer than it would ordinarily have done. Blake was the first poet in English literature, and so far as I know the first person in the modern world, to realize that the traditional authoritarian cosmos had had it, that it no longer appealed to the intelligence or the imagination, and would have to be replaced by another model. Blake gave us a complete outline of such a model, but unfortunately nobody knew that he had done so, and one has to read thousands of pages of poetry and philosophy since his time to pick up bits and pieces of his insight. Like its predecessor, Blake's cosmos is based on Biblical imagery and myth, but it turns the authoritarian structure upside down and makes it a revolutionary one.

By the Bible in its infernal or diabolical sense, Blake meant, first of all, replacing the original revolutionary impetus in the Bible which had got explained away by an establishment. This revolutionary impetus is primarily, in the Old Testament, the account of the exodus of Israel from

Egypt: in the New Testament it is the account of the execution of the prophet and martyr Jesus. Traditionally, the unique importance of Jesus' life has been thought to reside in his "sinlessness," his perfect conformity to established moral standards. For Blake, a conforming Jesus would have accomplished nothing: it was his open defiance of such standards that made him intolerable to society.

As for the Exodus, we have to distinguish two forces at work there, one revolutionary and the other reactionary. The revolutionary impulse, symbolized in Blake as the red and fiery Orc, inspired the Israelites to walk out of the Egyptian oppressive social system into the desert and set up their own society. Orc's "pillar of fire" guided them on their way. But as they went on, they became more and more hypnotized by the sense of predictable natural order, and so eventually congealed into the same kind of authoritarian structure that they had left behind. Opposed to Orc is the white Urizen, whose name echoes the word "horizon" and who belongs to the family of tyrannical old men in the sky that mankind has projected there since the beginning of history. Urizen's "pillar of cloud" eventually won out: the twelve (actually thirteen) tribes of Israel fell into the rhythm of the predictable revolution of the twelve signs of the Zodiac with its captive sun: a law of negative commandments was handed to Moses from the sky, and finally the story of the brazen serpent on the pole (Numbers 21) associates the defeated Orc with the serpent and the sinister tree that we find in the story of the fall of Adam and later in the Crucifixion.

Now, in Blake's day, there comes a revolt of the American colonies against the repressive government of "Albion," and we see them bearing flags with serpents, trees, and stars on them, as well as an alternation of red and white and a preoccupation with the number thirteen. Both tendencies, to freedom and to repression, are present in slave-owning America, and later both tendencies reappeared in France, producing both a revolution and Napoleonic imperialism. In England itself there is a constant conflict going on between creative and imaginative people and those who insist on rationalizing all the cruelty and injustice in the "dark Satanic mills."

The rebellion of Orc against Urizen produced the French and American Revolutions, but as Blake saw it such revolutions do not last, because the youthful Orc grows old, in other words turns into Urizen. History, as Blake saw it, breaks down into a series of cycles beginning with the birth of the terrible "Babe," the annunciation of a new era in time, and ending either with the Babe grown old, as in the poem called *The Mental Traveller*, or hung on a tree in youth like Absalom, the victim of youth's impotent protest against tyranny, as in *The Book of Ahania*. A much more permanent human resource is the creative faculty in man that begins by controlling and binding the energy of Orc and then proceeds to transform nature into the home of humanity. The arts themselves—poetry, painting, music—are in the forefront of this transformation, and its presiding genius is Los the blacksmith, the worker in iron, iron being regarded in the Old Testament as a new and suspicious substance, not to be used in constructing altars to the sky-god. Los's name is, I should think, taken from the old English word *los* or *loos*, meaning praise or glory, used by Chaucer and not quite extinct, at least as an archaism, in Blake's day.

Thus Blake's mythological universe neatly turns the traditional one on its head. On top is Blake's Satan, the death principle, the mechanical energy which whirls the stars around in their courses and sets up a model of predictability, or natural law, which is what the energies of man are expected to adjust to. Paul calls Satan the prince of the power of the air [Ephesians 2:2], implying that the traditional abode of the gods is really a place of alienation. Under Satan is Urizen's world of experience, the "fallen" world of the traditional Biblical reading, where morality tries to become as predictable as natural law; and Urizen sits on top of Orc, the revolutionary power latent in human energy.

In childhood man is in the state of innocence: that is, he assumes that the world makes human sense, and that there is a providential order, incarnate in his parents, that takes care of him. As he grows older, he enters Urizen's world of experience, which is a very different world, and his original childhood vision of innocence is driven underground into what we now call the subconscious, a boiling mass of frustrated and largely sexual desire. This conception of the human soul is commonplace enough to us now, but Blake grasped it before anyone else did. Still deeper down in the human spirit than the natural energy of Orc is Los, the creative power. This Los is the true God, the Holy Spirit who works only within human consciousness, and only as its creative potential. Los's home is in Atlantis, the primeval kingdom of human imagination, now submerged under what Blake calls the sea of time and space. It is with ideas like these that Blake attempts to make his pictures of the Bible intelligible to his contemporaries.

Blake's "Bible of Hell" probably began with the two poems called *The*

Book of Urizen and *The Book of Los*. Blake was aware that there were two accounts of the creation in Genesis, and he presents his own creation myth as a collision of opposing forces. Urizen is the tendency to stability and uniformity that finally reveals itself to be a tendency to death; Los is the tendency to expanding and growing life which fights against Urizen. The poems contain some striking anticipations of later theories about the evolving of forms of life and of the immense stretches of time that would be required for such growth. *The Book of Ahania* reshapes the Exodus into a story of revolution betrayed, except that Blake makes an Earth Mother or female principle, who is ignored in the Bible, the chief character. It is possible that the four poems on the continents, *America*, *Europe*, and the two parts of *The Song of Los* called "Africa" and "Asia," correspond to the historical books of the Old Testament: in any case the rather pedantic notion of what amounts to a series of parodies of the Bible was soon given up. The most interesting feature, perhaps, is the pictorial aspect of *The Book of Urizen*, where creation is not the work of an aloof deity commanding the world to exist, but the outcome of a battle of suffering titans.

We have already indicated that it is not always easy to say just what a Biblical illustration is in Blake. If it is not explicitly a picture referring to a specific text in the Bible, it may still illustrate Blake's infernal or diabolical Bible, and if it seems to illustrate something in Blake's contemporary world, it may still be a fulfilment or application of Biblical prophecy. One of Blake's most famous poems tells us that the real form of England, the "green and pleasant land," and the real Israel, the Garden of Eden, are the same place, and the object of Blake's art is to reunite them, to build Jerusalem in England. In his poem *Jerusalem* the tribes of Israel and the counties of England are superimposed on one another in the most laborious detail, and many events in his own time are seen as repetitions of the history of Israel.

The famous picture called *Glad Day* by Gilchrist, because he associated it with a sunrise image in *Romeo and Juliet*, is, according to Blake's own annotation, a portrait of Albion, that is, mankind in general and England in particular, in a sacrificial role (Luvah or Orc in Blake's symbolism), identified, as his phrase "at the mill with slaves" shows, with a regenerate or restored Samson.[7] This Samson figure, along with the identification with Albion, comes from a passage in Milton's *Areopagitica*,[8] not the Old Testament, but the picture has its roots in the Bible, as Blake read it, for all that. Again, there is a picture of an infant snatched up by a female in a chariot drawn by blind horses while another female, perhaps the mother, lies exhausted on the ground. The picture is called *Pity* because it is assumed to illustrate the metaphor in *Macbeth* about pity as a naked new-born babe.[9] Doubtless it does, but it also illustrates the infant who heralds a new era of time, and whose threatened and perilous birth comes into the story of Moses in the Old Testament and that of Jesus in the New. Another picture depicting the attempts of good and evil angels to get control of a similar infant is again not directly Biblical, but illustrates the two impulses, towards life and towards death, that have existed in every human being since the fall of Adam. This design appears in reverse in *The Marriage of Heaven and Hell* as a pictorial comment on the point the text is making: that morality, being founded on the forbidden knowledge of good and evil, is a perverted form of religion. At the other end of life such angels appear in the episode that Blake also illustrates, the legendary dispute mentioned in the New Testament of Michael with Satan over the body of Moses.[10]

Although Blake illustrates every part of the Bible, a large number of his most impressive pictures cluster around its beginning and end, the creation and the apocalypse. But, of course, to understand them we must first understand what creation and apocalypse meant to Blake. In the traditional version, God made a perfect world, free of corruption, and a garden in which he put Adam and Eve, who had only to enjoy themselves and not eat the fruit of a tree mysteriously called the "knowledge of good and evil." Naturally they did eat this fruit, and so were flung out of the garden into a lower world, while God retreated to the sky. So we now inhabit a savage and alienating order of nature, and it's all our fault. For Blake it is indeed all our fault, but the origin of the fault lies in believing in a nonhuman creation in the first place. In the picture called *God Judging Adam*, the only figure who is really there is Adam himself, being what Blake calls "idolatrous to his own Shadow."[11] The God in the chariot has been projected from the stupidest and most primitive part of Adam's brain. This picture was formerly identified with the ascent of Elijah, and it is something of a parody of that scene, where one prophetic power enters the spiritual world and another carries on in time. In another well-known picture, *The Elohim Creating Adam*, not in this exhibition, Adam lies prostrate with the serpent of morality coiled around him, while the alleged creator appears to be stuffing mud ("dust of the ground") into his head. All of which means that the creation, for Blake, is the world that registers on our closed up and filtering senses: creation and fall are the same thing. The powerful painting of the wise and foolish virgins contains for Blake an allusion to the five organized senses and their opposites.

What lies around us now is not God's creation but a quite ungodly mess, and it is the primary task of man to recreate it into a proper home for man, with the vision of the creative artists taking the lead. For most of the mess comes from the uncreative side of man, the side that wages war and supports parasitic rulers because it has accepted the knowledge of good and evil. This knowledge, or pseudo-knowledge, has two aspects. One is the belief in morality, which tells us that the "Mercy, Pity, Peace and Love" of the *Songs of Innocence* are virtues we may practice only as long as we are careful to keep on rationalizing the war and cruelty and hatred and exploitation that make them virtues. The other is the belief that sanity consists in sharply dividing the perceiving subject from the perceived object, and in regarding the subject as the source of illusion and the object as the source of reality.

In traditional Christianity God is male and a creator: the human society he redeems, men as well as women, is symbolically female, a "Bride" called Jerusalem, or, as Blake says, "a City, yet a Woman" [K362/E391]. In Blake all creative human beings are symbolically male: what is symbolically female is not human women but the objective world. Human beings, we saw, either try to help recreate the world or else stare at it passively: Blake calls the former attitude the "Imagination" and the latter one the "Spectre." Similarly there are two aspects of the object: the retreating elusive object and the responding or transformed object. Blake calls the former the "Female Will" and the latter the "Emanation," the total body of what one redeems by love. The "Spectre" cannot love; hence his "Emanation" is an object of possessive and panic-stricken jealousy. Such a possessed Emanation is illustrated in the frontispiece to *The Book of Ahania*, already mentioned, and in the poem *Visions of the Daughters of Albion*. The "Female Will" is Robert Graves's white goddess, represented in the painting called *Hecate*, the *diva triformis* who is also the elusive moon in the sky and the invisible virgin of the forest. *Hecate* is again a picture drawn from Shakespeare, but its roots are in the Biblical abhorrence of all worship of a female embodiment of nature. The female jealously possessed by an old man, and the female who is a disdainful or tantalizing mistress, are, for Blake, symbolic pictures of human consciousness, and are therefore more important as literary conventions than as facts of life.

The creation for Blake, then, was the imprisoning of human consciousness into the form in which we see the world, and the stories of the fall of man and of the flood of Noah are variations on the same theme. Blake speaks of the flood, in the poem *Europe*, as the time "when the five senses whelm'd / In deluge o'er the earth-born man" (K241/E63). The famous picture of the "Ancient of Days," which is the frontispiece to *Europe*, shows the traditional God, Urizen or the old man in the sky, setting his compasses on the face of the deep, in the phrase of the Book of Proverbs.[12] We see the sky as an overarching vault because we are looking at it with eyes underneath an overarching vault of bone, and Urizen's compasses are tracing the "horizon" both of the sky and of the human head. By contrast, the apocalypse is the recovery by man of his own proper vision, after he has, so to speak, blown his top and sees the world with his open mind and not with his skull. Blake's pictures of the Last Judgment, with the presence of God where the skull formerly was, indicate the kind of perspective that results. Another form of the skull image is the trilithon of Stonehenge and elsewhere that we see in Blake's *Jerusalem*, derived, as the exhibition shows us, from Stukeley's book on what he regarded as "Druid" temples. According to Blake the upright pillars represent two aspects of human creativity, known in the eighteenth century as the sublime and the beautiful, and the horizontal stone on top is the human "reason," or skull-bound view of reality.

The great apocalyptic visions in this exhibition are largely of monsters, because the passive view of the objective world sees it increasingly as monstrous, as more is known about the world of the stars. The huge mechanism held together with gravitation that stares silently at man from the night sky seems like a constant accuser of man, emphasizing his littleness, his unimportance in the scheme of things, and the inevitability of sin, misery, and the frustration of desire in his life. Ezekiel, according to Blake, saw this image as the "Covering Cherub," the angel who keeps us out of paradise, the Argus full of eyes who is the demonic parody of the vision of God with which Ezekiel's vision opens. Ezekiel identifies his Covering Cherub with the Prince of Tyre, which means with political tyrants of all kinds, and similarly Blake's demonic figures hold the swords and sceptres of temporal rule.

Elsewhere in the Bible such visions of consolidated evil, political tyranny embodying an alien cosmos, explicitly take the form of monsters. In the Book of Job there are two such creatures, a land monster called Behemoth and a sea monster called Leviathan, from whose power Job is delivered at the end of the book. Man's limited view of the cosmos is symbolically either subterranean, as in the story of Adam sent back to the red earth he was made from, or submarine, as in the story of Noah. As we saw, the flood for Blake was not the drowning of mankind but the limiting of man's perception, so that for most of us the flood has never receded, but remains as the "Sea of Time and Space" on top of Atlantis, already referred to. In Revelation 13 these two monsters again rise out of the sea and the earth. In that context they are politically connected with the Rome of Nero and other persecuting Caesars, but symbolically they are also the Pharaoh of Egypt whom Ezekiel identifies with Leviathan and the Nebuchadnezzar of Babylon who turns into Behemoth. This latter figure especially fascinated Blake, and he appears at the end of *The Marriage of Heaven and Hell*, as the final comment on the state of the world at the time of the French Revolution. It is also in the Book of Revelation that the vision of the old man clutching the young woman turns into its apocalyptic form, of a dragon trying to devour the woman crowned with stars who is the mother of the Messiah, or humanity become divine.

There is another type of apocalyptic subject in Blake, where the open vision taught by the seer on Patmos is applied to Blake's own time. For example, his Exhibition of 1809 contained pictures of the spiritual form of Pitt, the leader of Albion on land, guiding Behemoth, and the spiritual form of Nelson, the leader on the sea, guiding Leviathan. There was also a spiritual form of Napoleon, which has disappeared with no information about what beast he was involved with. A figure guiding such monsters would not always be a tyrant: he could be simply a leader doing what he can in a world where such monsters exist. Pitt and Nelson in Blake's pictures are neither examples of apotheosis, as Blake's commentary suggests, nor are they really demonic figures: they are states or functions of human action looked at from an apocalyptic perspective. They also, unfortunately, imply more understanding of Biblical symbolism than the public of 1809 was likely to possess, or attach to Blake's work if they did possess it.

A similar figure of this type is the picture of Newton, applying Urizen's compasses to a scroll on the ground, the rolled-up part of which forms a disappearing spiral, an image that Blake often employs in sinister contexts. In the more familiar Tate Gallery version, which is the more carefully finished one, Newton looks almost benignant: the version owned by a Lutheran church in America gives him a harder and more fanatical face. For Blake the apocalypse was, among other things, the separating of a world of life from a world of death, and everything in the latter forms a parody or mimicry of the former. Hence the consolidation of the passive view of existence is a necessary step in visualizing its opposite. So in the poem *Europe*, which describes the intellectual tyranny exerted over Europe between the birth of Christ and the end of the eighteenth century, the trumpet of the Last Judgment is blown by Newton [K243/E65]. This Newton, it is hardly necessary to add, is not the Sir Isaac who was Keeper of the Mint under George I, but the mighty angel Blake's picture presents, his spiritual form. Up to Newton's time, the worship of nature was still possible for some people, who might see, for example, a sun-god in a chariot at the rising of the sun, the presence of a being with whom some kind of "I–Thou" dialogue, to use a current phrase, would still be possible. But Newton had turned everything in nature into an "It," a part of a mechanistic force, and by doing so he achieved a negative deliverance of man from nature worship.

The genuinely apocalyptic form of such a Newton figure is the other mighty angel illustrated by Blake and mentioned in Revelation 10:6, who announces that "time should be no longer," a phrase Blake would have taken to mean just what it appears to mean. The apocalypse for Blake is the triumph of revelation and freedom over tyranny and mystery, and one of its central symbols is the ripping of seals from a scroll, the disclosing to the human mind the world that the human mind exists to see.

In *The Marriage of Heaven and Hell* there is a conflict of visions between the narrator and a panic-stricken conservative "angel" about what lies in store for man in the world beyond this life. The angel churns up a horrifying vision of black and white spiders (i.e., egos who are either "good" or "bad"), and of a serpentine or shark-like leviathan coiling and thrashing in the sea [K156/E41]. The angel then runs away, and the narrator, a "devil" who is mostly Blake himself, is left sitting on a pleasant river bank listening to a harper who tells him that the dogmatist, the man in the sleep of reason, breeds reptiles of the mind. For Blake the world that God is trying to reveal to man in the Bible, and the world Blake himself is trying to illustrate, is not a world of superstitious fantasy but a world in human shape that makes human sense. This is symbolized as a world where man lives in fire and yet is not burned, in water and yet is not drowned, a world above time where all the images of man's creative and charitable acts in the past move into the present, and his lost heritage turns into his regained home.

29

Blake's Bible

2 June 1987

Address to the Blake Society of St. James, London, from the annotated typescript in NFF, 1991, box 38, file 7, which also contains an earlier typed draft. First published in MM, *270–86. In Frye's typescript, a number of sentences or phrases are bracketed, but they are not crossed out as if for deletion, and are preserved without parentheses in the final version on Jane Widdicombe's disk; perhaps they represent possible shortenings for oral presentation. These bracketed passages are indicated here by braces { }.*

I

It is obvious that Blake is, even by English standards, an intensely Biblical poet. His approach to it is wholly that of a poet and painter: he has little of Milton's or Herbert's doctrinal content. As we all know, Blake developed a cosmic vision of a universe inhabited by dramatis personae of his own invention. His treatment of that vision remains remarkably consistent throughout his life, though it was not static: many vague and undeveloped areas of it become clearer and more detailed as he goes on. But at no time does he stray very far away from the Bible as his main source.

Blake never believed, strictly speaking, either in God or in man: the beginning and end of all his work was what he calls the "Divine Humanity." He accepted the Christian position because Christianity holds to the union of divine and human in the figure of Christ, and, in its conception of resurrection, to the infinite self-surpassing of human limitations. But any God Blake would accept would have to be not simply a personal God but an anthropomorphic one. A God who is not at least human is in practice only a scarecrow of superstition and cowardice scraped up from a subhuman nature and stuffed full of the malice and cruelty that man derives from nature. As for human societies in themselves, Blake regards them, or came to do so, as mostly aggregates of psychotic animals. A human being comes equipped with a potentially divine power centred in his ability to create, to love, to destroy his own grasping and clutching ego, and only such things make him human. In any case a divine being could communicate with a human being only in human language, and at the point of communication the difference between God and man would become an identity. Blake often has to speak for convenience of God *and* man, but either word separated from the other represents a sterile and sinister illusion. Traditionally, the Bible opens with an account of a creation by God followed by a fall of man, and man is responsible only for the consequences of his own fall. For Blake, the fall of man was a part of a badly bungled job of creation for which man is equally responsible, hence the primary duty of man at present is to recreate his world into something that makes more sense, human and divine.

We may take as our guide to Blake's development the famous passage from a poem in a letter written in 1802, where he speaks of having attained a "fourfold" vision:

> 'Tis fourfold in my supreme delight
> And threefold in soft Beulah's night
> And twofold Always. May God us keep
> From Single vision & Newton's sleep! [K818/E722]

Anyone trying to follow Blake biographically is bound to feel that he is on several time clocks at once: this statement is about six years later than the discovery at the beginning of the poem called *The Four Zoas* that "Four Mighty Ones are in every Man" [K264/E300]. Blake was one of a minority of visionaries in the West to think in fours and eights rather than the traditional constructs derived from the Trinity. His chief Biblical sources here are the four rivers of Eden [Genesis 2:10–14], the fourth figure who appears along with the three in Nebuchadnezzar's furnace [Daniel 3:24–5], and the "fourfold Gospel" [K677/E196], which is connected with his four "Zoas." Let us begin with what Blake meant by a "single vision," omitting the reference to Newton for the moment.

According to the Book of Genesis, Adam and Eve were placed in a garden with instructions to eat of every tree except one, which of course was the one that most attracted them. The tree was called the knowledge of good and evil, and in eating of it they became self-conscious about their sexual differences, which had not bothered them before. In short, what human beings acquired, at the dawn of history, was a repressive morality founded on a sexual neurosis. Such a knowledge had been forbidden because it is not a genuine knowledge of anything, even of good and evil.

When we look at the Bible as a sacred book, then, the worst way of misreading it is to take this neurotic repressiveness as the form of divine revelation, making moral taboos and sexual prudery the basis for behaviour acceptable to God. Such an attitude is really a form of devil-worship, as it enforces the exact opposite of what the same Genesis story presents as the original ideal. There is, it is true, some evidence that the Bible considers submission to arbitrary authority to be the best procedure for man. But there is better evidence that struggling against such authority is really what is required. The major pattern for this is the Exodus from Egypt, where revolution against a social establishment is the first and primary event in the history of Israel. {All through the Old Testament the historians and prophets keep returning to this Egyptian revolution as the essential factor in the relation, or what Blake would call the identity, of God and man.} In the New Testament the death and resurrection of a socially rejected Christ forms the counterpart to the Exodus, and completes the overcoming of the gap between the divine and the human. Clearly, one needs a counter-vision of the Bible, setting a gospel of freedom against the imbecile manifesto of moral inertia, social conformity, and sexual shame. Milton before Blake had spoken of the Bible as the charter of human liberty, and regarded all efforts to make it seem to endorse tyranny as perverse.

Blake speaks of the American Revolution as having a profound effect on his political and social thinking: with the fall of the Bastille in 1789 this expanded into a temporary conviction that after centuries of tyranny the world was coming into a new age of liberty. *The Marriage of Heaven and Hell* is a satire, partly political and partly religious, concerned with what we should now call left- and right-wing points of view. The left-wingers are called "Devils," the conservatives "Angels." The tone is light and good-natured throughout: the "Devils" are lively and amusing, and the "Angels," if sometimes stupid, are not really evil. At the end of this work Blake describes how he, taking the role of a "Devil," demonstrates to an "Angel" the true nature of Jesus. For the "Angel" what is unique about the life of Jesus was its conformity to moral virtue: he was the only man to have achieved the utterly futile goal of a life without sin. The "Devil" shows him that in fact Jesus broke all the ten commandments he is supposed to have endorsed, and that what was really significant about his life was that established moral authority found him intolerable. The "Angel" is converted, and the episode ends:

> Note. This Angel, who is now become a Devil, is my particular friend; we often read the Bible together in its infernal or diabolical sense, which the world shall have if they behave well.
>
> I have also The Bible of Hell, which the world shall have whether they will or no. [K158/E44]

We get a hint here of two levels of seriousness, one of good-humoured satire, and another that is more aware of the real depths of the conflict opening up in Blake's day between the forces of liberty and those of repression. The *Marriage* was engraved in 1793, but the text suggests that it was written around 1790. In a very short time Britain had gone to war with France and installed a repressive government, and the tone adopted by Blake becomes more bitter and denunciatory. What he thinks of the "single vision" of the Bible he puts into fairly explicit language in a couplet scribbled in the Rossetti Notebook:

> The Hebrew Nation did not write it.
> Avarice & Chastity did shite it. [K187/E516]

{Chastity, because the notion that sexual abstinence is a good thing in itself is a neurosis that is a fruitful breeder of further neuroses. Avarice, because this kind of perversion can be made only in the interests of some established authority, religious or secular.} At this period of his life, Blake regarded such radical figures as Voltaire, Rousseau, and Paine as fighters in the vanguard of freedom. Some of the most significant statements he made at this time occur in a series of marginalia he wrote on a book by Bishop Watson, a series of letters addressed to Tom Paine and denouncing Paine's *Age of Reason*. This was in 1798, at the height of the antirevolutionary hysteria in England. {All through his annotations Blake sees Paine and his iconoclastic attacks on the historical validity of the books of the Bible as the authentic voice of the Holy Spirit, fighting for rudimentary common sense against superstition.} One of his first comments runs: "Paine has not attacked Christianity. Watson has defended Antichrist" [K383/E612].

When Blake speaks of his fourfold vision as "twofold always," he means among other things that he is constantly aware of the contrast between a physical and a spiritual world. This could be translated into a Platonic construct, but it would be wrong to regard Blake as Platonic. The New Testament speaks of visible and invisible worlds, but for Blake the function of the invisible world is to make the genuine form of the world visible—the function that is carried out by poets and painters. It is called the spiritual world because spirit means air or breath, and the spiritual enables the invisible to become visible in the same way that the invisible air makes it possible to see the physical world. Hence Blake's counter-vision of the Bible makes it possible also to see what is really happening in the world at the end of the eighteenth century. {In the Watson notes Blake opposes the notion of an exclusive or peculiar Word of God, addressed only to whatever group, Jewish or Christian or what not, lays claim to it, with what he calls the "everlasting gospel" (Revelation 14:6), the proclamation of peace and liberty for man which, even if originally centred in Christianity, becomes the proclamation that, as he says, "all religions are one."} One of Blake's latest verbal works is the doggerel poem called *The Everlasting Gospel* (ca. 1818), which indicates in its opening lines[1] how little Blake's attitudes on this subject had changed over the years:

> The Vision of Christ that thou dost see
> Is my Vision's Greatest Enemy . . .
> Thine is the friend of All Mankind,
> Mine speaks in parables to the Blind . . .
> Both read the Bible day & night,
> But thou read'st black where I read white. [K748/E524]

Blake is the kind of writer who constantly seems to be anticipating later writers, and in this opposition of genuine Christianity to the infantile bourgeois morality that calls itself Christianity he may remind us of both Kierkegaard and Nietzsche. But one should be aware of differences as well as resemblances. Kierkegaard's *Attack Upon Christendom* has little of Blake's awareness of the worldwide political and social implications of a revolutionary view of the Bible: he thinks of his area of attack as primarily psychological. Again, in Nietzsche's ridiculing of the moral blinkers that man puts on to prevent himself from seeing what is there, there is no acceptance of resurrection as the symbol of man's self-transcendence {into an enlarged framework of existence}. So although Zarathustra tells us that man is something to be surpassed, he has to settle for conceptions of renewal and rebirth and cyclical return. Renewal and rebirth, for Blake, are only parodies of resurrection. Eventually Nietzsche came to contrast a life-denying Christ with a life-affirming Antichrist figure whom he identifies with Dionysus. As Dionysus was the most hypochondriac of all dying gods, and, even more strangely for Nietzsche, the most obsessed with the sexual impulses of females, it seems that Nietzsche had, from Blake's point of view, either lost control of his vision or gone over to what Blake would have considered the real Antichrist, namely Caesar or the authority of the "all too human" world.

II

Once Christianity had came to power in both spiritual and temporal areas, the Bible became the basis for a cosmology that helped to rationalize the existing structures of authority. The reason why the Bible became such a basis is that it is written mainly in poetic and metaphorical language, and cosmologies are essentially metaphorical structures. The language of logic and dialectic always suggests the possibility that the opposite of what it affirms may also be true, but the language of metaphor is far subtler and more pervasive. A metaphor will be "believed," that is, assumed as part of the framework of one's thinking, as long as it seems emotionally convincing, and is irrefutable until it ceases to be so.

According to the traditional cosmology, the universe is a hierarchy of authority stretching from God down through spiritual and human beings to animals, plants, the mineral world, and finally chaos. Creation was the establishing of an ordered hierarchy above chaos, and it contains four main levels. At the top is heaven in the sense of the place of the presence of God. Next comes the earthly paradise, the home God intended man to live in. Third is the present "fallen" world, which humanity has inhabited since the fall of Adam, and fourth is the demonic world. The ups and downs of this cosmos may sometimes be acknowledged to be metaphorical ups and downs, but until about Newton's time most people took the "up" of heaven and the "down" of hell to be more or less descriptive.

According to this construct, God is above nature, the demonic world below it, and in the middle are two levels of nature or creation itself. They are the levels of human and of subhuman or physical nature. Since Adam's fall, all of us are born in the lower world of subhuman nature, but we do not belong there. Our real place is on the upper level or human world. This was originally the Garden of Eden, which no longer exists as a place, but up to a point can be recovered as a state of mind. Many things are natural to man that are not natural to any other members of his environment, such as wearing clothes, using reason and consciousness, and being under social discipline. Man can do nothing by himself: all initiative has to come from above: however, the instruments of grace transmitted by a thoughtful establishment are all in place: obedience to law, the practice of moral virtue, and the sacraments of religion will bring him as close as he can get to his real level in the cosmos.

This cosmos had two by-products that for a long time were taken seriously as scientific concepts. One was the structure of the Ptolemaic universe. Heaven was somewhere outside this universe, and then we have the series of spheres, from the primum mobile down through the planets to the moon, and from the moon to the "sublunar" world of the four elements that since the fall are subject to decay. After Newton's time, these conceptions ceased to carry much conviction. For Dante, the planetary spheres could be guided in their courses by companies of angels, but the Newtonian laws of gravitation and motion suggested a gigantic mechanism without personality of any kind, regardless of Newton's own efforts to struggle against such a suggestion. That is why, in Blake's poem *Europe*, which covers the historical sequence from the birth of Christ to the coming of the French Revolution, it is Newton who blows the trumpet of the Last Judgment or the coming of a new age [K243/E65].

The other by-product was the chain of being, the ladder that was formed out of the two principles of form and matter, and stretched from God, who was pure form, through spiritual and human existence into the subhuman world until it reached chaos, which is as close as we can come to pure matter without form. The chain of being was firmly in place as late as the eighteenth century, in Pope's *Essay on Man*, but Voltaire was beginning to feel very doubtful about the *"échelle de l'infini,"* which he saw clearly to be a disguise for arbitrary authority.[2] For, of course, although in theory the authority it manifested was that of God, in practice the church and state reproduced that authority on earth, and demanded the same unquestioning obedience. The metaphorical kernel of the chain of being was the natural place, the "kindly stead," as Chaucer calls it,[3] which all the elements seek by instinct and which man should seek in his own society. It was, of course, only because it was a structure of authority that this construct had lasted so long, and the factor that was destroying it in Blake's day was the sequence of revolutions—American, French, Industrial—that exposed its skeleton of secular power.

One can find revolutionary ideas in many eighteenth-century writers; but there was one aspect of the situation that Blake was the first poet in English literature, and so far as I know the first person in the modern world, to understand. This was the fact that all the assumptions of the last eighteen centuries at least had been enclosed by a metaphorical framework, that this framework was obsolete, and that another was taking its place.

Blake's early works include the *Songs of Innocence*, where the symbol of innocence is the child. The child is innocent not because he is morally virtuous, but because he {is instinctively civilized: he} assumes that the world makes some kind of human sense, and was probably made for his own benefit. He grows up into the world of experience, and discovers that this is not true. What then happens to his childhood vision? The answer is easy enough now, but I know of no one before Blake who gives it. The childhood vision is driven into the metaphorical underworld that we call the subconscious, where it keeps seething and boiling with frustration, the frustration becoming increasingly sexual with puberty. The vision is of a world of objective experience sitting on top of a subjective furnace of frustrated desire.

The objective world, with which we all have to come to terms, is the source of the power of conservatism in human life that Blake calls Urizen. The subjective world squirming and writhing beneath it, a titan under a volcano, Blake calls Orc. In *The Marriage of Heaven and Hell*, "heaven" and "hell" are called that because they are the polemical terms used by the conservatives, or "Angels," who are terrified at the thought of human energies, especially sexual energies, getting loose. The "marriage" Blake speaks of is an explosion of revolutionary energy coming from Orc, the titan under the volcano, that will burn up the present world and restore to man his lost paradise.

This is the kernel, or middle division, of a metaphorical cosmos that grew more elaborate in Blake's later work, and finally became roughly the old authoritarian construct turned upside down into a revolutionary form. Instead of a heaven above, symbolized by the stars in their courses, the world up there becomes a world of outer space, {held together only by the mechanism of gravitation}: shapeless masses hanging on nothing, as Thomas Hardy says.[4] Below this comes the world of ordinary experience; below that a world of "nature" that seems to include human desire and energy, and yet, because of man's present alienation, excludes them as well. The true world corresponding to heaven can therefore only be metaphorically still further down. It is sometimes symbolized by Atlantis, the country that ought to be uniting America and England, but is now sunk underneath what Blake calls the "Sea of Time and Space."

Looking again at the centre of this inverted cosmic metaphor, we get something that looks like a Noah's ark of traditional human values tossing precariously on a sea of nature. It is a proto-Freudian vision of an ego threatened by suppressed desires, a proto-Marxist vision of an ascendant class threatened by an alienated one; a proto-Darwinian vision of moral values threatened by natural aggression; a proto-Schopenhauerian vision of a world as representation threatened by a world as will. To have turned a metaphorical cosmos eighteen centuries old upside down in a few poems, and provided the basis for a structure that practically every major thinker for the next century would build on, was one of the most colossal imaginative feats in the history of human culture. The only drawback, of course, was that no one knew Blake had done it: in fact Blake hardly realized he had done it either. One thing that is remarkable about Blake's construct, in any case, is that it is at least as solidly Biblical as its predecessor, something not true of later developments of it.

Around 1794 Blake began producing what were evidently intended to be parts of the "Bible of Hell" he had promised. They include *The Book of Urizen* and *The Book of Los*, both apparently parts of a Blakean version of the creation, and also *The Book of Ahania*, which is clearly a "deconstruction," as it might be called now, of the Exodus story. {There are also the four "continent" poems, *America*, *Europe*, and the two parts of *The Song of Los* called *Africa* and *Asia*. These may bear some analogy, although they are called Prophecies, to what we call the historical books of the Bible.} The somewhat pedantic scheme of Biblical parody was soon abandoned for the more comprehensive designs of *The Four Zoas* and its successors, but remained a part of Blake's total vision. The central parody theme in *The Book of Urizen*, where the seven days of the Biblical creation become seven long ages of "dismal woe," recurs in *The Four Zoas*, and, more perfunctorily, in the still later *Milton*.

As Blake knew, there are two accounts of creation in Genesis: the first or Priestly account, which covers the first chapter, and the second or Jahwist account, which starts in Genesis 2:4. {The Priestly account, though placed first, is historically later, and the two accounts are distinguished by the different names employed for God.} The Priestly account, as everyone knows, shows God creating the world in a sequence of six acts or "days," with a concluding comment that the seventh "day" was a day of rest. The Jahwist account also consists of six acts, though they are not so often counted. First, God creates a "mist," out of what is apparently dry ground; second comes the creation of the adam (he is not "Adam" until later); then the creating of the Garden of Eden, then the irrigating of the garden with four rivers, then the creation of all the nonhuman living creatures, and finally the creation of woman. The seventh episode is again not an act, but the comment that Adam and Eve were in the state of innocence, naked and unashamed.

The two accounts of creation emphasize two aspects of nature, the nature that is a structure or system and the nature that is the totality of life. They are sometimes distinguished as *natura naturata* and *natura naturans*: physical nature and biological nature.[5] {At the same time having two such different accounts caused trouble for some commentators.} In the first account, men and women are created on the sixth day along with the other land animals, whereas in the second the creation of human beings is quite separate from the other acts of creation and man and woman are created at different times. The difficulty bred the later legend of Lilith, Adam's first wife and mother of demons, a legend that failed to interest Blake. The story of the fall of man is attached to the Jahwist account, as such a story would have to be. God must have created a perfect or model world, and the alienation myth of a fall is needed to explain the contrast between such a model world and the chaotic mess we are in now. But no fall legend seems to be directly attached to the Priestly story of creation.

It emerges later, however, in the story of the fall of the rebel angels, whose leader is alluded to in Isaiah as Lucifer, or light-bearer. Of course traditionally this revolt is simply a revolt of evil against goodness, and if one accepts an omnipotent God, the war in heaven can be only some kind of practical joke on God's part, as it essentially is in *Paradise Lost*. But Classical legends tell us of a revolt of titans which the titans very nearly won, and they also strongly suggest that the supreme god of the skies is a usurper, {holding power by tyranny in the Greek sense of the word}.

Blake had already suggested, in *The Marriage of Heaven and Hell*, that there might be a devil's account of what happened as well as an angelic one, {and that one might get some notion of such an account even from the Bible}. For Blake, in any case, the first chapter of Genesis conceals a story of warring titanic beings, equally divine and human, whose struggles for power produced the world we are now in. It is from these wars that we got such things as the splendid ferocity of the tiger, who was created "When the stars threw down their spears" [K214/E25], stars meaning spiritual beings.

In Blake the word "reason" means the exact opposite of what the words "mental" and "intellectual" mean. The mind creates out of the world something with a human shape and sense, and thereby forms a model of the kind of world man should be living in, and was living in before "reason" started mucking it about. {Reason makes nothing out of the world: it merely stares at it, and then forms a squirrel-cage of logic to revolve in.} In *The Book of Urizen* we meet the titan of that name who should be, and once was, the mind or intellect of divine humanity, but who has transformed himself into reason, or passive consciousness. This immediately brings into the world {what genuine imaginative work tries to abolish:} the "Cloven Fiction" [K770/E268], as Blake calls it, of subject and object. The subject is reduced to a "soul-shudd'ring vacuum" [K222/E72], like the *tabula rasa* of Locke, the nothingness of a consciousness that {cannot act, but} can only be acted upon. The objective counterpart of this is a "world of solid obstruction" [K224/E72], or objectivity at its deadest. Urizen no longer understands the conception of unity, which he also turns into its opposite, or uniformity: "One King, One God, One Law," he says. Naturally this is not done all at once: one of the remarkable features of the poem is the emphasis Blake gives to the immense length of time in the prehistorical world.

Urizen is thus not so much a creator as the condition of creation: he is the world we have now, the ruin out of which we have to try to rebuild the original form. His great antagonist is the fire-demon Los, a Lucifer figure who retains a higher kind of energy. {Consciousness alone can see the world in any sort of human shape, and after seven ages of "dismal woe" Los does get some kind of intelligible human shape on Urizen. Some myths tell us how the world was made by the dismembering of a giant: here something of the same process in reverse seems to be going on as Urizen gradually becomes something of an objective counterpart to the humanity still present in Los.} Both the creation books emphasize the separation of the two figures of Los and Urizen. What separates with them are the more organic and the more mechanical aspects of both human and natural worlds. Urizen gives birth to the four elements, and, in the interests of trying to keep everything uniform, inspires man with a fascination for the quantitative and measurable, the "starry floor" [K210/E18], Blake calls it, the bedrock of recreation. Los creates the archetypal human family, a nuclear Freudian family of jealous father (Los himself), rebellious son (Orc), and anxious mother (Enitharmon). Both creation poems tell us of "many ages of groans" [K258/E92], where nothing very cheerful appears to be happening.

The Book of Ahania is Blake's version of the Exodus, which he sees as a betrayed revolution. Fuzon, the son of Urizen and a fire-demon like Los, leads a revolt against his father and leaves Egypt. {Urizen does not care whether his tyranny is Egyptian or Israelite in locale as long as it is tyranny, and} very soon Fuzon's pillar of fire has given place to the sky-god Urizen's pillar of cloud, the twelve tribes of Israel (actually thirteen, because of the division of the tribe of Joseph) fall into the cyclical rhythms of the zodiac, and the moral law is reimposed. Urizen acquires a poisonous serpent, the same serpent that introduced the tree of morality to Adam and Eve, and Fuzon is crucified on the Tree of Mystery (metaphorically the same tree) as a sacrifice to the serpent. This is what Blake reads into the story of the brazen serpent on the pole in Numbers 21.

The incident thus recalls the fall of Adam and Eve and anticipates the death of the rebellious son Absalom and the crucifixion of Christ, all of these being symbols of the completing of the triumph of tyranny and the martyrdom of the rebel against it. It remains the central image of human society for 1800 years until the red Orc appears in *America*, announces that he is the Orc who has been throughout history "wreath'd round the accursed tree" [K198/E54], and is ready to do battle with the white reactionary terror of Albion. We may recall that American flags at that period featured trees, serpents, stars, an alternation of red and white, and a preoccupation with the number thirteen.

The Oedipal trio of father, mother, and son reappears in *The Book of Ahania*, along with a very unusual fantasy of a primal scene. Fuzon throws his "pillar of fire" at Urizen, which divides Urizen's loins and separates from his body the female figure of Ahania, who is, in a manner of speaking, Fuzon's mother. The poem concludes with a beautiful lament of this Ahania, an earth-mother weeping for a dying god. Ahania has, of course, no counterpart in the Mosaic account of the Exodus, and her prominence here means that Blake is losing interest in the twofold stage of his Biblical vision and is moving into the threefold one of "soft Beulah's night." Beulah means married, and is the word applied by Isaiah to the land of Israel reunited with its God as bride to bridegroom [Isaiah 62:4].

III

Up to about 1795 Blake had apparently assumed that the revolution of human liberty, after spreading from America to France, would then spread over the rest of the world: {in that year he engraved the remarkable little poem *Asia*, describing its penetration into that traditionally benighted continent}. But it soon became clear to him that the reactionary powers would not disappear, but simply form an adversary relation with the revolutionary ones. This had happened before, Blake says, with the sixteenth-century Reformation, just as it was to happen again after 1917. An adversary situation, even if there is no war, impoverishes both sides, as both have to consolidate power on a basis of repression. This means that the apocalyptic contest of freedom and tyranny vanishes into dreamland, and the tactics of holding and gaining power emerge as the common ideology of both parties.

For Blake this common ideology was to be found in what he calls Deism or natural religion, and his opposition to it led him to denounce Voltaire and Rousseau on the same basis that he had already denounced {the empiricism of} Newton and Locke in England. Trying to explain why he hated "n.r." takes us into one of the most treacherous areas of symbolism, the male and female symbolism that recalls, but should not be confused with, the relations of men and women. It is also the most difficult area of Blake to explore, partly because Blake never shows much pictorial or verbal interest in what ought to have been his main Biblical source, the Song of Songs. {Some personal anxieties may also have obscured the clarity of this part of his vision.}

In traditional Christian symbolism, all Christian souls, whether of men or of women, are symbolically female, and make up the Bride of Christ, Christ being symbolically the only male. In Blake all human beings, both men and women, are symbolically male, and what is symbolically female is nature or the objective world. In Blake's myth of the creation-fall, one very unexpected event was the forming of two sexes among human beings. One of the "Eternals" in *The Four Zoas* says, "Humanity knows naught of sex: wherefore are sexes in Beulah?"[6] In *The Book of Urizen* we learn that the same Eternals shuddered at the appearance of the first separate female form. Blake seems to be taking quite seriously the hint dropped so lightly in Andrew Marvell's poem *The Garden*, that the real fall was the creation of Eve. Originally, in the second creation account, there was an androgynous "adam" and a garden which was itself the female principle. This symbolism recurs in the Song of Songs, where in the fourth chapter there is a male, that is a human, spirit or wind in the garden, and where the garden itself, "a garden enclosed, a fountain sealed," is what is female. A character in *The Four Zoas* recalls the happy days of eternity

> Where thou & I in undivided Essence walk'd about
> Imbodied, thou my garden of delight & I the spirit in the garden[7]

Elsewhere the symbolism becomes urban and focuses on the relation between a male God-Man and a female Jerusalem, "a city, yet a Woman," as Blake says [K362/E391]. This suggests that the individual is the sexual male and the social the sexual female. However, the present sexual relation within humanity provides the central imaginative focus for the kind of energy that rebuilds the creation. In any case, Blake does not mean that there is no sexual activity in his spiritual world, but that there is a tremendous heightening of it, a total merging of the creating and the responding aspects of the imagination.

There are two kinds of human subject, a positive subject that recreates the world and a negative one that just stares at it. The positive subject is the human imagination, which is constantly concerned with creation and love. The total body of what a human being loves is that being's "emanation," and emanations are symbolically female. The negative human subject is the ego or "selfhood," who withdraws from creative effort and, because full of desires and energies that have no outlet, is "in every man insane and most deformed," and "a ravening devouring lust continually."[8] Blake calls this ego-figure the "Spectre," and all Spectres, like all imaginations, are symbolically male. Confronting the Spectre is the negative aspect of the symbolically female, or what Blake calls the Female Will, the elusive, evasive, mysterious outside world as it appears to the ego, who keeps trying to grasp hold of what is actually inside him, waiting to be born from his body as Eve was from Adam's. All Spectres are symbolically dead, unless provided with "counterparts" or "concentering visions" that bring them to life [K330/E369].

We express one aspect of this symbolism, very misleadingly, when we speak of a Father God and a Mother Nature. In the actual relation the emanation is more like a daughter: we may remember the prominence of daughters in the restoration of Job. Thus the theme of Blake's poem *Jerusalem* is the union of Albion, the imagination of the human race, with his emanation or daughter Jerusalem, the totality of what Albion constructs, loves, and surrounds. The opposite relation, of Spectre and Female Will, is almost exactly what was later to be called the "ghost in the machine." There being no God apart from humanity, nature apart from humanity is the subhuman, hence "natural religion" is simply a worship of the machinery which is all that the Spectre can see in nature. The Spectre can respond to this vision of machinery, {most of which is in the stars,} only by building more machinery of its own, and so "natural religion" takes the form of an industrialism that builds up a system of exploiting other men on the basis of exploiting nature.

This threefold Beulah vision of the world is full of fairies and elemental spirits, which are not featured in the Bible but represent for Blake the original forms of what were later perverted into the heathen gods, nature-spirits turned monstrous and tyrannical. Blake's fairies appear in the most unexpected places: in the middle of the intensely political poem *The Song of Los* is an exquisite picture of Oberon and Titania resting upon lilies. The conventionally mocking, teasing, mischievous qualities of these creatures indicate that they are part of a genuine but still incomplete vision of nature where all natural objects are human entities "seen afar," {and where

> All the Wisdom which was hidden in caves & dens from ancient
> Time is now sought out from Animal & Vegetable & Mineral.}
>
> [K510/E121]

In the fourfold vision nature expands into the infinite worlds traditionally called heaven and hell, except that we have to remember that "Death & Hell / Team with Life" [K261/E673]. This is the apocalyptic vision at the end of *Jerusalem* in which "All Human Forms {are} identified" [K747/E258], as the entire universe turns inside out, going through the vortex of time and space to become the city and garden where man and nature are sexually at one. In the Bible the image for the fallen creation is the sea or watery deep that meets us at the beginning of Genesis and returns in the story of Noah's flood, a flood that has never really subsided. As the Atlantis story reminds us, the present world is symbolically submarine as well as subterranean. In Blake this watery chaos is the last of the four "Zoas" to become clear in his mind, the Tharmas who represents, Blake says, human strength and sublimity, and in the final vision turns from the water of death into the water of life. The Priestly account of creation also distinguishes the fire of life, the primordial light, from the sun created on the fourth day, and when man resumes his proper intelligence he can live in this fire as well as in the water of life.

With the fourfold vision we are in the world of full humanity: "The Sexual is Threefold: the Human is Fourfold," Blake says [K483/E97]. Hence if I go on talking about mankind and of what "man" does, it is because the English language, in its infinite and illogical unwisdom, compels me to do so. Blake's reading of the Bible from his "fourfold" point of view is not simply a reversal of traditional readings. What he reverses is the directional emphasis: he reads forward to the end instead of constantly looking back to the beginning. We start with a waste and void chaos, a fall, a flood, a descent to Egypt, and other images of being thrown into an alien world, {constantly subject to disaster, and} with nothing but an invisible God to depend on and a vague hope for a better world in some kind of future, in or out of time.

Blake's Bible tells us, as its essential revelation, not that man fell into chaos, but that he can climb out of it if he uses all his creative capacities to do so. {This means using everything he has that is imaginative, and the imagination, Blake says, is the human existence itself.} In our day Ezra Pound, by no means either a Biblical or a Blakean poet, also spoke near the end of his life of having tried to build a terrestrial paradise,[9] and of urging humanity to be men and not destroyers.[10] Blake, being both a Biblical and an English poet, speaks of the central task of man as building Jerusalem in England, of remaking the world into its genuinely human form.

We think we fall asleep at night into the illusions of dream, and wake up in our bedrooms in the morning facing reality again. But of course everything in the bedroom is a human construct, and whatever humanity has made it can remake. We gradually discover that this principle applies to everything: what is real is what we have made: *verum factum*, as Vico says. When Blake says that a man who is not a painter or poet is not a Christian,[11] he is putting into paradox his principle that the release of the imagination, in any human sphere whatever, creates human form, and cannot destroy anything except unreality. Blake also says that the notion that before the creation all was solitude and chaos is the most pernicious idea that can enter the mind.[12] In spite of the word "before," he is not talking about time but about a spiritual reality that has always been here, and that the imagination is constantly struggling to make more and more visible. The apocalypse at the end of the Bible is not simply a new heaven and earth, but the old heaven and earth restored in their original forms. Visions of what humanity could accomplish if the destructive side of man did not get in its way are common enough: in Blake, however, God and creative man being the same thing, his apocalypse is neither a humanistic vision of a better future nor a show of fireworks put on by God for an applauding or terrified human audience. It is the attaining of a divine and human identity whose creative powers are entirely without limits. Limits are in the forms of what is made, but the powers of making are infinite.

Notes

Introduction

1 See Denis Saurat, *Blake and Milton* (1920, rev. ed. 1935); Harold Bloom, *The Anxiety of Influence: A Theory of Poetry* (1973); Leslie Brisman, *Milton's Poetry of Choice and Its Romantic Heirs* (1973); J.A. Wittreich, Jr., *Angel of Apocalypse: Blake's Idea of Milton* (1975); Stephen C. Behrendt, *The Moment of Explosion: Blake and the Illustration of Milton* (1983); Jackie DiSalvo, *War of Titans: Blake's Critique of Milton and the Politics of Religion* (1983); Angela Esterhammer, *Creating States: Studies in the Performative Language of John Milton and William Blake* (1994).

2 Blackstone, *English Blake* (Cambridge: Cambridge University Press, 1949), 21.

1. Introduction to*"Paradise Lost" and Selected Poetry and Prose*

1 From *Elegia Sexta*: "Surgis ad infensos augur iture Deos" (l. 66) and "Diis etenim sacer est vates, divumque sacerdos, / Spirat et occultum pectus et ora Iovem" (ll. 77–8); apparently NF's translation.

2 "Et nunc sancta canit superum consulta deorum, / Nunc latrata fero regna profunda cane" (ll. 57–8).

3 Edward Phillips, *The Life of Milton*, in Merritt Y. Hughes, ed., *John Milton: Complete Poems and Major Prose* (New York: Macmillan, 1985), 1035.

4 This allusion, which NF also uses in the fourth essay of *The Return of Eden* (see no. 3 in this volume), seems to be a recollection of l. 50 of Aeschylus's *Prometheus Bound*: "For no one is free except Zeus" (ἐλεύθερος γὰρ οὔτις ἐστὶ πλὴν Διός). For NF, the verse encapsulates an important contrast between the Classical and Christian world view on the subject of human free will. But the idea that the gods are free is not generally representative of the Classical Greek, or the Homeric, world order.

5 *Tenure of Kings and Magistrates*, in *Works*, 5:1.

6 *Doctrine and Discipline of Divorce*, in *Works*, 3:472.

7 *Areopagitica*, in *Works*, 4:340.
8 *Readie and Easie Way*, in *Works*, 6:149.
9 *Of Education*, in *Works*, 4:277.
10 *Reason of Church Government*, in *Works*, 3:237.
11 The last plays of Jean Racine (1639–99) are *Esther* (1689) and *Athalie* (1690).
12 *Reason of Church Government*, in *Works*, 3:235.
13 Job 42:5, "I have heard of thee by the hearing of the ear: but now mine eye seeth thee," suggests a contrast between indirect knowledge (hearing *of*) and direct knowledge (seeing). The original quotation supports Frye's argument more strongly than the slight misquotation in the copy-text, which implies a straightforward contrast between aural and visual experience.

2. Literature as Context: Milton's *Lycidas*

1 "A god is he, a god, Menalcas!" (*Bucolica*, 5, l. 64; translation as in Loeb edition).
2 It is actually the "wolf" in l. 128, a symbol of the Roman Catholic Church, that Milton describes as "grim," not the mysterious "two-handed engine" of St. Peter in l. 130.
3 In his essay on Milton in *Lives of the English Poets*, Samuel Johnson denies that *Lycidas* contains "real passion" (*Lives*, 3 vols., ed. G.B. Hill [New York: Octagon Books, 1967], 1:163).
4 From Wordsworth's *A Slumber Did My Spirit Seal*, one of the short, elegiac lyrics grouped together as the "Lucy poems"; *The Poetical Works of William Wordsworth*, ed. E. de Selincourt (Oxford: Clarendon Press, 1963), 216.
5 Ibid., 216.
6 *The Complete Writings of Walt Whitman*, ed. Richard Maurice Bucke, Thomas B. Harned, and Horace L. Traubel (Grosse Pointe, Mich.: Scholarly Press, 1902), 94.
7 The "lunatic, lover, and poet" reference, used often by NF in various contexts, is from *A Midsummer Night's Dream*, 5.1.7–8.
8 The original version of the essay in the *Proceedings* and the Patrides volume contained two further sentences at this point: "When Thomas Rymer called *Othello* a bloody farce, he was not making a bad value-judgment; he was making a correct value-judgment based on impossibly narrow scholarship. Most of the famous howlers of criticism are of this kind." The passage was omitted when the essay was reprinted in *FI*. Thomas Rymer (1641–1713) was a historian, critic, and unsuccessful dramatist who supported extreme neo-Classical ideals. The reference is to Rymer, *A Short View of Tragedy* (1693; rpt. Yorkshire: Scolar Press, 1970), 146.

3. The Return of Eden

1 "You who read *Paradise Lost*, sublime poem of the great Milton, what do you read but the story of all things? This poem contains all things, the beginnings of all things, fate, the ends of all things" (*Paradise Lost*, ed. Roy Flannagan [New York: Macmillan, 1993], 106).

2 Sir Richard Blackmore came in for widespread critique for his epic *Prince Arthur: A Heroick Poem, in Ten Books* (1695). In the early 1960s, when Frye was writing this essay, the standard literary history for graduate students preparing for comprehensive exams in English at the University of Toronto was Albert Baugh's *A Literary History of England* (1948). The section on Restoration and eighteenth-century literature, by George Sherburn, explicitly contrasted Blackmore and Milton: "Milton had achieved greatness in the epic, but Sir Richard Blackmore in his repeated attempts showed piety, patriotism, and the desire to achieve greatness—but never true epic quality itself" (898); "At the end of the century, to be sure, Sir Richard Blackmore (ca. 1655–1729) was pouring forth interminable epic strains; but these were not highly regarded" (733).

3 *Gabriel Harvey's Marginalia*, ed. G.C. Moore Smith (Stratford-upon-Avon: Shakespeare Head Press, 1913), 161.

4 *A Discourse of English Poetrie* (1586; rpt., ed. Edward Arber, London, 1871), 25.

5 "Whoever had hoped for such a work could believe that it might be written, yet Britain can read this poem today" (*Paradise Lost*, ed. Flannagan, 106).

6 Matthew 25:14–30, the parable of the talents, to which Milton alludes most famously in Sonnet 19: "And that one Talent which is death to hide, / Lodg'd with me useless."

7 In Isaiah 6, the prophet sees a vision of Jehovah, and is sent out to prophesy after a seraph touches and purifies his mouth with a live coal from the altar.

8 Milton's friend Charles Diodati.

9 ". . . as, resplendent with holy vestments and with lustral waters, you rise, minded to go forth to face the angry gods" (*Works*, 1:213).

10 *The Life of the Renowned Sir Philip Sidney*, first published in 1652.

11 *An Apology for Poetry, Miscellaneous Prose of Sir Philip Sidney*, ed. Katherine Duncan-Jones and Jan van Dorsten (Oxford: Clarendon, 1973), 11. On Xenophon's *Cyropaedia*, cf. n. 13 to essay no. 4 in this volume.

12 "For this cause is Xenophon preferred before Plato, for that the one in the exquisite depth of his iudgement, formed a Commune welth such as it should be, but the other in the person of Cyrus and the Persians fashioned a gouernement such as might best be: So much more profitable and gratious is doctrine by ensample, then by rule" (*The Faerie Queene*, ed. A.C. Hamilton [London: Longman, 1977], 737). The reference to "ayrie Burgomasters" is in *Areopagitica* (*Works*, 4:316).

13 "As is painting, so is poetry" (Horace, *Ars Poetica*, l. 361). The idea that painting and poetry, as mimetic arts, are similar was widely repeated in Renaissance and later criticism, but began to be attacked in the eighteenth century by G.E. Lessing in his essay *Laokoön* (1766).

14 Rainer Maria Rilke's second *Duino Elegy* begins, "Jeder Engel ist schrecklich" ("Every angel is dreadful").

15 Probably an echo of the "better fortitude / Of Patience and Heroic Martyrdom" that Milton holds up against the more popular heroic subject of wars and battles in *PL*, 9.31–2.

16 *There Was a Child Went Forth*, in *The Complete Writings of Walt Whitman*, 135.

17 In Genesis 9:20–7, Ham is cursed by his father Noah for seeing Noah when he was drunk and naked. The punishment laid on Ham and his descendants, the Canaanites, is to be in servitude to the descendants of Noah's other sons Shem and Japheth.

18 Milton's line reads "This day *I have* begot," an inversion of the biblical source-text, Psalm 2:7: "Thou art my Son; this day *have I* begotten thee." NF misquotes Milton slightly, recalling the rhythm of the King James Bible instead.

19 Cf. Genesis 2:17, "in the day that thou eatest thereof thou shalt surely die," and *PL*, 7.544, "in the day thou eat'st, thou di'st."

20 Richard Hooker, *Of the Laws of Ecclesiastical Polity*, ed. A.S. McGrade (Cambridge: Cambridge University Press, 1989), 118 (bk. 1, chap. 4).

21 The description of the gates of horn and ivory—used by true and false dreams, respectively—is in *Odyssey*, bk. 19, ll. 562–7. In *Odyssey*, bk. 13, ll. 102–12, Odysseus finds himself in a sacred cave on the island of Ithaka that has two entrances: one of them, facing the north wind, for humans, the other, facing the south wind, for immortals. Porphyry (A.D. 233–305) integrates the "Cave of the Nymphs" into a Neoplatonist vision of the cosmos and the journey of the human soul. Yeats quotes from Porphyry in an essay on "The Philosophy of Shelley's Poetry" (in *Ideas of Good and Evil*) and in a note to *Among School Children*, and imagery reminiscent of Porphyry's description of the cave can be found in Yeats's *The Wild Swans at Coole* and Blake's *Book of Thel*.

22 *Of Education*, in *Works*, 4:277.

23 "God, or, at least, the Third Intelligence of emptied heaven . . . makes its way unseen through your throat, aye, makes its way, and graciously teaches mortal hearts the power to grow accustomed insensibly to sounds immortal. But, if all things are God, and God is transfused through all, yet it is in you alone that He speaks: to all else that He possesses He vouchsafes no voice" (*Works*, 1:229).

24 ". . . where there is singing, where the lyre revels madly, mingled with choirs beatific, and festal orgies run riot, in bacchante fashion, with the thyrsus of Zion" (*Works*, 1:317).

25 "So drive, rather, to the skies loathsome cowls, and as many insensate gods as Rome profane possesses, for, unless you aid each of them by such craft, or by some other, he will hardly—believe me—climb easily up the road to the skies" (*In Eadem*, in *Works*, 1:225).
26 In *Aeneid*, bk. 6, l. 126, the Sibyl tells Aeneas, "easy is the descent to Avernus" (i.e., the Underworld).
27 *Eikonoklastes*, in *Works*, 5:280.
28 "I love to lose my selfe in a mystery; to pursue my reason to an *o altitudo*!" Sir Thomas Browne, *Religio Medici*, in *The Works of Sir Thomas Browne*, ed. Geoffrey Keynes, 4 vols. (London: Faber & Faber, 1964), 1:18 (pt. 1, sec. 9).
29 *Tetrachordon*, in *Works*, 4:160.
30 Cf. n. 1 to essay no. 4 in this volume.
31 "Not *Babilon*, / Nor great *Alcairo* such magnificence / Equal'd . . ." (*PL*, 1.717–19).
32 Cf. Ezekiel chaps. 40–8, where the prophet experiences a vision of the temple in Jerusalem.
33 The notion of becoming that which one sees, or chooses to see, an idea that NF traces throughout this essay as it appears in the Bible and Milton, is prominent in Blake's work. Here at the end, NF explicitly echoes a phrase that Blake uses numerous times: "He became what he beheld" (e.g., K302, 305/E336, 338).
34 Cf. n. 4 to essay no. 1 in this volume.
35 Richard Baxter (1615–91) was an extremely learned and influential Puritan minister, and a prolific writer who produced over two hundred works. Taking a liberal stand on doctrinal matters, Baxter contributed to the evangelical tradition and worked to further the nonconformist cause. NF's quotation could not be located.
36 Blake, *Introduction* to *Songs of Experience* (K210/E18).
37 Malory, *Le Morte Darthur* (New York: University Books, 1961), 65 (bk. 10, chap. 36).
38 Dylan Thomas, *Altarwise by Owl-light*, in *Collected Poems, 1934–1952*, 65.
39 *Areopagitica*, in *Works*, 4:353.
40 *Reason of Church Government*, in *Works*, 3:196.
41 Cf. Blake, *The Marriage of Heaven and Hell*, pl. 6 (K35/E150).
42 *Of Reformation*, in *Works*, 3:34.
43 *Animadversions*, in *Works*, 3:172.
44 *History of Britain*, in *Works*, 10:33.
45 *Familiar Letters*, in *Works*, 12:33.
46 The preceding sentences replace the beginning of "The Typology of *Paradise Regained*" (the earlier version of this essay), which begins: "The second of three main episodes in the agon of Christ and Satan is presented in *Paradise Regained*. First is the original war in heaven recounted in *Paradise Lost*, and

third is the final binding of Satan in the second coming of Christ, prophesied in the Book of Revelation."

47 Preface to bk. 2, in *Works,* 3:237.

48 In "The Typology of *Paradise Regained,*" the preceding phrase reads, "might belong more naturally to the period immediately following Christ's death."

49 *Areopagitica,* in *Works,* 4:311.

50 The allusion to Jonah has been added in the revised version, and an allusion to *Paradise Lost* in the following sentence has been removed. In "The Typology of *Paradise Regained,*" it reads, "The Israelites conquer the Promised Land under '*Joshua* whom the Gentiles *Jesus* call' [*PL,* 12.310] (i.e., Joshua and Jesus are the same word), corresponding to Christ's victory over death and hell . . . ."

51 In place of this phrase, "The Typology of *Paradise Regained*" has an endnote: "*De doctrina Christiana,* bk. 1, chap. 26 (*Works,* 16:110–11)."

52 "The Typology of *Paradise Regained*" contains an extra sentence at this point: "In any case Eden, the Promised Land, and the inward Kingdom of Heaven proclaimed by Jesus are all the same place, and Jesus' victory as second Adam and Israel is identical with the central act of his ministry, the casting of devils out of the human mind."

53 "The Typology of *Paradise Regained*" has the following endnote: "For the homiletic tradition behind Milton's and Fletcher's treatment, see E.M. Pope, *'Paradise Regained': The Tradition and the Poem* (Baltimore, 1947). For Spenser's Despair, see also E. Sirluck, 'A Note on the Rhetoric of Spenser's Despair,' *Modern Philology,* 47 (1949): 8 ff."

54 "The Typology of *Paradise Regained*" has the following endnote at this point: "Giles Fletcher follows the Matthew order of temptations; Milton, of course, follows Luke."

55 "The Typology of *Paradise Regained*" has the following endnote: "This contrast is symbolized by the fact that the action of *Comus* moves up to the sprinkling of the Lady by Sabrina, an act with some analogies to Baptism, whereas the action of *Paradise Regained* follows Baptism (cf. A.S.P. Woodhouse, 'Comus Once More,' *University of Toronto Quarterly,* 19 [1950]: 218 ff.)."

56 The paragraph, up to this point, has been rewritten. "The Typology of *Paradise Regained*" reads: "The epic is traditionally a poem of heroic action, and a Christian poet must decide, before writing an epic, what in Christian terms a hero is and what an act is. For Milton all real acts are good, and there are no real evil acts. Christ in *Paradise Lost* illustrates the pattern of this positive or real act: all his acts are creative or recreative (i.e., redemptive). Adam's fall was thus not an act but a failure to act, the sham act of disobedience. Satan's fall was the parody act of rebellion, which, unlike disobedience, involves an attempt at rivalry with God. In the fallen world (since Nimrod, who introduced political authority and with it the pos-

sibility of imitating the demonic), man naturally turns to the demonic pseudo-hero as the pattern of heroic action. The genuinely heroic act is found only in the imitation of Christ, in endurance and obedience, and its pattern is illustrated in Abdiel, the faithful angel." NF adds an endnote after "there are no real evil acts": "*De Doctrina Christiana*, bk. 1, chap. 11 (*Works*, 15:198–9)."

57 "The Typology of *Paradise Regained*" contains an extra sentence at this point: "Some Milton scholars think that *Samson Agonistes* is earlier than *Paradise Regained*: if so, the latter is Milton's final poetic testament, and his treatment of this theme takes on an additional intensity and pathos."

58 This phrase originally read, "Milton goes to grotesque lengths in *Paradise Lost* in emphasizing this point . . . ."

59 Fyodor Dostoevsky, *The Brothers Karamazov*, pt. 2, bk. 5, chap. 5.

60 "The Typology of *Paradise Regained*" has the following endnote: "For an explicit assertion that Satan was right and Christ wrong, see the passage from the nineteenth-century anarchist Proudhon quoted in Karl Löwith, *Meaning in History* (Chicago[: University of Chicago Press], 1949), 64."

61 The beginning of the paragraph, up to this point, originally read: "In *Paradise Regained*, as to some extent in *Comus*, the dramatic and the dialectical aspects of the conflict are opposed and in a paradoxical relation to one another. Comus and Satan get our dramatic attention because they show such energy and resourcefulness; the tempted figures are either motionless or unmoved and have only the ungracious dramatic function of saying No. Yet, of course, the real relation is the opposite of the apparent one: the real source of life and freedom and energy is in the frigid figure at the centre."

62 *Animadversions*, in *Works*, 3:113.

63 This sentence is a shortened version of two sentences in "The Typology of *Paradise Regained*": "In the Classical epic, knowledge of the future is usually gained from a dark underworld, in contrast to the revelations of gods, which as a rule illuminate the present moment. Similarly in Dante the damned know the future but not the present, and in *Paradise Lost* Michael prophesies the future to Adam after he has gained his forbidden knowledge."

64 The two preceding sentences have been reworded from "The Typology of *Paradise Regained*," which reads: "For Milton what man can do for himself is negative and iconoclastic: man does not save himself, but, by clearing his world of idols, he can indicate his willingness to be saved. Christ has resisted the whole of Satan's world; he has done what man can do, and the only possible next step is for God to indicate acceptance of what he has done."

65 "The Typology of *Paradise Regained*" has the following endnote: "A.S.P. Woodhouse, 'Paradise Regained,' *University of Toronto Quarterly*, 25 (1956): 181."

66 "The Typology of *Paradise Regained*" adds, "and changed his mind for him."

67 The ending of the essay has been substantially rewritten. "The Typology of *Paradise Regained*" has one long paragraph in place of the last two paragraphs of the revised version: "In the *Christian Doctrine* Milton distinguishes between the literal and what he calls the "metaphorical" generation of the Son by the Father. By the latter he means what might more accurately be called "epiphany," the manifesting of Christ in a divine capacity to others. The showing of Christ to the angels in *Paradise Lost* is a metaphorical or epiphanic generation of him: the Father's phrase "This day have I begot" [*PL*, 5.603] can hardly refer to literal generation. The same distinction recurs in the Incarnation. Two of the Gospels, Matthew and Luke, are nativity Gospels, beginning with Christ's infancy or physical generation in the world. The other two, Mark and John, are epiphanic Gospels and begin with his baptism, where he is pointed out to man as the Son of God. (In the Western churches epiphany means particularly the showing of the infant Christ to the Magi, but in the Eastern churches it means particularly the baptism, though the date of observance is the same.) Epiphany is the theological equivalent of what in literature is called "anagnorisis" or "recognition." The Father recognizes Jesus as the Son at the baptism: Satan recognizes him on the pinnacle in a different, yet closely related, sense. That is, the action of *Paradise Regained* begins with the baptism, an epiphany which Satan sees but does not understand, and ends with an epiphany to Satan alone, the nature of which he can hardly fail to understand. Behind this is the still larger scheme in which *Paradise Regained* is the sequel of *Paradise Lost*. The epiphany of Christ to the angels, which caused the original revolt of Satan, was chronologically the first event in *Paradise Lost*, and, with the climax of *Paradise Regained*, the great wheel of the quest of Christ comes full circle, as far as Milton's treatment of it is concerned."

4. The Revelation to Eve

1 Keats, Letter to Benjamin Bailey, 22 November 1817. On the two gates of dreams, cf. n. 21 to essay no. 3 in this volume.

2 *Aeneid*, bk. 1, l. 47.

3 *Of Reformation*, in *Works*, 3:57.

4 *Eikonoklastes*, in *Works*, 5:185.

5 *Areopagitica*, in *Works*, 4:311.

6 Milton's Latin poem of 1638 to a Roman poet, *Ad Salsillum*.

7 Cf. *The Notebooks of Samuel Taylor Coleridge*, 4 vols., ed. Kathleen Coburn (London: Routledge, 1961), vol. 2, no. 2355: "Idly talk they who speak of Poets as mere Indulgers of Fancy, Imagination, Superstition, &c—They are the Bridlers by Delight, the Purifiers, they that combine them with *reason* & order, the true Protoplasts, Gods of Love who tame the Chaos."

8 Milton, *At a Solemn Musick*, in *Works*, 1:27.
9 "Eternal Feminine"; the term is associated with Goethe, who used it (most famously in the concluding lines of pt. 2 of *Faust*) to refer to an archetypal, inspiring female principle.
10 *Apology for Smectymnuus*, in *Works*, 3:287.
11 These conceptions of Eros and Agape have been drawn ultimately from *Agape and Eros*, by Bishop [Anders] Nygren, trans. Hebert and [Philip S.] Watson, 1932–39 [London: SPCK, 1953], but are very differently applied. [NF]
12 "And a song such as to send the Moon astray as she followeth her laborious course in the high heavens" (Sonnet 4, in *Works*, 1:55).
13 The original *Cyropaedia* of Xenophon dealt with the training of Cyrus of Persia, a heroic figure in both Classical and Biblical literature. This genre was revived during the Renaissance, when the prince emerged as both head and centre of his society; examples include Erasmus's *Institute of a Christian Prince*, Castiglione's *Il Cortegiano*, and Spenser's *Faerie Queene*, which is in one of its aspects an educational treatise on the qualities of the ideal prince, identified with the romance hero Prince Arthur.
14 *Areopagitica*, in *Works*, 4:316.
15 *Animadversions*, in *Works*, 3:171.
16 *Reason of Church Government*, in *Works*, 3:188–9.
17 Ibid., 3:268.
18 *Doctrine and Discipline of Divorce*, in *Works*, 3:420.
19 *Eikonoklastes*, in *Works*, 5:204.
20 Proverbs 8:30 [Vulgate]; *PL*, 8.10. [NF]

5. *Agon* and *Logos*

1 In a prefatory note to *Paradise Lost*, entitled *The Verse*, Milton describes his blank verse as "ancient liberty recover'd to Heroic Poem from the troublesom and modern bondage of Rimeing" (*Works*, 2:6).
2 Johan Huizinga, *Homo Ludens: A Study of the Play-Element in Culture* (1944; Boston: Beacon, 1955), discusses the relationship between play and deadly contest with reference to 2 Samuel 2:14 (pp. 41, 48–9).
3 William Prynne (1600–69) was a fanatical Puritan politician and pamphleteer who condemned the theatre.
4 The earlier version of the essay has an extra sentence at this point: "In fact, if he had been able to read T.S. Eliot's unfavourable contrasts between his aural Baroque rhetoric and the 'clear visual images' of Dante, he might even have said that the clear visual images of Dante indicated how badly Dante's version of Christianity, to say nothing of Eliot's, was in need of reformation." Eliot discusses the "clear visual images" of the "competent poet" in his essay *Dante*, and the "auditory imagination" of Milton in

Milton I; both are in *Selected Prose of T.S. Eliot*, ed. Frank Kermode (New York: Harcourt, 1975).

5 T.S. Eliot, *Four Quartets* (*Burnt Norton*, pt. 5); *The Complete Poems and Plays of T.S. Eliot* (London: Faber, 1969), 175.

6 Revelation 18:7: "I sit a queen, and am no widow."

7 Cf. Milton, *Works*, 3:276–7: "I cannot better liken the state and person of a King then to that mighty Nazarite *Samson* . . . ."

8 A probable reference is *SA*, ll. 1493–4: "And on his shoulders waving down those locks, / That of a Nation arm'd the strength contain'd."

9 The following two paragraphs were added in the *Spiritus Mundi* version of the essay.

10 The final sentence of Judges 16 (the story of Samson); also at the end of Judges 15.

11 The ally and heroine of Israel in Judges 4, who lures the enemy captain Sisera into her tent and kills him by driving a nail through his temples.

12 Chorus of Elders.

6. Tribute to Balachandra Rajan

1 Rajan has a chapter entitled "*Paradise Lost*: The Providence of Style" in his book *The Lofty Rhyme: A Study of Milton's Major Poetry* (London: Routledge, 1970), 100–12.

2 Ibid., 101.

3 Ibid., 111.

4 Merritt Y. Hughes, gen. ed., *A Variorum Commentary on the Poems of John Milton* (New York: Columbia University Press, 1970–).

5 Rajan, *The Lofty Rhyme*, 43.

6 *The Form of the Unfinished: English Poetics from Spenser to Pound* (Princeton: Princeton University Press), by Balachandra Rajan, was published in 1985, the same year NF wrote his tribute.

7 Rajan's two published novels are *The Dark Dancer* (London: Heinemann, 1958) and *Too Long in the West* (London: Heinemann, 1961).

7. Blake on Trial Again

1 Algernon Charles Swinburne (1837–1909), *William Blake: A Critical Essay* (London: Hotten, 1868).

2 Arthur Symons (1865–1945), *William Blake* (London: Constable, 1907).

3 John Middleton Murry (1889–1957), *William Blake* (London: Cape, 1933).

4 Jacob Bronowski (1908–74), *William Blake* (1944; republished 1965 by Harper & Row as *William Blake and the Age of Revolution*).

5 Mark Schorer, *William Blake: The Politics of Vision* (New York: Vintage, 1959), 403; this is the last line of Schorer's book.

6 Arthur Rimbaud, *Lettres du voyant* (Lettre à Paul Demeny du 15 Mai 1871), ll. 100–2.
7 In the preface to the 1959 edition, republished by Vintage Books, Schorer admits that the original 1946 edition was "too long . . . for its own good" and that he has cut it by one tenth.
8 This line appears several times in the opening section of Blake's *Milton* (the "Bard's Song").
9 Catherine Blake's remark, "I have very little of Mr. Blake's company; he is always in Paradise," is reprinted in G.E. Bentley, Jr., *Blake Records* (Oxford: Clarendon Press, 1969), 221.
10 The reference is to S. Foster Damon, *William Blake, His Philosophy and Symbols* (London: Constable, 1924).

9. Blake's Treatment of the Archetype

1 Immanuel Kant, *Critique of Practical Reason* (1788): "Two things fill the mind with ever new and increasing wonder and awe . . . the starry heaven above me and the moral law within me." The words are inscribed on Kant's grave. Alfred Kazin, whose *Portable Blake* NF had recently reviewed, also notes that Beethoven kept this quotation on his work table—while his contemporary Blake would have repudiated it (*The Portable Blake*, ed. Kazin [New York: Viking, 1946], 4).
2 Isaac Watts, *A Cradle Hymn*, from *Divine Songs for Children*, ed. J.H.P. Pafford (London: Oxford University Press, 1971), 267.
3 Annotations to Watson's *An Apology for The Bible*; K384/E612.
4 Ibid.; K390/E616.
5 Annotations to Lavater; K79/E594.
6 *FZ*, Night the Ninth, l. 222; K362/E391.
7 "Brave deeds of men." Cf. p. 157, above.
8 The "early book on the libido" is *Wandlungen und Symbole der Libido* (1912), translated in 1916 by Jung's disciple Beatrice M. Hinkle as *Psychology of the Unconscious: A Study of the Transformations and Symbolisms of the Libido.* Jung's later, revised version appeared in English as *Symbols of Transformation* (New York: Pantheon Books, 1956). NF read Hinkle in the 1930s, and annotated copies of both volumes are in the Northrop Frye Library.
9 "Service to women." Cf. p. 77, above.
10 Cf. no. 2, n. 8, in the present volume.

10. J.G. Davies' *The Theology of William Blake*

1 Rudolf Otto (1869–1937), *Mysticism East and West: A Comparative Analysis of the Nature of Mysticism* (New York: Macmillan, 1932).
2 Friedrich Freiherr von Hügel (1852–1925), *Essays & Addresses on the Philoso-*

phy of Religion (1921) and *The Mystical Element of Religion as Studied in Saint Catherine of Genoa and Her Friends* (1923).
3 Evelyn Underhill (1875–1941); her books include *Mysticism* (1911), *The Mystic Way* (1913), and *Man and the Supernatural* (1927).
4 Nikolai Berdyaev or Berdiaev (1874–1948); his books include *Freedom and the Spirit* (1927), *The Destiny of Man* (1931), and *The Beginning and the End* (1946).

11. Bernard Blackstone's *English Blake*

1 Alexander Gilchrist's *Life of William Blake* (1863) is the earliest full account of Blake's life, and a major source for biographers and critics during the early and mid-twentieth century.
2 From Theophrastus (322–287 B.C.), successor of Aristotle as the head of the "Peripatetic" school of Hellenistic philosophy. His *Characters* described thirty different moral types.
3 Blackstone, *English Blake*, 248.

12. Poetry and Design in William Blake

1 In his essay on "Blake" in *The Sacred Wood: Essays on Poetry and Criticism* (London: Methuen, 1920), Eliot criticizes the infelicitous "marriages of poetry and philosophy" in Blake's long prophetic poems, and argues that "you cannot create a very large poem without introducing a more impersonal point of view, or splitting it up into various personalities" (156). Although Eliot does not use the word "schizophrenia," it is likely that this is the passage NF is remembering.
2 A pictorial reproduction is inserted at this point in the original text with the following caption: "William Blake—Frontispiece to *Visions of the Daughters of Albion* (Courtesy National Gallery at Millbank, London)."
3 A pictorial reproduction is inserted at this point in the original text with the following caption: "William Blake—*The Book of Job: No. 8* (Courtesy Cleveland Museum of Art. Purchased by Income Charles W. Harkness Endowment Fund)."
4 *The Faerie Queene*, bk. 2, canto 12, stanza 1.
5 Darrell Figgis, *The Paintings of William Blake* (London: Benn, 1925). Pl. 4 is *The Four and Twenty Elders Casting Down Their Crowns before the Divine Throne* (1805). The "elaborate commentary" is Blake's prose text *A Vision of The Last Judgment*.

13. Introduction to *Selected Poetry and Prose of William Blake*

1 Letter to William Hayley, 28 May 1804; K847/E751.

2 Actually Anthony Stephen Mathew. The mistaken name "Henry" derives from Blake's nineteenth-century biographer, J.T. Smith, and was only corrected by H.M. Margoliouth in *Notes & Queries*, 196 (1951) at the time NF's essay was being written.
3 Now known by the title Blake himself gave the painting: *God Judging Adam*. The nineteenth-century identification of the subject as Elijah in the fiery chariot persisted until 1965.
4 Letter to Thomas Butts, 10 January 1802; K812/E724.
5 Housman, *Last Poems*—XII: "And how am I to face the odds / Of Man's bedevilment and God's? / I, a stranger and afraid / In a world I never made" (*The Poems of A.E. Housman*, ed. Archie Burnett [Oxford: Clarendon, 1997], 81).
6 Letter to George Cumberland, 19 December 1808; K865–6/E770.
7 John Wilson Croker's infamous attack on Keats's *Endymion* was published in 1818 in the *Quarterly Review*; Shelley, among others, claimed that it contributed to Keats's early death. John Ruskin's 1877 response to Whistler's paintings in *Fors Clavigera: Letters to the Workmen and Laborers of Great Britain*—which features such statements as "I have seen, and heard, much of Cockney impudence before now; but never expected to hear a coxcomb ask two hundred guineas for flinging a pot of paint in the public's face"—provoked a libel suit from Whistler.
8 The quoted phrase appears often in Blake's writing, but *A Descriptive Catalogue* is particularly relevant to NF's discussion.
9 Johann Heinrich Füssli or Fuseli (1741–1825), Swiss-born artist, whose interest in Gothic, psychological, and otherworldly themes gave him something in common with Blake. The two were friends from 1787 onward.
10 An Irish painter (1741–1806) affiliated with, but later expelled from, the Royal Academy and known primarily for history painting. His interest in print-making, his radical opinions and his situation as an "outsider" likely stirred Blake's admiration for him.
11 "William Blake, as we call him, was, before all things, an O'Neil . . . the very manner of Blake's writing has an Irish flavour, a lofty extravagance of invention and epithet, recalling the *Tain Bo Cuilane* and other old Irish epics, and his mythology brings often to mind the tumultuous vastness of the ancient tales of god and demon that have come to us from the dawn of mystic tradition in what may fairly be called his fatherland" (*The Works of William Blake*, 3 vols., ed. John Edwin Ellis and W.B. Yeats [London: Quaritch, 1893], 1:3–4).
12 James Boswell, *Boswell's Life of Johnson*, 6 vols., ed. G.B. Hill, rev. L.F. Powell (Oxford: Clarendon, 1934), 2:337.
13 Letter to John Flaxman, 19 October 1801; K811/E718.
14 Cf. Wordsworth, *To a Skylark*: "Type of the wise who soar, but never roam;

/ True to the kindred points of Heaven and Home!" *The Poetical Works of William Wordsworth*, ed. E. de Selincourt (Oxford: Clarendon Press, 1963), 2:266.

15 Annotations to Bacon; K410/E632.

16 Frederick Tatham, *Life of Blake* (ca. 1832), in *Blake Records*, 527.

17 The reference is to 2 Kings 4:35, where the Shunammite's son whom Elisha raises from the dead "sneezed seven times." The *Four Zoas* passage is Night the Eighth, ll. 16–17 (K341/E372).

18 Cf. *FZ*, Night the Ninth, l. 160 (K361/E390), and Joshua 2:18, where the "line of scarlet thread in the window" is the signal to the Israelite army that the prostitute Rahab's house is to be spared, since she helped the Israelite spies escape. Blake's Rahab, a symbol for the seductive world of nature, also has the potential to be redeemed in the apocalyptic moment of Blake's poem.

19 Milton, *Works*, 6:148: "Thus much I should perhaps have said though I were sure I should have spoken only to trees and stones; and had none to cry to, but with the Prophet, *O earth, earth, earth!* to tell the very soil it self, what her perverse inhabitants are deaf to."

20 Oliver Goldsmith, *The Vicar of Wakefield*, ed. Arthur Friedman (London: Oxford University Press, 1974), 75 (chap. 15).

21 Annotations to Wordsworth's *Poems*; K783/E666.

22 Blake's early-twentieth-century biographer, Mona Wilson, claims that "James Blake [William's father] may be credited with a certain imaginativeness since he was attracted by the doctrines of Emanuel Swedenborg" (*The Life of William Blake* [London: Nonesuch, 1927]). Wilson is likely responding to Ellis and Yeats, whose three-volume *Works of William Blake* (1893) reports that James Blake, though *not* "imaginative," nevertheless "permitted, if not encouraged, Swedenborgian doctrines to be studied in his family" (*The Works of William Blake: Poetic, Symbolic, and Critical*, 3 vols. [London: Quaritch, 1893], 1:4).

23 Henry Crabb Robinson, *William Blake* (in *Reminiscences*, 1852): "He declared his opinion that the Earth is flat not round and just as I had objected the circumnavig[ation]n dinner was announced." See *Blake Records*, 541.

24 Cf. Blake's annotations to Spurzheim's *Observations on the Deranged Manifestations of the Mind, or Insanity* (K772/E663).

25 Annotations to Watson's *An Apology for the Bible*; K383/E611.

26 *FZ*, Night the Seventh, l. 305; K327/E360.

27 *FZ*, Night the Ninth, l. 222; K362/E391.

28 *Laocoön*; K777/E274.

29 *Auguries of Innocence*, ll. 3–4; K431/E490.

15. Notes for a Commentary on *Milton*

1 In the *Aeneid*, Virgil compares Pyrrhus or Neoptolemus, the son of Achilles

and sacker of the palace of Troy, to a snake shedding its skin (*Aeneid*, bk. 2, ll. 627–35).

2 A volume of Chaucer containing *The House of Fame*, with an illustration engraved by Blake, was published in 1782. I also feel that *M*, 30.39 [28.39], "Ozoth here builds walls of rocks against the surging sea," has some reference to the *Franklin's Tale*. [NF]

3 The "incisive comment" NF has in mind is: "But in Milton; the Father is Destiny, the Son, a Ratio of the five senses. & the Holy-ghost, Vacuum!" (*MHH*, pl. 6, K150/E35). Blake, writing in 1790, could not have known Milton's *Christian Doctrine*, the manuscript of which was only rediscovered and published for the first time in 1825.

4 Johnson, *Lives of the Poets*, ed. G.B. Hill, 3 vols. (1905; rpt. New York: Octagon, 1967), 1:156 (par. 168).

5 Blake is alleged to have complained that Milton was grievously in error in saying that the pleasures of sex arose from the fall. Milton, of course, said nothing of the kind, as Blake, who made at least four illustrations of Satan watching the love-play of the unfallen Adam and Eve, knew very well. [NF]

6 Alonso de Ercilla y Zúñiga (1533–94), Spanish soldier and poet, was best known for his epic poem *La Araucana*, describing the difficulties encountered by the Spaniards during the insurrection of the natives in Arauco, Chile. Blake reports in a letter of 26 November 1800 that he has been reading Ercilla, among other Continental authors of epic (K806/E714).

7 The reference is to an entry in Blake's notebook: "Tuesday, Janry. 20, 1807, between Two & Seven in the Evening—Despair" (K440/E694).

8 "External world and vision everywhere coincided as it were in the object; in each a whole inner world was displayed, as though an angel who embraces space were blind and gazing into himself" (*Letters of Rainer Maria Rilke*, 2 vols., trans. Jane Bannard Greene and M.D. Herter Norton [New York: Norton, 1947–48], 1:145–6).

9 This phrase occurs throughout Blake's *Jerusalem*, referring to specific, individual expressions of universal forms—i.e., the material details of the real world.

10 Annotations to Swedenborg's *Divine Love and Divine Wisdom*; K91/E604.

11 The reference is to the well-known mantra OM MANI PADME HUM, one translation of which is "the jewel in the lotus."

12 David V. Erdman, *Blake: Prophet against Empire* (Princeton: [Princeton University Press], 1954), 387. [NF]

13 Hence Satan, at the crisis of *Milton*, appears as a sea-monster or leviathan (*M*, 43.9 ff. [38.9 ff.]), and Ololon as a "Moony Ark" (*M*, 49.7 [42.7]). For the iconography of the "moony ark" in Blake, see Keynes, *Blake Studies* (1949), 42; and Ruthven Todd, *Tracks in the Snow* (1946), 37. Similarly the "female will" aspect of Ololon disappears like the dove (*M*, 49.6 [42.6]; Genesis 8:12). [NF]

14 Lines 29–31 of Milton's *Nativity Ode*, "It was the Winter wilde, / While the Heav'n-born-childe, / All meanly wrapt in the rude manger lies," are echoed in Blake's *Europe*, pl. 3, ll. 1–3: "The deep of winter came; / What time the secret child, / Descended thro' the orient gates of the eternal day" (K239/E61). NF's parenthetical comment probably refers to the more general echo of stanza 12 of the *Nativity Ode* ("And bid the weltring waves their oozy channel keep") in *Milton* ("And the calm Ocean joys beneath & smooths his awful waves!" [K511/E123]). The phrase "Vision of beatitude" occurs in the previous line.

15 "Plac'd in the order of the stars," *Europe*, pl. 10 [K241/E63]; cf. Josephus, *Antiquities*, 3:7. An edition of Josephus, published in 1786, has illustrations engraved by Blake. The Classical tradition, attacked in the Preface to *Milton*, is thought of by Blake as much the same structure of natural religion as the Jewish priesthood, which is what Blake means by his *Laocoön* aphorism: "What we call Antique Gems are the Gems of Aaron's Breast Plate" [K777/E274]. The breastplate is also associated with the Covering Cherub (*M*, 9.31 ff.). [NF]

16 The line numbers for pl. 7 given in this paragraph and in an additional reference on p. 257 differ slightly from those given in Erdman. The corresponding references are *M*, 7.2, *M*, 7.1, and *M*, 7.31 in Erdman.

17 Annotations to Watson, *An Apology for the Bible*; K392/E617.

18 Numbers 11:29, "Would God that all the LORD's people were prophets," is quoted in Milton's *Areopagitica* as follows: "For now the time seems come, wherein *Moses* the great Prophet may sit in heav'n rejoycing to see that memorable and glorious wish of his fulfill'd, when not only our sev'nty Elders, but all the Lords people are become Prophets" (*Works*, 4:342–3).

19 Sotha, who has African connections, probably comes from Sothis, the Egyptian name for Sirius, the basis of Egyptian chronology. Ozoth appears to be derived from azoth, the alchemical panacea of Paracelsus. The sevens and eights of *M*, pl. 30 [28] are connected with the fact that the "Eyes of God" appear either as seven or as eight (see above [pp. 246 and 252], and cf. *M*, 17.5 ff. [15.5 ff.]). For this curious ambiguity between seven and eight, which runs all through the history of symbolism, see C.G. Jung, *Psychology and Alchemy* (1953), 66. Of other numbers in Blake, the number of consolidated error is usually one short of the imaginative number. Thus the awakened Albion has fifty-two counties and twenty-eight cities, hence error has fifty-one gods (*M*, 41.18 [37.18]) and twenty-seven churches (*M*, 41.35 [37.35]). [NF]

20 Other forms of the black but comely female in Blake are Oothoon, the heroine of *Visions of the Daughters of Albion*, and the Lyca of *The Little Girl Lost*. Lyca, like the little black boy, comes from the southern clime, and Oothoon, like the chimney sweep, is black in captivity and white in the

imaginative world. Oothoon makes her appearance just at the end of the poem, on pl. 49 [42], as one of the dark clouds of Los bearing the fertilizing rain. See Erdman, *Blake: Prophet against Empire*, 221, 367. Erdman sees in the sequence of place names at the end of pl. 49 [42] a parable of the Blakes returning from Felpham to London. Elynittria seems to be developed anagrammatically from artillery, in its original sense of a shower of arrows (cf. ll. 2 and 43 of *M*, pl. 5). "Arrows of desire" are appropriate to a Blakean Diana or moon-goddess. Ocalythron, goddess of the sun, may conceivably be from *ὁ καλὸς θρόνος* ["the beautiful seat"]. [NF]

21 The association of Robert with Rintrah is made clear by pl. 37, where the iconography is that of pure imagination (star entering *right* foot, *four* stone steps behind). For the significance of Satan's going over to Rintrah, a Saul among the prophets (*M*, 9.12), see *FS*, 329/*FS2*, 321–2. Blake's early letters from Felpham twice speak of Hayley as a brother. The conception of two brothers, one dead and one a murderer of the imagination, suggests Cain and Abel, who illustrate the conclusion of the Bard's Song at the top of pl. 15 [14]. For the origin of the "plough" and "harrow" symbols in Blake's mind, see the letter to Butts of 23 September 1800. Incidentally, if the plates of the Bard's Song are read in the order of the "C" copy (2, 7, 4, 6, 3, 8 ff., omitting 5), the narrative will be easier to follow. [NF]

22 Charles Wilkins, trans., *The Bhăgvăt-Găta or Dialogues of Krĕĕshnă and Ărjŏŏn; in Eighteen Lectures; with Notes* (London: Nourse, 1785).

23 In his edition of Blake's poetry, Geoffrey Keynes notes: "The first full-page illustration of 'Los entering Albion's bosom' has vestiges of lettering above, and at the sides of, the doorway through which Los is about to step. Most of this has been obliterated by Blake in the copies which he himself printed; I was able to read part of it, however, in a copy now in the Fitzwilliam Museum, Cambridge, printed from the original plates in 1832, and this was printed in the notes to the first Nonesuch edition. I afterwards found the whole text clearly printed in a proof of the plate which I acquired in 1943 (see *Blake Studies*, 1949, p. 110), so that it can now be put in its proper place" (K918). By "first Nonesuch edition" Keynes appears to mean the first revised edition published in 1957. The 1956 reprint of the 1927 edition (both of which were also Nonesuch editions) still has at the bottom of the first page of *Jerusalem* the following note: "All the words on this plate here printed in italic have been partially erased from the copper together with others which cannot be recovered" (433).

24 Cf. *M*, 13.39 [12.39] with *PL*, 2.760. Thomas Wright, *Life of William Blake*, 1:105, associates her in the personal allegory with Harriet Poole of Lavant; Erdman, *Blake: Prophet against Empire*, 396, in the political allegory with Marie Antoinette. [NF]

25 Ololon's remark is repeated in the frontispiece to *Jerusalem*, in the newly discovered inscription referred to above. I have nothing to add to my

explanation of the vortex in *FS*, 350/*FS2*, 341, except that its iconography is often serpentine: see the middle figure at the bottom of the plate of *America* beginning "Albion's Angel stood beside the Stone of night" [pl. 5]. [NF]

26 Letter to James Blake, 30 January 1803. Of Blake's knowledge of the Hebrew Bible two examples will suffice. The phrase translated "Lucifer, son of the morning" in Isaiah 14:12, is in Hebrew *Helal ben Sahar*, which underlies the identification of Lucifer with "Hillel" (*M*, 35.8 [32.8]) in a later plate. In Judges 18:30, the name Moses is written Manasseh, an editorial expurgation glanced at in *M*, 26.6 [24.6] (Tirzah was of the tribe of Manasseh). [NF]

27 *M*, 31.4 [29.4]; the tent is the symbol of the fact that the City of God is movable. The tent is pyramidal in shape, the pyramid being its demonic parody, its stony frozen form (cf. the pyramidal shape of the shepherds' tents in one of Blake's *Nativity Ode* illustrations). Blake regarded the story of Sisera [Judges 4] as a reminiscence of the fall of Albion, hence Albion is slain in his tent (*M*, 3.2). [NF]

16. William Blake (I)

1 Frederick Tatham, *Life of Blake* (ca. 1832), in *Blake Records*, 526.

2 Edward Dowden published a *Life of Percy Bysshe Shelley* (1886) and an edition of Shelley's *Poetical Works* (1895).

3 Cf. no. 11, n. 2, in the present volume.

4 Annette Vallon and Harriet Westbrook represent the romantic and sexual adventures of Wordsworth and Shelley, respectively. Vallon was Wordsworth's lover when he lived briefly in France at the time of the French Revolution. They planned to marry, but he was forced to leave her and their daughter in France in December 1792, when he ran short of funds and war broke out between France and England. Westbrook married Percy Shelley in 1811, at the age of sixteen; three years later, Shelley abandoned her and their two children in order to elope with Mary Wollstonecraft Godwin, and Westbrook committed suicide.

5 Algernon Charles Swinburne, *William Blake: A Critical Essay* (London: Hotten, 1868), 15.

6 Yeats, *William Blake and the Imagination*: *Essays and Introductions* (London: Macmillan, 1961), 112.

7 Nietzsche opposes *Herrenmoral*, or master morality, to *Sklavenmoral*, or slave morality, in sec. 260 of *Beyond Good and Evil.*

8 Cf. no. 15, n. 22, in the present volume.

9 Cf. Martin K. Nurmi, "Blake's 'Ancient of Days' and Motte's Frontispiece to Newton's *Principia*," in *The Divine Vision: Studies in the Poetry and Art of William Blake*, ed. Vivian de Sola Pinto (London: Gollancz, 1957), 207–16.

10 Natalis Comes (Natale Conti, 1520–82), who published his ten-book *Mythologiae* in the mid-sixteenth century; Scottish anthropologist James George Frazer (1854–1941), influential author of *The Golden Bough*; and Leo Frobenius (1873–1938), a German ethnographer who was one of the first European scholars of African cultures.
11 Rev. Edward Davies (1756–1831) was a largely self-educated Welsh scholar, schoolmaster, and cleric. In *Celtic Researches* (1804) and *The Mythology and Rites of the British Druids* (1809), he advanced the claim that British culture could be traced to Celtic and Druidical origins.
12 Jacob Bryant (1715–1804) was an antiquarian and scholar of mythology; Blake may have worked as the engraver for his *A New System, or, An Analysis of Ancient Mythology* (1774–76).
13 Rev. William Stukeley (1687–1765) was a doctor, later a vicar, and throughout his life an antiquarian with a keen interest in the prehistory of Britain. Stukeley dedicated himself to the archaeological work of recording and preserving ancient monuments; he is best known for two works on the prehistoric sites of Stonehenge and Avebury.
14 William Owen Pughe, born William Owen (1759–1835), was a contemporary and possibly an acquaintance of Blake's, a "Druidical mythologist," and the author of a Welsh dictionary. His *Cambrian Biography; or, Historical Notices of Celebrated Men among the Ancient Britons* (London, 1803), a biographical dictionary of figures in the ancient history of Britain, influenced Blake and other poets of the Romantic period.
15 Denis Saurat, *Blake and Milton* (New York: Russell & Russell, 1935), 15.
16 Cf. "Quest and Cycle in *Finnegans Wake*," *James Joyce Review*, 1 (February 1957): 39–47; rpt. in *FI*, 256–64.
17 Lawrence, *Introduction to these Paintings*, in *Phoenix: The Posthumous Papers of D.H. Lawrence*, ed. Edward D. McDonald (New York: Viking, 1936), 560.
18 Margaret Rudd, *Organiz'd Innocence: The Story of Blake's Prophetic Books* (London: Routledge & Kegan Paul, 1956), 12–13.

17. Blake After Two Centuries

1 In the *University of Toronto Quarterly* version of 1957, this sentence reads: "They make an instructive contrast to the Ruskin who cut up one of the two coloured copies of *Jerusalem* . . . ."
2 The reference is to the unsuccessful poet in Beerbohm's *Seven Men* (1919).
3 Cf. Kathleen Raine, *William Blake* (New York: Longmans, 1951), 3: "it is doubtful whether the discovery of a new drawing by Michelangelo could have caused more widespread delight than the discovery, in 1949, of a new Blake painting, among the lumber of an English country house in Devonshire."

4 *A Vision of The Last Judgment*; K605/E555.
5 Ibid.; K607/E556.
6 Smart, *Jubilate Agno*, Fragment B, ll. 718–62; *The Poetical Works of Christopher Smart*, ed. Karina Williamson (Oxford: Clarendon Press, 1980), 1:88–9.
7 Clare, *The Maid o' the West*, in *Poems of John Clare's Madness*, ed. Geoffrey Grigson (London: Routledge & Kegan Paul, 1949), 196.
8 *On Virgil* (K778/E270).
9 Cf. John Bunyan, *Grace Abounding to the Chief of Sinners* (1666), and John Keats, Letter to George and Georgiana Keats, 14 February–3 May 1819.
10 Thomas, *And Death Shall Have No Dominion*, in *Collected Poems, 1934–1952* (London: Dent, 1952), 62.
11 Cf. James Boswell, *Boswell's Life of Johnson*, 6 vols., ed. George Birkbeck Hill (Oxford: Clarendon, 1934), 2:9: "Hume owned to a clergyman in the bishoprick of Durham, that he had never read the New Testament with attention."
12 Cf. Bernard Shaw, *Back to Methuselah*, in *The Collected Works of Bernard Shaw*, 30 vols. (New York: Wise, 1930), 16:97: "BURGE-LUBIN: Then how did we get our reputation as the pioneers of liberty? CONFUCIUS: By your steadfast refusal to be governed at all." Shaw uses similar phrases in several other works.
13 *Public Address*; K600/E580.
14 John Keats, *The Fall of Hyperion*, canto 1, l. 199.
15 Cf. Eliot, *Preface* to *For Lancelot Andrewes: Essays on Style and Order* (London: Faber & Gwyer, 1928), ix: "The general point of view may be described as classicist in literature, royalist in politics, and anglo-catholic in religion."

18. Blake's Introduction to Experience

1 Cf. Marcel Proust, *Time Regained*, in *Remembrance of Things Past*, 3 vols., trans. C.K. Scott Moncrieff, Terence Kilmartin, and Andreas Mayor (London: Chatto & Windus, 1981), 3:903: "The true paradises are the paradises that we have lost."
2 *Laocoön*; K777/E274.
3 *A Descriptive Catalogue*; K579/E543.
4 Cf. Alfred, Lord Tennyson, *In Memoriam*, pt. 56: "Nature, red in tooth and claw / With ravine, shriek'd against his creed."
5 *A Vision of The Last Judgment*; K614/E563.
6 *FZ*, Night the Ninth, l. 222; K362/E391.

19. Preface to Peter Fisher's *The Valley of Vision*

1 "Blake and the Druids" appeared in the *Journal of English and Germanic*

Philology, 58 (1959): 589–612; "Blake's Attacks on the Classical Tradition" is in *Philological Quarterly*, 40 (1961): 1–18.

2 Henry David Thoreau, *Walden*, in *The Writings of Henry David Thoreau* (Houghton Mifflin, 1906), 2:112.

3 For the substance of many of NF's conversations with Fisher, see *The Diaries of Northrop Frye, 1942–1955*, vol. 8 of the Collected Works (Toronto: University of Toronto Press, 2001).

4 Thomas Taylor (1758–1835), translator and lecturer on Plato and the Neoplatonists, also had mystical experiences; he was probably acquainted with Blake and appears as "Obtuse Angle" in Blake's *Island in the Moon*.

5 *A Vision of The Last Judgment*; K607/E556.

20. The Road of Excess

1 Wallace Stevens, *The Man with the Blue Guitar*, in *The Collected Poems of Wallace Stevens* (New York: Knopf, 1955), 176: "Poetry is the subject of the poem, / From this the poem issues and / To this returns."

2 Stevens, *An Ordinary Evening in New Haven*, in *Collected Poems*, 486: "This endlessly elaborating poem / Displays the theory of poetry, / As the life of poetry."

3 Letter to Thomas Butts, 6 July 1803; K825/E730.

4 Letter to Rev. Dr. Trusler, 23 August 1799; K793/E702.

5 Matthew Arnold, "Wordsworth," in *Poetry and Criticism of Matthew Arnold*, ed. Dwight Culler (Boston: Houghton Mifflin, 1961), 33.

6 NF's original copy of Blake is no longer existent.

7 The last line of *The Remembrance of Things Past*: Marcel Proust, in *Time Regained, Remembrance of Things Past*, 3 vols., trans. C.K. Scott Moncrieff, Terence Kilmartin, and Andreas Mayor (London: Chatto & Windus, 1981), 3:1107.

8 Byron uses the term "longueurs" in *Don Juan*, canto 3, stanzas 97–8, in referring to a passage from Horace's *Art of Poetry*: "Nay, when good Homer drops into a nap, / His knuckles I feel half inclined to rap, / Though in long works 'tis no great sin, if sleep / O'er the tired poet now and then shall creep" (*The Works of Horace*, 2 vols., trans. Sir Theodore Martin [Edinburgh: Blackwood, 1881], 2:394–5).

9 Tachism, a European movement in abstract art, dates from the 1940s and 1950s. The term entered into common usage among art critics in 1952 with the publication of Michel Tapié's *Un art autre*. The "otherness" of tachism lies in the search for living rhythms expressed through the medium of paint.

10 See Lewis's *"The Diabolical Principle" and "The Dithyrambic Spectator"* (London: Chatto & Windus, 1931). In a student essay on Lewis, NF characterized the latter work as a "preposterous book" (*SE*, 354).

11 See *AC*, 89–92, where NF writes, "It is not often realized that all commentary is allegorical interpretation . . . ."
12 Preface to *Prometheus Unbound*, in *Shelley's Poetry and Prose*, ed. Donald H. Reiman and Sharon B. Powers (New York: Norton, 1977), 135.
13 Cf. Wilde's "The Portrait of Mr. W.H.," in *The Complete Works of Oscar Wilde* (New York: Harper & Row, 1989), 1150–1201.
14 *Laocoön*; K777/E274.
15 In *A Defence of Poetry*, Shelley quotes "the bold and true word of Tasso—*Non merita nome di creatore, se non Iddio ed il Poeta*" [None deserves the name of Creator except God and the Poet] (*Shelley's Poetry and Prose*, ed. Reiman and Powers, 506).
16 *A Defence of Poetry*, in *Miscellaneous Prose of Sir Philip Sidney*, ed. Katherine Duncan-Jones and Jan Van Dorsten (Oxford: Clarendon Press, 1973), 105.
17 *A Vision of The Last Judgment*; K609–10/E559.

22. The Keys to the Gates

1 S. Foster Damon, *William Blake, His Philosophy and Symbols* (London: Constable, 1924; rpt. Gloucester, Mass.: Smith, 1958).
2 *America*, 8.1–17; K198–9/E54. NF added the endnote: "Blake's punctuation is retained." NF's punctuation of the passage is retained, in turn, in the present edition. It corresponds most closely to the Erdman edition of Blake, although there are five times in the passage where Erdman has semicolons while NF's quotation has colons. This appears to be the first essay in which NF quotes from the Erdman edition, which was first published in 1965 under the title *William Blake: Poetry and Prose*. The Erdman edition is evidently used only for longer quotations from the prophetic books, however; phrases and quotations from Blake's lyrics and prose tend to follow the more normalized Keynes edition.
3 James Joyce, *Finnegans Wake* (London: Faber, 1939), 331.
4 *Europe*, 10.1–15, 24–31; K241–2/E63–4. Lines 16–23, omitted from this quotation, contain the image of the *ouroboros* that NF refers to below.
5 See also the pyramids in the design at the top of *The Marriage of Heaven and Hell*, pl. 21 (not in all copies). [NF]
6 Blake's "Little Girl Lost" in *Songs of Innocence* is located in the "southern clime" (K112/E20), but a more relevant reference seems to be the first line of *The Little Black Boy*: "My mother bore me in the southern wild" (K125/E9).
7 *FZ*, Night the Ninth, l. 222; K362/E391.
8 *A Vision of The Last Judgment*; K610/E559.
9 Letter to William Hayley, 6 May 1800 (K797/E705); "grammatically violent" in that Blake actually wrote, "The Ruins of Time builds Mansions in Eternity."

23. William Blake (II)

1 *A Vision of The Last Judgment*; K617/E565.

24. Comment on *Adam and Eve and the Angel Raphael*

1 *For the Sexes: The Gates of Paradise*; K770/E268. In the quotations used in this piece, Blake's spelling and punctuation were normalized to suit the public context and audience.

25. Blake's Reading of the Book of Job

1 S. Foster Damon, author of, among other things, *Blake's Job: William Blake's Illustrations of The Book of Job*, a commentated edition of the Job illustrations that appeared in 1967, shortly before NF's essay was written. Damon had also recently published *A Blake Dictionary: The Ideas and Symbols of William Blake* (Providence: Brown University Press, 1965), to which NF refers later in the present essay.
2 An engraving by Blake dating from 1793, also titled *Our End Is Come* and *A Scene in the Last Judgment Satans holy Trinity The Accuser The Judge & The Executioner*.
3 The illustration on pl. 93 of *Jerusalem* shows three figures pointing with outstretched fingers; the caption incorporated into it reads: "Anytus Melitus & Lycon thought Socrates a Very Pernicious Man" (K740/E253).
4 Cf. Bernard Shaw, "The Bible," in *A Treatise on Parents and Children*, in *The Collected Works of Bernard Shaw*, 30 vols. (New York: Wise, 1930–32), 13:99: "But the Bible is not sufficient . . . . The pleasure we get from the rhetoric of the book of Job and its tragic picture of a bewildered soul cannot disguise the ignoble irrelevance of the retort of God with which it closes, nor supply the need of such modern revelations as Shelley's Prometheus or The Niblung's Ring of Richard Wagner."
5 Cf. Shaw, *The Adventures of the Black Girl in Her Search for God* (London: Constable, 1932), 12–13.
6 *FZ*, Night the Third, l. 59, K293/E327; *J*, 29.46, K654/E192.

26. William Blake (III)

1 See Housman, *Last Poems*—IX: "We for a certainty are not the first / Have sat in taverns while the tempest hurled / Their hopeful plans to emptiness, and cursed / Whatever brute and blackguard made the world" (*The Poems of A.E. Housman*, ed. Archie Burnett [Oxford: Clarendon, 1997], 79).
2 *Europe*, pl. 15; K245/E66.

27. Blake's Reading of the Book of Job II

1 The original version of the essay appeared in a *Festschrift* for S. Foster Damon.
2 See no. 25, n. 6.
3 See no. 25, n. 2.
4 See no. 25, n. 3.
5 *America* 8.3–4; K198/E54.

28. Blake's Biblical Illustrations

1 David Bindman, *William Blake: His Art and Times* (London: Thames & Hudson [for] the Yale Center for British Art and the Art Gallery of Ontario, 1982).
2 The title of the etching and aquatint Francisco Goya intended as the frontispiece to his series of eighty *Caprichos* (1797).
3 See no. 16, n. 13.
4 See no. 16, n. 12.
5 *William Blake's Illustrations to the Bible: A Catalogue* (London: Trianon Press for the William Blake Trust, 1957).
6 Dylan Thomas, *Altarwise by Owl-Light*, in *Collected Poems, 1934–1952*, 66.
7 Blake's caption for the engraving, "Albion rose from where he laboured at the Mill with Slaves Giving himself For the Nations he danc'd the dance of Eternal Death," contains an allusion to *Samson Agonistes*, l. 41: "Eyeless in Gaza at the Mill with slaves."
8 See Milton, *Works*, 4:344: "Methinks I see in my mind a noble and puissant Nation rousing herself like a strong man after sleep, and shaking her invincible locks . . . ."
9 "And Pity, like a naked new-born babe, / Striding the blast, or heaven's Cherubins, hors'd / Upon the sightless couriers of the air, / Shall blow the horrid deed in every eye" (*Macbeth*, 1.7.21–4).
10 "Yet Michael the archangel, when contending with the devil he disputed about the body of Moses, durst not bring against him a railing accusation, but said, The Lord rebuke thee" (Jude 1:9).
11 *FZ*, Night the Third, l. 59, K293/E327; *J*, 29.46, K654/E192.
12 "When he prepared the heavens, I was there: when he set a compass upon the face of the depth" (Proverbs 8:27).

29. Blake's Bible

1 In the Erdman edition of *The Complete Poetry and Prose of William Blake*, which prints a different version of this manuscript poem, the quoted passage comes at the end, not the beginning—an interesting indication that NF continued to prefer the Keynes edition of Blake until the end of his career.

2 Cf. Voltaire, "Chaîne des Êtres Créés," in *Philosophical Dictionary*, ed. and trans. Theodore Besterman (Harmondsworth: Penguin Books, 1972), 107–9.

3 *House of Fame*, l. 731.

4 Cf. *The Dynasts*, "After Scene": "Monsters of magnitude without a shape, / Hanging amid deep wells of nothingness" (Thomas Hardy, *The Dynasts* [London: Macmillan, 1930], 522).

5 NF often used this distinction between nature as structure, order, or system (*naturata*), and nature as a process of growth (*naturans*). The two terms have medieval roots, but their modern usage in Schelling, Coleridge, and others descends from Spinoza.

6 The quotation is from *J*, 30.33, and should read: "Humanity knows not of Sex: wherefore are Sexes in Beulah?" (K656/E193).

7 *FZ*, Night the Seventh, ll. 271–2; K327/E359.

8 A near-quotation of two lines from *FZ*, Night the Seventh—"Thou knowest that the Spectre is in Every Man insane, brutish, / Deform'd, that I am a ravening devouring lust continually" (K664/E360)—but with an echo of *J*, 37.4, "The Spectre is, in Giant Man, insane and most deform'd" (K327/E179).

9 *The Cantos of Ezra Pound* (New York: New Directions, 1934), 803, *Canto* 120: "I have tried to write Paradise."

10 Ibid., 802, "Notes for CXVII et seq.": "To be men not destroyers."

11 *Laocoön*; K776/E274.

12 *A Vision of The Last Judgment*; K614/E563.

Emendations

page/line	
6/38	love freedom heartilie *for* love liberty heartilie
6/39	love not freedom *for* love not liberty
12/37	Odysseus *for* Ulysses
13/20	freedom or of *for* freedom and of
16/20	turning sphear *for* turning air
25/26	which is used *for* which are used
25/27	becomes conventional *for* become conventional
37/8	is contained *for* are contained
58/20	For wee have also our Eevning *for* We also have our evening (as in *Works*)
63/7–8	block of marble *for* block or marble
63/26	turn all *for* all turn
73/20	unconformed *for* unconform
76/28	Embraces are Cominglings *for* Embracings are comminglings
96/19	*Musikalisches Opfer* for *Musikalische Opfer*
98/1	wherein is no immaturity *for* where is no immaturity
109/8	either in *for* in either
123/23	While to their native land with joy they hast, (missing line restored in quotation)
161/21–2	who stood *for* which stood
161/22	l. 1659 *for* l. 1559
161/36–7	Prison within Prison *for* Prison within a Prison
171/30	then strenuous liberty *for* to strenuous liberty
174/28	serpent by the way *for* serpent in the way
180/17–18	the appropriateness of the style *for* the appropriate of style
181/18	has doubtless *for* had doubtless (as in earlier TS)
200/12	*κλέα ἀνδρῶν* for *κλέα ἀνδεῶν*
217/31	seventh plate *for* ninth plate
218/26–7	this goodly frame *for* the goodly frame

234/3 has preceded *for* had preceded
238/32 which made him *for* and which made him
242/30 in *Milton for* in Milton
248/37 *M*, 44.25–6 *for M*, 44.25
249/9 *M*, 9.25–6 *for M*, 9.2, 6
249/17 *M*, 28.41–2 *for M*, 28.41
255/23 *M*, 11.6–7 *for M*, 11.6
261/27 which lead *for* which leads
261/28 are not strong *for* is not strong
261/39 *M*, 14.48–9 *for M*, 14.48
262/10 *M*, 15.14–15 *for M*, 15.14
263/1 *M*, 43.29 ff. *for M*, 43.30 ff.
264/15 *M*, 29.8 ff. *for M*, 29.9 ff.
331/16–17 reproductions of *for* reproduction of
351/19–20 "bound or outward circumference" *for* "outward bound or circumference"
361/38 time and space *for* time and spaces
363/14 S. Foster Damon *for* Foster S. Damon
364/17 and were almost *for* and almost (as in TS)
365/27 his flaming sword *for* flaming sword (as in TS)
365/28 whole creation *for* whole of creation (as in TS)
398/19 What night *for* What time
407/20 have reached *for* has reached
416/4–5 five senses whelm'd *for* five senses rush'd
417/27 neither examples *for* examples neither
420/19 1802 *for* 1803 (as in Erdman)
430/27 appears in *America for* appears in America
435/13 nor a show *for* or a show
448/28–9 Visions of the Daughters of Albion *for* The Daughters of Albion (caption)
453/9 *θρόνος* for *θρός*

Index

Dates of first publication are given for works printed after 1600. Works by Blake which appear in the Pickering MS (ca. 1802–ca. 1807) are identified by (*PMS*), and those in the Notebook or Rossetti MS (ca. 1793–ca. 1818) by (*N*). Other abbreviations are given in the list of Abbreviations on pp. xiii–xiv.

www.ingramcontent.com/pod-product-compliance
Lightning Source LLC
LaVergne TN
LVHW040154080826
844660LV00014B/957/J

* 9 7 8 0 8 0 2 0 3 9 1 9 4 *